COLLINS COBUILD

GRAMMAR PATTERNS 1:VERBS

THE UNIVERSITY OF BIRMINGHAM

COLLINS COBUILD

HarperCollinsPublishers

HarperCollins Publishers
77-85 Fulham Palace Road
London W6 8JB

COBUILD is a trademark of William Collins Sons & Co Ltd

©HarperCollins Publishers Ltd 1996

First Published 1996

2 4 6 8 10 9 7 5 3 1

ISBN 0 00 375051 5 (HB)
ISBN 0 00 375062 0 (PB)

Corpus Acknowledgements

We would like to acknowledge the assistance of the many hundreds of
individuals and companies who have kindly given permission for
copyright material to be used in The Bank of English. The written
sources include many national and regional newspapers in Britain and
overseas; magazine and periodical publishers; and book publishers in
Britain, the United States, and Australia. Extensive spoken data has
been provided by radio and television broadcasting companies; research
workers at many universities and other institutions; and numerous
individual contributors. We are grateful to them all.

Note

Entered words that we have reason to believe constitute trademarks
have been designated as such. However, neither the presence nor absence
of such designation should be regarded as affecting the
legal status of any trademark.

Computer typeset by Tradespools Ltd, Frome, Somerset.

Printed and bound in Great Britain by
Caledonian International Book Manufacturing Ltd, Glasgow, G64

The COBUILD Series

Founding Editor-in-Chief   John Sinclair

Publishing Director   Gwyneth Fox

Editorial Team

Senior Editors	Gill Francis
	Susan Hunston
	Elizabeth Manning
Editorial Consultant	Eugene Gatt Winter
Editorial Assistant	Deborah Orpin
Publishing Manager	Debbie Seymour
Computer Officer	Tim Lane
Secretarial Staff	Sue Crawley
	Michelle Devereux

Production and Design

Jill McNair, Ted Carden

Acknowledgements

The editors would like to thank Dave Willis for his useful comments on the text, and would also like to acknowledge the contribution of the Masters degree students at the Universities of Birmingham and Aston.

Richard Thomas, who was Managing Director of Collins Dictionaries throughout most of the project, made valuable contributions to this book.

Foreword

I am very pleased to introduce this new COBUILD book, because I think that it is one of the most important and useful publications of the series. It is the first of a new range of books on grammar patterns, which present the structure of English in a fresh and innovative way, and will eventually cover all the major areas of the language.

To use words correctly and effectively, you have to arrange them in appropriate patterns. The patterns that are special to a particular word you will find in *Collins COBUILD English Usage*; this book, on the other hand, deals with the patterns associated with groups of words. It gives you a comprehensive account of the verb patterns of English, using the evidence of the Bank of English.

The Bank of English now stands at 250 million words of current English, and is thus large enough to give reliable information on all the verbs you are ever likely to need. Until it was available, the underlying regularities of the language were not clear.

The presentation of patterns is not new, of course, in language teaching. In the fifties and sixties the leading reference book for teachers and learners was A.S. Hornby's *A Guide to Patterns and Usage in English* (OUP 1954). In that book, the principal grammatical patterns of the language were set out using simple formulas, and the typical vocabulary for each pattern was shown in examples. Then for a number of years patterns went out of fashion in linguistics, but the advent of COBUILD in the eighties brought back an appreciation of the importance of the environment of a word to its usage, even its meaning.

This last point is very exciting, because it shows that these pattern grammars are much more than convenient ways of presenting the regularities of usage. During the early research days of COBUILD, I became convinced that the meaning of a word was closely related to the choice of which words occurred nearby, and their position. Twelve years ago this was actually difficult to think about; now the evidence is in front of you.

Through the reliability and objectivity of the computer evidence, verbs can be subdivided according to pattern, and patterns can be seen to correlate with meaning – that is to say, verbs with similar patterns have similar meanings. For example, in Chapter 2, Section 15 you will find the pattern consisting of a verb followed by the preposition *by* and a noun group indicating an amount. The verbs with this pattern indicate that an amount is exceeded or not reached, and the prepositional phrase indicates the size of the difference between the two amounts involved. The verbs fall into three closely related meaning groups: the 'increase' and 'decrease' group, the 'win' and 'lose' group, and the 'overrun' group:

*They expect the number of people emigrating this year to **increase** **by nearly 50 per cent**.*

*The government **lost** **by one vote**.*

*The meeting **overran** **by more than an hour**.*

We can now see that this relation between meaning and pattern is inevitable – that meaning and usage have a profound and systematic effect on each other.

So this book is not just a set of useful patterns of English that have to be learned. It is also a partial explanation of why the patterns are as they are, and why particular verbs have them – as the example above makes clear. This makes the patterns easier to understand and recall, and enables you to use the language accurately and productively.

John Sinclair
Professor of Modern English Language, University of Birmingham
Founding Editor-in-Chief, COBUILD

Contents

Contents

Introduction

This book presents all the patterns of English verbs, and relates these patterns to both structure and meaning. The patterns of a verb are important because they are not only crucial to its usage but also a pointer to its meaning.

What patterns are

A verb pattern is, in most cases, a verb and the words that come after it. These words might be a noun group, an adjective group, a prepositional phrase, an adverb group, or a finite or non-finite clause. In some cases, the Subject is restricted – for example it is always *it*, or always plural – and so can be considered part of the verb pattern.

In the Collins COBUILD English Dictionary (1995 edition), these patterns are encoded in a simple way whereby the elements in each pattern are set out in the order in which they occur. Thus, **V n** means 'verb followed by a noun group' and **V n that** means 'verb followed by a noun group and a that-clause'. The capital **V** indicates the verb that you are concerned with; any other verbal elements in a pattern have their own label. For example an '-ing' form has the label **-ing**, so **V -ing** means 'verb followed by the '-ing' form of another verb'. Note that in this pattern notation, no attempt is made to indicate the functional category of the elements (Object, Complement, or Adjunct). We have used this same pattern notation in this book.

A pattern of a verb includes only those words that are typical of or significant for that particular verb, not those that are just part of general clause structure. For example, most verbs in English can be followed by adverb groups or prepositional phrases indicating manner, time, or place. When information about manner, time, or place is not essential, the adverb group or prepositional phrase is not considered to be part of the pattern.

Some patterns occur very frequently; some are used with only one or two verbs. In this book, we cover over 700 patterns, including passive patterns and phrasal verb patterns. However, all these patterns are based on a very small number of simple elements – **n** (noun group), **adj** (adjective group), **prep** (prepositional phrase), **to-inf** (to-infinitive), **that** (that-clause), and so on. A list of the elements is given on the inside of the back cover of this book.

The chapters

In this book, we take each verb pattern in turn and present information about it, in most cases listing all the verbs in the Collins COBUILD English Dictionary which have the pattern. Chapters 1 to 4 contain information on 85 basic patterns. Chapter 5 contains information on link verbs, such as *be*, *become*, and *seem*. Chapters 6, 7, and 8 deal with verbs that have special combinations of patterns – reciprocal verbs, ergative verbs, and ergative reciprocal verbs. Chapter 9 deals with verb patterns in which the Subject or Object is always *it*. Chapter 10 deals with patterns beginning with *there*. Chapter 11 gives information on the patterns of auxiliaries, modals, and phrasal modals. Chapter 12 contains examples and lists of verbs which share two or more patterns.

The sections

In Chapters 1 to 4, each section deals with one particular pattern, and each section has the same basic arrangement. Below we give an outline of what you will find in each section. Much of this information also applies to the other chapters.

Structures

Each section begins with a heading showing the main pattern dealt with in the section, a simple description of each pattern, and information about how many structures it has, together with an example of each structure. The beginning of Section 2 in Chapter 1 is shown below:

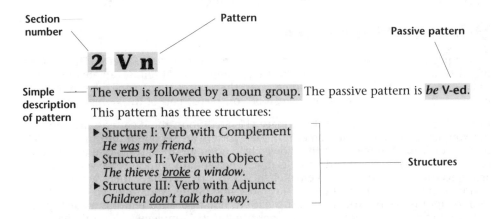

Section number — Pattern — Passive pattern

2 V n

Simple description of pattern — The verb is followed by a noun group. The passive pattern is *be* **V-ed**.

This pattern has three structures:

▶ Structure I: Verb with Complement
He was my friend.
▶ Structure II: Verb with Object
The thieves broke a window.
▶ Structure III: Verb with Adjunct
Children don't talk that way.

Structures

The structure of a pattern tells you whether the element or elements after the verb are, for example the Object, the prepositional Object, the Complement, or an Adjunct. For a full explanation of terms used when describing the structure of a pattern, see the Glossary (page xix). For a full list of the different structures, and information on which patterns have a particular structure, see the Structure Finder (page 623).

Within a section, each structure is dealt with separately. If there is more than one structure, the structures are numbered: I, II, III, IV. The structures are dealt with in this order:

Verbs in phase
Structures containing a Complement or prepositional Complement
Structures containing an Object or prepositional Object
Structures containing an Adjunct
Structures containing a Clause

For each structure, there is a table with a shaded area showing the pattern, a shaded area showing the structure and how the elements in the pattern relate to it, and simple examples of verbs used with this pattern and structure. There are also tables illustrating the passive pattern and the phrasal verb patterns, if these occur. Here is an example showing two tables for the structure 'Verb with Object and prepositional Object Complement' in the section on **V n** *as* **n**:

Structure I: Verb with Object and prepositional Object Complement

Active voice: V n *as* n/-ing

	Verb group	noun group	*as*	noun group/-ing clause
Subject	Verb	Object		prep. Object Complement
Joanna	did not dismiss	Maude	as	a fraud.
Goodliffe	mentions	this	as	being a safe alternative.
The government	has presented	these changes	as	major reforms.
He	regards	himself	as	being too old for the post.

Active pattern — (Verb group / noun group / *as* / noun group/-ing clause)
Structure — (Subject / Verb / Object / prep. Object Complement)
Examples —

Passive voice: *be* V-ed *as* n/-ing

	Verb group	*as*	noun group/-ing clause
Subject	Verb		prepositional Complement
A person's life	should be considered	as	beginning at the moment of birth.
A life sentence	is defined	as	being twenty-five years.
He	had been mentioned	as	a possible new Foreign Minister.
The liberators	were revealed	as	oppressors.

Passive pattern — (Verb group / *as* / noun group/-ing clause)
Structure — (Subject / Verb / prepositional Complement)
Examples —

Meaning groups

One of the most important features of this book is its identification of the link between pattern and structure on the one hand, and meaning on the other. This is the first time that this has been done systematically for all verb patterns.

The verbs with each structure have been divided into groups according to their basic meaning. For example, in the section on **V n into n**, there is a group of verbs with the structure 'Verb with Object and Adjunct' which are concerned with causing something or someone to have a quality or an idea. This group consists of the verbs *breathe, drum, hammer, implant, infuse, inject, instil,* and *strike*. There is also a group of verbs which are concerned with making someone do something. This group includes the verbs *bully, force, nag, con, trick, cajole, charm, persuade,* and *spur,* along with many others. Sometimes, as in this case, a group of verbs is divided into several sub-groups: making someone do something by using force, by deceiving them, by being nice to them, or by giving them motivation. This division into meaning groups means that this book can be used as a grammatically-based thesaurus.

Sometimes all the verbs with a particular pattern, or a particular structure within a pattern, have the same basic meaning. For example, in the section on **V n to n**, all the verbs with the structure 'Verb with Object and prepositional Object Complement' are concerned with changing something to something else. This group includes the verbs *change, convert, decrease, increase, reduce, shorten,* and *turn*.

Each meaning group is labelled with one (or more) of the verbs in it: for example, THE 'BORE' GROUP, THE 'START' AND 'STOP' GROUP. The meaning groups are numbered in a way that shows the structure they have. For example, meaning group II.3 is meaning group 3 within the section on Structure II.

If there are any verbs that do not belong to any of the meaning groups, they are put in a group called VERBS WITH OTHER MEANINGS at the end.

Sometimes we give additional information about the verbs in a particular meaning group, for example that they always have an inanimate Subject. Unless otherwise stated, the term **Subject** always refers to the Subject of an active clause.

Examples

Each meaning group has examples to show the verbs being used with the pattern in question. These examples are actual examples of current English, taken from the Bank of English. Enough context is given to make the meaning of the verb clear. The verb pattern is highlighted in bold, and the verb group itself is underlined.

This example illustrates the pattern **V** with the verb *suffer:*

verb group   *Your home life **may suffer** because of work pressures.*

This example illustrates the pattern **V adj** with the verb *prove:*

verb group   *The law **has proved** difficult to implement,* however.   adjective group

This example illustrates the pattern **V *for* n** with the verb *prepare:*

for

verb group   *The crew of the space shuttle Atlantis **is preparing** for*
the ride back to Earth tomorrow.   noun group

This example illustrates the pattern **V n prep/adv** with the verb *bring:*

noun group

verb group   *I **will bring** the tape to Paris and they will be able to*
check what is on it.   prepositional phrase

This example illustrates the pattern **V n *among* pl-n** with the verb *divide:*

verb group   noun group

plural noun   *Drain the noodles and **divide** them among*
group   *the individual serving bowls.*   among

Note that the verb group includes any auxiliaries (forms of *be, do,* and *have),* modals (for example *may* or *will),* and phrasal modals (for example *used to* or *have to).* See Chapter 11 for full information on auxiliaries, modals, and phrasal modals.

The negative word *not,* or its contracted form *n't,* is also included in the verb group.

> *She hastens to note that she **was not groomed** for a*
> *show business career.*

> *He **hasn't shown up** for work.*

A group of examples may contain active and passive examples, and examples of phrasal verbs, arranged so that the verbs being exemplified are in alphabetical order. Except for passives and questions, we have avoided giving examples where the elements of a verb pattern appear in a different order from the basic pattern. Circumstances when patterns appear in a different form are explained in the Appendix of this book (page 611).

We also mention and illustrate minor variations on the basic pattern, for example when a verb can be followed by a preposition and an '-ing' clause or a reflexive pronoun, rather than by a preposition and an ordinary noun group. For example, at **V** *of* **n**, meaning group 1, there is the following note and example:

Note   The preposition *of* is sometimes followed by an -ing clause

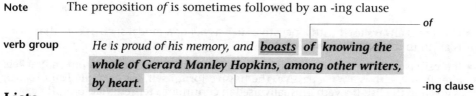

Lists

We have surveyed the patterns of over 4000 verbs, and this has enabled us to produce a valuable resource in the form of comprehensive lists of the verbs and phrasal verbs in each meaning group. In most sections, these lists show every sense of every verb in the Collins COBUILD English Dictionary which has a particular pattern. A unique feature is the giving of sense numbers, which means we can show that a less frequent sense of a verb has a particular pattern, rather than having to give information only about the most frequent or obvious sense.

In the two sections which deal with the most frequent patterns, not every verb can be listed: for **V**, the lists contain only verbs which are among the 500 most frequently occurring verbs in the Bank of English; for **V n**, Structure II, the lists contain only the top 400 verbs.

Sometimes we say that a pattern is productive with a particular meaning, that is, many verbs could be used with this pattern, or are used occasionally with this pattern. In this case, we list only the verbs which are most frequently used in that way.

The lists are set out in boxes as shown below.

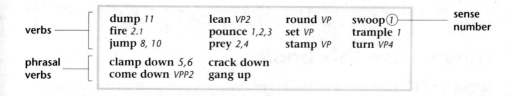

- If a verb has more than one sense in the Collins COBUILD English Dictionary, there is a number after it indicating which sense is meant. A number such as *1.2* means subentry 1, sense 2. If more than one sense of the verb has the pattern, all relevant sense numbers are given.

- If a phrasal verb was covered under an ordinary verb sense in the dictionary because it has the same meaning, a ▷ symbol is put before the sense number in the list. For example, you will find the verb *stand up* ▷ *2* under sense 2 of the verb *stand*.

- If a combination of a verb and a preposition or adverb was treated as a phrasal verb in the dictionary, but is treated in this book as an ordinary verb pattern, it has *VP* after it (this means it was treated under a Verb+Particle phrasal verb heading). For example, *turn on*, which was treated as a phrasal verb in the dictionary, is here treated as being the verb *turn* with the pattern **V** *on* **n**, because it has the same basic meaning as other verbs which are followed by *on* and are concerned with attacking or harming someone. Similarly, if a combination of a verb, an adverb, and a preposition was treated as a three-part phrasal verb, it has *VPP* after it. This information helps you if you want to look the verb up in the dictionary.

Below is another list, illustrating the use of bracketed information.

attract 1 *(people or animals)*	**call** 9 *(a witness) (usu passive)*	**force** 1	**work** 19
bind 2 *(Laws....people)*	**draw** 21 *(a lot of people)*	**push** 6	
call 5 *(a doctor)*	**(not) draw** 23 *(a person) (usa passive)*	**use** 1.7	

- If a verb is always used with a negative such as *not* or a modal such as *can*, that word is given in brackets before the verb.

- If a verb is usually passive with the pattern concerned, *usu passive* is put in brackets after it. If a verb is always passive, the passive form itself, for example *be rumoured*, is given in the list. If a verb is usually used in continuous tenses, that form, for example *be dying*, is given.

- Sometimes an Object that typically follows a verb is given in brackets after it, to make the meaning of the verb clearer. Similarly, a typical Subject is sometimes given in brackets after a verb, beginning with a capital letter. Sometimes both Subject and Object are indicated like this: *(Laws...people)*.

- If a verb is part of a phrase that appears in the dictionary in the entry for another word in the phrase, the information in brackets will direct you to the correct place in the dictionary. For example, the phrase *come to light* appears as sense 14 of *light*. When we refer to this sense of the verb *come*, the instruction *see light 14* is given in brackets.

Extra information

After all the meaning groups for a particular structure, we set out in words the structure information that is shown in the table at the beginning, and other information that has not been covered, for example about the possible order of the elements.

After all the structures and meaning groups have been explained, we deal with any other patterns which are related to the main pattern, for example patterns which contain an additional prepositional phrase or to-infinitive. For example, the pattern **V for n to-inf** is dealt with at the end of the section on **V for n**.

How to use this book

To find out which patterns a particular **verb** has, look it up in the **Verb Index** (page 631) and turn to the page(s) where it is listed, along with other verbs with the same pattern, structure, and meaning. The Verb Index also gives information about the frequency of each verb. If you want to know which verbs share two or more patterns, turn to **Chapter 12**.

To find out which verbs have a particular **pattern**, for example **V to n** or **V to n to-inf**, look it up in the **Contents** or the **Pattern Finder** (page 625) and turn to the section where it is dealt with.

To find out which patterns and verbs have a particular **structure**, for example 'Verb with two Objects', look it up in the **Structure Finder** (page 623) and turn to the relevant sections.

To find out which patterns and verbs are used when talking about a particular **type of action or activity**, for example 'Attacking' or 'Communication', look it up in the **Meaning Finder** (page 616) and turn to the relevant meaning groups.

An explanation of the grammatical terms used in this book is given in the **Glossary** (page xix). A list of abbreviations used in the patterns is given on the inside cover.

Advice for teachers

There are many ways in which this book can be used by teachers in planning teaching material, and by learners using self-access materials. Here we describe a few ideas which should inspire teachers and learners to think of more. First, we think about ways that this book can contribute to a lesson or self-access session. Then, we consider how this book can help the teacher or course designer implement syllabuses of various kinds.

The place of this book in a lesson or in a self-access session

This book can be used:

- to supplement work on a reading or listening text
- to extend vocabulary
- to check accuracy
- to encourage language awareness
- to write language learning materials

Supplementing a reading or listening text

Here is a short passage that might be used as a reading comprehension text:

Anger is a stress response, identical to fear. It is the 'fight or flight' syndrome, the body's arousal for action in the face of a threat. Suppressing anger is not healthy. <u>It is thought that</u> long-term, held-in anger can lead to longer-term raised blood pressure, ulcers and migraines. Insomnia, depression, and alcoholism have all been associated with suppressed anger. <u>It has</u> even <u>been suggested that</u> 75 per cent of breast cancer patients have an 'anger problem' - most of them bottling up their feelings.

The teacher may wish to draw learners' attention to the use of It is thought that and It has been suggested that in this text.

This pattern is **it be V-ed that**. It is described in this book in Chapter 9, Section 1. This section explains that you use the pattern to indicate that something is said, thought, or discovered by an unspecified group of people. Having read the description, the teacher can discuss with learners the meaning or significance of the pattern. The learners may then be invited to look at more examples of the same pattern, taken from this book (see pages 526-528):

It <u>can be argued</u> that human health would not suffer if we were to stop most animal research.

It <u>is claimed</u> that running helps to unleash hidden energies, both psychic and physical.

In 1990, it <u>was disclosed</u> that he had contracted the AIDS virus.

It <u>is estimated</u> that up to two million people around the country suffer from various forms of asthma.

A short time ago, it <u>was reported</u> that demonstrators had broken through the police lines and more vehicles were set alight.

The differences in meaning indicated by the different verbs chosen can be a topic for class discussion.

Finally, the learners can be asked to look at the list of verbs given for this pattern. Some of these verbs will be known to them, but not with this pattern. Other verbs may be unknown, and the learners can be asked to find out their exact meaning in a dictionary.

Extending vocabulary

Each list in this book contains words which have two things in common: they all have the same pattern, and they share an aspect of meaning. The lists therefore provide a resource for learners to extend their vocabulary by learning words concerned with a particular topic, function, or concept, and by learning the pattern of a group of words together with the words themselves. Learners can be encouraged to keep a record of new words learnt, in their meaning groups, and together with their patterns.

For example, a student of economics, management, or finance, may come across the following paragraph in the financial pages of a newspaper:

Britain's industrial production rose by 0.6 per cent in the year to December, while Holland's slumped by 5.7 per cent; Spain's fell by 2.6 per cent in the 12 months to November. America's retail sales rose by 6.6 per cent in the year to December; German sales increased by 4.6 per cent. In January Britain's retail sales jumped by 1.6 per cent, to give an annual increase of 2.3 per cent, the biggest rise since May 1989.

Any learner may well be intrigued by the range of different verbs meaning 'go up' or 'go down': *rise, slump, fall, increase,* and *jump,* and by the fact that they can all be followed by *by* and an amount. This pattern is **V by amount**. Looking at Chapter 2, Section 15 in this book (page 173), the learner can find a complete list of similar verbs, that is, verbs that are used in a financial context to mean 'go up' or 'go down' and which have the pattern **V by amount**:

climb 4	drop 1	rise 9	soar 1
decline 1	fall 5	shrink 2	surge 2
decrease 1	increase 1	sink 7	swell 1
depreciate	jump 6	slide 4	tumble 2
dip 7	plummet	slip 7	widen 4
dive 7	plunge 5	slump 1	
come down 1	go up 1		
go down 1	shoot up 1		

The lists in this book can be used as a basis for further vocabulary work. For example, a learner who already knows the phrases 'ask someone to do something' and 'tell someone to do something' might look at the pattern **V n to-inf** in Chapter 3, Section 4 of this book. The 'tell' group in that section includes verbs of communication, but with a variety of meanings, for example asking, advising, or telling someone to do something. Using the examples given, and a dictionary where necessary, the learner can be asked to pick out from the list in the 'tell' group those verbs that mean 'ask someone to do something', those that mean 'advise someone to do something', and those that mean 'tell someone to do something'. The learner would end up with three lists of his or her own:

'ask someone to do something'

ask 2	bid 2.2	request 2
beg 1	entreat	
beseech	implore	

'advise someone to do something'

advise 1	counsel 2
caution 2	warn 2

'tell someone to do something'

command *1*	**enjoin** *1*	**order** *2.1,2*
direct *12*	**instruct** *1*	**tell** *3*

Checking pattern accuracy

It is not always possible to tell from intuition whether a verb can be used with a particular pattern or not. If a verb is given in this book as having a particular pattern, this means that the verb and pattern occur reasonably frequently in the Bank of English. If a verb does not occur in the lists for that pattern, this means that the verb and pattern do not occur or occur only rarely in the Bank of English. Therefore, a teacher or learner can be confident that if a verb and pattern used by the learner is found in this book, the learner's usage is accurate. If the verb and pattern used by the learner is not found in this book, the learner should perhaps be advised to find an alternative verb or an alternative pattern.

For example, a learner, writing a story, wishes to indicate that one of the characters in the story advises another character to take a holiday. The learner decides that the verb *suggest* accurately represents the kind of advice she wants to talk about, so she writes: *Jennifer suggested Jim to take a holiday*, using the pattern **V n to-inf**. She now wishes to check whether this sentence is correct. If she looks at the verb *suggest* in the index to this book, she will find that it does not occur in the pattern **V n to-inf**, but that it does occur in the pattern **V that**. Alternatively, if she looks at the pattern **V n to-inf** in this book (Chapter 3, Section 4), she will find, not *suggest*, but some other possible words that indicate suggestions, notably *advise* and *counsel*. The learner then has two possible accurate versions of the incorrect sentence she had written: *Jennifer suggested that Jim should take a holiday* and *Jennifer advised Jim to take a holiday*.

One common source of difficulty for learners is knowing how far knowledge about one verb can be extended to another verb with a similar meaning. For example, a learner may know that the verb *promise* can be used in two patterns: **V that**, as in *I promised I would have a word with Nick when he returned*, and **V n that**, as in *He promised them that he'd change the way the government worked*. The learner may also know other verbs that have a similar meaning to *promise*, such as *assure, tell*, and *warn*. Chapter 12 in this book shows which verbs, or rather senses of verbs, share combinations of patterns. For example, the entry for **V n that; V that** (page 599) shows that of the verbs listed above only *warn* is like *promise* in that it has the same two patterns. In other words, the learner's knowledge about *promise* can be extended to *warn* but not to *assure* and *tell*.

Although it is possible to say what is correct in English, it is not always possible to say what is incorrect. There are at least two reasons for this. Firstly, the language is constantly changing, and one of the ways it changes is that verbs start to be used in patterns they were not used in before. Users of a language are creative, and may use verbs in unusual patterns, often because the meaning of the verb is similar to another verb that has that pattern.

Secondly, some patterns are very productive, that is, there are many verbs that are occasionally used with a particular pattern, so that it is not possible to distinguish completely between a verb that has that pattern and a verb that does not. Two patterns in this book that are particularly productive are **V way prep/adv**, in Chapter 4, Section 4, and **V n into -ing**, in Chapter 4, Section 17. Both patterns are used with a very wide range of verbs and, although some verbs can be said to be most frequently used with that pattern, it is not wise to state absolutely that a particular verb cannot be used with the pattern.

Encouraging language awareness

Several of the teaching ideas mentioned so far have as their immediate aim the raising of learners' awareness of patterns, the verbs they are used with, and the meaning of patterns. In general, this book is a useful resource for teachers who like to exploit reading or listening texts in order to raise learners' awareness of grammar and vocabulary. A useful exercise to raise the consciousness of learners who encounter English outside the classroom is to focus on one or two patterns at a time and ask learners to note down examples of those patterns that they hear or read between classes.

Three chapters in this book can be used to focus more specifically on the significance of a speaker or writer choosing one pattern rather than another. These chapters are Chapter 6: Reciprocal verbs, Chapter 7: Ergative verbs, and Chapter 8: Ergative reciprocal verbs. In each of these chapters, verbs which have more than one pattern are described, and the examples are given in groups, illustrating the two or more patterns together. For example, in Chapter 6, the following examples are given of the verb *fight*:

> Did he say why **they <u>were fighting</u>**?
> A man was injured after he **<u>fought</u> with a would-be thief tampering with his neighbour's BMW** yesterday.

And in Chapter 7, the following examples are given of the verb *change*:

> As society **<u>has changed</u>** in Java, the ways in which dancers are taught **<u>have</u>** also **<u>changed</u>**.
> Those who wish to **<u>change</u> society** have to create an active, political community.

In Chapter 8, the following examples are given of the phrasal verb *split up*:

> When **Ellen and her husband <u>split up</u>**, she took her three teenaged children and moved back to her hometown.
> She **<u>split up</u> with her husband** more than two years ago and now wants to divorce him.
> It's obvious she's being malicious and trying to **<u>split</u> us <u>up</u>** but it's not working.

These sets of examples can be used, at appropriate points in a course, to focus discussion on the distinctive meaning of each pattern, and on the significance of choosing one pattern when more than one is available. These choices are discussed briefly in the introduction to each chapter. The meaning groups and lists given in Chapters 6, 7, and 8 indicate the range of reciprocal, ergative, and ergative reciprocal verbs in English. When learners encounter one or more of these verbs in a text, they can be invited to consider the significance of the choice of pattern that was made. For example, in the first of each of the sets of examples above, no-one, or no one person, is presented as being responsible for the state of affairs being described, and thus a possible allocation of blame or responsibility is avoided.

Writing language learning materials

Many teachers like to supplement their course book with further practice materials. This book provides an excellent resource for writing materials of this kind. In addition to the types of exercises indicated above, it can be used in writing exercises which focus on a pattern itself, and, in particular, its meaning. Take, for example, the pattern **V way prep/adv**, which has a general meaning of someone doing something in order to achieve something, often something difficult. The achievement may be physical, as in *He inched his way up the cliff* or abstract, as in *She talked her way into a job in advertising*. This pattern can be found in Chapter 4, Section 4 of this book. There are many meaning groups, but the teacher might wish to focus on four or five, giving learners the examples given in this book for each meaning group. Here, for example, are the examples from meaning group 5:

> With nothing to do, the mind is unable to prevent negative thoughts from **<u>elbowing</u> their way to center stage**.
> The guardsmen who were now outside the walls **<u>had to fight</u> their way back** through the north gate.

The protesters __forced__ their way into the police headquarters, setting fire to parts of the building.

When he turned professional 11 years ago, Christie was expected to __storm__ his way to a world championship.

The teacher might also give the learners a list of the verbs in that meaning group which most frequently have this pattern: *claw, fight, force, push, smash,* and *work*.

Having been given this information, the learners might be asked to generalize about the meaning of the group. If this activity is repeated for four or five meaning groups in this pattern, the learners will begin to get a feel for the meaning of the pattern itself and the contexts in which it is used. This could then form the basis for further production tasks and exercises.

The place of this book in a syllabus

This book can be used by course designers, materials writers, and teachers who have the task of implementing a syllabus. Here we show how this book can be used in implementing:

- a grammatical syllabus
- a functional or notional syllabus
- a lexical syllabus

Implementing a grammatical syllabus

A grammatical syllabus gives a list of structures, tenses, and other grammatical points that the learner should know by the end of the course. The problems with such a syllabus are that it treats grammar as separate from vocabulary and from meaning, and that it gives little guidance on what vocabulary should be taught. This book can help to overcome such shortcomings.

For example, a syllabus may include an item such as 'verbs followed by a to-infinitive'. In pattern terms, this is **V to-inf**. Chapter 1, Section 8 of this book shows the various meanings that are commonly expressed using this pattern, and the particular verbs that are found with the pattern. The course designer can identify topics and concepts that would be likely to involve language using this pattern and, most importantly, can identify the vocabulary items that need to be taught with it. If the course is cyclical, introducing the same syllabus item at different points, the more frequent verbs can be taught first and the less frequent ones at a later stage.

Another item that often occurs in a grammatical syllabus is 'reporting structures'. The Meaning Finder in this book can be used to identify those patterns that are associated with reporting and, again, the necessary vocabulary can be identified.

Many grammatical syllabuses stress contrastive grammar. For example, they may call attention to the difference between 'remember doing' and 'remember to do'. In the Collins COBUILD English Dictionary, these two patterns are associated with different senses of *remember*. This indicates that the verb *remember* means something very different in the two patterns. The sections describing each pattern can be used to associate each sense of *remember* with other verbs. For example, Chapter 1, Section 7 groups 'remember doing' with *recall* and *regret*. This encourages the learner to associate this pattern of *remember* with the meaning of 'reflecting upon'. By contrast, Chapter 1, Section 8 groups 'remember to do' with *contrive* and *manage*. This encourages the learner to associate this pattern of *remember* with the meaning of 'achieving something'.

Implementing a functional or notional syllabus

A functional syllabus gives a list of communicative functions that the learner should be able to accomplish by the end of the course. A notional syllabus gives a list of conceptual notions that the learner should be able to express or talk about by the end of the course. Many syllabuses combine both functions and notions. The problem with functional or notional syllabuses is that they tend to be purely conceptual. They give little indication of the vocabulary or grammar that is to be taught.

Using the Meaning Finder, the course designer can identify the grammatical patterns and the vocabulary that express each function or notion. Although no-one would wish to present the learner with all this information at once, the course designer has access to the full range of means of expression for a function or notion, and can make a reasoned selection. If the course is designed cyclically, simple patterns can be presented before complex ones, or more frequent vocabulary before less frequent.

Implementing a lexical syllabus

A lexical syllabus takes as its starting point the vocabulary that the learner needs to know. This vocabulary is identified from a corpus consisting of the kind of language the learner is most likely to come across and to want to use. Because the grammar presented in this book is based on lexical items, it is ideally suited to provide the grammatical input to a lexically-organized course. As a result, a lexical syllabus could consist of a list of patterns as well as a list of vocabulary items.

Using this book, the course designer can identify target patterns, that is, those patterns that should be included in the course, at the same time as identifying target vocabulary. The course writer can ensure that learners become aware of how to use a word at the same time as learning the meaning of a word.

In addition, the patterns presented in this book provide a principle for the organization of vocabulary in the syllabus, in the sense that vocabulary items that share a pattern can be presented together. This is common practice in existing courses for the few patterns that are part of general knowledge. For example, many courses include a unit on verbs which are followed by the '-ing' form of another verb. This is the pattern **V -ing**. This book allows this organizational principle to be extended across a whole course.

By focusing on patterns as meaning, this book provides resources to help the learner guess the meaning of unknown words from their pattern. For example, a newspaper report that might be used as a reading text includes this sentence:

Elisabeth and Thomas were hailed yesterday as heroes.

A learner may well not know the meaning of *hail*, but may be encouraged to observe the pattern, which is the passive of **V n as n**. The learner may know other verbs that are used with that pattern, such as *see, consider*, or *describe*, and may have been made aware that the pattern is used to indicate that someone is thought of, or spoken about, in a particular way, usually as something good or as something bad. The general meaning of *hail* can therefore be guessed, and the specific meaning can be checked if necessary.

Finally, an awareness of pattern encourages teachers and learners to adopt the phrase, rather than the word, as the unit of learning. For example, these words are used in the patterns **V n for n** and **V n for -ing**: *admire, blame, congratulate, criticize, forgive, thank*. A learner developing vocabulary concerned with reactions to something that someone has done can learn, not just these words, but phrases such as *admire someone for doing something, blame someone for an action* and so on. In this way the learner builds up an idiomatic phraseology of English.

Glossary of grammatical terms

active voice If a verb is in the active voice, the Subject of the clause indicates the person or thing doing the action or responsible for it, e.g. *Anne **has given** me a tiny black kitten.* Compare **passive voice**.

adjective group An adjective group may consist of just one adjective, e.g. *I was **glad**.* Or the adjective may have words before it, such as an adverb, e.g. *I was **very happy**,* or words after it, such as a non-finite clause or a prepositional phrase, e.g. *I was **pleased to see her**... That was **kind of you**.* An adjective group is used to describe someone or something, or to give information about them.

Adjunct An Adjunct is a part of a clause that tells you something about the circumstances of an action, event, or situation. For example, it indicates the time or place of an action or event, its frequency, its degree, or the manner in which it occurs.
In this book we distinguish between two types of Adjunct. The first type is considered to be part of the pattern of the verb. This means that if it is omitted, the meaning of the verb changes or the verb makes no sense, e.g. *He's living **in Birmingham**... He behaved **badly**... He switched the television **off**.*
The second type is not considered to be part of the pattern of the verb: it is optional, e.g. *The children are playing **in the garden**.* In the tables showing patterns and structures, this kind of Adjunct is not given, or it is indicated as **Adjunct (optional)** on the second line of the table.
An Adjunct is typically either an adverb group or a prepositional phrase, but it may also be a noun group, e.g. *Very few people think **that way**,* or an amount, e.g. *Wales beat England **2-1**.*

adverb group An adverb group usually consists of just one adverb, e.g. *He swung **round** to see who was there... She is doing **well** at school,* but the adverb may also have another adverb before it, e.g. *Young skin burns **very easily**.* An adverb group indicates the time or place of an action or event, its frequency, its degree, or the manner in which it occurs. Adverb groups which are part of verb patterns are usually concerned with place or manner.

amount An amount is a word or phrase indicating an amount of something, for example *a lot, nothing, three percent, four hundred pounds, more, much,* e.g. *Her style of cooking owes **much** to her mother-in-law.*

auxiliary An auxiliary is one of the verbs *be, have,* and *do,* when they are used with a main verb to form tenses, passives, negatives, interrogatives, imperatives, etc. See Chapter 11, Section 1.

bare infinitive A bare infinitive is the infinitive without *to,* e.g. *Thomas did not dare **approach** the great man... She heard the girl **laugh**.*

colour A colour word refers to a colour. It behaves like an adjective, e.g. *The sky was **blue**,* and like a noun, e.g. *...several shades of **yellow**.*

Complement A Complement is a part of a clause that provides information about the Subject. It tells you what the Subject is or what it is like. It typically follows a link verb, e.g. *His father was **an accountant**... She looked **worried**.* A few verbs which are not link verbs are also followed by Complements, e.g. *He died **penniless**.*
A Complement occasionally follows the Object of a clause, again giving information about the Subject, e.g. *The dollar finished the day **lower**.*
A Complement is typically a noun group or an adjective group, but it may also be an amount, e.g. *Two and two make **four**.*
See also **Object Complement** and **prepositional Complement**.

Completive The term 'Completive' is used in the tables in this book as a general term covering anything that occurs after a verb, such as an Object, Complement, Adjunct, or new clause, wherever this cannot be specified exactly. For example, if a verb occurs in phase with another verb, these verbs form a complex verb group, and what occurs after this group varies according to the second verb. In the clause *The arrangements appeared to be **satisfactory**,* the complex verb group is *appeared to be,* and the Completive is the adjective *satisfactory* (the Complement). In the clause *No-one appeared to notice **her**,* the complex verb group is *appeared to notice,* and the Completive is the noun group *her* (the Object).

complex verb group A complex verb group consists of two verbs in phase. This means that the actions or states expressed by the two verbs cannot be separated from each other. For example, if you *begin to see* something, the *beginning* and the *seeing* are not two processes, but one. The second verb in the phase structure is typically a to-infinitive clause, e.g. *I'm **beginning to see** what you mean;* a bare infinitive, e.g. *I **helped save** those animals;* or an '-ing' clause, e.g. *He **kept saying** he was sorry.*
A complex verb group may also contain a preposition before an '-ing' form, e.g. *I **shall refrain from mentioning** who was involved.* Or it may consist of two verbs separated by *and,* e.g. *I'll **try and help** you.*

co-ordinated Two parts of a group or clause which are co-ordinated are joined together with a **co-ordinator** such as *and, or,* or *than,* e.g. *In his 68 years, **he and Diana** quarrelled only once.*

'-ed' clause An '-ed' clause is a non-finite clause beginning with the '-ed' form of a verb, e.g. *Rose had all her shops **decorated in pink**.*

'-ed' form The '-ed' form of a verb is its past participle form. This usually ends in '-ed' but it sometimes ends in '-en'. There are also several irregular verbs which have special forms, for example the past participle of *put* is *put*. The '-ed' form is used, for example, in all passive patterns, e.g. *The cliffs were **formed** when the sea level was higher.*

ergative link verb An ergative link verb behaves like an ergative verb in that it has one pattern which indicates that something happens to the Subject or that the Subject does something. This pattern is **V adj** or **V colour**, e.g. *They **kept** warm... The water **turned** pink.* It has another pattern which indicates that someone or something causes something to happen. This pattern is **V n adj** or **V n colour**, e.g. *The noise **kept** him awake... The lenses **turned** her eyes green.* In the patterns **V adj** and **V colour** only, the verb is a **link verb**. See Chapters 5 and 7.

ergative reciprocal verb An ergative reciprocal verb behaves both like an ergative verb and like a reciprocal verb. Like an ergative verb, it has some patterns which indicate that something happens to the Subject, or that the Subject does something, and other patterns which indicate that someone or something causes something to happen. You can say *The charities **should** all **combine*** and *The shower **combines** the hot and cold water.* In addition, like a reciprocal verb, an ergative reciprocal verb indicates that two or more people or things are mutually involved in a process. It has some patterns where both people or things are indicated together by the Subject, and some patterns where one person or thing is indicated by the Subject and the other is mentioned in another part of the pattern. You can say *Pinks and blues **combine** to give a stunning display* and *Other problems **may combine** with the loss of blood.* See Chapter 8.

ergative verb An ergative verb has two patterns, most commonly **V** and **V n**. The **V** pattern indicates that something happens to the Subject, or that the Subject does something, e.g. *The car **stopped**.* The **V n** pattern indicates that someone or something causes something to happen, e.g. *The driver **stopped** the car.* The Subject in the **V** pattern is the Object in the **V n** pattern. See Chapter 7.

finite clause In a finite clause, the verb group includes an indication of tense or modality, e.g. *A man was swimming fast to the canoe.* Compare **non-finite clause**.

fraction A fraction is a word like *half, quarter,* and *third,* e.g. *She cut the apple in **half**... It was divided into **thirds**.*

general it General *it* is used in some patterns and phrases to refer vaguely to a general situation, e.g. *It's raining... Cut it out.* See Chapter 9, Sections 3 and 4.

imperative When a clause is in the imperative, the base form of the verb is used and the clause usually has no Subject. The imperative is typically used to tell someone what to do, e.g. *Stand with your feet about a foot apart.*

'-ing' clause An '-ing' clause is a non-finite clause beginning with the '-ing' form of a verb, e.g. *His wife did not like him **drinking so much**... You should consider **supplementing your diet with vitamins and minerals**.*

'-ing' form The '-ing' form of a verb is the form that ends with '-ing'. It is used, for example, to form continuous tenses, e.g. *I've been **thinking** about it*; to make an action nominal, e.g. ***Swimming** is good exercise*; and in complex verb groups, e.g. *I kept **trying** to change the subject.*

introductory it Introductory *it* functions as a 'dummy' Subject or Object in a sentence, without contributing to its meaning. It points forward to another clause in the sentence, e.g. *It is not clear who will get the money... He made it clear that he would not negotiate.* See Chapter 9, Sections 1 and 2.

link verb A link verb is a verb like *be, become,* or *seem* which needs to be followed by a Complement. The Complement describes the person or thing indicated by the Subject. See Chapter 5.

modal verb There are eleven modal verbs in English: *can, could, dare, may, might, must, need, shall, should, will,* and *would.* They are used to add meaning to a main verb, for example to indicate how certain or possible something is, or whether a course of action is recommended or allowed. See Chapter 11, Section 2. See also **phrasal modal**.

non-finite clause In a non-finite clause, the verb group does not include an indication of tense or modality, e.g. *I can just see him **swimming in clear blue water**.* Compare **finite clause**.

noun group A noun group may consist of just one noun, e.g. ***Children** roamed the streets.* Or the noun may have words before it, such as a determiner, adjective, or other modifier, e.g. *He and **the children** drove down to the beach... She was raising **two little children**;* or words after it, such as a prepositional phrase or a relative clause, e.g. ***Children under twelve** are half-price... **Children who eat with their parents** can choose from an adult menu.* A noun group functions as an element in the clause, such as Subject, Complement, or Object, or it comes after a preposition in a prepositional phrase. A noun group may also consist of a pronoun, e.g. ***They** were enjoying **themselves**... **He** didn't say **anything**.* It may be an amount, e.g. *Jack owes his mother **a lot**.*

Object An Object is a part of an active clause that refers to the person or thing that is involved in an action but does not perform the action, e.g. *I was eating **my dinner**... They painted **the outside of the house**.*

An Object is typically a noun group, but it may also be a non-finite clause, e.g. *I'd like **to see you**.* When an Object is a clause it indicates a situation or action.

An Object typically comes after the verb, but in questions it may be a wh-word and occur at the beginning of the clause, e.g. ***What** do you want?* See also the Appendix for information on Objects which do not follow verbs.

Some verbs have two Objects, e.g. *He gave **his girlfriend a diamond ring**.* The noun group *his girlfriend* in this example is often known as the 'Indirect Object', but we do not use this term. The second Object may be a noun group or a non-finite clause. If it is a noun group, this Object has a direct relationship with the Subject of the clause. For example, in the clause *John brought Mary some tea, some tea* is directly related to *John* (the Subject): *John* is responsible for the action of bringing it.

If the second Object is a clause, however, this Object has a direct relationship with the first Object. For example, in the clause *Mary asked John to bring her some tea*, there is a direct relationship between *John* (the Object) and *to bring her some tea*: *John* is again responsible for the action of bringing it.

See also **prepositional Object**.

Object Complement An Object Complement is a part of a clause that provides information about the Object. It tells you what the Object is, is called, or is thought to be, e.g. *I found this puzzling... My children called him **Uncle Frank**.* An Object Complement is typically a noun group or an adjective group, but it may also be an '-ed' clause, e.g. *I couldn't make myself **understood**.* See also **prepositional Object Complement**.

ordinal An ordinal is a word such as *first, last,* or *tenth*. It is used to indicate where something comes in a sequence.

particle 'Particle' is the term used to refer to adverbs or prepositions such as *in, on, up,* or *down* when they combine with verbs to form phrasal verbs, e.g. *I set **up** the computer... A car ran them **down**... I'll look **after** it for you.*

passive voice If a verb is in the passive voice, the Subject of the clause is affected by the action and is not responsible for it, e.g. *He **was given** a bone marrow transplant.*

personal pronoun The personal pronouns are *I, me, you, he, him, she, her, it, we, us, they,* and *them.* They are used to refer to people or things whose identity is clear.

phase When two verbs are in phase, they together form a complex verb group. This means that the actions or states expressed by the two verbs cannot be separated from each other. For example, if you *start crying,* the *starting* and the *crying* are not two processes, but one. See also **complex verb group**.

phrasal modal A phrasal modal is a phrase which forms a single verb group with another verb and which affects the meaning of that verb in the same way that a modal verb does, e.g. *I **have to** go... You're **bound to** like him.* See Chapter 11, Section 3.

phrasal verb A phrasal verb consists of a verb and one or more particles. Its meaning is different from that of the verb and the particle(s) taken separately. Phrasal verbs have patterns that are similar to those of ordinary verbs, except for the presence of the particle(s). Some examples of phrasal verbs are *back down, die out, look after,* and *put up with.* See also **Verb**.

plural noun group With some verbs, the noun group which comes before the verb or after the verb has to be plural. A plural noun group may consist of one noun group which indicates two or more people or things, e.g. *Combine **all the ingredients** in a pan.* Or it may consist of two or more co-ordinated noun groups, linked by *and,* e.g. ***Molly and Simon** were always arguing.*

prepositional Complement A prepositional Complement functions like an ordinary Complement, but it begins with a preposition. A prepositional Complement typically follows a link verb, e.g. *A small deserted house served **for a temporary prison**... His grief turned **to joy**.* A few verbs which are not link verbs are also followed by prepositional Complements, e.g. *The plane broke **into pieces**.* A prepositional Complement occasionally follows the Object of the clause, e.g. *He struck me **as young, vigorous, and interesting**.* A prepositional Complement typically consists of a preposition and a noun group or an adjective group, but it may also consist of a preposition and an '-ing' clause, e.g. *They struck me **as being a happy and united couple**,* or a preposition and an amount, e.g. *The unemployment rate peaked **at 17 percent**.*

prepositional Object A prepositional Object functions like an ordinary Object, but it begins with a preposition, e.g. *I apologized **to him**.* A prepositional Object sometimes follows another Object in a clause. In this case, either the order of the noun groups is reversible, as in *He has confused fact **with fiction**,* or the prepositional Object is what is traditionally known as an Indirect Object, as in *He gave the money **to his mother**.* A prepositional Object typically consists of a preposition and a noun group, but it may also consist of a preposition and an '-ing' clause, e.g. *She attributes her coping ability **to growing up in a large family**,* or a wh-clause, e.g. *They argued **about what to wear**.*

prepositional Object Complement A prepositional Object Complement functions like an ordinary Object Complement, but it begins with a preposition, e.g. *They chose her **as their representative**... He saw the question **as crucial**.* A prepositional Object Complement typically consists of a preposition and a noun group or an adjective group, but it may also consist of a preposition and an '-ing' clause, e.g. *The card identified him **as having brown hair and eyes**.*

prepositional phrase A prepositional phrase typically consists of a preposition and a noun group, e.g. *He dived **into the river**,* but it may also consist of a preposition and an adjective group, e.g. *She is described **as critically ill**;* an '-ing' clause, e.g. *They will work **towards removing the underlying causes of famine**;* or a wh-clause, e.g. *They are preparing to vote **on whether to begin a full investigation**.* A prepositional phrase typically indicates the circumstances of an action or event, for example, its time or place, its frequency, its degree, or the manner in which it occurs. Prepositional phrases which are part of verb patterns are either concerned with place or manner, e.g. *Place the mixture **in a saucepan**,* or they indicate a person or thing that is directly involved in the action or state indicated by the verb, e.g. *A practical program of reform must be based **on firm principles**.*

quote clause A quote clause gives the words that someone has said, written, or thought.

There are usually quotation marks round a quote clause, e.g. *'I don't want you to leave,'* he said.

reciprocal pronoun There are two reciprocal pronouns, *each other* and *one another*. They indicate that what one person or thing does to another, the other does to them, e.g. *They looked at one another... They hated each other*.

reciprocal verb A reciprocal verb indicates a process which two or more people, groups, or things are involved in mutually, for example, they do the same thing to each other or they take part jointly in the same action or event. Reciprocal verbs are used in patterns with a plural Subject, where the Subject indicates both people, groups, or things, e.g. *We argued about politics... The two leaders met in New York yesterday*. They are also used in patterns with a singular Subject indicating one person, group, or thing, in which case the other participant is mentioned in another part of the pattern, e.g. *I argued with Dick about the rules... I met him in Switzerland*.

reflexive pronoun The reflexive pronouns are *myself, yourself, himself, herself, itself, ourselves, yourselves,* and *themselves*, e.g. *The government will continue to dedicate itself to peace*.

Subject In an active clause, the Subject is the part of the clause that refers to the person or thing that does the action indicated by the verb, or that is in the state indicated by the verb, e.g. *The children have eaten all the biscuits... The brain consists of billions of nerve cells*.

In a passive clause, the Subject typically indicates the person or thing that is affected by an action, e.g. *The house has been restored*. It may be something that is in the state indicated by the verb, e.g. *Her mother was known to be a rich woman... This factory is comprised of just three rooms*.

The Subject is typically a noun group, but it may also be a wh-word, e.g. *What happened?*; a clause beginning with *what* or *all*, e.g. *What I need is some accurate information*; a non-finite clause, e.g. *Thinking about it makes me feel unhappy*; or, infrequently, a that-clause or wh-clause.

The Subject typically begins the clause, and comes before the verb, but in questions it may come after an auxiliary verb such as *do* or *have*, e.g. *Do you think he will make a good president?*

subjunctive The subjunctive form of a verb is in most cases the base form, used in certain clauses in place of the present or past tense, e.g. *I suggested that he call me Pinky*. The subjunctive of *be* is *were* or *be*, e.g. *If I were you I'd complain... Eleanor suggested that she be hired*.

that-clause A that-clause is a finite clause that follows a verb group or a noun group and often, though not always, begins with *that*, e.g. *She thought that he was heading west... Gertrude told him he would soon be a father*.

to-infinitive A to-infinitive is the base form of a verb preceded by *to*, e.g. *The number of victims continues to rise*. A passive to-infinitive form consists of *to be*, and the '-ed' form of a verb, e.g. *He refused to be silenced*.

to-infinitive clause A to-infinitive clause is a clause beginning with the to-infinitive form of a verb, e.g. *She persuaded him to leave the office... The President agreed to be interviewed the next day*.

Verb The Verb is the part of a clause that tells you, for example, what someone or something does or what happens to them. The Verb is a verb group, e.g. *Her husband was waiting for her*. Phrasal verbs consist of a verb group and a particle. Sometimes there is an Object between the verb group and the particle, in which case the Verb element is discontinuous. In the tables showing structures this is represented by the notation 'Verb... ...Verb'. Thus the example *Theresa told him off* is analysed as 'Subject Verb... Object ...Verb'.

verb group A verb group may consist of just one verb, e.g. *I went to Wales last year*; or it may also contain one or more auxiliaries, e.g. *I have been thinking about your offer*; a modal, e.g. *Colleges should provide needed information*; a phrasal modal, e.g. *I have to leave immediately*; or the negative form *not*, e.g. *Grace did not answer the question directly*. A verb group tells you, for example, what someone or something does or what happens to them.

wh-clause A wh-clause is a finite clause that begins with a wh-word, e.g. *I wondered why the children weren't home yet... I asked her whether I should inform the police... Where and how they got the capital is not recorded*. A wh-clause indicates that something is uncertain or unknown. Wh-clauses usually follow verb groups or noun groups, although they occasionally occur as the Subject of a clause.

In this book, we sometimes use the term 'wh-clause' as a general term covering both the finite clause and the non-finite wh-to-inf clause. See wh-to-inf clause.

when/if clause The term 'when/if clause' is used in Chapter 9, Sections 1 and 2 to indicate a finite clause beginning with *when* or *if* which is not a wh-clause because it does not indicate that something is uncertain or unknown. It refers to a situation that occurs, or may occur, e.g. *I used to like it when you came round for coffee and a game of cards*.

wh-to-inf clause A wh-to-inf clause is a non-finite clause that begins with a wh-word and a to-infinitive, e.g. *I still have not decided what to spend the money on*. Wh-to-inf clauses refer to something that is uncertain or unknown.

wh-word A wh-word is a word such as *what, why, whether, how,* or *if*.

Chapter 1: Simple Patterns

In this chapter we describe simple verb patterns. The simplest of these is **V**, where the verb can be used on its own. In all the other patterns, the verb is followed by one other element, such as a noun group, an '-ing' clause, or a that-clause. Patterns in which the verb is followed by a prepositional phrase or adverb group are described in Chapter 2.

1 V

The verb can be used on its own, without anything following it.

	Verb group	
Subject	Verb	Adjunct (optional)
The meeting	had ended.	
The amount of desert in the world	is increasing.	
She	laughed	softly.

Phrasal verbs: V P

	Verb group	Particle
Subject	Verb	
The subject	didn't come	up.
All the lights	went	off.
He	sat	down.

Many verbs are used with this pattern only when something involved in the action, apart from the Subject, has already been mentioned or indicated. For example, in the case of *refuse*, you need to have been told what someone refuses to do, as in *A colleague urged him to see a psychiatrist, but he <u>refused</u>*. Some verbs of this kind fit into one of the meaning groups below; the remainder are listed in section (ii) of the 'Verbs with other meanings' group.

Verbs with this pattern belong to the following meaning groups:

1 THE 'MOVE' GROUP	13 THE 'OPERATE' GROUP
2 THE 'TURN' GROUP	14 THE 'START' AND 'BREAK' GROUP
3 THE 'LEAVE' GROUP	15 THE 'BEGIN' AND 'STOP' GROUP
4 THE 'HANG AROUND' GROUP	16 THE 'OCCUR' GROUP
5 THE 'JOIN IN' GROUP	17 THE 'COME BACK' GROUP
6 THE 'COMPETE' GROUP	18 THE 'THINK' AND 'WATCH' GROUP
7 THE 'CARRY ON' GROUP	19 THE 'SPEAK' GROUP
8 THE 'BACK OUT' GROUP	20 THE 'CALL' GROUP
9 THE 'CHANGE' GROUP	21 THE 'RING' GROUP
10 THE 'BENEFIT' GROUP	22 THE 'LAUGH' GROUP
11 THE 'MATTER' GROUP	23 THE 'KNOCK' GROUP
12 THE 'SUCCEED' AND 'FAIL' GROUP	24 VERBS WITH OTHER MEANINGS

V is the second most frequent verb pattern in English. The lists below contain only verbs which are among the 500 most frequently occurring verbs in the Bank of English. A typical Subject is indicated in brackets where this is helpful.

Many verbs have the pattern **pl-n V** or **pl-n V P**, and are **reciprocal verbs**. These are described in Chapter 6 and are not included in this section.

1 THE 'MOVE' GROUP

These verbs are concerned with moving or being somewhere. This includes:

- moving in a particular direction e.g. *advance, back up*
- moving in a particular way e.g. *run*
- being in a particular position e.g. *lie around*
- arriving somewhere e.g. *arrive, land, show up*
- staying somewhere e.g. *remain, stay, stick around*
- ceasing to move e.g. *stop*
- part of something breaking off e.g. *break off, fall off*

With many of these verbs, for example *arrive* and *close in*, the place involved must have been mentioned or indicated.

*As they **advanced**, the boys beamed their flashlights in every direction.*

*She returned to the cabin. George **had** just **arrived**.*

*He found a part of the arrow that **had broken off**.*

*The Ancients went to bed when the sun **went down** and arose as the sun **rose**.*

*I don't smoke, so there are no dirty ashtrays **lying around** to upset her.*

*The elevator began to **move** again, but now it moved up.*

*Now that you've reminded me I guess I **can stick around** for four or five days longer.*

*The car slowed and **stopped**.*

The verbs *gather* and *spread out* always have a plural Subject.

*The forces **will** then **spread out**, securing roads and protecting food convoys to the interior.*

advance *1*	fall *1,3*	run *1,17,33*
appear *3*	fly *2,4,7,9*	set *2.18 (The sun)*
approach *1*	follow *1*	settle *8 (The dust)*
arrive *1,2,3*	freeze *6*	(not) show *12*
back *3.2*	gather *1*	sit *1*
charge *10*	be hanging *1*	slip *1,2*
climb *1,3*	jump *1,2*	spread *5,6*
be closing *3.0*	land *6,7,14*	stand *1,7*
collapse *3,4*	mount *5*	stay *1*
collect *4*	move *1,2*	stick *2.9*
come *1*	pass *1*	stop *5*
dance *1,3*	remain *2*	swim *1,4*
drop *4*	return *1*	travel *1*
emerge *1*	rise *1,2,3,6*	be waiting *3 (A car)*
enter *1*	rise *4 (The sun)*	walk *1*
back up *5,6,7*	come up *6 (The sun)*	go down *7 (A ship)*
bear down *1*	fall away *1 (Part of something)*	go out *1,9*
break in *1*	fall back *1,2*	go under *2*
break off *1 (Part of something)*	fall in *1*	hang back *1*
break through *1,3*	fall off *1 (Part of something)*	be hanging up ▷*1*
check in *1,2*	fall out *1 (Your hair)*	knock around/about *3*
close in *1*	get about *1,2*	lie around/about *1*
come along *1,3*	get around	move about
come down *2*	get in *4*	move along *1*
come in *1,2,6*	get out *2*	move in *1,2*
come through *3*	get up *2*	pass by
come up *1*	go down *6 (The sun)*	pour in

press on *2*	run around	stick around
pull in *1*	show up ▷*12*	touch down *(An aircraft)*
pull over *1*	sign in	turn back *1*
pull up *1,3*	spread out *1*	turn in *1*
push in	stand aside *1*	turn off *1*
push on	stand up ▷*1*	turn out *8*
report back *2*	stay in	turn up *1*
roll in *1,2*	stay on	
roll up *2*	stay out *1*	

2 THE 'TURN' GROUP

These verbs indicate that someone or something changes posture, arrangement, or orientation, but does not move from one place to another. This includes:

- turning
- opening and closing
- continually moving e.g. *beat, shake*
- moving a limb or limbs e.g. *hit out, kick*
- standing up and sitting down
- falling down

*Kelly's heart **was beating** so hard she could barely breathe.*

*When I saw him lying on the floor, I thought he **had** just **fallen over** and hit himself on the head.*

*A hand groped swiftly and expertly in his bush-jacket pocket; he **hit out** wildly.*

*At this moment the screen door **opened** and John McGinnis emerged.*

*Her eyes were full of fear, and her hand **shook** slightly as she ate.*

*He **stood up** and went to the door.*

*She **turned** and stared at him.*

*Ross hit the brakes but the car **turned over** and crashed into a tree.*

beat *3 (Your heart)*	fly *6 (Your hair)*	shake *4,7*	struggle *3*
beat *8 (A bird's wings)*	kick *3*	shut *1,3*	turn *1,3,4*
close *1.1,3*	move *2*	sit *2*	
drop *5,6*	open *1,3,4*	stand *2*	
fall *2*	relax *2 (Your muscles)*	stretch *3*	
fall down ▷*2*	hit out *1*	open out ▷*3*	stand up ▷*2*
fall over	kick out ▷*3*	ride up	stretch out *1*
get down *2*	lie back	sit down ▷*2*	turn around/round ▷*1,2*
get up *1*	lie down	sit up *1*	turn over *1,2*

3 THE 'LEAVE' GROUP

These verbs are concerned with leaving a place, position, or situation. We include here *want out*, which indicates that someone wants to escape from a situation. With these verbs, the place, position, or situation involved must usually have been mentioned or indicated.

*'**Go away**!' Erin shouted.*

*Menti shook hands with her and **left**.*

*The senator said Arnett had been in Vietnam after the US troops **pulled out**.*

*The rebels are trying to force the President to **resign**.*

disappear *1,2*	go *1.2,13,14*	resign *1*
escape *1,7*	leave *1,2,3*	retire *1,2,4,5*
flee	move *5*	withdraw *2,4,5*

3

back away 2	get out 1,3	move up 1	stand down
back off 1	go away 1,2	pull away 1,2	step down
break away 1,2	lift off	pull back 2	take off 1,3
break out 2,3	make off 7.0	pull out 1,2,3	walk away
check out 1	move away	push off	walk out 1,2
clear off	move off	run away 1,3	want out
clear out 1	move on 1	set forth 2	
get away 1,2,3,4	move out	set off 1	
get off 2	move over 2,3	set out 1	

4 THE 'HANG AROUND' GROUP

These verbs are concerned with waiting, not doing much, or not acting.

*We **hung around** for an hour as an endless stream of young people came in and out of the shop.*

*'**Hang on**,' Joe said. 'I'll get you a bag.'*

*Isn't air travel too important for governments to **stand by** while the industry collapses?*

*What kept him? I'**ve been waiting** for hours.*

wait 1,5			
hang about 1	hold off 1	sit by	wait in
hang around/round 1	hold on 3	stand back	wait up 2
hang on 1	lie around/about 2	stand by 1,2	
hang out 2	sit around/about	wait around/about	

5 THE 'JOIN IN' GROUP

These verbs are concerned with getting involved in an activity or situation. The activity or situation must usually have been mentioned or indicated.

*She got up to prepare supper. '**Can** I **help**?' asked Polly.*

*People soon stop talking when I **join in**.*

*Those who were fit and of fighting age hurried to **join up**.*

*People were asking him to **step in** and save the country.*

help 1			
come in 3	join in	jump in	stand in
help out	join up 1	move in 3	step in

6 THE 'COMPETE' GROUP

These verbs are concerned with being involved in a competition of some kind. The competition must usually have been mentioned or indicated.

*Boys, grades 5-12, and girls, grades 9-12, are eligible to **compete**.*

*He is 'highly unlikely' to be fit to **run** in Birmingham in 10 days' time.*

*A presidential election is due in March. The current President, who has ruled the islands for 15 years, has judged it wise not to **stand**.*

compete 3	play 2	stand 19
enter 6	run 2,3,8	swim 2

7 THE 'CARRY ON' GROUP

These verbs are concerned with continuing to do something, or doing something you have planned. The activity or project involved must have been mentioned or indicated.

*It is understood that although Jo was not seriously hurt, she was too shaken to **carry on**.*

*If you are thinking of selling at auction, here are some key terms and points to bear in mind before you **go ahead**.*

carry on *1*	go ahead *1*	push ahead
follow through	go on *1,9*	push on
get on *2*	press on *1*	struggle on

8 THE 'BACK OUT' GROUP

These verbs are concerned with not doing something you had planned or promised to do, or being reluctant to get involved in something. The activity or situation involved must have been mentioned or indicated.

*It's too late, we made a deal and we're exchanging documents, we **can't back out** now.*

*After a month of increasingly violent student demonstrations, the government has decided, once again, to **climb down**.*

*Barron invited her to accompany him to the Kempton races and she agreed. But she caught 'flu and had to **cry off**.*

*GA's new plan is aimed at galvanising potential buyers who **have been holding back** for fear of getting caught in the same net.*

back away *1*	back out	drop out *1,2*	pull back *1*
back down	climb down	hang back *2*	pull out *2*
back off *3*	cry off	hold back *1,5*	

9 THE 'CHANGE' GROUP

These verbs are concerned with changing. This includes:

- increasing and decreasing
- improving and deteriorating e.g. *improve, suffer*
- becoming older e.g. *age, grow up*
- undergoing a physical or chemical change e.g. *break down, cook, set*

*These substances **break down** in the liver to form toxins.*

*Through the 10 million years of human evolution, the Earth's climate **has changed** considerably.*

*It is worth knowing that many hotel and tour prices **drop** dramatically after 1 May.*

*He can't face the fact that we**'re growing up** and that we want to do our own thing.*

*The construction business appears to **be picking up**.*

*Then he saw the line was perfect, and he **relaxed**.*

*Place the pan under a hot grill for a further three or four minutes until the omelette **has set** and the top is golden.*

*Your home life **may suffer** because of work pressures.*

advance *2*	cook *2 (Food)*	grow *1,4,6,8,11,12*	set *2.17*
age *4*	decline *1*	improve *1,2,3*	slip *7*
break *24,25 (Your voice)*	develop *1,3,4,7,11*	increase *1*	stretch *8*
build *6,8 (A quality)*	divide *1*	lift *5*	suffer *5*
burn *4 (Fuel)*	drop *1,8*	mount *2,3*	turn *7 (The tide)*
burn *5 (Food)*	expand *1,2*	recover *3*	turn *20 (A game)*
burn *11 (Your skin)*	fail *6 (Your health)*	reduce *5*	vary *2*
change *3*	fall *5*	relax *1,4*	wear *7*
climb *4*	freeze *1*	rise *9,13,14,17*	

break down *4*	draw in *1 (The nights)*	go off *6 (Food)*	move up *2*
build up *▷6,▷8,1*	drop off *3*	go up *1*	pick up *11,12*
clear up *4 (The weather)*	fall apart *3*	grow out	rise up *▷1,▷2,▷13*
close up *2*	fall away *3*	grow up *1,2,3*	shoot up *1*
come along *4*	fall off *2*	be looking up *3*	spread out *2*
come down *1*	fill out *2*	mount up *▷3*	turn down *3*
die back	freeze over	move along *2*	wear down *1*
die down	go down *1*	move down	wear out *1*

10 THE 'BENEFIT' GROUP

These verbs indicate that something happens to the Subject or is done to the Subject. For example, if a city *falls*, it is captured by an enemy. This includes something being learned about, perceived, or found. For example, if news *gets out*, it becomes known; if the sun *comes out*, clouds move away from it and it becomes visible. We include here *wait*: if you say that something *can wait*, you mean you will not deal with it until later.

> *If subsidies and tariffs are removed, each country can specialise in those things it grows or makes best, and everybody **will benefit**.*
> *The veins in the liver **block up**, and all sorts of damage follows.*
> *The sun **came out** briefly, and then dipped behind the dull grey clouds again.*
> *A top-level security investigation has been mounted to find out how the news **got out**.*
> *When there is a demand, a product **will sell**.*

benefit *3*	fall *6 (A president)*	freeze *3 (A pipe)*	sell *4*
break *17 (News)*	fall *7 (A city)*	hang *5 (A criminal)*	be showing *15 (A film)*
clear *18 (A cheque)*	fall *22 (A wicket)*	mark *2 (A surface)*	suffer *4*
emerge *3,4*	fill *1 (A container)*	run *30 (A newspaper article)*	(can) wait *4*
block up	come up *7 (A court case)*	get out *4 (News)*	lose out
come along *3*	fill up *▷1*	go around *3 (A story)*	open up *▷12,2,5*
come back *1*	fly *10 (Rumours)*	go in *(The sun)*	show up *1*
come out *2 (A fact)*	freeze up	go out *6 (A message)*	slip through
come out *8 (The sun)*	get about *3 (News)*	go out *7 (A programme)*	turn up *2*
come up *2 (A topic)*	get around *3 (News)*	go up *2 (A new building)*	wash out *2 (A stain)*

11 THE 'MATTER' GROUP

These verbs indicate that someone or something has a particular quality or is in a particular state. This includes:

- having a particular shape e.g. *fall away*
- being judged to have a particular quality e.g. *appeal, matter*
- being able to do something e.g. *extend, keep*

> *Well, you're alive, and that's what **counts**.*
> *If you need a table which **extends** to accommodate extra guests, look for one with an extra leaf or slot-in extension.*
> *To the south the garden **falls away** in terraces to an ornamental lake.*
> *She **was getting on**, but she could still see straight, believe you me.*
> *My throat **hurts**.*
> *The house was run down but that **didn't matter**, she was out every night.*
> *What makes her **stand out** is her personality.*

appeal *6*	freeze *5*	lie *2.3*	show *6,7*
burn *2,9,12*	go *1.16,3.4*	list *5 (A ship)*	smoke *2*
carry *11 (Sound)*	help *2*	(not) matter *9*	suffer *1*
count *6,7*	hold *3.6*	pay *7 (A job)*	swim *5 (The room)*
(will) do *2.16*	hurt *2 (Part of your body)*	pay *9 (Crime)*	swim *6 (Your head)*
be expecting *5*	be hurting *7*	ring *1.5*	turn *6 (A road)*
extend *6 (A table)*	keep *18 (Food)*	rise *7 (Land)*	vary *1,2*
fit *1.7*	last *12*	shake *9 (Your voice)*	(will not) wash *7*

add up *2,3*	drop away *(Land)*	jump out
beat down *1 (The sun)*	fall away *2 (Land)*	stand out *1,2,3*
come through *2 (A quality)*	be getting on *5*	stick out *2*

12 THE 'SUCCEED' AND 'FAIL' GROUP

These verbs are concerned with being successful, failing, or coping. The Subject may be human or inanimate. We include here verbs such as *hold* and *fall down*, which indicate how successful an argument or theory is. We also include *go down 4*, *go up*, *move down*, and *move up*, which indicate that someone or something moves to a lower or higher rank.

With many of these verbs, for example *fail 1* and *succeed 1* (which have a human Subject), the action or thing involved must have been mentioned or indicated.

*Many are finding it difficult to **cope** because of unpaid wages and lost savings.*

*New business schools at Oxford and Cambridge promise fresh methods of management education. **Can** they **deliver**?*

*Joseph's return looks the only likely change from the team which **drew** at Sheffield United in midweek.*

*Other swimmers got him ashore, but attempts to revive him **failed**.*

*This model **falls down**, though, when we look for real examples of the application of scientific knowledge to commerce and industry.*

*The gamble **has paid off**. Ratings have shot up beyond all projections.*

*I've made a big effort to improve my discipline and, to a large extent, I think I**'ve succeeded**.*

*Didn't I tell you things **would work out**?*

have arrived *8*	hold *3.11 (An argument)*	pass *13*	survive *1,2*
cope *1,3*	lead *1.4*	qualify *1,4*	win *1*
deliver *2*	lose *1*	recover *1,2*	work *12*
draw *24*	manage *4*	be struggling *7*	
fail *1,2*	miss *2.1,2*	succeed *1,2,3*	
bear up	get through *7 (A law)*	move up *2*	
break through *2*	go down *3*	pass out *2 (A cadet)*	
catch up *1,2*	go down *4 (A team)*	pay off *3*	
come off *1*	go through *5 (A law)*	pull through	
come out *7 (A photo)*	go under *1*	sell out *2 (A performance)*	
fall behind *1,2*	go up *5 (A team)*	stand up *2 (Evidence)*	
fall down *2 (An argument)*	hang on *2*	take off *2*	
fall through	hold on *2*	take over *4*	
get ahead	hold up *6*	turn around/round *3*	
get by	hold up *▷11 (An argument)*	win out	
get in *1 (A political party)*	keep up *1,2,3,4*	win through	
get on *4*	(not) measure up	work out *4*	
get through *4,5,6*	move down		

13 THE 'OPERATE' GROUP

These verbs indicate that something such as a machine, substance, or organization functions.

*The drug **acts** by binding fats coming through the digestive tract.*

*The bomb **went off** as a police vehicle was passing nearby.*

*Keep away from the cutters when the machine **is running**.*

*In severe weather, railways often continue to **operate** when roads and airports are closed.*

act *7 (A force or substance)*	**meet** *6 (A committee)*	**run** *11,12,13,14,23*	**work** *11,13,16*
focus *5 (Your eyes)*	**operate** *1,3*	**sit** *7 (Parliament)*	
go *3.2*	**roll** *4 (Cameras)*	**take** *2.40 (A dye)*	
go off *2 (A bomb)*			

14 THE 'START' AND 'BREAK' GROUP

These verbs indicate that something such as a machine, object, or organization starts to function, or ceases to function or exist. We include here verbs indicating that someone dies.

*I was worried that the rope **might break**.*

*Many of the victims are students who died when their university building **collapsed**.*

*The green light **went out**. A red light **came on**.*

*She looked frail and tired. I hoped the tablets **would kick in** soon.*

*His new shop **opens** today at 659 Fulham Road.*

*Each year from then on he helped with the harvesting and sorting until he **passed away** in 1981.*

*They climbed into the van and, for once, the engine **started** at the first turn of the key.*

blow *1.11 (A fuse)*	**die** *1,2,4,5,9*	**give** *3.1*	**shut** *4*
blow *1.12 (A tyre)*	**disappear** *3*	**go** *1.19 (Your sight)*	**start** *6*
break *1,2,3,4*	**fail** *4,5*	**go** *1.20 (A light bulb)*	**stop** *4*
close *1.4,5*	**fall** *17 (Someone)*	**go** *1.21 (Someone)*	
collapse *1,2,5*	**fire** *1.6 (An engine)*	**open** *12,18,19*	
blow out *12 (A tyre)*	**close down** *5*	**go down** *8*	**pack up** *2*
blow up *1*	**come on** *6*	**go off** *4*	**pass away** *(Someone)*
break down *1*	**cut out** *7*	**go on** *11*	**pass on** *3 (Someone)*
break up *1,3,4,5*	**fall apart** *1,2*	**go out** *4 (A light)*	**run down** *5*
burn down	**fall down** *▷2*	**go up** *3*	**shut down**
burn up *1*	**give out** *3*	**kick in**	**start up** *▷6*

15 THE 'BEGIN' AND 'STOP' GROUP

These verbs are concerned with beginning or stopping. They can be divided into two groups.

(i) Verbs with inanimate Subjects. This includes:

- events or situations beginning or ending e.g. *begin, finish*
- natural or abstract things coming into existence or disappearing e.g. *clear, develop*
- a type of thing coming into existence or disappearing e.g. *appear, die out*

*That year the first illustrated weekly **appeared** in London.*

*The talks **began** on Monday and continued late into Tuesday evening.*

*The fog **cleared** and the sun came out.*

*After the 18th treatment the symptoms **disappeared** completely.*

*Senior officials have said that oil supplies **will run out** at the end of the week.*

*The rain **had stopped**.*

*The initial euphoria **may wear off** quickly, however.*

appear *4,5*	**break** *26 (A storm)*	**emerge** *5*	**form** *3,9,10*
arrive *4,7*	**clear** *12 (Fog)*	**end** *2,5,11*	**lift** *11 (Fog)*
begin *2*	**develop** *2,8*	**fail** *9 (Your courage)*	**open** *20,23,26*
break *21 (Day)*	**die** *6 (An emotion)*	**fall** *17 (Night)*	**start** *2*
break *22 (A wave)*	**disappear** *3*	**finish** *3*	**stop** *3*

blow over	clear up 3	go out 5 (A fire)	set in
blow up 3 (A storm)	come on 4,7	kick off 2	wear away
break down 2	come out 1 (A new product)	let up	wear off
break off 2	die away (A sound)	run out 2,3	
break out 1,4	die out	sell out 3	

(ii) Verbs with human Subjects. This includes:

- starting or stopping in general e.g. *start over, stop*
- starting or stopping doing a particular kind of thing e.g. *shut up, strike up*

With verbs concerned with starting or stopping in general, the activity involved must have been mentioned or indicated.

*We'll never **finish** in time.*

*She **rang off** and Devlin replaced the receiver.*

***Shut up** and let me think, can't you?*

*So how can I quit and **start over** in another profession?*

*Just as we had finally fallen asleep, a street band **struck up** and firecrackers exploded on every corner.*

begin 1	start 1		
finish 1	stop 1,7		
get off 4	kick off 1	leave off 2	sign on
give over	knock off 4	ring off	start over
give up 1,2	lay off 2	shut up	strike up 2 (A band)
hang up 2	lead off 2	sign off 2	switch off 2

16 THE 'OCCUR' GROUP

These verbs indicate that something exists or happens. This includes:

- sounds and natural phenomena occurring e.g. *blow, play*
- something continuing to exist or happen e.g. *last*
- something being about to occur e.g. *approach, threaten*
- time passing e.g. *go by, wear on*

We also include here *be lacking*, which indicates that something does not exist.

*Evening **was approaching**.*

*Tonight the Palace was dark and a bitter wind **blew**.*

*They're not in a position to go back to their homes because their homes no longer **exist**.*

*But as the hours **went by**, they began to grow anxious.*

*'What's **going on**?' demanded Bunbury.*

*There had been a gentleness in Lonnie that **was lacking** in his twin brother.*

*The Loire Valley was beautiful, but Janet's contentment **didn't last**.*

*The accident **occurred** when the south-bound Number Four train on the Lexington Avenue line jumped the rails as the train switched tracks.*

*There was music **playing** on a lower floor.*

approach 6	continue 2,4	obtain 2	return 6
arrive 5	exist 1,2	occur 1	run 33 (A play)
be 2.8	grow 2 (Plants)	pass 9 (Time)	stand 5,12
blow 1.1 (The wind)	happen 1,2	play 12 (Music)	strike 6
burn 1 (A fire)	hold 3.9,10,12,13	remain 3	survive 3
burn 8 (A light)	be lacking 2	repeat 6	threaten 3
come 9	last 11	result 3	

beat down 2 *(The rain)*	come up 4,5	go by 1 *(Time)*	open up 3 *(An opportunity)*
close in 3.2	be coming up 3	go on 2,3,4	ring out *(A shot)*
come about	draw on 2 *(The evening)*	go up 4 *(A cheer)*	rise up ▷15 *(A cheer)*
come along 3	go ahead 2	last out ▷13	wear on *(Time)*
come around 3	go before 1	live on ▷1.6,2	

17 THE 'COME BACK' GROUP

These verbs indicate that a type of thing becomes popular or stops being popular. We include here *date*, which indicates that something comes to be regarded as old-fashioned.

*Tight trousers **are coming back**.*

*Liz has come up with some original eye-stopping designs that **won't date** and are super comfortable.*

date 6	
catch on 2	come in 4
come back 2	go out 8

18 THE 'THINK' AND 'WATCH' GROUP

These verbs are concerned with thinking, perceiving, and paying attention. The thing or matter involved must usually have been mentioned or indicated.

*'Are you going to the Christmas lunch? Or are you going to come straight back?' 'We **haven't decided** yet.'*

*Passers-by **looked on** aghast as the driver mowed her down.*

*Mack smiled, but she **didn't notice**.*

*She pauses and **thinks** for a moment.*

*If the players are interesting, people **will** turn out and **watch**.*

agree 1	hope 1	notice 1	see 1,4
believe 3	judge 3	observe 1	stare 1
care 1,2	know 1	realize 1	think 4
concentrate 1	listen 1,2,3	recall 1,2	watch 1.1,3
decide 1	look 1.1,3	reflect 4	wonder 1
follow 15	(not) mind 2.1	remember 1	worry 1
hear 1	mind 2.2	(cannot) remember 3	
catch on 1	look ahead	look round	
listen in	look back	sit up 4	
listen out ▷2	look on	think back	

19 THE 'SPEAK' GROUP

These verbs are concerned with saying something. The thing or matter involved must usually have been mentioned or indicated. We include here *break in* and *cut in*, which indicate that someone interrupts someone else.

*Arvo **cut in** swiftly. 'I know about quite a lot of things but I don't always talk about them.'*

*It matters more than you realize. Let me **explain**.*

*More companies than we know about get stung, but they are usually too embarrassed to **own up**.*

*'This is your last chance,' her father said. Erin **didn't reply**.*

*He never **spoke** unless he was spoken to.*

accept *1*	comment *1*	lie *2.2*	shout *1*
accuse *1*	complain *1*	promise *1*	sing *1*
agree *1,2*	conclude *2*	propose *6*	speak *1,2*
answer *1,4,6*	continue *5*	refuse *1*	talk *1,2,3,7,8,9*
argue *3*	decline *2*	reply *1*	tell *7*
(not) argue *6*	explain *1,2*	report *1*	
ask *1*	finish *6*	respond *1*	
begin *4*	insist *1*	order *2.5*	
answer back	fire away	open up	sound off
ask around	go on *7*	own up	speak out
break in *2*	hit back *2*	report back *1*	speak up *1,2*
carry on *3*	hit out *2*	shout out	strike back
cut in	let on	sign off *1*	talk back

20 THE 'CALL' GROUP

These verbs are concerned with visiting, phoning, or writing to someone. The person involved must have been mentioned or indicated.

Just before school closed yesterday afternoon two policemen in plain clothes __had called__.

In the evenings Beatty __would drop by__ to dine with her or take her out for a drive.

Hoffman said he __would ring back__ at 4 p.m.

'I'__ll write__,' he promised.

call *4,10*	ring *1.1*	write *5*	
reply *1*	visit *1*		
call back	drop by	ring in	stop off
call in *2*	drop in	ring round	write back
call up *1*	look in	ring up ▷*1*	write in *1*
come around *1*	ring back	stop by	write off *1*

21 THE 'RING' GROUP

These verbs indicate that something makes a sound.

When the final whistle __blew__, a lot of fans came onto the pitch.

Well, when the alarm __went off__, everyone ran for the door.

She could hear a record __playing__.

Davin pressed the button and heard a bell __ring__ inside.

beat *4*	knock *6* (Pipes)	ring *1.2,3*	strike *18* (A clock)
blow *1.6*	play *11* (A musical instrument)	sing *2*	
go *3.3*	play *12* (A record)	sound *1.5*	
go off *3*			

22 THE 'LAUGH' GROUP

These verbs indicate that someone makes a sound or puts on an expression, or that someone's body does something involuntarily.

If you find it hard to __drop off__ at night but are wary of sleeping pills, this could be the answer.

He launched into a fine imitation of Joan when she is nagging. We both __laughed__.

Then they both drank so much that they __passed out__ in their hotel.

She __smiled__ weakly.

cry *1*	laugh *1*	run *24 (Your nose)*	smile *1*
jump *5*	roll *9 (Your eyes)*	sleep *2*	start *7*
break down *5*	cry out	get off *5*	
come around *4*	drop off *2*	pass out *1*	
come to	fall about	throw up *1*	

23 THE 'KNOCK' GROUP

These verbs are concerned with hitting, holding, or exerting force on something. The thing involved must have been mentioned or indicated.

*Jupe caught his arm and **held on**.*

*Erin stopped outside Room 13 and **knocked**.*

*Wheeler clenched his jaw, caught Baker's shirt under the neck and **pulled** with all his strength, dragging Baker back from the edge.*

kick *1*	pull *1*
knock *1*	push *1*
bear down *2*	hit back *1*
hang on *4*	hold on *1*

24 VERBS WITH OTHER MEANINGS

There are many other verbs with this pattern. They can be divided into three groups.

(i) Verbs where something else involved in the action does not need to have been mentioned or indicated already. This includes:

- everyday activities e.g. *dress, wash*
- ways of earning a living e.g. *act, teach*

The Subject usually indicates a human being.

*At 16, she failed to graduate, left school and announced to her family that she wanted to **act**.*

*I **blew up** sometimes, told him to shut up, 'cause he was so nasty.*

*From an early age he loved to **draw** and **paint**.*

*Rupert Welch **scored** twice for Southgate.*

*But before you **sell up** and move, you should look long and hard at your hopes and motives.*

*Members of the third group have a tendency to **show off**, to dramatize almost every situation.*

*I unpacked my small case, **washed** and **changed**.*

*I got up early every morning and went to work and **worked** hard all day.*

act *1,8*	dress *3*	negotiate *1*	settle *2,6*
advertise *1*	drink *2*	operate *4*	shoot *2,9*
blow *1.3*	drive *1*	pack *1*	smoke *3*
break *13*	earn *1*	paint *3,4*	strike *2 (Workers)*
breed *3*	feed *3,4*	perform *3*	strike *7 (A criminal)*
change *5,9*	fight *4,9*	play *1,13*	struggle *1*
clean *5*	fire *2.1*	read *1,3*	teach *3*
conduct *5*	fish *3,5*	ride *1*	trade *2*
cook *1*	hide *2*	rise *18 (A people)*	train *2.1,3*
count *1*	hold *3.4*	run *26 (Dye)*	wash *2*
demonstrate *3*	indicate *6 (A driver)*	save *2*	work *1,3*
direct *11*	lay *1.5 (Hens)*	score *1,12*	write *1,3*
draw *1*	mix *6*	serve *6,8,11*	

act up *1,2*	come forward	play up *2,3*	slip up
add up ▷*2*	come out *3*	rise up ▷*18*	step back
blow up *4*	dress down *1*	sell out *4,5*	stay out *2 (Strikers)*
carry on *4*	dress up *1*	sell up	strike out *1,2,4*
cast off *2*	fight back *1*	settle down *1,2,4*	sweep up
change down	give in *1,2*	settle in	(cannot) turn back *2*
change up	move on *3*	settle up	turn over *6*
clean up *1*	pack up *1*	shoot up *2*	walk out *3 (Workers)*
clear away	pay out *2 (An insurance policy)*	show off *1*	wash up *1,2*
clear up *1*	pay up	sit up *3*	watch out
come around *2*	play around *1,3*	sleep around	work out *7*

(ii) Verbs where something else involved in the action must have been mentioned or indicated already.

The Subject usually indicates a human being.

*I actually went and had a look round the school, but I didn't particularly like the people and I decided I wasn't going to **apply**.*

*We are prepared to **attack**, if necessary, tomorrow.*

*Oh God. Patients' records are sacrosanct. Hilde will go berserk when she **finds out**.*

*For Kirston it was very definitely a relief to be away from her old school where she felt she really **didn't fit in**.*

*When the police **investigated** they could find no one among the neighbours who had noticed anything wrong.*

*Suppose we meet somewhere for a drink? I**'ll pay**.*

*I went to Dent's to get some more books 'cos I**'ve run out**.*

The verbs *demand* and *go around* have this pattern mainly in one fairly fixed phrase, as shown in the examples below.

*She could be very charming **when the occasion demanded**.*

*The food queues have become a daily occurrence across the country. There is never **enough to go round** and tempers are frayed.*

apply *1,3*	contribute *1,2*	move *3*	sell *1*
attack *1,5*	count *2*	pass *21*	sign *7*
attend *1,2*	defend *3*	pay *1,5,10*	stick *2.7 (A name)*
belong *10*	demand *2*	prepare *2*	stick *2.8 (A charge)*
bother *1*	dominate *1,2*	publish *2*	sweep *1*
cast *9*	drink *1*	qualify *2,3*	switch *2*
celebrate *1*	eat *1*	receive *5*	tell *9 (The strain)*
charge *1*	follow *4,6,7,13*	repeat *5*	try *1*
check *1*	hurt *4,5*	reply *3 (A team)*	vote *5*
choose *1,2*	investigate	respond *1*	
claim *9*	lead *1.1*	rule *5*	
compete *1*	learn *1*	search *1*	
change over	find out *1*	lock up *3*	sing along
check up *1*	fit in *2,3*	miss out *1*	strike back
cut back	go around *4*	move over *1*	switch off *1*
cut down *1*	go without	play along	switch on
do without *1*	hit back *2*	run out *1*	switch over ▷*2,1*
drink up	hold out *2,3,4*	sell out *1*	take over *3*

(iii) Verbs where the other thing or person involved is unspecified or general. For example, if people want to *adopt*, they want to adopt an unspecified child; people who *steal* take things in general.

Some of the verbs in the previous lists sometimes have this meaning, especially when they are used in the present tense or in the to-infinitive form. The verbs listed here are ones which frequently have this meaning.

> He could build a two-story addition to the rear of the house, providing he **didn't add on** at ground level.
> Under the present law only married couples or single people are allowed to **adopt**.
> '**Have** you **eaten** yet?' 'Yes, thanks. I had dinner on the road.'
> Her book analyses why women **kill** and how the law treats them.

adopt *2*	(can) hear *1*	learn *1*	sell *5*
eat *3*	injure	marry *1*	share *7*
be dating *10*	invest *2*	please *5*	steal *1*
deliver *1*	kill *1*	(can) see *1*	study *1*
add on *3*			

Structure information

a) This structure has no passive.

b) The phrasal verb pattern is the same except that there is a particle, P, which comes after the verb.

2 V n

The verb is followed by a noun group. The passive pattern is **be V-ed**.

This pattern has three structures:

▶ Structure I: Verb with Complement
He was my friend.
▶ Structure II: Verb with Object
The thieves broke a window.
▶ Structure III: Verb with Adjunct
Children don't talk that way.

Structure I: Verb with Complement

V n

	Verb group	noun group
Subject	**Verb**	**Complement**
My husband	is	a doctor.
He	can leave	a free man.
I	won't play	the hypocrite.

Verbs with this structure belong to the following meaning groups:

I.1　THE 'BE' GROUP
I.2　THE 'BECOME' GROUP
I.3　THE 'SEEM' GROUP

I.1 THE 'BE' GROUP

These verbs indicate that a person or thing is something. They are all **link verbs** (see Chapter 5). We include here verbs such as *comprise 2* and *make up*, where the Subject indicates the parts, members, or elements of something, and *comprise 1*, where the Complement indicates the parts of something.

> That story *is a good example of Crane's greatness as a writer*.
> How many players *comprise a team* in netball?
> The information pack *comprises 15 single sheets*, each devoted to a separate subject.
> The proposal said the expanded brigade *could form the nucleus of a European army*.
> Do you think he*'d make a good president*?
> French President François Mitterrand said the treaty *represented a major breakthrough in disarmament and arms control*.

The verbs *form 6* and *represent* have the passive pattern **be V-ed by n**. The verbs *comprise 2* and *compose* have the passive pattern **be V-ed of n**. The verb *constitute* has two passives: **be V-ed by n** and **be V-ed of n**. The phrasal verb *make up* has the passive pattern **be V-ed P of n**.

> The brain *is composed of billions of nerve cells called neurons*.
> The Chinese character for 'wise leader' *is made up of three symbols*.

Note that because *comprise 1* and *comprise 2* represent the relationship between a whole and its parts in opposite ways, the active of *comprise 1* and the passive of *comprise 2* have the same meaning.

> The flat *comprised a sitting room, bedroom, kitchen and bathroom*.
> This factory *is comprised of just three rooms*.

be *2.1*	constitute *1,2*	prove *1*	stay *3*
compose *1*	form *6,7*	remain *1*	
comprise *1,2*	make *4.1*	represent *5*	

V n P and V P n (not pron)

make up *1*

I.2 THE 'BECOME' GROUP

These verbs indicate that a person or thing becomes something. They are all **link verbs** (see Chapter 5).

> She eventually gave up her job and *became a full-time singer*.
> After about 10-15 minutes, the police quietly began *forming a line across the road*.

In the case of *turn*, the noun group is always singular but without a determiner.

> Both *turned informer* and were the main prosecution witnesses in the trial of the other men.

become *1*	make *4.2*
form *3*	turn *15*

I.3 THE 'SEEM' GROUP

These verbs indicate that a person or thing seems to be something. The verb *feel* indicates how someone seems to themselves. They are all **link verbs** (see Chapter 5).

> For the first year after the divorce I *felt a real failure*.

15

*He **seems** a reasonable man.*

*That **sounds** a good idea.*

appear *1,2*	look *2.1*	sound *8*
feel *1*	seem *1*	

I.4 THE 'ACT' GROUP

These verbs indicate that someone behaves like a kind of person they are not. They are both **link verbs** (see Chapter 5). The noun group after the verb always begins with *the*.

*The more the parents **act** the boss, the less control they seem to have and the more miserable they are.*

act *5*	play *9*

I.5 THE 'DEPART' GROUP

These verbs are concerned with living, dying, or leaving somewhere. The Complement describes the condition or situation of the Subject during his or her life or at the time of dying or leaving. This is a productive use. The verbs listed here are the ones which are most frequently used in this way.

*Lloyd **departed** a shaken man.*

*It is better to fight and run away than to **die** a hero.*

depart *1*	leave *1*	retire *1*
die *1*	live *2*	

Structure information: Verb with Complement

a) The noun group is the Complement.

b) Only a few verbs are used in the passive, as indicated in meaning group I.1 above. The prepositional phrase ***by*** n or ***of*** n is the prepositional Complement.

c) There is only one phrasal verb with this structure, *make up*. The active patterns are **V P n (not pron)** and **V n P**. The passive pattern is *be* **V-ed P** *of* n.

Structure II: Verb with Object

Active voice: V n

		Verb group	noun group
	Subject	Verb	Object
I		fear	no-one.
A number of insurgent groups		have formed	an alliance.
Uniformed police on motor cycles		headed	the procession.

Passive voice: *be* V-ed

	Verb group	
Subject	Verb	Adjunct (optional)
She	had been freed	on humanitarian grounds.
This venue	is directly funded	by the City Council.

Phrasal verbs

Active voice: V n P, V P n, V P P n

	Verb group	noun group	Particle
Subject	Verb...	Object	...Verb
	Eat	the biscuits	up.
A car	ran	them	down.

	Verb group	Particle	noun group
Subject	Verb		Object
We	must close	up	the house.
I	was gaining	on	him.
I	set	up	the computer.

	Verb group	Particle	Particle	noun group
Subject	Verb			Object
Albert	is coming	up	to	his 30th birthday.
The food	lives	up	to	the restaurant's reputation.

Passive voice: *be* V-ed P

		Verb group	Particle	
Subject		Verb		Adjunct (optional)
The photos		must have been blown	up.	
Thousands of operations		are carried	out	each year.

Most phrasal verbs have the patterns **V n P** and **V P n (not pron)**. That is, the noun group comes either between the verb and the particle or after the particle. If the noun group comes after the particle, it cannot be a personal pronoun. You say

He **<u>filled</u> it <u>up</u>**
or He **<u>filled up</u> the barrel**

but you do not say *He filled up it*.

However, some phrasal verbs have the pattern **V P n** only. That is, the noun group comes after the particle and it is sometimes a personal pronoun. You say

He **<u>went without</u> his lunch**
or He **<u>went without</u> it**.

The two kinds of phrasal verbs are shown separately in the lists below.

Verbs with this structure cover a very wide range of meanings. There are also many types of relationship between the verb and the noun group. The meaning groups in this section are grouped into larger groups, each showing one kind of relationship between the verb and the noun group:

II.1   THE 'KILL', 'EAT', AND 'FIX' GROUPS: concrete actions which change or affect the thing indicated by the noun group.
The soldiers destroyed the building.

II.2   THE 'BRING', 'BUY', AND 'OPERATE' GROUPS: concrete or abstract actions which involve moving something, physically or metaphorically.
He sold his books.

II.3   THE 'COVER', 'FOLLOW', AND 'RECORD' GROUPS: concrete actions which do not change, move, or affect the thing indicated by the noun group.
They recorded the bird's song.

II.4   THE 'BUILD' GROUP: concrete actions which create the thing indicated by the noun group.
They built a large tower.

II.5   THE 'CHANGE', 'CONCERN', AND 'ARRANGE' GROUPS: abstract actions which change or affect the thing indicated by the noun group.
They increased the price.

II.6   THE 'WATCH', 'BREAK A RECORD', AND 'APPROVE' GROUPS: abstract actions which do not affect the thing indicated by the noun group.
She watched her favourite television programme.

II.7   THE 'FORM' GROUP: abstract actions which create the thing indicated by the noun group.
She established a hostel for battered wives.

II.8   THE 'START' AND 'STOP' GROUP: starting, finishing, or doing an action in a particular way.
They abandoned the climb.

II.9   THE 'DO' AND 'TAKE', 'TURN A CORNER', AND 'OPEN YOUR EYES' GROUPS: concrete and abstract actions expressed by the verb and the noun group together.
I had a bath.

II.10   THE 'FACE', 'TAKE THREE DAYS', AND 'SEE' GROUPS: relations of place and time expressed by the verb and the noun group together.
The meeting lasted an hour.

II.11   THE 'TOP', 'DEVELOP', AND 'INCLUDE' GROUPS: qualities or roles of the Subject expressed by the verb and the noun group together.
The child developed several bad habits.

II.12   THE 'SHOW', 'ALLOW', AND 'IDENTIFY' GROUPS: logical relations between the Subject and the Object.
The experiments confirm our theory.

II.13   THE 'HEAR', 'INTEREST', AND 'GIVE AN IMPRESSION' GROUPS: thoughts, feelings, and perceptions.
They heard a loud cry.

II.14   THE 'SAY', 'DESCRIBE', AND 'CALL' GROUPS: acts of communication.
I asked three questions.

V n is by far the most frequent verb pattern in English. The lists below contain only verbs which are among the 400 most frequently occurring verbs in the Bank of English. A typical Object is indicated in brackets where this is helpful.

Not all the verbs with this structure are used in the passive. Verbs which never or rarely occur in the passive are indicated with * in the lists below.

II.1 THE 'KILL', 'EAT', AND 'FIX' GROUPS

These verbs are concerned with a concrete action or event which changes or affects the person or thing indicated by the Object. They can be divided into eight groups:

(i)   The 'kill' group
(ii)   The 'touch' group
(iii)   The 'eat' group
(iv)   The 'prepare' group
(v)   The 'fix' group
(vi)   The 'change' group
(vii)   The 'feed' group
(viii) The 'protect' group

(i) The 'kill' group

These verbs are concerned with harming, breaking, attacking, or destroying something or someone. We include here *abandon*, which indicates that someone is harmed by being left by someone.

Wobbly teeth in unsound gums are as much of a problem in adults as tooth decay. Toxins that **attack** *the connective tissue and bone which support the teeth are to blame.*

When I **broke** *my left leg, I went to the gym for rehabilitation.*

He **filled in** *the hole the mine had left and resumed his search.*

Summoned by his wife to remove a large, agile fly from the bathroom, Mr. Kiam admits to a frustrating time. 'It finally lit on the door and I **got** *it.'*

One civilian and one soldier **were killed***.*

Suddenly some ruffians **laid into** *him and left the poor soul half dead.*

In all, 18 warships, 187 aircraft and 2,400 servicemen **were lost** *in an attack lasting no more than two hours.*

The dog almost **pulled** *the fence* **down** *to reach him.*

I certainly feel stiff, as if I **have been worked over** *by a few toughs.*

The phrasal verb *hit back* has the pattern **V n P** only.

*If somebody hits you you***'ve got to hit** *them* **back***, haven't you?*

abandon 1 *(a child)*	**fell** 2 *(a tree) (usu passive)*	**injure**
attack 1,3	**fell** 3 *(a person)*	**jump** 8 *(a person)*
attack 5 *(the opponent's goal)*	**fight** 3,4 *(an army)*	**kill** 1,7
beat 1,2,4,7	**fight** 5 *(a person)*	**kill** 4 *(pain)*
bind 3,4	**fight** 9 *(a boxer)*	**lose** 12 *(usu passive)*
blow 1.11 *(a fuse)*	**fill** 3	**miss** 2.1
blow 1.12 *(a tyre)*	**force** 5 *(a lock)*	**oppose** *(a person)*
break 1,2,3,4,16	**get** 2.15 *(an animal)*	**reject** 5 *(a transplanted organ)*
burn 3,5,6,11,12	**hang** 5 *(a criminal)*	**remove** 3 *(a stain)*
cut 1,2,3	**hit** 1 *(something deliberately)*	**shoot** 1 *(a person or animal)*
destroy 1	**hit** 2 *(something by accident)*	**strike** 3,4 *(a person or thing)*
destroy 3 *(an animal) (usu passive)*	**hurt** 1,4	**strike** 19 *(words)*

V n P and **V P n (not pron)**

beat out 2 *(a fire)*	**burn off** 2 *(waste)*	**eat away**
beat up *(a person)*	**burn up** 1	**fight off** 2 *(an enemy)*
blow out 1 *(a flame)*	**cross off** *(words)*	**fill in** ▷3 *(a hole)*
blow up 1 *(a building)*	**cross out** *(words)*	**finish off** 2 *(an injured animal)*
break down 4 *(a substance)*	**cut down** 2 *(a tree)*	**hit back** 1
break down 6 *(a door)*	**cut up** 1	**kill off** 2
break up 1 *(something whole)*	**do in** *(a person)*	**lay out** 6 *(a person)*
bring down 2 *(an aeroplane)*	**do over** 2 *(a place)*	**let down** 3 *(a tyre)*
burn down *(a building)*	**do over** 3 *(a person)*	**pick off** *(people or aircraft)*

pull down *(a building)*	**shoot down** *1 (an aeroplane)*	**take out** *4 (an enemy)*
push over	**shoot down** *2 (a person)*	**wear away**
put down *5 (an animal)*	**strike down** *1 (a person)*	**wear down** *1*
put out *2 (a fire)*	**strike out** *▷19 (words)*	**wear out** *1*
run down *4 (a pedestrian)*	**take apart** *1 (something whole)*	**work over** *(a person)*
run over *(a pedestrian)*	**take down** *2 (a structure)*	**write off** *4 (a vehicle)*
shake down *(a victim)*	**take on** *5 (an opponent)*	

V P n and **V P P n**

beat up on *(a person)*	**lay into** *(a person)*
go for *3 (a person)*	**set upon** *(a person) (usu passive)*

(ii) The 'touch' group

These verbs are concerned with touching something. We include here *avoid*, which indicates that something is not touched, and *get off*, which is used to tell someone to stop touching you.

> I **felt the blankets**, estimated their warmth.

> Thousands of birds died because they **could not get at** their normal prey in water covered with a layer of ice.

> The thieves **did not touch** the other paintings.

avoid *4 (a vehicle)*	**hit** *3 (a target)*	**press** *2*	**touch** *1,2,4*
feel *5 (an object)*	**hold** *1.3 (a person)*	**press** *3 (a button)*	**(not) touch** *6 (a person or thing)*
handle *8*	**meet** *14 (an object)**	**(can) reach** *4*	

V P n

get at *1*	**get off** *4*

(iii) The 'eat' group

These verbs are concerned with consuming something, or not consuming something.

> Astronauts **burn up** a lot of calories just moving because they work hard against the pressurised suits.

> The children went in, and **ate the biscuits**.

> She made a brief attempt to give up smoking, but was said to **be getting through** 30 cigarettes a day.

> Princess Anne **won't touch** alcohol, even at official functions, and toasts her mother in mineral water.

> The waters of the River Ural **have been used up** by numerous industrial enterprises.

burn *4 (fuel)*	**have** *2.2 (food)**	**(not) touch** *7 (food or drink)*
drink *1 (liquid)*	**leave** *11 (food)*	**use** *1.2 (a supply of something)*
eat *1,2 (food)*	**take** *2.35 (food)*	**use** *1.3 (drugs)*

V n P and **V P n (not pron)**

burn off *1 (energy)*	**eat up** *1 (food)*	**get down** *4 (food)*	**take in** *7 (air or food)*
burn up *2 (fuel)*	**finish off** *1 (food)*	**keep down** *3 (food)*	**use up** *2 (a supply of something)*
drink up *(liquid)*	**finish up** *2 (food)*	**shoot up** *2 (heroin)*	

V P n

> **get through** 3 *(a supply of something)*

(iv) The 'prepare' group

These verbs are concerned with preparing something for use.

> The battery **can** even **be charged**, without having to take it out.
> **Cook** *the spring onions and mushrooms* until soft.
> I **used to make** my own bed **up** when I was at school.
> **Prepare** *the salad ingredients*, but do not mix the salad until about 20 minutes before it is to be served.
> I have had no difficulty in operating my VCR since I discovered that the technicians who **set** it **up** had done so incorrectly.

charge 11 *(a battery)*	**fire** 1.5 *(a pot)*	**prepare** 3 *(food)*	**work** 24,25 *(clay or metal)*
cook 2 *(food)*	**fix** 22 *(a dye or photograph)*	**sign** 6 *(a document)*	
develop 12 *(photographs)*	**lay** 1.2 *(the table)*	**sort** 3 *(laundry)*	
dress 9 *(meat)*	**make** 1.7 *(a bed)*	**turn** 24 *(wood)*	

V n P and V P n (not pron)

blow up 2 *(a tyre)*	**lay out** 4 *(a corpse)*	**set up** 3 *(a machine)*
break in 4 *(something new)*	**make up** 8 *(a bed)*	
charge up ▷11 *(a battery)*	**put on** 6 *(food)*	

(v) The 'fix' group

These verbs are concerned with mending something that is not in good condition. We include here *bring round* and *bring to*, which indicate that an unconscious person is returned to consciousness.

> Ralph told me, after I'd passed out and he'**d brought** me **round**, that I'd taken off my shoes and danced on the table.
> Mechanics took time off from building racing cars to **fix** the broken axle.
> The house **had been** lovingly **restored** by a builder three years earlier, using only the best materials.

fill 12 *(a tooth)*	**maintain** 4 *(a vehicle)*	**(not) touch** 5 *(usu passive)*
fix 4 *(something broken)*	**point** 19 *(a wall)*	
fix 15 *(hair or clothes)*	**restore** 3 *(something)*	

V n P and V P n (not pron)

bring round 1 *(an unconscious person)*	**clear up** 1 *(a place)*	**fix up** 2 *(something)*
bring to *(an unconscious person)*	**do up** 2 *(a building)*	

The verbs *mend* and *repair*, which are not among the 400 most frequent verbs in English, also belong in this group.

(vi) The 'change' group

These verbs are concerned with making something different in some other way. This includes:

- opening or closing something e.g. *close, open*
- changing the appearance of something e.g. *mark, paint*
- making something larger or smaller e.g. *extend, reduce*
- changing the shape or arrangement of something e.g. *gather, throw*

*I am proud that we helped **change** the world.*

*I went to my dad's desk and I **opened up** his drawer.*

*She even **painted** the outside of the house, climbing up scaffolding.*

*She **had taken in** the grey dress so that it hugged her thin body more closely.*

*Lovelock **threw** a switch and water began to pump up into the ballast tanks.*

*The mountains are rich in marble and **have been worked** for at least two thousand years.*

affect *1*	**draw** *5 (a curtain)*	**press** *9 (clothes)*
age *4 (a person's appearance)*	**extend** *5*	**press** *10 (fruit)*
break *8 (a silence)*	**gather** *7 (cloth)*	**reduce** *5 (liquid)*
change *3*	**mark** *2 (a surface)*	**score** *11 (a surface)*
change *7 (a bed)*	**open** *1,2,3*	**throw** *16 (a switch)*
clear *9 (an area)*	**open** *17 (your shirt)*	**try** *6 (a door)*
close *1.1,2,3,8*	**paint** *3 (a wall)*	**work** *20,21 (land)*
cut *10 (a pack of cards)*	**paint** *6 (your nails)*	
divide *1,2 (people or things)*	**pick** *7 (a lock)*	

V n P and **V P n (not pron)**

clear out *2 (a building or room)*	**do up** *1 (clothing)*	**open up** *▷2,▷3*
close up *1 (a building)*	**fill in** *2 (a shape)*	**open up** *5 (a building)*
close up *2 (a gap)*	**make up** *3 (your face)*	**take in** *9 (a dress)*

(vii) The 'feed' group

These verbs are concerned with giving something to someone. The Object indicates the person who receives the thing given.

*But if you **arm** the police isn't the likelihood that more criminals will go armed?*

*When I gave birth and **fed** my first baby, I felt the most intense emotion, and sense of happiness and pride, that I'd ever felt in my life.*

arm *2.2*	**feed** *1,2,4*	**supply** *1*
change *8 (a baby)*	**feed** *10 (a plant)*	**treat** *2 (a patient)*
dress *4 (a child)*	**serve** *8*	**treat** *4 (a child)*

(viii) The 'protect' group

These verbs are concerned with doing something concrete to help or protect someone or something.

*If persons are having difficulty getting started at a particular physical task, **help** them **out**.*

*The T cells would stop attacking the joint tissue and **protect** it instead.*

cover *6 (a person under attack)*	**help** *1*	**save** *1*
defend *1*	**protect** *1*	

V n P and **V P n (not pron)**

help out

II.2 THE 'BRING', 'BUY', AND 'OPERATE' GROUPS

These verbs are concerned with concrete or abstract actions which involve moving or holding something, physically or metaphorically, or with operating machinery or a vehicle. They can be divided into three groups:

(i) The 'bring' group
(ii) The 'buy' group
(iii) The 'operate' group

(i) The 'bring' group

These verbs are concerned with moving or holding something. This includes:

- putting something somewhere e.g. *add, arrange, hang up*
- throwing or sending something somewhere e.g. *drive (a ball), launch (a rocket)*
- carrying something e.g. *bear, carry*
- accompanying someone or something e.g. *deliver, drive (a passenger)*
- pulling something e.g. *attract, pull*

*Heat the butter and oil in a large saucepan, then **add the onion and crushed garlic**.*

*The North pole **will attract** another magnet's North pole.*

*We requested an interview. He agreed, but we **could not bring** a tape recorder.*

*The boxes **were to be carried** by camels, of which Haig had three.*

*We found the house easily, just across a little bridge on the main road into the village, and George **dropped** me **off**.*

*Then I **fitted** the new door casings.*

*Opening her bag again, Nancy **handed over** another envelope.*

*After **hanging up** the overcoat, Rickmore said: 'I'll just tell my wife what's happening.'*

*Michelle remembers the first time he **held** the new baby.*

*Each soldier **was** mounted and **leading** a horse.*

*If you **pull a gun**, I'll shoot you!*

*The prison director was murdered by a prisoner who **had been released** on leave for the day.*

*The assistant took the twenty-five guineas from him briskly, and asked whether they **should send the suit** when it was ready.*

*They **should be able to take** their kids **out** and walk down the street and not have to worry about getting shot or whatever.*

*His truck is seen by school children. From above, they **throw a huge rock**.*

The phrasal verb *get away* has the pattern **V n P** only.

*He **got** me **away** within a week.*

add *1*	**fire** *2.1,3 (a bullet or arrow)*
apply *6*	**fit** *1.6*
arrange *4 (objects)*	**fly** *7 (a flag)*
attract *5 (iron)*	**gather** *2*
bear *1.2 (a weapon)*	**gather** *3 (information)*
bring *1,3*	**get** *2.3 (something (from somewhere))*
carry *1,2,3*	**hang** *1*
catch *21*	**head** *19 (a ball)*
change *4 (a fuse)*	**hide** *1*
collect *4,5 (a substance or energy)*	**hold** *1.1,4*
deal *2.5 (cards)*	**hold** *3.1 (a prisoner)*
deliver *1*	**launch** *1,2 (a rocket or ship)*
draw *6 (a gun)*	**lay** *1.3 (carpets or foundations)*
draw *7 (a cart)*	**lead** *1.2*
draw *12 (money)*	**lift** *1*
drive *2 (a passenger)*	**lift** *12 (vegetables)*
drive *9 (a ball)*	**move** *1*
drop *2,7*	**pick** *3 (fruit)*

produce 5	send 1
pull 1	serve 11 (a ball)
pull 3 (a cart)	settle 8 (a residue)
pull 8 (a gun)	shake 1,7
push 1	spread 5
raise 1,2	strike 20 (a match)
reflect 2 (light)	take 2.1
release 1 (a prisoner) (usu passive)	throw 1 (an object)
release 6 (a person or thing)	throw 6 (a rider)
release 8 (a gas)	turn 3,4 (a wheel or key)
remove 1,2	turn 9 (a page)
replace 4	upset 4 (an object)
restore 4 (something stolen) (usu passive)	walk 8 (the dog)
return 3 (something borrowed)	withdraw 1,3
ride 1 (a horse)	

V n P and **V P n (not pron)**

add in (an ingredient)	hang out 1 (clothes)	send off 1 (a letter)
add on 1 (usu passive)	hang up ▷1,3	send on (a document)
add on 2 (an item)	hang up 2 (the phone)	send out 1 (letters)
break off 1 (a piece)	hold back 3	set out 3 (things)
bring along	hold up 2 (an object)	shake off 3 (a person's hand)
bring up 3 (food)	keep back 1	shake out (a cloth)
clear away (dishes)	lay aside 1	sit down 3 (a person)
collect up (things)	lay out 1 (things)	sit up 2 (a person)
count out 1 (money)	leave behind 1	sort out 1 (things)
cut off 1 (a piece)	lift up ▷1	spread out ▷1 (a cloth)
cut out 1 (a piece)	pass around/round	take away 1 (a thing)
deal out ▷5 (cards)	pass on 1	take away 2 (a number)
draw off (a liquid)	pick up 1,3,4	take away 3 (a person)
draw up 2 (a chair)	pull in 2 (a criminal)	take down 1
drop off ▷9 (a passenger)	pull up 2 (a chair)	take on 3 (goods or people)
fish out	put aside 1	take out 1 (a tooth)
gather up ▷2 (things)	put away 1 (something)	take out 3 (a friend)
get away 3 (a person)	put away 2 (a criminal)	throw away/out 1
give back	put by (money)	throw up 2 (dust or stones)
give out 1	put out 4 (things to be used)	try on 1 (clothes)
hand back (something borrowed)	put up 2 (a poster)	turn around/round 2
hand out 1	roll up 1 (your sleeves)	turn out 7 (contents)
hand over 1	send in 1 (an application)	turn over 1
hand round/around	send in 2 (troops)	

(ii) The 'buy' group

These verbs are concerned with changes in ownership or possession. This includes:

- commercial transactions e.g. *buy, sell, spend*
- voluntarily exchanging goods e.g. *accept, offer, share*
- temporarily transferring possession e.g. *check (luggage)*
- losing and keeping e.g. *find, keep, lose*
- selecting one item from a range e.g. *choose, draw*
- being able to buy something e.g. *(can) afford, (cannot) run to*

*Tamsin **accepted** the bulky packet of letters, held together with a rubber band, and returned the postman's cheery greeting.*

*When I left the army I came back home and **bought** a house.*

*If you **choose** a real Christmas tree this year, the Christmas Tree Stand could help to keep it looking good for longer.*

*A child may want to do well only to **earn** praise.*

*Everyone who is modern tells me to **get a word processor** as it would make my chore so much easier.*

*A man who overheard the conversation sprang from his seat in the crowd and said, 'You **can have** my ticket, son.'*

*The thieves **kept** my credit card, which the bank immediately stopped.*

*I decided I **would** never **own** a TV.*

*Mr Patrick **had** signed nothing and **put up** no money.*

*Dillinger's has just reissued the Schubert songs as a three-volume set on 21 CDs. If you **can't run to** that, consider the recording of Wolf's complete Spanish Songbook.*

*The nation's most famous fish and chip shop, Harry Ramsden's in West Yorkshire, last year **sold** 264,000lb of haddock.*

*They began their marriage in a communal flat which demanded a lot of adjustment on the part of Karen, an only child who **had** never **had to share** her belongings.*

accept 1 (something offered)	**lose** 2,3
adopt 2 (a child)	**lose** 16 (money)
adopt 4 (a country)	**offer** 1
(can) afford 1 (something for sale)*	**order** 2.5 (some food)
blow 1.9 (money)	**own** 4
buy 1	**pick** 1
catch 1,2,19	**present** 4.1 (a gift)
change 14 (money)	**provide** 1
check 5 (luggage)	**push** 9 (drugs)
choose 1	**receive** 1
claim 9 (money)	**receive** 6 (stolen goods)
collect 1,2,3,6	**recover** 4,6
deal 2.3 (drugs)	**refuse** 3 (something offered)
discover 2,3 (something lost or unknown)	**save** 4
draw 14 (a lottery number)	**score** 12 (drugs)
earn 1,3 (money or praise)	**sell** 1
find 1 (something lost)	**serve** 6 (food)
gain 4	**serve** 9 (a summons)
get 2.1 (something you need)*	**share** 7 (something you have)
get 2.2 (a present)*	**spend** 1 (money)
get 2.16 (a newspaper)*	**steal** 1,2 (things or ideas)
have 3.9*	**take** 2.2,8
hold 2.7 (shares)	**take** 2.15 (something offered)
keep 9 (a possession)	**take** 2.26 (something (from a range))
let 14 (your house)	**take** 2.28 (a house)

V n P and **V P n** (not pron)

buy up (land)	**lay in** (supplies)	**sell up** (possessions)
carry off 2 (a prize)	**lay on** (food)	**serve up** 6 (food)
check in ▷5 (luggage)	**lay out** 5 (money)	**set aside** 1 (something useful)
divide up 2 (a whole)	**let out** ▷14 (your house)	**share out**
fix up 3 (a person)	**pass on** 2 (costs)	**sign away**
get back 3 (something lost or stolen)	**pay back** 1 (money)	**sign over**
give away 1	**pay out** 1 (money)	**take back** 1 (something bought)
give out 2 (information)	**pick out** 2	**throw in** 2 (something extra)
give up 3 (a job)	**put down** 2 (money)	**trade in** (a car)
give up 4 (something deserved)	**put on** 7 (money)	**turn in** 3 (homework)
hand down 1 (knowledge or a possession)	**put up** 4 (money)	**turn in** 4 (something borrowed)
hand in 1 (homework or something found)	**sell off**	**turn over** 4,5
hand on	**sell on**	**win back** (something lost)

V P n and **V P P n**

buy into *(a company)*	**come up with** 2 *(a sum of money)**	**settle on**
come by*	**hold on to** 1,2*	
come into 1 *(money)**	**(cannot) run to** 3 *(something for sale)**	

(iii) The 'operate' group

These verbs are concerned with operating machinery or vehicles.

*Edna O'Brien can't swim, **can't drive** a car, **can't work** an answering machine.*

*Charles came and **operated** the security lock.*

*The second time we **played** the record, it sounded twice as fast.*

*Well, you **can't ride** your bicycle today, and that's final.*

*Eileen smiled, and **started up** the engine without speaking.*

apply 7 *(brakes)*	**fire** 1.1 *(a gun)*	**ride** 2 *(a bicycle)*	**start** 6 *(an engine)*
back 3.2 *(a car)*	**fly** 4 *(an aircraft)*	**ring** 1.3 *(a bell)*	**stop** 4 *(a machine)*
blow 1.6 *(a horn)*	**handle** 6 *(a weapon or vehicle)*	**run** 13 *(a tape)*	**work** 22 *(a machine)*
control 5 *(equipment)*	**operate** 3 *(a machine)*	**run** 14 *(a machine)*	
drive 1 *(a car)*	**play** 11 *(an instrument)*	**set** 2.5 *(a clock)*	
drive 5 *(a machine)*	**play** 12 *(a record)*	**sound** 1.5 *(a horn)*	

V n P and **V P n (not pron)**

back up 6 *(a car)*	**play back** *(a tape)*	**put out** 3 *(a light)*	**start up** ▷6 *(an engine)*
let off 3 *(a gun)*	**put on** 5 *(a record)*	**set off** 2 *(a bomb)*	**turn out** 4 *(a light)*

II.3 THE 'COVER', 'FOLLOW', AND 'RECORD' GROUPS

These verbs are concerned with a concrete action or event which does not change or affect the person or thing indicated by the Object, but where the Object is involved in the action or event. They can be divided into five groups:

(i)   The 'cover' group
(ii)   The 'meet' group
(iii)   The 'follow' group
(iv)   The 'record' group
(v)   The 'use' group

(i) The 'cover' group

These verbs are concerned with moving something so that it is on, under, or around the Object, or so that it is no longer in that position. The person or thing indicated by the Object is not moved or changed, although it is covered, revealed, or supported. We also include here *cover 2,3, hide, support,* and *surround,* where the Subject indicates the thing that is over, under, or around the Object.

*The light became so bright she automatically **covered** her eyes.*

*I had driven Jowan to the hospital, where they **had** examined and **dressed** his wound.*

*She was dressed in a black cape that she removed to **reveal** a red petticoat.*

The verbs *cover 2,3, hide,* and *support* have inanimate Subjects.

*Thick smoke **covered** the prison.*

*The beams that **supported** the roof had jagged ends.*

cover 1,2,3	**fill** 1 (a container)	**ring** 2.8 (a bird)	**surround** 2
dress 7 (a wound)	**hide** 5	**show** 6 (something hidden)	**treat** 3 (a surface)
dress 8 (a salad)	**reveal** 2 (something hidden)	**support** 6	

V n P and **V P n** (not pron)

cover up 1	**fill up** ▷1 (a container)	**stop up** (a hole)

(ii) The 'meet' group

These verbs are concerned with meeting or getting to know someone, or visiting someone or a place. We include here *lay*, *go with*, and *sleep with*, which mean 'have sex with', and *avoid*, which is concerned with deliberately not meeting someone.

> *I'll see you tomorrow for that coffee you promised. **Call for** me at four.*

> *I **was to meet** Dad as the car pulled up and not let him enter the house in the usual manner through the backdoor.*

> *When she said, 'Are you **seeing** somebody else?' he said, 'I'm sorry,' and burst into tears.*

> *I did all the things you do when you **visit** relatives – ate their food, used their bathtub, washing machine and telephone.*

avoid 3	**lay** 1.9	**pull** 15	**see** 15 (a boyfriend)*
catch 12	**meet** 1,2,3,4,5	**see** 2 (a friend)	**visit** 1,3

V n P and **V P n** (not pron)

look up 2 (a friend)

V P n

call for 1 (a friend)	**go with** 3*	**run into** 2*
come upon 1*	**run across**	**sleep with***

(iii) The 'follow' group

These verbs are concerned with going in a particular direction or to or from a particular place. The Object indicates a direction, a place, a road, or a person who is in a particular place.

> ***Cross** the road and walk on the other side.*

> *If he's the killer, he'll have to go out, and then we **can follow** him and call the police.*

> *They made their way back up before going on upstream, **following** the upper path.*

> *He went back to Yorkshire to **join** his loyal, long-suffering wife.*

> *It was not enough for tired drivers to switch on the radio and open the window. They **should pull off** the road and sleep.*

> *Ginette **stuck to** me like a leech and accompanied Red and me on all our outings.*

> *Daniels **had** never even **visited** Canada.*

approach 1 (a place)	**follow** 1 (a friend)	**join** 1 (your family)	**negotiate** 2 (an area of land)
cross 1.1 (a road)*	**follow** 2 (a suspect)	**join** 4 (a queue)*	**take** 2.27 (a route)
enter 1 (a room)	**follow** 8 (a path)	**leave** 1 (a place)*	**visit** 2 (a place)

V P n

drop by *(a place)*	**keep to** 2 *(a path)**	**stick with** 2 *(a person)**
fall behind 1 *(a person)**	**pull into** *(a place)**	**stop by** *(a place)*
gain on *(a person)**	**pull off** 2 *(a road)**	**turn off** 1 *(a road)**
get off 3 *(a piece of land)**	**stick to** 1 *(a person or thing)**	

(iv) The 'record' group

These verbs are concerned with recording, measuring, indicating, or copying something or someone.

> As Zara guides us on a tour of the house, she stops to **point out** a large portrait on the dining room wall.
> Dozens of local reporters were waiting to **record** his every word.
> I mentioned my admiration for General Gordon and they **sent** him **up** and made jokes about his death – they've no decency at all.

cover 21 *(a song)*	**indicate** 5 *(a measurement)*	**paint** 4	**record** 6 *(a measurement)*
draw 1	**mark** 7 *(a student's work)*	**realize** 3 *(a design)*	**test** 1
indicate 3	**mark** 11 *(a place or position)*	**record** 3,4 *(speech or music)*	

V n P and **V P n (not pron)**

act out	**point out** 1 *(a landmark)*	**take off** 7 *(a person)*
blow up 6 *(a photograph)*	**send up** *(a person)*	

The verbs *copy*, *film*, and *measure*, which are not among the 400 most frequent verbs in English, also belong in this group.

(v) The 'use' group

These verbs are concerned with using something.

> To understand the whole chain of events leading to the Aurora, scientists **have to employ** a wide range of methods, from space satellites to ground stations.
> Transfer the cookies to cooling racks, **using** a wide spatula.

employ 2 *(materials or methods)*	**try** 4 *(something new)*	**use** 1.1 *(a knife)*

V n P and **V P n (not pron)**

try out *(something new)*

II.4 THE 'BUILD' GROUP

These verbs are concerned with a concrete action or event which creates something or brings it into being.

> If Mother and Grandma **can build** a house, so can I.
> I **have completed** my greatest work of art.
> The cliffs are made of volcanic rocks and **were formed** when the sea level was higher.
> She was likely to be home in good time to **get** the lunch.
> He had offered her his scarf, wrapping it round so that just a space **was left** for breathing and talking.

*The play **wasn't performed** until 1965.*

*He **has** selected thirty posters as examples of his best work and **run off** 500 copies of each, every one numbered and hand signed.*

*The explosions were thought to have been caused by a gas leak, which **started** a fire and blew up one of the refinery's gas separation units.*

*These small breweries **turn out** some really traditional beer.*

bear *1.12 (a child)*	**grow** *3 (a plant)*	**mix** *7 (a piece of music)*
blow *1.5 (bubbles)*	**grow** *5 (a beard)*	**perform** *3 (a play)*
be born *1,5*	**grow** *12 (a crystal)*	**place** *21 (an order)*
build *1 (a building)*	**have** *3.11 (a baby)**	**prepare** *1*
complete *8 (a book)*	**lay** *1.4 (a trap)*	**prepare** *3 (a meal)*
cook *1 (a meal)*	**lay** *1.5 (an egg)*	**produce** *2,3*
create *1,2*	**leave** *12 (a mark)*	**roll** *6 (a cigarette)*
deliver *5 (a baby)*	**leave** *14 (a space)*	**rule** *8 (a line)*
design *1 (a garment or building)*	**make** *3.1*	**set** *2.19 (a trap)*
fix *14 (a meal)*	**make** *3.2 (a television programme)*	**shoot** *7 (a film)*
form *9 (a natural feature) (usu passive)*	**make** *3.3 (a meal)*	**start** *2 (a fire)*
get *2.4 (a meal)**	**mix** *2 (cement)*	**strike** *22 (a coin) (usu passive)*

V n P and **V P n** (not pron)

beat out *1 (sounds)*	**put up** *1 (a building)*	**set up** *2 (a structure)*
cook up *3 (a meal)*	**roll up** ▷*6 (a cigarette)*	**throw off** *2 (a substance)*
give off/out *(gas or heat)*	**run off** *2 (a copy)*	**throw up** *3 (a building)*
make up *7 (food)*	**send out** *2 (a signal or light)*	**turn out** *5 (products)*
mark out *1 (an area or shape)*	**send out** *3 (roots)*	

II.5 THE 'CHANGE', 'CONCERN', AND 'ARRANGE' GROUPS

These verbs are concerned with an abstract action or event which changes or affects the person or thing indicated by the Object. They can be divided into nine groups:

(i)   The 'change' group
(ii)   The 'end' group
(iii)   The 'beat an illness' group
(iv)   The 'concern' group
(v)   The 'help' group
(vi)   The 'control' group
(vii) The 'beat' group
(viii) The 'call out' group
(ix)   The 'arrange' group

(i) The 'change' group

These verbs are concerned with doing something abstract that makes the Object different.

*They were going to use some kind of mind-altering drugs to **break** him.*

*When he lost confidence after Christmas I tried to **build** him **up** and give him my support.*

*This method of electing the president **was changed** by the referendum of October 1962.*

*The bank lost so much that it **had to close** the operation.*

*Killing people from the air may make some people feel better but it **will not improve** the lives of anyone in Bosnia.*

*We were instructed that the depth of the Penguin Pool was to be reduced to **keep down** the costs of regularly changing the water.*

*Parents often invest large sums of money in their children's education in an attempt to **raise** their intellectual capacity.*

*We also found out how she **had been able to turn** the business **around** so dramatically.*

affect 1	**destroy** 2 *(a person)*	**limit** 5
arrange 5 *(a piece of music) (usu passive)*	**develop** 5 *(land)*	**open** 18,19 *(a shop)*
bind 1	**develop** 7 *(a skill or relationship)*	**raise** 4,5 *(a rate or standard)*
break 12 *(a person)*	**divide** 5 *(people)*	**reduce** 1
change 3	**drop** 1 *(a level)*	**score** 8 *(a piece of music)*
clear 5 *(your mind)**	**extend** 7 *(a meeting)*	**train** 2.1,4 *(a person or animal)*
close 1.4,5 *(a shop)*	**feed** 9 *(an emotion)*	**train** 2.2 *(a talent)*
control 6,7 *(prices or feelings)*	**increase** 1 *(a price)*	**train** 2.3 *(an athlete)*
cut 7 *(costs)*	**improve** 1,2	**turn** 20 *(a game)*
cut 8 *(a text)*	**lift** 10 *(an amount)*	**upset** 3 *(a situation)*

V n P and V P n (not pron)

break down 3 *(an idea)*	**divide off** *(an area)*	**roll back**
break in 3 *(a recruit)*	**divide up** 1 *(an area or institution)*	**run down** 2,3 *(an industry or amount)*
build up 1 *(a thing)*	**drive out**	**shake up** 1 *(an organization)*
build up 2 *(a person)*	**feed up** *(a person)*	**step up**
close down ▷1.5 *(a factory)*	**fill up** 2 *(a person)*	**train up** *(a person)*
cut back *(expenditure)*	**keep down** 1 *(costs)*	**turn around/round** 3 *(a business)*
cut down ▷7 *(costs)*	**keep up** 6 *(costs)*	**turn around/round** 5 *(a sentence)*
cut down 1 *(an activity)*	**pick out** 3 *(usu passive)*	
cut out 2 *(part of a text)*	**put up** 5 *(the price)*	

(ii) The 'end' group

These verbs are concerned with bringing a situation to an end. With some verbs, such as *end*, the Object indicates the situation itself. With other verbs, such as *open up (a border)*, the verb and the Object together indicate a situation that is brought to an end.

*East Germany, Poland and Czechoslovakia were beginning to **break** their links with any form of communist orthodoxy.*

*The police pumped tear gas into the building in an effort to **end the siege**.*

*The 86-year-old elder statesman has been struggling to ensure that the more conservative figures in the leadership **do not** completely **kill off** his reform programme in the next five-year plan.*

*Still far from resolved are key issues such as how to reduce military confrontation, **open up the border** and, ultimately, how to end forty five years of division.*

*The justices **struck down the law** by a vote of eight to nothing.*

break 10 *(links)*	**complete** 9 *(a degree)*	**end** 2 *(a situation)*	**open** 12 *(a border)*
close 1.6,7	**cut** 9 *(a supply)*	**kill** 3 *(a project)*	**settle** 4 *(plans) (usu passive)*

V n P and V P n (not pron)

break off 3 *(a relationship)*	**grow out** *(a hairstyle)*	**work off** 1 *(a feeling)*
break up 3 *(a marriage)*	**kill off** ▷3 *(a project)*	**work off** 2 *(a debt)*
break up 4 *(a meeting)*	**open up** ▷12 *(a border)*	**write off** 2 *(a debt)*
bring down 1 *(a government)*	**pay off** 1 *(a debt)*	**write off** 5 *(a project)*
cut off 3 *(a supply)*	**strike down** 2 *(a law)*	

V P n

back off 2 *(a claim)**

(iii) The 'beat an illness' group

These verbs are concerned with improving a bad situation, solving a problem, or surviving an unpleasant situation.

> Since a lack of confidence was still an issue for him, Sean **attacked this problem** daily.
>
> Thousands of women **are beating breast cancer** and I plan to be one of them.
>
> The strikes did play an important role in **fighting the social injustice caused by the totalitarian system**.
>
> She admitted to herself she didn't know how to **handle the problem** and was tired of trying.
>
> It is obvious that socialism **meets a fundamental need of modern man**, or its attraction would not be so widely felt.
>
> His art enabled him to **rise above the horror of life in the trenches** in the First World War.
>
> If you could get the electricity turned on tomorrow somehow, **would** that **save the situation**?
>
> I don't care what you do. It's your problem, **work** it **out** somewhere else.

address 6 *(a problem)*	**control** 8 *(pollution)*	**remove** 5 *(an obstacle)*
answer 13 *(a need)*	**fight** 1 *(something unpleasant)*	**save** 5 *(a bad situation)*
attack 4 *(a problem)*	**fill** 7 *(a need)*	**settle** 1,2 *(an argument or problem)*
beat 11 *(a problem)*	**fix** 5 *(a problem)*	**sort** 4 *(a problem) (usu passive)*
break 7 *(a difficult situation)*	**handle** 3 *(a situation)*	**survive** 1,2,3 *(a dangerous or difficult situation)*
break 11 *(a habit)*	**improve** 1 *(a situation)*	**treat** 2 *(an illness)*
break 23 *(a code)*	**meet** 9,10 *(a need or a challenge)*	

V n P and **V P n (not pron)**

break down 7 *(barriers)*	**hold off** 2 *(a challenge)*	**shake off** 1 *(an illness)*
clear up 2 *(a problem)*	**live down** *(a mistake)**	**sort out** 2 *(a problem)*
clear up 3 *(an illness)*	**make up** 6 *(a quarrel)*	**sort out** 3 *(a person)*
fight off 1 *(an illness)*	**put down** 3 *(a riot)*	**throw off** 1 *(a bad situation)*
head off 2 *(an unpleasant situation)*	**ride out** *(a crisis)*	**work out** 1 *(a problem)*

V P n and **V P P n**

get around/round 1,2 *(a problem or rule)*	**rise above** *(a problem)**
get over 1,2 *(an experience or problem)*	**stand up to** 1 *(something unpleasant)*

The verb *solve*, which is not among the 400 most frequent verbs in English, also belongs in this group.

(iv) The 'concern' group

These verbs are concerned with someone being affected, usually negatively, by something. The Subject is usually inanimate and the Object usually indicates a person or a group of people.

> His eyes had begun to glaze over, the effects of the heavy drinking **were catching up with him**.
>
> I don't want to talk about something that **doesn't concern** me.
>
> The report said rising oil prices were likely to **hit many developing nations** hard, complicating the task faced by countries with debts or low incomes.
>
> Nationalism **can threaten democracies**.

The phrasal verbs *be playing up* and *put out* have the pattern **V n P** only.

> Kershaw was at that moment bent over the potato-peeling machine, which **had been playing him up** since he had been introduced to it that morning.

The phrasal verbs *let down* and *put out* have animate as well as inanimate Subjects.

*Suddenly he became a betraying, hopeless man, just like all the others who **had let** Sylvia **down**.*

affect *2*	dominate *2 (a person or country)*	hurt *8*	strike *6*
burn *13 (usu passive)*	fail *7,9*	(not) move *12 (usu passive)*	surprise *4,6*
concern *9**	hit *4*	rule *6 (your life)*	threaten *2*

V n P and **V P n (not pron)**

lay up	be playing up *2**
let down *1,2*	put out *6*

V P n and **V P P n**

catch up with *2**	do for *(usu passive)*

(v) The 'help' group

These verbs are concerned with doing something abstract to benefit someone or something.

*The US effort to boost economic activity **will** in itself **help** business confidence in an otherwise subdued economic outlook.*

The phrasal verb *pull through* has the pattern **V n P** only.

*We all hoped that since he'd managed to survive so far, proper treatment **would pull** him **through**.*

help *1,2*	serve *1 (your country)*

V n P

pull through

(vi) The 'control' group

These verbs are concerned with having a particular role in an organization or among a group of people. This role is usually controlling or leading.

*The telephone workers' union **is controlled** by the President's own supporters.*

*They now own and **operate** a 300-acre working farm 50 miles south of Rochester.*

*Since then the country **has** mostly **been ruled** by tyrants, even by tyrant dynasties.*

*He bought one of the most prized buildings in Hong Kong's Central district, in 1980, and in the following year he **took over** Laker Airways.*

control *4 (an organization)*	lead *1.8 (an organization)*	present *4.9 (a TV programme)*
head *10 (an organization)*	lead *1.14 (a conversation)*	present *4.10 (a play)*
hold *3.2 (An army...a place)*	manage *1 (an organization)*	rule *5 (a country)*
introduce *4 (a TV programme)*	occupy *3 (a country)*	run *10 (a business)*
keep *16 (a business)**	operate *1 (a business)*	

V n P and **V P n** (not pron)

> **take over** *1,2 (a company or country)*

(vii) The 'beat' group

These verbs are concerned with competition. The Subject indicates one competitor, the Object indicates another.

> *I want to run against the best athletes in the world and I think I **can beat** them.*
>
> *Becker opens his Olympic campaign today against Norway's Christian Ruud and is then expected to **play** Britain's Chris Wilkinson.*
>
> *This is the second time that Ruby Tiger **has seen off** her juniors in this race.*

> **beat** 9   **meet** 18*   **play** 3*

V n P and **V P n** (not pron)

> **beat out** 3   **put out** 7
> **face down*   see off** 1

(viii) The 'call out' group

These verbs are concerned with making someone go somewhere or behave in a certain way. The Object indicates the person or people affected.

> *Family doctors are fed up with **being called out** on home visits late at night.*
>
> *The spokesman refused to **be drawn**. 'We do not comment on the reasons for people either joining or leaving the company,' he said.*
>
> *I told them that twenty-three was a bit higher than we wanted to pay. Before I could attempt to **talk** them **down**, the president said, 'Perhaps it is, but that's the price.'*

The verb *bind* has an inanimate Subject.

> *The rules that **bind** societies are the identical rules that **bind** individual humans.*

> **attract** 1 *(people or animals)*   **call** 9 *(a witness) (usu passive)*   **force** 1   **work** 19
> **bind** 2 *(Laws...people)*   **draw** 21 *(a lot of people)*   **push** 6
> **call** 5 *(a doctor)*   **(not) draw** 23 *(a person) (usu passive)*   **use** 1.7

V n P and **V P n** (not pron)

> **beat down** 3 *(a seller)*   **order around/about**   **set off** 4
> **buy off**   **pick up** 6   **start off** 2,3 *(a person or activity)*
> **call out** *(a doctor)*   **pull back** 2 *(troops)*   **talk down** 1 *(a pilot)*
> **draw out** 2   **pull in** ▷9 *(crowds)*   **talk down** 3 *(a seller)*
> **head off** 1 *(a person or vehicle)*   **pull out** 3 *(troops)*   **talk up** 2 *(a buyer)*
> **hold back** 1,2   **pull over** 2 *(a driver)*   **throw out** 3
> **move along** 1   **pull up** 4   **turn back** 1
> **move on** 2   **push around**   **turn out** 6

(ix) The 'arrange' group

These verbs are concerned with making different not the Object itself but the circumstances surrounding the Object. This includes:

- arranging for someone to take up a job or a position, or to leave a job or a position e.g. *admit, elect, fire*

- providing a home, money, or education for something or someone e.g. *house, keep*
- making arrangements about something such as the time of an event e.g. *fix (a date), move (an event)*

*She was one of the first girls at the school to **be accepted** by Oxford University.*

*His bankers **had arranged** a breakfast meeting.*

*The assembly meeting **will** also **elect** a new president.*

*She still **wouldn't fix** a date for the wedding.*

*A homeless mother of two has spent two years living in squalor while waiting to **be housed** by the city council.*

*What **kept** him? I've been waiting for hours.*

*In spite of your mother's rejection there was always someone to **look out for** you.*

*It is easy to forget that both parents have an equal obligation to **provide for** their children.*

*I never actually **put** a meeting **off** because I had to go to the toilet.*

*Dr Wilkinson wants to talk to you. I**'ll put** you **through**.*

*They're your babies and you'll find a way to **raise** them.*

*Aymes is now fit and has the right temperament, but it would be a gamble to **recall** him.*

*Now I was beginning to feel impatient with his loyalty and wanted to **shake** him **off**.*

*He had been slightly disappointed when the Red Sox turned out to be the only team that wanted to **sign** him.*

*She died of influenza a year later and I **was taken in** by her only relative.*

The phrasal verbs *set back* and *set up 7* have an inanimate Subject.

*Although the tunnel could be finished by the end of the century, the problems of attracting private sector cash are likely to **set** it **back** further.*

The phrasal verb *set up 7* has the pattern **V n P** only.

*A win on Saturday **would set** us **up** nicely.*

accept 6 *(a person)*	**leave** 3 *(your partner)*
accept 10 *(a transplanted organ)**	**maintain** 5 *(a person)*
accept 11 *(coins)*	**mark** 16 *(a player)*
admit 2 *(a patient) (usu passive)*	**marry** 1,2
admit 3,4 *(a person)*	**mind** 2.6 *(a child)*
appoint	**move** 6 *(a person)*
arrange 1,3 *(a meeting)*	**move** 9 *(an event)*
arrest 1 *(a suspect)*	**place** 25 *(an employee)*
ban 3 *(a person)*	**promote** 3,4 *(usu passive)*
buy 4 *(a person) (usu passive)*	**publish** 2 *(an article)*
commit 3 *(resources)*	**raise** 12 *(a child)*
commit 6 *(a patient) (usu passive)*	**raise** 13 *(a type of animal or crops)*
confirm 4 *(a church member) (usu passive)*	**recall** 4,6 *(a person or product)*
drop 11 *(a team member) (usu passive)*	**recall** 5 *(a team member)*
elect 1	**receive** 3 *(a visitor)*
employ 1	**refer** 4 *(a patient) (usu passive)*
enter 7 *(a competitor)*	**refuse** 2 *(a person)*
fire 3.0 *(an employee)*	**reject** 3,4 *(a person)*
fix 2 *(a date)*	**release** 3 *(a person under an obligation)*
fix 3 *(an arrangement)*	**remove** 4 *(an official) (usu passive)*
fix 23 *(a person)*	**run** 3 *(a horse)*
hold 3.8 *(something delayed)*	**sign** 7 *(a person)*
house 12 *(a person)*	**stop** 5 *(a vehicle)*
keep 13 *(a person)*	**support** 4 *(a person)*
keep 15 *(an animal)*	**tend** 4 *(something delicate)*
keep 17 *(a delayed person)**	

V n P and V P n (not pron)

bind over *(a criminal)*	**miss out** *2*
bring forward *1 (a meeting)*	**open up** ▷*2 (a place or economy)*
bring in *3 (an outsider)*	**pass over** *1 (a person)*
bring up *1 (a child)*	**pay back** *2 (an enemy)*
buy out *1 (an owner)*	**pay off** *2 (a debtor)*
buy out *2 (a soldier)*	**pull up** *3 (a person)*
call off *(an event)*	**put back** *(a meeting)*
call up *2 (a recruit)*	**put off** *2 (a meeting)*
catch up *5 (a person) (usu passive)*	**put through** *1 (a caller)*
check in *1 (a hotel guest)*	**put up** *6 (a guest)*
check out *1 (a hotel guest)*	**put up** *7 (a candidate)*
close off *(an area)*	**send down** *1 (a student) (usu passive)*
cut off *2 (a person or place)*	**send down** *2 (a prisoner) (usu passive)*
cut off *4 (a caller)*	**send off** *2 (a player)*
cut up *2 (a driver)*	**set back** *1 (a project)*
cut out *5 (a person)*	**set up** *7 (a person)*
draw in *2 (a person)*	**set up** *8 (a victim)*
fit in *1 (a person or task)*	**shake off** *2 (a person following)*
fit out/up	**show around/round**
fix up *1*	**sign up**
give away *5 (the bride)*	**stand up** *3 (a boyfriend)*
give up *5 (a criminal)*	**strike off** *(a doctor or lawyer) (usu passive)*
hand over *2 (a prisoner)*	**strike out** *4 (a batter)*
hold down *2 (a person)*	**take back** *3 (a boyfriend)*
hold over *2 (a meeting)*	**take in** *1 (a visitor)*
hold up *3 (a person or process)*	**take in** *2 (a suspect)*
keep down *2 (a group of people)*	**take off** *8 (a service)*
keep on *2 (an employee)*	**take on** *4 (an employee)*
lay off *1 (workers)*	**throw off** *3 (people following)*
leave out	**throw up** *4 (a person or thing)*
let off *2 (a criminal)*	**turn away** *1 (a person)*
mark up *(a product)*	**turn in** *2 (a suspect)*
mark down *3 (a product)*	**vote in** *(a party)*
mark down *4 (a student)*	**vote out** *(a party)*
marry off	

V P n and V P P n

come for*	**provide for** *1*	**stick by** *1**
look after *1,2*	**see about** *(something to happen)**	**walk over** *(a person)*
look out for *2*	**sit on** *(something to be dealt with)**	
pick on *2*	**stand by** *3**	

II.6 THE 'WATCH', 'BREAK A RECORD', AND 'APPROVE' GROUPS

These verbs are concerned with an abstract action or event which does not change or affect the person or thing indicated by the Object. They can be divided into seven groups:

(i)   The 'watch' group
(ii)   The 'break a record' group
(iii)   The 'win' group
(iv)   The 'approve' group
(v)   The 'answer' group
(vi)   The 'count against' group
(vii)   Verbs with other meanings

(i) The 'watch' group

These verbs are concerned with directed mental activity.

> *Open University students have to be dedicated enough to get up early to <u>catch</u> the Open University programmes on radio and TV.*

*What surprised me was that nobody **checked** my papers.*

*They **check** the company **out** fully, they talk to the competition, they talk to academics.*

*He took her home for dinner and **went over** her manuscript line by line.*

*Lucy Jennings **is reading** catering management and sociology at Oxford Brooks.*

*Read for a while or **watch** a television program that doesn't require much intellect.*

catch 11 *(a TV programme)*	**read** 14 *(a subject)*
check 1 *(a document)*	**review** 5 *(troops)*
examine 1,2 *(a person or thing)*	**seek** 1,2,3
follow 16 *(a sport)*	**study** 1 *(a subject)*
follow 18 *(a musical score)*	**study** 5,6
hear 2 *(a lecture)*	**test** 7 *(a person with a disease) (usu passive)*
investigate *(an event or situation)*	**watch** 1.1,4,5
read 1,3,4 *(a book, words, or music)*	**watch** 1.2 *(a TV programme)*
read 12 *(a measuring device)*	

V n P and V P n (not pron)

check out 2	**look up** 1 *(information)*	**seek out**
look over	**pick over**	

V P n

go over *(a document or problem)*	**look round/around***	**watch over**

(ii) The 'break a record' group

These verbs focus on the fact that the Subject achieves success. We include here *buy (time)*, *make 3.7*, and *sell (a product)*, which indicate that the Subject contributes to the success of something else.

*Since he turned 18 he has won the European Cup, the World Cup, and the Commonwealth Games. He **has** also **broken** the world record three times.*

*The company is having trouble **filling** the vacancy for a new chairman.*

*It is not Ms Jones's colourful career that **will sell** the book, but the face that stares out from the front cover.*

*Lisa successfully argued that the students were doing field work in sociological studies, an assertion that **won** credit for the teachers and recognition for her program.*

achieve *(success)*	**fill** 11 *(a theatre)*	**reach** 5 *(a person (by phone))*
beat 10 *(a record)*	**find** 2 *(something needed)*	**sell** 5 *(product)*
beat 15 *(a time limit)*	**hit** 6 *(a high point)*	**stand** 15 *(a test)**
break 20 *(a record)*	**make** 3.7 *(something)*	**strike** 21 *(oil)*
buy 3 *(time)**	**make** 5.1 *(the team)**	**win** 4 *(something you need)*
claim 6 *(a record)*	**pass** 13 *(a test)*	
fill 8,9 *(a role or vacancy)*	**reach** 2 *(a stage)**	

V P n

get through 6 *(an examination)**	**get through** 7 *(parliament)**

(iii) The 'win' group

These verbs are concerned with winning, losing, or taking part in a competition. The Object indicates the competition or the thing that is won or lost.

*If Republicans don't do well in rural Illinois, I don't think they have much of a chance of **carrying** this state.*

*Wednesday night marks the recording industry's Grammy Awards; and if the predictions hold up, Eric Clapton is sure to **walk off with** a bevy of awards.*

*He only **won** fourteen of the eighty races.*

carry 12 *(a political district)*	**drop** 12 *(a game)*	**take** 2.9 *(a political district)*
defend 4 *(a title)*	**enter** 6 *(a competition)*	**throw** 17 *(a competition)*
draw 24 *(a match)*	**lose** 1 *(a contest)*	**win** 1,3 *(a contest or medal)*

V P P n

run away with 2 *(a competition or prize)*	**walk off with** 2 *(a competition or prize)*
walk away with *(a competition or prize)*	

(iv) The 'approve' group

These verbs are concerned with the practical demonstration of approval or disapproval.

*Despite some mutinous mutterings, they are likely to **approve** the deal eventually.*

*The Berlin Wall was breached a year ago this Friday and in Berlin a series of events is being held this week to **mark** that anniversary.*

*Who knows if I'll still be running in 1998. I am not saying I will but I **won't rule** it **out** either.*

accept 3 *(a plan)*	**confirm** 6 *(a position)*
accept 5 *(a document)*	**discover** 5 *(a performer) (usu passive)*
adopt 1 *(a plan)*	**follow** 19 *(a religion)**
allow 1 *(an activity)*	**fund** 3 *(an organization)*
allow 2 *(a gift) (usu passive)*	**mark** 13 *(an event)*
approve 3,4 *(a plan or product)*	**pass** 15 *(something (as correct))*
back 3.3 *(a person or what they do)*	**promote** 1 *(something)*
back 3.4 *(a horse)*	**push** 8 *(an idea)*
ban 1 *(a film)*	**support** 1,4 *(an idea or person)*
clear 19 *(a document) (usu passive)*	**support** 9 *(a team)*
clear 20 *(an accused person)*	

V n P and **V P n (not pron)**

back up 1,2,3,4 *(a person)*	**rule out** 1 *(a course of action)*	**vote down** *(a proposal)*
bear out *(a person)*	**show off** 2 *(a possession or attribute)*	
build up 3 *(a person or thing)*	**throw out** 2 *(a legal case)*	

V P n

drink to *(a person or thing)**

(v) The 'answer' group

These verbs are concerned with responding or reacting to something.

*For a while, she was unable to look at him, and she **answered** his attempts at conversation softly and distractedly.*

*Until recently this research formed rather a backwater, and few astronomers wanted to **follow up** the discoveries.*

*Men are slightly more likely than women to start swooning over someone who **does not return** their feelings.*

answer 6 *(the telephone)*	**return** 5 *(a call)*
answer 11	**return** 5 *(feelings)*

V n P and **V P n (not pron)**

follow up *(a suggestion or discovery)*

V P n

fall for 2 *(a trick)*

(vi) The 'count against' group

These verbs are concerned with making people think of someone or something in a particular way. The Object indicates the person or thing that is thought of.

All of these verbs, except *blow up, dress up*, and *show up*, have inanimate Subjects.

*Only you would think of that colour. It **becomes you**.*

*If you live in rented accommodation and have moved around a lot, this **will count against you**.*

*As far as the locals are concerned, you are a foreigner. Even the way you walk **will give you away**.*

*La Noblesse restaurant has much to **recommend it**.*

*He'd call me things, humiliate me and try to **show me up**.*

become 2 *(a person)**	**recommend** 3 *(a person)**

V n P and **V P n (not pron)**

blow up 5 *(an incident)*	**give away** 4 *(a person)*	**show off** 3 *(a feature)*
dress up 3 *(a situation)*	**set off** 5 *(a colour)*	**show up** 2 *(a person)*

V P n

count against *(a person)**	**tell against** *(a person)**

(vii) Verbs with other meanings

These verbs are concerned with a wide range of other abstract actions. The Object indicates the focus or target of the action, but this is not directly affected by the action.

*Do you believe that Adam **fixed that race**, maybe even murdered the trainer?*

*At least 300 people were evacuated from a variety store this afternoon when a gunman **held up a nearby bank** and took two hostages.*

*In certain parts of the world some people are known to live to well over 100 years old but they mainly **live off the land**, in mountainous areas where the air is cleaner.*

*The typical employee spends as much as seven hours a week in these meetings and often works late into the night to **make up the time**.*

*Your child is probably using his friend as a vehicle for **releasing any strong feelings that are troubling him**.*

*The next day Roberto packed his bags. Ingrid went with him to the railway station to **see him off**. He was finally leaving for India.*

*She checked into a hotel in Victoria two days ago, then promptly **settled the bill** and moved without explanation in the middle of the night.*

*It's a good idea to spend the first night of your holiday **sleeping off the jet lag** in a hotel.*

*Tell me, honey, and maybe I can help. I'd like to help, just **try me**.*

The Subject of *replace 1* is one of the people or things involved in the exchange, whereas the Subject of *replace 2,3* is a person who arranges the exchange.

Will *corn starch **replace** plastic foam?*

*I wonder if we **can** ever **replace** such a tremendous array of talent.*

apply 4 *(a rule)*	**meet** 12 *(a situation)**
attend 1,2 *(a meeting or school)*	**name** 2 *(a person)*
break 5 *(a rule)*	**offer** 5 *(friendship)*
carry 9 *(a motion) (usu passive)*	**offer** 7 *(a service)*
claim 10 *(money)*	**pay** 1 *(a bill)*
clear 18 *(a cheque)*	**promote** 2 *(a product)*
cost 4 *(a proposal) (usu passive)*	**realize** 2 *(fears) (usu passive)*
declare 3 *(goods)*	**release** 4 *(feelings)*
enter 2 *(an organization)*	**release** 5 *(documents)*
examine 4 *(a student) (usu passive)*	**release** 9 *(a new record)*
experience 4 *(a situation)*	**replace** 1,2,3
face 2.3 *(a person or group)*	**represent** 1,2 *(a group of people)*
fill 13 *(a prescription)*	**represent** 3 *(a town or country)*
fix 17,18 *(a race or prices)*	**be represented** 4
follow 12 *(advice)*	**restore** 2 *(a condition)*
follow 13 *(what someone else has done)**	**save** 2 *(money)*
follow 14 *(a person's profession)*	**serve** 4 *(an area)*
handle 5 *(an area of work)*	**settle** 3 *(a bill)*
impose 1 *(a rule)*	**show** 17 *(a work of art)*
introduce 1 *(something new)*	**spread** 8 *(wealth)*
join 2 *(an organization)*	**test** 3 *(a student)*
launch 4 *(a new product)*	**test** 5 *(a person)*
leave 2 *(an organization)*	**try** 5 *(a shop or person)**
manage 2 *(time or money)*	**try** 7 *(a suspected criminal)*
match 3 *(two things)*	**use** 1.6 *(a name)*

V n P and **V P n (not pron)**

catch out *(a person)*	**hold up** 4 *(a bank)*	**see off** 2 *(a traveller)*
check off *(things on a list)*	**lay out** 3 *(an area)*	**sit out** *(an activity)**
cost out 4 *(a proposal)*	**make up** 5 *(time or hours)*	**sleep off** *(ill effects)*
cover up 2 *(the truth)*	**save up** ▷2 *(money)*	

V P n and **V P P n**

come on to 2 *(a person)**	**live off** *(a person)**	**trade off** 2 *(something)*
draw on 1 *(skills or experience)*	**live on/off** 2,3,4 *(something)**	**trade on** *(something)*
go against 1 *(wishes or expectations)*	**play on** *(a person's fears)*	
go on 10 *(information)**	**run through** 2 *(a performance)*	

II.7 THE 'FORM' GROUP

These verbs are concerned with an abstract action or event which creates something or brings something into being. The Object indicates the thing that is created.

*A Japanese garden next to the drive **adds** a touch of the exotic.*

*Attacks of asthma **can** also **be brought on** by emotional distress, reactions to some drugs such as aspirin, and physical exertion.*

*High-impact aerobics, such as jogging, is now known to **cause** more problems than it solves.*

They were not allowed to join any of the smart Los Angeles country clubs, so they decided to **_form_ a club of their own.**

Make a firm rule about weighing yourself; be consistent.

I would have liked to **_make out_ a stronger case** by providing some scientific evidence.

Ersted showed that an electric current **_could produce_ a magnetic effect**.

He **_will raise_ huge amounts of money**.

They are expected to **_ring up_ big profits** for the third quarter.

He **_had started up_ his own business**, was working all hours and had lots of other pressures.

Then, when I **_have worked up_ an appetite**, I sit down with the family and tuck in to a huge bowl of cornmeal porridge, which I love.

add 4 *(a quality)*	**finish** 2 *(something made)*	**produce** 4 *(an argument)*
build 3 *(an organization)*	**form** 8 *(an organization)*	**produce** 6 *(a film)*
build 6 *(someone's confidence)*	**form** 10 *(a relationship)*	**publish** 1,3 *(a book)*
call 8 *(a meeting)*	**form** 11 *(someone's character)*	**pull** 9 *(crowds)*
cause 2 *(something bad)*	**found** 2 *(an institution)*	**raise** 9 *(money)*
complete 4 *(a group)*	**found** 3 *(a city) (usu passive)*	**raise** 10 *(an emotion)*
create 1	**get** 2.5 *(a particular result)*	**reach** 7 *(an agreement)*
cut 12 *(a record)*	**make** 3.5 *(rules)*	**restore** 1 *(a situation)*
design 2 *(a system)*	**open** 24 *(a bank account)*	**set** 2.19 *(a trap)*
develop 4 *(a business)*	**open** 26 *(opportunities)*	**show** 7 *(an attitude or feeling)*
develop 10 *(a new product)*	**order** 2.2 *(an investigation)*	**show** 8 *(a quality)*
develop 11 *(an idea or story)*	**pass** 16 *(a law)*	**start** 5 *(a business)*
establish 1 *(an organization)*	**place** 22 *(an advertisement)*	**strike** 13 *(a deal)*
establish 4 *(a reputation)*	**produce** 1 *(an effect)*	**strike** 15 *(a pose)*

V n P and **V P n (not pron)**

bring about *(an event)*	**draw up** 1 *(a document)*	**ring up** 3 *(an amount of money)*
bring back 1 *(a memory)*	**finish off** ▷2 *(something made)*	**run up** 1 *(a debt)*
bring back 2 *(a fashion)*	**fix up** 1 *(an event)*	**set down** 1 *(rules)*
bring in 1 *(a law)*	**lay down** 2 *(rules)*	**set up** 1 *(a procedure)*
bring in 2 *(money)*	**make out** 4 *(a case)*	**start up** ▷5 *(a business)*
bring in 4 *(a verdict)*	**make up** 4 *(an amount)*	**throw down** *(a challenge)*
bring on *(an illness or problem)*	**mark off** 1 *(a part of something)*	**work up** 2 *(enthusiasm)*
bring out 1 *(a new product)*	**open up** 3 *(opportunities)*	**work up** 3 *(an appetite)*
bring out 2 *(a kind of behaviour)*	**push through** *(a law)*	**work up** 4 *(a piece of writing)*
build up ▷6 *(confidence)*	**put on** 2 *(a show or service)*	
build up ▷8 *(pressure or speed)*	**ring up** 2 *(a sale)*	

II.8 THE 'START' AND 'STOP' GROUP

These verbs and Objects together indicate that an activity is started, finished, or carried out in a particular way. This includes:

- starting an activity e.g. *join, start*
- finishing or leaving an activity e.g. *abandon, finish*
- continuing an activity e.g. *continue, repeat*
- not doing or preventing an activity e.g. *avoid, escape, prevent*
- doing something persistently or with difficulty e.g. *attempt, manage, press*

At first Mark tried to watch surreptitiously for any vehicle that might be tailing them. But on the main highway it was impossible to be certain, and he **_abandoned_ the attempt**.

Tony and Richard were facing each other, as if they had just stood up to **_continue_ their stroll** and had paused to exchange a last remark.

She beseeched him to **_cut_ his drinking, his smoking**, to sleep more.

White **_could_** still **_manage_ a smile** when he came into his after-match press conference.

Diplomatic efforts to **_prevent_ a civil war** have so far been unsuccessful.

*The military and the civilian administration **would start** the arduous task of bringing these people to book.*

*It is questionable whether the agreement **will stop** the killing.*

The phrasal verbs *carry on, finish up, leave off* and *strike up* have the pattern **V P n (not pron)** only.

*From this research it is difficult to draw general conclusions because some of the patients **left off** treatment for reasons that were not connected with the treatment itself.*

*They all meet at the supermarket where, under the guise of checking the sell-by dates on the strawberry yoghurts, they **strike up** light conversation.*

abandon *2,3 (a process)*	**cut** *15 (bad behaviour)**	**open** *20 (a meeting)*
(cannot) afford *2 (a situation)**	**drop** *10 (an activity)*	**press** *6 (a claim)*
arrest *2 (a process)*	**escape** *3 (injury)**	**prevent** *1,2 (an event)*
attempt *1 (a task)*	**finish** *1,3 (an activity)*	**repeat** *5 (an action)*
avoid *1,2 (an event or activity)*	**join** *3 (an activity)*	**run** *12 (an experiment)*
begin *2 (talks)*	**launch** *3 (an activity)*	**start** *1 (the work)*
check *3,4 (a process)*	**lift** *4 (a rule)*	**start** *2 (the day)**
contain *5 (a process)*	**maintain** *1 (a process)*	**stop** *1,2 (an activity)*
continue *2,4 (something)**	**manage** *3 (an improvement)**	
cut *14 (classes)**	**manage** *6 (a response)**	

V n P and V P n (not pron)

break off *2 (an activity)*	**leave off** *2 (an activity)**
bring off *(something difficult)*	**move along** *2 (a process)*
carry off *1 (something difficult)*	**play out** *(an event) (usu passive)*
carry on *1,2 (an activity)*	**pull off** *1 (a difficult task)*
carry out *(a threat or instruction)*	**put off** *1 (an activity)*
carry through *(a difficult task)*	**put on** *9 (behaviour)**
cut out *4 (a behaviour)**	**start over** *(an activity)**
do over *1 (a task)*	**strike up** *1 (a conversation or friendship)*
finish up ▷*1 (an activity)*	**strike up** *2 (a piece of music)*
follow through *(an action)*	**take up** *1,3,7 (an activity, job or task)*
give up *1 (an activity)**	**throw aside** *(a way of life)*
keep up *5 (an activity)**	**turn on** *3 (behaviour)**
lead off *2 (an activity)**	

V P n and V P P n

build up to *(an activity)**	**get up to** *(an activity)**	**go through** *4 (an activity)*
come off *3 (medication)**	**give over** *(an activity) (imperative)*	**go through with** *(an action)**
fall back on *(an activity)**	**go about** *2 (normal activities)**	**play at** *1,2 (an activity)*
get in on *(an activity)**	**go at** *(an activity)**	**stick at** *(an activity)**
get through *1 (a task)*	**go in for** *(an activity)**	**stick to** *2 (an activity)**

II.9 THE 'DO' AND 'TAKE', 'TURN A CORNER', AND 'OPEN YOUR EYES' GROUPS

These verbs are concerned with both concrete and abstract actions and events. The verbs and the Objects do not indicate separate entities; the verb and the Object together express the action or event. They can be divided into three groups:

(i)   The 'do' and 'take' group
(ii)   The 'turn a corner' group
(iii)   The 'open your eyes' group

(i) The 'do' and 'take' group

These verbs and Objects are not separable and it is not possible to replace the Objects by pronouns. For example, it does not make sense to say 'they wanted a verdict so we returned it', or 'he offered me a sip and I took it'. This means that the clause does not focus attention on what is done to the Object but on what the Subject does, or on something that happens to the Subject. The verb and the Object together describe an action by the Subject.

Many of these verbs, especially *do, get, give, have,* and *take,* have little meaning in themselves but take their meaning from the Object.

> *He was sick with a muscular disease that __would claim__ his life.*
>
> *In psychotherapy, as in life, it is not unusual to __come up against__ what seems to be a brick wall.*
>
> *__Have__ you __done__ your homework, Gemma?*
>
> *He also warned Whitlock not to talk to any of the residents, as his accent __would__ only __draw__ an angry reaction.*
>
> *The regiment __fought__ this battle in the coveted position on the right of the line.*
>
> *When __do__ I __get__ the time to go to Rio, Mike?*
>
> *Cosmo __gave__ a sympathetic grin in the direction of Dick Dempsey.*
>
> *Tanya __had__ a hot bath, hoping it would relax her.*
>
> *Last month he __held__ a big party to mark his 60th birthday.*
>
> *She continued to __live__ the life of an invalid until the end.*
>
> *Last month David Rusev __lost__ his grandmother. She died at the age of 81.*
>
> *'I need to __make__ a phone call,' he said. 'It won't take long.'*
>
> *Ben was trying to impress his girlfriend by __performing__ somersaults.*
>
> *He __did not run__ a perfect race last night but it was good enough.*
>
> *The war continues to __run up against__ the obstacles typical of an air war.*
>
> *I took the Tube from Heathrow to __save__ time.*
>
> *The partners expect the company to __show__ its first profit next year.*
>
> *__Could__ you __take__ a screen test?*
>
> *They're committed to making a good life for their four children, who __turn__ cartwheels in the grass as we talk.*
>
> *Hilda was regarded as one of Hollywoood's most powerful women, but she __wore out__ her welcome in town and became despised.*
>
> *She __has to work out__ her notice, then she'll be joining me.*

The phrasal verbs *hold out, open up, put up,* and *set up* have the pattern **V P n (not pron)** only.

> *Troops of the peace-keeping force took control of the airport on Friday, but the rebel forces __put up__ stiff resistance.*

The verb *do 2.9* is used in questions beginning with *what.*

> *What __does__ your father __do__?*

accept 8 *(responsibility)**	collect 7 *(your thoughts)**	draw 20 *(a reaction)**
adopt 3 *(a position)*	commit 1 *(a crime)*	be expecting 5 *(a baby)*
aim 7 *(a kick)*	commit 2 *(suicide)**	fight 3,4 *(a battle)*
assume 2 *(responsibility)*	cost 8 *(jobs)**	fill 8 *(a role)*
attract 4 *(support)**	deliver 6 *(a blow)*	find 11 *(time)**
bear 1.8 *(responsibility)*	die 3 *(a death)**	follow 11 *(a course)*
bear 1.11 *(interest)**	do 2.1 *(your teeth)*	force 13 *(a smile)**
carry 14 *(a child)*	do 2.6 *(harm)*	get 2.7 *(the time or chance)**
catch 6 *(a train)**	do 2.9	get 2.14 *(a train)**
change 5 *(your clothes)**	do 2.10 *(an activity)*	get 2.17 *(a TV channel)*
change 9 *(buses)**	do 2.12 *(a service or product)*	give 1.1 *(a smile)**
change 10 *(gears)**	do 2.14 *(a subject at school)*	give 1.2 *(a service)*
charge 1 *(interest)*	do 2.15 *(an accent)**	give 1.10 *(a party)*
claim 3 *(responsibility)*	draw 8 *(a deep breath)*	have 2.1 *(a bath)**
claim 11 *(someone's life)*	draw 11 *(blood)*	have 3.3 *(a lot of room)**

have *3.9 (some help)** | move *7 (jobs)** | strike *14 (a balance)*
(can) hold *1.13 (drink)** | offer *6 (a sacrifice)* | survive *4 (a relative)*
hold *1.14 (the road)** | pass *22 (urine)** | take *1.1,2 (a sip, an attitude)*
hold *2.3 (office)* | pay *11 (a visit or attention)* | take *2.12 (damage)*
hold *2.5 (a party)* | perform *1,2 (an action or function)* | take *2.18 (a prize)*
hold *3.4 (the line)* | pick *6 (a fight)** | take *2.19 (the blame)**
jump *7 (a queue)** | place *23 (a telephone call)* | take *2.20 (patients)*
keep *8 (a watch)* | play *4 (a shot)* | take *2.21 (a telephone call)*
kill *9 (time)** | play *5 (a joke)* | take *2.29 (a newspaper)*
lay *1.6 (a basis or plans)* | play *13 (a concert)* | take *2.30 (a car)*
lead *1.10 (a life)** | pull *12 (a muscle)* | take *2.31 (a subject)*
leave *21 (a wife)* | pull *14 (a stunt)* | take *2.32 (a test)*
live *1.2 (a life)** | receive *2 (blame or injuries)* | take *2.34 (drugs)*
lose *7 (blood)* | return *10 (a verdict)* | take *2.36 (a letter)**
lose *9 (a part of the body)** | run *2 (a race)* | take *2.37 (a measurement)*
lose *10 (your life)* | save *3 (time or money)* | throw *12 (a fit)**
lose *11 (a relative)** | score *5 (a success)* | throw *14 (a punch)*
lose *13 (time)* | serve *3 (a purpose)* | throw *15 (a party)*
lose *14 (an opportunity)* | serve *5 (your interests)* | turn *8 (a cartwheel)*
make *1.1 (a phone call)* | set *2.20 (the table)* | turn *21 (a profit)*
make *3.6 (money)* | shoot *10 (pool)** | use *1.4 (the toilet)**
make *2.9 (a friend)** | shoot *9 (a goal)* | work *15 (its magic)**
move *5 (house)** | show *11 (a profit or loss)*

V n P and V P n (not pron)

deal out *(a punishment)* | offer up ▷*6 (a sacrifice)* | take up *2 (a cause)*
fire off *1 (a shot)* | open up *4 (a lead)* | take up *3 (a job)*
hand in *2 (your notice)* | put up *3 (resistance)* | take up *4 (an offer)*
hand over *3 (a responsibility)* | set up *5 (home)** | take up *6 (a position)*
hold out *5 (hope)** | take in *6 (a museum)** | wear out *3 (a welcome)**
lay down *3 (your weapons)* | take on *1 (a job)** | work out *6 (your notice)**
leave behind *2 (a situation)* | take out *2 (a loan)*

V P n and V P P n

come under *1 (attack)** | go against *2 (someone)** | sign off *2 (the dole)*
come up against *(a problem)** | run into *1 (problems)** | sign on *(the dole)*
come up for *(consideration)* | run up against *(problems)**

(ii) The 'turn a corner' group

The verbs and Objects in this group are not competely separable. The Objects can be replaced by pronouns, but as with the verbs in the preceding group the clause does not focus attention on what is done to the Object but on what the Subject does. For example, it does not make sense to ask 'What did the baby cut?' or 'What did the baby do to the tooth?' but only 'What did the baby do?' or 'Did the baby cut a tooth?'

*The system let her **get away with** cold-blooded murder.*

*You were smart enough to run, but then you **gave away** your advantage.*

*The court will start **hearing the case** next week but no date was fixed.*

*Select a location where you can be alone for 10 to 15 minutes at a time. That may mean disconnecting the telephone for a while or telling your secretary to **hold calls**.*

***Does** your bank current account **pay interest** when in credit?*

*These transactions would help the company to **realize** the value of its assets.*

*It was hard enough trying to keep a home and **run a car** on a teacher's salary.*

*There has been been no progress in **setting** a date for a top-level meeting on the crisis.*

*I didn't get anybody to fill the job. I **took it over** myself.*

*He watched her gray car pass under dull streetlamps until it **turned** a **corner** and disappeared.*

act 8 *(a role)*	**hear** 4 *(a case)*	**play** 11 *(a tune)*
bear 1.3 *(weight)*	**hold** 3.5 *(calls)*	**realize** 4 *(potential)*
bear 1.7 *(a cost)*	**keep** 11 *(a promise)*	**realize** 5 *(an amount of money)*
blow 1.10 *(a chance)*	**meet** 11 *(the cost)*	**resign** 1 *(your post)**
break 27 *(a serve)*	**miss** 2.2 *(a shot)**	**run** 16 *(a car)**
claim 4 *(an inheritance)*	**miss** 2.5 *(a chance)*	**run** 22 *(water)*
cross 1.4 *(a line)*	**miss** 2.8 *(a train)**	**save** 6 *(a goal)*
cut 13 *(a tooth)*	**miss** 2.9 *(a meeting)**	**score** 1,2 *(a goal or points)*
deliver 2 *(something promised)*	**move** 16 *(a motion)*	**set** 2.6 *(a date or goal)*
draw 13 *(a salary)*	**pay** 6 *(interest)*	**show** 15 *(a film or programme)*
earn 2 *(interest)*	**play** 2 *(tennis)*	**sit** 5 *(an exam)*
fight 12 *(a court action)*	**play** 8 *(a role)*	**turn** 5 *(a corner)**

V n P and V P n (not pron)

cut out 6 *(the light)*	**live out** 2 *(a dream or fantasy)*	**take over** 3 *(a role)*
give away 2 *(an advantage)*	**pass up** *(an opportunity)*	**throw away** 2 *(an opportunity)*

V P n and V P P n

come under 2 *(an authority)**	**get away with** *(a crime)**	**go without** *(something)**
do without 1 *(something)**	**go towards** *(something bought)**	

(iii) The 'open your eyes' group

These verbs are concerned with actions done with and to your own body.

*And then we **cross** our **fingers**. We hope for the best.*

*She **opened** her **eyes** and smiled at me.*

*Kemp merely nodded but the child **put out** his **hand** to be shaken.*

blow 1.7 *(your nose)**	**lift** 2 *(a part of your body)**	**roll** 9 *(your eyes)**
cross 1.11 *(your fingers)**	**lift** 3 *(your eyes or head)**	**set** 2.16 *(your face or jaw)**
drop 8 *(your voice)**	**open** 4 *(your eyes)**	**shake** 2,3,6 *(a part of your body)**
extend 9 *(your hand)*	**open** 5 *(your arms)**	**spread** 2 *(your arms or legs)**
focus 5 *(your eyes)**	**pick** 5 *(your teeth)**	**turn** 1 *(a part of your body)**
hide 3 *(your face)**	**raise** 6 *(your voice)**	**work** 27 *(a part of your body)*

V n P and V P n (not pron)

hold out 1 *(your hand)**	**spread out** ▷2 *(your arms or legs)**
hold up 1 *(your hand)**	**stick out** 1 *(a part of your body)**
lift up ▷2 *(a part of your body)**	**turn round/around** ▷1 *(a part of your body)**
put out 5 *(your hand)**	

II.10 THE 'FACE', 'TAKE THREE DAYS', AND 'SEE' GROUPS

These verbs and Objects together are concerned with place or time. They can be divided into three groups:

(i)   The 'face' group
(ii) The 'take three days' group
(iii) The 'next week sees' group

(i) The 'face' group

The verb and the Object together indicate place or extent. This includes:

- where something or someone is relative to something else e.g. *meet, pass*
- the direction something or someone is pointing or facing e.g. *face*
- how big or extensive something is e.g. *fill*

*Gunnell's face was painfully contorted as she **cleared the final hurdle**.*

*The Canadian tour was scheduled to **cover 16,000 miles** in nine weeks.*

*A flicker of real alarm **crossed his face**.*

*Each atom was seen to have three proper motions of its own: spinning on its axis like a top, **describing a small circle** with its axis like a top, contracting and expanding like a heart.*

*He turned on the bed until he **was facing her** directly and spoke in a tight voice.*

*We didn't want players **running the length of the field**, stretching themselves unnecessarily.*

The verbs *cross, divide, follow, join, meet, pass,* and *run* 4 have an inanimate Subject.

*There were a few small fir trees where the sand dunes **met the cobble beach**.*

*Beyond the pub, the road **passes a farmyard** and becomes a grass track.*

clear 17 (an object)	**head** 4 (a procession)	**pass** 3 (an area)*
cover 5 (a distance)	**head** 5 (a list)	**reach** 1 (a place)*
cross 1.2,3 (an area or line)	**join** 7 (a river)*	**ring** 2.7 (something) (usu passive)
cross 1.5 (your face)*	**jump** 3 (a fence)	**run** 1,4*
describe 3 (a circle)	**lead** 1.1 (a procession)	**settle** 6 (an area)
divide 4 (an area)	**meet** 16 (an area)*	**surround** 1 (a person or thing)
face 2.1,2 (a thing or direction)*	**meet** 17 (a line)	**top** 14
fill 2 (a space)	**occupy** 1 (a building)	**travel** 1 (a distance)
fish 4 (a river)	**occupy** 2 (a seat) (usu passive)	**travel** 3 (the world)*
fit 1.1*	**occupy** 7 (an area)	**walk** 1 (a distance or place)*
follow 9 (a route)	**pass** 1	**work** 18 (an area or place)

V n P and **V P n (not pron)**

fill up ▷2 (a space)	**pass by***

V P n and **V P P n**

cut across (a division)*	**lead off** 1 (a place)*	**lead on to** 2 (a place)*

(ii) The 'take three days' group

The verb and the Object together indicate a point in time, the duration of something, or a sequence of events.

*The men, who last month **began their seventeenth year in prison**, have always maintained their innocence.*

These verbs often have inanimate Subjects.

*Today's talks **follow the summit meeting of Community leaders at the weekend**.*

*He predicted that the current parliament **would not last the full term**.*

*The journey **took thirty-nine days**.*

The phrasal verb *serve out* has the pattern **V P n (not pron)** only.

*Barlow refused to be interviewed after making clear his intention to **serve out the last year of his contract**.*

approach *7 (a future time)**   occupy *8*
begin *2*   pass *10**
end *4**   serve *10 (a sentence)*
enter *5 (a situation or period of time)**   stay *2**
fill *6*   succeed *4 (a person)*
follow *4 (an event)*   succeed *5 (an event) (usu passive)*
last *13**   take *2.13**
(can) manage *5 (an amount of time or money)**   wait *1,6**
mark *14 (a point or stage)*

V n P and **V P n** (not pron)

fill in *5*   last out ▷*13**   serve out*
fill up ▷*6*   put in *1*

V P P n

be coming up to *(a time or state)**

(iii) The 'next week sees' group

These verbs indicate that an action, state, or event occurs. The Subject indicates a time or place, the Object indicates an action, state, or event. We include here *go into*, where the Subject indicates the length of time required to achieve the Object.

*Not only is cash in limited supply, but each day **brings** new efforts to separate people from their money.*

*The album has been a work in progress since 1987, although it's hard to see how six years **went into** its creation.*

*Next week **sees** the first (and long overdue) conference on sickle cell disease sufferers.*

bring *8*   see *9*

V P n

go into *3*

II.11 THE 'TOP', 'DEVELOP', AND 'INCLUDE' GROUPS

These verbs and Objects together give information about the qualities, attributes, or role of the Subject. They can be divided into three groups:

(i) The 'top' group
(ii) The 'develop' group
(iii) The 'include' group

(i) The 'top' group

These verbs and Objects indicate how good, big, or important something or someone is. We include here *(cannot) beat*, which indicates how good the Object is, and *buy* and *cover*, which indicate that an amount of money is enough to pay for something.

*Nothing **beats** a refreshing shower to wake you up first thing in the morning, or to revitalise you before an evening out.*

*Under Lloyd George £10,000 **could buy** a knighthood and ten times that secured a peerage.*

*Legal aid itself is money to **cover** all or part of the cost of having a solicitor to represent you in court, either in a civil or a criminal case.*

Brazil **had left** Argentina far **behind** in industrialization but it had failed to expand its internal market.

Stevie Wonder **topped** the UK chart with 'I Just Called To Say I Love You' for six consecutive weeks.

approach 8 (a level or state)*	**fill** 4 (the air)	**take** 2.39 (a size in clothes)*
beat 13*	**fit** 1.7,8*	**top** 12 (a list)
(cannot) beat 14	**hold** 2.8 (the lead)	**(cannot) touch** 12 (a person)
buy 2 (a quantity)	**lead** 1.4 (the competition)	**touch** 13 (a point or level)
cover 14	**match** 7 (something good)	**turn** 22 (an age)*
dominate 1 (a situation)	**pass** 12 (a level or figure)	
dominate 3 (an area)	**reach** 6 (a point or level)	

V n P and **V P n (not pron)**

eat up 2 (resources)	**leave behind** 3

V P n and **V P P n**

fall behind 1*	**make up for***	**run to** 2 (an amount or size)*
live up to (a reputation)*	**match up to***	

(ii) The 'develop' group

These verbs and Objects indicate what something or someone has, what they are like, or what they become. This includes:

- getting an illness or characteristic e.g. *adopt, catch (a disease), develop*
- having a quality e.g. *bear (no resemblance), catch (the light), have (red hair)*
- changing e.g. *gain (weight), gather (speed)*

After a few years of marriage I found that my husband **bore** no resemblance to the man I thought I loved.

You will soon realize when something is wrong because your youngster will either go off her food or **develop** a tummy or headache.

Muriel was all sweetness and light. She **took after** her mother.

By the age of thirty he **had taken on** the manner and appearance of an eccentric academic.

adopt 1 (an attitude)	**develop** 9 (a fault)*	**hold** 3.6 (its value)*
affect 4 (an interest)*	**enjoy** 3 (a benefit)	**lose** 4,5 (a quality or ability)*
assume 3,4 (a quality or manner)	**gain** 1 (an ability)	**lose** 6 (heat)
bear 1.4 (a mark)	**gain** 3 (weight or speed)	**lose** 8 (weight)*
bear 1.9 (no resemblance)*	**gather** 5 (strength or courage)*	**occupy** 4 (a place in a system)
bear 1.10 (flowers)	**gather** 4 (speed)*	**present** 4.2 (a difficulty)
carry 4 (a disease)	**get** 2.11 (a type of weather)*	**present** 4.7 (an appearance)
carry 14 (a child)*	**get** 2.13 (an illness)*	**recover** 5 (consciousness)*
catch 18 (a disease)*	**have** 2.2 (something)*	**run** 35 (a temperature)*
catch 20 (the light)*	**have** 3.1 (red hair)*	**sell** 2 (goods)
develop 6 (a habit)*	**have** 3.10 (an illness)*	**wear** 1,2,3
develop 8 (an illness)	**hold** 2.4 (a permit)	

V n P and **V P n (not pron)**

> **gather up** ▷5 *(strength or courage)**   **pick up** 7 *(an illness)*   **take on** 2 *(an appearance)**
> **hold down** 1 *(a job)**   **put on** 3 *(weight)*

V P n and **V P P n**

> **come down with** *(an illness)**   **go down with** *(an illness)**
> **come in for** *(criticism)**   **take after** *(someone)**

The verb *have* is also used like an auxiliary, without an Object, following comparatives or in phrases with *neither, nor,* and *so* (see Chapter 11).

> *Maybe the kid would have more luck than he **had**. He hoped so.*
> *He has the character to fight back. So **have** I.*

(iii) The 'include' group

These verbs and Objects indicate what something contains or is about.

> *On one level, the play **concerns** the tactics of survival.*
> *The law **covers** religions in general.*
> *The Guardian has a whole page **covering** the issue, with each republic dealt with separately.*
> *The first of a series of anthologies features three novellas **following** the life and crimes of Eastender Joe Hawkins.*
> *The dish further **included** a variety of rice which I had not previously tasted.*
> *Figure 1 **shows** the structure of your back in graphic detail.*

> **carry** 8 *(a picture)*   **cover** 11 *(A law...people)*   **house** 13 *(an office)*
> **concern** 8 *(a topic)**   **cover** 12 *(a topic)*   **include** 1 *(a component)*
> **contain** 1,2,4   **feature** 3   **involve** 2 *(someone)*
> **contain** 3 *(information)*   **follow** 17 *(someone's life)**   **show** 2 *(something)*
> **cover** 9 *(Insurance...something)*   **hold** 1.9,11

V n P and **V P n (not pron)**

> **take in** 8 *(something smaller)**

V P n and **V P P n**

> **come down to** *(an issue)**   **run to** 4*
> **deal with** 3 *(a topic)*

II.12 THE 'SHOW', 'ALLOW', AND 'IDENTIFY' GROUPS

These verbs indicate a logical relation between the inanimate Subject and the Object. They can be divided into three groups:

(i)   The 'show' group
(ii)   The 'allow' group
(iii) The 'identify' group

(i) The 'show' group

The thing indicated by the Subject provides evidence for the truth of the fact indicated by the Object. We include here *bear out*, where the Object indicates a person who has said something, rather than the thing they have said.

Time and again, Crosby relates, Europeans in America showed their robust health. Statistics certainly **bear** him **out**.

The latest experiments **have** also **confirmed** earlier results that there are fewer neutrinos than expected according to our understanding of the nuclear physics of the sun.

The death of a family of three who were overcome by fumes **shows** the importance of having gas appliances serviced regularly.

If you ask the parents who have children enrolled in Wisconsin's Parental Choice Program, they say it's working beautifully. But the test scores **tell** a different story.

confirm 1	mean 1.4*	reveal 1	support 5
indicate 1,4	prove 2	show 1	tell 8*
mark 12	reflect 1 (a situation)	suggest 4	

V n P and V P n (not pron)

bear out

(ii) The 'allow' group

The thing indicated by the Subject:

- causes the state of affairs indicated by the Object e.g. *decide, make for*
- makes possible or impossible the thing indicated by the Object e.g. *afford, allow, rule out*
- makes necessary the thing indicated by the Object e.g. *need, require, take*

Sun terraces and private balconies **afford** a relaxing corner for simply doing nothing.

Only a 60 to 90 per cent reduction in acid rain **would allow** recovery of fisheries, wildlife and fishing birds such as dippers.

Ultimately, it's likely to be sale of tickets that finally **decides** the Festival's future.

Simple safety precautions **should make for** a safer mechanical environment.

Serious collecting also **takes** a lot of money and time.

afford 3*	decide 3	ensure	need 2*
allow 4	demand 2	invite 3 (trouble)*	require 2
carry 5 (a consequence)*	determine 1	involve 1*	take 2.14*
carry 10 (a punishment)	encourage 4	mean 1.5*	

V n P and V P n (not pron)

rule out 2 (a situation)	set up 6 (a process)
set off 3 (an event)	touch off (a process)

V P n and V P P n

call for 3	enter into 2*	lead up to 1,2 (an event)
count towards (an achievement)*	go with 1*	lie behind*
cry out for*	lead on to 1*	make for 2*

(iii) The 'identify' group

The Subject and the Object are associated with each other in people's minds. This includes:

- identifying someone or something e.g. *identify, mark out*

- representing someone or something e.g. *represent, stand for*
- being a part of a situation e.g. *come into, surround*
- applying to a person or situation e.g. *go for*

This general absence of fuss __catches__ the mood of the occasion.

They both said yes, and that __goes for__ me, too.

Buy a separate strap in case the zip breaks – a bright colour will help __identify__ luggage, too.

Two factors __mark__ her __out__. She listens and she knows her brief.

The party __should stand for__ what people want.

Remote Easter Island has for generations __been surrounded__ by an aura of mystery.

catch 15 *(a mood)**	represent *6,7*
identify *4*	surround *3*

V n P and **V P n (not pron)**

mark out *2*	set apart	show up *1*

V P n

come into *2**	go for *4**
come under *3 (a heading)**	stand for *1,2**

II.13 THE 'HEAR', 'INTEREST', AND 'GIVE AN IMPRESSION' GROUPS

These verbs, or verbs and Objects together, are concerned with processes that take place in the mind, such as thinking, perceiving, or feeling. They can be divided into four groups:

(i) The 'hear' group
(ii) The 'interest' group
(iii) The 'give an impression' group
(iv) The 'eyes follow' group

(i) The 'hear' group

The Subject indicates a person or something that shares certain characteristics with a person, such as a radio receiver which can 'hear'. The Object indicates something that is thought, perceived, or felt. This includes:

- ways of thinking about something or someone e.g. *decide, expect, plan*
- ways of perceiving something or someone e.g. *experience, feel, hear, see*
- attitudes towards something or someone e.g. *accept, believe, buy, like, love, mean*
- ways of finding out or knowing about something e.g. *learn, remember*

We also include here *count*, which sometimes has an inanimate Subject and which indicates a metaphorical form of thinking, and *force back*, which indicates that a feeling is not expressed openly.

It is difficult to __accept__ my son's death, but he's alive in my heart.

It's a common belief that one of the ways in which men and women differ emotionally is that women __experience__ a strong drive to become mothers.

Nancy __forced back__ tears. No way was she going to cry in front of all those people.

'You look a little under the weather, Ralph.' 'So would you if you'd had the night I had.' 'I've already __gathered__ that.'

At that point the skies over the city lit up with a shower of fireworks and you **could hear** the **cheering** for miles around.

I sat down and thought hard about what I liked doing most – trudging through woods in search of animals – and **hit on** the idea of becoming a wildlife photographer.

What we've accomplished is the development of a whole system that **can be learned** by any able farmer who is interested in preserving and improving his land.

If you**'d like** a copy of those recipes, we can easily let you have one.

I put my eyes to the crack in the door. I could hear him muttering to himself and I **could** just **make out** his tall figure.

I**'d planned** a weekend away with a friend, only everything had gone wrong and I came back after only one night.

'You **read me**, Ben?' the operator asked.

Both loudspeakers **receive the same signal**, carrying both left and right sound channels, but each is preset to decode only one of the channels.

Black holes **cannot be seen** directly, so determining how many of them there are in the Galaxy is a tough task.

She was witty but the audience **didn't take to her**.

The girls may of course not actually be asleep, they **may be** reading, writing or drawing, **thinking** beautiful thoughts.

The verb *mind 2.4* is always imperative or used to report an imperative.

'**Mind** my heart,' he gasped. 'I've got a heart problem.'

accept 2 (an idea)	fix 12 (the position of something)
accept 4 (an unpleasant fact)	follow 15 (an explanation)
accept 9 (advice)	forget 1,2,3,4
bear 1.5 (an experience)	gather 6
(cannot) bear 1.6 (something unpleasant)*	get 2.8 (an idea)*
bear 1.13 (an emotion)	get 2.9 (a warm feeling)*
believe 2 (what someone says)	get 2.10 (a look)*
blame 1	get 2.12 (a joke)*
(not) blame 3	guess 1,2 (information)
buy 5 (an idea)*	hang 8 (problems)*
catch 9 (a glimpse)*	hate 1,2
catch 10 (what someone said)	(will not) have 3.12 (something unpleasant)*
consider 2,3	hear 1,3,7,8
(cannot) contain 6 (a feeling)*	hide 4 (a feeling or knowledge)*
count 2 (things)	hold 2.1 (an opinion)*
count 8 (a factor)	identify 1,3
decide 2	ignore 1 (a person)
determine 2 (a fact)	ignore 2 (an argument)
determine 3 (a plan)	imagine 1,3
discover 1,3,4	intend 3 (a meaning)
draw 17 (a conclusion)	know 1,2,5,6,9
enjoy 1	learn 1,5
establish 3 (a fact)	like 2.1,2,3
estimate 1	(would) like 2.5,7,8*
examine 3 (an idea)	love 1,3,5,6
expect 1,2,3	(would) love 9*
(not) expect 4	mean 1.7 (what you say)*
experience 5 (a feeling)	(not) mean 1.9 (harm)
face 2.4 (a problem)	(not) mind 2.1*
face 2.5 (the truth)	mind 2.4*
(cannot) face 2.6 (something unpleasant)*	miss 2.3,4,6,7
fear 2,4	need 1
feel 1 (a pain)	note 9 (a fact)
feel 6 (a hand)	notice 1
feel 7 (something happen) (usu passive)	(cannot) place 26 (a person)*
feel 9 (a presence)	plan 2,4
feel 14 (the effect of something)	prefer
fight 14 (an emotion)*	read 9,10 (someone's mind or gestures)

read *11 (someone talking by radio)**
realize *1 (a fact)*
recall *1*
receive *5 (a signal)*
regard *3 (someone)*
remember *1,2*
(cannot) remember *3*
require *1*
review *2 (a situation)*
see *1,3,5,8*
see *17 (the next chapter)**
share *5 (an opinion)*
stand *16 (a situation)**

(cannot) stand *17**
suffer *1,3*
suspect *2*
(cannot) take *2.11 (something difficult)**
take *2.24 (someone's point)*
think *8 (a thought)**
understand *1,2,3,4*
want *1,3,4,8,9*
want *7 (a criminal) (usu passive)*
watch *1.3,6 (a situation)*
welcome *3 (a situation)*
welcome *5 (actions or people)*

V n P and V P n (not pron)

cook up *1 (a plan)*
cook up *2 (a story)*
count up *▷2 (things)*
drink in *(something seen or heard)**
fight back *2 (a feeling)**
fight down *(a feeling)**
find out *1 (a fact)*
find out *2 (a person)*
force back *(a feeling)*
hear out *(a person)*
hold back *5 (tears or laughter)*
hold in *(a feeling)*
lay aside *2 (a feeling)*
make out *1,2 (something unclear)*
make up *2 (a story)*
pick out *1 (a person or thing)*
pick up *5 (a skill or idea)*

pick up *8 (a signal or sound)*
pick up *9 (a pattern)*
plan out *(the future)*
push aside *(an idea)*
put aside *2 (a feeling or disagreement)*
set aside *2 (a feeling)*
take apart *2 (an idea)*
take in *4 (information)*
take in *5 (sights)*
tell apart *(people or things)*
think out
think over
think through
think up *(a plan)*
work out *2 (a sum)*
write off *3 (a person)*

V P n and V P P n

bear with*
buy into *▷5**
come across *1*
come up with *1**
decide on
(could) do without *2**
face up to *▷2.5 (a fact or problem)*
fall for *1*
fall on
fix on
get at *2 (the truth)**
get off on*

give up on
go by *2**
go for *2*
go off *1**
hit on
hold on to *3 (beliefs)*
(not) hold with*
look down on
look forward to *1,2*
look through *3*
look to *2 (something in the future)*
look up to

plan on
put up with
run away with *3 (an idea)**
see through
stand by *4 (a decision)*
(not) stand for *3**
stick by *2 (a decision)*
take against
take to *1**
turn against*

(ii) The 'interest' group

The Subject usually indicates the person or thing that makes someone think or feel in a particular way. The Object usually indicates a person. With some verbs, the Object indicates something such as someone's attention.

*Jarvis looked at Kate as he prised himself up from the chair. She shook her head, indicating a half-full glass in front of her. 'This **will do** me,' she said.*

*William **was driven** by an overriding passion for power.*

*Everything about her grandchildren seemed to **interest** Sara.*

*I lived with Mike for six months and then I arranged the wedding. Two failed marriages **didn't put** me **off**.*

*These stories **surprised** and **moved** me, and sometimes they made me laugh.*

In the case of *come over, come upon, be eating, enter, fill, get into, go out of,* and *run away with,* the Subject indicates the feeling itself or a sign of it.

*Joe jumped up impetuously. 'What**'s eating** you?' Frank asked.*

*She sighed, the tension **going out of** her.*

The phrasal verb *get into* is always used with *what* as the Subject.

*I don't know what **got into** him. It really seems as if he doesn't recognize me anymore.*

The phrasal verbs *get down, lead on,* and *take back* have the pattern **V n P** only.

*Little things **get** me **down**.*

*'That **takes** me **back**,' he said. 'You used to drive me crazy with that stuff.'*

affect 3	**do** 2.16*	**get** 1.17*	**shake** 10,11
arrest 3 *(your attention)*	**draw** 19 *(attention)*	**hit** 5	**strike** 10,12
attract 2,3	**draw** 22	**hold** 2.9 *(your attention)*	**surprise** 3
catch 14 *(your eye)*	**drive** 14	**hurt** 5	**throw** 13
claim 8 *(your attention)**	**be eating** 3*	**interest** 3	**touch** 9,10
concern 2*	**enter** 3 *(your mind)**	**lift** 5 *(your spirits)*	**upset** 2
convince 1,2	**escape** 6 *(your attention)**	**move** 14	**worry** 2
cross 1.12	**fill** 5	**occupy** 5,6	**(not) worry** 3*
decide 5*	**fire** 1.8	**please** 5	

V n P and **V P n (not pron)**

bring round 2	**shake up** 2	**throw off** ▷13	**wear out** 2
get down 1*	**take back** 4	**turn off** 3,4	**win over**
lead on	**take in** 3	**turn on** 2	
put off 3,4	**talk round**	**wear down** 2	

V P n and **V P P n**

come over 1*	**get into** 3*	**grow on** *
come upon 2*	**go out of** *	**run away with** 1

(iii) The 'give an impression' group

The Object indicates an idea or feeling. The Subject indicates the reason for that idea or feeling.

*He **gave** the impression of great physical strength without a mind to direct it.*

*Earth tones, such as dark greens, browns and greys, represent stability, while bright greens, yellows and turquoises **suggest** dynamism.*

give 1.6 *(an impression)**	**hold** 2.2 *(no fear)**	**suggest** 5 *(an impression)**
give 1.7 *(a feeling)**	**leave** 12 *(an impression)*	

(iv) The 'eyes follow' group

The Subject indicates someone's eyes. The Object indicates a person or thing that is watched or seen.

*My eyes **followed** the track as it weaved between the boulders, disappeared under the stream, and emerged to join the road on the far side of the bridge.*

*Mrs. Keely was saying this into the rear-view mirror, where her eyes **met** Mrs. Dambar's.*

53

```
follow 10*    meet 15*
```

II.14 THE 'SAY', 'DESCRIBE', AND 'CALL' GROUPS

These verbs are concerned with communication, especially speaking or writing. They can be divided into three groups:

(i)   The 'say' group
(ii) The 'describe' group
(iii) The 'call' group

(i) The 'say' group

The Object indicates what is said or written. The verb and the Object together indicate the process of speaking or writing. This includes:

- verbs which themselves indicate communication e.g. *ask, say, speak*
- verbs which indicate communication only when used with particular noun groups e.g. *draw, make, pass*

*Mothers **come out with** remarks like that and there's not a thing sons can do about it.*

*He **gave out** a scream of pain.*

*Some letters are either full of praise or downright rude but **don't make** any constructive suggestions.*

*On that day, the Hopi leaders arrived at a deserted strip of coastline near Laguna, California, to gather salt and **offer** their prayers.*

*When booking the flight, **put in** your request for high-protein low-fat meals.*

*The News of the World **ran** a story about the manager of pop group Take That.*

*Shirley took me into a separate room where, clipboard in hand, she **ran through** various personal details she'd need.*

*I took some of my drink. I **didn't say** anything.*

*I can't believe that Paul **wrote** that letter.*

add 5 *(a remark)*	**lay** 1.7 *(blame or charges)*	**sign** 3 *(a word)*
adopt 5 *(a tone of voice)*	**leave** 5 *(a message)*	**sing** 1 *(a song)*
ask 1 *(a question)*	**make** 1.1 *(a suggestion)*	**smile** 3 *(thanks)*
call 3 *(someone's name)*	**make** 3.4 *(a note)*	**sound** 1.6 *(a warning)*
complete 10 *(a form)*	**offer** 4 *(advice)*	**speak** 1 *(a word)*
cross 1.10 *(a cheque) (usu passive)*	**offer** 6 *(prayer)*	**speak** 4 *(a language)*
deliver 4 *(a speech)*	**paint** 7 *(a picture)*	**supply** 5 *(a word)*
draw 18 *(a comparison)*	**pass** 17 *(sentence)*	**talk** 10 *(a language)*
employ 2 *(a word)*	**pass** 18 *(comment)*	**talk** 12 *(rubbish)*
enter 8 *(some figures)*	**propose** 5 *(a toast)*	**tell** 2 *(a joke or story)*
enter 9 *(information)*	**put** 9 *(a question)*	**use** 1.5 *(a word)*
fire 2.4 *(questions)*	**put** 12 *(a word)*	**withdraw** 6 *(a remark)*
give 1.8 *(a speech)*	**relate** 4 *(a story)*	**write** 1 *(a word)*
hold 2.6 *(a conversation)*	**run** 30 *(a story)*	**write** 2,4 *(a book or letter)*
hold 3.7 *(a musical note)*	**say** 1 *(something)*	**write** 6 *(a cheque)*
issue 4 *(a statement)*	**send** 4 *(a signal)*	
keep 12 *(a record)*	**set** 2.10 *(an exam)*	

V n P and **V P n (not pron)**

call out ▷3 *(words)*	**give out** 4 *(a sigh or scream)*	**take back** 2 *(something said)*
cry out ▷2 *(words)*	**hand out** 2 *(advice)*	**throw in** 1 *(a remark)*
draw out 1 *(a sound)*	**let out** 2 *(a sound)*	**write down** *(a word)*
fill in 1 *(a form)*	**make out** 5 *(a cheque)*	**write out** 1 *(a report)*
fill out 1 *(a form)*	**put about** *(a rumour)*	**write out** ▷6 *(a cheque)*
fire off 2 *(a letter or question)*	**put in** 2 *(a request)*	**write up** *(notes)*
get down 3 *(words)*	**sing out** *(words)*	

V P n and V P P n

| come out with *(a remark)* | fall into *(a conversation)* | run through *1 (a list)* |

(ii) The 'describe' group

The Object indicates the topic or content of the communication.

*Each market was opened by a town crier who **would announce** the market's rules.*

*Grace **did not answer** the question directly.*

*He courageously voiced his political convictions and **argued** the case for a poetry with a purpose.*

*She **described** the building where the man and woman responsible for the theft were.*

*The pilots, as well as the police, **have indicated** their view that the hijackers should immediately be handed over to the authorities.*

*A journalist from the Washington Post asked if Wilder, who is divorced, had plans to marry. The governor **laughed off** the suggestion.*

*Miss Hoare stood in the middle of the crush, clutching a sheaf of papers as she called out names and **marked** them **off**.*

*No, I **didn't mean** a French teacher, I **mean** a teacher who teaches French.*

*A trainee journalist, Mr William Giles, has been fined five thousand pounds for refusing to **name** the source of information about a company's finances which he had gathered for an article in the London-based Engineer magazine.*

*During a lecturing trip to Australia, I **had to play down** my enthusiasm for the plants shown in some of my slides because, out there, they have become noxious weeds.*

*Twelve-year-old Sammy Hicks wrote to the World Book people to **point out** an error in their encyclopedia.*

*Why **do** you **raise** this subject if you don't understand anything about it?*

*In his estimation, the soldiers have become too comfortable for a fighting force. He **recommended** tougher and more demanding training.*

*He **rejects** the suggestion that he might have felt like an outsider.*

*They walked back down Piccadilly and looked in at an exhibition at the Royal Academy. Afterwards, she **suggested** a walk in St James's Park.*

*The president and his top advisers started their Christmas holiday at Camp David **talking** logistics.*

accuse *1,2 (a suspect)*	give *1.3 (an opinion)*	publish *4 (an opinion)*
admit *1 (a crime)**	identify *2*	put *10 (an opinion)*
announce *1,3,4*	indicate *2 (a fact or opinion)*	qualify *5 (a statement)*
announce *5 (dinner) (usu passive)*	indicate *6 (a turn)*	quote *1 (what someone said)*
answer *4,9 (a letter or question)*	leave *19*	quote *3 (a fact)*
argue *1 (a point)*	maintain *2 (a fact)*	quote *4 (a price)*
argue *2*	mean *1.2**	raise *11 (a subject)*
ask *6 (permission)*	mention *1*	read *2 (poetry)*
attack *2*	mention *3 (a person) (usu passive)*	recall *1*
break *18 (some news)*	name *4,6*	recommend *1,2*
charge *5 (a suspect)*	name *5 (a price)*	record *2 (a piece of information)*
claim *1 (something advantageous)*	negotiate *1 (terms)*	reject *1,2 (a proposal or belief)*
confirm *2 (what someone has said)*	note *10,11*	repeat *1,2*
confirm *3 (an appointment)*	offer *9*	report *1*
cover *13 (an event)*	predict *(an event)*	reveal *1*
declare *1,2*	present *4.4 (information)*	review *4*
defend *2,3 (a person)*	present *4.11 (a person)*	say *6 (the time)**
deny *1 (an accusation)*	promise *1,2 (something)*	strike *18 (the time)*
deny *2 (a person)*	propose *1,2 (a plan)*	suggest *1,2*
describe *1*	propose *3 (a theory)*	take *2.23 (a topic)*
discuss *1,2*	propose *4 (a candidate)*	talk *11,13 (politics)**
explain *1,2*	propose *6 (marriage)*	teach *3 (a subject)*
express *1 (an idea)*	prove *2 (a theory)*	urge *3 (a course of action)*

V n P and V P n (not pron)

argue out *(a point)*	**mark off** *3 (a date or item)*	**set down** *2*
bring forward *2 (an argument)*	**note down**	**set forth** *1 (information)*
bring up *2 (a subject)*	**pass on** ▷*7 (information)*	**set out** *4 (information)*
do down *(a person)*	**pick up** *10 (a topic)*	**shoot down** *3 (someone's ideas)*
explain away *(a mistake)*	**play down**	**take apart** *2 (an idea)*
give away *3 (information)*	**play up** *1*	**take down** *3 (information)*
give away *4 (a criminal)*	**point out** *2*	**talk down** *2*
get across *(an idea)*	**put across/over** *(information)*	**talk out** *(a problem)*
hand down *2 (a decision)*	**put down** *1,4*	**talk over** *(a problem)*
hold back *4 (information)*	**put forth** *(a plan)*	**talk through** *1 (a problem)*
keep back *2 (informatioon)*	**put forward**	**talk up** *1*
laugh off	**put out** *1 (a story)*	**throw around** *(a name)*
lay out *2 (ideas)*	**read out** *(a piece of writing)*	**turn down** *1 (a request)*
leave off *1**	**report back** *1*	**write in** *2 (a candidate)*
mark down *1*	**run down** *1*	**write out** *2 (a character)*

V P n and V P P n

ask after	**get at** *3**	**lay into**	**pick up on** *10*
come down on *1 (a side of an argument)*	**get on to** *1**	**lead up to** *3**	**sign for**
come on to *1**	**go into** *1 (a topic)*	**pass over** *2 (a topic)*	

(iii) The 'call' group

The Object indicates the hearer or reader.

> Maria whispered, 'How did he get in?' Then she **answered** herself. 'He could have taken a spare key. When he came last time.'
>
> She has no phone or I**'d call** her.
>
> 'I think it's worth looking at what Tim does.' 'We**'ve got to get on to** him, haven't we, on other matters.'
>
> My father tried to teach me to toughen up and retaliate because boys **were** always **picking on me** since I was the weakest.
>
> Despite being behind schedule he took the time to **ring me**.
>
> If rows break out between the children, pull over and explain to them that the journey will take even longer if you have to keep stopping the car to **tell** them **off**.
>
> Yang Tsiao seemed to be suffering. I **urged** him **on** but I was beginning to worry.

address *3,4*	**call** *4,6*	**invite** *1,2*	**thank** *5 (a person)*
answer *1*	**encourage** *1,3*	**persuade** *1*	**threaten** *1*
approach *3*	**fight** *6**	**ring** *1.1*	**welcome** *1*

V n P and V P n (not pron)

answer back	**dress down** *2*	**ring up** ▷*1.1*	**warn away**
call back	**fill in** *3 (a person)*	**sound out**	**warn off**
call up *1*	**ring around/round***	**tell off**	
cut off *5 (a speaker)*	**ring back***	**urge on**	

V P n and V P P n

get on to *2**	**pick on** *1*
get round *2**	**run to** *1**

Structure information: Verb with Object

a) The noun group is the Object.

b) This structure has a passive, with the pattern *be* V-ed. Verbs which never or rarely occur in the passive are shown by * in the lists above. Some verbs, when used in the passive, always have the pattern *be* V-ed *by* n (see page 58). The passive of some verbs is usually or often formed with *get* instead of *be* (see pages 58-59).

c) Phrasal verb patterns are the same except that there is also a particle, P. The Object comes either between the verb and the particle or after the particle. Most phrasal verbs have both these patterns, and if the Object comes after the particle, it is not a personal pronoun. You say

I looked them up
or *I looked up some old friends*

but you do not say *I looked up them.*
This first type of phrasal verb is included in the lists with the heading **V n P** and **V P n (not pron)**. However, with some phrasal verbs, the Object comes after the particle only and it may be a personal pronoun. You say

I ran into some old friends
or *I ran into them.*

This second type of phrasal verb is shown under the heading **V P n** or, if the verb has two particles, **V P P n**.

Structure III: Verb with Adjunct

V n

	Verb group	noun group
Subject	**Verb**	**Adjunct**
I	have to act	a certain way.
Very few people	think	that way.

Verbs with this structure are all concerned with doing something. The Adjunct indicates how the action is done. In most cases, the Adjunct contains the noun *way*. This pattern is productive: many verbs occur in the pattern **V n** if the noun group contains the word *way*. The verbs listed here are the ones which are most frequently used in this way.

> It's standard procedure not to reveal sources if you're working alone. The resistance forces always *operated* that way during the war.

> Once nine out of 10 people realise they will be better off, then I think they will be inclined to *vote* Labour.

act *3*	play *1*	vote *6 (a political party)*
live *1.2*	talk *1*	walk *1*
operate *2*	think *3,5*	work *12*

Structure information: Verb with Adjunct

a) The noun group is an Adjunct.

b) This structure has no passive.

Other related patterns

be V-ed *by* n

The passive of **V n** is always *be* **V-ed**, and the person or thing responsible for the action can always be indicated by *by* **n**. However, some verbs, when they are passive, are always followed by a prepositional phrase beginning with *by*. The pattern is *be* **V-ed** *by* **n**. The phrasal verb pattern is *be* **V-ed P** *by* **n**. The list below shows all verbs with this pattern, not just those among the most frequent 400 verbs.

afflict	edit *2*	greet *2,3*	punctuate
back *3.5*	embody *1,2*	grieve *2*	rack *2*
barrage *3*	encourage *2*	herald *3*	reclaim *4*
beset	encumber *2*	infect *3*	replace *1*
bind *2*	enrage	inform *3*	represent *1,2,3,5,6*
bombard *1*	epitomize	inspire *3*	screen *5*
bound *2.2,3*	evidence *4*	introduce *4*	shackle *1*
buoy *2*	father *2*	leaven *1*	staff *3*
characterize *1*	flank *4*	maul *1*	strike *12*
chasten	follow *7*	partner *5*	tear *2.8*
choke *3*	form *3,6*	people *4,5*	top *14*
colonize *3*	frame *8*	plague *5*	undo *3*
confront *1,3*	girdle *2*	poison *3*	
debilitate *1*	govern *2*	precede *1,2*	
deluge *2*	grace *5*	be prefixed	
weigh down *2*			

get V-ed

The passive voice is sometimes formed with *get* instead of *be*. Most of the verbs with the passive pattern *get* **V-ed** also have the passive *be* **V-ed**. The list below shows the verbs most frequently used with the pattern *get* **V-ed** and the phrasal verbs most frequently used with the pattern *get* **V-ed P**.

Many of the verbs that often have a passive with *get* indicate that something unpleasant is happening, such as *attack, criticize, hit, injure, penalize, rape,* and *wound*.

> Eric seems to be the one paying for his incredible talent because defenders are getting away with it while he **gets penalised**.

> And sometimes, of course, innocent bystanders **get wounded**.

Other verbs have a passive with *get* to emphasize that someone else, not the person indicated by the Subject, does the action and is responsible for it, even if the person indicated by the Subject wishes the action to be done.

> I applied for college and **got accepted** but I can't go now because it would cost too much to put Christopher in a creche.

> They're wise enough to know they have to play by the rules to **get noticed**.

> Anyone that has any concerns, we do advise that they **get tested**.

accept *6*	ask *1*	block *4*	cane *4*
activate	attack *1*	book *5*	catch *1*
add *1*	ban *1*	break *1,2*	change *5*
admit *3*	bash *2*	burgle	cheat *3*
advertise *1*	beat *1,9*	burn *7,13*	choose *1*
affect *3*	bend *4*	bust *2*	clamp *5*
approach *3*	bite *1*	call *4*	clean *4*
arrest *1*	blame *1*	cancel *1*	clobber *3*

clog *1*	hit *1,2*	play *11*	shoot *1*
complete *4*	hurt *1,5*	poison *3*	sign *7*
criticize	ignore *1*	print *2*	smack *1*
crush *1*	infect *1*	promote *3,4*	smash *1*
cut *2*	injure *1*	prosecute *1*	solve
damage *1*	interview *4*	publish *2*	spend *1*
destroy *1*	kick *1*	punch *1*	sponsor *1*
distort *1*	kidnap *1*	punish *1*	stab *1*
divorce *2*	kill *1*	push *1,8*	steal *1*
do *2.1*	lay *1.9*	rape *1*	sting *1*
draft *3*	lynch	rehabilitate *1*	stop *5*
drench	make *1.1,3.2*	reject *4*	strand *3*
drop *11*	marry *1*	release *1*	sue
eat *1*	mention *3*	relegate *2*	suspend *2*
educate *1*	move *6*	report *2*	tangle *2,4*
elect *1*	mug *2*	rescue *1*	tax *2*
establish *4*	murder *2*	review *4*	tease *1*
feed *2*	nab	reward *3*	test *7*
fine *2.2*	nail *4*	rob *1*	thump *2*
fire *3.0*	neglect *2*	sack *2*	trap *7,8*
fix *4*	nick *2*	scratch *2*	vaccinate
freak *5*	nominate *3*	screw *9*	wash *2*
fund *3*	notice *1*	select *1*	waylay
hammer *5*	overheat *1*	sentence *3*	weigh *2*
hassle *2*	overlook *2*	separate *6*	wound *2*
hear *6*	pay *1,2*	serve *6*	write *2*
hire *1*	penalize	shell *8*	
beat up	kick out	pick up *4,6*	tangle up *1*
block in	knock around/about *1*	psych up	tell off
blow up *1,5*	knock down/over *1*	rip off	throw out *3*
break down *4*	knock up *3*	run over	trip up
get/be caught up *5*	lay off *1*	slag off	turn on *2*
clog up	leave behind *3*	sort out *2*	turn down *1*
cut off *4*	lock up *2*	steam up *1*	wipe out
find out *2*	mess up *1*	take in *3*	
fob off	pick on *1*	take over *1*	

V colour

See pages 75 and 79.

3 V pl-n

The verb is followed by a **plural noun group**. This may consist either of one noun group indicating two or more people or things, or of two or more co-ordinated noun groups. The passive pattern is *be* **V-ed**.

This pattern has one structure:

▶ Verb with Object
The research <u>will compare</u> two drugs.

Active voice: V pl-n

	Verb group	plural noun group
Subject	Verb	Object
A cook	can blend	raspberries and asparagus.
Jim	introduced	us.
I	can't separate	the threads of my life and my work.

Passive voice: *be* V-ed

	Verb group	
Subject	Verb	Adjunct (optional)
The two styles	may be contrasted.	
Their problems and ours	are dovetailed.	
Tales like this	will be swapped	tomorrow.

Phrasal verbs

Active voice: V pl-n P, V P pl-n (not pron)

	Verb group	plural noun group	Particle
Subject	Verb...	Object	...Verb
	Add	the numbers	up.
The teacher	lined	the children	up.

	Verb group	Particle	plural noun group
Subject	Verb		Object
They	added	up	the numbers.
I	muddled	up	the pedals.

Passive voice: *be* V-ed P

	Verb group	Particle
Subject	Verb	
The letters	have been mixed	up.
Non-smokers	are paired	up.

Verbs with this pattern belong to the following meaning groups:

1 THE 'COMBINE' AND 'SEPARATE' GROUP
2 THE 'COMPARE' GROUP
3 THE 'ALTERNATE' GROUP
4 THE 'INTRODUCE' AND 'COME BETWEEN' GROUP

1 THE 'COMBINE' AND 'SEPARATE' GROUP

These verbs are concerned with joining, combining, or separating two or more things, either physically or metaphorically. We include here *clink*, which is concerned with making two or more things touch, and *line up*, which is concerned with arranging two or more things in relation to each other.

> *They **clinked** glasses.*
>
> ***Combine** all the ingredients for the soup in a pan.*
>
> *Eventually, an understanding of the brain might allow pleasure and addiction to **be decoupled**.*
>
> *Bands like Orbital and The Orb **are fusing** dance and rock and creating a new set of ideas, sound and lifestyles.*
>
> *In order to cover a double bed, you'll need to **join** two widths of fabric.*
>
> *Reggie finished polishing the cocktail glasses and **lined** them **up** behind the bar.*
>
> *I had long felt that the departments of trade and industry **should be merged**.*
>
> *He did not touch the face of the pictures but used a pair of tongs from the desk drawer to **separate** them.*

The verb *combine 3* often has an inanimate Subject.

> *Photographer Bob Sidaman says he wanted to create an image that **combined** technology and innocence.*

aggregate 3	decouple	intertwine 1	(not) mix 5
amalgamate	dovetail 1	interweave	overlap 1
blend 1	entwine 1,2	join 5,6	separate 3,4,6,9
clink	fuse 4,5	lace 6	tie 8 (usu passive)
combine 1,2,3,5	integrate 2	link 9	touch 2
conjoin	interlink	merge 1	unify
connect 1,4	interlock 1,2	mix 1	
add up ▷2	link up 2 (usu passive)		
line up 3	mix up 2		

2 THE 'COMPARE' GROUP

These verbs are concerned with seeing a similarity, difference, or connection between two or more things.

> *They undertook a study to **compare** levels of income across countries.*
>
> *There are people who **equate** those two terrible video tapes.*
>
> *The Seeker can ask questions and weigh answers, free to **juxtapose** whatever ideas come his or her way.*
>
> *I think we **should not mix up** the hostages and the detainees.*

compare 1	distinguish 1	mismatch 2	separate 7
conflate	equate	muddle 2	
connect 7,8	juxtapose	reconcile 1	
contrast 5	match 3,4,5	relate 2	
mix up 1	muddle up ▷2		

3 THE 'ALTERNATE' GROUP

These verbs are concerned with making a connection between two things or activities. This includes:

- doing two things at the same time or at different times e.g. *alternate, synchronize*
- breeding two things together e.g. *cross-breed, hybridize*

- exchanging two things e.g. *exchange, swap*
- taking account of two things e.g. *balance, co-ordinate*

*An independent radio station set up hastily in Leningrad **is alternating** local and Baltic news in an attempt to keep people informed.*

*The state has got to find some way to **balance** these two needs.*

*The deal was we **would swap** keys, and when one family went away the other would water their plants.*

*There is some evidence that attempts were made to **synchronize** lunar and solar time.*

alternate *1*	co-ordinate *2*	hybridize	swap *1,3*
balance *3*	cross-breed *1*	interchange *2*	switch *2,4*
combine *4*	exchange *1*	multiply *3*	synchronize

4 THE 'INTRODUCE' AND 'COME BETWEEN' GROUP

These verbs are concerned with making or breaking a relationship between two or more people.

*Alice was there and so was David and I remember **introducing** them.*

*Mother and I **were reconciled** soon afterwards, but somehow the relationship was never quite the same again.*

The phrasal verb *come between* has the pattern **V P n** only.

*Clearly, Sarah loved that young man and someone cruelly **came between** them.*

bond *2*	be parted *2.4*	reconcile *3*
introduce *3*	be reconciled *2*	
come between	pair up *(usu passive)*	

Structure information: Verb with Object

a) The plural noun group is the Object.

b) This structure has a passive, with the pattern **be V-ed**.

c) Phrasal verb patterns are the same except that there is also a particle, P. The Object comes either between the verb and the particle or after the particle. Most phrasal verbs have both these patterns, and if the Object comes after the particle, it is not a personal pronoun. You say

*I nearly **mixed** them **up***
or *I nearly **mixed up** the two twins*

but you do not say *I nearly mixed up them*.
However, in the case of one phrasal verb, *come between*, the Object comes after the particle only and it may be a personal pronoun.

d) Many of the verbs which have this pattern are **ergative reciprocal verbs** (see Chapter 8).

4 V pron-refl

The verb is followed by a **reflexive pronoun**.

This pattern has one main structure:

▶ Verb with Object
Lise severely <u>injured</u> herself in a fall.

V pron-refl

	Verb group	reflexive pronoun
Subject	**Verb**	**Object**
I	asserted	myself.
He	couldn't kid	himself.
She	might scratch	herself.

Phrasal verbs: V pron-refl P

	Verb group	reflexive pronoun	Particle
Subject	**Verb...**	**Object**	**...Verb**
	Pull	yourself	together.
Moira	stretched	herself	out.
Things	will work	themselves	out.

Verbs with this pattern belong to the following meaning groups:

1 THE 'HANG' GROUP
2 THE 'FLAUNT' GROUP
3 THE 'DEMEAN' GROUP
4 THE 'EXERT' GROUP
5 THE 'COMPOSE' GROUP
6 THE 'DELUDE' GROUP
7 THE 'EXCEL' GROUP
8 THE 'EXPLAIN' GROUP
9 THE 'OCCUPY' GROUP
10 THE 'STRETCH OUT' GROUP
11 THE 'REPRODUCE' GROUP
12 THE 'ENJOY' GROUP
13 THE 'HIDE' GROUP
14 THE 'ABSENT' GROUP
15 THE 'PRESENT' GROUP
16 VERBS WITH OTHER MEANINGS

1 THE 'HANG' GROUP

These verbs are concerned with doing physical harm to yourself. This includes:

- injuring yourself accidentally e.g. *burn, cut*
- killing yourself in some way e.g. *drown, electrocute*

*As we know from whenever we **cut** ourselves, blood darkens as it gets older.*

*If she'd wanted to **drown** herself there was a swimming pool handy.*

*Children had seen a man up a tree with a noose round his neck. He was threatening to **hang** himself.*

burn *6*	hang *5*	kill *1*	scratch *1*
cut *2*	hurt *1*	nick *4*	starve *2*
drown *1*	inject *1*	prick *2*	
electrocute *1*	injure	rupture *3*	

2 THE 'FLAUNT' GROUP

These verbs are concerned with a person's self-image. In most cases, the person involved has a better self-image than he or she deserves, or is trying to make a better impression than he or she deserves. This includes:

- trying to make a good impression on other people e.g. *aggrandize, flaunt*
- thinking well of yourself e.g. *fancy, flatter*

- trying to improve your appearance e.g. *doll up, preen*
- congratulating yourself

*Dressing for success doesn't mean **dolling yourself up** in suits and shoulder pads.*

*I **would be flattering myself** if I believed I could snap my fingers and force a Swiss bank to jump.*

*The president, the government, parliament – they all **flaunt themselves** on the television and make pretty speeches about reform and democracy. But what have they actually done?*

*Despite his eagerness to **ingratiate** himself, he remained an outsider without the full, honest support of the people in his own political party.*

aggrandize	flatter *2*	preen *1*
congratulate *3*	flaunt *2*	
fancy *1.5*	ingratiate	
doll up	dress up *1*	make up *3*

3 THE 'DEMEAN' GROUP

These verbs are concerned with doing harm to your dignity, freedom, or image.

*The American people support capital punishment; that's wrong, too. We **demean ourselves** and we betray the ideals of our country when we do things like that.*

*Two of the fundamental bases of British justice are that no one should be forced to **incriminate** himself and that neither should he face trial twice.*

*It's sad to see so many artists **prostituting themselves**. Once rebellious rock 'n' roll has become nothing more than a corporate marketing game.*

*They come here because the staff are more helpful, and we'**ll put ourselves out** to help them.*

compromise *3*	forget *5*	overreach	prostitute *2,3*
demean *1*	incriminate	overstretch	
disgrace *4*	lower *7*	perjure	
put out *6*			

4 THE 'EXERT' GROUP

These verbs are concerned with doing something with a great deal of effort, enthusiasm, or commitment.

*Try not to **exert yourself** while working.*

*I found I was having a hell of a good time with various girlfriends without **committing** myself.*

*I taught there for five years and I **killed myself** over the students because they just needed so much.*

apply *2*	commit *4,5*	kill *6*
assert *4*	exert *2*	stir *5*
burn out *2*	wear out *2*	

5 THE 'COMPOSE' GROUP

These verbs are concerned with controlling, or failing to control, your feelings or behaviour. This includes:

- keeping calm under difficult circumstances e.g. *collect, compose*
- preparing yourself for a difficult situation e.g. *brace*
- failing to keep calm and becoming agitated e.g. *(cannot) contain, work up*
- adapting to new conditions e.g. *acclimatize, assimilate*

● organizing yourself e.g. *organize, pace*

*India was much hotter than Tibet, and they had difficulty in **acclimatizing** themselves.*

*He **will** suppress his own fears, **brace** himself, and step forward to defend the weak.*

*By now, she was crying. She tried to **compose** herself, but could be seen visibly shaking.*

*At the moment I **have to pace** myself until I am 100 per cent fit.*

*If something is weighing heavily on your mind, don't just lie there **working yourself up**, get up and do something about it.*

acclimatize	check *4*	control *7*	orient *1*
assimilate *1*	collect *7*	discipline *5*	pace *5*
behave *2*	compose *5*	limit *6*	steady *6*
brace *1*	(cannot) contain *6*	organize *4*	
cheer up	psych up	sort out *4*	
pick up *2*	pull together *2*	work up *1*	

6 THE 'DELUDE' GROUP

These verbs are concerned with having the wrong idea about something.

*When one wants to believe something, it's easy to **delude** oneself.*

*Somebody's making an awful lot of money out of this. **Don't** you **kid yourself**.*

deceive *2*	delude *1*	fool *3*	kid *6*

7 THE 'EXCEL' GROUP

These verbs are concerned with being successful, becoming successful, or showing yourself to be successful.

*After a few years, I became a production secretary in radio: I wanted to **better** myself and found it a wonderful apprenticeship.*

*Sheppard **excelled** herself, breaking her own 50m time and setting a new British record.*

*You are going to have to fight for your honour and good name. Others will demand that you **prove yourself**, you cannot demand their respect without it.*

*Although country ministers generally suffered from declining status and income, expansion helped some **pull themselves up**.*

better *9*	excel
distinguish *4*	prove *3*
pull up *4*	

8 THE 'EXPLAIN' GROUP

These verbs are concerned with talking, often about yourself.

*They were asked to leave the room when the affair was discussed and were refused an opportunity to **explain** themselves.*

*Johnson pretended not to be able to hear anything Shaw said, so Shaw **had to repeat** himself in a louder voice.*

*If we'd had another week together, Neville might have told me all manner of things. He was struggling to **unburden** himself, but couldn't quite screw himself up to it.*

excuse *5*	express *1*	repeat *3*
explain *2*	introduce *3*	unburden

9 THE 'OCCUPY' GROUP

These verbs are concerned with occupying time.

> You **are** only **busying yourself** at home to avoid dealing with certain larger issues.
>
> To **occupy myself**, I returned to my reading.

amuse *2*　busy *4*　occupy *5*

10 THE 'STRETCH OUT' GROUP

These verbs are concerned with moving your body, doing an action involving your body, or changing your position.

> She **crossed** herself because she wanted divine protection for her husband.
>
> The old woman glared at him, **drew herself up** and stormed into the building.
>
> Linda rushed round with pots of steaming tea or coffee as soon as they **had seated themselves**.
>
> 'Nothing is wrong now,' laughed Bess as she **stretched** herself **out** lazily.

cross *1.7*	preen *3*	seat *3*
expose *5*	prostrate *1*	shake *2*
flatten *3*	raise *3*	support *8*
draw up *3*	plop down	stretch out *1*

11 THE 'REPRODUCE' GROUP

These verbs are concerned with reproduction.

> Computer organisms no longer just **replicate themselves**, they evolve in much the same way that real ones do.
>
> We **are reproducing ourselves** at such a rate that our sheer numbers threaten the ecology of the planet.
>
> In early summer there's sweet rocket, a cottage garden flower that **seeds itself** year by year.

replicate *2*　reproduce *4*　seed *2*

12 THE 'ENJOY' GROUP

These verbs are concerned with enjoying yourself or treating yourself well.

> I **do enjoy myself**, I love sports, travelling and socializing, but when I'm at work I like to be kept busy.
>
> This is the time to **indulge yourself**. Go on, treat yourself to a new dress, splash around all the perfume you've been hoarding since Christmas.
>
> Go through the whole scene a second time, changing the words to **suit yourself** while getting the same message across.

enjoy *2*	help *4,7*	spoil *3*
fortify *3*	indulge *1*	suit *7*
fulfil *3*	pig *4*	sun *3*
fill up *1*		

13 THE 'HIDE' GROUP

These verbs are concerned with hiding or keeping away from other people.

*His first instinct was to **hide** himself.*

*Williams **locked** himself **away** for 10 days with his producer to turn out a detailed filming schedule.*

*Billy tends to keep things to himself and **shut** himself **off**.*

hide 2	isolate 2	
lock away 3	shut away	shut off 2

14 THE 'ABSENT' GROUP

These verbs are concerned with leaving somewhere or not being somewhere.

*With his waiting and cooking experience, Akhtar can fill the void when staff **absent** themselves.*

*You are, of course, free to depart when you wish – but be warned, after such a restful break you will probably find it very difficult to **tear** yourself **away**.*

absent 3	uproot 1
take off 3	tear away

15 THE 'PRESENT' GROUP

These verbs are concerned with something happening. This includes:

- something occurring e.g. *manifest, present*
- something becoming established e.g. *entrench, establish*
- something happening again e.g. *repeat*

*He **established** himself in the team before this match.*

*An opportunity soon **presented** itself, which he eagerly seized.*

*History **didn't have to repeat** itself. This time, we'd get it right.*

*Just how this situation **will work** itself **out** remains to be seen.*

assert 4	manifest 2	repeat 6
entrench	present 4.3	
establish 4	reassert 2	
work out 5		

16 VERBS WITH OTHER MEANINGS

There are a number of other verbs which have this pattern.

*She had decided to **avenge** herself and all the other women he had abused.*

*One day when I **locked** myself **out** I discovered I could put my arm through the back-door catflap and turn the key on the inside.*

*She lay still for a few seconds, trying to **orient** herself.*

*Pamela was beginning to **reproach** herself for letting Rosie down.*

The Subject of all the verbs typically indicates a person, except for *burn out*, where the Subject indicates fire.

*The fire commissioner said either the fire **will burn** itself **out** or the sprinklers will get it.*

avenge	dress *3*	reproach *3*
disarm *2*	orient *2*	soap *2*
disguise *2*	relieve *7*	
burn out *1*	dust down *2*	lock out *2*
dig in *2*	give up *5*	

Structure information

a) The reflexive pronoun is the Object.

b) This structure has no passive.

c) The phrasal verb pattern is the same except that there is a particle, P, which comes after the Object.

Other structures

In the case of one verb, *be*, the reflexive pronoun is a Complement. Only the forms *be* and *being* are used.

> *'What do I have to do?' I asked. Tony laughed. 'Just **be yourself**. Nothing more.'*
>
> *With George she felt completely at ease, capable of **being herself** in his company.*

> be *2.9*

---

5 V amount

The verb is followed by a word or phrase indicating an amount, such as *three dollars, a lot, much, two per cent*. The passive pattern is **be V-ed**.

This pattern has three structures:

▶ Structure I: Verb with Complement
  Two and two don't always make four.
▶ Structure II: Verb with Object
  The canoes held two people.
▶ Structure III: Verb with Adjunct
  I had to walk four miles.

Structure I: Verb with Complement

V amount

	Verb group	amount
Subject	**Verb**	**Complement**
Two and two	make	four.
He	weighed	18 stone.

Verbs with this structure belong to the following meaning groups:

I.1 THE 'EQUAL' GROUP

These verbs are used when indicating how big an amount is. They are all **link verbs** (see Chapter 5).

*The trust banks' joint investment in the firm **equals** 23 per cent of their total capital.*

*The bill **could** easily **run into** hundreds of pounds.*

*The amount involved is said to **total** up to four thousand million dollars.*

be *2.1*	make *4.3*	total *4*
equal *6*	number *5*	
run into *4*		

I.2 THE 'MEASURE' GROUP

These verbs are used when indicating the size or weight of something or someone. They are all **link verbs** (see Chapter 5).

*Twenty years ago, supermarkets **averaged** 20,000 square feet.*

*The skirt **measures** 32 inches from waistline to hem.*

*The fattest cat ever was an Australian called Himmy, who **weighed** 21.3kg.*

average *6*	extend *1*	weigh *1*
cover *3*	measure *3*	

Structure information: Verb with Complement

a) The **amount** is the Complement.

b) This structure has no passive.

c) There is only one phrasal verb with this structure, *run into*. The pattern is **V P amount**.

Structure II: Verb with Object

Active voice: V amount

	Verb group	amount
Subject	**Verb**	**Object**
The scheme	could cost	millions of pounds.
A mysterious bidder	offered	1.5 million dollars.
The dining room	could seat	394 passengers.

Passive voice: *be* V-ed

	Verb group	
Subject	**Verb**	**Adjunct (optional)**
An extra £6	is charged	for express transfer.
£4000	was taken	in one night.

Phrasal verbs: V P amount

	Verb group	Particle	amount	
Subject	**Verb**		**Object**	**Adjunct (optional)**
He	lives	on	eight pounds a week.	
An agent	takes	in	£300	for each holiday.

Verbs with this structure belong to the following meaning groups:

II.1 THE 'PAY' GROUP
II.2 THE 'HOLD' GROUP
II.3 THE 'DO' GROUP
II.4 THE 'GAIN' AND 'LOSE' GROUP
II.5 VERBS WITH OTHER MEANINGS

II.1 THE 'PAY' GROUP

These verbs are concerned with financial transactions such as buying, selling, or earning a living.

> He **is charging** a hefty £3.95 plus VAT, more than double the going rate.
>
> Sophisticated locals patronise the well-established jewellers, who quote fair prices; when pressed they **knock off** 10 per cent.
>
> Dental charges are also to rise, with patients having to **pay** 80 per cent rather than 75 per cent of the cost of treatment.
>
> I only **pull in** £15,000 a year before taxes as a social worker, which is like nothing to live on.

The phrasal verb knock off also has the pattern **V amount P**.

> They **should knock** £2,000 **off**.

The verbs cost and pay 6 have an inanimate Subject.

> Things are expensive: a jar of black caviar **costs** 1,700 roubles.
>
> The job now **pays** £135,000 a year.

```
ask 8        cost 2        make 3.6      take 2.17
average 6    earn 1        offer 9
charge 1     get 2.2       pay 1,6

cough up     knock off 1   pull in 3
fork out     live on 1.1   take in ▷2.17
```

II.2 THE 'HOLD' GROUP

These verbs are concerned with the capacity of something.

> The Vacutank is a combined hand pump and tank which **can hold** 8.3 litres of oil or other fluids.
>
> The bungalow **sleeps** four.

```
hold 1.12    seat 4    sleep 4
house 14     serve 7   take 2.38
```

II.3 THE 'DO' GROUP

These verbs are concerned with the speed of something.

> Having driven that highway, I knew they **were doing** 70 miles an hour, at a minimum.

average 6	**do** 2.13

II.4 THE 'GAIN' AND 'LOSE' GROUP

These verbs are concerned with gaining or losing something.

> *The group has since opened its doors to everyone and __gained__ 250,000 members.*
>
> *The Fidelity fund has a different charging structure. Investors __lose__ only 2 per cent in an initial charge.*

gain 3	**lose** 8,16

II.5 VERBS WITH OTHER MEANINGS

There are a few other verbs which have this structure. We include here *average*, which can indicate how much someone or something gets or produces. It can also indicate the speed or price of something, and is included in meaning groups II.1 and II.3 above.

> *All biopsies are performed by a radiologist and helpers. The time is highly variable, but __allow__ two hours.*
>
> *The city now __averages__ three or four murders every year.*
>
> *Jones __has made__ 4,690 runs in one-day international matches.*
>
> *The cut in interest rates __does not mean__ a lot financially.*

allow 5	**make** 1.4
average 6	**mean** 1.3

Structure information: Verb with Object

a) The **amount** is the Object.

b) This structure has a passive, with the pattern **be V-ed**. However, not all verbs with this structure are used in the passive. The following verbs are the ones most frequently passive.

ask 8	**gain** 3	**make** 1.4	**pay** 1
charge 1	**lose** 8,16	**offer** 9	**take** 2.17

c) Phrasal verb patterns are the same except that there is also a particle, P. In most cases, this particle comes after the verb, but in the case of *knock off*, the particle can also come after the Object. No phrasal verbs occur in the passive.

Structure III: Verb with Adjunct

V amount

	Verb group	amount
Subject	**Verb**	**Adjunct**
Pretax profit	climbed	11 per cent.
His team	lost	3-0.
Paul	swam	16 lengths.

Phrasal verbs: V P amount

	Verb group	Particle	amount
Subject	**Verb**		**Adjunct**
The current law	dates	back	250 years.
The crime rate in Rio	went	down	37.4 percent.

A wider range of words and phrases indicating an amount are used in this structure than in the others. These include *ten-fold* and *a bit*.

Verbs with this structure belong to the following meaning groups:

III.1 THE 'INCREASE' GROUP
III.2 THE 'WALK' GROUP
III.3 THE 'WIN' GROUP
III.4 VERBS WITH OTHER MEANINGS

III.1 THE 'INCREASE' GROUP

These verbs are concerned with changes in value, amount, or degree.

*The nation's industrial production **declined** 2 percent last month.*

*In Paris, the dollar **fell** a fifth of a cent.*

*If you have five stocks, and three **go down** 75 percent, one **goes up** ten-fold, and one **goes up** 20 percent, you still have good performance for those five.*

*Antibodies **increase** two- to three-fold in experimental animals fed on excess vitamin E.*

*Income **rose** a bit for families without children.*

*The Dow Jones industrial average, which **slid** 37.55 points on Friday, finished up 25.94 points at 3,276.26.*

climb 4	fall 5	rise 9	surge 2
decline 1	increase 1	shrink 2	swell 1
decrease 1	jump 6	sink 7	tumble 2
dive 7	plummet	slide 4	
drop 1	plunge 5	slip 7	
go down 4.1	go up 4.1		

III.2 THE 'WALK' GROUP

These verbs are concerned with moving or travelling. The amount indicates the distance travelled. This is a productive use: most verbs which involve moving or travelling can be used with this pattern. The verbs listed here are those which are most frequently used in this way.

*Bud said he'**d back up** a hundred yards, hide his truck off the road in the bushes, and head for where the action was.*

*You **could travel** a long way and have nothing to show for it.*

*Joseph **walked** over four miles in 90 degree heat.*

ascend 3	jump 1,2	run 1	travel 1
go 1.1	march 1	swim 1	walk 1
back up 3.5,7			

III.3 THE 'WIN' GROUP

These verbs are concerned with winning or losing. The amount indicates the score.

She then lost her serve to __trail__ 3-5 and the match was effectively over.

Maple Leafs began with a handicap goal, but Ellerston __won__ 7-6.

lead *1.4*	**trail** *8*
lose *1*	**win** *1*
go down *3*	

III.4 VERBS WITH OTHER MEANINGS

There are a few other verbs which have this structure.

There is evidence of human settlement __dating back__ 5,000 years.

Although coins are more expensive to manufacture than bills, they __last__ much longer in circulation.

last *11,12*			
date back	**go back** *1,2*	**move down**	**move up** *2*

Structure information: Verb with Adjunct

a) The **amount** is an Adjunct.

b) This structure has no passive.

c) The phrasal verb pattern is the same except that there is a particle, P, which comes after the verb.

Other related patterns

V amount adj/adv

The verb is followed by an **amount** and an adjective group or adverb group. Verbs with this pattern are used when indicating the size of someone or something. They are **link verbs** (see Chapter 5).

The fence __was__ two and a half metres high and had triple strands of barbed wire at the top.

The river __was__ only fifty yards across and we were over in a minute.

The cushion __measures__ 16 inches square.

be *2.1*	**measure** *3*	**stand** *14*

These verbs also have the pattern **V amount *in* n**. The prepositional phrase beginning with *in* indicates the dimension concerned.

The brooch __measures__ 2 inches in length, and the clip-on earrings __are__ 1 inch in diameter.

V amount *in* n

See **V amount adj/adv** above.

6 V adj

The verb is followed by an adjective group.

This pattern has one structure:

▶ Verb with Complement
I was hungry.

V adj

	Verb group	adjective group
Subject	**Verb**	**Complement**
Poe	died	penniless.
Mother's cheeks	glowed	red.
She	looked	happy.
I	stood	perfectly still.

Phrasal verbs: V P adj

	Verb group	Particle	adjective group
Subject	**Verb**		**Complement**
	Sit	up	straight.
Matching sets	work	out	cheaper than separate items.

Some verbs with this pattern are generally considered to be **link verbs** because they need an adjective after them to complete their meaning (see Chapter 5). Others are not considered to be link verbs, because they have a complete meaning in themselves, for example they indicate an action such as moving. However, for both kinds of verb, the adjective group after the verb describes the person or thing indicated by the Subject.

Verbs with this pattern belong to the following meaning groups:

1 THE 'BE' GROUP	8 THE 'SLIDE OPEN' GROUP
2 THE 'BECOME' GROUP	9 THE 'BREAK FREE' GROUP
3 THE 'SEEM' GROUP	10 THE 'JUMP' GROUP
4 THE 'ACT' GROUP	11 THE 'CLOSE HIGHER' GROUP
5 THE 'DIE' GROUP	12 THE 'GLEAM' GROUP
6 THE 'SIT' GROUP	13 THE 'SET' GROUP
7 THE 'STARE' GROUP	14 VERBS WITH OTHER MEANINGS

1 THE 'BE' GROUP

These verbs indicate that someone or something has a particular quality or is in a particular state. We include here *keep*, *remain*, and *stay*, which indicate that someone or something remains in a particular state. The verbs in this group are all **link verbs** (see Chapter 5). *Keep* is an **ergative link verb** (see Chapter 7).

She __was not__ young, but she __was__ beautiful.

I __was feeling__ a bit lonely.

They had been burning charcoal to __keep__ warm after their electricity had been cut off.

The law __has proved__ difficult to implement, however.

The United States __stands__ ready to take whatever military action is appropriate to bring things under control.

The verbs *go 2.3* and *pass* are followed by negative adjectives such as *unnoticed* and *undetected*.

> *Adler wasn't going to let such behaviour **go unnoticed**.*

The verbs *rank* and *rate* are used with *high* and *low*. The adjective is usually followed by a prepositional phrase. This pattern is **V adj prep**.

> *The technology on which the machine is based, called parallel supercomputing, **ranks high on the research agenda of every big computer company**.*

The phrasal verb *work out* is used with the adjectives *cheap* and *expensive*.

> *Check washing instructions before you buy – some fabrics are 'dry-clean only' which **can work out expensive**.*

be *2.1*	keep *1*	prove *1*	remain *1*
feel *1*	lie *1.4*	rank *4*	stand *11*
go *2.2,3*	pass *19*	rate *6*	stay *3*
work out *3*			

2 THE 'BECOME' GROUP

These verbs indicate that someone or something starts to have a particular quality or be in a particular state. They are all **link verbs** (see Chapter 5).

> *If your boss is opposed to your idea, your task **becomes** more difficult.*
>
> *He **came over** all dizzy, he said, when he stood up.*
>
> *People who've tried that in the past **have ended up** dead.*
>
> *She **fell** silent suddenly and cast an uneasy glance over her shoulder.*
>
> ***Does** your father ever **get** cross?*
>
> *The audience **went** crazy, booing, screaming, clapping hands, some even standing on their seats and shaking their fists.*

become *1*	get *1.1,2*	turn *16,18*
come *6*	go *2.1*	
fall *9*	grow *7*	
come out *4*	end up *2*	turn out *1*
come over *2*	finish up *1*	wind up *3*

The verb *turn 17* is only followed by colour adjectives and has the pattern **V colour**. It is an **ergative link verb** (see Chapter 7). See also meaning group 12 below.

> *Swanson's face **turned** white as he realized what was about to happen.*

Turn can also be used with a noun group indicating a colour.

> *Erin watched as the sun **turned** a deep pink-orange on the western horizon.*

turn *17*

3 THE 'SEEM' GROUP

These verbs indicate that someone or something seems to have a particular quality or be in a particular state. They are all **link verbs** (see Chapter 5). The verb *feel 1* indicates how someone seems to themselves.

> *He **felt** ridiculous.*
>
> *The Government **seems** unable to take control of the situation.*
>
> *In principle, it **sounds** great: no pollution, free energy, and everyone lives happily ever after.*

Bottled fruit not only __tastes__ delicious but it also __looks__ terrific displayed in the kitchen.

appear *1,2*	**seem** *1*	**taste** *4*
feel *1,2,3*	**smell** *3*	
look *2.1,4*	**sound** *7,8,9*	

4 THE 'ACT' GROUP

These verbs indicate that someone pretends to have a particular quality or be in a particular state. They are both **link verbs** (see Chapter 5).

Claire decided not to __act__ surprised at the mention of Walker's name.

act *5*	**play** *9*

5 THE 'DIE' GROUP

These verbs are concerned with actions or processes.

This is a productive use: many verbs referring to an action or process can be used with this pattern. The verbs listed here are the ones which are most frequently used in this way and are used with a wide variety of adjectives.

My father __died__ young.
What does it mean to __grow up__ poor in this rich society?
None of them __returned__ alive.

arrive *1*	**emerge** *1,2*
die *1*	**return** *1,9*
grow up *1*	

With most verb-adjective combinations of this kind, it is the adjective that is frequently used in this way and that makes the combination possible, rather than the verb. Negative adjectives such as *unharmed*, *unnoticed*, *intact*, and *barefoot* are most frequently used in this way.

She __walks__ __barefoot__ through the kitchen, brushing her hair and looking for Allen.
He is a fascinating talker and Freddy and I __listen__ __entranced__.
I considered __showing__ __up__ __unannounced__ at his front door, then rejected the idea as undignified.
The man's car was hit by rifle fire but he __escaped__ __unhurt__.

The following adjectives are frequently used after verbs indicating actions or processes.

ashen-faced	poker-faced	unassisted	unimpeded
barefoot	red-faced	unattended	uninterrupted *1*
bareheaded	sober *1*	unbidden	uninvited
blindfold *3*	spellbound	unchallenged *1,2,3*	unmolested
breathless *1*	stark naked	unchecked	unnoticed
drunk *1*	stony-faced	unclothed	unobserved
empty-handed	straight-faced	uncontrolled *1*	unplugged
entranced	topless *1*	uncovered	unprotected *1,2*
expressionless	unabated	undetected	unpunished
flat-footed *1,2*	unaccompanied *1,3*	unescorted	unread
free *4*	unafraid	unhampered	unrecognized *1,2,3*
incognito	unaided	unharmed	unscathed
intact	unaltered	unheard *1*	unseen *2*
knee-deep *2*	unannounced	unheeded	untouched *2,3*
naked *1,3*	unarmed	unhurt	untreated *1*
nude *1*	unasked *2*	unimpaired	

In addition, the comparative adjective *closer* is used after verbs of movement such as *come* and *draw*.

> As they **drew <u>closer</u>**, the forms of three black-and-white police cars could be seen.

6 THE 'SIT' GROUP

These verbs indicate the position or posture of someone or something.

> Behind him a man **was <u>lying</u> dead**, struck in the head by the bullet intended for Sharpe.
>
> Her Bronco still **<u>sits</u> unused** in the garage.
>
> He put the phone down and Jessica **<u>stood</u> motionless**, waiting.

hang *3*	sit *1*
lie *1.1,2*	stand *1,4*

The following adjectives are frequently used with one or more of these verbs.

awake *1*	helpless	speechless	undisturbed *1,2,3*
comatose *2*	motionless	sprawled	unfinished
crooked *1*	neglected *2*	still *1.1*	unopened
dead *1*	prone *2*	stock-still	untouched *1,4*
defenceless	prostrate *2*	straight *1*	unused *1*
flat *3*	proud *5*	transfixed	upright *1*
forlorn *1*	senseless *2*	unconscious *1*	

7 THE 'STARE' GROUP

These verbs are concerned with looking. They are used with adjectives describing the expression or emotion of the person who is looking at something.

> Others cling to older children who **<u>stare</u> wide-eyed** at the scene unfolding before them.
>
> Jerry Hall **<u>watched</u> aghast** as her drunken friend leapt on to an historic four-poster bed, setting off alarms and creating mayhem in a packed museum.

gaze *1*	stare *1*	watch *1.1*

The following adjectives are used with these verbs. In addition, some adjectives from the lists in meaning groups 5 and 6 above, for example *entranced* and *transfixed*, can be used with these verbs.

aghast	goggle-eyed	wide-eyed *2*
amazed	open-mouthed	
appalled	unseeing	

8 THE 'SLIDE OPEN' GROUP

These verbs indicate that something such as a door moves, or makes a sound as it moves. They are used with adjectives such as *open* and *shut*.

This is a productive use: other verbs with similar meanings, for example *squeak* and *yawn*, can be used with this pattern. The verbs listed here are the ones which are most frequently used in this way.

> As Adam and Zelikov entered, the heavy steel doors **<u>banged</u> shut** behind them.
>
> The door **<u>slid</u> open** to admit Blake.

bang *3*	clang	slide *1*	swing *1*
blow *1.2*	creak	snap *2*	
burst *4*	slam *1*	spring *5*	

9 THE 'BREAK FREE' GROUP

These verbs indicate that a person manages to get free from a restraint, or that an object comes away from or out of something. They are used with *free* or *loose*.

This is a productive use: other verbs with similar meanings, for example *jerk, scramble,* and *twist,* can be used with this pattern. The verbs listed here are the ones which are most frequently used in this way.

The more I struggled to __break free__, the more I became entangled.

He gave a feeble shrug and tried to __squirm free__.

One of the pins __had worked__ loose from the outer plate.

break *6*	roll *1,2*	squirm *1*	wrench *2*
pull *4*	shake *8*	struggle *6*	wriggle *2*
rattle *1*	spring *5*	work *23*	

10 THE 'JUMP' GROUP

These verbs indicate movement upwards or downwards. They are used with *high* or *low*.

The chef __bent__ low to ignite the burners beneath the table.

She could run faster and __jump__ higher than her brothers.

| bend *1* | fly *2,4* | leap *1* | stoop *2* |
| crouch *1* | jump *1* | soar *2* | swoop *2* |

11 THE 'CLOSE HIGHER' GROUP

These verbs are used when talking about the level of share prices or currencies. They are used with the adjectives *higher* and *lower*. *Close, end, finish,* and *open* are also used with *firmer, weaker,* and *unchanged*. These verbs are all **link verbs** (see Chapter 5).

Stocks __closed__ lower on Wall Street today.

The pound __edged__ higher against the dollar, to close up .15 cents at £1.68.

On Tuesday, London __opened__ firmer on a technical bounce after Monday's broad decline.

close *1.9*	edge *3*	inch *2*
creep *4*	end *7*	move *11*
drift *2*	finish *4*	open *22*

12 THE 'GLEAM' GROUP

These verbs indicate that something gives out or reflects light. They are used with adjectives indicating colour, and with adjectives such as *bright* and *clear*. We include here *run*, which is used when indicating the appearance of a liquid.

This is a productive use: other verbs with similar meanings, for example *glimmer, glitter, shimmer,* and *sparkle,* can be used with this pattern. The verbs listed here are the ones which are most frequently used in this way.

The metal box __gleamed__ silver in the sun.

Behind us the white cliffs of Dover __shone__ bright in the morning sun.

flash *2*	gleam *1,3*	glisten *1*	run *21*
flicker *5*	glint *1*	glow *4,6,7*	shine *1,3*

Verbs which are used with colour adjectives, and not other adjectives, have the pattern **V colour**.

*Laidi **blushed** scarlet and looked at me.*

blush *1*	flame *2*	flush *1*

Both these groups of verbs can also be used with a noun group indicating colour.

*Taken off guard, Charlie **flushed** a dark red.*

*The water **glowed** a faint yellow from the reflected lights of the city.*

13 THE 'SET' GROUP

These verbs indicate that something becomes solid. They are used with *solid* or *hard*.

*It was bitterly cold and my underwear **had frozen** solid.*

*The mixture **will** soon **set** hard.*

freeze *1*	set *2.17*

14 VERBS WITH OTHER MEANINGS

There are a number of other verbs which have this pattern. With the exception of *dawn* and *wax*, they are used with only one or two adjectives, as indicated in the list below.

*The fire **had burned** low and they had been sitting in semi-darkness.*

*Easter Sunday **dawned** bright and clear.*

*Hell, they**'d fall down** dead if they ran six steps, most of 'em.*

*The chair has eight adjustable positions and **folds** flat for easy storing.*

*In court today, Mr Alleyne **pleaded** guilty and was jailed for thirty days.*

*Writers **have been waxing** lyrical about the country house hotel for years.*

*Stay indoors, **wrap up** warm and don't venture out.*

burn *1 (low)*	marry *1 (young)*	stoop *3 (so low)*	weigh *5 (heavy)*
dawn *4*	plead *2 (guilty/innocent)*	strip *4 (naked)*	
fold *4 (flat)*	run *8 (unopposed)*	wax *5*	
hang *6,7 (heavy)*	stand *19 (unopposed)*	wear *7 (thin)*	
fall down ▷*2 (dead)*	stand up *1 (straight)*		
sit up *1 (straight)*	wrap up *1 (warm)*		

Sometimes verb and adjective combinations are regarded as phrases, for example *lie low*, *loom large*, and *run wild*.

Structure information

a) The adjective group is the Complement.

b) This structure has no passive.

c) The phrasal verb pattern is the same, except that there is a particle, P, which comes after the verb.

Other productive uses

In informal and non-standard English, adjective groups are sometimes used after verbs as Adjuncts, as in *Why does he act so mean?*, *He continued to talk tough*, and *You've got to think positive*.

Other related patterns

V adj prep

See meaning group 1 above.

V amount adj

See page 73.

V colour

See meaning groups 2 and 12 above.

V -ed

The verb is followed by an '-ed' clause – that is, a clause introduced by the '-ed' form of another verb. The '-ed' clause indicates the state that something is in, starts being in, or seems to be in. These verbs are all **link verbs** (see Chapter 5).

*The dog was on a chain, which **was attached to another chain that stretched the width of the yard**.*

*The tanks then **became trapped between barricades**, and were eventually abandoned.*

*He **felt betrayed**.*

appear *1,2*	feel *1*	seem *1*
be *2.1*	lie *1.4*	
become *1*	look *2.1*	

7 V -ing

The verb is followed by an '-ing' form.

This pattern has three structures:

▶ Structure I: Verbs in phase
  She started walking.
▶ Structure II: Verb with Object
  He liked dancing with her.
▶ Structure III: Verb with Adjunct
  They ended up fighting.

Structure I: Verbs in phase

V -ing

	Verb group	-ing	
Subject	**Verb**		**Completive**
The sea	came	rushing	in.
The government	ceased	funding	the bank.
He	kept	saying	he was sorry.
Jane	cannot resist	buying	kitchen gadgets.

Phrasal verbs: V P -ing

	Verb group	Particle	-ing	
Subject	**Verb**			**Completive**
I	carried	on	walking.	
I	gave	up	trying	to sleep.
He	left	off	setting	the breakfast table.

Verbs with this structure belong to the following meaning groups:

I.1   THE 'START' AND 'STOP' GROUP
I.2   THE 'AVOID' GROUP
I.3   THE 'TRY' GROUP
I.4   THE 'GO RIDING' GROUP

I.1 THE 'START' AND 'STOP' GROUP

These verbs are concerned with starting, stopping, continuing, or doing an action.

*Then she **burst out** crying.*

*They **came stalking** in here yesterday and demanded to see me.*

*When I **went around** asking people how they felt about America, I was a little apprehensive about the answers.*

*Rather than correct her, I **kept trying** to change the subject.*

*I hope you're not going to **start** crying.*

***Stop** treating me like a schoolgirl.*

begin *1*	continue *1,3*	go *1.4*	resume *1*
cease *2*	discontinue *1*	(not) go *1.7*	start *1*
come *1*	finish *1*	keep *7*	stop *1*
commence	get *1.12*	quit *2*	
burst out *14*	fall to *2*	go about *1,3*	keep on ▷*7*
carry on *1*	give over	go around/round *2*	leave off *2*
fall about	give up *1*	go on *1*	take to *2*

I.2 THE 'AVOID' GROUP

These verbs are concerned with not doing an action.

*Farling studiously **avoided** looking at Piercey.*

*I thought, I **won't bother** washing my hair – I'll wash it tomorrow.*

*Some teens simply **hold off** speaking to their parents.*

*He left word that he had rung, but carefully **omitted** leaving his own number.*

avoid *1,2*	escape *3*	forbear	(cannot) resist *3*
(not) bother *1*	evade *1,2*	omit *2*	shun
hold off *1*			

I.3 THE 'TRY' GROUP

These verbs are concerned with doing something even though it may be dangerous or may not bring success.

*People are still very concerned at their employment prospects, and they are not prepared to **risk** moving house yet.*

*I **tried** ringing his home, but they told me he wasn't there.*

chance *5*	risk *6*	try *1,4*

I.4 THE 'GO RIDING' GROUP

These verbs are concerned with taking part in an activity, often shopping or a leisure activity.

*Next time you **come** shopping in Safeway, why not bring with you any unwanted clean carrier bags from previous shopping trips?*

*The next afternoon Amy **went** riding with Gerald.*

come *2*	go *1.3*

Structure information: Verbs in phase

a) The verb and the '-ing' form are two verbs **in phase**, and together form a **complex verb group**. This means that the actions or states expressed by the two verbs cannot be separated from each other. For example, if you *start laughing*, the *starting* and the *laughing* are not two processes but one.

The complex verb group is followed by a group, phrase or clause which completes the pattern of the second verb. In the structure tables above this is called a **Completive**. For example, if the second verb is normally followed by a noun group, then the Completive of the complex verb group will be a noun group.

b) This structure has no passive, but the '-ing' form may be passive, consisting of *being* and an '-ed' form.

*To **avoid** being caught, the gang sometimes cut off the phone.*

c) The phrasal verb pattern is the same, except that there is a particle, P, which comes after the verb.

Structure II: Verb with Object

V -ing

	Verb group	-ing clause
Subject	**Verb**	**Object**
Only one person	admitted	seeing him that night.
She	may fear	being left on her own.
He	likes	walking his dogs.

Phrasal verbs: V P -ing

	Verb group	Particle	-ing clause
Subject	**Verb**		**Object**
She	had counted	on	riding home with Norman.
The couple	are looking	into	getting a three-month visa.
I	didn't take	to	teaching.

Verbs with this structure belong to the following meaning groups:

II.1   THE 'LIKE' AND 'DISLIKE' GROUP
II.2   THE 'DREAD' AND 'LOOK FORWARD TO' GROUP
II.3   THE 'CONSIDER' GROUP
II.4   THE 'REMEMBER' GROUP
II.5   THE 'RECOMMEND' GROUP
II.6   THE 'INVOLVE' GROUP
II.7   THE 'POSTPONE' GROUP
II.8   THE 'NEED' GROUP
II.9   THE 'RISK' GROUP
II.10 VERBS WITH OTHER MEANINGS

II.1   THE 'LIKE' AND 'DISLIKE' GROUP

These verbs are concerned with liking or disliking something.

*I **don't appreciate** being treated like a suspect.*

*I hate the sight of guns and **dislike** touching them.*

*I **don't** really **like** having people round.*

*He **preferred** being an audience rather than an entertainer.*

*Many other people today said they **could not tolerate** doing nothing.*

adore 2	dislike 1	loathe	relish 1
appreciate 3	(cannot) endure 1	love 5	resent
(cannot) bear 1.6	enjoy 1	(not) mind 2.1	(cannot) stand 16,17
(not) begrudge 2	hate 2	mind 2.2	(cannot) stomach 5
detest	like 2.1,2,3	prefer	(not) tolerate 1
take to 1			

II.2 THE 'DREAD' AND 'LOOK FORWARD TO' GROUP

These verbs are concerned with attitudes towards the future. This includes:

- not wanting something to happen e.g. *dread, fear*
- wanting something to happen e.g. *fancy, favour, look forward to*

*I would like to meet him but at the same time I **dread** meeting him.*

*She was hungry, but she **couldn't face** eating.*

*Angelina has spent all her primary school years in Britain and **is looking forward to** going on to senior school.*

dread *1*	fancy *1.1*	fear *8*
(not) face *2.6*	favour *4*	
look forward to *1*		

II.3 THE 'CONSIDER' GROUP

These verbs are concerned with ideas about what is going to happen in the future.

*In the early part of December, you **can anticipate** making a major purchase.*

*You **should consider** supplementing your diet with vitamins and minerals.*

*He **debated** taking his car, but decided to go on foot.*

*I haven't been in any trouble and I **don't intend** getting into any.*

*I'**d reckoned on** having nine thousand pounds and I haven't – I've only got six thousand.*

anticipate *1*	debate *4*	imagine *1*
consider *3*	envisage *1*	intend *1*
contemplate *1*	fantasize *1*	visualize
count on/upon *1*	look into	reckon on
figure on	plan on	see about

II.4 THE 'REMEMBER' GROUP

These verbs are concerned with attitudes and ideas about the past. This includes:

- remembering or forgetting e.g. *forget, recall*
- having a feeling about something in the past e.g. *miss, regret*

*I'**ll** never **forget** going to Sunday school as a kid.*

*When they had calmed down they were sure to **regret** having revealed themselves so unguardedly when there was a stranger present.*

*She **can't remember** committing the murder, although all the evidence points to her guilt.*

forget *1,4*	recollect	(cannot) remember *3*
miss *2.7*	regret *1*	
recall *1*	remember *1*	

II.5 THE 'RECOMMEND' GROUP

These verbs are concerned with speaking or writing. This includes:

- talking about something done in the past e.g. *admit, deny, report*
- making a suggestion about the future e.g. *advise, recommend*
- discussing something e.g. *debate*

*Members **had debated** changing the law to fight disease.*

*He **denied** causing death by reckless driving.*

*The judges **recommended** giving more modest prizes.*

acknowledge *1*	debate *4*	mention *1*	report *1*
admit *1*	deny *1*	prohibit	suggest *1*
advise *1*	describe *1*	propose *1*	urge *1*
advocate *1*	forbid *1*	recommend *2*	

II.6 THE 'INVOLVE' GROUP

These verbs are concerned with a logical relation between two actions, events, or states. One is indicated by the Subject and one is indicated by the '-ing' clause.

*The job of a choreologist **entails** teaching dancers the technique and performance of dance movements.*

*Fusion **involves** forcing nuclei together rather than fragmenting them.*

*Taking the engine out **necessitates** removing the front panel.*

*My brother had suggested that I take the bus because it **would save** having to find a place to park in Manhattan.*

allow *1*	justify	permit *1*	save *5*
entail	mean *1.6*	preclude *1*	
involve *1*	necessitate	prevent *1*	

II.7 THE 'POSTPONE' GROUP

These verbs are concerned with postponing the time when something is done.

*These goods are also expensive, so people **defer** buying them when they are hard-up.*

*Many young couples **have postponed** having families because of the recession.*

defer *1*	delay *1*	postpone
put off *1*		

II.8 THE 'NEED' GROUP

These verbs are concerned with needing or deserving action or treatment of some kind.

*Surely our feet **deserve** pampering all year round.*

*I asked if there were any more problems that **needed** sorting out.*

*Miles is in good health and doesn't cry unless he **wants** feeding or changing.*

deserve *1*	require *1*
need *2*	want *5*

II.9 THE 'RISK' GROUP

These verbs are concerned with doing something that may have bad results. The '-ing' clause indicates the possible result of the action.

*The advertisers **chance** alienating the customers they hope to woo.*

*Since race cars aren't insured, you **risk** losing everything if you hit something solid.*

chance *5*	risk *5*

II.10 VERBS WITH OTHER MEANINGS

There are a number of other verbs which have this structure.

He has abandoned a fitness regime which __encouraged__ dining on muesli and bananas.

The vast majority of patients still __have to endure__ being cut open and having several weeks off work, even for quite simple operations.

In many companies more effort __went into__ generating profits than into long-term planning.

The profits __will go towards__ fighting pollution and the destruction of rainforests.

They say that when you're playing chess you __can go without__ eating.

__Practise__ changing your behaviour in situations which are relatively neutral for you.

discourage *2*	endure *1*	practise *1*
encourage *3,4*	mime *2*	
get away with	go towards	play at *1,2*
go into *2*	go without	

Structure information: Verb with Object

a) The '-ing' clause is the Object. The first verb and the '-ing' clause express two closely-related but separate actions or states. For example, if you *regret leaving*, the *regretting* and the *leaving* are two processes.

b) This structure has a passive, with the pattern *be* **V-ed**. However, it does not often occur.

c) The phrasal verb pattern is the same except that there is a particle, P, which comes after the verb. The phrasal verbs *look forward to* and *get away with* have the pattern **V P P -ing**, with two particles after the verb.

Structure III: Verb with Adjunct

V -ing

	Verb group	-ing clause
Subject	**Verb**	**Adjunct**
I	'd die	feeling guilty.

Phrasal verbs: V P -ing

	Verb group	Particle	-ing clause
Subject	**Verb**		**Adjunct**
We	ended	up	having dinner.
I	was hanging	around	hoping to see him.

Verbs with this structure are all concerned with beginning, ending, or spending time in a particular way.

The soldiers reasoned that they'd prefer to __die__ fighting rather than waiting.

Their boat __finished up__ pointing the wrong way.

I __started off__ doing languages, which I quite enjoyed, but I switched to law and qualified as a solicitor.

> die *1,9*
>
> end up *2*   hang around *1*   wind up *3*
> finish up *1*   start off *1*

Structure information: Verb with Adjunct

a) The '-ing' clause is an Adjunct.

b) This structure has no passive.

c) The phrasal verb pattern is the same except that there is a particle, P, which comes after the verb.

8 V to-inf

The verb is followed by a to-infinitive.

This pattern has three structures:

▶ Structure I: Verbs in phase
  The number of victims <u>continues</u> to rise.
▶ Structure II: Verb with Object
  He <u>expects</u> to fly to Beijing soon.
▶ Structure III: Verb with Adjunct
  He <u>hurried</u> to catch up with his friend.

Structure I: Verbs in phase

V to-inf

	Verb group	to-infinitive	
Subject	Verb		Completive
The arrangements	appeared	to be	satisfactory.
Prison officers	continued	to patrol	the grounds.
He	refused	to comment.	

Phrasal verbs: V P to-inf

	Verb group	Particle	to-infinitive	
Subject	Verb			Completive
Dr Carey	went	on	to spell out	his views.
These theories	may turn	out	to contain	elements of truth.

Verbs with this structure belong to the following meaning groups:

I.1   THE 'BEGIN' GROUP
I.2   THE 'APPEAR' GROUP
I.3   THE 'TRY' GROUP
I.4   THE 'MANAGE' GROUP

Chapter 1: Simple Patterns

I.1 THE 'BEGIN' GROUP

These verbs are concerned with starting, stopping, or continuing an action.

Edgar **began to laugh** again.

The social activities patients enjoyed before they became sick **will continue** to be enjoyed during the course of their illness.

He treated us okay but I never **got to like** him.

Phil **went on** to enjoy more success at cricket than he had at football.

The verb come on is always used with verbs indicating the weather, with the Subject it.

It **was coming on** to rain when finally Mac's lorry arrived.

begin 1	commence	grow 7
cease 2	continue 1	proceed 1
come 7	get 1.10	start 1
come on 7	go on 5	settle down 3

I.2 THE 'APPEAR' GROUP

These verbs are concerned with an activity being real or appearing to be real. We include here make, which indicates that someone appears to be about to do something, but does not do it.

He listens to five different conversations simultaneously, while **appearing to give** each one 100 per cent of his attention.

She **made to move** past him. He placed himself in her way.

He**'d** only **pretended to be sleeping**. He'd really been watching her all the time.

The great storm of 1987 **proved to be** a blessing in disguise for Chepsea Gardens in Sussex.

The diagnosis **turned out** to be her worst nightmare.

affect 4	make 1.3	seem 1,2
appear 1,2	pretend 1,2	
feign	prove 1	
turn out 3		

I.3 THE 'TRY' GROUP

These verbs are concerned with trying to achieve something.

Though I**'ve attempted to buy** a soundtrack album, no shop seems to have heard of it.

For a further nine years Gladstone **laboured to reverse** that decision.

A lot of people **struggled to understand** why they were doing this.

That's what he's doing, though he **tries to ignore** it.

attempt 1	fight 2,14	scrabble 2	strive
battle 4,5	grapple 1	scramble 3	struggle 1,5,7
endeavour 1	labour 3	strain 8	try 1

I.4 THE 'MANAGE' GROUP

These verbs emphasize that something is successfully done, especially something that is difficult or easily forgotten.

> *The whole of the Great Lakes was exerting a strange hold on me, which I **couldn't begin** to **understand**.*

> *I still cannot understand how you **contrived** to **get** into the room with a gun.*

> *With some difficulty he **managed** to **stretch out** an arm and get hold of the chocolate.*

> *A gust of wind caught the parachute, dragging him along the ground until he **remembered** to **hit** the release catch at his waist.*

The verbs *serve* and *suffice* have an inanimate Subject.

> *What he learned **served** to **improve** the managerial skills needed in his present employment.*

(cannot) begin *8*	manage *3*	suffice *1*
contrive *3,4*	remember *4*	
get *1.11*	serve *3*	

I.5 THE 'FAIL' GROUP

These verbs are concerned with not doing an action. We include here *remain*, which indicates that something has not yet been dealt with, and *(not) need*, which has this structure when it is used to tell somebody not to do something.

> *The peace talks collapsed when the rebels **failed** to **turn up**.*

> *Jane went back to bed and fell promptly asleep, **forgetting** to **turn off** the light.*

> *You **don't need** to **respond** right now.*

> *He completely lost his head, told a number of lies and **omitted** to **mention** one or two things that might have helped him.*

In the case of *remain*, the verb is always followed by a passive to-infinitive.

> *A lot of questions **remain** to **be answered**.*

(not) bother	fail *1,3*	(not) need *4,5,6,8*	refuse *1*
decline *2*	forbear	neglect *3*	remain *4*
disdain *3*	forget *2*	omit *2*	(not) trouble *10*

I.6 THE 'REGRET TO SAY' GROUP

These verbs are concerned with the manner or attitude of the person doing the action. We include here *choose*, *elect*, and *opt*, which have this structure when they are used to indicate that someone does something by choice. We also include here *hate*, *want*, and *wish* which have this structure when they are used in phrases such as *I hate to be rude but...*

> *I gave you some new information, some different ways of looking at and thinking about your life situation, and you **chose** to **believe** what I told you.*

> *They finally **condescended** to **give** her a form to be filled in by a doctor.*

> *Each time the phone rings I **hesitate** to **answer**.*

> *I **regret** to **tell** you that very many American lives have been lost.*

care *6,7*	deign	(not) need *9*	venture *3*
choose *2*	elect *2*	opt	(not) want *16*
come *8*	hate *3,4,6,7*	presume *2*	(not) wish *3*
condescend *1*	hesitate *2,3*	regret *3*	
dare *1*	mean *1.8*	tend *3*	

I.7 THE 'HASTEN' GROUP

These verbs are concerned with doing something without delay.

The agent __hastened__ to reassure him.

hasten *2,3*	hustle *2*	scurry *2*
hurry *2*	rush *2*	

I.8 THE 'CHANCE' GROUP

These verbs are concerned with something happening by chance.

She and Nancy did not speak, hardly glanced at each other if they __chanced__ to pass in the hospital corridor.

It was a light-hearted wartime affair which had come about because they both __happened__ to be in the same place at the same time.

chance *4*	happen *4*

I.9 THE 'TEND' GROUP

These verbs are concerned with how probable something is or how frequently something happens.

This year's competition __promises__ to be the best ever.

The front line states __stand__ to gain from a democracy in South Africa.

Low-heeled comfortable shoes are best, too, as feet __tend__ to swell if you sit still for too long.

incline *1*	stand *18*
promise *4*	tend *1*
shape up *1*	

I.10 VERBS WITH OTHER MEANINGS

There are a few other verbs which have this structure.

In the industrial Midlands, pollution and weather __conspired__ to create a perfect canopy of impenetrable cloud.

The religious background binds people together and __helps__ to promote the moral and ethical standards in the school.

'You __may live__ to regret those words, Archdeacon,' said the chaplain.

conspire *2*	live *1,4*
help *1,2*	stop *7*

Structure information: Verbs in phase

a) The first verb and the to-infinitive are two verbs **in phase**, and together form a **complex verb group**. This means that the actions or states expressed by the two verbs cannot be separated from each other. For example, if you *begin to see* something, the *beginning* and the *seeing* are not two processes, but one.

The complex verb group is followed by a group, phrase, or clause which completes the pattern of the second verb. In the structure tables above this is called a **Completive**. For example, if the second verb is normally followed by a noun group, then the Completive of the complex verb group will be a noun group.

b) This structure has no passive, but the to-infinitive may be passive, consisting of *to be* and an '-ed' form.

He __refused__ to be admitted to the hospital.

c) The phrasal verb pattern is the same except that there is a particle, P, which comes after the verb.

Structure II: Verb with Object

V to-inf

	Verb group		to-infinitive clause
Subject	Verb		Object
The President	agreed		to be interviewed.
Turkish airlines	has offered		to lay on a dozen flights starting next week.
He	pleaded		to speak with me privately.

Phrasal verbs: V P to-inf

	Verb group	Particle	to-infinitive clause
Subject	Verb		Object
He	didn't go	out	to injure opponents.
Governments	queue	up	to buy US spy satellites.

Verbs with this structure belong to the following meaning groups:

II.1 THE 'PROMISE' GROUP
II.2 THE 'DEMAND' GROUP
II.3 THE 'HOPE' GROUP
II.4 THE 'LIKE' GROUP
II.5 THE 'CLAIM' GROUP
II.6 THE 'NEED' GROUP
II.7 VERBS WITH OTHER MEANINGS

II.1 THE 'PROMISE' GROUP

These verbs are concerned with being committed to a future action. This includes:

- talking or writing about a future action e.g. *agree, promise*
- thinking about a future action e.g. *choose, decide*
- doing something about a future action e.g. *arrange, prepare*

We __should not be looking__ to increase salaries across the board.
I __had planned__ to stay longer, but something came up.
Chloe __had promised__ to take her shopping as soon as she arrived.
Jones __had set out__ to intimidate and dominate Paul.

agree *2,3*	fix *24*	pledge *2*	threaten *1,3*
arrange *2*	guarantee *3*	plot *2*	undertake *2*
choose *2*	intend *1*	prepare *2*	volunteer *3*
consent *2*	be looking	promise *1,4*	vote *5*
contract *2*	mean *1.10*	propose *2*	vow *1*
decide *1*	offer *2*	resolve *2*	
determine *4*	opt	scheme *3*	
elect *2*	plan *2*	swear *2*	
go out *3*	set out *2*		

II.2 THE 'DEMAND' GROUP

These verbs are concerned with persuading someone to do something or with obtaining permission from someone to do something.

*The police **asked** to use Keith's video as evidence.*

*He **demanded** to be flown to Sweden, but the pilot landed instead at Helsinki.*

*They were so concerned about the Pacific yew tree that they **petitioned** to have it included on the endangered species list.*

apply *1*	bid *1.3*	demand *1*	pray *1*
ask *3*	campaign *2*	petition *3*	
beg *1*	clamour *1*	plead *1*	

II.3 THE 'HOPE' GROUP

These verbs are concerned with attitudes towards a future action or event. This includes:

- wanting to do something e.g. *hope, long, want*
- not wanting to do something e.g. *dread, fear*
- expecting to do something e.g. *expect, reckon*

*We **expect** to see her back on the screen in the autumn.*

*She **hoped** to find an English audience receptive to her watercolors and her images of contemporary life.*

*Graduates with first-class degrees still **queue up** to teach in Ulster's grammar schools.*

*He'd had his eyes on the telephone all during breakfast and he **couldn't wait** to get out of his chair and get at it.*

*He **yearned** to sleep.*

ache *3*	be dying *8*	hope *1*	seek *4*
aim *1*	dread *1*	(cannot) hope *2*	(cannot) wait *8*
aspire	expect *1,3*	hunger *4*	want *1,2,3,4,6*
burn *10*	(not) expect *4*	itch *2*	wish *2,3*
crave	fear *8*	long *4.0*	yearn
desire *2*	hanker	reckon *3*	
queue up			

II.4 THE 'LIKE' GROUP

These verbs are concerned with liking or disliking something.

*She **likes** to entertain, shop and go to the theatre.*

*Douglas **preferred** to do his own driving.*

(cannot) bear *1.6*	like *2.1,3,4,5,6,7,8*	prefer
hate *2*	love *5,9*	(cannot) stand *16*

II.5 THE 'CLAIM' GROUP

These verbs are concerned with saying that something is true when it may not be.

*He **claims** to have had no inside knowledge.*

*Dianne **may** well **profess** to admire Grace, but I suspect that deep down her attitude borders on jealousy, resentment and dislike.*

claim *1*	profess *1,2*
(not) pretend *3*	purport

II.6 THE 'NEED' GROUP

These verbs are concerned with needing or deserving to do something or to have something done.

Women __deserve__ to be treated as professionals.

The players __need__ to rest more than train at the moment.

> deserve *1*   need *1,2*

II.7 VERBS WITH OTHER MEANINGS

There are two other verbs which have this structure.

I want my books to be as cheap as possible so that more people __can afford__ to buy them.

She never __learned__ to read or write.

> (can) afford *1,2*   learn *1,3*

Structure information: Verb with Object

a) The to-infinitive clause is the Object. The first verb and the to-infinitive clause express two closely-related but separate actions or states. For example, if you *promise to pay* something, the act of *promising* is separate from the act of *paying*. Indeed, you may promise to pay but then not pay.

b) This structure has no passive, but the to-infinitive clause may itself be passive, beginning with *to be* and an '-ed' form.

Everyone leaving the library __can__ now __expect__ to be searched.

c) The phrasal verb pattern is the same except that there is a particle, P, which comes after the verb.

Structure III: Verb with Adjunct

V to-inf

	Verb group	to-infinitive clause
Subject	**Verb**	**Adjunct**
He	paid	to go to classical concerts.
She	qualified	to join a special team.
The paramedics	rush	to help.

Phrasal verbs: V P to-inf

	Verb group	Particle	to-infinitive clause
Subject	**Verb**		**Adjunct**
He	sat	back	to wait.
Another plane	was standing	by	to take her to Rome.

Verbs with this structure belong to the following meaning groups:

III.1 THE 'COLLABORATE' GROUP

These verbs are concerned with reaching an agreement or doing something jointly with someone else. The verbs in this group are **reciprocal verbs** (see Chapter 6) and in this pattern have a plural Subject.

*Three researchers **collaborated** to investigate how a ewe's brain changes to accommodate her need to recognise her own lamb.*

*The other parties **ganged up** to keep him out of power.*

collaborate *1*	connive *1*	negotiate *1*
collude	conspire *1*	
gang up		

III.2 THE 'FLOCK' GROUP

These verbs are concerned with going somewhere in order to do something.

*Audiences **flocked** to see The Beatles in their screen appearances.*

*Franklin **hurried** to catch the last train back to Washington.*

come *2*	go *1.4*	rush *1*
flock *3*	hurry *1*	
go around/round *1*		

III.3 THE 'VIE' GROUP

These verbs are concerned with doing something in competition with other people. The verbs in this group are **reciprocal verbs** (see Chapter 6) and in this pattern have a plural Subject.

*She was cheered and clapped by tourists who **jostled** to see her.*

*To keep customers loyal, the two firms **are vying** to provide the best sales and service backup.*

compete *1,2*	jostle *1*
jockey *2*	vie

III.4 THE 'WAIT' GROUP

These verbs are concerned with waiting to do something.

*The entire household **waited** to greet them.*

*I **waited around** to speak to the doctor.*

queue *3*	wait *1,3*
stand by *1*	wait around

III.5 THE 'QUALIFY' GROUP

These verbs are concerned with preparing for a job or activity.

*The two experiences helped convince Robb that he **should qualify** to become a doctor.*

*Women **can** also **train** to become fast jet pilots.*

> qualify *1,2*   register *2*   train *2.1*

III.6 THE 'PAY' AND 'CHARGE' GROUP

These verbs are concerned with paying to do something or charging someone to do something.

*Now they **charge** to take the stuff away.*

*Retailers **will pay** to occupy the premises the property company has built.*

> charge *1*   pay *1*
>
> fork out   pay out *1*   shell out

III.7 THE 'WAKE' GROUP

These verbs are concerned with waking. The to-infinitive indicates what happens at the time of waking.

*One night he **awoke** to find her crying softly.*

> awake *3*   awaken *3*   wake *1*
>
> wake up ▷*1*

III.8 VERBS WITH OTHER MEANINGS

There are a number of other verbs which have this structure.

*Parliament responded by **legislating** to prohibit corporal punishment in state schools.*

*She **lives** to perform.*

*Money is tight and the older children's godparents **are pitching in** to pay their school fees.*

*We **sat back** to wait for the phone to ring.*

*She **survived** to record her experiences as a cave dweller in the beleaguered city.*

> legislate   live *1.3*   survive *1,2*
>
> pitch in   sit back   sit down *2*

Structure information: Verb with Adjunct

a) The to-infinitive clause is an Adjunct.

b) This structure has no passive.

c) The phrasal verb pattern is the same except that there is a particle, P, which comes after the verb.

Productive uses

The to-infinitive clause is used with two additional meanings. These uses are productive, that is, they occur with a wide range of verbs.

1 The to-infinitive clause has the meaning 'in order to do something'. An example is *He smiled to hide his fear*, which means that hiding his fear was the purpose of his smiling.

2 The to-infinitive clause has the meaning 'because something happens'. An example is *She smiles to see her grandson*, which means that seeing her grandson is the cause of her smiling.

---

9 V inf

The verb is followed by a **bare infinitive**.

This pattern has one structure:

▶ Verbs in phase
I <u>didn't dare</u> disagree with them.

V inf

		Verb group	infinitive	
Subject		**Verb**		**Completive**
No politician	would dare	take on		the mighty tobacco industry.
I	'll go	see		what's happening.
I	helped	save		those animals.

Verbs with this pattern belong to the following meaning groups:

1 THE 'COME' AND 'GO' GROUP
2 THE 'DARE' AND 'NEED' GROUP
3 VERBS WITH OTHER MEANINGS

1 THE 'COME' AND 'GO' GROUP

These verbs indicate that the action indicated by the second verb is done. Only the base forms of the verbs, *come* and *go*, are used in this pattern, and only in American English.

*Why <u>**don't**</u> you <u>**come**</u> see me any more?*
*What I did was reach for my bathrobe and <u>**go**</u> **open** my front door.*

> come *2*   go *1.4*

2 THE 'DARE' AND 'NEED' GROUP

These verbs are concerned with daring or needing to do something.

*Thomas <u>**did not dare**</u> **approach** the great man.*
*People should know, with absolutely no doubt, no-one <u>**needs**</u> **starve** in the world.*

> (not) dare *1*   (not) need *4,5*

3 VERBS WITH OTHER MEANINGS

There is one other verb which has this pattern.

*A fever isn't always cause for concern and you can do a number of things to <u>**help**</u> **reduce** it.*

help *1,2*

Structure information

a) The first verb and the infinitive are two verbs **in phase**, and together form a **complex verb group**. This means that the actions or states expressed by the two verbs cannot be separated from each other. For example, if you *come see* someone, the *coming* and the *seeing* are not two processes, but one.

The complex verb group is followed by a group, phrase, or clause which completes the pattern of the second verb. In the structure table above this is called a **Completive**. For example, if the second verb is normally followed by a noun group, then the Completive of the complex verb group will be a noun group.

b) This structure has no passive.

10 V that

The verb is followed by a that-clause.

This pattern has one structure:

▶ Verb with Clause
*I *said* that I would do it.*

V that

	Verb group	that-clause
Subject	Verb	Clause
I	agree	that the project has possibilities.
The president	ordered	that the conference be suspended.
He	said	the country was unstable.

Phrasal verbs: V P that

	Verb group	Particle	that-clause
Subject	Verb		Clause
I	found	out	they were planning to erase the tapes.
Most of them	reported	back	that they were continuing to enjoy good health.

Verbs with this pattern belong to the following meaning groups:

1 THE 'SAY' GROUP
2 THE 'ADD' GROUP
3 THE 'SCREAM' GROUP
4 THE 'THINK' GROUP
5 THE 'DISCOVER' GROUP
6 THE 'CHECK' GROUP
7 THE 'SHOW' GROUP
8 THE 'ARRANGE' GROUP

1 THE 'SAY' GROUP

These verbs are concerned with speaking, writing, and other forms of communication. They indicate what kind of function the speech or writing is performing. This includes:

- guessing or predicting something e.g. *estimate, predict, prophesy*
- putting forward a suggestion or theory e.g. *postulate, suggest*
- saying something in a way that shows your attitude e.g. *crow, sneer*

The that-clause indicates the event or situation that is mentioned.

*The president **boasted** that it would be by far the biggest service program in American history.*

*She **claims** she paid no money for it.*

*Many passengers **complained** that once they emerged from the train, there were no emergency personnel to greet them.*

*I **explained** that you were upset and wanted to be alone.*

*However, the article **points out** that trade with Britain's European partners has risen considerably since 1973.*

*He **predicted** that the terms would be rejected and the war would continue.*

*Taylor **said** he was delighted to be at the festival.*

*The kids have loved him for years while their cynical elders **sneered** that he was just a pretty face.*

*We all felt hungry, so I **suggested** that we stop for an early lunch.*

*Mr Lightman **wrote** that there had been a number of misapplications of funds and breaches of duty.*

Agree and *concur* are **reciprocal verbs** (see Chapter 6) which have a plural Subject with this pattern and meaning.

*We **agreed** that she was not to be told.*

accept 2	confide	indicate 2	profess 1
acknowledge 1	conjecture 2	insinuate 1	promise 1
admit 1	contend 2	insist 1,2	pronounce 3
advise 1	crow 3	instruct 1	prophesy
advocate 1	declare 1,2	intimate 7	propose 1,3,4
affirm 1	decree 2	joke 2	protest 3
agree 1,3	demand 1	lament 1	quip 2
allege	deny 1	maintain 2	radio 6
allow 6	dictate 2	mandate 5	reason 4
announce 1,2,3	direct 12	marvel 1	recall 1
argue 1	disclose	mention 1	recollect
ask 2,3	divulge	moan 2	recommend 2
assert 1	emphasize	move 16	recount 1
attest	enthuse 1	muse 1	reflect 5
aver	estimate 1	note 10,11	regret 1
beg 1	explain 1,2	observe 3	remark 1
boast 1	forecast 2	opine	remonstrate
brag	foretell	ordain 2	report 1
caution 2	grant 3	order 2.2	request 1
certify 1	groan 3	plead 1,4	reveal 1
claim 1	grouse 2	pledge 2	rule 7
command 1	grumble 1	posit	say 1,2
comment 1	guarantee 3	postulate 1	signal 2
complain 1	guess 1	pray 1	signify 2
concede 1	hazard 3	preach 2	sneer
conclude 1	hint 2	predict	specify 2
concur	hypothesize	pretend 3	speculate 1
confess 1	imply 1	proclaim 1,2	state 8

stipulate	swear 2,3	underscore 1	wager 2
stress 1	testify 1	urge 3	warn 1
submit 2	theorize	venture 3	warrant 4
suggest 1,3,4	threaten 1	volunteer 4	write 5
surmise 1	underline 1	vow 1	
(not) let on	point out 2	report back 1	
make out 3	put down 1		

2 THE 'ADD' GROUP

These verbs indicate the relationship of something that is said or written to something else that has been said or written. This includes:

- saying something after you have said something else e.g. *add, repeat*
- saying something after someone else has said something e.g. *interject, reply*

*He said the air campaign will continue and might, in fact, intensify, but he **added** that other forces will probably be brought in to supplement the air campaign.*

*The opponents of this view **countered** that the unwillingness to carry out strategic attacks would weaken deterrence by showing a lack of resolve.*

*I said: 'What a lovely morning,' and he **replied** that it would be very hot later.*

add 5	counter 4	reaffirm	respond 1
agree 1,3	disagree 1	reiterate	retort
answer 1	dispute 2	rejoin 4	verify 2
concur	interject	repeat 1	
confirm 2	object 5	reply 1	

3 THE 'SCREAM' GROUP

These verbs indicate how something is said, for example how loudly or at what pitch.

*According to the legend, she **cried out** that no storm was going to stop her from finishing her ride.*

*Francis **murmured** that he would do anything he could and left the room.*

*She **screamed** that they'd killed her sons.*

bellow 1	cry 2	mutter	wail 2
bleat 3	declaim	scream 2	whine 2
burble 2	exclaim	shout 1	whisper 1
chant 3	murmur 1	squawk 2	yell 1
cry out ▷2			

4 THE 'THINK' GROUP

These verbs are concerned with thinking. This includes:

- having a belief
- knowing or understanding something
- hoping and fearing

*He was fantastically short of money, so everyone just **assumed** he sold the pictures.*

*Once I realized how much time I was spending at work, and how little I was enjoying life, I **decided** that things had to change.*

*The students **fear** that the government does not intend to fulfil this demand.*

*'I **didn't know** you owned a camera,' said Michael.*

*It was a calculated risk. They probably **reasoned** that without proof the fuss would die down.*

Nobody __suspected__ that the comet might contain much smaller particles.
I __thought__ you were dead.

Agree and *concur* are **reciprocal verbs** (see Chapter 6) which often have a plural Subject with this pattern and meaning.

Scientists __agree__ that these lumps of matter must originate in the asteroid belt.

accept 2,4	disbelieve 1	grasp 4	reflect 5
acknowledge 1	doubt 2	guess 1	regret 1,3
agree 1	dread 1	hallucinate	rejoice 1
anticipate 1	dream 2,4	hold 2.1	remember 1,5
appreciate 2	(never) dreamed 10	hope 1	resolve 2
assume 1	envisage	hypothesize	see 5
believe 1	envision	imagine 1,2,3	speculate 1
(cannot) believe 6	estimate 1	intend 1	suppose 1,2
bet 3	expect 1	know 1,8	surmise 1
calculate 1,2	fancy 1.7	marvel 1	suspect 1,2
(cannot) conceive 1	fantasize 1	(not) mind 2.1	theorize
concur	fear 4,9	muse 1	think 1,2,14,15,16,17
conjecture 2	feel 9,10,11	pray 1,2	trust 7
consider 1	figure 11	prefer	understand 5
(cannot) credit 10	foresee	presume 1	vow 1
decide 1	forget 2,4	realize 1	wish 4
determine 3,4	fret 1	reason 4	wonder 2
disagree 1	gather 6	reckon 1	worry 1

5 THE 'DISCOVER' GROUP

These verbs are concerned with coming to know or think something. We include here verbs which indicate that someone remembers something they had forgotten or not thought about for some time.

We soon __discovered__ that almost everything we had hidden had been found, and either carried off or wantonly destroyed.
My boyfriend left me as soon as he __found out__ I was pregnant.
I __noticed__ that a pane of glass was missing.
Suddenly she __realized__ that the only people she could ask were in Granville.
Rigid with fear, Jessica __remembered__ that the window was open.
Oh, I __see__ you've already started.

ascertain	establish 3	notice 1	remember 2
calculate 1	find 7	observe 2	see 1,4,16
conclude 1	gather 6	perceive 1	sense 2
decide 4	guess 2	read 1	suss
deduce	hear 7	realize 1	(can) tell 5
determine 2	infer 1	recall 1,2	twig 2
discern 1	intuit	recognize 2	
discover 1,3	learn 2	recollect	
divine 4	note 9	register 7	
figure out	find out 1	work out 1	

6 THE 'CHECK' GROUP

These verbs are concerned with checking something you believe is true.

Montagu stood up and __checked__ that the door was closed.

check 1	double-check	verify 1

7 THE 'SHOW' GROUP

These verbs are concerned with indicating a fact or situation. These verbs usually have an inanimate Subject.

> The large size *implies* that the gaps were created by a star rather than a planet.
> An argument with a friend or relative *doesn't mean* that you don't get on with anyone.
> Research *shows* that the more children are hit, the more likely they are to be aggressive themselves.

confirm *1*	imply *2*	reveal *1*	underline *1*
demonstrate *1*	indicate *1,5*	show *1,7*	underscore *1*
denote *1*	mean *1.1,2,4*	signal *4*	
illustrate *1*	prove *2,3*	signify *1*	

8 THE 'ARRANGE' GROUP

These verbs are concerned with causing something to happen. This includes:

- people making arrangements for the future e.g. *arrange, fix, see*
- situations determining the future e.g. *guarantee, mean*

> He *had arranged* that all calls from there would be charged to the police.
> They are anxious to *ensure* that emergency assistance is efficiently distributed.
> In 1981 he was appointed Provincial Superior. This *meant* he had to leave Huddersfield and take responsibility for over 100 priests in England, Wales and New Zealand.

The verb *mind* is used only in the imperative.

> *Mind* you don't slip.

arrange *2*	fix *3*	mind *2.5*	see *12*
dictate *3,4*	guarantee *1*	ordain *2*	
ensure	mean *1.5*	provide *2*	

9 THE 'GO' GROUP

These verbs are used when you are quoting something. We include here *say 6*, which you use when indicating the information given by something such as a clock or a map. These verbs have an inanimate Subject.

> The story *goes* that the dish was invented by Kaiser Franz-Joseph's cook, who had promised to make his master something delicious to tempt his jaded appetite.
> The map *says* there's six of them.

go *3.5*	say *3,6*

10 VERBS WITH OTHER MEANINGS

There are a number of other verbs which have this pattern.

> Like Clinton, he *is gambling* that a recovering economy will swell the government's coffers.
> The notion of self-sacrifice is a nonsense. It *presupposes* that we can give to others something which we do not have ourselves.
> Anastasia *pretended* she hadn't heard his question.
> Federal law *requires* that consumers be informed whenever an investigative report is ordered.

In the case of *get out* and *remain*, the that-clause is really part of the pattern of the noun that comes before the verb.

When word **_got out_** *that we had spent nearly £1.6 million on a single sixty-second* **_commercial_**, *irate shareholders began firing off letters.*

The fact **_remains_** *that you can produce steel much more cheaply here than you can in* **_Germany or the rest of the European Community._**

gamble *2*	presuppose	remain *8*
presume *3*	pretend *1,2*	require *2*
get out *4*		

Structure information

a) The that-clause is a new clause, with its own structure.

b) This structure has a passive with the pattern **be V-ed**, where the that-clause is the Subject, but it very rarely occurs. However, there is a related passive structure beginning with introductory *it*, as in *It* <u>*was claimed*</u> *that she often turned up more than an hour late*. This pattern is discussed in more detail in Chapter 9, Section 1 (see pages 526-528). The pattern **it V that** is also discussed in Chapter 9, Section 1 (see pages 519-520).

c) The phrasal verb pattern is the same except that there is a particle, P, which comes after the verb.

Omitting *that*

1 After the more frequent, more basic verbs such as *say, think*, and *notice*, the word *that* is often left out, especially in speech.

I <u>*said*</u> *there was to be no talk of divorce.*

I <u>*think*</u> *he made a tactical blunder by announcing it so far ahead of time.*

However, *that* tends to be used when the that-clause is separated from the Subject by a prepositional phrase, adverb group, or subordinate clause.

A Foreign Ministry spokesman <u>*said*</u> *at a press briefing* **that relations with the Community were strained**.

That is less often left out after more formal or less frequent words such as *demand, estimate*, and *brag*, and is retained when the rhythm of the sentence requires it.

They <u>*demanded*</u> *that he step down immediately*.

The 14-year-old <u>*brags*</u> *that he has escaped from custody 31 times.*

2 In the case of meaning groups 1-5, the Subject and verb can, as with a quote clause, come within or after the that-clause, except with verbs expressing a statement or request that something should be done. The word *that* is not used.

Things didn't, he <u>*admitted*</u>, *look good in Russia.*

Italian striker Gianluca Vialli will play for Juventus next season, Sampdoria president Paolo Mantovani <u>*confirmed*</u> *today.*

3 Some of the more frequent verbs concerned with speech, writing, and thought are also used in clauses beginning with *as*, which usually come before or within a main clause without *that*. This structure implies that, in the opinion of the user, what was said or thought is true, or turned out to be true.

As Eamonn McCabe <u>*says*</u>, *now it's up to the industry to prove him wrong.*

He had, as he <u>*predicted*</u>, *immediately assumed an non-executive chairmanship.*

4 Some of these verbs can be used in a clause beginning with *as* or *than* when making a comparison between what people say or think about a situation and what it is really like.

I'm not as disheartened **as people** <u>**think**</u>.

*When the doorbell rang, Marianne thought it might be Jake arriving earlier **than he <u>had</u> <u>promised</u>**.*

5 Some verbs that have the pattern **V that** also have the pattern **V *so*** or **V *so/not***, where *so* or *not* acts as a substitute for a that-clause. See pages 119-121.

Words in inverted commas

Sometimes some of the words in the that-clause are put in inverted commas. The inverted commas indicate that the words inside them are the actual words used, or have had only an appropriate change of tense and reference. Compare **V with quote** (pages 113-119).

On our most recent trip, our luncheon hostess commented on his attractiveness. I <u>replied</u> that we were 'only friends'.

He now <u>murmured</u> that 'he needed a drink or he would die'.

Should or subjunctive in that-clause

Some verbs can have *should* or a subjunctive in the that-clause. They are concerned with statements or requests that something should be done.

The government <u>has ordered</u> that people should not gather in groups of more than two on the streets.

I <u>propose</u> that we examine two basic trends, moving in opposite directions.

I <u>suggested</u> that we taper off the counseling sessions.

advise *1*	demand *1*	order *2.2*	rule *7*
advocate *1*	direct *12*	plead *1*	specify *2*
agree *3*	insist *1*	prefer	stipulate
ask *2,3*	instruct *1*	propose *1*	suggest *1*
beg *1*	intend *1*	recommend *2*	urge *3*
command *1*	move *16*	request *1*	
decree *2*	ordain *2*	require *2*	

Indicating the speaker's intention

Verbs are usually used with the pattern **V that** in order to describe what someone else has said or thought. However, some verbs with this pattern are often used in the simple present tense, with *I* or *we* as the Subject, as a preface to a statement, in order to indicate what kind of statement the speaker intends to make.

I <u>confess</u> I'm sorry for her.

I <u>insist</u> that the funds be returned.

Except in the case of verbs concerned with statements or requests that something should be done, and the verb *disagree*, the Subject and verb can come after or within the clause. The word *that* is not used.

This, I <u>admit</u>, is still an open question.

I'll come back for that, I <u>promise</u>.

acknowledge *1*	confirm *1,2*	maintain *2*	recommend *2*
admit *1*	contend *2*	move *16*	submit *2*
advise *1*	declare *1,2*	pledge *2*	suggest *1,3,4*
agree *1*	demand *1*	pray *1*	swear *2,3*
bet *3*	disagree *1*	predict	
concede *1*	guarantee *3*	promise *1*	
confess *1*	insist *1,2*	propose *1*	

Some verbs are used in this way with a modal: usually *would, must,* or *could* in a statement, and *may, can,* or *could* in a request.

> I **must stress** that this is an exceedingly rare complication.

> **May** I just **say** that we appreciated the understanding and help of all those who felt for us in our misfortune.

add *5*	comment *1*	insist *1,2*	stress *1*
admit *1*	confess *1*	mention *1*	testify *1*
agree *1*	contend *2*	observe *3*	
argue *1,7*	deny *1*	say *2*	
claim *1*	emphasize	state *8*	

Note that the verbs *deny* and *disagree* add a negative meaning to what you are saying.

> I **disagree** that it is a relatively easy matter to negotiate over hostages.

> I phone twice a day but I **can't deny** I miss them.

Other related patterns

V *the fact* that

Verbs concerned with feeling or thinking which do not have the pattern **V that** can be followed by *the fact* and a that-clause, to form a structure which has a similar function to that of **V that**.

> But then the moment comes when they **have to face** the fact that they will never, ever see their child again.

> I decided to give up because I **can** no longer **ignore** the fact that it is bad for my health.

Some verbs with the pattern **V that** can also be followed by *the fact that*, for extra emphasis.

> You **must accept** the fact that you are older than you used to be.

V *into* n that

The verb is followed by a prepositional phrase beginning with *into*, and a that-clause. The prepositional phrase indicates the person who is addressed.

> He**'s** always **drumming** into us that we must be consistent.

drum *VP*

V *on/upon* n that

The verb is followed by a prepositional phrase beginning with *on* or *upon*, and a that-clause. The prepositional phrase indicates the person who is addressed.

> But the C.O. continues to **impress** on me that I am too old for this job. I think he wants to force me to relinquish my commission.

impress 2

V *to* n that

The verb is followed by a prepositional phrase beginning with *to*, and a that-clause. The prepositional phrase indicates the person who is addressed, or the person to whom a fact is demonstrated. The phrasal verb pattern is **V P *to* n that**.

David __admitted__ to the clerk that he had been at the scene and had lent the other youth a knife to get into cars.

You __will have to demonstrate__ to the court that the repairs are reasonably necessary to preserve your property.

admit 1	demonstrate 1	prove 2,3	stress 1
announce 1,2,3	disclose	recommend 2	submit 2
boast 1	explain 1	remark 1	suggest 1
brag	grumble 1	repeat 1	swear 3
comment 1	hint 2	report 1	whisper 1
complain 1	indicate 1,2,5	reveal 1	write 5
confess 1	intimate 7	say 1,2	
confide	mention 1	show 1,7	
declare 1,2	pray 1	signal 2	
(not) let on	point out 2		

V *with* n that

See page 471.

---

11   V wh

The verb is followed by a finite **wh-clause**.

This pattern has one structure:

▶ Verb with Clause
   Can you __suggest__ what I should say to her?

V wh

	Verb group	wh-clause
Subject	**Verb**	**Clause**
We	cannot estimate	what the local interest will be.
Statistical facts	illustrated	how dreadful conditions have become.
People	don't notice	whether it's winter or summer.
She	understood	why her mother just gave up and died.

Phrasal verbs: V P wh

	Verb group	Particle	wh-clause
Subject	**Verb**		**Clause**
She	couldn't figure	out	what was wrong with her.
No-one	has set	out	how the scheme will work.
	Think	through	what you need.

Verbs with this pattern belong to the following meaning groups:

1 THE 'ASK' GROUP
2 THE 'THINK' GROUP
3 THE 'DISCOVER' GROUP
4 THE 'SHOW' GROUP
5 THE 'DETERMINE' GROUP
6 VERBS WITH OTHER MEANINGS

If a verb is usually used with only one or two wh-words, this is indicated in the lists below.

1 THE 'ASK' GROUP

These verbs are concerned with speaking or writing. This includes:

- asking for information e.g. *ask*, *query*
- agreeing or discussing e.g. *argue*, *discuss*
- giving information e.g. *disclose*, *explain*

Don't ask *who my informant was, because I'm not going to tell you.*

The government **is** *also* **debating** *what sort of treaty it wants.*

She began to **explain** *where each muscle was, and urged him to concentrate on that particular spot as she worked it.*

A passer-by **inquired** *why the television cameras were there.*

Note down *when you first became noticeably fatigued.*

Toy companies **suggest** *what age of child a toy would be suitable for.*

During his visit, he **underlined** *how critical the grain credits are to the Soviet Union.*

He also **warned** *how such a law could be used in an oppressive manner against the interests and rights of minorities.*

The verbs *agree*, *argue 4*, *debate*, and *discuss* are **reciprocal verbs** (see Chapter 6) and often have a plural Subject with this pattern.

We **can argue** *whether we should have a press conference or not.*

acknowledge *1*	describe *1*	illustrate *1*	reveal *1*
advise *1*	detail *6 (how)*	indicate *2*	say *1*
affirm *1*	dictate *2*	inquire *1*	see *16*
agree *1,3*	disclose	intimate *7*	specify *1*
announce *1,2,3*	discuss *1*	mention *1*	state *8*
argue *1,4 (how/whether)*	dispute *2*	note *11*	stipulate
articulate *2*	divulge	proclaim *1,2*	stress *1*
ask *1*	emphasize *(how)*	propose *1 (how)*	suggest *1,2*
chronicle *1*	explain *1*	query *3*	underline *1*
confess *1*	explain *2 (why)*	recall *1*	underscore *1*
confirm *2*	forecast *2*	recommend *2*	warn *1*
debate *3*	guarantee *3*	recount *1*	
declare *1,2*	hint *2*	remark *1 (how)*	
demand *1*	hypothesize	report *1*	

106

| let on | point out 2 | set out 4 |
| note down | put down 1 | |

2 THE 'THINK' GROUP

These verbs are concerned with thinking about something. This includes:

- knowing or understanding something
- forgetting or remembering something
- understanding something wrongly e.g. *mistake, underestimate*
- having an attitude towards a situation e.g. *care, mind*
- wondering or speculating about a situation e.g. *consider, surmise*
- thinking about the future e.g. *foresee, predict*

I've never known her __not__ to __care__ what she looked like before.

Observers __doubt__ if this Sunday's elections will produce a government able or willing to tackle the economic crisis.

They __can__ accurately __foretell__ whether a marriage will work or not.

I rarely went to the movies and I __forgot__ what it was like to eat in a fancy restaurant.

The last time I saw him, he said he was going to try and get to America. But I __don't know__ whether he made it or not.

No one __should mistake__ how serious it is.

It's too early to __speculate__ where the problem occurred.

They don't stop to __think__ who's going to do the actual basic work.

Brand __wondered__ what thoughts were going through her mind.

The verb *agree* is a **reciprocal verb** and often has a plural Subject with this pattern.

They are furious. They want action. But they __don't agree__ what the problem is or what the action should be.

accept 2,4	determine 3,4	know 1,7	see 5
acknowledge 1	doubt 2 (if/whether)	marvel 1 (how)	speculate 1
agree 1	envisage	mind 2.2 (if)	surmise 1
anticipate 1	envision	(not) mind 2.3	suspect 2
appreciate 2	fantasize 1	mistake 4	think 6,8
(cannot) believe 6	figure 11	misunderstand	underestimate 1
care 1	foresee	ponder	understand 1,3,4
(cannot) conceive 1	foretell	predict	visualize
conjecture 2	forget 1	reflect 5 (how)	wonder 1
consider 2	guess 1	rehearse 2	worry 1
debate 4	hypothesize	remember 1	
decide 1	imagine 1	resolve 2	

3 THE 'DISCOVER' GROUP

These verbs are concerned with coming to know something or bringing something to mind. This includes:

- working something out e.g. *analyse, calculate*
- finding something out e.g. *discover, investigate*
- realizing something e.g. *realize, twig*
- remembering something you had forgotten
- finding something out through the senses e.g. *catch, feel*

Keep a record of how much you watch each week and __calculate__ what it amounts to a year.

'Is this really necessary?' he shouted, after failing twice to __catch__ what he was being told.

*An inquiry was underway last night to **discover** why Evans was not handcuffed to his police escort.*

*I wanted to have a look at the book on my own to **find out** what was going on.*

*You **can judge** how warm your cat is by the posture he adopts.*

*The study is following the health of over a million people to **learn** who gets cancer and why.*

*How easy is it to **pinpoint** what makes a face appealing to us?*

*After meandering down endless country lanes like the bottoms of ditches I **realized** why we were led astray: someone had turned a signpost around.*

*Several times she heard her name being called but when she turned around to **see** who it was, no one was in the room.*

*It's been nagging away at me for ages, but now I**'ve** finally **twigged** who Noel Edmonds reminds me of.*

*You **have to weigh up** whether a human life is more important than an animal's life.*

The verb *look* is used only as an imperative.

*Hey, Mom, **look** what I can do.*

analyse *1,2*	divine *4*	note *9*	register *7*
ascertain	establish *3*	notice *1*	remember *2*
assess *1,2*	estimate *1*	observe *1,2*	(cannot) remember *3*
calculate *1,2*	(cannot) fathom *2*	perceive *1*	see *1,4,10*
catch *10*	feel *5*	pinpoint *1,2*	sense *2*
check *1*	find *7*	prove *2*	suss
decide *4*	guess *2*	read *1*	(can) tell *5*
deduce	hear *7*	realize *1*	tell *6*
detect *1*	investigate	recall *1*	think *4*
determine *2*	judge *4,5*	recognize *2*	twig *2*
discern *1*	learn *1,2,3*	recollect	verify *1*
discover *1,3*	look *1.10*	reconstruct *3*	weigh *3*
fathom out ▷*2*	make out *1,2*	puzzle out	weigh up ▷*3*
figure out	piece together *1*	suss out ▷	work out *1*
find out *1*	pin down *1*	think through	

4 THE 'SHOW' GROUP

These verbs are concerned with showing that a situation exists or showing what it is like.

*People **can** provide practical help or **demonstrate** how you can overcome a particular problem.*

*The director prefers to **show** what a hideous and futile business fighting a war can be.*

The verbs *indicate, show 2, underline,* and *underscore* always have inanimate Subjects. The other verbs in this group sometimes have inanimate Subjects.

*A hormone profile **will indicate** whether there is a possible problem.*

*The incident **underlines** how easily things can go wrong on holiday.*

confirm *1* (whether)	illustrate *1*	reveal *1*	underline *1*
demonstrate *1*	indicate *1,5*	show *1,2*	underscore *1*
demonstrate *4* (how)	prove *2* (whether)	signal *4*	

5 THE 'DETERMINE' GROUP

These verbs are concerned with influencing a situation.

*Vacant land taxes enable the government to **influence** where development occurs.*

The verbs *decide, define, determine 1,* and *dictate* always have an inanimate Subject. The verb *influence* sometimes has an inanimate Subject.

*The final exam **determines** whether you can sit for university entrance or not.*

Apart from habits we picked up as children, there are many other factors which __influence__ what we choose to eat.

decide *3*	determine *1*	influence *4*
define *1*	dictate *3*	plan *2*

6 VERBS WITH OTHER MEANINGS

There are two other verbs which have this pattern.

The verb *see* is followed by a clause beginning with *if* or *what*.

I'll give you a cool wash, and then we__'ll see__ if we can make your bed more comfortable.

In the case of *remain*, the wh-clause is really part of the pattern of the noun that comes before the verb.

But the question __remains__ whether science is capable of ensuring that bad research is caught and bad researchers punished.

remain *8*	see *11*

Structure information

a) The wh-clause is a new clause, with its own structure.

Not all verbs that are sometimes followed by a clause beginning with a wh-word have the pattern **V wh**. For example, the following sentence is not an example of a **V wh** pattern:

Revson knew what it takes many people a lifetime to learn.

In this example, *what it takes many people a lifetime to learn* occurs in the place of an ordinary noun group. It could be paraphrased as *the thing that it takes many people a lifetime to learn*.

Compare this with a sentence that does have a **V wh** pattern:

I __knew__ what his job was.

In this example, *what his job was* does not occur in the place of an ordinary noun group. It indicates that something was unknown, and could be paraphrased as *what it was that his job was*.

b) This structure has a passive, with the pattern **be V-ed**. The wh-clause is the Subject. However, the passive does not often occur, and not all verbs with this structure occur in the passive at all. The following verbs are the ones that are most frequently used in the passive.

decide *3*	detect *1*	discuss *1*	reveal *1*
demonstrate *1*	determine *1*	explain *1,2*	underline *1*
describe *1*	dictate *3*	indicate *1*	

c) The phrasal verb pattern is the same except that there is also a particle, P, which comes after the verb.

Other related patterns

V *of* n wh

The verb is followed by a prepositional phrase beginning with *of*, and a wh-clause. The prepositional phrase indicates the hearer or reader.

Kay __inquired__ of Seaton how things were these days over in Cremorne.

inquire *1*

V *on/upon* n wh

The verb is followed by a prepositional phrase beginning with *on* or *upon*, and a wh-clause. The prepositional phrase indicates the hearer or reader.

I __impressed__ on him what a huge honour he was being offered and urged him to accept it.

impress *2*

V *to* n wh

The verb is followed by a prepositional phrase beginning with *to*, and a wh-clause. The prepositional phrase indicates the hearer or reader. The phrasal verb pattern is **V P *to* n wh**.

I don't like people __dictating__ to me what I should do and what I shouldn't do.
Let me __explain__ to you how this works.

admit *1*	dictate *2*	indicate *1,2,5*	reveal *1*
confess *1*	disclose	mention *1*	show *1*
demonstrate *1*	explain *1*	prove *2*	suggest *1,2*
(not) let on			

---

12 V wh-to-inf

The verb is followed by a to-infinitive clause introduced by a wh-word.

This pattern has one structure:

▶ Verb with Object
I __knew__ what to do.

V wh-to-inf

	Verb group	wh-to-infinitive clause
Subject	Verb	Object
I	've forgotten	what to say.
We	have to discuss	how to divide the land.

Phrasal verbs: V P wh-to-inf

	Verb group	Particle	wh-to-infinitive clause
Subject	**Verb**		**Object**
I	couldn't figure	out	what to do.
I	couldn't work	out	how to do it.

Verbs with this pattern belong to the following meaning groups:

1   THE 'DESCRIBE' GROUP
2   THE 'DISCOVER' GROUP
3   THE 'DECIDE' GROUP
4   THE 'REMEMBER' GROUP

1   THE 'DESCRIBE' GROUP

These verbs are concerned with showing or telling someone how to do something. The Subject is usually a person or something that has been written, but in the case of *indicate*, it may also be an experiment.

With most of the verbs in this group the to-infinitive is most frequently introduced by *how*, but in the case of *indicate* it is most frequently introduced by *where*.

*The book **describes** how to set up a self-help group.*

*Medical studies can never prove causation but **can** only **indicate** where to look for the real cause.*

*Are your cosmetics past their sell-by date? We **reveal** how to make them last longer.*

*Some American reviewers have criticised him for failing to **suggest** how to govern a modern society without a belief in progress.*

advise *1*	explain *1*	instruct *1*	show *2,5*
demonstrate *4*	illustrate *1*	reveal *1*	specify *1*
describe *1*	indicate *1*	say *1*	suggest *1,2*

2   THE 'DISCOVER' GROUP

These verbs are concerned with finding out how to do something or whether to do something.

With most of the verbs in this group the to-infinitive is most frequently introduced by *how*.

*The computer **calculates** how to move each individual joint of each finger, and the joints in the arm.*

*People **discovered** how to cultivate cereals thousands of years ago.*

*In every library and bookshop there's a mass of information if you want to **find out** what to do for your children.*

*The Environmental Protection Agency **is investigating** whether to make these tests compulsory.*

*The team boss **was weighing up** what to do about the drastic rule changes.*

ask *1*	check *1*	establish *3*	learn *1,2,3*
assess *1,2*	determine *2*	guess *1,2*	see *1,10*
calculate *1*	discover *1,3*	investigate	think *4*

> figure out   puzzle out   work out *1*
> find out *1*   weigh up ▷*3*

3 THE 'DECIDE' GROUP

These verbs are concerned with thinking or talking about how to do something or whether to do something.

With most of these verbs, the to-infinitive is most frequently introduced by *whether* or *how*, but in the case of *argue* it is most frequently introduced by *whether* alone, whereas in the case of *imagine, plan,* and *rehearse, whether* is never or rarely used.

> *The Prime Minister **is** now **deciding** whether to continue to fight to retain her position as party leader.*

> *How to implement such tactics **was discussed** on Birmingham's local radio station.*

> *She began to **plan** how to get out of town without being caught.*

The verbs *argue, debate 3,* and *discuss* are **reciprocal verbs** (see Chapter 6) and have a plural Subject.

> *It's like people **arguing** whether to put out a fire in the house while the house burns down.*

argue *4*	decide *1,4*	figure *11*	plan *2*
consider *2*	determine *3*	imagine *1*	ponder
debate *3,4*	discuss *1*	judge *4*	rehearse *2*

4 THE 'REMEMBER' GROUP

These verbs are concerned with knowing, remembering, forgetting, and understanding what to do or how to do something. With most of the verbs in this group the to-infinitive is most frequently introduced by *how* or *what*, but in the case of *know*, it is sometimes also introduced by *whether*.

> *I**'ve forgotten** what to say.*

> *Kemp **didn't know** whether to believe her or not.*

> *I just **couldn't remember** how to spell the most simple of words.*

> *I **couldn't see** how to make money.*

forget *1*	recall *1*	see *5*
know *1,7*	remember *1*	think *6,8*
realize *1*	(cannot) remember *3*	understand *1,3,4*

Structure information

a) The wh-word and the to-infinitive clause together form the Object.

b) This structure has a passive, with the structure *be* **V-ed**. However, the passive does not often occur.

c) The phrasal verb pattern is the same except that there is also a particle, P, which comes after the verb.

13 V with quote

The verb is used with a quote clause.

This pattern has one structure:

▶ Verb with Clause
'Hello,' he <u>said</u>.

V with quote

The Subject, Verb, and Clause can be arranged in five different ways.

quote clause	Verb group	
Clause	Verb	Subject
'But the blood on the back seat?'	objected	Parslow.
'Don't be silly, Dawn!'	said	Quaver.

quote clause		Verb group
Clause	Subject	Verb
'No, no, no,'	she	cried.
'Someone in your family?'	Browne	suggested.

quote clause...	Verb group		...quote clause
Clause...	Verb	Subject	...Clause
'Yes,'	replied	the man,	'I am.'
'This,'	said	Anthony,	'is going to take some time.'

quote clause...		Verb group	...quote clause
Clause...	Subject	Verb	...Clause
'Yes,'	she	admitted,	'it will.'
'So why,'	he	asked,	'don't they just leave?'

	Verb group	quote clause
Subject	Verb	Clause
He	replied:	'It's nothing.'
A police spokesman	said:	'It is a mystery.'

113

Phrasal verbs: V P with quote

The Subject, Verb, and Clause can be arranged in the same five ways as for verbs with the pattern **V with quote**. One way is shown below.

	Verb group	Particle	quote clause
Subject	**Verb**		**Clause**
I	shouted	out	'I'm OK!'

Note that the only verb that is frequently used with the pattern **V with quote** in conversation is *say*, as shown in the example in meaning group 1 below.

Verbs with this pattern belong to the following meaning groups:

1 THE 'SAY' GROUP
2 THE 'ADD' GROUP
3 THE 'SCREAM' GROUP
4 THE 'GASP' GROUP
5 THE 'SNEER' GROUP
6 THE 'THINK' GROUP
7 THE 'GO' GROUP

1 THE 'SAY' GROUP

These verbs are concerned with speaking, writing, and other forms of communication. They indicate what kind of function the speech or writing is performing. We include here *read 1* which indicates that someone understands something written.

'Mr McClintock,' she <u>announced</u>, 'has decided to go and visit the bank in London.'

'What's the matter?' she <u>asked</u>, backing away a step.

'I'm sorry,' Meg <u>blurted out</u>. 'I won't do it again, I promise.'

'We have been told nothing,' <u>claims</u> Mr Matveyev.

The note had slipped down behind the teapot. She <u>read</u>, 'Ta for these things, but I don't need them yet. Thanks for everything.'

'How he lost, I shall never know,' <u>remarked</u> Lord Howard somewhat wistfully.

'Perhaps I should get the others,' he <u>said</u>, and made for the door.

'Where the hell did these guys come from?' Kravis <u>wondered</u> aloud.

'How depressed I am,' he <u>wrote</u> in his diary.

When *say* is used in conversation, the Subject and verb nearly always come before the quote clause.

Yeah 'cos somebody over there <u>said</u>, erm, 'Oh somebody at number a hundred and seventy-something has found a cat,' and I <u>said</u>, 'Oh, is it white?', and he <u>said</u>, 'Yeah, I think so, I'm not sure,' and it was all like this, and I <u>was saying</u>, 'Oh, it must be her, it must be her.'

admit *1*	avow	claim *1*	deduce
advise *1*	banter *2*	command *1*	demand *1*
affirm *1*	beg *1*	comment *1*	entreat
allege	beseech	complain *1*	estimate *1*
announce *2*	blurt	concede *1*	exhort
apologize	bluster	conclude *1*	explain *1,2*
argue *1*	boast *1*	confess *1*	go *3.7*
ask *1*	brag	confide	grouse *2*
assent *2*	cable *5*	console *1*	grumble *1*
assert *1*	caution *2*	contend *2*	guess *1*
attest	challenge *4*	counsel *2*	hazard *3*
aver	chorus *6*	declare *1*	hedge *4*

114

implore	order *2.1*	recall *1*	tease *1*
inquire *1*	philosophize	remark *1*	telegraph *2*
insist *2*	plead *1*	reminisce	temporize
instruct *1*	pray *1*	report *1*	urge *1*
jest *2*	predict	reprove	venture *3*
joke *2,4*	proclaim *2*	request *2*	volunteer *4*
maintain *2*	promise *1*	say *1*	vow *1*
marvel *1*	pronounce *3*	scold	warn *1,2*
moan *2*	protest *3*	scrawl *1*	wheedle
muse *1*	put *12*	speculate *1*	whinge
note *11*	query *3*	state *8*	wonder *1*
observe *3*	quip *2*	stress *2*	write *5*
offer *2*	read *1,2*	suggest *1*	
opine	reason *4*	summarize	
blurt out	burst out *15*		

2 THE 'ADD' GROUP

These verbs indicate the relationship of something that is said or written to something else that has been said or written. This includes:

- saying something first or last e.g. *begin, finish*
- saying something after you have said something else e.g. *add, repeat*
- saying something after someone else has said something e.g. *interject, reply*

Mr Brown __added__: 'We are a very broadly spread business. We are not dependent on the UK market.'

'The fire seems to be behind that door,' Judy __began__.

'All this publicity helps build the brand's renown,' __chipped in__ Frederik Zimmer.

'You're -' 'Please,' she __interjected__. 'Let me tell you in my own way.'

'You knew her?' he asked. 'Of course,' she __replied__.

add *5*	continue *5*	interpose *2*	rejoin *4*
agree *1*	correct *6*	interrupt *1*	repeat *1*
amend *1*	counter *4*	intervene *2*	reply *1*
answer *1*	echo *4*	object *5*	respond *1*
begin *4*	end *6*	persist *2*	resume *3*
conclude *2*	finish *6*	prompt *2*	retort
concur	interject	reiterate	riposte *2*
break in *2*	chime in	cut in	pipe up
butt in	chip in *2*	go on *7*	put in *3*

3 THE 'SCREAM' GROUP

These verbs indicate how something is said, for example how loudly or quickly, or at what pitch. Some verbs, such as *wail* and *rasp*, also indicate the feeling that the speaker has (see also meaning group 5 below).

Most of these verbs are usually used in fiction rather than in journalism or conversation.

She __called out__, 'Nina, come in here and look at this.'

'I guess you guys don't mind if I smoke?' he __drawled__.

She hesitated before __gabbling__, 'I bought them this afternoon. I was trying them on.'

When he came back I asked him whether it was still raining. 'Don't know,' he __muttered__. 'I didn't notice.'

'Traitor!' she __screamed__.

'He's coming,' Egan __whispered__.

115

babble *1*	croak *2*	mouth *5*	slur *2*
bark *2*	croon *2*	mumble	splutter *1*
bawl *1*	cry *2*	murmur *1*	sputter *3*
bellow *1*	declaim	mutter	squawk *2*
bleat *2*	drawl	pipe *4*	squeal
boom *6*	ejaculate *2*	purr *3*	stammer *1*
bray *2*	exclaim	rasp *1*	thunder *6*
breathe *2*	gabble	roar *4*	trill *2*
burble *2*	growl *2*	scream *2*	twitter *2*
call *3*	hiss *2*	screech *2*	wail *2*
chant *3*	holler	shout *1*	wheeze *1*
chirp *2*	howl *4*	shriek *2*	whine *2*
chirrup	intone	shrill *4*	whisper *1*
coo *2*	lisp *2*	sing *1*	yell *1*

boom out ▷*6*	holler out ▷	sing out
call out ▷*3*	rap out	
cry out ▷*2*	shout out	

4 THE 'GASP' GROUP

These verbs are used to express speech accompanied by an expression, gesture, or non-verbal sound. They are usually used in fiction rather than in journalism or conversation.

'Do you know what this means?' I __gasped__, *laying a hand on Sauter's shoulder.*

'Go ahead,' she __smiled__.

'Oh, Dennis,' she __sobbed__. *'I'm sorry. I really am.'*

beam *1*	giggle *1*	nod *1*	sniffle *1*
cackle	grunt *1*	pout *2*	snigger
chortle	guffaw *2*	sigh *2*	snort *2*
chuckle	gulp *2*	smile *3*	sob *2*
gasp *2*	laugh *1*	sniff *3*	wince

5 THE 'SNEER' GROUP

These verbs indicate the feeling expressed or felt by the person speaking, for example anger, enthusiasm, surprise, scorn, or unhappiness. Many of these verbs also indicate the way that something is said, to some extent.

Most of these verbs are usually used in fiction rather than in journalism or conversation.

'This is great!' __enthused__ *Francis.*

'It's monstrous!' Jackie __fumed__. *'I've got a good mind to – '*

'Takes some of the heat off you, doesn't it?' he __sneered__.

'Take him to the checkpoint!' Bykov __spat out__.

crow *4*	groan *2*	mock *1*	snarl *2*
enthuse *1*	gush *3*	rage *3*	sneer
explode *2*	huff *1*	rant *1*	spit *5*
expostulate	jeer *1*	rave *1,2*	storm *5*
exult	jibe *2*	rhapsodize	whimper *2*
froth *3*	lament *1*	scoff *1*	
fume *2*	moan *1*	snap *4*	

spit out ▷*5*

6 THE 'THINK' GROUP

These verbs are concerned with thinking. Sometimes quotation marks are not used around the quote clause.

> *What a terrible scenario, I <u>thought</u>.*
>
> *Boisi was puzzled to see senior executives such as Cohen and Robinson darting about. 'Who's in charge here?' he <u>wondered</u>.*

muse *1*	think *8*	wonder *1*

7 THE 'GO' GROUP

These verbs are used when quoting a piece of writing or something such as a song or poem. They have an inanimate Subject.

> *'You can't kill the spirit, she is like a mountain,' <u>went</u> the Greenham women's chant.*
>
> *The sign <u>read</u>: SPEED ZONE AHEAD 35 MPH.*

go *3.5*	run *31*
read *5*	say *3*

Structure information

a) The quote clause is a new clause, with its own structure. It may be one word, such as *yes*, or it may be much longer. The Subject and verb most frequently come after the quote clause or in the middle of it, but they sometimes come before it.

b) The order of Subject and verb is also variable; the Subject may come before or after the verb. Before a quote, the Subject usually comes first, although in journalism, the verb sometimes comes before the Subject:

> *<u>Said</u> Mr. Fellmeth: 'We don't necessarily need more lawyers. We need more competent ones.'*

After a quote, the Subject may come first or second, unless it is a personal pronoun. If the Subject is a personal pronoun, in modern English it always comes first.

c) This structure has no passive.

d) The phrasal verb pattern is the same except that there is a particle, P, which comes after the verb.

Other related patterns

V *after* n with quote

The verb is used with a quote clause and is followed by a prepositional phrase beginning with *after*. The Subject always comes before the verb.

Most verbs with this pattern indicate that someone is speaking loudly. The prepositional phrase indicates who is being addressed. The person being addressed is moving away from the speaker.

> *'And don't forget to send Kenny for those items!' the Duchess <u>called</u> after her.*

call *3*	shout *1*	yell *1*

The verb *repeat* indicates that someone repeats what someone else has just said. The prepositional phrase indicates the first speaker.

Then Bishop Paulk asked everyone to __repeat__ after him, 'The Lord is God' and 3,000 voices affirmed that He was.

repeat 2

V *at* n with quote

The verb is used with a quote clause and is followed by a prepositional phrase beginning with *at*. The Subject usually comes before the verb.

These verbs indicate that someone is speaking loudly, angrily, or forcefully. The prepositional phrase indicates who is being addressed.

'Don't panic,' I __yelled__ at him.

bark 2	hiss 3	shout 1	snarl 2
bawl 1	holler	shriek 2	yell 1
bellow 1	scream 2	snap 4	

V *of* n with quote

The verb is used with a quote clause and is followed by a prepositional phrase beginning with *of*. The Subject usually comes before the verb. The prepositional phrase indicates who is asked a question. This pattern does not often occur.

'Who am I?' I __inquired__ of myself.

ask 1	inquire 1

V *to* n with quote

The verb is used with a quote clause and is followed by a prepositional phrase beginning with *to*. The phrasal verb pattern is **V P *to* n with quote**. The Subject usually comes before the verb. The prepositional phrase indicates who is being addressed.

'Your cat isn't very friendly,' a woman __complained__ to Reggie.
'This is all very well,' he __muttered__ to himself, 'but what about my dinner?'
I __said__ to Al, 'Wait a minute. What time did Steve call you?'

In the case of *muse, reason, say 4, think,* and *wonder,* the noun group following the preposition is always a reflexive pronoun. This pattern is **V *to* pron-refl with quote**. These verbs indicate that someone is thinking. Sometimes quotation marks are not used around the quote clause.

'No,' he __said__ to himself. 'It's not going to be like that.'
Just what I was afraid of, Tatiana __thought__ to herself.

admit 1	crow 4	groan 2	mumble
announce 2	cry 2	grouse 2	murmur 1
boast 1	declare 1	grumble 1	muse 1
brag	exclaim	gush 3	mutter
cable 5	explain 1,2	hiss 2	observe 3
call 3	explode 2	holler	proclaim 2
comment 1	expostulate	insist 2	protest 3
complain 1	exult	joke 2,4	quip 2
confess 1	fume 2	lament 1	rage 3
confide	go 3.7	moan 2	reason 4

remark 1	shout 1	wail 2	write 5
report 1	suggest 1	whimper 2	yell 1
say 1,4	telegraph 2	whisper 1	
scream 2	think 8	wonder 1	
call out ▷3			

Most of the verbs in meaning group 3 can have this pattern, but it is most frequent with the ones included in the above list.

V with sound

The verb is used with a word or group of letters representing a sound, which is not usually written in inverted commas. The Subject and verb may come before or after the sound word. If the sound word comes first, the Subject usually comes after the verb, unless it is a personal pronoun.

The verb indicates that a thing or an animal makes a sound.

> *The television **went** bang and then I heard an explosion in the kitchen and it was the new microwave.*

> ***Grrrr went** the dog.*

> **go** 3.6

V as quote

The verb is followed by a prepositional phrase consisting of *as* and a quote clause, which may be a single word. The quote clause indicates the meaning of a word or phrase. The Subject indicates the word or phrase concerned.

> *Two enterprising Neopolitan journalists are launching the game of Tangentopoli tomorrow. The name roughly **translates** as 'Bribe City'.*

> *The exhibition will be called 'Suite Substitute', which loosely **translates** as 'Art to Replace Favourite Pieces of Furniture'.*

> **translate** 2,4

14 V *so/not*

The verb is followed by *so* or *not*.

This pattern has one structure:

▶ Verb with Object
  *I **don't think** so.*

V *so/not*

	Verb group	*so/not*
Subject	Verb	Object
I	believe	so.
He	hopes	not.
I	should imagine	so.
I	wouldn't have thought	so.

Most of the verbs with this pattern are used to indicate what someone thinks or believes about something that has already been mentioned. The pattern is used widely in conversation, where the Subject is often *I* or *you*.

We include here the verb *say*, which is used to report what someone said. It is also used to express an opinion, as in *I would say so*. The phrase *if I may say so* is used to introduce or accompany an opinion, as in *Utter nonsense, if I may say so*.

These verbs have the affirmative **V *so*** and the negative **V *not***. In the case of the verbs *think*, *believe*, and *imagine*, the negative is also often formed with *do not* or another auxiliary or modal, and *so*, as in *I don't think so*.

In the case of the verbs *assume, fear, hope, presume,* and *suspect*, the negative is always formed with *not*, as in *I hope not*. You do not say *I don't hope so*.

> Can anyone who eats bacon sandwiches campaign with integrity against people who eat whale meat? The Norwegians **do not believe** so.

> 'You don't really suspect I'd be involved in something like that, do you?' 'I certainly **hope not**, Tony.'

> 'What is he doing here on a weekday? Is something wrong?' 'From his expression I **would say** so.'

> She admired him because he was clever and adroit, and because everyone whom she knew **thought** so too.

assume *1*	hope *1*	say *1,3*
believe *1*	imagine *2*	suspect *1*
fear *9*	presume *1*	think *1,2,16*

VERBS WITH OTHER MEANINGS

There is one verb, *do*, which does not fit into the above meaning group. This has the affirmative *do so* only – the negative is formed with an auxiliary or modal.

Do so can be used to stand for any verb group. It usually refers back to another verb group, which may be one in a previous sentence. *Do so* has an important function in repeating given information while introducing something new. In the first example below, *were doing so* repeats the information *majored in education* while the new information in the clause is *in 1983 only 15 percent*.

> In 1963 about half of all women undergraduates majored in education. In 1983 only 15 percent **were doing** so.

> A stewardess said the plane was vibrating so much that she presumed the captain was going to declare an an emergency, but he **did not do** so.

Do so occasionally refers forwards to a verb group in the same sentence.

> If patients wish to **do so**, they can buy their own needles and bring them to the acupuncturist to use for their own treatment.

do *2.2*

Structure information

a) *So* or *not* is the Object.

b) This structure has no passive.

---

15 V as if, V as though

The verb is followed by a finite clause beginning with *as if* or *as though*. In informal English, the clause sometimes begins with *like*, although some people think this is incorrect.

This pattern has one structure:

▶ Verb with Clause
  I *felt* *as if I'd been hit.*

V as if/as though

	Verb group	as if/as though-clause
Subject	**Verb**	**Clause**
He	acted	as if he was expecting me.
You	look	as if you've seen a ghost.
He	sounds	as though he's enjoying it.

Verbs with this pattern belong to the following meaning groups:

1 THE 'LOOK' GROUP
2 THE 'ACT' GROUP

1 THE 'LOOK' GROUP

These verbs are used to indicate how someone or something seems. They are all **link verbs** (see Chapter 5). The verb *feel* indicates how someone seems to themselves. The clause after the verb indicates a situation that would make someone or something have the qualities they appear to have.

*He **felt** as though he had run five miles.*
*You **look** like you need a rest.*
*Isabel's voice **sounded** as if she had been crying.*

appear *2*	**look** *2.1*	**sound** *7,8,9*
feel *1*	**smell** *3*	**taste** *4*

2 THE 'ACT' GROUP

These verbs are concerned with behaving or speaking. The clause indicates a situation in which the behaviour or what is said would be expected or appropriate.

This is a productive use: any verb which indicates behaviour or action can be used with this pattern. The verbs listed here are the ones which are most frequently used in this way.

**Act** as if nothing had happened.

Some activists now **speak** as though any attempt to clarify the law is a denial of justice which demands compensation.

act _1_	speak _1_
behave _1_	talk _1_

Structure information

a) The clause after the verb is a new clause, with its own structure.

b) This structure has no passive.

Other related patterns

V _as if_ to-inf

The verb is followed by the conjunction _as if_ and a to-infinitive clause. The clause indicates what someone seems to be about to do.

She **made** as if to leave.

make _1.3_

16 V _and_ v

The verb is followed by the conjunction _and_ and another verb of the same tense or form.

This pattern has two structures:

▶ Structure I: Verbs in phase
Try and lift it.
▶ Structure II: Co-ordinated verbs
Go and find him.

Structure I: Verbs in phase

V _and_ v

	Verb group	_and_	verb group	
Subject		**Verb**		**Completive**
I	'll try	and	help	you.

Phrasal verbs: V P _and_ v

	Verb group	Particle	_and_	verb group	
Subject		**Verb**			**Completive**
I	went	ahead	and	bought	it.

Verbs with this structure have a variety of meanings.

> Then he __goes__ *and* __spoils__ *it all by saying that just because something shows up on the graph doesn't mean it will happen.*

> They __could go on__ *and* __win__ *the trophy.*

> *I feel that if I say how tired I get and how much I long to stay at home sometimes, David* __will turn around__ *and* __say__*, 'I told you so.'*

> *One day he just* __upped__ *and* __left__*.*

In the case of *try*, both verbs are always in the base form.

> *He has started a privatisation programme to* __try__ *and* __win__ *support from the business community.*

go 3.15	try 2	up 3.2
go ahead 1	go on 5,9	turn around 4

Structure information: Verbs in phase

a) The verb is followed by *and* and another verb group of the same tense or form, without a Subject or any auxiliary verbs. The verbs are **in phase**, and together form a **complex verb group**. This means that the actions or states expressed by the two verbs cannot be separated from each other. For example, if you *try and remember* something, the *trying* and the *remembering* are not two processes, but one.

The complex verb group is followed by a group, phrase, or clause which completes the pattern of the second verb. In the structure tables above, this is called a **Completive**. For example, if the second verb is normally followed by a noun group, then the Completive of the complex verb group will be a noun group.

b) This structure has no passive.

c) The phrasal verb pattern is the same except that there is a particle, P, which comes after the verb.

Structure II: Co-ordinated verbs

V *and* v

	Verb group	*and*	clause
Subject	**Verb**	**Co-ordinator**	**Clause**
I	'll go	and	see him.

Phrasal verbs: V P *and* v

	Verb group	Particle	*and*	clause
Subject	**Verb**		**Co-ordinator**	**Clause**
We	've got to sit	down	and	sort things out.

This pattern is productive: any two verbs can be co-ordinated with *and*. The verbs listed here are the ones for which this pattern is most significant, that is, the two verbs are very closely linked, with the focus of information on the second verb.

> __Come__ *and* __sit down__*.*

*He was 'greatly troubled' by the use of imitation weapons 'because if you are on the receiving end, there isn't time to **look** and see if the gun is real or not'.*

*We **are not going to stand by** and watch when they gun our people down.*

*When you **stop** and think about it, the achievements of the last 20 years in the Classic Car world are stunning.*

In the case of *wait*, the conjunction *and* is nearly always followed by the base form *see*.

*A spokesman said the surgeons could now only **wait** and see how things went.*

come *2*	sit *1*	wait *11*
go *1.4*	stay *1*	
look *1.1*	stop *7*	
---	---	---	---
go along *1*	sit by	sit up *4*	stand by *2*
go out *3*	sit down *2*	stand back	step back

Structure information: Co-ordinated verbs

a) The verb is followed by *and* and a clause whose verb group has the same tense or form as the first verb, but has no auxiliary verbs or Subject. The verb group and the clause are co-ordinated.

b) This structure has no passive.

c) The phrasal verb pattern is the same except that there is a particle, P, which comes after the verb.

Chapter 2: Simple Patterns with Prepositions and Adverbs

In this chapter we describe simple verb patterns in which the verb is followed by a prepositional phrase or an adverb group. In Sections 1 to 4 we describe patterns in which the verb is followed either by a prepositional phrase introduced by a wide variety of prepositions, or by an adverb group. In Sections 5 to 34 we describe patterns in which the verb is followed by a prepositional phrase introduced by a specific preposition, such as *about, to* or *with*. These sections are ordered alphabetically, by preposition.

1   V prep/adv, V adv/prep

The verb is followed by a prepositional phrase beginning with a variety of prepositions, or an adverb group. Some verbs listed here are also included in sections relating to verbs followed by specific prepositions.

Here we treat all verbs with this pattern as having one structure:

▶ Verb with Adjunct
  He __ran__ across the road.

Some verbs with some prepositions have other structures, however. For example, some prepositional phrases beginning with *into* are prepositional Objects and some prepositional phrases beginning with *as* are prepositional Complements.

Most verbs in English can be followed by Adjuncts of manner, time, or place. When information about manner, time, or place is not essential, the Adjunct is not part of the pattern. The verbs dealt with below are those which are always or typically followed by an Adjunct.

V prep/adv, V adv/prep

	Verb group	prep. phrase/adverb group	
Subject	Verb	Adjunct	Adjunct (optional)
I	behaved	very stupidly.	
I	lived	there	for ten years.
He	ran	down the path.	

Phrasal verbs: V P prep/adv, V P adv/prep

	Verb group	Particle	prep. phrase/adverb group
Subject	Verb		Adjunct
Everything	is coming	along	nicely.
He	had moved	on	to Poland.

Verbs with this pattern belong to the following meaning groups:

1 THE 'GO' GROUP	12 THE 'LOOK' AND 'GESTURE' GROUP
2 THE 'WANDER' GROUP	13 THE 'SEARCH' GROUP
3 THE 'WALK' GROUP	14 THE 'LURCH' GROUP
4 THE 'DRIVE' GROUP	15 THE 'BEHAVE' GROUP
5 THE 'FLOW' GROUP	16 THE 'SHAPE UP' GROUP
6 THE 'FLOCK' GROUP	17 THE 'COME OVER' GROUP
7 THE 'ROAR' GROUP	18 THE 'BEGIN' AND 'END' GROUP
8 THE 'TURN' GROUP	19 THE 'LAST' GROUP
9 THE 'LIVE' GROUP	20 THE 'BREAKFAST' GROUP
10 THE 'FACE' GROUP	21 VERBS WITH OTHER MEANINGS
11 THE 'ECHO' GROUP	

1 THE 'GO' GROUP

These are general verbs concerned with moving, going, or arriving somewhere. This includes starting a journey e.g. *set off*.

*Lee and I **arrived** in Panama City suffering terribly from jet lag.*

*Ron became so ill with worry that he **ended up** in hospital.*

*She didn't want to **go** home.*

*Mr Baker **will go on** to Tunisia tomorrow.*

*They plan to **set off** for Baghdad on Thursday.*

arrive *1,2*	get *1.6,7*	move *1,2*	return *1*
come *1*	go *1.1*	pass *2*	travel *1*
continue *7*	journey *3*	proceed *4*	
end up *1*	go on *6*	set off *1*	
finish up *1*	move on *1*	set out *1*	

2 THE 'WANDER' GROUP

These verbs are concerned with movement or arrival of a more specific kind. This includes:

- going in a particular direction e.g. *advance, spiral, turn*
- going somewhere quickly or slowly e.g. *drift, whizz*
- going somewhere in an enjoyable or unenjoyable way e.g. *slog, swan*
- going somewhere for a reason or for no reason e.g. *barnstorm, wander*
- becoming attached to something or detached from something e.g. *screw, tear*

We also include here *drain, filter, percolate,* and *seep,* which indicate that something abstract such as news goes somewhere.

*The hairs are tipped by tiny sacs filled with a substance that sticks to any insect that **alights** on the leaf.*

*The Democrats **barnstormed** through the heartland in what appears to be a very successful campaign road trip.*

*They **clambered** over the low fence, shouting encouragement to each other.*

*Results from Ivory Coast's first free elections are beginning to **filter** through.*

*The camera **screws** onto a detachable plate.*

*I began to worry about rainstorm chills myself as I **slogged** up the sticky chalk track.*

I grabbed a can of beer, pulled the tab and of course, the tab __snapped off__.

__Turn right__ at the lights.

I was allowed to __wander around__ quite freely.

He was passing the woods when a bullet of some sort __whizzed__ past his ear.

adhere 3	fit 1.4	plunge 1	squirm 1
advance 1	flash 4	poke 4	stand 3
adventure 3	flee	pop 7	start 7
alight 3,4	flick 1	promenade 2	stray 1
arc 3	flicker 4	push 2	streak 4
arch 6	flit 1,3	ramble 2	struggle 6
ascend 1	float 1,5	rampage 1	swan 2
barnstorm	flop 2	range 7	sweep 4,7
blow 1.2	flounder 3	retreat 1	swerve
bob 1,2	flutter 2	ricochet	swim 1,4
bounce 1,5	fly 2	roam	swing 2
brush 6	fork 7	roll 1,2	swoop 2
buck 7	gallivant	rove 1	tear 2.1
bump 6	glide 2	rush 1	toil 2
burrow 2,4	go 1.16,17	sail 4	tootle 1
call 10	grovel 2	sally 2	trail 7
careen	head 16	schlep 2	traipse 1,2
cartwheel 2	hike 2	scorch 3	travel 5
circle 5	hurry 1	scramble 1,2	trek 1,2
clamber	inch 2	screw 2,4	trespass 1,2
climb 1,2	jerk 1	scud	trundle 3
come 5	jink	seep 2	tumble 1
crawl 3	jolt 1	shift 1	tunnel 2
creep 2,3	jump 1,2,4	shoot 3,4	turn 5
cross 1.1	land 6,11	shrink 3	twirl
curl 6	lash 3	shuttle 3	veer 1,3
dash 1	leap 1,3	skitter	venture 2
dip 3	lock 4	slew 2	wade 1
dive 3,5	lodge 7	slide 1	wander 1,2
dodge 1	loop 3	slip 2,3	wash 3
drain 7,9	meander 3	slither 1,2	whip 4,6
draw 3	migrate 1,2	slog 3	whirl 1
drift 1,3,5	mosey	snap 1,2	whizz 1
drop 3,4	navigate 4,5	snuggle	whoosh 2
duck 5	nestle 1	soar 2	wing 9
ease 5	nip 1	speed 5	wobble 1
encroach 2	nuzzle	spiral 2	wriggle 2
fall 1	perch 4	spread 5	zigzag 2
feint 1	percolate 1	spring 4	zip 3
filter 5	pitch 3	squeeze 4	zoom 1
beam down	buzz off 1	land up	strike out 3
beam up	fall in 2	pop off 2	turn back 1
branch off	fetch up	roll up 2	

3 THE 'WALK' GROUP

These verbs are concerned with walking or running somewhere. This includes:

- verbs indicating the speed of the movement e.g. *amble, race*
- verbs indicating how gracefully or clumsily someone moves e.g. *glide, stagger*
- verbs indicating the emotion or attitude of the person moving e.g. *flounce, storm*
- verbs indicating that someone is trying not to be noticed e.g. *slink, sneak*

On the second floor, he __raced down another corridor__, rounded a sharp turn, and found himself facing a closed door.

We __had to sneak out__ because it was after nine at night.

As the other officers pounced on the attacker, the injured policeman **_staggered_ into the street.**

He **_stormed_ out of the apartment**, slamming the door furiously behind him.

Mrs. Madrigal **_walked_ to the window**, where she stood motionless.

amble	gallop *1,2*	race *6*	steal *3*
belt *5*	gambol	reel *3*	step *2*
blunder *4*	glide *1*	run *1*	stomp
bolt *5*	hare *2*	sashay	storm *4*
bounce *7*	hasten *4*	saunter	stride *1*
bound *2,4*	hobble *1*	scamper	stroll
breeze *2*	hop *1,2,3*	scoot	strut *1*
burst *5*	jig *2*	scurry *1*	stumble *1*
bustle *1*	leap *2*	scuttle *1*	stump *4*
buzz *2*	limp *1*	shamble *2*	swagger
canter	lollop	shimmy	sweep *9*
caper *2*	lope	shuffle *1*	tear *2,7*
charge *10*	lumber *2*	sidle	teeter *2*
chase *6*	lurch *1*	skip *1*	tiptoe *1*
clump *3*	march *1,2,3*	slide *2*	toddle
crawl *1*	mince *3*	slink	totter *1*
creep *1*	pace *4*	slip *3*	tramp *2*
dance *7,8*	pad *3*	slope *6*	trip *6*
dart *1*	parade *8*	slouch *2*	trot *1,2*
edge *3*	pelt *4*	sneak *1*	trudge
float *7*	plod *1*	sprint *4*	twirl *2*
flounce *1*	pound *6*	stagger *1*	waddle
flutter *4*	prance *1,2*	stalk *3*	walk *1*
fly *8*	prowl *1*	stamp *5*	waltz *4*

4 THE 'DRIVE' GROUP

These verbs indicate that a form of transport, or someone using a form of transport, goes or arrives somewhere.

She slowed the cab to avoid an old Chevy sedan which **_was backing_ into a parking space.**

A veterinary officer escaped injury when her jeep exploded and burst into flames as she **_was driving_ to work.**

After the plane **_landed_ in Miami**, the man surrendered peacefully.

Pete got on his bike and **_pedalled_ off.**

Pull in here and let's have a look at the map.

She **_sailed_ from Sydney** on her second New Guinea voyage on May 12.

accelerate *2*	cruise *2,3*	jet *2*	roll *3*
back *3,2*	cycle *1*	land *7*	row *2,0*
barrel *4*	dive *4*	motor *5,6*	sail *2,3*
bicycle *2*	draw *2*	navigate *1,3*	skate *3*
bike *2*	drive *1*	nose *5*	ski *2*
bowl *10*	fly *3*	paddle *2*	swing *3*
bucket *4*	freewheel	parachute *2*	tack *4*
bus *2*	glide *2*	park *2*	taxi *2 (An aircraft)*
call *11*	grind *4*	pedal *2*	terminate *3*
career *4*	hack *7*	punt *2*	trundle *1*
coast *2*	hitchhike	ride *1,2,3*	voyage *2*
pull in *1*	put in *4 (A ship)*		

5 THE 'FLOW' GROUP

These verbs indicate that a liquid, gas, or other substance goes somewhere. We include here verbs indicating that light, sound, or a signal goes somewhere, and the verb *lick*, which indicates that flames go somewhere.

*Mahoney flung open the saloon door and black smoke **billowed** out.*

*The warming sound of Brian's laughter **drifted** through the window.*

*Blood is the vital substance that **flows** through the body, carrying oxygen and nutrients and removing waste materials from the tissues.*

*Flames **were licking** around the door to the toy shop.*

*The rain **spattered** on the uppermost leaves and **dripped** miserably from the lower.*

*Light **was streaming** into Dr Denny's office from the door connecting it to the waiting room.*

beam *3,5*	drive *11*	radiate *1*	spout *1*
billow *2*	eddy *2*	run *21*	spray *3,4*
bubble *4*	float *6*	rush *10*	spurt *4*
carry *11*	flood *8*	seep *1*	squirt *1*
cascade *3*	flow *1*	settle *8*	stream *5,8*
collect *4*	funnel *4*	slop *1*	surge *5*
course *10*	gush *1*	slosh *1*	swirl
diffuse *4*	leak *1*	sluice *2*	travel *4*
drain *1*	lick *3*	soak *3*	trickle *1*
dribble *1*	ooze *1*	spatter	waft
drift *6*	percolate *3*	spill *1,5*	
drip *1*	pour *3*	splash *2*	

6 THE 'FLOCK' GROUP

These verbs indicate that a number of people, or sometimes things, go somewhere.

*The jury **filed** out, silent, reverent.*

*The wild and beautiful west coast of Ireland has captured the imagination of Hollywood film directors as well the ordinary tourists who **flock** there.*

*Police **swarmed** into the area within moments and searched for other devices.*

cluster *2*	flow *2,3*	snake *2*	swarm *2,3*
dribble *6*	gather *1*	spill *3,4*	trickle *2*
file *7*	huddle *2*	straggle *1*	troop *5*
flock *3*	parade *2*	stream *7*	
flood *5*	pour *5,6*	surge *3*	

7 THE 'ROAR' GROUP

These verbs are concerned with going somewhere in a way that makes a particular noise. The Subject can be a vehicle, person, animal, or thing, depending on the verb.

*There was still a solitary fly **buzzing** around the classroom.*

*The rain **pattered** on the glass roof.*

*The jeep **roared** off.*

*He **squelched** through the mud and disappeared round the corner of a wall.*

burble *1*	gurgle *1*	rumble *2*	thud *2*
buzz *1*	patter *1*	scream *3*	thump *3*
chug	plop *2*	screech *1*	thunder *4*
clatter *1*	purr *2*	slosh *2*	
crash *3*	rattle *5*	squelch *1*	
crunch *3*	roar *1*	swish *1*	

8 THE 'TURN' GROUP

These verbs indicate that someone or something changes posture, arrangement, or orientation, but does not move from one place to another. This includes:

- turning
- reaching out
- sitting down
- falling over

His motorcycle __fell__ on top of him.

Pat __reached__ up and grasped one of the water pipes above his head.

Sylvia and I __sat down__ on the bench by the fountain.

He __turned__ away before the tears came again.

bend *1*	fold *4*	reach *3*	swing *1*
crane *3*	hunch *2*	recline *1*	swivel *2*
crouch *1,2*	jut *2*	rock *4*	thrash *3*
curl *5*	kneel	settle *7*	tilt *1*
drop *5*	lash *8*	shuffle *2*	topple *1*
duck *3*	lean *1*	sink *6*	turn *1*
fall *2*	loll *2*	sit *2*	twist *3*
flip *3*	lunge	slump *3*	yaw
flop *1,2*	perch *1*	squat *1*	
fly *6*	pivot *2*	sway *1*	
crouch down ▷*1*	sprawl out ▷*1*	stretch out *1*	
sit down ▷*2*	squat down ▷*1*		

9 THE 'LIVE' GROUP

These verbs are concerned with being or staying somewhere, or originating somewhere. This includes doing something somewhere, e.g. *operate, work*.

The restaurant __was__ in Cork Street, Mayfair.

This place is just too decadent. I __could__ never __live__ here.

The study of handwriting, or graphology, __originated__ in Italy in the seventeenth century.

In 1969, he __settled down__ in Tuscaloosa, Alabama, where he spent the rest of his life playing on the local blues circuit.

She __was sitting__ at the kitchen table when I came in.

He __worked__ in a travel agent's.

balance *1*	huddle *1*	navigate *2*	sit *1,8*
bathe *1*	idle *7*	nestle *2*	skulk
be *2.1*	keep *2,3*	occur *2*	slouch *1*
belong *10*	kip *2*	operate *5*	slump *1*
bivouac *2*	kneel	originate	snoop *1*
browse *1*	languish *1*	perch *2*	sprawl *1*
centre *10*	laze	recline *1*	sprout *2,5,6*
crouch *1*	lean *2*	remain *2*	stand *1,4*
dangle *1*	lie *1.1,2,3,6,7,8,9*	repose *2*	stay *1,2*
doss	linger *1,2*	reside *1*	stop *10*
dwell *2*	live *1.1*	rest *2.6*	vacation *4*
fly *10 (Rumours)*	locate *2*	roost *2*	winter *2,3*
hang *1,6*	lodge *5*	serve *2*	work *1*
holiday *5*	loll *1*	settle *6*	
hover *1,2*	lounge *4*	shelter *4*	
bed down	hang out *2*	loll about	set up *4*
doss down ▷	knock around *2*	put up *6*	settle down *1*

10 THE 'FACE' GROUP

These verbs indicate the shape of something, or where it is in relation to something else. The Adjunct usually indicates direction.

*She was a beautiful woman, with long blonde hair that **cascaded** down her back.*

*Presently, the land started to **drop away** to precipitous cliffs.*

*The garden **faces** south and does not suffer from late frosts.*

*The pool and terrace **look out** over the sea.*

*They saw a series of stones **projecting** from the outside wall near the window.*

*On the first leg of the trek the road **wound** through a forest.*

arc *3*	face *2.1*	point *16*	stick *2.3*
arch *6*	fall *15*	project *7*	straggle *2*
ascend *2*	flow *7*	radiate *1*	stream *9*
begin *6*	fork *6*	rear *7*	stretch *1*
bulge *1*	go *1.6*	rise *5,7*	sweep *12*
cascade *4*	hang *2*	run *4*	taper *1*
coil *6*	jut *1*	shelve *2*	thrust *3*
continue *8*	lead *1.3*	slant *1*	tower *2*
curve *2*	loll *2*	slope *3,4*	trail *6*
dip *4*	look *1.11*	snake *2*	twist *6*
droop	loom *1*	soar *3*	wind *2.1*
end *11*	meander *1*	splay	
extend *1,2,4*	pass *3*	sprawl *2*	
branch off	lead off *1*	rise up ▷*5*	
drop away	look out ▷*1.11*		

11 THE 'ECHO' GROUP

These verbs indicate that a sound is heard somewhere. The Adjunct usually indicates direction. The Subject is inanimate.

*There was confusion and panic as the sound of gunfire **echoed** round the city.*

*The insistent hum of jet engines **reverberates** through these ultra-modern hangars.*

boom *6*	resound *1*
echo *2,8*	reverberate *1,2*
boom out ▷*6*	

12 THE 'LOOK' AND 'GESTURE' GROUP

These verbs are concerned with looking, gesturing, and communicating. We include here *pan*, which indicates that a camera is viewing something; *scroll*, which indicates that someone looks at text on a computer screen; and *wander 3*, which indicates that someone thinks about something. The Adjunct usually indicates direction.

*He **gestured** towards the two Englishmen. 'How much do they know?'*

*I **looked** at her and shrugged.*

*Higgins shifted uncomfortably in his seat as the camera **panned** over the scene.*

*Houston's eyes **roved** restlessly about the room.*

*He let his mind **wander** lazily over the events of the night before.*

dart *2 (Your eyes)*	leer	radio *6*	stare *1*
gaze *1*	look *1.1*	rove *2 (Your eyes)*	sweep *11 (Your eyes)*
gesture *3*	pan *4*	scroll *3*	swivel *3 (Your eyes)*
glance *1*	peep *2*	signal *2*	wander *3 (Your mind)*
glower	peer *1*	squint *1*	wander *4 (Your eyes)*

13 THE 'SEARCH' GROUP

These verbs are concerned with searching. The Adjunct indicates the place, container, or group of things in which someone is searching.

> She **rummaged** *through her beach bag*, *trying to find something thin and made out of metal.*
>
> He dropped the shell and grovelled on the floor, inhaling carpet dust as he **searched** **under the bed**.

burrow *3*	ferret *2*	look *1.5*	scavenge
delve *2*	fumble *1*	probe *2,4*	search *2*
dig *2*	grope *1*	root *9*	shop *2*
feel *5*	grub *3*	rummage *1*	

These verbs also have the patterns **V prep/adv** *for* **n** and **V** *for* **n prep/adv**. The prepositional phrase beginning with *for* indicates what someone is trying to find.

> Police **are looking** *in nearby buildings for other firebombs*.
>
> She looked away and **rummaged** *for a hankie in her handbag*.

14 THE 'LURCH' GROUP

These verbs are concerned with progressing or coming to be in a different state. We include here *hold* and *hover*, which indicate that someone or something remains in a particular state for a while, and *loom*, which indicates that something is about to happen.

> The World Health Organization **went** *even further during its 1988 session held in Geneva*, *urging the testing of all children.*
>
> For three weeks I **hovered** *between life and death*.
>
> What they do is prompted by a passionate desire to warn humanity about the danger **looming** *over it*.
>
> In 1861, this country **lurched** *into a civil war from which it has never fully recovered*.
>
> Marseille **romped** *to a 4-1 win over Lille* yesterday.
>
> This is the main reason why the divorce rate **is spiralling** *upwards*.

ascend *5*	go *1.8,9*	loom *2*	squeak *2*
bubble *6*	gyrate *3*	lurch *2*	stagger *2*
crawl *3*	hold *3.6*	romp *1*	stutter *3*
creep *3*	hover *3,4*	spiral *3,4*	tilt *4*
get *1.13*	limp *2*	sputter *1,2*	veer *2*

15 THE 'BEHAVE' GROUP

These verbs are used to describe people's behaviour. The Adjunct indicates the way someone behaves. In the case of *eat*, it indicates the kind or amount of food someone eats; in the case of *dress* and *wrap up*, it indicates the type of thing someone wears. The prepositional phrase often begins with *like* or is something like *in an unusual way*.

> They **were behaving** *like animals*.
>
> Rownall drove jerkily, **cornering** *too fast* and fumbling the gears.
>
> Forget gimmicky diets; **eat** *sensibly* and fill up with fresh fruit and vegetables.
>
> Always **wrap up** *warmly* after a spa bath.

act *1,3*	dress *5*	react *1*
behave *1*	eat *2*	think *3,5*
corner *11*	live *1.2*	tread *2,4*
wrap up *1*		

Some of these verbs also have the pattern **V as if** (see pages 121-122).

The verbs *behave* and *react* also have the pattern **V prep/adv** *towards/toward* **n**. The prepositional phrase beginning with *towards* or *toward* indicates who or what a person's behaviour involves or relates to.

> *They take drugs, get drunk, and **behave** sadistically towards younger schoolmates.*

The verb *react* also has the patterns **V prep/adv** *to* **n** and **V** *to* **n prep/adv**.

> *But afterwards shareholders **reacted** angrily to the deal.*

16 THE 'SHAPE UP' GROUP

These verbs are used when talking about how something behaves when it is used, or how successful something or someone is. Most of them are used with adverbs such as *well* and *nicely*. The phrasal verb *come off* is used with *worst* and *best*.

> *Her English **is coming along** well.*
>
> *In negotiations with European partners, they invariably **come off** worst.*
>
> *For once, the show **went off** without technical hitches.*
>
> *This is a magnificent machine which rides well at low speed and which **handles** faultlessly when driven fast.*
>
> *If the book **sells** well, and we think it will because it's an excellent read, they stand to make a lot of money.*
>
> *Heather Edwards, recently appointed as the Chancellor's parliamentary private secretary, **is shaping up** nicely.*
>
> *I'm convinced that everything's **going to work out** well in the end.*

act *4*	fit *1.1*	progress *3*	sell *4*
behave *3*	handle *7*	read *6*	work *11*
corner *11*	operate *2*	run *11*	
come along *4*	get on *3*	make out *6*	work out *4*
come off *2*	go along *2*	pass off	
come on *5*	go off *5*	shape up *2*	

17 THE 'COME OVER' GROUP

These verbs are used when talking about how someone or something is perceived or received.

> *The supposedly normal people **came over** like loonies while the religious weirdos seemed reasonable and well-balanced.*
>
> *His joke **went down** well. Even Blake smiled.*

come across *2*	come over *3*	go down *5*

18 THE 'BEGIN' AND 'END' GROUP

These verbs are concerned with beginning or ending. The Adjunct indicates the circumstances that existed at the beginning or end of something, or the state of the Subject at that time.

> *Clinton's campaign **began** well.*
>
> *The year **ended** on a high note with the biggest attendance (39 members and 12 visitors) enjoying some excellent films presented by Alan Wilmott.*
>
> *The driver of the car **escaped** with cuts and bruises.*

begin *2,3*	continue *6*	finish *4*
close *1.9*	end *4,7,18*	open *22*
conclude *3*	escape *3*	start *2*

19 THE 'LAST' GROUP

These verbs are used when indicating how long something lasts or when it started and ended.

*The mixture **will keep** for 2-3 days in the fridge and can be served hot, warm or cold.*

*The strike **did not last** long.*

*Robert Heath MP, who **lived** from 1806 to 1893, created the magnificent gardens there.*

keep *18*	live *1.4*
last *11,12*	run *33*

20 THE 'BREAKFAST' GROUP

These verbs are concerned with having a meal. The Adjunct indicates the circumstances in which the meal is eaten.

*She **breakfasted** alone in her cell.*

breakfast *3*	dine	lunch *2*

21 VERBS WITH OTHER MEANINGS

There are a few other verbs which have this pattern.

*The statement **came** at the end of the council's annual summit in Qatar on Tuesday.*

*Much of the working mother's hard-earned salary **goes** on expensive toys and treats.*

*Sir Philip now **lives** in luxury in Kent. But he has never forgotten his roots.*

*British Rail says its services **are** more or less **running** to time this lunchtime.*

*He was determined to **stay up** until twelve o'clock and watch the people celebrating in Times Square, New York.*

come *9*	go *1.10*	live *1.2*	run *34*
stay up			

Structure information

a) The prepositional phrase or adverb group is usually an Adjunct, although some prepositional phrases are prepositional Objects or prepositional Complements.

b) This structure has a passive with the pattern **be V-ed prep** (**prep** here means a preposition, not a prepositional phrase). However, it does not often occur. Usually there can be a passive structure only with one or two particular prepositions. The Subject refers to something directly affected by or involved in the action.

*Even old and venerable rugs **are walked** on by all and sundry.*

*The cottage **has not been lived** in for several years.*

The following verbs from the lists above are the ones most frequently used in the passive, with the preposition(s) indicated.

jump *1 (on)*	**look** *1.1 (at)*	**stand** *1 (on)*	**walk** *1 (on/over/through)*
leap *1 (on/upon)*	**peer** *1 (at)*	**stare** *1 (at)*	
live *1.1 (in)*	**sit** *1,2 (on)*	**step** *2 (on)*	

c) Phrasal verb patterns are the same except that there is a particle, P, which comes after the verb. The passive pattern, *be* **V-ed P prep**, does not often occur.

Other related patterns

V adv prep

Most verbs with the pattern **V prep/adv** also have the pattern **V adv prep**. The verb is followed by an adverb and a prepositional phrase.

> *They got into the lorries which were waiting for them and __drove__ off into the forest.*

> *He __walked__ over to his desk.*

V prep prep

Many of the verbs described in this section also have the pattern **V prep prep**. The verb is followed by two prepositional phrases.

> *The state government __has lurched__ from one budget crisis to another.*

> *He __ran__ down the stairs to the living room.*

Sometimes verbs are followed by more than two prepositional phrases.

> *The dams will regulate the flow of water on the flood-prone Souris River, which __flows__ from southeastern Saskatchewan across the Canada-U.S. border into North Dakota.*

V prep/adv *for* n, V *for* n prep/adv

See meaning group 13 above.

V prep/adv *to* n, V *to* n prep/adv

See meaning group 15 above.

V prep/adv *towards/toward* n

See meaning group 15 above.

V prep/adv n

The verb is followed by a prepositional phrase or an adverb group, which is followed by a noun group describing the Subject. This is a productive pattern: many verbs of movement can be used in this way.

> *You__'re going__ out a youngster, but you__'ve got to come__ back a star.*

2 V adv

The verb is followed by an adverb group.

This pattern has one structure:

▶ Verb with Adjunct
They __did__ well.

V adv

	Verb group	adverb group	
Subject	**Verb**	**Adjunct**	**Adjunct (optional)**
She	is doing	well	at school.
My skin	was peeling	off.	

Most verbs can be followed by adverbs of manner or place. When information about manner or place is not essential, the adverb group is not part of the pattern. The verbs dealt with below are the ones which are always or typically followed by a particular adverb or small group of adverbs.

Many verbs which can be followed by an adverb group can also be followed by a variety of prepositions. These verbs are dealt with in Section 1 above (see pages 125-135). Verbs which can also be followed by one or two specific prepositions are dealt with in the sections on verbs followed by individual prepositions (see Sections 5 to 34).

Verbs with the pattern **V adv** belong to the following meaning groups:

1 THE 'DO WELL' GROUP
2 THE 'CLEAN' GROUP
3 THE 'BRUISE' GROUP
4 THE 'SCARE' GROUP
5 THE 'SWING' GROUP
6 THE 'GET SOMEWHERE' GROUP
7 THE 'PHONE' GROUP
8 VERBS WITH OTHER MEANINGS

1 THE 'DO WELL' GROUP

These verbs are used with adverbs such as *well* and *badly*. Most of them are concerned with success or failure. We include here *rank* and *rate*, which are used with *highly*.

I've seen quite a few of the recent gangster films and this __compares__ very favourably.

The Republicans __did__ badly in the election.

Many defence chiefs feel they __might fare__ better under Labour, which is keen to protect Britain's conventional armed forces.

Friendships __rate__ highly in Amanda's scheme of things.

augur	do *1.11*	pay *2,6*	rate *6*
bode	fare *3*	perform *4*	work *12*
compare *3*	go *3.1*	rank *4*	

The verbs *bode* and *augur* also have the pattern **V adv *for* n**. The prepositional phrase beginning with *for* indicates who or what is likely to be fortunate or unfortunate.

With delivery scheduled for 1994, a Boeing spokesman says this latest order __bodes__ __well for__
__the airline industry__.

The verb *compare* also has the pattern **V adv with n**. The prepositional phrase beginning
with *with* indicates what something is better than or worse than.

While Britain's overall road safety record __compares__ __favourably with__ that of other
European countries, Britain's child accident rates are no better than average.

2 THE 'CLEAN' GROUP

These verbs are used to indicate that something has a desirable quality, such as being
easily cleaned, prepared, or moved. They are all **ergative verbs** (see Chapter 7).

This use is productive: many verbs which have the pattern **V n** and indicate something
you want to do to something can be used with the pattern **V adv**. The verbs listed here are
the ones which are most frequently used in this way.

Our wood flooring not only looks smart, feels comfortable and __cleans__ easily, but it's
environmentally friendly into the bargain!

Buy a canvas beach bag that __folds__ easily and leave your cumbersome straw shopping bag at
home.

Apart from peppers and aubergines, many other vegetables __grill__ well.

apply *6*	display *1,4*	glue *2*	read *1,6*
clean *4*	drain *2*	grill *4*	wash *1*
cut *1*	fold *4*	lift *1*	wear *8*

3 THE 'BRUISE' GROUP

These verbs are used to indicate that something is easily damaged. These are all **ergative**
verbs (see Chapter 7).

This use is productive: any verb which has the pattern **V n** and is concerned with damage
can be used with the pattern **V adv**. The verbs listed here are the ones which are most
frequently used in this way.

Hands are gentler than spoons for tossing salad leaves that __bruise__ easily.

Sarah has typically British fair skin that __burns__ easily.

break *1,3,4*	crack *1.1*	rip *1*	shatter *1*
bruise *2,3*	damage *1*	scorch *2*	snap *1*
burn *5,11,12*	fracture *2*	scratch *2*	tear *2.1*
chip *6*	mark *2*	scuff *1*	

4 THE 'SCARE' GROUP

This verb indicates that someone feels an emotion easily.

This use is productive: any verb which has the pattern **V n** and indicates that someone is
made to feel an emotion, especially fear, can be used with the pattern **V adv**. The verbs
given here are the ones which are most frequently used in this way.

I __don't scare__ easily but I have to say I was terrified.

scare *1*	spook *3*

5 THE 'SWING' GROUP

These verbs are concerned with movement or progress. They are used with one particular
adverb of direction, or with a restricted set, as indicated in the list below. (The pattern **pl-n**
V together is described separately in Section 3 below, see pages 139-141.)

Chapter 2: Simple Patterns with Prepositions and Adverbs

*After 1 mile, **bear right** at Rooksnest Farm.*

*They **crowded round**, inspecting, touching, laughing.*

*In spite of the recession, profits **have galloped ahead**.*

*We hurried across the wet concrete, flung our cases into the big Parks vehicle and **piled in**.*

*He **swung round** to see who was there.*

bear *1.15 (left/right)*	**creep** *4 (up)*	**jiggle** *2 (around/about)*	**pull** *6 (ahead/away)*
belch *▷2 (out)*	**crowd** *3 (round/around)*	**lag** *1 (behind)*	**race** *7,9 (ahead)*
billow *1 (out)*	**delve** *1 (deeper)*	**pass** *8 (back)*	**run** *19 (over/down)*
bounce *4 (up and down)*	**dive** *1 (in)*	**peel** *3 (off/away)*	**splash** *1 (around/about)*
bound *2.6 (ahead)*	**drag** *7 (past)*	**pelt** *3 (down)*	**stay** *4 (away)*
brush *6 (by/past)*	**filter** *5 (through/in/out)*	**pile** *6 (in/out)*	**swill** *2 (around/about)*
bum *6 (around)*	**flash** *7 (up)*	**pour** *4 (down)*	**swing** *4 (round/around)*
climb *1 (up/down)*	**gad** *(about/out)*	**press** *3 (down)*	**wheel** *7 (round/around)*
coast *3 (home)*	**gallop** *4 (ahead)*	**pull** *4 (away)*	**writhe** *(around/about)*

6 THE 'GET SOMEWHERE' GROUP

These verbs are used with adverbs of distance, such as *far*, or general adverbs of place, such as *somewhere* or *there*.

*Fairbairn had then questioned Arnold closely, but **had not got** very far.*

*Both Otto's and the Lockwood Inn use the same style of open, wood fire pit, but the similarity **stops** there.*

end *16*	**stop** *8*
get *1.14*	**stretch** *10*

7 THE 'PHONE' GROUP

These verbs are concerned with phoning or writing a letter. They are used with the adverb *home*.

*On four or five occasions, she **had phoned** home and said she was staying with friends.*

*Give my compliments to your lovely wife when you **write** home.*

call *4*	**ring** *1.1*	**write** *4*
phone *4*	**telephone** *3*	

8 VERBS WITH OTHER MEANINGS

There are a few other verbs which have this pattern. They are used with a particular adverb or pair of adverbs.

*If Leaphorn **had guessed** right about the lake, the chance of catching George there looked a little better.*

*First-borns generally **score higher than later-born children** on tests of intellectual performance.*

The phrasal verb *come in* is used only in questions or clauses beginning with *where*.

*After a short pause, Rose asked again, 'But **where do** we **come in**, Henry?'*

guess *1 (wrong/right)*	**score** *2 (low/high)*	**weigh** *6 (heavily)*
come in *5*		

Structure information

a) The adverb group is an Adjunct.

b) This structure has no passive.

c) There is only one phrasal verb associated with this pattern, *come in* (see meaning group 8 above).

Other related patterns

V adv *for* n

See meaning group 1 above.

V adv *with* n

See meaning group 1 above.

V amount adv

See page 73.

V ord

The verb is followed by an ordinal, such as *first*, *second*, or *last*. These verbs are concerned with the position of someone or something in a competition or list.

> He **came** **third** in the 1967 Eurovision Song Contest with 'Eldorado'.

> France **ranked** **fourth** in 1990 in terms of total spending on science as a percentage of gross domestic product.

| come | 18 | lie | 1.5 |
| finish | 5 | rank | 3 |

The verb *rank* also has the pattern **V ord prep**. The prepositional phrase after the ordinal indicates the group of things or people in which the Subject holds a particular position.

> Newly-released official statistics indicate that Hong Kong still **ranks** **first among the Chinese mainland's top ten trading partners**.

---

3 pl-n V *together*

The verb is followed by the adverb *together*. The Subject is a **plural noun group**.

This pattern has one structure:

▶ Verb with Adjunct
  The cells <u>clump</u> together.

pl-n V *together*

plural noun group	Verb group	*together*
Subject	**Verb**	**Adjunct**
They	clung	together.
The whole team	must pull	together.

Phrasal verbs: pl-n V P *together*

plural noun group	Verb group	Particle	*together*	
Subject	**Verb**		**Adjunct**	**Adjunct (optional)**
We all	mucked	in	together.	
They	ran	away	together	to America.

The Subject refers to two or more people, things, or groups. Note that verbs with this pattern are similar in meaning to **reciprocal verbs** (see Chapter 6), but they are not regarded as true reciprocal verbs because they must have the adverb *together* when used with a plural Subject.

Verbs with this pattern belong to the following meaning groups:

1 THE 'CLUSTER' GROUP
2 THE 'LIVE' GROUP
3 THE 'BAND' GROUP
4 VERBS WITH OTHER MEANINGS

1 THE 'CLUSTER' GROUP

These verbs indicate that two or more people or things move closer to each other or touch each other.

> *Someone suggested coffee, as* **they <u>clustered</u> together** *outside the Underground in Tottenham Court Road.*

> **The edges** *are ready-gummed and when moistened* **<u>will stick</u> together**.

> **Tree limbs** *which* **<u>rub</u> together** *can cause weakness through deformation, and disease infection is likely.*

cling *1*	gather *1*	stick *2.5*
clump *4*	knit *3*	
cluster *2*	rub *5*	
cuddle up		

2 THE 'LIVE' GROUP

These verbs indicate that two or more people live together, start living together, or spend time with each other. We include here *get*, which indicates that two or more people meet by arrangement.

> *They usually* **<u>hung around</u> together** *most of the time.*

> *The relationship blossomed.* **They** *decided to* **<u>live</u> together** *the following year.*

> *We'd been seeing each other for a year when he suggested we* **<u>should move in</u> together**.

get *VP1*	room *4*	
live *VP*	sleep *VP*	
hang around/round *2*	move in *1*	run off *1*
knock around/about *4*	run away *2*	

3 THE 'BAND' GROUP

These verbs indicate that people form a group, do something together, or support each other.

Several meat producers in my area <u>have banded</u> together to form a lobbying group.
We men <u>have got to stick</u> together.

band *VP*	hang *VP1*	stick *VP*
club *VP*	hold *VP*	
group *6*	pull *VP1*	
muck in		

4 VERBS WITH OTHER MEANINGS

There are two other verbs which have this pattern.

We <u>belonged</u> together. Even when we hated each other, which was most of the time, we needed each other too.

In the case of *hang*, the Subject is occasionally a singular noun group.

There are a few bright spots, but the show as a whole <u>doesn't hang</u> together.

belong *9*	hang *VP2*

Structure information

a) The adverb *together* is an Adjunct.

b) This structure has no passive.

c) The phrasal verb pattern is the same except that there is a particle, P, which comes after the verb.

4 V prep

The verb is followed by a prepositional phrase which consists of a preposition and a noun group. The passive pattern is **be V-ed prep** (**prep** here means a preposition, not a prepositional phrase). The verbs described in this section are used with a variety of prepositions. Some verbs listed here are also included in sections relating to verbs followed by specific prepositions (see Sections 5 to 34).

This pattern has two structures:

▶ Structure I: Verb with prepositional Object
They <u>will vote</u> on it.
▶ Structure II: Verb with Adjunct
He <u>disappeared</u> into the kitchen.

Both these structures are dealt with together because both structures can occur with the same verb, depending on the preposition (see 'Structure information' below for further details).

Structure I: Verb with prepositional Object

Active voice: V prep

	Verb group	prepositional phrase
Subject	Verb	prepositional Object
She	chewed	on her pencil rubber.
I	grieved	for all that had been lost.
He	would not speculate	on what actions might follow.

Passive voice: *be* V-ed prep

	Verb group	preposition	
Subject	Verb	Preposition	Adjunct (optional)
That measure	will be voted	on	later today.

Phrasal verbs: V P prep

	Verb group	Particle	prepositional phrase
Subject	Verb		prepositional Object
Smaller mammoths	could get	by	on less food.
He	was thinking	back	to the scenes of his childhood.

Structure II: Verb with Adjunct

V prep

	Verb group	prepositional phrase
Subject	Verb	Adjunct
The small convoy	descended	into the valley.
She	disappeared	through the door.

Phrasal verbs: V P prep

	Verb group	Particle	prepositional phrase
Subject	Verb		Adjunct
The van	pulled	out	from the line of parked cars.

Verbs with this pattern belong to the following meaning groups:

1 THE 'RECEDE' GROUP
2 THE 'RISE' AND 'DROP' GROUP

1   THE 'RECEDE' GROUP

These verbs are concerned with moving, arriving, or being somewhere.

*I don't remember what happened after I **collapsed** onto the settee.*

*Two steamers **used to ply** between Sakhalin and Yuzhno Kurilsk, the main town on the the southernmost island.*

*He got into the car and **pulled out** into the traffic.*

*Because the Universe is expanding, a distant galaxy **recedes** from us faster than a nearby one.*

*Her brother was killed when his car went out of control on a bend and **somersaulted** into a field.*

backtrack 2	diffuse 1	ply 4	sledge 2
catapult 3	disappear 1	rake 4	somersault 3
circulate 3	fall 4	recede 1	spread 6
climb 3	flow 4 (An emotion)	rip 4	tumble 3
collapse 4	gust 2	ripple 4	weave 4
crumple 2	hiss 1	run 17	
descend 1	pirouette 2	rustle 1	
detour 2	play 14	sigh 3 (The wind)	
pull out 1			

2   THE 'RISE' AND 'DROP' GROUP

These verbs indicate that someone or something starts being in a different situation or doing something different. We include here *change*, as in *change from fourth to fifth gear*.

*Havant, the former champions, **dropped** to fourth place when they suffered their second defeat of the season by Slough.*

*Earlier, Mr Ryzhkov said the two sides **were moving** towards a solution to their confrontation.*

*Not a single woman **has risen** to the rank of Agent.*

change 10	leap 5	rise 19
drift 2	leapfrog 2	slide 4
drop 1,13	move 10	swing 9
branch out	rise up ▷19	

3   THE 'SHOOT' GROUP

These verbs are concerned with sending something or gesturing in a particular direction. The prepositional phrase indicates direction. We include here *whisper*, which indicates that someone sends their voice in a particular direction.

*He **blew** on his chilled, purple fingers and put his mittens back on.*

*'Do you recognize this man?' He **nodded** towards Hubbard.*

*Its drivers were climbing out of the cab and **shooting** in the general direction of the chopper.*

*The players claimed they **had been spat** on and had objects thrown at them.*

*As Mr Evans put her down, Meg tugged at his hand and **whispered** in his ear.*

blow *1.3*	gob *3*	pitch *5*	spit *2*
gesticulate	nod *2*	shoot *2*	whisper *1*

4 THE 'SCRAPE' GROUP

These verbs are concerned with physical contact, connection, or damage. The prepositional phrase indicates the thing that is touched or damaged.

*Josef **is hacking** at the trunk of a tree he chopped down in his back yard.*

*There is an optional grass box which **hooks** onto the back of the mower.*

*After a while the only audible sound is that of knives and forks **scraping** against china.*

bite *7*	froth *2*	rasp *2*	slobber
chew *4*	hack *1*	saw *3*	tap *2*
chomp	hook *2*	scrape *2*	tighten *1*
fasten *1*	lap *5*	scribble *1,2*	twine *2*

5 THE 'DELIBERATE' GROUP

These verbs are concerned with speech, writing, thought, or emotion. The prepositional phrase indicates the topic or issue involved.

*At the same time his colleagues in parliament **have been deliberating** about constitutional change.*

*But I understand Wright is adamant he did not act irresponsibly and **is seething** at the accusation.*

*If I saw a prisoner being beaten by a prison officer, then I **would speak up** about it.*

*The extent to which under-urbanization has resulted from such labour practices **is speculated** on below.*

In the case of the following verbs, the preposition is sometimes followed by a wh-clause: *adjudicate, deliberate, differ, disagree, discourse, speculate, vote, waver.*

*The ethics committee is preparing to **vote** on whether to begin a full investigation.*

adjudicate	discourse *3*	generalize *1*	smart *6*
deliberate *3*	drool *1*	grieve *1*	speculate *1*
differ *2*	eulogize	gush *3*	vote *5*
disagree *1*	fuss *2*	seethe *1*	waver *1*
come out *5*	speak up *1*		
speak out	think back		

6 THE 'WORK' GROUP

These verbs are concerned with action or endeavour. The prepositional phrase indicates the field of the action or endeavour.

*Twelve boats from ten countries **will compete** in the Americas Cup.*

*You see, Tim, we **have been working** on this project, Henry and I, for a long time.*

In the case of *persevere* and *work*, the preposition is sometimes followed by an '-ing' clause.

*They say they **will work** towards removing the underlying causes of famine.*

compete *3*	serve *2*	work *5*
enrol	slog *1*	
persevere	struggle *1*	

7 VERBS WITH OTHER MEANINGS

There are a number of other phrasal verbs which have this pattern.

*Thousands of broadcasters **came out** on strike.*

*In the computer manufacturing industry, they're learning to **get by** with fewer employees.*

*Let your child **go around** with bare feet for as long as possible.*

come out 6	go about 3	line up 5
get along 2	go around 2	
get by	go round 2	

Structure information

a) If the prepositional phrase indicates something that is directly affected by or involved in an action, it is considered to be a prepositional Object. If it indicates the circumstances of an action, it is considered to be an Adjunct. Verbs with the pattern **V prep** are followed by three or more different prepositions, and in some cases the prepositional phrase may be an Adjunct or a prepositional Object, depending on the preposition.

b) This structure has a passive, with the pattern **be V-ed prep** (**prep** here means a preposition, not a prepositional phrase). However, it does not often occur. Usually there can be a passive structure for a verb only with one or two particular prepositions. The Subject refers to something directly affected by or involved in the action.

*The proposals **are** still **being worked** on.*

The following verbs from the lists above are the ones most frequently used in the passive, with the preposition(s) indicated.

adjudicate *(on)*	**gob** 3 *(at)*	**hack** 1 *(at)*	**spit** 2 *(on/at)*
compete 3 *(for)*	**grieve** 1 *(for)*	**rummage** 1 *(through)*	**vote** 5 *(on/for)*
drool 1 *(over)*	**gush** 3 *(over)*	**speculate** 1 *(on/upon/about)*	**work** 5 *(on/at/for)*

c) The phrasal verb pattern is the same except that there is a particle, P, which comes after the verb. The passive pattern does not often occur.

5 V *about* n

The verb is followed by a prepositional phrase which consists of the preposition *about* and a noun group. With most verbs, the preposition is sometimes followed by an '-ing' clause or a wh-clause. In Structure I, the preposition is followed by an '-ing' form. The passive pattern is **be V-ed *about***.

This pattern has three structures:

▶ Structure I: Verbs in phase
Don't bother about clearing up.
▶ Structure II: Verb with prepositional Object
He was grumbling about the weather.
▶ Structure III: Verb with Adjunct
David rang about the meeting tomorrow.

Structure I: Verbs in phase

V *about* -ing

	Verb group	*about*	-ing	
Subject	**Verb**			**Completive**
	Forget	about	being	friendly.

There are only two verbs with this structure. They are concerned with not doing something.

> As the Indians **did not bother** about **digging** *very deep graves, many skeletons had been found.*

(not) bother *1*   **forget** *2,4*

When the preposition *about* is followed by a noun group, these verbs have Structure II (see meaning groups II.2 and II.4 below).

Structure information: Verbs in phase

a) The verb is followed by the preposition *about* and the '-ing' form of another verb. The verbs are **in phase**, and together form a **complex verb group**. This means that the actions or states expressed by the two verbs cannot be separated from each other. For example, if someone is told to *forget about getting* something, the *forgetting* and the *not getting* are not two processes, but one.

The complex verb group is followed by a group, phrase, or clause which completes the pattern of the second verb. In the structure table above, this is called a **Completive**. For example, if the second verb is normally followed by a noun group, then the Completive of the complex verb group will be a noun group.

b) This structure has no passive.

Structure II: Verb with prepositional Object

Active voice: V *about* n/-ing/wh

	Verb group	*about*	noun group/-ing clause/wh-clause
Subject	**Verb**		**prepositional Object**
You	didn't agonize	about	whether or not to do it?
I	dream	about	winning the 100 meters.
Other players	are grumbling	about	unpaid wages.
I	heard	about	the accident.

Passive voice: *be* V-ed *about*

	Verb group	*about*	
Subject	**Verb**	**Preposition**	**Adjunct (optional)**
These children	are not being forgotten	about.	
Nothing else	had been talked	about	for weeks.

Phrasal verbs: V P *about* n

	Verb group	Particle	*about*	noun group
Subject	**Verb**			**prepositional Object**
Successive ministers	have droned	on	about	the need for cuts.
She	's found	out	about	the money.

Verbs with this pattern belong to the following meaning groups:

II.1 THE 'TALK' GROUP
II.2 THE 'THINK' GROUP
II.3 THE 'LEARN' GROUP
II.4 VERBS WITH OTHER MEANINGS

II.1 THE 'TALK' GROUP

These verbs are concerned with speaking or writing. This includes:

* verbs that indicate the function of what is said e.g. *argue, ask, complain*
* verbs that indicate how something is said e.g. *mutter, wail*
* verbs that indicate the feeling of the speaker e.g. *enthuse, fulminate*

All the phrasal verbs (as well as some of the ordinary verbs) indicate that someone speaks for longer than you consider acceptable, and sometimes that there is something else that you dislike about what they are saying, for example that it is boring or stupid. The prepositional phrase indicates the topic involved.

*He seemed to have forgotten that I **had asked** about his car.*

*She**'s not complained** about the conditions or anything.*

*I have not heard her **enthuse** about a resort so enthusiastically ever before.*

*Some of them could be heard **muttering** about the high prices of the clothes.*

*He **talked** about all kinds of things.*

*He **witters on** about how rising paper and print costs have made this regrettable increase unavoidable.*

The verbs *argue 4, bicker, chat, dicker, fight, haggle, quarrel, row, squabble,* and *talk 2* always or often have a plural Subject with this pattern because they are **reciprocal verbs** concerned with having an argument or discussion (see Chapter 6).

*My parents **were quarrelling** about me though I could not quite tell why.*

With most of the verbs in this group, the preposition *about* is sometimes followed by an '-ing' clause.

*He **had boasted** about stabbing a woman.*

With some of these verbs, particularly *complain, joke,* and *go on,* the preposition *about* is sometimes followed by a noun group and an '-ing' clause. This pattern is **V about n -ing**.

*Terrified residents **complained** about aircraft flying low over their homes.*

In the case of the following verbs, the preposition *about* is sometimes followed by a wh-clause: *argue, ask, bicker, chat, chatter, equivocate, fight, haggle, inquire, joke, lie, quarrel, quibble, row, squabble, talk, waffle.*

*He and Patra **argued** about what to wear.*

argue *4,5*	dicker	moan *2*	swank *1*
ask *1*	discourse *3*	mutter	talk *2,3,4,8*
bellyache *2*	enthuse *1*	pontificate *1*	testify *1*
bicker	equivocate	preach *2*	trumpet *2*
bitch *3*	fight *6*	protest *1*	tut-tut *2*
blab	fulminate	quarrel *3*	twitter *2*
blather	generalize *1*	quibble *1*	waffle *1*
bleat *3*	gripe *1*	rant *1*	wail *2*
boast *1*	groan *3*	rap *2*	whine *2*
brag	grouse *2*	rave *2*	whinge
burble *2*	grumble *1*	rhapsodize	whisper *2*
carp *2*	gush *3*	row *3.3*	witter
chat	haggle	sing *1*	write *3*
chatter *1*	inquire *1*	snigger	yap *2*
complain *1*	joke *2*	speak *1*	
crow *3*	lie *2.2*	squabble	
babble on	carry on *3*	prattle on	sound off
bang on *VPP*	drone on ▷*2*	rabbit on	spout forth ▷*3*
blather on	go on *8*	ramble on	spout off ▷*3*
bleat on *VPP*	harp on	rant on	waffle on ▷*1*
burble on	keep on *VPP*	rattle on	witter on ▷

II.2 THE 'THINK' GROUP

These verbs are concerned with thought or feeling, or the expression of thought or feeling. The prepositional phrase indicates the topic of the thought or feeling.

*It's a problem that **has been known** about for years.*

*For the most part, people **think** about themselves rather than others.*

With most verbs, the preposition *about* is sometimes followed by an '-ing' clause.

*He told me he **had** always **dreamed** about being a star when he was a kid.*

With some of these verbs, particularly *know*, *think*, and *worry*, the preposition *about* is sometimes followed by a noun group and an '-ing' clause. This pattern is **V *about* n -ing**.

*I think he still **worries** about me being the youngest.*

In the case of the following verbs, the preposition *about* is sometimes followed by a wh-clause: *agonize, bother, brood, care, cogitate, deliberate, differ, disagree, dither, fret, know, muse, philosophize, puzzle, ruminate, theorize, think, wonder, worry*.

*It averages out so that you don't need to **dither** about when to buy.*

agonize	differ *2*	gloat	speculate *1*
agree *1*	disagree *1*	know *1,4,8*	theorize
bother *4*	dither	muse *1*	think *4,11*
brood *3*	dream *2,4*	obsess	waffle *2*
care *1,2*	fantasize *1,2*	philosophize	waver *1*
cogitate	forget *2,3,4*	puzzle *2*	wonder *1*
daydream *1*	fret *1*	rage *3*	worry *1*
deliberate *3*	fume *2*	ruminate *1*	

See also Structure I above.

II.3 THE 'LEARN' GROUP

These verbs are concerned with acquiring knowledge. The prepositional phrase indicates what the knowledge concerns.

*We **found out** about these changes by pure accident.*

*I **heard** about the trouble on the television early this morning, so I hurried on over.*

The preposition *about* is sometimes followed by an '-ing' clause.

The players __learned__ about competing against quality opposition and *improved each game.*

In the case of *learn*, the preposition *about* is sometimes followed by a wh-clause.

Even in school, Hewitt __was learning__ about how to use time.

In the case of *hear* and *read*, the preposition *about* is sometimes followed by a noun group and an '-ing' clause. This pattern is **V *about* n -ing**.

And that's how you __heard__ about Ron Hythe fighting with Doyle?

> **hear** *7*   **learn** *1*   **read** *1*
>
> **find out** *1*

II.4 VERBS WITH OTHER MEANINGS

There is one other verb which has this structure.

I'll be late, __don't bother__ about supper.

> **(not) bother** *1*

See also Structure I above.

Structure information: Verb with prepositional Object

a) The prepositional phrase is the prepositional Object.

b) This structure has a passive, with the pattern **be V-ed *about***. However, not all verbs with this structure are used in the passive. The following verbs are the ones which are most frequently passive.

> **argue** *4,5*   **know** *1*   **talk** *4,8*
> **forget** *2,3*   **lie** *2.2*   **think** *4*
> **joke** *2*   **speak** *1*   **write** *3*

c) The phrasal verb pattern is the same except that there is a particle, P, which comes after the verb. There is no passive pattern.

Structure III: Verb with Adjunct

V *about* n

	Verb group	*about*	noun group
Subject	Verb		Adjunct
I	'm phoning	about	the arrangements for tomorrow.

Phrasal verbs: V P *about* n

	Verb group	Particle	*about*	noun group
Subject	Verb			Adjunct
Thousands of people	write	in	about	their experiences.

These verbs are concerned with communication by telephone or letter. The prepositional phrase indicates the topic which is the reason for the communication.

> Hello? I'*m calling* about the ad for the car.
> I don't know if you can remember, a few months ago I *rang up* about some housing problems I and my husband were having with the landlord.

call *3*	phone *4*	ring *1.1*
phone up	ring up *1*	write in *1*

Structure information: Verb with Adjunct

a) The prepositional phrase is an Adjunct.

b) This structure has no passive.

c) The phrasal verb pattern is the same except that there is a particle, P, which comes after the verb.

Other related patterns

V *about* n *to* n, V *to* n *about* n

See page 245.

V *about* n *with* n, V *with* n *about* n

See page 471.

V adj/adv *about* n

The verb is followed by an adjective group or an adverb group, and a prepositional phrase beginning with *about*.

> He *felt* good about the show.
> He *felt* differently about this scaled-down plan.

This pattern may occur as part of a question or wh-clause.

> Look, I know how you *feel* about James.

The preposition *about* is sometimes followed by an '-ing' clause, or by a noun group and an '-ing' clause.

> Obviously one *should feel* depressed about being 60.
> How *do* you *feel* about me being a policeman?

feel *12*

6 V *across* n

The verb is followed by a prepositional phrase which consists of *across* and a noun group.

This pattern has one structure:

▶ Verb with Adjunct
I cut across the field.

V *across* n

	Verb group	*across*	noun group
Subject	**Verb**	**Adjunct**	
She	cut	across	the grass.
Birds	skimmed	across	the water.

Verbs with this pattern are all concerned with crossing or passing from one side of a place to the other, either physically or metaphorically.

*Nancy, out of the corner of her eye, saw the shadow that suddenly **fell** across the doorway.*

*A cold, dead smile **flickered** across Vincent's grey features, and for a brief second his eyes sparked to life.*

*Hurricane Dean **swept** across Bermuda with torrential rains and winds as strong as 113 miles per hour, flooding some coastal roads.*

brush 5	fall 14	flit 4	skim 2
cut 6	flicker 3	plane 7	sweep 8

Structure information

a) The prepositional phrase is an Adjunct.

b) This structure has no passive.

7 V *after* n

The verb is followed by a prepositional phrase which consists of the preposition *after* and a noun group.

This pattern has one structure:

▶ Verb with prepositional Object
They lust after power.

V *after* n

	Verb group	*after*	noun group
Subject	**Verb**	**prepositional Object**	
The attendants	chased	after	him.
Americans	hanker	after	the big gas-guzzling cars of yesteryear.

Phrasal verbs: V P *after* n

	Verb group	Particle	*after*	noun group
Subject	**Verb**		**prepositional Object**	
I	had to clean	up	after	her.

Verbs with this pattern belong to the following meaning groups:

1 THE 'HANKER' GROUP
2 THE 'GO' GROUP
3 THE 'FOLLOW' GROUP
4 THE 'CLEAR UP' GROUP

1 THE 'HANKER' GROUP

These verbs are concerned with wanting something or someone very much.

*He still **hankers** after high office.*
*But even as a professional, she felt treated like a little girl, a piece of fluff to **be lusted** after.*

hanker	lust *VP*	yearn
hunger *4*	thirst *4*	

2 THE 'GO' GROUP

These verbs are concerned with trying to get something or someone.

*I **was** always **chasing** after men who just couldn't handle intimacy.*
*It gives you the credibility you'll need if you want to **go** after a managerial position elsewhere.*

chase *2,3*	go *VP*	run *VP*

3 THE 'FOLLOW' GROUP

These verbs are concerned with following someone.

*She grabbed a towel and **followed** after him.*

chase *1*	follow *1*

4 THE 'CLEAR UP' GROUP

These verbs are concerned with doing something, usually cleaning or tidying, which has been made necessary by someone else. The prepositional phrase indicates the other person.

*He had a reputation for leaving bathrooms in an appalling state, safe in the knowledge that his minions **would clear up** after him.*

clean up *1*	run around *VPP*
clear up *1*	tidy up *1*

Structure information

a) The prepositional phrase is the prepositional Object.

b) This structure has a passive, with the pattern **be V-ed *after***. However, the passive does not often occur. The verb that is most frequently used in the passive is *lust*.

   *He wanted to **be lusted after**.*

c) The phrasal verb pattern is the same except that there is a particle, P, which comes after the verb. There is no passive pattern.

Other related patterns

V *after* n with quote

See pages 117-118.

8 V *against* n

The verb is followed by a prepositional phrase which consists of *against* and a noun group. With some verbs, the preposition is sometimes followed by an '-ing' clause. The passive pattern is **be V-ed *against***.

This pattern has one structure:

▶ Verb with prepositional Object
   Thousands of people __demonstrated__ against the tax.

Active voice: V *against* n/-ing

	Verb group	*against*	noun group/-ing clause
Subject	Verb		prepositional Object
He	campaigned	against	arranged marriages.
You	're competing	against	younger workers.
They	have decided	against	boycotting the referendum.
Their bullets	slammed	against	the fuselage.

Passive voice: *be* V-ed *against*

	Verb group	*against*	
Subject	Verb	Preposition	Adjunct (optional)
They	are discriminated	against	by their employers.

Phrasal verbs: V P *against* n/-ing

	Verb group	Particle	*against*	noun group/-ing clause
Subject	Verb			prepositional Object
Several countries	have come	out	against	holding official celebrations.
He	has fought	back	against	the hardliners.
He	lashed	out	against	the proposal.

Verbs with this pattern belong to the following meaning groups:

1. THE 'COMPETE' GROUP
2. THE 'CAMPAIGN' GROUP
3. THE 'PREACH' GROUP
4. THE 'BUMP' GROUP
5. THE 'INSURE' GROUP
6. THE 'OFFEND' GROUP
7. VERBS WITH OTHER MEANINGS

1 THE 'COMPETE' GROUP

These verbs are concerned with opposing someone, competing with someone, or doing something to harm someone. We include here *draw, lose, prevail, win, win out,* and *win through,* which indicate the result of a contest. Some of these verbs are **reciprocal verbs** and have a plural Subject in this pattern (see Chapter 6).

*The competition gave junior players the chance to **compete against members of other clubs**.*

*When I started at college, all the girls in my class seemed to **gang up against me** and talk and laugh about me.*

*I can't wait to **play against them** because we are capable of giving United a real run for their money.*

*She also began to have aggressive and murderous thoughts about her family, thinking that they **were plotting against her**.*

*Sir Geoffrey Howe made clear through friends on the evening of his resignation that he **would not stand against Mrs Thatcher**.*

*In the quarter-finals, Notts beat Essex, Worcestershire beat Glamorgan, Lancashire disposed of Surrey and Somerset **won against Middlesex**.*

The verb *stack up* usually has this pattern in a clause beginning with *how*.

*A favorite theme of Perot's is **how the US stacks up against its foreign competitors**.*

battle *4*	lose *1*	rebel *3,5*	side *16*
compete *1,3*	mutiny *2*	retaliate	sin *2*
conspire *1,2*	play *3*	revolt *2,4*	spy *3*
discriminate *2*	plot *2*	rise *18*	stand *19*
draw *24*	prevail *3*	run *8*	testify *1*
fight *4*	race *2*	scheme *3*	win *1*
fight back *1*	rise up ▷*18*	win out	
gang up	stack up *1*	win through	

2 THE 'CAMPAIGN' GROUP

These verbs are concerned with trying to stop something that is happening or is planned.

*He **has campaigned against apartheid** all his life.*

*Most EC countries **have** already **legislated against excessive overtime**.*

*The students **are protesting against a cut in the education budget**.*

campaign *2*	fight *1*	protest *1*
crusade *2*	legislate	strike *2*
demonstrate *3*	lobby *1*	vote *5*

3 THE 'PREACH' GROUP

These verbs are concerned with saying that something is bad in some way. We include here *appeal*, which indicates that someone makes a formal complaint about a decision.

> Both Warren Beatty and Billy Crystal **have lashed out** against studios for not pushing their films hard enough.

> Here was a man who **preached** against the gun, yet had friends who were notorious gunmen.

The preposition *against* is sometimes followed by an '-ing' clause.

> Doctors **advise** against putting a thermometer into your child's mouth because it may cause him to choke.

advise *1*	caution *2*	protest *1*	rule *7*
appeal *4*	fulminate	rage *3*	warn *2*
argue *2*	inveigh	rail *5*	
blaspheme	preach *1,2*	rant *1*	
come out *5*	lash out *2*		
hit out *2*	speak out		

4 THE 'BUMP' GROUP

These verbs indicate that something hits or touches something else.

> After what seemed eternity, there was a jerk as the boat **bumped** against something.

> A cat came into the room and **rubbed** against its mistress's legs.

beat *2*	clatter *2*	knock *2*	smash *3*
brush *5*	clink	rest *2.7*	strike *5*
bump *1*	clunk *2*	rub *2,5*	
chafe *1*	grate *3*	slam *4*	

5 THE 'INSURE' GROUP

These verbs are concerned with taking precautions against possible harm. The person or thing that is being protected is not explicitly mentioned. We include here the verb *guard*, which is used to indicate that someone avoids doing something or letting something happen.

> While many **insure** against death, far fewer take precautions against long-term or permanent loss of income because of sickness.

> It is exactly the right time to **spray** against the potato blight fungus.

In the case of *guard*, the preposition *against* is sometimes followed by an '-ing' clause.

> He warned the jury to **guard** against returning a tough verdict out of sympathy with relatives.

guard *VP*	insure *1,2*	spray *7*
hedge *2*	protect *1,2*	

6 THE 'OFFEND' GROUP

These verbs are concerned with breaking something such as a rule or convention.

> The policy seems to offer several aspects that **offend** against the constitution.

> It is about a teacher who **rebels** against hidebound practices in an American school.

go *VP1*	rebel *3,5*	transgress
offend *2*	revolt *4*	

7 VERBS WITH OTHER MEANINGS

There are a number of other verbs which have this pattern.

*He warned today that the plan **could backfire** against the allies.*

*I had toyed with the idea of dyeing my hair black, but **decided** against it.*

*I have always saved. And I always like to pay bills as soon as they arrive. My father never saved and perhaps I **reacted** against that.*

In the case of *decide*, *militate*, and *react*, the preposition *against* is sometimes followed by an '-ing' clause.

*We **decided** against having a midday meal so as to save time.*

backfire *1*	chafe *2*	harden *4*	struggle *1*
battle *5*	decide *1*	militate	weigh *6*
boomerang *2*	depreciate	react *2*	

Structure information

a) The prepositional phrase is the prepositional Object.

b) This structure has a passive, with the pattern **be V-ed *against***. However, not all verbs with this structure are used in the passive. The verbs that are most frequently passive are *discriminate* and *sin* (usually in the phrase *more sinned against than sinning*).

c) The phrasal verb pattern is the same, except that there is a particle, P, which comes after the verb.

9 V *around/round* n

The verb is followed by a prepositional phrase which consists of *around* or *round* and a noun group.

This pattern has two structures:

▶ Structure I: Verb with prepositional Object
*Her life **centres** around her family.*
▶ Structure II: Verb with Adjunct
*They **clustered** around me.*

Structure I: Verb with prepositional Object

V *around/round* n

	Verb group	*around/round*	noun group
Subject	**Verb**	**prepositional Object**	
The plot	centres	around	a baffling murder.
I	was skirting	around	the real issues.

Verbs with this structure belong to the following meaning groups:

I.1 THE 'CENTRE' GROUP

These verbs are used when indicating what the focus of something is.

*Their disagreements **have centred** around the make-up of a proposed guerilla leadership council.*

*Community life here **revolves** around churches and schools.*

*Set on a ranch in Mexico early in the 20th century, the film **revolves** around Tita, the youngest of three sisters.*

centre *9*   revolve *1,2*

I.2 THE 'SKATE' GROUP

These verbs are concerned with avoiding a subject.

*Both of them like to **skate** around the subject of what they can do for African-Americans.*

*The Prime Minister tried to **skirt** round the trickier issues.*

skate *5*   skirt *4*

I.3 THE 'FUSS' GROUP

These verbs indicate that a person or group of people pays someone or something too much attention.

*He was getting cross with the doctors for **fussing** around him and wanted to come back home.*

cluck *2*   fawn *3*   fuss *3*

Structure information: Verb with prepositional Object

a) The prepositional phrase is the prepositional Object.

b) This structure has no passive.

Structure II: Verb with Adjunct

V *around/round* n

	Verb group	*around/round*	noun group
Subject	**Verb**	**Adjunct**	
The bird	was circling	around	the house.
The children	clustered	around	me.

Verbs with this structure belong to the following meaning groups:

II.3 THE 'HANG' GROUP
II.4 THE 'MOVE' GROUP

II.1 THE 'CIRCLE' GROUP

These verbs indicate that someone or something moves in a circle or curve round someone or something else.

> *Because the firing was still going on, I __circled__ **around the building** and came in from the other direction.*
>
> *I __skirted__ **round the north of Brighton and Hove**, avoiding them as Jeremy had instructed.*

circle *6*	revolve *3*	skirt *3*

II.2 THE 'CROWD' GROUP

These verbs indicate that a number of people move so as to surround someone or something.

> *Inside, the paparazzi __cluster__ **around any hapless celebrity they can find**.*
>
> *The boys __crowded__ **round the detailed map of the area**.*

cluster *2*	flock *3*	throng *2*
crowd *3*	gather *1*	

II.3 THE 'HANG' GROUP

These verbs indicate that someone or something is in a particular place, not doing much or not being used.

> *All the boys who are out of work __hang around__ **the five or six cafes there** and drink endless cups of tea.*
>
> *He says the gun __had been lying__ **around the house**, and he just wanted to get rid of it.*

hang *VP1,2*	lie *VP1,2*	stick *VP*

II.4 THE 'MOVE' GROUP

These verbs indicate that someone goes to a lot of different places.

> *In our ailing jobs market, people __must move__ **around the country** in order to find work.*

move *VP*	run *VP*

Structure information: Verb with Adjunct

a) The prepositional phrase is an Adjunct.

b) This structure has no passive.

---

10 V *as adj*

The verb is followed by a prepositional phrase which consists of the preposition *as* and an adjective group.

This pattern has one structure:

▶ Verb with prepositional Complement
That <u>counts</u> as old.

V *as* adj

	Verb group	*as*	adjective group
Subject	**Verb**	**prepositional Complement**	
A large number of plants	qualify	as	medicinal.

Phrasal verbs: V P *as* adj

	Verb group	Particle	*as*	adjective group
Subject	**Verb**		**prepositional Complement**	
He	comes	over	as	smug and arrogant.

Verbs with this pattern indicate that someone or something is perceived as having a particular quality or status, or hopes to be perceived in that way. All these verbs except *count* and *emerge* are **link verbs** (see Chapter 5).

*I'm told that I **come across** as hard and intimidating but I don't feel hard and intimidating.*

*In Italy, many women **count** as unemployed even if they have a perfectly respectable 'black market' job.*

*Parents can try to set good examples without trying to **masquerade** as perfect.*

*But with such a narrow definition, entire branches of knowledge **would not qualify** as useful.*

count 7	masquerade 1	qualify 3
emerge 4	pass 20	
come across 2	come over 3	

Structure information

a) The prepositional phrase is the prepositional Complement.

b) This structure has no passive.

c) The phrasal verb pattern is the same, except that there is a particle, P, which comes after the verb.

11 V *as* n

The verb is followed by a prepositional phrase which consists of the preposition *as* and a noun group.

This pattern has one structure:

▶ Verb with prepositional Complement
His wife <u>works</u> as a designer.

159

V *as* n

	Verb group	*as*	noun group
Subject	**Verb**		**prepositional Complement**
The bacterium	acts	as	a natural carrier for the gene.
The scandal	began	as	a family feud.
She	trained	as	a teacher.

Phrasal verbs: V P *as* n

	Verb group	Particle	*as*	noun group
Subject	**Verb**			**prepositional Complement**
I	signed	up	as	midshipman on a cruiser.
She	started	out	as	an assembly line worker.

Verbs with this pattern belong to the following meaning groups:

1 THE 'WORK' GROUP
2 THE 'FUNCTION' GROUP
3 THE 'BEGIN' AND 'END' GROUP
4 THE 'RANK' GROUP
5 THE 'MASQUERADE' GROUP
6 VERBS WITH OTHER MEANINGS

1 THE 'WORK' GROUP

These verbs are concerned with doing, getting, leaving, or training for a job. The noun group after *as* contains a job title such as *doctor* or *president*.

> She **has** recently **qualified** *as a doctor* and is hoping to practise in Pakistan.
> Mr Guerra **resigned** *as deputy prime minister* in January.
> After a spell as a volunteer in the RAF, he **signed up** *as a steward* with P&O Lines.
> He intends to **step down** *as chairman* in 1997.
> He **worked** *as a kitchen assistant* for the Ministry of Defence.

enlist *1*	practise *4*	run *8*	train *2.1*
freelance *3*	qualify *1*	serve *2*	volunteer *3*
moonlight *2*	resign *1*	stand *19*	work *1*
put up *7*	sign up	step down	
shape up *2*	stand down		

2 THE 'FUNCTION' GROUP

These verbs are concerned with having a role or a function. The prepositional phrase indicates what someone or something is. All these verbs are **link verbs** (see Chapter 5).

> Players **act** *as their own referees*, and altercations and bad language are virtually unknown.
> A basic walking boot with tough leather uppers **can double up** *as a digging boot*.
> Monosodium glutamate is a food additive that **functions** *as a flavour enhancer*.

act *4*	figure *13*	operate *2*
double *11*	function *3*	serve *3*
double up ▷*11*		

3 THE 'BEGIN' AND 'END' GROUP

These verbs are concerned with beginning, continuing, and ending. The prepositional phrase indicates what someone or something was at the beginning or end of something, or what they continue to be. All these verbs are **link verbs** (see Chapter 5).

*The camp **began** **as a maze of tents**, but over 14 years it has grown into a proper village.*

*Mr. Barker **will continue** **as chairman of the company's corporate finance division**.*

*All of the other county games **ended** **as draws**.*

*People like me are facing poverty and **may** even **end up** **as social welfare cases**.*

begin *3,5*	finish *4,5*	start *4*
continue *6*	originate	
end *4*	remain *1*	
end up *2*	start off ▷*4*	
finish up *1*	start out *1*	

4 THE 'RANK' GROUP

These verbs indicate that someone or something is perceived as a particular thing. All these verbs except *count*, *emerge*, and *qualify* are **link verbs** (see Chapter 5).

*The MP **came across** **as a genuine, committed socialist, a forthright man**, honest and to be trusted.*

*Payment for transportation necessary for medical care **qualifies** **as a medical expense**.*

*The view through the columns and turrets over the surrounding gardens and parkland **must rank** **as one of the most strangely beautiful and evocative in the land**.*

*The world Olympiad final between the British women's team and Austria **was shaping up** **as one of the most dramatic on record** when play ended last night.*

The preposition *as* is occasionally followed by an '-ing' clause.

*If you are homeless through no fault of your own and you **qualify** **as being in priority need**, the council is obliged to find you somewhere to live.*

count *7*	pass *20*	rank *4*
emerge *4*	qualify *3*	rate *6*
come across *2*	go down *VPP*	
come over *3*	shape up *1*	

5 THE 'MASQUERADE' GROUP

These verbs indicate that someone is trying to be perceived as something they are not or that something is intended to be perceived as something it is not. All these verbs except *dress up* are **link verbs** (see Chapter 5).

*As a youngster he loved **dressing up** **as Superman**.*

*It denounces the use of taxpayer funds 'to subsidise obscenity and blasphemy **masquerading** **as art**.'*

*Jones and his accomplice **posed** **as police officers** to gain entry to the house.*

masquerade *1*	parade *10*	pose *3*
dress up *1*		

6 VERBS WITH OTHER MEANINGS

There are two other verbs which have this pattern. The verb *come* is a **link verb** (see Chapter 5).

> *His promotion __came as a surprise__ to some MPs since Mr Gummer, aged 53, has tended to be underestimated by opponents.*
>
> *Stephanie __came out__ as a **lesbian** when she was 21.*

```
come 20
come out 3
```

Structure information

a) The prepositional phrase is a prepositional Complement.

b) This structure has no passive.

c) The phrasal verb pattern is the same except that there is a particle, P, which comes after the verb.

Productive uses

The use of *as* and a noun group is productive. Many verbs in addition to the ones listed above are sometimes followed by such a prepositional phrase, which indicates the role of the Subject; for example someone can *compete as an amateur*, *live as a recluse*, or *testify as a witness*. The verbs listed in this section are the ones which are most frequently used in this way.

12 V *as to* wh

The verb is followed by a prepositional phrase which consists of *as to* and a wh-clause or occasionally a noun group.

This pattern has one structure:

▶ Verb with prepositional Object
  I __inquired__ as to whether any solution had been reached.

V *as to* wh/n

	Verb group	*as to*	wh-clause/noun group
Subject	**Verb**		**prepositional Object**
We	advise	as to	whether the group has a good legal case or not.
Analysts	differ	as to	how profitable the company will eventually be.
She	will be testifying	as to	his mental condition.

This pattern is rather formal, and is used in writing more often than in speech. Verbs with this pattern belong to the following meaning groups:

1 THE 'INQUIRE' GROUP
2 THE 'ADVISE' GROUP
3 THE 'AGREE' GROUP

1 THE 'INQUIRE' GROUP

These verbs are concerned with trying to find out about something. We include here verbs such as *inquire*, which involve speaking, and verbs such as *speculate*, which involve thinking.

> The journalist **inquired** as to sales. 'It has sold twelve thousand copies in three weeks,' said Ford.

> I wanted to **speculate** as to how it feels being in the middle of a revolution, to have history overtaking you.

enquire *1*	inquire *1*	think *4*
guess *1*	speculate *1*	

2 THE 'ADVISE' GROUP

These verbs are concerned with giving advice or information.

> **Can** you **advise** as to why this should be happening?

> Officials **wouldn't comment** as to whether any new agreements about a trading range for the dollar were made at Saturday's meeting.

advise *1*	comment *1*	testify *1*

3 THE 'AGREE' GROUP

These verbs are concerned with agreeing, disagreeing, or arguing about something.

> They **do not agree** as to the pronunciation of some of the simplest and commonest words in the English language.

> To this day historians **disagree** as to whether he was hero or villain.

agree *1*	differ *2*
argue *4*	disagree *1*

Structure information

a) The prepositional phrase is a prepositional Object.

b) This structure has no passive.

13 V *at* n

The verb is followed by a prepositional phrase which consists of *at* and a noun group. With some verbs, the preposition is sometimes followed by an '-ing' clause or a wh-clause. The passive pattern is **be V-ed *at***.

This pattern has two main structures:

▶ Structure I: Verb with prepositional Complement
*Unemployment **is running** at 17 per cent.*
▶ Structure II: Verb with prepositional Object
*They **swore** at him.*

Structure I: Verb with prepositional Complement

V *at* amount

	Verb group	*at*	amount
Subject	**Verb**	**prepositional Complement**	
The unemployment rate	peaked	at	11 per cent.
Inflation	is running	at	around sixty per cent.

Phrasal verbs: V P *at* amount

	Verb group	Particle	*at*	amount
Subject	**Verb**		**prepositional Complement**	
The two CDs	clock	in	at	just under 100 minutes.
The price	works	out	at	£10 a cup.

In this structure, the noun group following the preposition is always an **amount**.

Verbs with this structure belong to the following meaning groups:

I.1   THE 'STAND' GROUP
I.2   THE 'PEAK' GROUP

I.1 THE 'STAND' GROUP

These verbs are used to indicate the size, level, or weight of something. They are all **link verbs** (see Chapter 5).

> *The cost of the fighter programme now __stands__ at more than four thousand million dollars.*

> *The average rise __works out__ at 6.5 per cent.*

run *32*	**stand** *13*
average out	**weigh in** *2*
clock in *VPP*	**work out** *3*

I.2 THE 'PEAK' GROUP

These verbs are used to indicate that something has a certain size, level, or price at a certain time or point.

> *The Confederation of British Industry has predicted that unemployment __will bottom out__ at between 2.25 million and 2.5 million.*

> *The dollar __closed__ at DM1.4917, compared with Wednesday's New York close of DM1.4868.*

> *Temperatures __have peaked__ at over thirty degrees Celsius and a drought may shortly be declared in the region.*

close *1.9*	**finish** *4*	**peak** *2*
end *7*	**open** *22*	**stabilize**
bottom out	**level off** *1*	**level out** *1*

Structure information: Verb with prepositional Complement

a) The prepositional phrase is the prepositional Complement.

b) This structure has no passive.

c) The phrasal verb pattern is the same except that there is a particle, P, which comes after the verb.

Structure II: Verb with prepositional Object
Active voice: V *at* n/-ing

	Verb group	*at*	noun group/-ing clause
Subject	**Verb**		**prepositional Object**
He	glanced	at	his watch.
They	have protested	at	being underrepresented in government.
The rivals	shouted	at	each other.
The kid	tugged	at	the cuff of his sweater.

Passive voice: *be* V-ed *at*

	Verb group	*at*
Subject	**Verb**	**Preposition**
Men in shorts	are laughed	at.
His car	has been shot	at.

Phrasal verbs: V P *at* n

	Verb group	Particle	*at*	noun group
Subject	**Verb**			**prepositional Object**
The recession	is eating	away	at	their revenues.
A senior judge	hit	out	at	the new law.

Verbs with this structure belong to the following meaning groups:

II.1 THE 'BAY' GROUP

II.2 THE 'SHOUT' GROUP

II.3 THE 'WINK' GROUP

II.4 THE 'LOOK' GROUP

II.5 THE 'GRUMBLE' GROUP

II.6 THE 'REJOICE' GROUP

II.7 THE 'BALK' AND 'JUMP' GROUP

II.8 THE 'PROD' AND 'PULL' GROUP

II.9 THE 'CHEW' GROUP

II.10 THE 'EAT AWAY' GROUP

II.11 THE 'SHOOT' GROUP

II.12 THE 'HIT BACK' GROUP

II.13 THE 'WORK' GROUP

II.14 THE 'SELL' GROUP

II.15 VERBS WITH OTHER MEANINGS

II.1 THE 'BAY' GROUP

These verbs indicate that an animal makes a noise. The prepositional phrase indicates who or what the noise is directed at.

*A small dog **barked** at a seagull he was chasing.*

*Somewhere in the streets beyond a dog suddenly howled, **baying** at the moon.*

bark *1*	growl *1*	screech *3*
bay *7*	howl *1*	snarl *1*

II.2 THE 'SHOUT' GROUP

These verbs are concerned with shouting at someone, making noises at someone, or speaking in an unpleasant way to someone. The prepositional phrase indicates who is being addressed.

*They're frightened of **being laughed** at in the street.*

*Charley won't like it. He'**ll go on** at me for telling.*

*He **used to shout** at people and sometimes even hit his assistants.*

*I'm sorry, love, I didn't mean to **snap** at you like that.*

bark *2*	holler	rant *1*	sneer
bawl *1*	hoot *1*	scream *2*	swear *1*
bellow *1*	jeer *1*	screech *2*	whistle *2*
cluck *3*	laugh *2*	shout *1*	wolf-whistle
coo *2*	preach *3*	shriek *2*	yap *2*
cuss	rage *3*	snap *4*	yell *1*
hiss *3*	rail *5*	snarl *2*	
blow up *4*	go on *8*	keep on *VPP*	

II.3 THE 'WINK' GROUP

These verbs are concerned with communicating with a facial expression or a gesture. The prepositional phrase indicates who the person is communicating with.

*She looked back at Michael. 'You don't think I'll do it, do you?' Michael just **grinned** at her, maddeningly.*

*I saw my parents **waving** at me through the window.*

*Cross **winked** at Menti and Menti smiled.*

beam *1*	grimace	nod *3*	smirk
blink *1*	grin *1*	scowl	wave *1*
frown	leer	smile *1*	wink *1*

II.4 THE 'LOOK' GROUP

These verbs are concerned with looking at something or someone. Most of them indicate the manner of the looking or the attitude or emotion of the person looking.

*Betty **glared** at her in disgust.*

*'**Look** at this,' one of the guests said. 'The dial on this intercom's turned all the way down.'*

*Then he burst into sobs and covered his face with his hands. Alberg **stared** at him.*

gape *1*	glance *2*	look *1.2,3,7,10*	peer *1*
gawk	glare *1*	ogle	squint *1*
gawp	glower	peek	stare *1*
gaze *1*	goggle *1*	peep *1*	

II.5 THE 'GRUMBLE' GROUP

These verbs are concerned with speaking, usually to express an opinion. The prepositional phrase indicates what is being talked about. We include here *hint*, which indicates that someone mentions something indirectly.

*The council also **hit out** at incompetence among the officials in charge of distribution.*

Councillor Mani <u>scoffed</u> at government claims that sufficient funds are unavailable for programmes for the aged.

In the case of *grumble, hint,* and *protest,* the preposition *at* is sometimes followed by an '-ing' clause.

We cooked them so well they were burnt and we couldn't eat them and we threw them out to the hens and our mothers <u>grumbled</u> at wasting good food.

In the case of *protest,* the preposition *at* is occasionally followed by a noun group and an '-ing' clause. This pattern is **V *at* n -ing**.

It is understandable that many women <u>have protested</u> at money being spent on sex offenders.

carp *2*	exclaim	laugh *2*	rant *1*
cavil	fume *2*	protest *1*	scoff *1*
cluck *3*	grumble *1*	rage *3*	sneer
coo *2*	hint *2*	rail *5*	snipe *1*
hammer away	lash out *2*		
hit out *2*	strike out *2*		

II.6 THE 'REJOICE' GROUP

These verbs are concerned with having a particular feeling in reaction to something, or expressing this feeling.

He <u>chuckled</u> at my expression of dismay.

Science fiction fans in Britain <u>have been rejoicing</u> at the return of 'Thunderbirds' to their TVs.

What would Sarah do to her then? She <u>shuddered</u> at the thought and hurriedly put the problem away in the back of her mind.

With many of these verbs, especially *bridle, bristle, chafe,* and *rejoice,* the preposition *at* is sometimes followed by an '-ing' clause.

Elsewhere parents <u>chafe</u> at paying school fees and would rather see their children start earning as soon as possible.

blanch *1,2*	despair *2*	marvel *1*	smart *6*
boggle	drool *1*	quail *2*	smirk
bridle *2*	exult	rage *3*	snicker
bristle *5*	fume *2*	recoil *2*	(not) sniff *4 (usu passive)*
cackle	grieve *1*	rejoice *1*	snigger
chafe *2*	grimace	salivate *2*	thrill *2*
chuckle	guffaw *2*	seethe *1*	wince
cringe	laugh *1*	shudder *1*	wonder *2*

II.7 THE 'BALK' AND 'JUMP' GROUP

These verbs are concerned with being willing or unwilling to do something.

To our surprise we were told that as they were about to change the display we could buy it for £500. Naturally, we <u>jumped</u> at the chance.

In the case of *balk* and *jib,* the preposition *at* is sometimes followed by an '-ing' clause.

The prospect of higher taxes will make employers <u>balk</u> at hiring workers and consumers will be reluctant to spend.

balk	jump *9*
jib *2*	leap *7*

II.8 THE 'PROD' AND 'PULL' GROUP

These verbs are concerned with touching something. This includes:

- hitting something or trying to hit it
- grasping something or trying to grasp it
- pulling something

*Graham **clawed** at the chain as it dug into his neck but he could make no impression on Lemmer's stranglehold.*

*I **knocked** at the front door.*

*Her announcement was intended to make a forceful impact but she was totally unprepared when Ricky immediately **lashed out** at her with his fists.*

*Cathy **was prodding** at a boiled egg, staring into space.*

*'Maria?' he said again and **pulled** at her wrist.*

beat *2*	hammer *3*	prod *1*	tap *2*
claw *4*	jab *1*	pull *1*	tear *2.6*
clutch *1*	knock *1*	slash *2*	thrash *4*
dab *1*	lap *5*	snatch *1*	tug *1*
grab *2,6*	paw *3,4*	stab *2*	yank
grasp *1*	pluck *VP*	swing *5*	
hack *1*	poke *VP*	swipe *1*	
hack away ▷*1*	lash out *1*		
hit out *1*	strike out *2*		

II.9 THE 'CHEW' GROUP

These verbs are concerned with biting or consuming something. We include here *puff*, which is concerned with smoking.

*He **chewed** at the end of his pencil, thinking out the next problem.*

*It was winter and the sparrows **were pecking** at whatever they could find under the trees.*

*The men **puffed** at their cigars.*

*He **sipped** at his coffee and spread butter and marmalade on a roll.*

chew *1*	nip *2*	puff *1*	suck *1*
gnaw *1,2*	peck *1*	sip *1*	
nibble *1,2,3*	pick *VP*	snap *6*	
munch away	nibble away ▷*3*		

II.10 THE 'EAT AWAY' GROUP

These verbs are concerned with gradually reducing or weakening something.

*They just **have to chip away** at some of the prosecution's evidence.*

*Enzymes begin to **eat away** at the cells.*

chip away *VPP1,2*	nibble away ▷*4*
eat away	whittle away

II.11 THE 'SHOOT' GROUP

These verbs are concerned with attacking someone in some way. This includes:

- sending something towards someone e.g. *shoot, spit*
- moving towards someone e.g. *rush*

We also include here *strike*, which indicates that something is attacked in a non-physical way.

> *Official sources said a police patrol **was fired** at by some people from inside a place of worship.*
> *Now Chuck, armed with a wrench, jumped down from the truck, and **rushed** at Hans.*
> *The soldiers **were shooting** at anything that moved now.*
> *Such a policy **strikes** at the very heart of the aircraft industry.*

aim *5*	fly *VP*	shoot *2,9*	strike *9*
come *VP*	gob *3*	snipe *2*	
fire *2.2*	rush *9*	spit *2*	

II.12 THE 'HIT BACK' GROUP

These verbs are concerned with retaliating. The prepositional phrase indicates who the retaliation is against.

> *Okay, I guess I wanted to **get back** at Junior for what he did to you, too.*

get back *4*	hit back *2*	strike back

II.13 THE 'WORK' GROUP

These verbs are concerned with working. The prepositional phrase indicates what the work is concerned with.

> *Not surprisingly in a large organisation, some scientists **beaver away** at what are, as far as the company is concerned, even quirkier projects.*

In the case of *work*, the preposition *at* is sometimes followed by an '-ing' clause.

> *There is no magic cure. It's up to you. You just **have to work** at breaking the habit.*

toil *1*	work *5*	
beaver away	toil away ▷*1*	work away

II.14 THE 'SELL' GROUP

These verbs are used when indicating the price that is paid for something.

> *Tickets **were selling** at twice their face value.*

retail *3*	sell *3*

II.15 VERBS WITH OTHER MEANINGS

There are a number of other verbs which have this structure.

> *If and when they decide to reconsider the situation they will obtain your views before **arriving** at any decision as to cessation of operations.*
> *So we looked in the back of Melody Maker and the advert for Von's studio was the one that **jumped out** at us.*

In the case of *aim*, *connive*, and *excel*, the preposition *at* is sometimes followed by an '-ing' clause.

> *The Government **must aim** at getting Britain back to work.*
> *Hayloft Woodwork make anything their customers want and **excel** at finding solutions to difficult problems.*

In the case of *guess*, the preposition *at* is sometimes followed by a wh-clause.

*From a distance, Mark had no way of **guessing** **at what they were saying***.

aim *1*	excel	niggle *1,2*	sniff *2*
arrive *6*	guess *1*	point *14*	
connive *2*	nag *2*	rush *6*	
jump out	leap out		

Structure information: Verb with prepositional Object

a) The prepositional phrase is the prepositional Object.

b) This structure has a passive, with the pattern **be V-ed *at***. However, not all verbs with this structure are used in the passive. The following verbs are the ones which are most frequently passive.

fire *2.2*	look *1.2,3,7,10*	sneer	wonder *2*
guess *1*	marvel *1*	sniff *4*	work *5*
hint *2*	scoff *1*	stare *1*	
laugh *2*	shoot *2*	swear *1*	

Sniff occurs in the passive in the expression *not to be sniffed at*, and *wonder* in the expression *not to be wondered at*.

*The rewards for those who reach the chief executive's office are **not** to **be sniffed** **at***.

c) Phrasal verb patterns are the same except that there is a particle, P, which comes after the verb. The passive pattern, **be V-ed P *at***, does not often occur.

Other structures

With three verbs, the prepositional phrase is an Adjunct. Only one noun, or a very restricted range of nouns, can occur in the prepositional phrase.

*He was wearing a grey cotton jacket and a shirt which **was fraying** **at the collar***.

*Marie would cook a meal for them and Jean **would wait** **at table***.

fray *1 (at the edges/collar/cuffs)*	froth *3 (at the mouth)*	wait *7 (at table)*

Other related patterns

V *at* n prep/adv

The verb is followed by a prepositional phrase beginning with *at*, which is followed by another prepositional phrase or an adverb indicating manner. Two senses of the verb *look* have this pattern.

*Miss Leon was driving very slowly. McKee **looked** **at her impatiently***.

Look** **at it from their point of view.

look *1.4,8*

V *at* n to-inf

The verb is followed by a prepositional phrase beginning with *at*, which is followed by a to-infinitive clause. The phrasal verb pattern is **V P *at* n to-inf**.

Verbs with this pattern are concerned with loudly, angrily, or forcefully telling someone to do something. The prepositional phrase indicates the hearer.

They were firing. I __screamed__ at them to stop.
I __shouted__ at her to run.

bark 2	hiss 3	screech 2	yell 1
bawl 1	holler	shout 1	
bellow 1	scream 2	snap 4	
go on 8	keep on VPP		

V *at* n with quote

See page 118.

---

14   V *between* pl-n

The verb is followed by a prepositional phrase which consists of the preposition *between* and a **plural noun group**.

This pattern has one structure:

▶ Verb with prepositional Object
She __alternated__ between anger and depression.

V *between* pl-n

	Verb group	*between*	plural noun group
Subject	**Verb**		**prepositional Object**
Many customers	cannot distinguish	between	psychiatrists and other psychotherapists.
I	liaise	between	these groups.

Verbs with this pattern belong to the following meaning groups:

1   THE 'ARBITRATE' GROUP
2   THE 'DIFFERENTIATE' GROUP
3   THE 'ALTERNATE' GROUP
4   THE 'RANGE' GROUP
5   VERBS WITH OTHER MEANINGS

1 THE 'ARBITRATE' GROUP

These verbs are concerned with sorting out or helping the relationship between two people or groups.

Any community contains conflicting interests within it and it is the politician's job to __arbitrate__ between them.
I've been instructed to __liaise__ between my chief and the Branch and to assist where I can.

adjudicate	liaise
arbitrate	mediate *1*

2 THE 'DIFFERENTIATE' GROUP

These verbs are concerned with recognizing the difference between two or more things.

*It's difficult to **differentiate** between chemical weapons and chemicals for peaceful industrial use.*

differentiate *1*	discriminate *1*	distinguish *1*

3 THE 'ALTERNATE' GROUP

These verbs are concerned with doing, being, or using two things alternately.

*The weather **alternated** between warm sunshine and chilling showers that left the moorland climbs streaming with water.*

*His canvassing had found many Conservative voters **wavering** between defection and abstention.*

alternate *1*	oscillate *3*	waver *1*
flit *2*	vacillate	

4 THE 'RANGE' GROUP

These verbs indicate that something has a range of values. The noun group following the preposition is always two co-ordinated amounts, indicating a minimum and a maximum value. This pattern is **V** *between* **pl-amount**.

*Prices **range** between £30 and £50.*

*Estimates of its population **varied** between 300 and 500.*

hover *4*	range *4*
oscillate *2*	vary *1*

5 VERBS WITH OTHER MEANINGS

There are two other verbs which have this pattern.

*A senior official of the World Wildlife Fund said that world leaders **do not have to choose** between economic growth and protecting the environment.*

*Now based in London, she and her French husband **commute** between London and Paris while their son is at Westminster public school.*

choose *1*	commute *1*

Structure information

a) The prepositional phrase is the prepositional Object.

b) This structure has no passive.

15 V *by* amount

The verb is followed by a prepositional phrase which consists of the preposition *by* and a noun group indicating an amount.

This pattern has one structure:

▶ Verb with Adjunct
Their incomes <u>have dropped</u> by 30 per cent.

V *by* amount

	Verb group	*by*	amount
Subject	Verb		Adjunct
The overall number of jobs	decreased	by	1000.
The Reds	were leading	by	two runs.

Phrasal verbs: V P *by* amount

	Verb group	Particle	*by*	amount
Subject	Verb			Adjunct
Farm production	went	down	by	4.2 per cent.

Verbs with this pattern belong to the following meaning groups:

1 THE 'INCREASE' AND 'DECREASE' GROUP
2 THE 'WIN' AND 'LOSE' GROUP
3 THE 'OVERRUN' GROUP

1 THE 'INCREASE' AND 'DECREASE' GROUP

These verbs indicate that a quantity or level increases or decreases. The prepositional phrase indicates the size of the increase or decrease.

*The price of petrol at Shell garages <u>**is coming down**</u> by more than four pence a gallon.*

*The number of women killing men <u>**has decreased**</u> by 25 per cent in the last few years.*

*Sales <u>**went up**</u> by 0.1 per cent last month as consumers began to shop early for Christmas.*

*They expect the number of people emigrating this year to <u>**increase**</u> by nearly 50 per cent.*

climb 4	drop 1	rise 9	soar 1
decline 1	fall 5	shrink 2	surge 2
decrease 1	increase 1	sink 7	swell 1
depreciate	jump 6	slide 4	tumble 2
dip 7	plummet	slip 7	widen 4
dive 7	plunge 5	slump 1	
come down 1	go up 1		
go down 1	shoot up 1		

2 THE 'WIN' AND 'LOSE' GROUP

These verbs are concerned with winning and losing. The prepositional phrase indicates the difference between the score of the winner or loser and their competitor, or the nearest competitor.

*The government **lost** by one vote.*
*In the event, Cambridge **won** by fifteen points.*

lead *1.4*   lose *1*   win *1*

3 THE 'OVERRUN' GROUP

These verbs indicate that an amount that was set is exceeded. The prepositional phrase indicates how much extra time or money is involved.

*The meeting, which **overran** by more than an hour, was dominated by the crisis besetting the European exchange rate mechanism.*

*An accounting mix-up has allowed programme makers to **overspend** by about £50 million so far this year.*

overrun *3*   overspend *1*

Structure information

a) The prepositional phrase is an Adjunct.

b) This pattern has no passive.

c) The phrasal verb pattern is the same, except that there is a particle, P, which comes after the verb.

Other related patterns

V *by* amount prep

The verb is followed by a prepositional phrase which consists of *by* and a noun group indicating an amount. This is followed by another prepositional phrase.

*They **voted** by 80 per cent in favour of privatisation.*

vote *4*

V *by* amount to-inf

The verb is followed by a prepositional phrase which consists of *by* and a noun group indicating an amount. This is followed by a to-infinitive clause.

*The national committee **has voted** by seventeen to five to wind up the party.*

vote *4*

16   V *by* -ing

The verb is followed by a prepositional phrase which consists of the preposition *by* and an '-ing' clause.

This pattern has one structure:

▶ Verb with Adjunct
They <u>responded</u> by ordering him to go home.

V *by* -ing

	Verb group	*by*	-ing clause
Subject	**Verb**		**Adjunct**
She	began	by	telling me what the exhibition was about.
The fans	retaliated	by	pelting them with plastic chairs.

Phrasal verbs: V P *by* -ing

	Verb group	Particle	*by*	-ing clause
Subject	**Verb**			**Adjunct**
All of them	started	out	by	defying a long-established authority.

Verbs with this pattern belong to the following meaning groups:

1 THE 'START' AND 'FINISH' GROUP
2 THE 'RECIPROCATE' GROUP
3 VERBS WITH OTHER MEANINGS

1 THE 'START' AND 'FINISH' GROUP

These verbs are concerned with starting or finishing. The prepositional phrase indicates what someone does at the beginning or end of a task, session, or period of time.

*The Chairman **finished** by thanking us and reminding us that the decision of his committee on the listing of a company was final.*

***Start** by listing randomly all the ideas you want to include.*

*She **started off** by breeding budgerigars and cockatiels, and then gradually progressed to the larger parrots and parrot-like birds.*

begin *3*	**end** *6,18*	**open** *21*
close *1.7*	**finish** *4*	**start** *3*
finish off *4*	**start off** *1*	
finish up *4*	**start out** *2*	

2 THE 'RECIPROCATE' GROUP

These verbs are concerned with responding to something that has been done, or compensating for it. The prepositional phrase indicates what someone does in response or as compensation.

This is a productive use: many other verbs which involve a response to an action or situation sometimes have this pattern. The verbs listed here are the ones which are most frequently used in this way.

*In hot, dry and windy weather, water evaporates from the leaves of plants which in turn **compensate** by taking more up through their roots.*

*On Thursday he **will reciprocate** by entertaining the Queen to a fabulous banquet at the hotel.*

175

atone	counter 2,4	reciprocate	respond 1,2
compensate 2,4	react 1	reply 4	retaliate

3 VERBS WITH OTHER MEANINGS

There are two verbs which have the pattern **V by -ing/n**. The verb *live* is followed by *by* and an '-ing' clause or noun group which indicates a means by which someone gets the money or food that they need to live. The verb *profit* is followed by *by* and an '-ing' clause or noun group which indicates the source of profit or benefit for someone.

> *Many people were forced to __live__ by their wits or to tramp about the country looking for work.*
> *Their aim is to __profit__ by buying replacement shares later at a lower price.*

live 1.5	profit 2,3

Structure information

a) The prepositional phrase is an Adjunct.

b) This structure has no passive.

c) The phrasal verb pattern is the same except that there is a particle, P, which comes after the verb.

Other related patterns

V *by* n

See meaning group 3 above.

---

17 V *for* n

The verb is followed by a prepositional phrase which consists of *for* and a noun group. With some verbs, the preposition is sometimes followed by an '-ing' clause. The passive pattern is **be V-ed for**.

This pattern has two structures:

▶ Structure I: Verb with prepositional Complement
  She __could pass__ for a much younger woman.
▶ Structure II: Verb with prepositional Object
  He __longed__ for death.

Structure I: Verb with prepositional Complement

V *for* n

	Verb group	for	noun group
Subject	Verb		prepositional Complement
She	could pass	for	a man.
A shelf	served	for	a desk.

Verbs with this structure are concerned with seeming to be something or functioning as something. These verbs are **link verbs** (see Chapter 5).

Is this what __passes__ for wit among college students these days?

We were close to a small deserted chateau which it was thought __would serve__ for a temporary prison.

pass 20	serve 3

In the case of *pass*, the preposition *for* is sometimes followed by an adjective or by a number indicating an age. These patterns are **V *for* adj** and **V *for* num**.

The six-hour long drama focuses in the main on her own personal story – the trials and tribulations of a mixed-race woman who __could pass__ for White.

Before I was 50 I looked absurdly young, __could pass__ for 25.

Structure information: Verb with prepositional Complement

a) The prepositional phrase is the prepositional Complement.

b) This structure has no passive.

Structure II: Verb with prepositional Object

Active voice: V *for* n/-ing

	Verb group	*for*	noun group/-ing clause
Subject	Verb		prepositional Object
I	apologized	for	wasting his time.
I	longed	for	a sister.
The new president	opted	for	the toughest plan.
She	works	for	the Medical Research Council.

Passive voice: *be* V-ed *for*

	Verb group	*for*	
Subject	Verb	Preposition	Adjunct (optional)
Most Alzheimer's victims	are cared	for	by their spouses.
The tests	are paid	for	by the National Health Service.

Phrasal verbs: V P *for* n

	Verb group	Particle	*for*	noun group
Subject	Verb			Adjunct
	Look	out	for	original Fifties party dresses.
His deputy	had to stand	in	for	him.

Verbs with this structure belong to the following meaning groups:

Chapter 2: Simple Patterns with Prepositions and Adverbs

II.1 THE 'ASK' GROUP

These verbs are concerned with trying to get something. This includes:

- asking for something
- trying to get a job or position e.g. *audition, stand*
- taking action in order to obtain something

We also include here the verb *gasp*, as in *gasping for breath*.

*'No payment was offered and none **was asked** for,'* he says.

*You know what to do. And don't let up till they**'re begging** for mercy.*

*Then he paid tribute to all those who**'d campaigned** for his release.*

*During the war the first floor was occupied by the Ministry of Food and it was there that we all **had to queue up** for our ration books.*

*So fill in the coupon and **send off** for your stencils now.*

*Michel Rocard first **stood** for the presidency in 1969.*

*The episode also holds important lessons for investment bankers **touting** for business in emerging markets.*

advertise *2*	claim *9*	pitch *VP*	send *VP1,2*
agitate *1*	clamour *1*	plead *1*	shout *1*
aim *1*	crusade *2*	ply *3*	stand *19*
angle *5*	demonstrate *3*	pray *1*	strike *2*
appeal *1*	fight *2*	press *4*	strive
apply *1*	file *5*	push *7*	subscribe *4*
ask *4,5*	fish *3,5*	queue *3*	tender *2.2*
audition *2*	gasp *2*	register *2*	tout *2*
bay *6*	holler	ring *1.1,4*	try *3*
beg *1,2*	howl *2*	roar *4*	wail *1*
bid *1.3,4*	lobby *1*	run *8*	wish *5*
call *VP2*	negotiate *1*	scrabble *2*	
campaign *2*	panhandle *2*	scream *2*	
canvass *1*	petition *3*	scrounge	
hold out *2*	queue up ▷*3*	send off *VPP*	stick out *VPP*
put in *2*	send away *VPP*	send out *VPP*	try out *VPP*

II.2 THE 'COMPETE' GROUP

These verbs are concerned with competing for something: that is, two or more people or groups of people are trying to get the same thing. These are **reciprocal verbs** (see Chapter 6) and have a plural Subject with this pattern.

*This means that schools and universities **have to compete** for pupils.*

*You seem to be the centre of attraction this week, with suitors **vying** for your attention.*

compete *1,2,3*	jostle *2*	vie
contend *3*	struggle *4*	
jockey *2*	tussle *2*	

These verbs also have the patterns **V *with* n *for* n** and **V *for* n *with* n** (see page 471).

II.3 THE 'WORK' GROUP

These verbs are concerned with doing something for someone. This includes:

- working for someone
- doing something on someone's behalf e.g. *act, speak*

We also include here *sign*, which indicates that someone agrees to work for someone.

This is a productive use: any verb which involves doing something for someone can be used with this pattern. For example, you can <u>*cook*</u> *for someone* or <u>*sing*</u> *for someone*. The verbs listed here are the ones which are most frequently used in this way.

> *The lawyer who **acted** for some of the detainees is Mr Peter Cathcart.*
> *I**'m canvassing** for the Conservative Party.*
> *I**'m** always **having to cover up** for her and lie to my father.*
> *Billy Davies, the mid-field player who joined Leicester City from St Mirren in the summer, is to **sign** for the Scottish Premier Division side Dunfermline.*
> *In 1907, the year after Picasso's famous Cubist portrait of Gertrude Stein, Felix Vallotton approached her to ask if she **would sit** for him.*
> *He **works** for a local heavy engineering firm.*

In the case of *fend*, the noun group following the preposition is always a reflexive pronoun. This pattern is **V *for* pron-refl**.

> *More and more young children were left to **fend** for themselves after school.*

act *6*	collect *6*	play *2,11*	stump *5*
babysit	cover *19*	sign *7*	work *1*
caddie *2*	fend	sit *4*	write *3*
canvass *1*	fight *4*	slave *3*	
char *2*	guest *4*	speak *3*	
clerk *3*	model *11*	spy *3*	
cover up *2*			

II.4 THE 'DEPUTIZE' GROUP

These verbs are concerned with replacing someone who is absent and performing their duties.

> *Suppose your boss is going to be away from the office and you **have to deputise** for her.*
> *Then someone rang and asked if I **would stand in** for Frank Bough and do the Sunday cricket on BBC2.*

cover *20*	deputize	substitute *1*
fill in *4*	stand in	

II.5 THE 'VOLUNTEER' GROUP

These verbs are concerned with offering or arranging to do something, or going somewhere to do something. The prepositional phrase indicates the activity or work involved.

He **hasn't shown up** for work. He hasn't been at his apartment. No one has heard from him.

She later **signed up** for an arts/law course at Queensland University of Technology.

On his return to England in 1950, he **volunteered** for service with the Parachute Regiment and joined the 2nd Battalion as a company commander.

enrol	report 8	volunteer 3
report back 2	sign on VPP	turn out 8
show up ▷12	sign up	

II.6 THE 'ARGUE' GROUP

These verbs are concerned with supporting or defending someone or something.

Most ministers **argued** for a strengthening of ties between the two institutions.

The president of Chile said he **would intercede** for me with Castro.

Sometimes this means learning to **stand up** for yourself and your own needs by saying no to family and friends after a lifetime of saying yes.

In the case of argue and vote, the preposition for is sometimes followed by an '-ing' clause.

The poll showed 42 per cent **would vote** for ratifying the treaty, with 32 per cent against.

argue 2	demonstrate 3	pray 1	testify 1
declare VP	intercede	root VP	vote 5
speak up 1	stand up VPP	stick up VPP	

II.7 THE 'OPT' GROUP

These verbs are concerned with choosing.

The other big question is whether to **go** for a fixed rate mortgage.

None of the children **has opted** for farming as a career.

The preposition for is sometimes followed by an '-ing' clause.

I wanted to be a dancer but my father said I couldn't possibly do that, so instead I **settled** for getting married and having children.

go VP1	plump 3
opt	settle VP

II.8 THE 'YEARN' GROUP

These verbs are concerned with wanting something.

I**'m dying** for a breath of fresh air. I've been two whole days indoors.

It's probably the best that **can be hoped** for in the circumstances.

People **weren't** exactly **queuing up** for the job when Andy Roxburgh was appointed in 1986.

I **yearned** for something new.

ache 3	hope 1,2	lust VP	thirst 4
crave	hunger 4	pine 3	wish 2,6
be dying 8	itch 2	pray 2	yearn
hanker	long	be spoiling VP	
queue up			

II.9 THE 'CARE' GROUP

These verbs are concerned with feeling an emotion. The prepositional phrase indicates who or what the emotion relates to.

*He **did not care** for the place*.

*He fled on Friday, saying he **feared** for his life*.

*But, I'll tell you this much, Doug: I **feel** for people who don't know Christ, because they don't know what they're missing*.

*Meanwhile, several houses away, widows and bereaved mothers **mourned** for loved ones who would never come home*.

care *2,7*	feel *VP2*	pine *2*
(not) care *5*	grieve *1*	
fear *6*	mourn *1,2*	

II.10 THE 'COMPENSATE' GROUP

These verbs are concerned with compensating for or balancing an action or situation in some way. We include here *claim*, which indicates that someone asks for compensation.

*You **won't be able to claim** for damage to your car if you have third-party cover only*.

*The government has always said that it will raise salaries to try to **compensate** for the price increases*.

With all these verbs except *retaliate*, the preposition *for* is sometimes followed by an '-ing' clause.

*I **apologized** for disturbing him and held out the cassette. 'I thought you ought to have this.'*

answer *VP1,2*	atone	compensate *2,3,4*	pay *10*
apologize	claim *9*	expiate	retaliate
make up *VPP*			

II.11 THE 'SEARCH' GROUP

These verbs are concerned with looking for something or being alert for something.

*They continued to argue that with advances in technology it might be possible to **drill** for oil without causing environmental damage*.

*She leaned and **groped** for the lamp switch beside the bed*.

*Always **look** for other ways of managing difficult situations*.

*Meanwhile, the band **are searching** for an appropriate venue for a special festive show*.

***Watch out** for pests and disease*.

check *1*	hunt *1,2,3*	scout *3*
dig *1*	listen *2*	scrabble *1*
divine *5*	look *1.5,6*	scramble *3*
dowse	pan *5*	screen *6*
drill *3*	probe *1*	search *1*
explore *3*	prospect *4*	shop *2*
feel *VP1*	be questing	trawl *2*
forage *1,2*	rummage *1*	watch *VP*
fumble *1,2*	scan *3*	
grope *1,3*	scavenge	
cast around/about *VPP*	rummage about	shop around
ferret around/about	rummage around/round	watch out *VPP*
listen out ▷2	scout around/round	
look out *VPP1*	scrabble around/about ▷1	

If a verb in the list above also has the pattern **V prep** or **V prep/adv**, these patterns can be combined, with the prepositional phrase beginning with *for* coming either after or before the other prepositional phrase or the adverb.

> I **rummage** *in my suitcase* **for** *a tie.*

> I**'ve been looking** **for** *you everywhere.*

II.12 THE 'PREPARE' GROUP

These verbs are concerned with preparing for something, for example an exam or a sports event.

> *Right now, the Army **is gearing up** for a recruitment drive in Bay Area high schools from January through April.*

> *The crew of the space shuttle Atlantis **is preparing** for the ride back to Earth tomorrow.*

> *Sally from Gloucester wants to say hullo to everybody who**'s revising** for their geography exam in Swansea on Friday.*

> *McCullough, aged 22, who gave up his job to **train** for the Olympics, will fight Joel Casamayor.*

cram *4*	read *14*	revise *4*	swot *1*
prepare *2*	rehearse *1*	study *1*	train *2.3*
gear up			

II.13 THE 'PAY' GROUP

These verbs are concerned with paying for something. We include here *save* and *save up*, which are concerned with accumulating money to pay for something.

> *They want us to **pay** for services we don't use.*

> *It took me 15 years to **save up** for my bike and now I am a happy man.*

> *And to make matters worse, new car safety laws could mean drivers **having to shell out** for complete new windscreens.*

overpay	pay *1,5*	save *2*
cough up	pony up	shell out
fork out	save up ▷*2*	

II.14 THE 'PLAN' GROUP

These verbs are concerned with making plans or taking things into account. The prepositional phrase indicates a factor in a plan or analysis, or something that occurs or is provided as the result of a plan.

> *The study shows that, after meteorological factors **are allowed** for, the distribution of certain sicknesses among trees 'was uniquely attributable to pollution'.*

> *He **hadn't bargained** for the intervention of the stock exchange.*

> *They **are planning** for growth rather than decline.*

allow *VP*	bargain *VP*	cater *2*	plan *2*
arrange *3*	budget *VP*	legislate	provide *VP2,3*

II.15 THE 'STOP' GROUP

These verbs are concerned with stopping doing something for a period of time. The prepositional phrase indicates what takes place in the meantime or how long the break is.

> *The United States Senate **has adjourned** for the year after passing three major bills in its final hours.*

*It will be published later this month before MPs **break up** for the summer recess*.
*Let's **stop** for lunch now*.

adjourn	pause *1*	stop *1,10*
break *13*	recess *2*	
break up *5*		

II.16 THE 'WAIT' GROUP

These verbs are concerned with waiting for someone or something.

*If he's there, bring him in. And if he's not there yet, then stick around and **wait** for him*.
*She washes his clothes and, when he's late, she **waits up** for him in the kitchen*.

wait *1,3*	
stand by *1*	wait in
wait around	wait up *1*

II.17 THE 'HEAD' GROUP

These verbs are concerned with moving, travelling, or leaving. The prepositional phrase indicates the person's destination.

*He spun around and **headed** for the door*.
*My wife and I **are leaving** for Mexico next month*.

depart *1*	leave *1*	run *1*
head *16,17*	make *VP1*	scramble *2*

II.18 THE 'LAST' GROUP

These verbs are used when indicating the duration or size of something. The noun group following the preposition *for* is always an **amount**. This pattern is **V *for* amount**.

This is a productive use: any verb indicating a continuing activity can be used with this pattern. For example, you can *talk for half an hour* or *drive for days*. The verbs listed here are the ones which are most frequently used in this way.

*The French coastline **extends** for some 5500 km and constitutes a highly coveted and pressurized environment*.
*This effect **can last** for several days after the treatment session*.

endure *2*	last *11,12*	stretch *1*
extend *1*	run *33*	

II.19 THE 'SELL' GROUP

These verbs are used when indicating the price that is paid for something. The noun group following the preposition *for* is always an **amount**. This pattern is **V *for* amount**.

*Fresh-picked morel mushrooms **can go** for up to 25 dollars a pound*.
*His paintings **sell** for between £5000 and £12000*.

go *1.13*	retail *3*	sell *3*

II.20 VERBS WITH OTHER MEANINGS

There are a number of other verbs which have this structure.

*That dream came true when the house **came up** **for sale** and the couple realised they could just about afford it.*

*For some weeks the baby **was cared** for in the Convent of St Sulpice.*

*Thus equipped, I again **entered** for the annual English Festival of Spoken Poetry competition.*

*Come on, Frank, let's **go** for a walk.*

In the case of *speak*, the noun group following the preposition is always a reflexive pronoun. This pattern is **V for pron-refl**.

*His record **speaks** for itself. He is a tremendous manager and I have found him to be a charming man.*

In the case of *count*, the noun group following the preposition is always an **amount**. This pattern is **V for amount**.

*What about us? **Do** our feelings **count** for nothing?*

care 3	dress 6	insure 1	speak 8
cater 1,3	enter 6	live 1.3	
count 6	go 3.3	qualify 2,4	
come through 4	come up 5		

Structure information

a) The prepositional phrase is the prepositional Object.

b) This structure has a passive, with the pattern **be V-ed for**. However, not all verbs with this structure are used in the passive. The following verbs are the ones which are most frequently passive.

aim 1	bid 3,4	compete 1,2	pray 1
allow VP	budget VP	fight 2	send VP1
apply 1	care 3	hope 1,2	vote 5
ask 4,5	cater 1,3	look 1.5,6	
atone	compensate 2,3,4	pay 1,5	

c) Phrasal verb patterns are the same except that there is a particle, P, which comes after the verb. The passive pattern is **be V-ed P for**, but it does not often occur.

Other related patterns

V *for* adj

See Structure I above.

V *for* num

See Structure I above.

V *for* n prep/adv

See meaning group II.11 above.

V *for* n to-inf

The verb is followed by a prepositional phrase beginning with *for*, and a to-infinitive clause. The phrasal verb pattern is **V P *for* n to-inf**.

Verbs with this pattern belong to the following meaning groups:

1 THE 'ASK' GROUP
2 THE 'LONG' GROUP
3 THE 'WAIT' GROUP
4 THE 'ARRANGE' GROUP

1 THE 'ASK' GROUP

These verbs are concerned with asking for something to be done or to happen. We include here *motion* and *gesture*, which indicate that someone communicates a request by using a gesture.

*She got up from her desk and **motioned** for Wade to follow her.*

*They **are pressing** for the government to implement the electoral promises of job creation and land reform as a first priority.*

In the case of *ask* and *campaign*, the to-infinitive is usually passive.

*The Minister responsible for Indian Affairs in Quebec **has** now **asked** for the plans to be delayed until the matter is settled.*

agitate *1*	campaign *2*	petition *3*	push *7*
appeal *1*	gesture *3*	plead *1*	shout *1*
ask *4*	holler	pray *1*	
call *VP2*	motion *4*	press *4*	

2 THE 'LONG' GROUP

These verbs are concerned with wanting something to happen or be done.

*All the women **will be dying** for you to make a mistake.*

*He **longed** for the winter to be over.*

be dying *8*	pray *2*
long *4.0*	yearn

3 THE 'WAIT' GROUP

These verbs are concerned with waiting for something to happen.

*I don't want to sit around **waiting** for the phone to ring.*

wait *1*
wait around

4 THE 'ARRANGE' GROUP

These verbs are concerned with making arrangements so that something happens or is done.

*'What about our baggage?' 'Don't worry. I'**ll arrange** for it to be sent direct to the property when it is unloaded.'*

> arrange *2,3*   fix *3*

V *for* n *with* n

See Chapter 6.

V *with* n *for* n

See Chapter 6.

V prep/adv *for* n

See meaning group II.11 above.

---

18   V *from* n

The verb is followed by a prepositional phrase which consists of *from* and a noun group. With some verbs, the preposition is sometimes followed by an '-ing' clause. In Structure I, the preposition is followed by an '-ing' form.

This pattern has three structures:

▶ Structure I: Verbs in phase
  He __refrained__ from making any comment.
▶ Structure II: Verb with prepositional Object
  We __will__ all __benefit__ from this change.
▶ Structure III: Verb with Adjunct
  The train __emerged__ from the tunnel.

Structure I: Verbs in phase

	Verb group	*from*	-ing	
Subject	Verb			Completive
Finney	does not flinch	from	portraying	the cruelty of this period.
He	has not shrunk	from	facing	the challenges.

These verbs are concerned with not doing something.

> *The incident occurred in the late Seventies, so I __shall refrain__ from naming the school involved.*
> *Sometimes we __shrink__ from making decisions, not out of fear but from sheer confusion.*
> *So far police and riot troops __have shied away__ from using physical force to break the strikers.*

> abstain *1*   forbear   refrain *1*   shirk
> desist   keep *5*   retire *1,2*   shrink *4*
> flinch *2*   recoil *2*   retreat *3*   withdraw *5*
>
> shy away *VPP*

When the preposition is followed by a noun group, these verbs have Structure II (see meaning group II.8).

Structure information: Verbs in phase

a) The verb is followed by the preposition *from* and the '-ing' form of another verb. The verbs are **in phase**, and together form a **complex verb group**. This means that the actions or states expressed by the two verbs cannot be separated from each other. For example, if you *refrain from saying* something, the *refraining* and the *not saying* are not two processes, but one.

The complex verb group is followed by a group, phrase, or clause which completes the pattern of the second verb. In the structure table above, this is called a **Completive**. For example, if the second verb is normally followed by a noun group, then the Completive of the complex verb group will be a noun group.

b) This structure has no passive.

c) There is only one phrasal verb with this structure, *shy away*. The pattern is **V P *from* -ing**.

Structure II: Verb with prepositional Object

V *from* n/-ing

	Verb group	*from*	noun group/-ing clause
Subject	**Verb**		**prepositional Object**
She	could borrow	from	her family.
Fitness	comes	from	working against gravity.
Much of the instability	stems	from	the economic effects of the war.

Phrasal verbs: V P *from* n

	Verb group	Particle	*from*	noun group
Subject	**Verb**			**prepositional Object**
He	shied	away	from	violence.
They	stand	out	from	the crowd.

Verbs with this structure belong to the following meaning groups:

II.1 THE 'RESULT' GROUP
II.2 THE 'DERIVE' GROUP
II.3 THE 'BORROW' GROUP
II.4 THE 'DRINK' GROUP
II.5 THE 'BENEFIT' GROUP
II.6 THE 'SUFFER' AND 'RECOVER' GROUP
II.7 THE 'DIFFER' GROUP
II.8 THE 'ABSTAIN' AND 'WITHDRAW' GROUP
II.9 THE 'BACKTRACK' GROUP
II.10 THE 'DETRACT' GROUP
II.11 VERBS WITH OTHER MEANINGS

II.1 THE 'RESULT' GROUP

These verbs are concerned with resulting. The prepositional phrase indicates the cause of the thing or situation indicated by the Subject.

> *Alzheimer's is a complex disease and is probably unlikely to **result** from a defect in a single human gene.*

*I made that journey with increasing hate in my heart. The hatred **sprang** from fear*.

The preposition *from* is sometimes followed by an '-ing' clause.

*The major difficulty in putting your skills to work elsewhere is the inertia which **stems** from being bored all day*.

In the case of *arise*, *come*, and *result*, the preposition *from* is sometimes followed by a noun group and an '-ing' clause. This pattern is **V *from* n -ing**.

*All cultural innovation **comes** from cultures mixing*.

*Conflict **results** from A trying to grab something belonging to B*.

arise *2*	develop *1,2,6*	follow *6*	spring *7*
come *16*	flow *5*	result *3*	stem *1*

II.2 THE 'DERIVE' GROUP

These verbs are used to state the place of origin of a person or thing, or the source of something.

*She **comes** from Wiltshire and lives in London*.

*The term 'cannibalism' **derives** from the Spanish 'canibal', meaning 'savage'*.

come *15*	derive *2*	hail *5,6*

II.3 THE 'BORROW' GROUP

These verbs are concerned with getting something from a source. The thing that is obtained is not explicitly mentioned. We include here the verbs *extrapolate* and *generalize*, which indicate that someone derives a conclusion from a fact or set of facts.

*That's why it's so expensive to **borrow** from finance companies*.

***Don't generalize** from one example. It's bad science*.

*While he is happy to **import** from abroad, he regrets that European fruit growers show more enthusiasm for their heritage than their counterparts here*.

*In his very last lecture, he **quoted** from a famous medieval lament, where the poet expresses his shock and pain on the death of his prince*.

borrow *2*	crib *2*	generalize *1*	plagiarize
copy *3*	extrapolate	import *1*	quote *1*

II.4 THE 'DRINK' GROUP

These verbs are concerned with eating and drinking. The prepositional phrase indicates the container the food or drink is in.

*The mechanic **drank** from the bottle with enthusiasm*.

drink *1*	eat *1*	sip *1*

II.5 THE 'BENEFIT' GROUP

These verbs are concerned with getting a benefit of some kind. The prepositional phrase indicates what produces the benefit.

*Many areas of the world **would** actually **gain** from global warming*.

*We **should learn** from their experience and change to the type of system they have*.

The preposition *from* is often followed by an '-ing' clause.

*I'm sure our players **would benefit** from having fewer matches*.

benefit *3*	learn *4*
gain *2*	profit *2,3*

II.6 THE 'SUFFER' AND 'RECOVER' GROUP

These verbs are concerned with having or recovering from something such as an illness, shock, or disappointment.

*He **is** still **recuperating** from his recent operation and undertaking only essential duties*.

*He**'s been suffering** from a niggling shoulder injury*.

In the case of *recover, reel, smart*, and *bounce back*, the preposition *from* is sometimes followed by an '-ing' clause.

*Leeds never **recovered** from losing to Rangers*.

convalesce	recuperate	suffer *2,4*
die *1,2*	reel *4*	
recover *1,2,3*	smart *6*	
bounce back		

II.7 THE 'DIFFER' GROUP

These verbs are concerned with being or becoming different. In most cases, the Subject and the noun group following the preposition refer to different things. In the case of *evolve*, the Subject and the noun group following the preposition refer to the same thing at different stages of its development. The verbs *differ*, *diverge*, and *grow apart* are **reciprocal verbs** (see Chapter 6).

*The culture of the south **differs** from that of the north in many ways*.

*Mammals **evolved** from reptiles called cynodonts about 220 million years ago*.

*They**'re** now getting rich quick and **growing away** from the audience they once purported to represent*.

*Make your advertisement **stand out** from all the others by having it printed in bold type or put in a box*.

differ *1*	diverge *1,2*	evolve *1,2*
grow apart	stand out *2*	
grow away *VPP*	stick out *2*	

II.8 THE 'ABSTAIN' AND 'WITHDRAW' GROUP

These verbs are concerned with not doing something. This includes:

- not wanting to do something e.g. *flinch, shrink*
- stopping doing something or being involved in something e.g. *desist, withdraw*

*They **abstained** from meat because they believed that killing life injured the spirit within*.

*But he stressed he had no intention of **retiring** from politics yet*.

*He never **shrank** from a fight, and he actively sought new challenges*.

*A woman with her own income is no longer dependent. She **can walk away** from an impossible situation*.

*This hurtful allegation led him to **withdraw** from public life*.

abstain 1	forbear	retire 1,2	shrink 4
desist	recoil 2	retreat 3	withdraw 5
flinch 2	refrain 1	shirk	
shy away	stand aside 1	walk away	

See also Structure I above.

II.9 THE 'BACKTRACK' GROUP

These verbs are concerned with changing your plans, your position on something, or your way of doing something. We include here *digress*, which indicates that someone stops saying what they had planned to say and talks about something else.

*The committee **has backed away** from a plan to put a legal limit on credit card rates.*

*Lufthansa's decision to **backtrack** from the imposition of a new pay structure means that its staff will continue to enjoy among the highest salaries paid in the airline business.*

*Mr Gorbachev said that the party **would not deviate** from the course outlined in his radical programme document.*

*She **digressed** from her prepared speech to praise President Havel of Czechoslovakia.*

*We want to **get away** from the politics of outdated dogmatism and class confrontation.*

back-pedal 2	depart 2	digress
backtrack 1	deviate	waver 1
back away 1	get away 4	turn away 2
back off 2	pull back 1	

II.10 THE 'DETRACT' GROUP

These verbs indicate that something makes something else seem less good or impressive.

*It is important that written communications are well presented, as bad presentation **can detract** from your message.*

*The theory of Galileo and Newton has now been largely replaced by relativity and quantum theory, but this **does not take away** from their achievement.*

detract
take away VPP

II.11 VERBS WITH OTHER MEANINGS

There are a number of other verbs which have this structure.

*You **will** also **be able to choose** from a range of topics such as Business Language, Language in the Media, and Grammar.*

*You **haven't heard** from Mona, have you?*

*It was necessary to **step back** from the project and look at it as a whole.*

*Later today the British Prime Minister, Mr Major, begins his first visit to Washington since he **took over** from Mrs Thatcher.*

choose 1	dissent 2
date VP	hear 5,6
step back	take over 3,4

Structure information: Verb with prepositional Object

a) The prepositional phrase is the prepositional Object.

b) This structure has a passive with the pattern *be* **V-ed** *from*, but it does not often occur. The only verb that is frequently used in the passive is *hear 5*.

   *They **have not been heard** from since.*

c) The phrasal verb pattern is the same except that there is a particle, P, which comes after the verb.

Structure III: Verb with Adjunct

V *from* n

	Verb group	*from*	noun group	
Subject	**Verb**		**Adjunct**	**Adjunct (optional)**
He	escaped	from	prison	on Saturday.
Gales of laughter	issued	from	the classroom.	

Phrasal verbs: V P *from* n

	Verb group	Particle	*from*	noun group	
Subject	**Verb**			**Adjunct**	**Adjunct (optional)**
Spray	rose	up	from	the surface of the water.	
He	's run	away	from	home	twice.

Verbs with this structure are all concerned with leaving or coming from a place, group, thing, person, or position. The Subject can be animate or inanimate. We include here verbs such as *emanate* and *radiate* which indicate that a quality is strongly shown by someone. The verbs *part* and *separate 5* are **reciprocal verbs** (see Chapter 6).

   *Smoke **belched** from the steelworks in the background.*

   *Special units have been set up to search for Lithuanians who **have defected** from the Soviet army.*

   *The service **will depart** from Inverness at 10.15, calling at principal stations to Edinburgh, before returning north at 15.35.*

   *She snaps photos of the buckled floors and the plaster that **has fallen away** from the walls.*

   *She's going to destroy me. I **have to get away** from her.*

   *I **have parted** from my wife by mutual agreement.*

   *Restlessness **radiated** from him.*

abscond 1	disengage 2	fall 6	recoil 1
arise 4	diverge 3	graduate 3,4	return 1
ascend 7	divert 1	haemorrhage 4	rise 1,2,15
belch 2	drain 6	immigrate	secede
break 10	eject 3	issue 6	separate 3,4,5
commute 1	emanate 1,2	part 2.3	(not) stir 3
defect 2	emerge 1,2	peel 3	transfer 1,2,4,5,8
depart 1,3	emigrate	puff 2	vanish 1,2
desert 7	escape 1	radiate 2	withdraw 2
detach 1	exit 5	rebound 1	
disembark	fade 3,4	recede 3	

back away *2*	fall back *1*	rise up ▷*1*,▷*2*
break away *1,2*	get away *1*	run away *1,3*
fall away *1*	pull away *2*	split off

Structure information: Verb with Adjunct

a) The prepositional phrase is an Adjunct.

b) This structure has no passive.

c) The phrasal verb pattern is the same except that there is a particle, P, which comes after the verb.

Other related patterns

V *from* amount

See **V** *from* **amount** *to* **amount** below.

V *from* colour to colour

See **V** *from* **n** *to* **n** below.

V *from* n *into* n

See **V** *from* **n** *to* **n** below.

V *from* n *to* n

The verb is followed by a prepositional phrase beginning with *from* and another prepositional phrase beginning with *to*. The phrasal verb pattern is **V P** *from* **n** *to* **n**.

Verbs with this pattern belong to the following meaning groups:

1 THE 'SWITCH' GROUP
2 THE 'CHANGE' GROUP
3 THE 'RANGE' GROUP
4 THE 'LAST' GROUP
5 VERBS WITH OTHER MEANINGS

1 THE 'SWITCH' GROUP

These verbs are concerned with stopping doing, using, or dealing with one thing and starting to do, use, or deal with another.

> *The plan is for the crop drier to __change over__ from heating oil to 80 per cent home-grown fuel by 1995.*
>
> *I find it easy to __switch__ from one role to the other.*
>
> *Health is another reason for __turning__ from tap water to mineral water.*

The prepositions are sometimes followed by '-ing' clauses.

> *Soon Jimmy and John __graduate__ from selling stolen shirts to selling guns.*

change *4*	graduate *5*	move *7,8*	switch *2*
flit *2*	lurch *2*	skip *5*	turn *14*
change over			

2 THE 'CHANGE' GROUP

These verbs indicate that something becomes different.

*The mood of the demonstrators **changed** from outrage to jubilation as they chanted 'Orlando for mayor'.*

In the case of *turn 17*, the prepositions are both followed by a noun or adjective group indicating a colour. This pattern is **V *from* colour *to* colour**.

*We stretch our newly exercised limbs and watch the sky **turn** from pink to golden.*

change *3*	graduate *5*	turn *15,17*
evolve *2*	metamorphose	

With all these verbs except *turn 17*, the second preposition is sometimes *into* instead of *to*. This pattern is **V *from* n *into* n**.

*The group **is having to metamorphose** from a loose collection of businesses into a fully integrated multinational.*

*For six months we had lived with the agony of watching our baby **turn** from a healthy, happy child into a sad creature with a distended stomach and wasted limbs.*

3 THE 'RANGE' GROUP

These verbs are concerned with range. The prepositional phrases indicate the two extremes of a range or scale.

*Hundreds of them were given expert advice on problems **ranging** from debt to credit card management.*

*The fee **can vary** from 0.5 per cent to around 3 per cent or more, depending on the size and bargaining power of the retailer.*

range *4*	stretch *7*	vary *1*

4 THE 'LAST' GROUP

These verbs are concerned with duration. The prepositional phrases indicate the times when something begins and ends.

*We are now in the peak hay fever season, which **lasts** from May to July.*

extend *3*	last *11*	stretch *6*

5 VERBS WITH OTHER MEANINGS

There is one other verb which has this pattern.

*It has appeared very difficult for such diseases to **pass** from one species to another.*

pass *6*

V *from* amount *to* amount

The verb is followed by a prepositional phrase which consists of *from* and a noun group referring to an amount, and another prepositional phrase which consists of *to* and a noun group referring to an amount. The phrasal verb pattern is **V P *from* amount *to* amount**.

Verbs with this pattern indicate that a quantity or level increases or decreases. The prepositional phrase with *from* indicates the original quantity or level; the prepositional phrase with *to* indicates the final quantity or level.

My wages <u>will come down</u> from just under £270 a week to about £210.

The top income tax rate <u>would go up</u> from 31 to 33 percent.

Inflation <u>has increased</u> from 8.9 per cent to 9 per cent.

Average starting salaries for graduates are forecast to <u>rise</u> from £12,300 to £12,700, according to the survey by Incomes Data Services.

balloon *3*	drop *1*	plunge *5*	slump *1*
climb *4*	fall *5*	rise *9*	soar *1*
decline *1*	increase *1*	shrink *2*	surge *2*
decrease *1*	jump *6*	sink *7*	swell *1*
dip *7*	mushroom *2*	slide *4*	swell *1*
dive *7*	plummet	slip *7*	widen *4*
come down *1*	go up *1*		
go down *1*	shoot up *1*		

Some of these verbs occasionally have the pattern **V *from* amount**, in clauses such as *Trading volumes <u>have plummeted</u> from their 1987 peaks* where the original amount is not specified. However, it is much more usual for both amounts to be specified.

---

19 V *in* n

The verb is followed by a prepositional phrase which consists of *in* and a noun group. With some verbs, the preposition is sometimes followed by an '-ing' clause. In Structure I, the preposition is followed by an '-ing' form.

This pattern has three structures:

▶ Structure I: Verbs in phase
  He <u>succeeded</u> in catching the bus.
▶ Structure II: Verb with prepositional Complement
  The secret <u>lies</u> in planning ahead.
▶ Structure III: Verb with prepositional Object
  They <u>believe</u> in democracy.
▶ Structure IV: Verb with Adjunct
  They <u>were wallowing</u> in the mud.

Structure I: Verbs in phase

V *in* -ing

	Verb group	*in*	-ing	
Subject	**Verb**			**Completive**
Drugs	can help	in	lowering	the level of cholesterol.
He	did not succeed	in	obtaining	a suspension of the boycott.

Verbs with this structure belong to the following meaning groups:

I.1 THE 'PARTICIPATE' GROUP

These verbs are concerned with helping to do something or taking part in an activity together with other people.

*We hope to **be able to assist** in **safeguarding** the future of the Leyland plant in Lancashire.*

*People want to **participate** in **making** decisions.*

aid *6*	collude	participate
assist *1,2,3*	help *1,2*	
collaborate *1*	join *3,VP*	

When the preposition is followed by a noun group, these verbs have Structure III (see meaning group III.5 below).

I.2 THE 'PERSIST' GROUP

These verbs are concerned with deliberately continuing to do something.

*Yet, oddly enough, we **persist** in **thinking** of our culture as morally superior.*

persevere	persist *2*

When the preposition is followed by a noun group, these verbs have Structure III (see meaning group III.9 below).

I.3 VERBS WITH OTHER MEANINGS

There are two other verbs with this structure.

*He indeed liked to play cards and is said to **have indulged** in **playing** poker twice a week.*

*Many collectors wanted to own the picture but Queen Victoria **succeeded** in **buying** it.*

indulge *1*	succeed *1*

When the preposition is followed by a noun group, these verbs have Structure III (see meaning groups III.5 and III.6 below).

Structure information: Verbs in phase

a) The verb is followed by the preposition *in* and the '-ing' form of another verb. The verbs are **in phase**, and together form a **complex verb group**. This means that the actions or states expressed by the two verbs cannot be separated from each other. For example, if you *succeed in creating* something, the *succeeding* and the *creating* are not two processes, but one.

The complex verb group is followed by a group, phrase, or clause which completes the pattern of the second verb. In the structure table above, this is called a **Completive**. For example, if the second verb is normally followed by a noun group, then the Completive of the complex verb group will be a noun group.

b) This structure has no passive.

Structure II: Verb with prepositional Complement

V *in* n/-ing

	Verb group	*in*	noun group/-ing clause
Subject	**Verb**		**prepositional Complement**
Holiness	consists	in	doing God's will joyfully.
The country's only hope	lay	in	the restitution of its monarchy.

These verbs indicate what something abstract consists of or involves. They are all **link verbs** (see Chapter 5).

As with so many other aspects of a relationship, the solution <u>lies</u> in communication.

The greatness of this team <u>resides</u> in its ability to cover up for its missing players.

The preposition *in* is sometimes followed by an '-ing' clause.

It is, everybody likes to think, a huge, secretive bureaucracy whose only pleasure <u>consists</u> in producing rules to prevent people from doing things.

> consist 2   lie *1.6*   reside 2

Structure information: Verb with prepositional Complement

a) The prepositional phrase is the prepositional Complement.

b) This structure has no passive.

Structure III: Verb with prepositional Object

V *in* n

	Verb group	*in*	noun group
Subject	**Verb**		**prepositional Object**
I	believe	in	regulation.
They	would intervene	in	quarrels and crisis situations.
She	lectures	in	economics.
She	rejoiced	in	each achievement.

Phrasal verbs: V P *in* n

	Verb group	Particle	*in*	noun group
Subject	**Verb**			**prepositional Object**
He	broke	out	in	a rash.
I	used to dress	up	in	my Mum's clothes.

Verbs with this structure belong to the following meaning groups:

   III.1 THE 'DELIGHT' GROUP

   III.2 THE 'BELIEVE' GROUP

   III.3 THE 'LECTURE' GROUP

III.1 THE 'DELIGHT' GROUP

These verbs are concerned with enjoying something or feeling good about something.

He stretched his limbs slightly, ***luxuriating in the warmth****.*

Soviet journalists ***revelled in their new freedom to probe and to criticize****.*

The preposition *in* is sometimes followed by an '-ing' clause.

He ***delights in stirring up controversy and strife****.*

bask *2*	exult	luxuriate	revel *1*
delight *5*	glory *5*	rejoice *1*	wallow *1*

III.2 THE 'BELIEVE' GROUP

These verbs are concerned with belief or agreement.

The shadow spokesman for Defence agreed, although most other Conservatives were still unwilling to ***acquiesce in these plans****.*

I ***don't believe in coincidences****.*

acquiesce	concur	trust *8*
believe *3,4,5*	disbelieve *2*	

III.3 THE 'LECTURE' GROUP

These verbs are concerned with learning or teaching a subject.

As well as accepting commissions for her own designs, Karen ***lectures in Fine Craft Design*** *at the University of Ulster.*

I ***majored in psychology*** *at Hunter College and taught elementary school in New York City.*

There are an increasing number of historians and sociologists ***specialising in sport****.*

graduate *3,4*	qualify *1*	tutor *3*
lecture *2*	specialize	
major *5*	train *2.1*	

III.4 THE 'DEAL' GROUP

These verbs are concerned with trading or work. The prepositional phrase indicates what goods or substances are involved. We include here *work*, in the sense of using a material to create something.

He ***deals in antiques and fine art****.*

Annie Boursot ***specialises in decorative yet affordable silverware****.*

Some ***have*** *never* ***worked in clay*** *before; others are among the world's leading potters.*

In the case of *specialize*, the preposition *in* is sometimes followed by an '-ing' clause. The prepositional phrase indicates what activity someone's work involves.

He ***specializes in treating epileptics and schizophrenics****.*

deal *2.2*	speculate *2*	traffic *4*
specialize	trade *2*	work *26*

III.5 THE 'PARTICIPATE' GROUP

These verbs are concerned with being involved in something or taking part in an activity. This includes:

- helping to do something
- interfering

*You do not have the right to **interfere** in our internal affairs.*

*The job gave her a chance to **participate** in sales and product development.*

*He has not yet announced whether he **will stand** in the election.*

act *8*	connive *2*	indulge *1*	overindulge
aid *6*	co-star *2*	interfere *1*	partake *2*
appear *6*	dabble	intervene *1*	participate
assist *1,2,3*	engage *1*	invest *1,2,3*	share *VP*
collaborate *1*	feature *4*	join *3,VP*	stand *19*
collude	figure *13*	meddle	star *5*
compete *3*	help *1,2*	officiate *2*	

See also Structure I above.

III.6 THE 'SUCCEED' GROUP

These verbs are concerned with doing something successfully or unsuccessfully.

*Local residents **had failed** in an attempt to have the march banned.*

*The United States sent in 28,000 troops last December in a bid to help the UN **succeed** in its aim.*

In the case of *excel*, the preposition *in* is sometimes followed by an '-ing' clause.

*To reach senior positions, you will also need to **excel** in managing people, finances, facilities and time.*

excel	fail *1,8*	succeed *1*

See also Structure I above.

III.7 THE 'ABOUND' GROUP

These verbs indicate that something or someone has a large quantity of something.

*The books **abound** in social comedy.*

*These are normal people like you or me who gradually find themselves **drowning** in debt.*

abound	drown *2*	swim *7*

III.8 THE 'ERUPT' GROUP

These verbs indicate that something or someone suddenly starts to be in a different state. The range of noun groups used after *in* is quite restricted. The verbs *erupt 5*, *break out*, and *come out* are followed by phrases such as *in spots* and *in a sweat*; *erupt 4* and *burst out* are followed by phrases such as *in laughter*; *go up* is followed by *in flames* and *in smoke*.

*They either **come out** in spots, grow too much hair where they don't want it or go bald!*

*When she proudly displayed the cheese dispenser, the thirteen assembled men **erupted** in gales of laughter.*

*Her flat in St John's Wood **went up** in flames along with her passport on the day she was to go abroad.*

---

erupt *3,4,5*

break out *4*   **come out** *VPP*
burst out *14*   **go up** *3*

III.9 VERBS WITH OTHER MEANINGS

There are a number of other verbs which have this structure.

*Developed in America, these enamel polymer paints **come** in 24 colours.*

*I wish she **would confide** in me.*

*She always **dresses** in black.*

*People **dress up** in costume, parade around the village, and dance to the music of sound trucks.*

*The uppermost leaves **end** in curious tendrils that are very attractive.*

*It was too beautiful a day to **persist** in such efforts.*

*The operation **resulted** in the arrest of one alleged kidnapper and the death of another from gunshot wounds.*

In the case of *result*, the preposition *in* is sometimes followed by a noun group and an '-ing' clause. This pattern is **V *in* n -ing**.

*Disturbing your regular sleep pattern **could result** in you losing out on your 'deep sleep' phase.*

---

come *19*   end *10*   result *2*
confide   persevere
dress *5*   persist *2*

dress up *1*

See also Structure I above.

Structure information: Verb with prepositional Object

a) The prepositional phrase is the prepositional Object.

b) This structure has a passive, with the pattern **be V-ed *in***. However, it does not often occur.

c) The phrasal verb pattern is the same except that there is a particle, P, which comes after the verb.

Structure IV: Verb with Adjunct

V *in* n

	Verb group	*in*	noun group
Subject	**Verb**		**Adjunct**
He	enlisted	in	the army.
Government bonds	have fallen	in	value.

Phrasal verbs: V P *in* n

	Verb group	Particle	*in*	noun group
Subject	**Verb**			**Adjunct**
Cigarettes and petrol	will go	up	in	price.
Strong feelings of pride	welled	up	in	me.

Verbs with this structure belong to the following meaning groups:

IV.1 THE 'LIE' GROUP
IV.2 THE 'RISE' GROUP
IV.3 THE 'INCREASE' AND 'DECREASE' GROUP
IV.4 THE 'BEGIN' AND 'END' GROUP

IV.1 THE 'LIE' GROUP

These verbs are concerned with being in or entering a thing, group, or situation, either physically or metaphorically.

*He saw a package **floating in the bay**.*

*World champion Lance Armstrong **is** currently **lying in third place**.*

*It is not true, as some Labor promoters suggest, that all wisdom **resides in their party**.*

*Over the past few years, he **has sat in Parliament** as an independent Social Democrat.*

appear *7*	enlist *1*	land *9*	ride *3*
assemble *1*	enrol	lie *1.5*	rise *17*
bask *1*	float *1*	move *15*	sit *6*
belong *4*	go *1.15*	rank *3*	stick *2.2,6*
catch *5*	implant *3*	reside *2*	wallow *2*

IV.2 THE 'RISE' GROUP

These verbs indicate that someone has a feeling or thought. The feeling or thought is the Subject.

*It is something that **will live in my memory** for the rest of my life.*

*A slight hope **rose in me**. Perhaps she's at my place, I said to myself, she may have got there just after I left.*

*The telephone continued ringing and an inordinate anger **welled up in him**.*

live *1.6*	rise *16*	surge *7*
lodge *8*	stir *7*	well *6.2*
live on ▷*6*	surge up ▷*7*	well up *2*

IV.3 THE 'INCREASE' AND 'DECREASE' GROUP

These verbs are concerned with increasing, decreasing, or being different. The prepositional phrase indicates what quality, for example size or value, the increase, decrease, or difference relates to.

*Now that VCRs with hi-fi Nicam stereo **have come down in price**, they are worth considering if your budget allows it.*

*Since 1945 air forces **have decreased in size** but vastly **increased in capability and complexity**.*

*This frees manufacturers from relying on natural supplies, which **can vary in quality**.*

change 3	double 9	increase 1	triple 2
decline 1	drop 1	lessen	tumble 2
decrease 1	fall 5	rise 9	vary 1,2
differ 1	gain 1	shrink 2	
come down 1	go down 1	go up 1	

IV.4 THE 'BEGIN' AND 'END' GROUP

These verbs are concerned with beginning and ending. The prepositional phrase indicates the situation or event at the beginning or end of something.

*His tenure of office **began** in confusion when his predecessor refused to go.*

*The first flight nearly **ended** in disaster when, at 500 feet, a large section of the leading edge broke away from the upper wing.*

In the case of *culminate* and *end*, the preposition *in* is sometimes followed by a noun group and an '-ing' clause. This pattern is **V in n -ing**.

*They had an argument, which **culminated** in Tom getting drunk and beating her in front of all the customers.*

begin 2,3	culminate	end 7

Structure information: Verb with Adjunct

a) The prepositional phrase is an Adjunct.

b) This structure has no passive.

c) The phrasal verb pattern is the same except that there is a particle, P, which comes after the verb.

Other related patterns

V *in* n *from* amount *to* amount

The verb is followed by prepositional phrases beginning with *in*, *from*, and *to*. The prepositional phrases beginning with *from* and *to* indicate the two extremes of a range of values or qualities. The prepositions are usually followed by **amounts**, but they are sometimes followed by ordinary noun groups, adjectives, or colours. These patterns are **V in n from n to n**, **V in n from adj to adj**, and **V in n from colour to colour**.

The prepositional phrase beginning with *in* indicates what quality, for example size, colour, or age, is involved.

*The victims **ranged** in age from 60 to 89.*

*This oil **varies** in colour from pale yellow to light green.*

range 4	vary 1,2

20 V *in favour of* n

The verb is followed by a prepositional phrase which consists of *in favour of* and a noun group. With some verbs, the preposition is sometimes followed by an '-ing' clause.

This pattern has one structure:

▶ Verb with prepositional Object
He spoke in favour of the plan.

V *in favour of* n/-ing

	Verb group	*in favour of*	noun group/-ing clause
Subject	**Verb**	**prepositional Object**	
The majority	have argued	in favour of	waiting.
A GATT panel	has ruled	in favour of	the Americans.
More than 350 deputies	voted	in favour of	the proposals.

Phrasal verbs: V P *in favour of* n/-ing

	Verb group	Particle	*in favour of*	noun group/-ing clause
Subject	**Verb**		**prepositional Object**	
They	came	out	in favour of	setting up a new party.
He	stood	down	in favour of	his friend.

Verbs with this pattern also have the pattern **V *in poss favour*** – that is, the verb can be followed by *in*, a possessive determiner such as *his* or *their*, and *favour*, as in *The court ruled in his favour.*

Verbs with this pattern belong to the following meaning groups:

1 THE 'SPEAK' GROUP
2 THE 'DISCRIMINATE' GROUP
3 THE 'STAND DOWN' GROUP

1 THE 'SPEAK' GROUP

These verbs are concerned with saying that someone or something is good or right, deciding that someone or something is good or right, or showing support for someone or something.

*It would be intolerable for Labour to block a referendum if the party conference clearly **came out** in favour of it.*

*Crowds surged through the streets of every town, **demonstrating** in favour of the King.*

*And at Hereford a short while ago, an inspector at the public inquiry into the bypass **ruled** in favour of the anti-road campaign.*

*President Kaunda **spoke** in favour of a referendum but he reaffirmed his strong opposition to any change to multiple parties.*

The preposition *in favour of* is sometimes followed by an '-ing' clause.

*The other chamber, the Council of the Union, **voted** in favour of adopting the bill.*

argue *2*	demonstrate *3*	vote *5*
campaign *2*	rule *7*	
decide *1*	speak *2*	
come down	come out *5*	speak out

2 THE 'DISCRIMINATE' GROUP

These verbs are concerned with helping or benefiting someone.

*Many universities <u>**discriminate**</u> in favour of minorities in awarding academic tenure.*

In the case of *work*, the pattern **V in poss favour** is more frequent than **V in favour of** n.

*She said all the weather delays <u>**worked**</u> in her favour*.

discriminate *2*	work *14*

3 THE 'STAND DOWN' GROUP

These verbs indicate that someone resigns. The prepositional phrase indicates who they allow to take their place.

*Labour commissioner Bruce Millan, 65, is prepared to <u>**stand down**</u> in favour of 50-year-old Mr Kinnock.*

resign *1*	
stand down	step down

Structure information

a) The prepositional phrase is the prepositional Object.

b) This structure has no passive.

c) The phrasal verb pattern is the same, except that there is a particle, P, which comes after the verb.

21   V *into* n

The verb is followed by a prepositional phrase which consists of *into* and a noun group.

This pattern has three structures:

▶ Structure I: Verb with prepositional Complement
His smile <u>turned</u> into a grin.
▶ Structure II: Verb with prepositional Object
The tax people <u>are inquiring</u> into his affairs.
▶ Structure III: Verb with Adjunct
He <u>dived</u> into the river.

Structure I: Verb with prepositional Complement

V *into* n

	Verb group	*into*	noun group
Subject	**Verb**		**prepositional Complement**
The plane	broke	into	pieces.
The rally	developed	into	a riot.

Verbs with this structure belong to the following meaning groups:

I.1   THE 'TURN' GROUP
I.2   THE 'BREAK' GROUP

I.1 THE 'TURN' GROUP

These verbs are concerned with becoming. The prepositional phrase indicates what something becomes. We include here *segue* and *shade*, which indicate either that something becomes something else or that it is next to or followed by something else. The verbs *convert*, *shade*, *transmute*, and *turn* are **link verbs** (see Chapter 5).

> *The year before, a number of senior generals had been muttering that the Czech business must be stopped before it **blew up** into a world war.*
>
> *He wanted to **curl** into a tiny ball, smaller, smaller, so small they couldn't find him.*
>
> *With her care, he **grew** into a normal, healthy child.*
>
> *He's **shaping up** into a very nice horse.*
>
> *The downturn in television advertising **has turned** into a collapse.*

The verbs *amalgamate*, *coalesce*, and *merge* always have a plural Subject with this pattern because they are **reciprocal verbs** concerned with two or more things becoming one thing (see Chapter 6).

> *Another group of Algeria's twenty or so opposition parties **has coalesced** into an alternative third force.*

amalgamate	condense 2	evolve 1,2	mushroom 2
ball 3	convert 1	fizzle	mutate 1,2
bloom 4	curl 7	form 3	ossify
blossom 2	decompose	gel 2	segue
broaden 1	degenerate 1	germinate 2	shade 7
build 8	develop 1	grow 9	transmute
change 3	erupt 3	merge 1	turn 15
coalesce	escalate	metamorphose	
blow up 5	curl up ▷7	shape up 1	

A few of these verbs also have the pattern **V** *from* **n** *into* **n** (see pages 192-193).

I.2 THE 'BREAK' GROUP

These verbs are concerned with breaking or dividing. The prepositional phrase refers to pieces or subgroups. The verb *resolve* is a **link verb** (see Chapter 5).

> *The oil tanker grounded in the Shetland Islands **has broken** into several pieces.*
>
> *Gradually, over the centuries, the buildings **will crumble** into dust.*
>
> *Let's **separate** into smaller groups.*
>
> *When the BMW hit the barrier head on, the windscreen **shattered** into a thousand crazy fragments.*

break 1	fragment 2	separate 10	splinter 2
crumble 2	polarize	shatter 1	split 1
divide 1	resolve 4	smash 1	

Structure information: Verb with prepositional Complement

a) The prepositional phrase is the prepositional Complement.

b) This structure has no passive.

c) There are only three phrasal verbs with this structure, *blow up*, *curl up*, and *shape up*. The pattern is **V P** *into* **n**.

Structure II: Verb with prepositional Object

V *into* n

	Verb group	*into*	noun group
Subject	**Verb**		**prepositional Object**
You	're prying	into	police matters.
Mike	sank	into	suicidal depression.
The car	slammed	into	a van.

Verbs with this structure belong to the following meaning groups:

II.1 THE 'CRASH' GROUP
II.2 THE 'BITE' GROUP
II.3 THE 'INQUIRE' GROUP
II.4 THE 'ENTER' GROUP
II.5 THE 'LAPSE' GROUP
II.6 THE 'CHANGE' GROUP
II.7 VERBS WITH OTHER MEANINGS

II.1 THE 'CRASH' GROUP

These verbs are concerned with collisions. The prepositional phrase indicates the thing or person that someone or something hits.

*He led them rapidly past many branching passages, until he stopped so abruptly Bob **bumped into him**.*

*At least ten people were killed on Monday when a freight train **crashed** into a passenger train at Mangra railway station.*

bang 7	cannon 3	run *VP3*
barge 3	crash 2	slam 4
bump 1	plough *VP1*	smash 3

II.2 THE 'BITE' GROUP

These verbs are concerned with exerting pressure or making a dent or hole in something. We include here *bore*, as in *Her eyes bored into his*.

*Weatherby **bit into a digestive biscuit**.*

*His fingers **dug into my arm** like pincers.*

bite 1,7	dig 3	sink 11
bore 6	drill 2	
crunch 1	eat *VP1,2*	

II.3 THE 'INQUIRE' GROUP

These verbs are concerned with research and inquiry. The prepositional phrase indicates the subject of the research or inquiry.

*They see no reason to **delve into the origins of international economic inequality**.*

*Although he had no criminal record, police **are inquiring** into some of Wilson's business deals.*

*I told him I **would look** into the story and get right back to him.*

delve *1*	look *VP*	research *2*
dig *4*	probe *1*	
inquire *2*	pry *1*	

II.4 THE 'ENTER' GROUP

These verbs indicate that someone becomes involved in something.

Always seek professional legal advice before __entering__ into any agreement.

I'd like to __get__ into management.

If I __had__ unwisely __intruded__ into his affairs, he would surely understand that my intentions had been good.

It's a difficult situation and I have to think things over very carefully. I__'m not rushing__ into anything.

blunder *3*	get *VP1*	plunge *4*	venture *4*
break *VP3*	go *VP2*	rush *8*	wade *VP*
diversify	hook *6*	settle *VP*	walk *VP1,2*
enter *VP1*	intrude *1,2*	tumble *4*	

In the case of *rush*, the preposition is sometimes followed by an '-ing' form. In this pattern, the verbs are **in phase**.

__Don't rush__ into buying any watering equipment. Take time to work out which is the best for you that you can afford.

II.5 THE 'LAPSE' GROUP

These verbs indicate that someone or something starts being in a different state, usually a bad one, or starts doing something.

She __burst__ into tears.

Jeremy __burst out__ into peals of laughter as he wagged a finger at us.

The Senate's public gallery was packed with Judge Hastings' supporters, who __erupted__ into applause after he finished his argument.

They __lapsed__ into silence, each caught in his own private world of guilt.

After celebrating the so-called 'economic miracle' of the 1980s, the country __plunged__ into recession in 1990.

Such people often __slide__ into a melancholic state as they age.

Three days later he __slipped__ into a coma and died.

break *VP2*	erupt *3,4,5*	launch *VP*	sink *9*
burst *VP1,2,3*	fall *9*	plunge *3*	slide *3*
come *6*	fly *VP*	regress	slip *6*
descend *6*	get *1.2*	relapse *1*	
dissolve *VP*	lapse *3,4*	retreat *3*	
burst out *1*	get back *1*		

II.6 THE 'CHANGE' GROUP

These verbs are concerned with putting on different clothes.

This is a productive use: other verbs of movement, for example *get*, *scramble*, and *squeeze*, occur with this pattern. The verbs given here are the ones which are most frequently used in this way.

Then I put on a new pair of army running shoes and __changed__ into a clean shirt and trousers.

change *5*   slip *8*

II.7 VERBS WITH OTHER MEANINGS

There are a number of other verbs which have this structure.

*The report suggests that consumers **dipped** into their savings for holiday spending.*
*The report **lashes** into the police for ignoring the warning signs.*
*The alley **opened** into the unlit plaza just above the mission church.*
*We'll help you **tap** into your creative energy.*
*The question for many Americans, though, is whether these higher profits **will translate** into new jobs.*

dip *11,12*	lash *4*	tap *4*
grow *VP*	open *13*	translate *3*
open out ▷*13*		

Structure information: Verb with prepositional Object

a) The prepositional phrase is the prepositional Object.

b) This structure does not often have a passive. However, *bite* (II.2) and *look* (II.3) sometimes have the passive *be* **V-ed** *into*.

*He said that the matter **was being looked** into.*

c) There are only three phrasal verbs with this structure, *burst out*, *get back*, and *open out*. The pattern is **V P** *into* n.

Structure III: Verb with Adjunct

V *into* n

	Verb group	*into*	noun group
Subject	**Verb**		**Adjunct**
They	barged	into	my house.
The sound of the engine	faded	into	the distance.

Verbs with this structure belong to the following meaning groups:

III.1 THE 'INFILTRATE' GROUP
III.2 THE 'DIP' GROUP
III.3 THE 'FADE' GROUP
III.4 VERBS WITH OTHER MEANINGS

III.1 THE 'INFILTRATE' GROUP

These verbs indicate that someone or something enters a place, group, or thing, physically or metaphorically.

*This lack of finesse **carried over** into his dealings with customers.*
*More than 300 guests **crowded** into the ornate gothic rooms for a sit-down dinner.*
*Irrationally, another image from the past **flashed** into her mind.*
*The organizers said they believe pro-military thugs **had infiltrated** into the crowd and started the violence.*
*You can buy plastic divider strips which **slot** into the trays to form compartments.*

207

ascend 6	crowd 4	hack 6	push 3
assimilate 1	crumble 2	infiltrate 1	put VP4 (A ship)
barge 2	dive 1	integrate 1	roll VP1,2
bleed 2	empty 7 (A river)	intrude 3	slot 2
book VP	fall 10	jam 5	splash 1
break VP1	filter 4	marry 1	throng 2
check VP1	fit 1.7,VP1,2	move VP	tumble 4
cram 2	flash 5	pack 3	withdraw 4
creep 3	get VP2	pile 6	
cross 1.1	go 1.15	plug VP1,3	
carry over			

III.2 THE 'DIP' GROUP

These verbs indicate that someone puts their hand in a container in order to get something.

*Theodora Adams **dug into her purse**, extracted a folded square of notepaper and smoothed it on the leg of her pants.*

*Nancy **dipped** into a bowl of popcorn that Hannah had made for them before she'd gone to bed.*

dig 2	dip 2,12	dive 6

III.3 THE 'FADE' GROUP

These verbs are concerned with disappearing or not being noticeable.

***Does** the new housing stick out like a sore thumb or **blend** into its surroundings?*

*They immediately engaged in animated conversation, and I **faded** into the background, finished my orange juice, and left.*

*Margaret Thatcher **will not fade away** into quiet retirement.*

*They jumped over the lowest part of the wall and **vanished** into the night.*

blend VP	melt 3	recede 2
fade 2,3,4	merge 2	vanish 1
fade away ▷3,▷4		

III.4 VERBS WITH OTHER MEANINGS

There are three other verbs which have this structure.

*The debate is expected to be a lengthy one. Officials say it **will** probably **stretch** into next week.*

In the case of *spark* and *spring*, only a very restricted range of nouns can occur in the prepositional phrase.

*As both parties recognise the signal, neurons in the brain **spark** into life.*

*Suddenly all the alarms go off and the Special Branch protection people **spring** into action.*

spark 3 (into life, activity)	spring 6 (into action, life, existence, being)	stretch 5

Structure information: Verb with Adjunct

a) The prepositional phrase is an Adjunct.

b) This structure rarely has a passive. However, *break* (III.1) sometimes has the passive *be V-ed into*.

*Our house **was broken** into earlier this year.*

c) There are only two phrasal verbs with this structure, *carry over* and *fade away*. The pattern is **V P** *into* **n**.

Other related patterns

V *into* n that

See page 104.

22   V *like* n

The verb is followed by a prepositional phrase which consists of *like* and a noun group.

This pattern has two main structures:

▶ Structure I: Verb with prepositional Complement
  *She **looked** like Alex.*
▶ Structure II: Verb with Adjunct
  *You're **acting** like a fool.*

Structure I: Verb with prepositional Complement

V *like* n

	Verb group	*like*	noun group
Subject	**Verb**	**prepositional Complement**	
Music	is	like	a living thing.
This place	feels	like	a prison.

Verbs with this structure are all used to indicate how someone or something seems. They are all **link verbs** (see Chapter 5). The verb *feel 1* indicates how someone seems to themselves.

With all these verbs except *be* and *seem*, you may be saying that one person or thing resembles another, as in *She **looks** like her mother*, or you may be indicating what you think someone or something is, as in *They **look** like a good team*.

*He **was** like any other kid any of us knew.*
*I **feel** like a new person.*
*From a distance, it **looked** like a haystack.*
*In retrospect, the whole trip **seems** like a darkening nightmare.*
*That **sounds** like a good idea.*

In the case of *be* and *look 2.4*, the preposition *like* is sometimes followed by an '-ing' clause. With *look*, the '-ing' clause indicates what someone or something seems likely to do or experience.

*It **was** like being in a dream.*
*He **looks** like being made president for another year.*

be *2.1*	seem *1*	taste *4*
feel *1,2,3*	smell *3*	
look *2.1,4*	sound *7,8,9*	

Structure information: Verb with prepositional Complement

a) The prepositional phrase is the prepositional Complement.

b) This structure has no passive.

Structure II: Verb with Adjunct

V *like* n

	Verb group	*like*	noun group
Subject	**Verb**		**Adjunct**
He	didn't act	like	a 13-year-old.
We	lived	like	fugitives.

Most verbs with this structure are used to describe the behaviour of someone or something. The prepositional phrase indicates whose behaviour it resembles.

This is a productive use: any verb which indicates behaviour or action can be used with this pattern. The verbs listed here are the ones which are most frequently used in this way.

> *I never wanted to be a star. I **don't act** like a star, I **don't dress** like a star. It's just not my thing.*
> *If Sid wanted to **behave** like a lunatic, that was his choice.*

act *1,3,4*	dress *5*	think *3,5*
behave *1,3*	live *1.2*	

VERBS WITH OTHER MEANINGS

There is one other verb with this structure. With this verb, the preposition *like* is always followed by *this*.

> *The story **goes** like this.*

go *3.5*

Structure information: Verb with Adjunct

a) The prepositional phrase is an Adjunct.

b) This structure has no passive.

Other structures

In the case of *feel 13*, the prepositional phrase is the prepositional Object. It indicates something that someone would like to have or do. This structure has no passive.

> *'D'you **feel** like a coffee?' 'I wouldn't say no to a cuppa.'*

The preposition *like* is sometimes followed by an '-ing' clause.

> *I **don't** really **feel** like doing any work 'cos I'm dog-tired.*

feel *13*

23 V *of* n

The verb is followed by a prepositional phrase which consists of the preposition *of* and a noun group. With some verbs, the preposition is sometimes followed by an '-ing' clause. The passive pattern is *be* **V-ed** *of*.

This pattern has one main structure:

▶ Verb with prepositional Object
  She *complained* of a headache.

Active voice: V *of* n/-ing

	Verb group	*of*	noun group/-ing clause
Subject	**Verb**		**prepositional Object**
I	do not approve	of	this change.
He	despaired	of	finishing it.
The bar	stank	of	sweat and beer.
She	talked	of	killing herself.

Passive voice: *be* V-ed *of*

	Verb group	*of*
Subject	**Verb**	**Preposition**
Laziness	is disapproved	of.

Verbs with this pattern belong to the following meaning groups:

1 THE 'TALK' GROUP
2 THE 'THINK' GROUP
3 THE 'KNOW' GROUP
4 THE 'REEK' GROUP
5 VERBS WITH OTHER MEANINGS

1 THE 'TALK' GROUP

These verbs are concerned with talking. The prepositional phrase indicates what is being talked about.

He *__complained__ of a ringing in his ears*.

In November 1966, Adenauer __spoke__ of the need for a new, major West German effort to reach gradual agreement with the Soviet Union.

The preposition *of* is sometimes followed by an '-ing' clause.

He is proud of his memory, and __boasts__ of knowing the whole of Gerard Manley Hopkins, among other writers, by heart.

The preposition *of* is also sometimes followed by a noun group and an '-ing' clause, especially in the case of *speak*, *talk*, and *tell*. This pattern is **V** *of* n -ing.

*We **talked** of him getting a summer job.*

boast *1*	speak *1,2,5*	tell *1*
complain *1,2*	talk *2,8*	warn *1*

2 THE 'THINK' GROUP

These verbs are concerned with thinking or having an opinion. The prepositional phrase indicates the topic of the thought or opinion.

*She was very much concerned that her parents **did not approve** of her decision.*

*She's not even trying. I **despair** of her!*

The preposition *of* is sometimes followed by an '-ing' clause.

*Peter **is thinking** of giving up teaching to become a full-time politician.*

In the case of *approve, conceive 1, disapprove, dream,* and *think,* the preposition is sometimes followed by a noun group and an '-ing' clause. This pattern is **V of n -ing**.

*He **couldn't conceive** of anyone arguing with his results.*

*She **disapproves** of me talking to you.*

approve *1,2*	daydream *1*	dream *2,4,9,10*
(cannot) conceive *1*	despair *3*	repent
conceive *3*	disapprove	think *6,7,11,12,13,15*

3 THE 'KNOW' GROUP

These verbs are concerned with getting or having knowledge.

*I **had heard** of this band before, but I had never witnessed a performance or heard their music.*

*They also **knew** of the link between Lathan and the two journalists.*

In the case of *hear,* the preposition *of* is sometimes followed by an '-ing' clause.

*I've **heard** of looking on the bright side of life, but this is ridiculous!*

In the case of *hear* and *know,* the preposition is sometimes followed by a noun group and an '-ing' clause. This pattern is **V of n -ing**.

*The president admitted that he **did not know** of any rebels having surrendered so far.*

hear *7,8*	know *3*	learn *2*

4 THE 'REEK' GROUP

These verbs indicate that something resembles something else or seems to be something. This includes:

- smelling like something else
- tasting like something else
- being similar in some other way

Smell and *taste* are **link verbs** (see Chapter 5).

*The hall **reeked** of cigar smoke.*

*The West's response to the crisis **smacks** of appeasement, the Post says.*

*The water was refrigerated and **tasted** of metal.*

reek *1,2*	smell *3*	stink *1,2*
smack *3*	speak *7*	taste *4*

5 VERBS WITH OTHER MEANINGS

There are a number of other verbs which have this pattern.

*It appears he **died** of natural causes.*

*The rest **can be disposed** of safely by controlled incineration or secure landfill.*

The verb *beware* is only used in the imperative and infinitive.

***Beware** of food which has been left to stand in warm temperatures, such as in buffets*.

In the case of *beware*, *come 16*, *tire*, and *weary*, the preposition *of* is sometimes followed by an '-ing' clause.

*One of the disembarking passengers **had tired** of waiting for the coach and set off at a smart pace.*

beware	dispose *VP*	permit *3*
come *16,17*	drain *6*	tire *2*
die *1,2,7,9*	partake *1,3*	weary *3*

Structure information

a) The prepositional phrase is the prepositional Object.

b) This structure has a passive, with the pattern **be V-ed of**. However, not all verbs with this structure are used in the passive. The following verbs are the ones which are most frequently passive.

approve *1,2*	despair *3*	hear *7,8*	think *6,7*
boast *1*	disapprove	partake *1*	
complain *1,2*	dispose *VP*	speak *1,2,5,7*	
conceive *1,3*	dream *2,4,9,10*	talk *8*	

Other structures

In the case of *consist*, which is a **link verb** (see Chapter 5), the prepositional phrase is a prepositional Complement. The preposition *of* is sometimes followed by an '-ing' clause.

*The crew **consisted** of pilot, co-pilot, navigator and flight engineer.*

consist *1*

Other related patterns

V *of* n *as* n/-ing/adj

The verb is followed by a prepositional phrase beginning with *of*. This is followed by another prepositional phrase which consists of *as* and a noun group, '-ing' clause, or adjective group. The passive pattern is **be V-ed of as n/-ing/adj**.

These verbs are concerned with regarding or describing someone or something as a particular thing.

*She **speaks** of her family as a 'great support system'.*

*Now he **is being talked** of as the party's next leader.*
*I **don't think** of myself as abnormal, just unusual.*

conceive *2*	talk *2,8*
speak *1,2,5*	think *9*

V *of* n wh

See page 110.

V *of* n with quote

See page 118.

---

24   V *off* n

The verb is followed by a prepositional phrase which consists of *off* and a noun group.

This pattern has two structures:

▶ Structure I: Verb with prepositional Object
  *He **sponged** off friends.*
▶ Structure II: Verb with Adjunct
  *The ball **rebounded** off a tree.*

Structure I: Verb with prepositional Object

V *off* n

	Verb group	*off*	noun group
Subject	**Verb**	**prepositional Object**	
All the components	can run	off	battery power.
I	don't sponge	off	women.

There are two verbs with this structure.

*The Biotrace Hygiene Monitor is totally portable and **runs** off both mains and batteries.*
*Saying immigrants have come to **sponge** off the state is ridiculous.*

run *15*	sponge *6*

Structure information: Verb with prepositional Object

a) The prepositional phrase is the prepositional Object.

b) This structure has no passive.

Structure II: Verb with Adjunct

V *off* n

	Verb group	*off*	noun group
Subject	**Verb**	**Adjunct**	
The ball	cannoned	off	the post.
The light	reflected	off	the stone.

Most verbs with this structure indicate that an object, or light or sound, hits something and comes back from it.

> The sunlight **glinted** *off the distant mountains* in a dazzling silver-white radiance.
>
> Another bullet **ricocheted** *off a rock behind him*.

bounce 3	glint 1	reflect 2
cannon 3	rebound 1	ricochet

VERBS WITH OTHER MEANINGS

There is one other verb which has this structure.

> The paint **was peeling** *off the door*.

peel 3

Structure information: Verb with Adjunct

a) The prepositional phrase is an Adjunct.

b) This structure has no passive.

---

25 V *on* n

The verb is followed by a prepositional phrase which consists of *on* and a noun group. With some verbs, the preposition is sometimes followed by an '-ing' clause or a wh-clause. In Structure I, the preposition is followed by an '-ing' form.

Some verbs are sometimes followed by *upon* instead of *on*. *Upon* is a more formal or literary word.

The passive pattern is *be* V-ed *on*.

This pattern has three structures:

▶ Structure I: Verbs in phase
  She <u>insisted</u> *on paying*.
▶ Structure II: Verb with prepositional Object
  He <u>remarked</u> *on the heat*.
▶ Structure III: Verb with Adjunct
  Police <u>are converging</u> *on the area*.

Structure I: Verbs in phase

V *on* -ing

	Verb group	*on*	-ing	
Subject	**Verb**			**Completive**
The dog	insisted	on	coming	with me into the room.

There are only two verbs with this structure. The verb *embark* indicates that someone starts doing something, and the verb *insist* indicates that someone does something even though this is not wanted or not reasonable.

> If we win the elections, we **will not embark** **on reforming** the constitution before the presidential elections.

> She **insisted** **on giving** Nina her telephone number, just in case.

The verb *insist* is sometimes followed by *upon* instead of *on*.

> We tried our best, but he **insisted** **upon leaving**.

```
embark 1     insist 1
```

When the preposition *on* is followed by a noun group, these verbs have Structure II (see meaning groups II.26 and II.27 below).

Structure information: Verbs in phase

a) The verb is followed by the preposition *on* and the '-ing' form of another verb. The verbs are **in phase**, and together form a **complex verb group**. This means that the actions or states expressed by the two verbs cannot be separated from each other. For example, if you *insist on wearing* something, the *insisting* and the *wearing* are not two processes, but one.

The complex verb group is followed by a group, phrase, or clause which completes the pattern of the second verb. In the structure table above, this is called a **Completive**. For example, if the second verb is normally followed by a noun group, then the Completive of the complex verb group will be a noun group.

b) This structure has no passive.

Structure II: Verb with prepositional Object

Active voice: V *on* n/-ing/wh

	Verb group	*on*	noun group/-ing clause/wh-clause
Subject	**Verb**		**prepositional Object**
They	cannot agree	on	what they want done.
He	is concentrating	on	getting himself re-elected.
I	knocked	on	the door.
My husband	remarked	on	her marvellous sense of humour.
The authorities	reneged	on	the deal.

Passive voice: *be* V-ed *on*

	Verb group	*on*	
Subject	Verb	Preposition	Adjunct (optional)
His car	was fired	on.	
One toddler	was trodden	on	in the scuffle.

Phrasal verbs: V P *on* n

	Verb group	Particle	*on*	noun group
Subject	Verb			prepositional Object
Big American firms	were muscling	in	on	the two companies' markets.
	Swot	up	on	local sites.

Verbs with this structure belong to the following meaning groups:

II.1   THE 'COMMENT' GROUP
II.2   THE 'ENLARGE' GROUP
II.3   THE 'REFLECT' GROUP
II.4   THE 'DOTE' GROUP
II.5   THE 'READ UP' GROUP
II.6   THE 'BEAT' GROUP
II.7   THE 'IMPINGE' GROUP
II.8   THE 'INTRUDE' GROUP
II.9   THE 'POUNCE' GROUP
II.10 THE 'SPY' GROUP
II.11 THE 'INFORM' GROUP
II.12 THE 'WALK OUT' GROUP
II.13 THE 'BACK-PEDAL' GROUP
II.14 THE 'BACKFIRE' GROUP

II.15 THE 'DEPEND' GROUP
II.16 THE 'GAMBLE' GROUP
II.17 THE 'WORK' GROUP
II.18 THE 'BUILD' GROUP
II.19 THE 'FEED' GROUP
II.20 THE 'LIVE' GROUP
II.21 THE 'ECONOMIZE' GROUP
II.22 THE 'OVERSPEND' GROUP
II.23 THE 'FOCUS' GROUP
II.24 THE 'CALL' GROUP
II.25 THE 'CHECK' GROUP
II.26 THE 'START' GROUP
II.27 VERBS WITH OTHER MEANINGS

II.1 THE 'COMMENT' GROUP

These verbs are concerned with speaking or writing. The prepositional phrase indicates the topic involved. We include here verbs such as *legislate*, *rule*, and *vote*, which are concerned with expressing your decision or judgement about something.

*The government **has not** yet **commented** on his release*.

*They are not supposed to interfere in local politics but **can report back** on what is going on*.

*Parliament is due to **vote** on the peace plan on Wednesday*.

Many of these verbs are sometimes followed by *upon* instead of *on*, especially *comment*, *dwell*, *pronounce*, *remark*, *report*, *touch*, and *vote*.

*The question of prisoners of war **will** no doubt **be touched** upon by the two foreign ministers*.

In the case of *advise* and *vote*, the preposition *on* is sometimes followed by an '-ing' clause.

*The Parliament is also due to **vote** on lowering the legal voting age from twenty-one to eighteen*.

In the case of the following verbs, the preposition *on* (or *upon*) is sometimes followed by a wh-clause: *adjudicate*, *advise*, *comment*, *discourse*, *dwell*, *pronounce*, *report*, *report back*, *rule*, *touch*, *vote*.

*Mr. Potter declined to **comment** on why he left the company and said he doesn't yet know what he will be doing*.

adjudicate	dwell *1*	pontificate *1*	speak *2*
advise *2*	generalize *1*	preach *1*	talk *4*
comment *1*	harp *VP*	pronounce *3*	touch *8*
commentate	lecture *2*	remark *1*	vote *5*
counsel *3*	legislate	report *2*	write *3*
discourse *3*	philosophize	rule *7*	
report back *1*	sound off		

II.2 THE 'ENLARGE' GROUP

These verbs are concerned with saying more about a topic or adding details.

> *Mr Dienstbier **was enlarging** on proposals he made last night to members of the Royal Institute of International Affairs.*

These verbs are sometimes followed by *upon* instead of *on*.

> *Georg Simmel, a colleague of Weber's, **expanded** upon this concept in his essay, 'The Web of Group Affiliations'.*

elaborate *4*	enlarge *3*
embroider *2*	expand *VP*

II.3 THE 'REFLECT' GROUP

These verbs are concerned with thought, or the expression of thought. The prepositional phrase indicates the topic of the thought. We include here verbs concerned with agreeing and disagreeing.

> *It gave me a chance to **reflect** on what I was doing.*

Many of these verbs are sometimes followed by *upon* instead of *on*, especially *agree, dwell, meditate,* and *reflect.*

> *The student **must** carefully **meditate** upon the symbols and concepts that relate to the element of Earth.*

The verbs *agree, differ,* and *disagree* are **reciprocal verbs** (see Chapter 6), and have a plural Subject with this pattern.

> *Meeting on February 11th, the two men failed to **agree** on anything.*

The preposition *on* (or *upon*) is sometimes followed by a wh-clause.

> *But they rarely **agree** on how to act and often attack each other, personally and politically.*

In the case of *reflect*, the preposition *on* (or *upon*) is sometimes followed by an '-ing' clause.

> *Many long-term prisoners are in their twenties and have already had plenty of time to **reflect** on losing their most vigorous years.*

agree *1,3*	differ *2*	muse *1*	speculate *1*
brood *3*	disagree *1*	ponder	
cogitate	dwell *1*	reflect *4*	
deliberate *3*	meditate *1*	ruminate *1*	

The verbs *agree, differ,* and *disagree* also have the pattern **V with n on n** (see page 471).

II.4 THE 'DOTE' GROUP

These verbs are concerned with someone's attitude towards someone or something. We include here *smile*, which usually has something like *fortune* or *the gods* as its Subject.

> *Marie's parents **dote** on her and devote much of their time and resources towards making her happy.*

*This time fortune **smiled** on us and there were no hitches. The weather was beautiful, the breeze was good, we caught the tide.*

These verbs are sometimes followed by *upon* instead of *on*.

*It was a time when rock'n'roll **was frowned** upon and dismissed as juvenile rubbish.*

dote	frown *VP*
fawn *3*	smile *4*

II.5 THE 'READ UP' GROUP

These verbs are concerned with learning about a subject because you feel you need to.

*Get a copy of your company's employee handbook and **mug up** on the relevant sections.*

*Mark **had read up** on opals in Bess's encyclopedia.*

bone up *VPP*	gen up *VPP*	read up *VPP*
catch up *2*	mug up	swot up ▷*1*

II.6 THE 'BEAT' GROUP

These verbs are concerned with touching something. This includes:

- hitting something
- pressing something

*The rain **was beating** on the windowpanes.*

*With this in mind, she **knocked** on the door and waited.*

***Press** on the wound firmly with your fingers to flatten the cut blood vessels.*

*The most common foot fracture occurs in contact sports where feet **can** easily **be trodden** on.*

Many of these verbs are sometimes followed by *upon* instead of *on*, especially *beat, knock, rest*, and *tread*.

*His legs were stretched out and his feet **rested** upon a sofa.*

bang *4*	grate *3*	press *3*	strum
beat *2*	hammer *3*	pull *1*	tap *2*
clatter *2*	impact *4*	rap *4*	thump *1*
clunk *2*	knock *1*	rest *2.7*	trample *3*
drum *6*	pound *6*	stamp *6*	tread *1*
bear down *2*	beat up *VPP*		

II.7 THE 'IMPINGE' GROUP

These verbs are concerned with affecting or beginning to affect someone or something, often negatively. The Subject often refers to a worrying thought or situation. We include here *grate* and *jar*, where the effect is very negative.

*All these problems seem to **be crowding in** on him right now.*

*A gloomy silence once again **descended** on the room.*

*There was an edge to her voice that **grated** on Gretchen's nerves.*

*Sometimes the thought of my husband's wartime ordeals **weighed** on me dreadfully.*

Most of these verbs are sometimes followed by *upon* instead of *on*, especially *act, fall, impact, impinge*, and *weigh*.

*It was perhaps the first time that public affairs **had impinged** upon him in a personal way.*

act 7	grate 4	jar 4	tell 9
descend 2	impact 3	press 7	weigh 5
fall 12	impinge	prey 5	
creep up VPP2	crowd in	sneak up VPP2	

II.8 THE 'INTRUDE' GROUP

These verbs are concerned with interrupting someone or something, or getting involved in something, sometimes when this is unwelcome.

*They would like the Czechs to **come in** on this, but they are hesitating.*

*They wrote letters from time to time, but **did not intrude** on his privacy.*

*European governments are thus rightly wary of allowing the commission to **muscle in** on such projects.*

*If you were to **walk in** on the man you love, and he was with somebody else, what would you feel?*

The verbs *encroach*, *infringe*, and *intrude* are sometimes followed by *upon* instead of *on*.

*'Oh, Dr. Stockton, I'm not trying to **encroach** upon your duties,' Houston said.*

encroach 1	intrude 1,2		
infringe 2	trespass 2		
barge in	come in 3	move in 3	walk in VPP
break in 2	cut in	muscle in	weigh in 1
butt in	get in VPP	sit in VPP	

II.9 THE 'POUNCE' GROUP

These verbs are concerned with attacking or harming someone, or treating them in a bad or hostile way. This includes:

- physically attacking someone
- criticizing someone
- stopping someone's activities

*A new scheme has been launched by police in Coventry to **crack down** on youngsters who play truant.*

*The girl, who **was pounced** on while waiting for a train, was treated in hospital for head wounds.*

*Speaker after speaker **rounded** on ministers from the floor, with Dr Clifford Lutton, an Edinburgh GP, saying the party appeared to have lost the confidence of its own supporters.*

Many of these verbs are sometimes followed by *upon* instead of *on*, especially *fire*, *pounce*, *prey*, and *turn*. *Set* is nearly always followed by *upon*.

*They **prey** upon the community and **are**, in turn, **preyed** upon by its most perverted and malign forces.*

*I took the short cut, over the fields, and I **was set** upon by a gang of boys.*

dump 11	lean VP2	round VP	swoop 1
fire 2.1	pounce 1,2,3	set VP	trample 1
jump 8,10	prey 2,4	stamp VP	turn VP4
clamp down	crack down		
come down VPP2	gang up		

II.10 THE 'SPY' GROUP

These verbs are concerned with secretly watching, listening to, or finding out about someone.

> *Sloan mingles with the crowd waiting to go inside and likes to **eavesdrop on their conversations**.*
>
> *But they'**ll** read your post, and **listen in on your telephone calls**.*
>
> *They portrayed him as a temperamental tyrant who employed private detectives to **snoop on adversaries**.*

The verb *spy* is sometimes followed by *upon* instead of *on*.

> *They felt that they **were being spied** upon.*

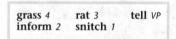

eavesdrop	snoop 2	spy 3,4
listen in		

II.11 THE 'INFORM' GROUP

These verbs are concerned with telling people in authority that someone has done something wrong. The prepositional phrase indicates who that person is. The implication is usually that the person referred to by the Subject betrays the other person by giving this information.

> *This is a tense thriller about a diamond heist that goes badly wrong because someone **has grassed on the thieves**.*
>
> *They had to attend indoctrination sessions at which they were urged to **inform on suspected 'separatists'**.*

grass 4	rat 3	tell VP
inform 2	snitch 1	

II.12 THE 'WALK OUT' GROUP

These verbs are concerned with abandoning someone. We include here *hang up*, which indicates that someone ends a telephone conversation abruptly.

> *When I told him that you'd be negotiating for me, he said he'd call again, and **hung up on me**.*
>
> *His first wife **walked out on him**.*

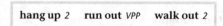

hang up 2	run out VPP	walk out 2

II.13 THE 'BACK-PEDAL' GROUP

These verbs are concerned with not having a fixed attitude. This includes:

- changing a plan
- breaking a promise
- not making a decision

> *The government **has backed down on plans to introduce national tests for seven-year-old children**.*
>
> *Last week he appeared to **back-pedal on that statement**, but it was too late.*
>
> *The President has begun to **renege on promises he made when the talks began**.*
>
> *He legalised opposition parties, and granted an amnesty to political exiles, but tried to **stall on the question of a national conference**.*

In the case of *compromise* and *stall*, the preposition *on* is sometimes followed by an '-ing' clause.

The government is unlikely to __compromise__ on ending emergency rule there.

back-pedal *1,2*	flip-flop *2*	renege	waffle *2*
backtrack *1*	prevaricate	soft-pedal	waver *1*
compromise *2*	procrastinate	stall *2*	
default *1*	rat *4*	stonewall	
back down	climb down	hang back *2*	
cave in *2*	go back *VPP*		

II.14 THE 'BACKFIRE' GROUP

These verbs indicate that a plan or action has a different result from the one intended, often harming the person who planned or did it. The prepositional phrase refers to that person.

Such attacks __could backfire__ on Yeltsin's opponents, however.

The verb *rebound* is sometimes followed by *upon* instead of *on*.

The very success of that policy now threatens to __rebound__ upon the government.

backfire *1*	boomerang *2*	rebound *2*

II.15 THE 'DEPEND' GROUP

These verbs are concerned with depending or relying on something or someone, or hoping to have something.

I hope we __can count__ on your support.
A great deal __hangs__ on the answer to these questions.

Many of these verbs are sometimes followed by *upon* instead of *on*, especially *count*, *depend*, *rely*, and *rest*.

This system of legalised extortion __rests__ upon a whole system of political control.

In the case of *bank*, *count*, *depend*, *hinge*, *rely*, and *rest*, the preposition *on* (or *upon*) is sometimes followed by an '-ing' clause.

People __can__ no longer __rely__ on doing their chosen job for life.

In the case of *depend*, *hinge*, *rest*, and *turn*, the preposition *on* (or *upon*) is sometimes followed by a wh-clause.

Much __will hinge__ on how well the Free Democrats do tonight.

In the case of *bank*, *count*, *depend*, *hinge*, and *rely*, the preposition *on* (or *upon*) is sometimes followed by a noun group and an '-ing' clause. This pattern is **V on n -ing**.

In the case of spacecraft such as the Space Shuttle, lives __depend__ on such systems working properly.

bank *VP*	hang *VP6*	pivot *VP*	ride *5*
count *VP1,2*	hinge *VP*	rely *1,2*	turn *VP5*
depend *1,2,3*	lean *VP1*	rest *2.3*	

The verbs *count 2*, *depend 2*, and *rely 1* also have the pattern **V on n for n**. The prepositional phrase beginning with *for* indicates what the person referred to provides or ensures.

She, too, __relied__ upon him for her safety.

These three verbs also have the pattern **V *on* n to-inf**, which is dealt with at the end of this section.

II.16 THE 'GAMBLE' GROUP

These verbs are concerned with gambling.

A greyhound trainer has won £200,000 from the bookies by __betting__ on his own dog.

The preposition *on* is sometimes followed by a wh-clause.

Interest rates might go up again, so people __are__ sort of __gambling__ on what's going to happen in the next five or ten years from now.

In the case of *gamble*, the preposition *on* is sometimes followed by an '-ing' clause.

They __gambled__ on getting stronger western backing and, this time, they won.

In the case of *bet* and *gamble*, the preposition *on* is sometimes followed by a noun group and an '-ing' clause. This pattern is **V *on* n -ing**.

Some day the company may pay for the failure to diversify, but __do not bet__ on it happening soon.

bet *1,3*	speculate *2*
gamble *2,3*	wager *1*

II.17 THE 'WORK' GROUP

These verbs are concerned with working. The prepositional phrase indicates what the work relates to.

He __was operated__ on immediately and the assailant's knife removed from his back.

The verb *collaborate* is a **reciprocal verb** (see Chapter 6), and has a plural Subject with this pattern.

After his return to Edinburgh, we __collaborated__ on a musical version of Kingsley Amis's 'Lucky Jim'.

In the case of *collaborate* and *work*, the preposition *on* is sometimes followed by an '-ing' clause.

Mr Waldegrave said British diplomats __were working__ on solving these problems.

collaborate *1*	operate *4*	work *3,5,9*
experiment *2*	toil *1*	
beaver away	toil away ▷*1*	

The verb *collaborate* also has the patterns **V *with* n *on* n** and **V *on* n *with* n** (see page 471).

II.18 THE 'BUILD' GROUP

These verbs are concerned with using something as a basis or exploiting it. We include here *act*, which indicates that someone follows advice or instructions, and *improve*, which indicates that someone produces something better than a previous thing.

So, __acting__ on our director's instructions, we drove off the highway down a rough track that led through the dunes.

I think I was too naive at the time. I __didn't capitalize__ on opportunities.

His classic cocoon-shaped coat with ruched velvet shawl collar simply __cannot be improved__ on.

Many of these verbs are sometimes followed by *upon* instead of *on*, especially *act*, *build*, *capitalize*, and *improve*.

This year we __are building__ upon that success to provide an even better and bigger show.

In the case of *cash in*, the preposition *on* is sometimes followed by an '-ing' clause.

*In 1979 he was accused of **cashing in** on being part of the Royal Family.*

act *2*	capitalize *1*	improvise *2*	trade *VP*
build *7*	improve *4*	piggyback *2*	work *17*
cash in *1*			

II.19 THE 'FEED' GROUP

These verbs are concerned with eating or consuming something. We include here *draw*, *puff*, and *pull*, which are concerned with smoking, and *choke* and *overdose*, which are concerned with the harmful effects of consuming something.

*He **chewed** on his toast, taking his time.*

*She **had** nearly **choked** on the tiny nibble of wedding cake she had tasted.*

*Slugs **feed** on decaying plant and animal material, as well as living plant material such as seedlings and flowers.*

*'So what are the options?' Mr Clarke asks, **puffing** on his small cigar.*

Some of these verbs are occasionally followed by *upon* instead of *on*, especially *feast* and *feed*.

*Mrs Drake wondered if an alligator **were feasting** upon Leo's fish.*

binge *2*	dine *VP*	gorge *2*	puff *1*
browse *3*	draw *9*	live *VP3,4*	pull *13*
chew *1*	feast *2*	munch	snack *3*
choke *1*	feed *3,11*	nibble *1,2,3*	suck *1*
crunch *1*	gnaw *1*	overdose *2,4*	
fill up *1*	munch away ▷	nibble away ▷*3*	

II.20 THE 'LIVE' GROUP

These verbs are concerned with living or functioning. The prepositional phrase indicates what resources someone or something has which enable them to live or function.

*She **is getting by** on borrowed money.*

*They may not look for work once they are accustomed to **living** on benefit.*

*I got the idea of making a car that **runs** on clean gas when visiting a factory where many facilities were operated by air pressure.*

In the case of *thrive*, the preposition *on* is sometimes followed by an '-ing' clause.

*Switzerland **has thrived** on being different from its neighbours.*

exist *2*	run *15*	survive *2*
live *VP2*	subsist	thrive *2*
get by		

II.21 THE 'ECONOMIZE' GROUP

These verbs are concerned with spending less on something or using less of it.

*Pregnant women are still advised to **cut down** on coffee.*

*I **shall have to economize** on clothes, food and other necessities that I've worked for all my life.*

economize	scrimp
save *3*	skimp
cut back	cut down *1*

II.22 THE 'OVERSPEND' GROUP

These verbs are concerned with spending a lot of money, or too much money, on something.

> **_Don't overspend_ on your home** and expect to get the money back when you sell.
> And why not **_splash out_ on the ultimate luxury of linen sheets**?

overspend *1*	splurge	
fork out	shell out	splash out

II.23 THE 'FOCUS' GROUP

These verbs are concerned with having or starting to having a particular thing as your focus of attention. A number of these verbs have someone's eyes as the Subject.

> As he sipped his drink, his eye **_fell_ on a child's alphabet chart lying on the table**.
> Chomsky tends to **_focus_ on well-studied languages like English rather than languages from far afield**.
> Critics **_have zeroed in_ on his plan to raise gasoline taxes 10 cents a gallon every year for five years**.

These verbs are sometimes followed by *upon* instead of *on*.

> The film **_centres_ upon two prisoners**: Gerry Conlon and his father Giuseppe.

In the case of *centre*, *concentrate*, and *focus*, the preposition *on* (or *upon*) is sometimes followed by an '-ing' clause.

> He gave up his party duties to **_concentrate_ on clearing his name**.

alight *5 (Your eyes)*	fall *16 (Your eyes)*	focus *1,5*
centre *9*	fasten *3,4*	rest *9 (Your eyes)*
concentrate *1*	fix *7 (Your eyes)*	settle *9 (Your eyes)*
home in *1,2*	zero in *VPP1,2*	zoom in

II.24 THE 'CALL' GROUP

These verbs are concerned with visiting someone.

> He went to **_call_ on Gianni**, who was out.
> Actually, I can't stay late. I said I'**_d drop in_ on someone**. A patient.

call *VP*		
call in *2*	drop in	look in

II.25 THE 'CHECK' GROUP

These verbs are concerned with checking a fact or situation.

> I'll get somebody to **_check_ on the luggage**.

check *2*
check up *1,2*

II.26 THE 'START' GROUP

These verbs are concerned with starting to do or deal with something.

*We're ready to **start** on the runways.*

The verb *embark* is sometimes followed by *upon* instead of *on*.

*We want to dispel the idea that at 40, people are too old to **embark** upon a political career.*

embark *1*	start *VP*

See also Structure I above.

II.27 VERBS WITH OTHER MEANINGS

There are a number of other verbs with this structure.

*I mean, even your own personal behavior as a teacher, outside of school hours, **reflects** on the school itself.*

*Some of Snape's caution **had rubbed off** on me.*

Many of these verbs are sometimes followed by *upon* instead of *on*, especially *insist*.

*He began to **insist** upon a bullet-proof limousine, just for peace of mind.*

In the case of *miss out*, the preposition *on* is sometimes followed by an '-ing' clause.

*Reggae band Inner Circle said they were very upset to **have missed out** on performing at the Carnival.*

In the case of *insist 1*, the preposition *on* is sometimes followed by a noun group and an '-ing' clause. This pattern is **V on n -ing**.

*They **insist** on three conditions being met.*

abut	insist *1,2*	ride *1,2,3*
foreclose	pass *21*	sponge *6*
impose *4*	reflect *6*	wait *7,VP*
catch up *3,4*	follow through	miss out *1* tighten up ▷*6*
come through *4*	hold out *3*	rub off
ease up *3*	lose out	stock up *2*

See also Structure I above.

Structure information: Verb with prepositional Object

a) The prepositional phrase is the prepositional Object.

b) This structure has a passive with the pattern **be V-ed on**. However, not all verbs with this structure are used in the passive. The following verbs are the ones which are most frequently passive.

act *2*	improve *4*	rely *1,2*	vote *5*
agree *3*	jump *8,10*	set *VP*	wait *7*
comment *1*	lean *VP2*	stamp *VP*	work *3,5,9*
count *VP1,2*	operate *4*	touch *8*	
depend *1,2,3*	pounce *1,2,3*	trample *1*	
fire *1*	prey *2,4*	tread *1*	

c) The phrasal verb patterns are the same except that there is a particle, P, which comes after the verb. The passive pattern, *be* **V-ed P *on***, does not often occur.

Structure III: Verb with Adjunct

V *on* n

	Verb group	*on*	noun group
Subject	**Verb**		**Adjunct**
He	appeared	on	weekend TV talk shows.
Looters	have descended	on	the suburb where the plane crashed.

Phrasal verbs: V P *on* n

	Verb group	Particle	*on*	noun group
Subject	**Verb**			**Adjunct**
The crowd of onlookers	closed	in	on	her.

Verbs with this structure belong to the following meaning groups:

    III.1 THE 'CONVERGE' GROUP
    III.2 THE 'SQUAT' GROUP
    III.3 THE 'APPEAR' GROUP
    III.4 VERBS WITH OTHER MEANINGS

III.1 THE 'CONVERGE' GROUP

These verbs are concerned with going towards or onto something or someone, literally or metaphorically.

> *Up to 20,000 fans are expected to __converge on Sweden__ for the first games on June 10.*
> *As the elephants shake the palms, the nuts __rain down on their backs__.*
> *There was clearly no way to __sneak up on the house__.*

Many of these verbs are sometimes followed by *upon* instead of *on*, especially *descend*, *devolve*, and *rain down*.

> *Most of the administrative work __devolved upon a more junior minister__.*

close *3.0*	devolve	fall *11,14*	trespass *1*
converge *1*	embark *2*	rain *4*	
descend *3*	encroach *2*	settle *10*	
bear down *1*	creep up *VPP1*	rain down *▷4*	
close in *1*	move in *2*	sneak up *VPP1*	

III.2 THE 'SQUAT' GROUP

These verbs indicate that someone takes up a squatting or kneeling position.

> *She __got down on her knees__ and began praying.*
> *He pulled out some matches, __squatted on his heels__, struck a match and held it towards the wood.*

> squat *1*
>
> get down *2*   go down *2*

III.3 THE 'APPEAR' GROUP

These verbs indicate that someone takes part in a television or radio programme, or in a film.

*He frequently **appeared** on television, and wrote regular columns in newspapers on every subject from clothing fashions to the afterlife.*

> appear *6*   go *1.12*
> feature *4*   guest *4*

III.4 VERBS WITH OTHER MEANINGS

There are a number of other verbs which have this structure.

*'Well, we took it to the garage for its MOT test and it failed.' 'Did it **fail** on the clutch?'*

*The report **falls down** on analysis and background.*

*No police representatives **will sit** on the investigation committee.*

*Local fishermen had complained that their nets kept **snagging** on some underwater objects.*

*Suddenly she **tripped** on a clump of grass and pitched forward, clutching vainly at a branch to save herself.*

In the case of *fall*, the noun group following the preposition *on* refers to a day or date.

*Derby Day **fell** on the 40th anniversary of the coronation.*

In the case of *teeter*, only a restricted range of nouns are used after the preposition *on*, mainly *brink* and *edge*.

*Their economy **is teetering** on the brink of collapse.*

> catch *5*   sit *6*   trip *2*
> fail *1,10*   snag *2*
> fall *13*   teeter *1*
>
> fall down *2*   trip up ▷*2*

Structure information: Verb with Adjunct

a) The prepositional phrase is an Adjunct.

b) This structure has a passive with the pattern *be* V-ed *on*. However, the passive does not often occur.

c) Phrasal verb patterns are the same except that there is a particle, P, which comes after the verb.

Other related patterns

V on/upon n as n/-ing/adj

The verb is followed by a prepositional phrase beginning with *on* or *upon*. This is followed by another prepositional phrase which consists of *as* and a noun group, '-ing' clause, or adjective group. The second prepositional phrase indicates what someone regards someone or something as being. The passive pattern is *be* V-ed *on/upon as* n/-ing/adj.

**Look** on it as a challenge.

People who put their own pleasure higher up on the list of priorities **are** often **looked** on as selfish or immature.

> look *VP*

V *on/upon* n *for* n

See meaning group II.15 above.

V *on/upon* n *that*

See pages 104-105.

V *on/upon* n to-inf

The verb is followed by a prepositional phrase beginning with *on* or *upon*, which is followed by a to-infinitive clause. The passive pattern is *be* **V-ed** *on/upon* **to-inf**.

Verbs with this pattern belong to the following meaning groups:

1 THE 'RELY' GROUP
2 THE 'CALL' GROUP

1 THE 'RELY' GROUP

These verbs are concerned with hoping or being certain that someone will do something.

> _One lesson they may have learned is that they **cannot rely** on anyone else to fight their battles for them_.

> bank *VP*   depend *2,3*
> count *VP2*   rely *2*

2 THE 'CALL' GROUP

These verbs are concerned with asking or persuading someone to do something.

> _So we **call** on everyone to seize this opportunity and to look at it positively_.

> _Then I stepped down, and John, in fact, **had been prevailed** upon to take over for a year_.

> call *VP1*   prevail *4*

V *on/upon* n wh

See page 110.

V *on* n *with* n, V *with* n *on* n

See pages 471-472.

26 V *on to* n, V *onto* n

The verb is followed by a prepositional phrase which consists of *on to* or *onto* and a noun group.

This pattern has one structure:

▶ Verb with prepositional Object
   I <u>held</u> on to the rail.

V *on to* n, V *onto* n

	Verb group	*on to*	noun group
Subject	**Verb**	**prepositional Object**	
His garden	backs	onto	a school.
She	was clinging	on to	his arm.

Verbs with this pattern belong to the following meaning groups:

1 THE 'HOLD' GROUP
2 THE 'BACK' GROUP
3 THE 'GET' GROUP
4 VERBS WITH OTHER MEANINGS

1 THE 'HOLD' GROUP

These verbs are concerned with holding onto something or becoming attached to something, physically or metaphorically.

*The Socialists seem desperate to **cling** onto power*.

*The pilot was sucked part of the way out of the window but was saved by two stewards who **held** on to his legs*.

*We had one of those can openers that **hooked** onto the wall*.

*Amanda Fairchild **had latched** on to us on the boat from Newcastle to Bergen the night before*.

cling *1,2*	hold *VP1,VPP1*	slot *2*
fasten *4,5*	hook *2*	
hang *VP3,4,5*	latch *VP1,2,3*	

2 THE 'BACK' GROUP

These verbs are used when indicating what is next to a building or room.

*We live in a ground floor flat which **backs** on to a busy street*.

*On the second floor, two shuttered French doors **opened** onto the balcony*.

*French windows **open out** onto the garden from the dining room*.

back *3.1*	lead *VPP2*
front *13*	open *13*
open out *▷13*	

3 THE 'GET' GROUP

These verbs are concerned with starting to talk about a new topic.

*Let's **get** on to more important matters*.

> come *VPP1*   get *VPP1*   move *VP3*
> get back *2*

4 VERBS WITH OTHER MEANINGS

There are a few other verbs which have this pattern.

*From the moment Lee Atwater first **burst** onto the national political scene at age 28, he seemed like an incredible character from a best-selling novel.*

***Get** on to the freight agents and hustle up a cargo for Australia.*

> burst *6*   get *VPP2*
> come *VPP2*   lead *VPP1*

Structure information

a) The prepositional phrase is the prepositional Object.

b) This structure has no passive.

c) There are only two phrasal verbs with this pattern, *get back* and *open out*. The pattern is **V P *on to* n** or **V P *onto* n**.

27   V *out of* n

The verb is followed by a prepositional phrase which consists of *out of* and a noun group. In Structure I, the preposition is followed by an '-ing' form.

This pattern has three structures:

▶ Structure I: Verbs in phase
*She **backed** out of accompanying him.*
▶ Structure II: Verb with prepositional Object
*We **ran** out of money.*
▶ Structure III: Verb with Adjunct
*I **checked** out of the hotel.*

Structure I: Verbs in phase

V *out of* -ing

	Verb group	*out of*	-ing	
Subject		**Verb**		**Completive**
She	chickened	out of	confessing.	
Insurance companies	wriggle	out of	paying	just claims.

Verbs with this structure are all concerned with not doing something. This includes:

- not doing something you had planned or promised e.g. *chicken*, *get*
- stopping doing something e.g. *drop*

*The banks **may drop** out of lending to sovereign governments.*
*I found myself trying to scheme how I **could get** out of taking my kid to the beach.*

*America had decided to **pull** out of financing the proposed construction of the Aswan Dam.*

back VP	**drop** VP1	**get** VPP	**pull** VP2
chicken VP	**duck** VP	**opt** VP	**wriggle** VPP

When the preposition is followed by a noun group, these verbs have Structure II (see meaning group II.1).

Structure information: Verbs in phase

a) The verb is followed by the preposition *out of* and the '-ing' form of another verb. The verbs are **in phase**, and together form a **complex verb group**. This means that the actions or states expressed by the two verbs cannot be separated from each other. For example, if you *opt out of voting*, the *opting* and the *not voting* are not two processes, but one.

The complex verb group is followed by a group, phrase, or clause which completes the pattern of the second verb. In the structure table above, this is called a **Completive**. For example, if the second verb is normally followed by a noun group, then the Completive of the complex verb group will be a noun group.

b) This structure has no passive.

Structure II: Verb with prepositional Object

V *out of* n

	Verb group	*out of*	noun group
Subject	**Verb**	**prepositional Object**	
He	had changed	out of	his work clothes.
They	've run	out of	ideas.

Verbs with this structure belong to the following meaning groups:

II.1 THE 'DROP' GROUP
II.2 THE 'FALL' GROUP
II.3 THE 'CHANGE' GROUP
II.4 THE 'GROW' GROUP
II.5 THE 'ARISE' GROUP
II.6 THE 'RUN' GROUP

II.1 THE 'DROP' GROUP

These verbs are concerned with not being involved in something. This includes:

- not doing something you had planned or promised e.g. *back, chicken*
- removing yourself from a situation e.g. *bow, drop*

We include here *want*, which indicates that someone wants to escape from a situation.

*Actress Julia Roberts **has backed** out of a £1.8 million movie deal.*
*He began drinking and **dropped** out of school.*

back VP	**chicken** VP	**get** VP3, VPP	**walk** VP1
bow VP	**contract** VP2	**opt** VP	**want** VP
break VP3	**drop** VP1	**pull** VP2	**wriggle** VPP
butt VP	**duck** VP	**stay** 5	

See also Structure I above.

II.2 THE 'FALL' GROUP

These verbs indicate that someone or something stops being in a particular state.

> *After the First World War, when heating became very expensive, conservatories **fell** out of favour.*
>
> *Big computers **are going** out of fashion.*
>
> *Most economists predict that the economy **will pull** out of the recession by mid-year.*

fall *9*	go *VP8*	snap *VPP*
get *1.2*	pull *VP4*	

II.3 THE 'CHANGE' GROUP

These verbs are concerned with taking off your clothes.

This is a productive use: other verbs of movement, for example *get*, *step*, and *wriggle*, occur with this pattern. The verbs given here are the ones which are most frequently used in this way.

> *Then she went into the bathroom to get a robe and **change** out of her wet clothes.*

change *5*	slip *8*

II.4 THE 'GROW' GROUP

This group consists of two senses of the verb *grow*.

> *Most girls go through a phase of loving ponies, and most **grow** out of it.*
>
> *I had to have my older sister's clothes when she **grew** out of them.*

grow *VPP1,2*

II.5 THE 'ARISE' GROUP

These verbs indicate that one thing develops or results from another.

> *The trouble appears to **have arisen** out of demands that several senior police officers should be forced to stand down.*
>
> *This book **grew** out of three experiences which happened in 1968.*

arise *2*	develop *1,2,6*	grow *10*

II.6 THE 'RUN' GROUP

These verbs are concerned with using or selling all you have of something.

> *Her doctor was supportive – but the health authority **had run** out of money.*
>
> *A sign of increased consumer demand is that some retailers **have sold** out of popular items.*

run *VP1*	sell *VP1*

Structure information: Verb with prepositional Object

a) The prepositional phrase is the prepositional Object.

b) This structure has no passive.

Structure III: Verb with Adjunct

V *out of* n

	Verb group	*out of*	noun group
Subject	**Verb**	**Adjunct**	
He	had to bail	out of	the aircraft.
Everyone	piled	out of	the car.

Verbs with this structure all indicate that someone or something comes out of or leaves a place or thing.

> On the same day a former police chief **broke** out of prison and took over police headquarters.
> He **checked** out of his hotel room at nine this morning.
> However, reports of unrest have continued to **filter** out of the capital.
> 'If we ever **move** out of this house, we'll sell everything with it,' he resolves.

bail VP3	**clear** VP1	**get** VP1	**poke** 3
belch 2	**clock** VP	**go** VPP	**pull** VP3
break VP2	**condense** 2	**move** VP	
check VP1	**filter** 5	**pile** 6	

Structure information: Verb with Adjunct

a) The prepositional phrase is an Adjunct.

b) This structure has no passive.

Other related patterns

V *out of* n adv/prep

The verb is followed by a prepositional phrase beginning with *out of*. This is followed by an adverb or another prepositional phrase which indicates the state someone is in at the end of a process or event.

> She knew she had to control the situation and **come** out of it well.

come VP4

---

28 V *over* n

The verb is followed by a prepositional phrase which consists of *over* and a noun group. With some verbs, the preposition is sometimes followed by a wh-clause. The passive pattern is **be** V-ed *over*.

This pattern has two structures:

▶ Structure I: Verb with prepositional Object
   <u>Don't **fret**</u> over things you can't change.

▶ Structure II: Verb with Adjunct
The plane <u>skimmed</u> over the trees.

Structure I: Verb with prepositional Object

Active voice: V *over* n/wh

	Verb group	*over*	noun group/wh-clause
Subject	Verb		prepositional Object
They	argued	over	whether to extend the deadline.
She	brooded	over	what had happened.
He	ruled	over	a vast kingdom.

Passive voice: *be* V-ed *over*

	Verb group	*over*	
Subject	Verb	Preposition	Adjunct (optional)
The Council	is presided	over	by a senior judge.

Phrasal verbs: V P *over* n

	Verb group	Particle	*over*	noun group
Subject	Verb			prepositional Object
Emotion	won	out	over	reason.

Verbs with this structure belong to the following meaning groups:

I.1   THE 'ARGUE' GROUP
I.2   THE 'GRIEVE' GROUP
I.3   THE 'FUSS' GROUP
I.4   THE 'PORE' GROUP
I.5   THE 'DAWDLE' GROUP
I.6   THE 'BACK DOWN' GROUP
I.7   THE 'SKATE' GROUP
I.8   THE 'PREVAIL' GROUP
I.9   VERBS WITH OTHER MEANINGS

I.1   THE 'ARGUE' GROUP

These verbs are concerned with speaking or making sounds. The prepositional phrase indicates what you are talking or making sounds about.

He <u>was</u> still <u>chuckling</u> over the letters with Judith and Chris Fortyne when the telephone rang.

From her first moments in cabaret in the early 1950s, everyone who saw Georgia Brown <u>enthused</u> over her professionalism and her potential.

The Consumers' Association says people will get the best deal if they <u>haggle</u> over prices.

The verbs *argue 4, bicker, dicker, fight, haggle, quarrel, row, squabble, tussle,* and *wrangle* always or often have a plural Subject with this pattern because they are **reciprocal verbs** concerned with having an argument or discussion (see Chapter 6).

*We **argued** over household chores.*

In the case of the following verbs, the preposition *over* is sometimes followed by a wh-clause: *argue, bicker, equivocate, fight, haggle, quarrel, quibble, row, squabble, tussle, wrangle.*

*The Senate **has been quibbling** over how much money each state receives as compared to how much each state pays in gas taxes.*

argue *4,5*	**dicker**	**haggle**	**squabble**
bicker	**enthuse** *1*	**quarrel** *3*	**tussle** *2*
chuckle	**equivocate**	**quibble** *1*	**wrangle**
coo *2*	**fight** *6*	**rhapsodize**	
crow *3*	**gush** *3*	**row** *3.3*	

Some of these verbs also have the pattern **V *with* n *over* n**: see page 472.

I.2 THE 'GRIEVE' GROUP

These verbs are concerned with thinking or feeling. The prepositional phrase indicates what the thought or feeling relates to. We include here *differ* and *disagree*, which indicate that people have different views on something.

*Fashion editors **drooled** over every item, from the black wool shaped jackets to the tie-dyed velvet trousers.*

*They have assembled a list of helpful hints for families who **are grieving** over the death of a loved one.*

Differ and *disagree* are **reciprocal verbs** (see Chapter 6) and always have a plural Subject with this pattern.

*The two **have disagreed** over the pace of economic reforms.*

In the case of the following verbs, the preposition *over* is sometimes followed by a wh-clause: *agonize, brood, deliberate, differ, disagree, dither, fret, muse, ponder, puzzle, ruminate, speculate, waffle, waver.*

*Many **agonized** over whether to take the offer.*

*But yesterday Baker said the two sides still **disagree** over when those meetings should be held.*

agonize	**fantasize** *2*	**muse** *1*	**slaver** *2*
brood *3*	**fret** *1*	**obsess**	**smart** *6*
deliberate *3*	**fume** *2*	**ponder**	**speculate** *1*
differ *2*	**fuss** *2*	**puzzle** *2*	**swoon**
disagree *1*	**gloat**	**ruminate** *1*	**waffle** *2*
dither	**grieve** *1*	**salivate** *2*	**waver** *1*
drool *1*	**moon** *3*	**seethe** *1*	

I.3 THE 'FUSS' GROUP

These verbs are concerned with paying someone too much attention.

*Today they lounge at their record company's UK office as staff **fuss** over them.*

cluck *2*	**fawn** *3*	**fuss** *3*

I.4 THE 'PORE' GROUP

These verbs are concerned with reading or studying something.

*We **pore** over maps and photos, and plot fabulous journeys.*

> browse 2   pore 3

I.5 THE 'DAWDLE' GROUP

These verbs are concerned with delaying. The prepositional phrase indicates the issue or thing involved in the delay.

> *Don't fuss him if he __dawdles__ over his food.*
>
> *But ministers __have been prevaricating__ over the matter since the outbreak of the crisis.*

> dally 1   prevaricate   stall 2
> dawdle 2   procrastinate

I.6 THE 'BACK DOWN' GROUP

These verbs are concerned with changing your attitude or plans. The prepositional phrase indicates the issue or topic involved.

> *The British Government has been forced to __back down__ over controversial plans to impose a code of impartiality on independent television broadcasters.*

> compromise 2
>
> back down   climb down

I.7 THE 'SKATE' GROUP

These verbs are concerned with not saying something or not dealing with something properly or thoroughly. The prepositional phrase indicates the words or issue involved.

> *He was scathing in his criticism of the way important evidence __had been__ rejected or __skated over__.*
>
> *In addition, he __stumbles__ over words, and it's not uncommon for him to lose his train of thought.*

> gloss VP   skip 4
> skate 5   stumble 2

I.8 THE 'PREVAIL' GROUP

These verbs are concerned with being in a superior or powerful position. The prepositional phrase indicates who or what the Subject is in charge of or is more powerful than.

> *Today, Mr. Corry __presides__ over a company whose fortunes have changed abruptly.*
>
> *In the end, good __prevailed__ over evil.*
>
> *Free-market liberals __have won out__ over soft-hearted social democrats.*

> preside   reign 2,3   triumph 3
> prevail 1,3 rule 5   tyrannize
>
> win out

I.9 VERBS WITH OTHER MEANINGS

There is one other verb with this structure.

> *When you're busy all day the last thing you want to do is spend hours __slaving__ over a hot stove.*

slave 3

Structure information: Verb with prepositional Object

a) The prepositional phrase is the prepositional Object.

b) This structure has a passive with the pattern **be V-ed *over***. However, not all verbs with this structure arc used in the passive. The following verbs are the ones which are most frequently passive.

agonize	fawn 3	pore 3
argue 4,5	fight 6	preside
coo 2	fuss 2,3	skate 5

c) Phrasal verb patterns are the same except that there is a particle, P, which comes directly after the verb. The passive pattern is **be V-ed P *over***, but it does not often occur.

Structure II: Verb with Adjunct

V *over* n

	Verb group	*over*	noun group
Subject	**Verb**	**Adjunct**	
A slight smile	flickered	over	his face.
Sheer walls of limestone	towered	over	us.

Verbs with this structure are all concerned with movement, position, or extent, either physical or metaphorical. The prepositional phrase indicates the place, thing, or field of activity involved. With most of these verbs, the Subject is inanimate.

*A discernible gloom **descended** over the former drill hall.*

*Speaking to reporters in a lengthy address after their talks, the two foreign ministers said their talks **ranged** over many issues.*

*Soon we **were skimming** over the water.*

*Make sure trailing flexes are kept out of the way behind the furniture so you **don't trip up** over them.*

*The hair on the back of Luther's neck bristled and a wave of temper **washed** over him.*

descend 2	flicker 3	reign 1	tower 2
extend 1,3	hang 7	skim 2	trip 2
fall 12,14	range 5	stoop 2	wash 5
trip up ▷2			

Structure information: Verb with Adjunct

a) The prepositional phrase is an Adjunct.

b) This structure has no passive.

c) There is only one phrasal verb with this structure, *trip up*. The pattern is **V P *over* n**.

29 V *through* n

The verb is followed by a prepositional phrase which consists of *through* and a noun group. The passive pattern is **be V-ed *through***.

This pattern has two structures:

▶ Structure I: Verb with prepositional Object
  She <u>was looking</u> through a magazine.
▶ Structure II: Verb with Adjunct
  He <u>barged</u> through the crowd.

Structure I: Verb with prepositional Object

Active voice: V *through* n

	Verb group	*through*	noun group
Subject	**Verb**	**prepositional Object**	
Some of the activists	broke	through	a security cordon.
She	sailed	through	her exams.
Lloyd	sorted	through	the entire batch.

Passive voice: *be* V-ed *through*

	Verb group	*through*	
Subject	**Verb**	**Preposition**	**Adjunct (optional)**
The floor	will have to be drilled	through.	
Every available Russian magazine	was flicked	through	over the weekend.

Verbs with this structure belong to the following meaning groups:

    I.1   THE 'LIVE' GROUP
    I.2   THE 'LOOK' GROUP
    I.3   THE 'SMASH' GROUP

I.1 THE 'LIVE' GROUP

These verbs are concerned with experiencing something or coping with something in a particular way.

> The third seed Jennifer Capriati **breezed through her opening match** to beat Erika de Lone of the United States 6-4, 6-love in just 50 minutes.

> Life was unbelievably hard. 'I **wouldn't go** through that again,' says Gill with feeling. 'I honestly didn't realise how rough it would be.'

> Another day to **be lived** through.

battle 5	**go** VP1	**pass** 11	**sit** VP
breeze 3	**live** VP	**pull** VP	**sleep** VP
come VP1	**muddle** VP	**sail** VP	
get VP2	**navigate** 6	**scrape** VP	

I.2 THE 'LOOK' GROUP

These verbs are concerned with reading or searching, usually in a careful or casual way, which involves looking at a lot of items.

*Walsh took the note, **glanced** **through the text**, then handed it back without comment.*

*When she was out, Sylvie **had gone** **through her cases** and found the black wig, a hypodermic syringe and ampoules.*

*I've **been looking** **through this handbook**, but it doesn't mention anything that fits the description.*

*Mysteriously, nothing had been stolen, though their drawers **had been rifled** **through**.*

browse 2	leaf VP	riffle	thumb VP
comb 4	look VP1,2	rifle 2	trawl 1
flick 5	plough VP1	scan 1	wade 2
flip 2	pore 3	sift 2	
glance 2	rake 6	skim 3	
go VP2,3	read 1	sort 3	

I.3 THE 'SMASH' GROUP

These verbs are concerned with making a hole or breaking a barrier. We include here *poke*, which indicates that part of something appears through a hole or opening.

***Drill** **through the joint** from below.*

*I could see a rifle **poking** **through an open door**.*

*The thieves used a sledgehammer to **smash** **through barred and shuttered dining room windows** at 11pm on Saturday.*

bore 5	cut 1	drill 2	poke 3	
break VP1,2,3	dig 1	pierce 1,3,5	smash 2	

Structure information: Verb with prepositional Object

a) The prepositional phrase is the prepositional Object.

b) This structure has a passive with the pattern **be V-ed *through***. However, it does not often occur. The verbs most frequently used in the passive are *go* and *live* in meaning group 1, the verbs in meaning group 2, and *cut* and *drill* in meaning group 3.

Structure II: Verb with Adjunct

V *through* n

	Verb group	*through*	noun group
Subject	**Verb**	**Adjunct**	
Thoughts of arson	flitted	through	my head.
The other swimmers	plough	through	the water.

Verbs with this structure belong to the following meaning groups:

II.1 THE 'FILTER' GROUP
II.2 THE 'FLASH' GROUP

II.1 THE 'FILTER' GROUP

These verbs are concerned with moving or travelling through a place, thing, or group of things. We include here *permeate 1* and *run 29*, which indicate that something exists throughout a place, thing, or group.

> He **can cut** **through backyards** *and end up on Royal Avenue. But he's not supposed to.*

> *The sunlight* **filtered** **through the trees** *onto soggy green vegetation.*

> *Indeed the theme that* **runs** **through his entire oeuvre** *is that of role play.*

barge *2*	permeate *1,2*	shoulder *6*	thread *6*
cut *5,6*	plough *VP2,3*	slice *5*	
filter *4,5*	run *28,29*	sweep *8*	

II.2 THE 'FLASH' GROUP

These verbs indicate that someone has a thought or feeling, usually briefly. The Subject indicates the thought or feeling, and the noun group after *through* is usually something like *my mind* (in the case of a thought) or *me* or *my body* (in the case of a feeling).

> *A ludicrous thought* **flashed** **through Harry's mind**: *what on earth was he going to do even if he did manage to stop them?*

> *A convulsive shudder* **ran** **through his body**.

flash *5*	race *9*	surge *7*
flit *4*	run *27*	wash *5*

Structure information: Verb with Adjunct

a) The prepositional phrase is an Adjunct.

b) This structure has no passive.

30 V *to* n

The verb is followed by a prepositional phrase which consists of *to* and a noun group. With some verbs, the preposition is sometimes followed by an '-ing' clause. The passive pattern is **be V-ed to**.

This pattern has three structures:

▶ Structure I: Verb with prepositional Complement
  Her expression <u>changed</u> *to one of horror.*
▶ Structure II: Verb with prepositional Object
  I <u>apologized</u> *to him.*
▶ Structure III: Verb with Adjunct
  We <u>moved</u> *to London.*

Structure I: Verb with prepositional Complement

V *to* n

	Verb group	*to*	noun group
Subject	**Verb**		**prepositional Complement**
The club's deficit	amounted	to	£6596.
Inflation	has fallen	to	4.1 per cent.
His embarrassment	turned	to	anger.

Verbs with this structure belong to the following meaning groups:

I.1 THE 'CHANGE' GROUP

I.2 THE 'INCREASE' AND 'DECREASE' GROUP

I.3 THE 'AMOUNT' GROUP

I.4 VERBS WITH OTHER MEANINGS

I.1 THE 'CHANGE' GROUP

These verbs indicate that something changes to something else. The verbs *convert*, *shade*, and *turn* are **link verbs** (see Chapter 5).

Stir until the mixture __changes__ to a smooth paste.

It has a tennis court that effortlessly __converts__ to an ice hockey rink in the winter.

Her voice __dropped__ to a whisper.

A couple of months later, their euphoria __had turned__ to gloom.

change *3*	drop *8*	shade *7*
convert *1*	extend *6*	sink *8*
crumble *2*	rise *14*	turn *15*

The verbs *change* and *turn* also have the pattern **V *from* n *to* n**. See pages 192-193.

I.2 THE 'INCREASE' AND 'DECREASE' GROUP

These verbs indicate that a quantity, level, or thing increases or decreases. The prepositional phrase indicates the final quantity or level. The noun group following the preposition *to* is always an **amount**. This pattern is **V *to* amount**.

We are pushing for interest rates to __come down__ to 8 per cent at least and perhaps even 5.

Sales __decreased__ to £2.1 billion.

The number of people injured __has increased__ to almost a thousand.

balloon *3*	drop *1*	plunge *5*	soar *1*
build *8*	explode *3*	rise *9*	surge *2*
climb *4*	fall *5*	shrink *2*	swell *1,2*
decline *1*	increase *1*	sink *7*	tumble *2*
decrease *1*	jump *6*	slide *4*	widen *4*
dip *7*	mushroom *2*	slip *7*	
dive *7*	plummet	slump *1*	
build up ▷*8*	creep up	go up *1*	
come down *1*	go down *1*	shoot up *1*	

I.3 THE 'AMOUNT' GROUP

These verbs are used when indicating a total or the result of a calculation. They are **link verbs** (see Chapter 5). The noun group following the preposition *to* is always an **amount**. This pattern is **V *to* amount**.

*He said defence spending **amounted** to 17,600 million rupees this year.*

*In 1894 Hamilton scored 196 runs, which **averaged out** to slightly more than 1 per game.*

amount 2	come 14
add up *VPP*	average out

I.4 VERBS WITH OTHER MEANINGS

There are two other verbs which have this structure. The verb *amount* is a **link verb** (see Chapter 5).

*This **amounts** to a major concession by the authorities.*

amount *VP*
boil down *VPP*

Structure information: Verb with prepositional Complement

a) The prepositional phrase is the prepositional Complement.

b) This structure has no passive.

c) The phrasal verb pattern is **V P *to* amount**.

Structure II: Verb with prepositional Object

Active voice: V *to* n/-ing

	Verb group	to	noun group/-ing clause
Subject	**Verb**		**prepositional Object**
He	admits	to	having self-doubts.
I	apologized	to	her.
Joe	beckoned	to	his brother.
He	did not return	to	the subject.

Passive voice: *be* V-ed *to*

	Verb group	to	
Subject	**Verb**	**Preposition**	**Adjunct (optional)**
These rules	must be adhered	to.	
We	're being lied	to	every day.

Phrasal verbs: V P *to* n/-ing

	Verb group	Particle	*to*	noun group/-ing clause
Subject	**Verb**			**prepositional Object**
	Don't give	in	to	their demands.
Half of them	owned	up	to	having revealed their friends' secrets.
She	never talked	down	to	students.

Verbs with this structure belong to the following meaning groups:

II.1 THE 'TALK' GROUP	II.14 THE 'COME' GROUP
II.2 THE 'ADMIT' GROUP	II.15 THE 'PROGRESS' AND 'SWITCH' GROUP
II.3 THE 'SWEAR' GROUP	II.16 THE 'TURN' GROUP
II.4 THE 'POINT' GROUP	II.17 THE 'ADAPT' GROUP
II.5 THE 'REFER' GROUP	II.18 THE 'REACT' GROUP
II.6 THE 'CONDESCEND' GROUP	II.19 THE 'ATTEND' GROUP
II.7 THE 'BECKON' GROUP	II.20 THE 'KNUCKLE DOWN' GROUP
II.8 THE 'SUBMIT' GROUP	II.21 THE 'LEND' GROUP
II.9 THE 'AGREE' GROUP	II.22 THE 'COTTON ON' GROUP
II.10 THE 'SUBSCRIBE' GROUP	II.23 THE 'LISTEN' GROUP
II.11 THE 'STICK' GROUP	II.24 THE 'CORRESPOND' GROUP
II.12 THE 'CLING' GROUP	II.25 THE 'RELATE' GROUP
II.13 THE 'AFFILIATE' GROUP	II.26 VERBS WITH OTHER MEANINGS

II.1 THE 'TALK' GROUP

These verbs are concerned with speaking or writing. The prepositional phrase indicates who someone speaks or writes to. We include here *propose*, which indicates that someone asks someone else to marry them; *read*, which indicates that someone reads something aloud to someone; and *whistle*, which indicates that someone calls an animal by whistling. The verbs *chat*, *speak 6*, and *talk* are **reciprocal verbs** (see Chapter 6).

*'Don't **lie** to me,' she shouted.*

*She was certain that in the next few months he **would propose** to her.*

*You **had better** attend to the issue of the unauthorized cleaning and **report back** to me in writing.*

*Hello. **Can** I **speak** to the doctor on call, please.*

*He needed to **talk** to someone.*

In the case of *mumble* and *mutter*, the noun group following the preposition is usually a reflexive pronoun. This pattern is **V *to* pron-refl**.

*Finally the woman closed her eyes and began to **mumble** to herself.*

apologize	lie *2.2*	read *2*	transmit *1*
blab	mumble	reply *1*	whisper *1*
boast *1*	mutter	report *2*	whistle *2*
brag	natter	sing *1*	write *4*
chat	pray *1*	speak *1,2,6*	
complain *1*	preach *1*	talk *2,3,4,6,7*	
confess *1,2*	propose *6*	telegraph *2*	
open up	write back	write off *1*	
report back *1*	write in *1*		

Most of these verbs also have the patterns **V *to* n *about* n** and **V *about* n *to* n**. A prepositional phrase beginning with *about* is used after or, less frequently, before the prepositional phrase beginning with *to*. It indicates the topic of the speech or writing.

> *She says when she **complained** to her supervisor **about the behaviour**, no action was taken.*

> *He was forced to change his plea after he **bragged about the killing to a pal** in jail.*

A few of these verbs also have the pattern **V *to* n *for* n**, which is explained at the end of this section.

II.2 THE 'ADMIT' GROUP

These verbs are concerned with admitting something. The prepositional phrase indicates what someone admits doing.

> *Within a week two young men **had confessed** to the crime and been arrested.*

> *Unfortunately, for obvious reasons officials who are responsible for public safety **do not** always **own up** to their shortcomings.*

The preposition *to* is sometimes followed by an '-ing' clause.

> *The most co-operative men in Europe are to be found in the former East Germany, where only 42.7 per cent **admitted** to being useless around the house.*

```
admit 1    confess 1,2
own up
```

II.3 THE 'SWEAR' GROUP

These verbs are concerned with saying firmly or formally that something happened, exists, or is true.

> *But he didn't plant that key here, or make you an anonymous call. I'm prepared to **swear** to that.*

The preposition *to* is sometimes followed by an '-ing' clause.

> *Eva **testified** to having seen Herndon with his gun on the stairs.*

```
attest    swear 3    testify 1
```

II.4 THE 'POINT' GROUP

These verbs are concerned with showing that something happened, exists, or is true. The Subject is inanimate.

> *She can't remember committing the murder, although all the evidence **points** to her guilt.*

> *The range of products available also **testifies** to a widespread dissatisfaction with traditional remedies.*

```
attest    point 17    testify 2
```

II.5 THE 'REFER' GROUP

These verbs are concerned with referring to something.

> *The spokesperson also **referred** to the traumatic effects of the arrest on the mother and children.*

```
allude    refer 1,2,3
```

These verbs also have the pattern **V to n as n**. The prepositional phrase beginning with *as* indicates what someone or something is called.

*She always **referred** to the murder as 'that business'.*

II.6 THE 'CONDESCEND' GROUP

These verbs are concerned with speaking to someone in a way that shows a superior or disrespectful attitude towards them.

*Although Moffett makes his field attractive through the pictures and a simple, lively style, he **does not condescend** to his readers.*

*We're willing to work with them. But we**'re not going to be dictated** to by them.*

*He was also an excellent teacher, who never **talked down** to his pupils, and who was invariably courteous, kind, and considerate.*

condescend *2*	dictate *2*
talk back	talk down *VPP*

II.7 THE 'BECKON' GROUP

These verbs are concerned with communicating with someone by means of a gesture or movement.

*He **beckoned** to Egan, who followed him out into the hall.*

*Surya **bowed** to Danlo and said, 'I'm honoured to make your acquaintance.'*

beckon *1*	mime *3*	wave *1*
bow *1.1*	nod *3*	
curtsy	signal *2*	

II.8 THE 'SUBMIT' GROUP

These verbs are concerned with submissive behaviour. This includes:

- behaving in a humble or ingratiating way e.g. *grovel, suck up*
- giving in on an issue e.g. *submit, yield*

*The Government **will not bow** to pressure from the Right.*

*He's repeated that France **will not give in** to US demands to reduce EC agricultural subsidies.*

*You strongly imply that we **kowtow** to advertisers. Nothing could be further from the truth.*

*We **cannot and will not submit** to those forces who wish to panic our city and who disregard the value of human life.*

*She kept **sucking up** to the teachers, especially Mrs Clements and Miss Pearson.*

bend *7*	genuflect *2*	submit *1*	yield *1,5*
bow *1.3*	grovel *1*	succumb *1*	
capitulate	kowtow	surrender *1*	
defer *2*	pander	toady *2*	
bow down *2*	give in *2*	sell out *4*	
cave in *2*	knuckle under	suck up	

II.9 THE 'AGREE' GROUP

These verbs are concerned with agreeing that something can happen.

*With characteristic astuteness, he spoke separately to all those involved, leading them to believe that he **would** soon **accede** to their request.*

*A scheme to share the costs between insurers and taxpayers **has been agreed** to, but Parliament has yet to approve it.*

*Doctors faced with an adult patient's refusal to **consent** to proposed treatment had to consider the true scope and basis of that refusal.*

accede *1*	agree *2*	consent *2*
acquiesce	assent *2*	
come around/round *2*		

II.10 THE 'SUBSCRIBE' GROUP

These verbs are concerned with holding a particular belief.

*They regard anyone who **does not adhere** to their beliefs as being 'inferior.'*

*I**'ve** personally never **subscribed** to the view that either sex is superior to the other, but I do believe that we're different.*

adhere *2*	cling *6*	subscribe *1*
cleave *2*	hold *3.14*	

II.11 THE 'STICK' GROUP

These verbs are concerned with obeying a rule or keeping an agreement.

*If the appropriate codes of practice or building codes **had been adhered** to, then, in fact, the damage that was sustained in this event could have been significantly reduced.*

*He concedes that there are no firm guarantees that the different political parties **will stick** to their agreement.*

adhere *1*	hold *3.15*	stick *VP3,4*
conform *1,2*	keep *VP1*	

II.12 THE 'CLING' GROUP

These verbs are concerned with holding onto something, or being or becoming attached to something, either physically or metaphorically.

*Delegates at the Conference have accused the President of attempting to **cling** to power by any means possible, including assassinating his opponents.*

*This rattle with three bears will keep babies amused for longer. It **clips** to buggies and carrycots.*

*The stuff **sticks** to your teeth.*

adhere *3*	cleave *2*	connect *1*
attach *3,4*	cling *1,2,3,4,5*	mould *5*
bind *5*	clip *2*	stick *2.5*

The verbs *hang on* and *hold on* are included in Section 26 above (**V on to n**). See page 230.

II.13 THE 'AFFILIATE' GROUP

These verbs are concerned with joining a group or organization.

*But the government recently liberalised industrial relations, allowing trade unions the option not to **affiliate** to the Congress of Trade Unions.*

*The Liberal Democrats were reeling last night after one of their candidates **defected** to Labour just a day before polling.*

affiliate 2	sign 7
defect 2	transfer 4
go over VPP2	

II.14 THE 'COME' GROUP

These verbs indicate that something comes to someone or someone gets something. We include here *come 11*, *occur*, and *come back*, which indicate that a thought comes into someone's mind.

*The attention they deserve **will come** to them quite naturally. No problem.*

*I had rather forgotten what the garden looked like, but as Patty described it, it all **came back** to me.*

*At the end of the lease, the properties **revert** to Community Housing, which can sell them on the open market.*

accrue 2	fall VP1	occur 3	revert 4
come 11,12	go 1.5	pass 6	transfer 2
come back 1			

II.15 THE 'PROGRESS' AND 'SWITCH' GROUP

These verbs are concerned with starting to be in a different situation. This includes:

- doing something different
- starting to have, use, or deal with something different e.g. *switch*
- going back to a previous situation e.g. *return, revert*

*Of all the conventional farmers around here, he's the best. In his heart I know he'd like to **change over** to the organic method we're using.*

*Daniel forced himself to concentrate. But it was no use. His mind kept **flashing back** to the previous night.*

*In various interviews with the media today, he explained why he agreed to **return** to his old job as foreign minister.*

*He **shot** to fame with 'Hello Darling', but his follow-up releases failed to achieve the same success.*

*Eat as much freshly prepared or raw food as you can and **switch** to low-fat, wholemeal foods wherever possible.*

The preposition *to* is sometimes followed by an '-ing' clause.

*The graduate trainee **may progress** to dealing i.e. working in the trading office of a broker.*

accede 2	convert 5	progress 3	succeed 4
ascend 4,7	descend 5	regress	switch 2
attain 2	fast forward 2	return 7,9	switch 3 *(Your attention)*
catapult 4	get 1.13	revert 1,3	turn 14
change 4	graduate 5	shoot 6	
come 6	move 7	stoop 3	
change down	get back 1	move over 1	
change over	go over VPP1	switch over ▷2,1	
flash back *(Your mind)*	move on 3	win through	

II.16 THE 'TURN' GROUP

These verbs are concerned with starting to talk about a different topic. We include here *keep*, which indicates that someone continues talking about the same topic, and *skip*, which indicates that someone misses out part of an account they are giving or something they are reading.

<u>Going back</u> to sentencing, I think magistrates' courts in particular are much too inconsistent with their sentencing.

Before you say that you know your skin type, and <u>skip to the next chapter</u>, let me tell you that the odds are in favor of your being wrong in your assessment.

Let us now <u>turn</u> to the problem of compensating the population for higher food prices.

come *21*	move *8*	revert *2*	switch *2*
keep *VP3*	return *8*	skip *4*	turn *12*
come back *VPP*	go back *VPP2*		
get back *2*	switch over ▷*2*		

II.17 THE 'ADAPT' GROUP

These verbs are concerned with adapting to a new situation.

NATO is clearly trying to show it <u>can adapt</u> to the changes in Europe.

At first Maria <u>could not adjust</u> to life in London.

acclimatize	adapt *1*	readjust *1*
accommodate *5*	adjust *1*	

II.18 THE 'REACT' GROUP

These verbs are concerned with reacting or responding to something that has happened or been done.

One of the first world leaders to <u>react</u> to the news from Moscow was the British Prime Minister.

By the end of the day, Sri Lanka, <u>replying</u> to Australia's 256, had made 265 for three wickets.

overreact	reply *3 (to a score)*
react *1,3*	respond *1,2,3*

The verbs *react 1* and *respond 1* also have the pattern **V to n with n**. The prepositional phrase beginning with *with* indicates what someone does in response to something.

The government <u>responded</u> to the rebellion with the declaration of a state of emergency.

II.19 THE 'ATTEND' GROUP

These verbs are concerned with dealing with something or serving someone.

He added that the President had left the meeting early to <u>attend</u> to other matters.

He <u>ministered</u> to the survivors and explored the uninhabited island.

He told me, 'Well, don't worry about it, I'<u>ll see</u> to it.'

attend *3*	minister *4*	tend *5*
cater *1*	see *VP*	

II.20 THE 'KNUCKLE DOWN' GROUP

These verbs are concerned with starting or continuing a task.

*If you'll excuse me, I really **have to get back** to work.*

*Right, lads, let's **get down** to work.*

*He then **returned** to his examination of the distant vessel*.

The preposition *to* is sometimes followed by an '-ing' clause.

*I knew I needed a house for Rebecca to be independent in, so I **knuckled down** to getting it for her*.

return 9	turn 14	
buckle down	get down VPP	settle down 3
get around/round VPP	go back VPP1	
get back VPP	knuckle down	

II.21 THE 'LEND' GROUP

These verbs are concerned with giving, lending, or selling something to someone. The thing given or sold is not explicitly mentioned.

*The results of a survey released today show that Americans **are** still **giving** to charity despite hard economic times*.

*However, although he has recovered from recent ill-health, he has decided the time is right to **hand over** to a younger man*.

*In this climate, banks were eager to **lend** to anybody with a good business idea*.

*The vendor finally agreed to **sell** to me for £158,000, provided contracts could be exchanged within a week*.

contribute 2,4	lend 1	sell 1
give 2.1	pass 8	subscribe 2,3
hand over 3		

II.22 THE 'COTTON ON' GROUP

These verbs are concerned with becoming aware of something.

*Others later **cottoned on** to the song's potential*.

*Sun-worshippers **have wised up** to the fact that a tan is an indicator of skin damage*.

awaken 2		
catch on 1	tune in 2	wise up
cotton on	wake up VPP	

II.23 THE 'LISTEN' GROUP

These verbs are concerned with listening to something or someone.

*I don't concentrate on what songs mean when I **listen** to them*.

*When I joined the Post Office, I signed a formal notice to say I **would not listen in** to telephone conversations*.

listen 1,3	
listen in	tune in 1

II.24 THE 'CORRESPOND' GROUP

These verbs indicate that one thing is similar to another or is linked to it in some way. This includes:

- resembling something
- matching a description, idea, or standard
- having a connection with something

The verbs *correlate, correspond, relate,* and *match up* ▷5 are **reciprocal verbs** (see Chapter 6) or **ergative reciprocal verbs** (see Chapter 8).

> *The hitchhiker was on the Portmarnock to Balgriffin road, and he **answered** to Rory's description.*
> *It consists of three slabs inscribed on both sides with a text that **approximates** to Latin.*
> *That number **corresponds** to a telephone number on this list he gave me.*
> *How **does** your job **measure up** to your ideal?*

answer *14*	correlate *1*	relate *2*
approximate *3*	correspond *1*	
conform *1,3*	equate	
hark back *VPP1*	measure up	
match up ▷*3,*▷*5,VPP*	stack up *1*	

II.25 THE 'RELATE' GROUP

These verbs indicate that one thing relates to another.

> *The perjury charge **relates** to allegations that Berry lied under oath to an insurance company investigator.*

apply *3*	pertain	relate *1*

II.26 VERBS WITH OTHER MEANINGS

There are a number of other verbs which have this structure.

> *This is money which **belongs** to the members and should be carefully nurtured.*
> *He said that his main task at the moment was to retake the town of Tappita which **fell** to the rebels on the 28th of March.*
> *What **happened** to James?*
> *These men worry that when it comes time to compete for loans, these small farmers **will lose out** to urban businessmen.*
> *Britain **objected** to the idea when it was first put forward by President Mitterrand at the G7 summit in Munich.*

In the case of *aspire, commit, object,* and *resort,* the preposition *to* is sometimes followed by an '-ing' clause.

> *This law was prompted by fears that poor people **might resort** to selling their body parts for hard cash.*

In the case of *lead,* the preposition *to* is sometimes followed by a noun group and an '-ing' clause. This pattern is **V *to* n -ing**.

> *The popularity of the fax **has led** to large sums being invested in its development.*

add *3*	contribute *1,3*	(not) matter *9*	speak *7*
appeal *6*	fall *7*	object *5*	succumb *1,2*
aspire	get *1.16*	point *14,18*	turn *11,13*
belong *1,2,3,4,5,6,7,8*	happen *3*	refer *7*	warm *6*
cater *2*	incline *1*	relate *3*	yield *3*
commit *4*	lead *1.11*	report *9*	
connect *5,6*	look *VP1*	resort *1*	

add on *3*	get through *4,5*	lose out	square up
get across	go back *2*	open up *2*	stand up *2*

Structure information: Verb with prepositional Object

a) The prepositional phrase is the prepositional Object.

b) This structure has a passive, with the pattern *be V ed to*. However, not all verbs with this structure are used in the passive. The following verbs are the ones which are most frequently passive.

adhere *1,2*	attest	listen *1,3*	see *VP*
agree *2*	cater *1,2*	object *5*	speak *1*
allude	dictate *2*	refer *1,3*	
attend *3*	lie *2.2*	respond *1*	

c) Phrasal verb patterns are the same except that there is a particle, P, which comes after the verb. The passive pattern, *be V-ed P to*, does not often occur.

Structure III: Verb with Adjunct

V *to* n

	Verb group	*to*	noun group
Subject	**Verb**		**Adjunct**
He	lived	to	the age of 80.
Daniel	had moved	to	Los Angeles.

Phrasal verbs: V P *to* n

	Verb group	Particle	*to*	noun group
Subject	**Verb**			**Adjunct**
Our association	goes	back	to	the early 1970's.
They	went	round	to	Sue's house.

Verbs with this structure belong to the following meaning groups:

III.1 THE 'MOVE' GROUP

III.2 THE 'STRETCH' GROUP

III.3 THE 'BLEED TO DEATH' AND 'SWEEP TO VICTORY' GROUP

III.4 THE 'WAKE' GROUP

III.5 VERBS WITH OTHER MEANINGS

III.1 THE 'MOVE' GROUP

These verbs are concerned with going to or reaching a place. We include here *come up* and *cuddle up*, which indicate that someone moves close to someone else.

*What does make me uncomfortable is when people **come up** to me and say: 'I love your clothes.'*

*The flats are well positioned for young couples or single people who **commute** to London.*

*As soon as I heard this I **went round** to his mother's house to give what comfort I could.*
*We **were going to move** to Florida, but then he got sick so now I'm going alone.*

ascend *6*	emigrate	immigrate	return *1*
come *3*	escape *1*	journey *3*	rise *1*
commute *1*	flock *3*	move *5*	throng *2*
cross *1.1*	get *1.7*	repair *4*	transfer *1,5,8*
defect *2*	go *1.11*	report *8*	withdraw *2,4*
divert *1*	gravitate	retire *3*	
back up *5*	cuddle up	report back *2*	
come around/round *1*	go along *1*	rise up ▷*1*	
come up *1*	go around/round *1*	run away *1*	

III.2 THE 'STRETCH' GROUP

These verbs are used to indicate that something extends to a particular point or lasts until a particular time. We include here *date back* and *go back*, which are used to indicate that something began or was made at a particular time in the past.

> *The beautiful gardens **date back** to the 14th century and are the same age as the original building.*
> *I **may live** to a ripe old age, but who knows.*
> *The waters **stretched** to the horizon, marred only by the twenty-four-mile Causeway.*

extend *1,3,4*	reach *6*
live *1.4*	stretch *5,11*
date back	go back *1*

III.3 THE 'BLEED TO DEATH' AND 'SWEEP TO VICTORY' GROUP

With each of these verbs, only one or two specific nouns can occur in the prepositional phrase.

The verbs *bleed, choke, freeze, haemorrhage,* and *starve* are followed by *to death*.

> *Reports say he **bled** to death after a bullet severed a main artery in his thigh.*

The verbs *brake, grind, pull,* and *shudder* are followed by *to a halt* or *to a stop*.

> *Egan **braked** to a halt at the end of a pier overlooking an old boat basin.*

The verbs *drift off, drop off,* and *nod off* are followed by *to sleep*.

> *She **drifted off** to sleep before he could reply.*

The verbs *coast, cruise,* and *sweep* are followed by *to victory* or *to a win*.

> *His socialist government **swept** to victory in the general election in June.*

The verb *come* is followed by *to court*.

> *When this case **comes** to court the owners face a maximum penalty of £800.*

The verb *open* is followed by *to the public*.

> *The show **opens** to the public at 3.45 pm.*

The verb *retire* is followed by *to bed*.

> *Some time after midnight, he **retired** to bed.*

The verb *spring* is followed by *to life*.

> *He says the economy **won't spring** to life on its own.*

bleed *1*	come *13*	haemorrhage *2*	shudder *2*
brake *2*	cruise *4*	open *19*	spring *6*
choke *1*	freeze *5*	pull *5*	starve *1*
coast *3*	grind *9*	retire *5*	sweep *14*
drift off	drop off *2*	nod off	

III.4 THE 'WAKE' GROUP

These verbs are concerned with waking up. The prepositional phrase indicates what is happening when someone wakes up.

One night I __woke__ to the sound of policemen banging on the door.

awake	awaken *3*	wake *1*

III.5 VERBS WITH OTHER MEANINGS

There are a number of other verbs which have this structure.

The city __resounds__ to the heavy thud of artillery and tank fire.

When I was about five years old, I remember very vividly __singing along__ to a Loretta Lynn record along with my mother.

dance *1*	redound	thrill *2*
rally *2*	resound *2*	
carry over	sing along	

Structure information: Verb with Adjunct

a) The prepositional phrase is an Adjunct.

b) This structure has no passive.

c) The phrasal verb pattern is the same except that there is a particle, P, which comes after the verb.

Other related patterns

V *about* n *to* n

See meaning group II.1 above.

V *for* n *to* n

See **V** *to* n *for* n below.

V *to* n *about* n

See meaning group II.1 above.

V *to* n *as* n

See meaning group II.5 above.

V *to* n *for* n

The verb is followed by two prepositional phrases, the first beginning with *to* and the second beginning with *for*. The phrasal verb pattern is **V P *to* n *for* n**.

Most verbs with this pattern are concerned with asking someone for something.

> Detectives **have appealed** *to the public for information on the missing girl.*
> **Write** *to the appropriate tourist office for details*.

appeal *1*	pray *1*
apply *1*	write *4*
write off *1*	

There is one other verb which has this pattern. The prepositional phrase beginning with *for* indicates why someone apologizes.

> She **apologized** *to them for the delay.*

apologize

Appeal and *apply* also have the pattern **V *for* n *to* n**, but this does not often occur.

V *to* n that

See page 105.

V *to* n to-inf

The verb is followed by a prepositional phrase beginning with *to*, and a to-infinitive clause.

Verbs with this pattern are concerned with saying or indicating with a gesture that you want someone to do something.

> He **appealed** *to them not to go in for revenge and provoke civil war*.
> He **gestured** *to Marcia to sit down*.

appeal *1,4*	motion *4*	signal *2*
gesture *3*	nod *2*	

V *to* n *with* n

See meaning group II.18 above.

V *to* n with quote

See pages 118-119.

V *to* num

The verb is followed by a prepositional phrase consisting of *to* and a number.

> Chavez and all the others **counted** *to ten before coming back up*.

count *1*

31 V *towards/toward* n

The verb is followed by a prepositional phrase which consists of *towards* or *toward* and a noun group. With some verbs, the preposition is sometimes followed by an '-ing' clause.

This pattern has one structure:

▶ Verb with prepositional Object
We __are heading__ towards war.

V *towards/toward* n/-ing

	Verb group	towards/toward	noun group/-ing clause
Subject	**Verb**	**prepositional Object**	
Britain	was leaning	towards	the French view.
We	are racing	towards	complete economic collapse.
Bernard	worked	towards	reversing these attitudes.

Verbs with this pattern belong to the following meaning groups:

1 THE 'HEAD' GROUP
2 THE 'TEND' GROUP
3 THE 'STRIVE' GROUP
4 THE 'HELP' GROUP
5 THE 'COOL' GROUP
6 VERBS WITH OTHER MEANINGS

1 THE 'HEAD' GROUP

These verbs indicate that someone or something is going to be in a particular state or situation, or is going to do a particular thing.

The ruling party seems to __be heading__ towards a resounding defeat.

The steady increase in asthma deaths is one reason why doctors __are shifting__ towards greater use of preventative drugs, rather than short-term relief.

With most of these verbs, the preposition *towards* is occasionally followed by an '-ing' clause.

The two political parties which form Liechtenstein's government __have been edging__ towards joining the UN for twenty years.

edge *3*	move *10*	shift *2*
evolve *2*	race *7*	turn *14*
head *17*	rush *8*	veer *2*

2 THE 'TEND' GROUP

These verbs indicate that someone or something is likely to have a particular characteristic or opinion, or to do a particular thing.

They're very anxious, and they __tend__ towards depression.

incline *1*   lean *VP*   tend *2*

3 THE 'STRIVE' GROUP

These verbs are concerned with trying to achieve something.

*Vision scientists **are groping** towards an understanding of what the brain does when it sees – or conjures up – an image.*

*Students participating in the programme are encouraged to **strive** towards a high level of achievement.*

The preposition *towards* is sometimes followed by an '-ing' clause.

*We need to **work** towards giving women and children the power and resources to protect themselves.*

grope *3*   strive   work *5*

4 THE 'HELP' GROUP

These verbs indicate that something is partly responsible for something happening or being achieved. We include here *contribute 3*, which indicates that someone is partly responsible for paying for something.

*People from the neighbourhood **have contributed** towards the cost of the shrine.*

*The slowing down of the domestic economy **helped** towards the improvement in exports.*

The preposition *towards* is sometimes followed by an '-ing' clause.

*The document they have drafted **should help** towards finding a solution to the crisis.*

contribute *2,3*   help *2*
count *VP*   lead *11*

5 THE 'COOL' GROUP

These verbs are concerned with a change in someone's attitude. The prepositional phrase indicates the person or thing their attitude relates to.

*When Stephanie didn't return his calls, David thought she **had cooled** towards him.*

cool *6*   soften *3*   warm *6*

6 VERBS WITH OTHER MEANINGS

There are two other verbs which have this pattern.

*These men **gravitate** towards trendy clubs.*

*Steve Homans and his colleagues **are looking** towards ways in which arthritis could be prevented.*

gravitate   look *7*

Structure information

a) The prepositional phrase is the prepositional Object.

b) This structure has no passive.

32 V *under* n

The verb is followed by a prepositional phrase which consists of *under* and a noun group.

This pattern has one structure:

▶ Verb with prepositional Object
He is smarting under his recent humiliation.

V *under* n

	Verb group	*under*	noun group
Subject	**Verb**	**prepositional Object**	
Franklin	chafed	under	this arrangement.
Many campaigners	have been labouring	under	an illusion.

Most verbs with this pattern indicate that someone is experiencing something trouble-some, worrying, or upsetting, or indicate how they are coping with it.

*Did your informant say how the cosmonauts **were bearing up** under this psychological pressure, which must be quite considerable?*

*Mr White resigned two weeks ago amid reports that he **was chafing** under the company's new ownership.*

*But last summer's recovery was aborted for one simple reason: consumers **were groaning** under the weight of cripplingly high interest rates.*

```
chafe 2    labour 3
groan 6    smart 6

bear up
```

VERBS WITH OTHER MEANINGS

There are two other verbs which have this pattern.

*The bar counter **groans** under the weight of huge plates of the freshest fish, giant crabs and live lobsters.*

*Despite their radically different backgrounds, both authors **labour** under the strange delusion that the world is run by feminists.*

```
groan 5    labour 8
```

Structure information

a) The prepositional phrase is the prepositional Object.

b) This structure has no passive.

c) There is only one phrasal verb with this pattern, *bear up*. The pattern is **V P *under* n**.

33 V *with* n

The verb is followed by a prepositional phrase which consists of *with* and a noun group. In Structure I, the preposition is followed by an '-ing' form. The passive pattern is **be** V-ed **with**.

Many verbs with this pattern are **reciprocal verbs**. With these verbs, the prepositional phrase indicates one of the people, things, or groups involved in an activity or situation. These verbs are dealt with in Chapter 6, and are not included in the lists in this section.

This pattern has three structures:

▶ Structure I: Verbs in phase
They will proceed with building the model.
▶ Structure II: Verb with prepositional Object
I sympathize with them.
▶ Structure III: Verb with Adjunct
They screamed with laughter.

Structure I: Verbs in phase

V *with* -ing

	Verb group	*with*	-ing	
Subject	**Verb**			**Completive**
The volunteers	will help	with	teaching	English.
NATO	will not proceed	with	modernising	existing short-range weapons.

Phrasal verbs: V P *with* -ing

	Verb group	Particle	*with*	-ing	
Subject	**Verb**				**Completive**
The EC commission	will go	ahead	with	drafting	a formal proposal.
We	should press	on	with	identifying	our requirements.

Verbs with this structure belong to the following meaning groups:

I.1 THE 'PROCEED' GROUP
I.2 THE 'HELP' GROUP

I.1 THE 'PROCEED' GROUP

These verbs are concerned with doing something that you had planned to do.

*I **couldn't get on** with **clearing up** in the kitchen because they kept quarrelling.*

*A Treasury spokesman said the consultant's list of options would give a clearer idea on how to **proceed** with **overhauling** the Treasury building.*

proceed 2		
get on 2	go through VPP	push ahead
go ahead 1	press on 1	

When the preposition is followed by a noun group, these verbs have Structure II: see meaning group II.11.

I.2 THE 'HELP' GROUP

These verbs are concerned with helping someone to do something.

*They **can** also **assist** with **organising** car hire, ferry tickets, and flights to Geneva.*
*They **help** with **feeding** the cows.*

assist *1,2,3*	help *1*
help out	muck in

When the preposition is followed by a noun group, these verbs have Structure II: see meaning group II.13.

Structure information: Verbs in phase

a) The verb is followed by the preposition *with* and the '-ing' form of another verb. The verbs are **in phase**, and together form a **complex verb group**. This means that the actions or states expressed by the two verbs cannot be separated from each other. For example, if you *proceed with making* something, the *proceeding* and the *making* are not two processes, but one.

The complex verb group is followed by a group, phrase, or clause which completes the pattern of the second verb. In the structure tables above, this is called a **Completive**. For example, if the second verb is normally followed by a noun group, then the Completive of the complex verb group will be a noun group.

b) This structure has no passive.

c) The phrasal verb pattern is the same except that there is a particle, P, which comes after the verb.

Structure II: Verb with prepositional Object

Active voice: V *with* n

	Verb group	*with*	noun group
Subject	**Verb**	**prepositional Object**	
The plane	collided	with	a pine tree.
I	can't cope	with	relationships.
The place	was crawling	with	people.
I	fiddled	with	the radio.

Passive voice: *be* V-ed *with*

	Verb group	*with*
Subject	**Verb**	**Preposition**
The matter	has been dealt	with.
The phone	had been tampered	with.

Phrasal verbs

Active voice: V P *with* n

	Verb group	Particle	*with*	noun group
Subject	**Verb**		**prepositional Object**	
We	're going	ahead	with	the project.
I	can't go	along	with	this plan.

Passive voice: *be* V-ed P *with*

	Verb group	Particle	*with*
Subject	**Verb**		**Preposition**
The present system	should be done	away	with.

Verbs with this structure belong to the following meaning groups:

II.1 THE 'BRIM' GROUP	II.12 THE 'DABBLE' GROUP
II.2 THE 'GLISTEN' GROUP	II.13 THE 'ASSIST' GROUP
II.3 THE 'ECHO' GROUP	II.14 THE 'INTERFERE' GROUP
II.4 THE 'FIT IN' GROUP	II.15 THE 'TWIDDLE' GROUP
II.5 THE 'AGREE' AND 'DISAGREE' GROUP	II.16 THE 'ABSCOND' GROUP
II.6 THE 'REMONSTRATE' GROUP	II.17 THE 'BREAK' GROUP
II.7 THE 'CHECK' GROUP	II.18 THE 'CATCH UP' GROUP
II.8 THE 'SYMPATHIZE' GROUP	II.19 THE 'RANKLE' GROUP
II.9 THE 'ASSOCIATE' GROUP	II.20 THE 'COLLIDE' GROUP
II.10 THE 'COPE' GROUP	II.21 VERBS WITH OTHER MEANINGS
II.11 THE 'CONTINUE' GROUP	

II.1 THE 'BRIM' GROUP

These verbs indicate that something has or contains a lot of something else, or that someone is full of a quality or feeling. We include here *fill* and *fill up*, which indicate that something becomes full of something else.

> By the end of the day, Juliana **_was brimming over_** with new-found confidence.
>
> The town **_was crawling_** with visitors today.
>
> Both horse and rider **_were dripping_** with sweat within five minutes.
>
> Catherine's eyes **_filled_** with tears.

abound	bustle *2*	groan *2*	seethe *2*
brim *2,3,4*	buzz *3,4*	hum *3*	swarm *5*
bristle *6*	be crawling *4*	ooze *2*	be swimming *7*
bubble *5*	drip *2,5*	overflow *2,3*	teem
bulge *3*	fill *1*	resonate *2*	
burst *7*	flow *8*	run *25*	
brim over ▷*2*,▷*3*	fill up ▷*1,1*		

II.2 THE 'GLISTEN' GROUP

These verbs indicate that something is bright or shining. The prepositional phrase indicates the cause or nature of the brightness.

> The room **_was blazing_** with light.

*The tanned skin of his arms and face **glistened** with sweat.*

blaze *3*	glisten *1*	glow *5,7*
gleam *1*	glitter *1*	sparkle *1*

II.3 THE 'ECHO' GROUP

These verbs indicate that a place has a lot of sound in it.

*After dark, the pubs and inns **echo** with music and laughter.*

echo *3*	ring *1.5*
resound *2*	throb *2*

II.4 THE 'FIT IN' GROUP

These verbs are concerned with being compatible with something else, or like something else. We include here *comply* and *conform*, which indicate that something is done in accordance with a rule or someone's wishes.

*The state where a ship is registered is also responsible for seeing that all its craft **comply** with international regulations.*

*Nearly all chores can wait or be organised to **fit in** with a weekly schedule.*

*Her economic and social class **did not square** with her socialism.*

*Choose shades which **tone in** with your natural colouring* – warm browns for dark skins, peach for medium skins and dusky pinks for fair skins.

accord *3*	(not) compare *4*	conform *1,2*	square *8*
chime *VP*	comply	equate	tone *8*
blend in *1,2*	fit in *3*	tone in ▷*8*	
chime in *VPP*	tie in *VPP*		

II.5 THE 'AGREE' AND 'DISAGREE' GROUP

These verbs are concerned with agreeing or disagreeing with something such as a plan. We include here *play along*, which indicates that someone pretends to agree with something.

*Not everyone **agreed** with his conclusions.*

*I **do not disagree** with this viewpoint.*

*The three main political parties are likely to **go along** with the plan, despite some private reservations.*

agree *1,4*	disagree *1,2*	quibble *1*
(not) argue *7*	quarrel *5*	
fall in *VPP1*	go along *VPP1,2*	play along

II.6 THE 'REMONSTRATE' GROUP

These verbs are concerned with speaking to someone in a particular way.

*You **can't** actually **reason** with those people because they don't want to **be reasoned** with.*

*A man **remonstrated** with them but they shouted obscenities at him, so he fetched two policemen.*

(not) argue 6	expostulate	level 14	visit VP
bargain 3	intercede	plead 1	
commiserate	joke 2	reason VP	
consult 1	laugh 1	remonstrate	

Many other verbs with this meaning, for example *gossip*, *speak*, and *talk*, are **reciprocal verbs** (see Chapter 6).

II.7 THE 'CHECK' GROUP

These verbs are concerned with checking something. The prepositional phrase indicates who you ask about the thing you are checking.

> *Remember, these signs do not necessarily mean malignant melanoma but it's best to **check with your doctor** to make sure.*

| check 1 | double-check |

II.8 THE 'SYMPATHIZE' GROUP

These verbs are concerned with feeling sympathy or feeling a connection with someone else.

> *I really **sympathize** with the two officers that had to make that decision.*

| empathize | identify 5 | sympathize 1,2,3 |

II.9 THE 'ASSOCIATE' GROUP

These verbs are concerned with associating with someone, or beginning to have an association with them.

> *The point is, I'm not supposed to **associate** with Westerners, except in the way of business.*
>
> *His wife says she'd have known if he **was carrying on** with any other woman.*
>
> *Many of them had sympathised with the occupation and **had** even **collaborated** with the invading army.*
>
> *Before you **register** with a new doctor, ask around to find one who is good with children.*
>
> *Finally, the young man and I parted and he **took up** with a 20-year-old, and later I learned they had two children.*

affiliate 2,3	collaborate 2	engage 4	socialize 1
align 1	commune 3	hobnob	visit VP
assimilate 1	consort 1	integrate 1	
associate 3	co-operate 2	register 2	
cavort	dally 2	sign 7	
carry on 4	get off VPP	play around 3	take up VPP1
fall in VPP2	go around VPP	run around	
fool around 2	keep in VPP	sleep around	
get in VPP	move in 1	tag along	

II.10 THE 'COPE' GROUP

These verbs are concerned with dealing or coping with a problem.

> *Riots on the main university campus **have been dealt** with by the security forces, who showed little or no mercy.*
>
> *What is astonishing is that the Government refuses to **grapple** with the problem of over-production in meat and milk.*

In the case of *cope*, the preposition *with* is sometimes followed by an '-ing' clause.

*She **has had to cope** with losing all her previous status and money.*

battle *5*	deal *VP1,2*	juggle *1*	wrestle *1*
contend *1*	fight *14*	struggle *5,7*	
cope *1,2,3*	grapple *1*	tussle *3*	

II.11 THE 'CONTINUE' GROUP

These verbs are concerned with continuing to do something, or doing something that has been planned.

*I want to **continue** with my career as a TV presenter, to make the most of my abilities and my brain and to do something worthwhile.*

*In the New Year, the district board will vote on whether to **go ahead** with the plan.*

continue *1,3*	persist *2*	stick *VP1*	
persevere	proceed *2*		
carry on *1*	get on *2*	go through	push ahead
follow through	go ahead *1*	plough on	struggle on
forge ahead	go on *1*	press on *1*	

See also Structure I above.

II.12 THE 'DABBLE' GROUP

These verbs are concerned with getting involved with something or someone, or doing something to something or someone. This includes:

- getting involved in something in a superficial way e.g. *dabble*
- altering something slightly e.g. *fiddle, tinker*
- using something to do or make something e.g. *experiment, work*
- treating someone badly e.g. *mess, trifle*

We also include here *flirt* and *toy*, which indicate that someone is considering an idea.

*He **dabbled** with jazz rock and heavy metal.*

*Well, I **didn't experiment** with drugs until I was in my mid-20s.*

*For a brief period, Macmillan **flirted** with the idea of a new centre party to rally progressive opinion.*

*We were jamming, **playing around** with a melody.*

*Margaret Thatcher talked tough on benefits, but she merely **tinkered** with the system when it was reviewed in the mid-1980s.*

*He was not a man to **be trifled** with.*

*Sometimes Hammons even **works** with materials created by other artists.*

(not) bother *1*	experiment *2,4*	tangle *VP*	work *10,26*
dabble	fiddle *2*	tinker *1*	
deal *VP4*	flirt *3*	toy *VP1*	
engage *4*	mess *VP*	trifle *VP*	
fiddle about *2,3*	play around *2*		

II.13 THE 'ASSIST' GROUP

These verbs are concerned with helping someone to do something. The prepositional phrase indicates the task involved or the thing that needs dealing with.

*For the rest of the time he was left to his own devices, though expected to do his quota of domestic chores and to **assist** **with the gardening**.*

*She loved **helping out** with amateur dramatic productions.*

assist *1,2,3*	help *1*
help out	muck in

See also Structure I above.

II.14 THE 'INTERFERE' GROUP

These verbs are concerned with interfering in a situation, or making something worse in some way.

*They say, however, they **will not interfere** **with press freedom**.*

*And the other problem is where people are too keen and try to **muck about** **with the system**.*

*He maintained that official records **had been tampered** with to create proof.*

fool *4*	meddle	tamper
interfere *1,2*	mess *VP*	
fool around *1*	mess about *2*	muck about *2*

II.15 THE 'TWIDDLE' GROUP

These verbs are concerned with touching, playing with, or physically doing something to something, often with no clear purpose.

*Chef had finished **fiddling about** **with his pots and pans**, and was serving out the vegetables.*

*Do you want to come and **play** **with my electric train**?*

*'I don't have many possessions,' he says, **twiddling** **with his thin, goatee beard**.*

fiddle *1,3*	fumble *1*	play *1,6*	toy *VP2,3*
fidget *2*	fuss *2*	tinker *1*	twiddle *1*
fiddle about *1*	mess about *1*	play around *1*	

II.16 THE 'ABSCOND' GROUP

These verbs are concerned with taking something without permission.

*Unfortunately, his partners were crooks and **absconded** **with the funds**, leaving Taylor to face the creditors.*

*They bought all this gear and people **walked off** with it, they never saw it again.*

abscond *2*	decamp
go off *VPP2*	make off *VPP* walk off *VPP1*

II.17 THE 'BREAK' GROUP

These verbs are concerned with ending a connection or getting rid of something.

*He was sacked from the shadow cabinet in 1968 for his alleged racism, and eventually **broke** **with the party** over the Common Market.*

*The long-range goal must be to **do away** with nuclear weapons altogether.*

break *10*	finish *VP*
dispense *VP*	part *VP*
break off *3*	do away *VPP*

II.18 THE 'CATCH UP' GROUP

These verbs are concerned with reaching or remaining at a particular level or position. The prepositional phrase indicates who you are following, or what topic or action is involved. We include here *fall behind*, which indicates that someone fails to remain at a particular level.

*If children are removed from their poor environments, they **can catch up** with other children.*

*Hard-pressed homeowners can soon expect even tougher action from banks and building societies if they **fall behind** with mortgage repayments.*

catch up *1,2,3,4*	fall behind *2*	keep up *1,2,3,4*

II.19 THE 'RANKLE' GROUP

These verbs indicate the effect of something on someone. The prepositional phrase indicates the person involved. The Subject indicates the thing that has the effect.

*Well, I must say, this place seems to **agree** with you. You all look very healthy.*

*The memories of that game **will live** with me forever.*

*Losing to Manchester United the way we did still **rankles** with everyone.*

agree *6,7*	live *1.6*	(not) wash *7*
disagree *3*	rankle	

II.20 THE 'COLLIDE' GROUP

These verbs indicate that one thing hits or joins another.

*Two people were killed today when their car **collided** with a roadblock set up by protesting French truckers.*

collide *1*	dock *3*	impact *4*

II.21 VERBS WITH OTHER MEANINGS

There are a number of other verbs which have this structure.

*The continuing process of patient negotiation **has met** with limited success.*

*The decision to free him **rests** with the Belgian Justice Minister.*

*In some other spheres, the Conservatives **have sided** with consumers against special-interest groups, and have won.*

*Weathermen advised people to **stock up** with food and fuel.*

belong *9*	gamble *2*	rest *2.4*
bind *5*	meet *8,13*	settle *2,3*
connect *5*	rank *5*	side *16*
stock up *2*		

Structure information: Verb with prepositional Object

a) The prepositional phrase is the prepositional Object.

b) This structure has a passive, with the pattern **be V-ed with**. Not all verbs with this structure are used in the passive, although most of the verbs in meaning groups II.6, II.10, II.12, and II.14 are. The following verbs are the ones which are most frequently passive.

cope *1,2,3*	do away *VP*	mess *VP*	tinker *1*
deal *VP1,2*	experiment *2,4*	reason *VP*	toy *VP1*
dispense *VP*	interfere *1,2*	tamper	trifle *VP*

c) The phrasal verb patterns are the same except that there is a particle, P, which comes after the verb.

Structure III: Verb with Adjunct

V *with* n

	Verb group	*with*	noun group
Subject	**Verb**		**Adjunct**
He	responded	with	a stream of abuse.
He	was trembling	with	excitement.

Phrasal verbs: V P *with* n

	Verb group	Particle	*with*	noun group
Subject	**Verb**			**Adjunct**
Simon	chipped	in	with	a story about his father.
She	doubled	up	with	laughter.

Verbs with this structure belong to the following meaning groups:

III.1 THE 'TREMBLE' GROUP
III.2 THE 'BEGIN' AND 'END' GROUP
III.3 THE 'RESPOND' GROUP
III.4 THE 'CHIP IN' GROUP
III.5 VERBS WITH OTHER MEANINGS

III.1 THE 'TREMBLE' GROUP

These verbs indicate that someone does something or has a particular appearance or physical sensation because of what they feel. This includes:

- moving e.g. *squirm, tremble*
- making a noise e.g. *hoot, snort*
- someone's eyes having a particular appearance e.g. *blaze, glisten*

*Her eyes **blazed** with fury*.

*The boys **hooted** with laughter as they watched the man in the water being hauled into the motorboat, drenched and dripping.*

*His face **lit up** with pleasure.*

*Eve fell into her chair. She **was trembling** with rage.*

beam *1*	explode *2*	reel *4*	snort *1*
blaze *4 (Your eyes)*	gleam *5 (Your eyes)*	roar *3*	sparkle *1 (Your eyes)*
boil *5*	glisten *1 (Your eyes)*	scream *1*	sparkle *3*
brighten *2 (Your eyes)*	glitter *2 (Your eyes)*	seethe *1*	squeak *1*
bristle *5*	glow *8*	shake *4*	squeal
bubble *7*	groan *1*	shake *9 (Your voice)*	squirm *2*
burn *10,12*	hoot *2*	shine *3 (Your eyes)*	swell *3*
cackle	howl *5*	shriek *1*	throb *1*
cloud *5 (Your eyes/face)*	laugh *1*	shudder *1*	tingle *2*
crow *4*	quake *2*	sigh *1*	tremble *1*
cry *1*	quiver *2*	smoulder *3*	
bubble over ▷*7*	fall about		
double up	light up *2 (Your eyes/face)*		

III.2 THE 'BEGIN' AND 'END' GROUP

These verbs are concerned with beginning or ending. The prepositional phrase indicates what happens or is done at the beginning or end of something.

*The proceedings **began** **with a minute's silence** in memory of those who died in the revolution.*

*It's non-stop music right through until ten thirty and we'**ll kick off** **with Def Leppard**.*

The preposition *with* is sometimes followed by a noun group and an '-ing' clause. This pattern is **V** *with* **n -ing**.

*An earlier attempt by police to remove the demonstrators **ended** **with a policeman being shot dead**.*

begin *3,7*	end *6,7*	start *3*
climax *2*	finish *4*	
culminate	open *21*	
kick off *2*	start off *1*	

III.3 THE 'RESPOND' GROUP

These verbs are concerned with responding to something that has been done, or compensating for it. The prepositional phrase indicates what someone does in response or as compensation. We include here *oblige*, which indicates what someone does in response to a request or a need.

*We called up three economists today to ask how to eliminate the deficit and they **obliged** **with very straightforward answers**.*

*When that war ended and people demanded the restoration of their rights, the government **responded** **with arrests and some police intimidation**.*

compensate *2,4*	oblige *2*	respond *1*
counter *2,4*	reply *4*	retaliate

III.4 THE 'CHIP IN' GROUP

These verbs are concerned with making a contribution to a conversation or activity.

*Brett Allison **chipped in** **with another goal for North Melbourne**.*

*I was telling an anecdote when an Irishman **interrupted** **with 'You talk too much'**.*

interrupt *1*		
butt in	chip in *1,2*	pitch in
chime in	join in	

III.5 VERBS WITH OTHER MEANINGS

There are three other verbs which have this structure.

__Hurry up__ with that coffee, will you?

She sipped ice-cream soda, ate more candies, and __sang along__ with the records.

| come through 4 | hurry up | sing along |

Structure information: Verb with Adjunct

a) The prepositional phrase is an Adjunct.

b) This structure has no passive.

c) The phrasal verb pattern is the same except that there is a particle, P, which comes after the verb.

Productive uses

A prepositional phrase beginning with *with* is used with two additional meanings. These uses are productive, that is, they occur with a wide range of verbs.

1 The prepositional phrase indicates what someone uses to do something. An example is *I __shave__ with an old-fashioned Gillette razor.*

2 The prepositional phrase indicates what company someone uses, for example when travelling or investing money. Examples are *We __flew__ with British Airways* and *My husband __has banked__ with the Co-op since before the war.*

Other related patterns

V *with* n to-inf

The verb is followed by a prepositional phrase beginning with *with*, and a to-infinitive clause. Most of the verbs with this pattern are **reciprocal verbs** and are dealt with in Chapter 6.

The non-reciprocal verbs with this pattern are concerned with asking someone to do something. The verb *contract* is also used to indicate that someone agrees to do something, as in the second example below.

If you prefer, you __can contract__ with us to deliver your cargo in our airship, which will be much cheaper than any other means.

We __contract__ with airlines to take their excess capacity and then retail it as efficiently and cheaply as we can.

I __pleaded__ with her to stop but she wouldn't.

| contract 2 | plead 1 |

V *with* n that

See page 471.

34 Less frequent patterns

There are some patterns with prepositions which apply to a very small number of verbs. They are collected together in this section.

V *among* pl-n

The verb is followed by a prepositional phrase which consists of *among* and a plural noun group. The prepositional phrase is an Adjunct. This structure has no passive.

*Citizens were forced to **choose** among candidates from one ruling party.*

*He is a happily unconventional genius who **ranks** among the great scientists of history.*

choose *1*	rank *3,4*

V adj *among* pl-n

The verb is followed by an adjective group and a prepositional phrase which consists of *among* and a plural noun group.

*His prices **rank** high among contemporary photographers'.*

rank *4*	rate *6*

V *before* n

The verb is followed by a prepositional phrase which consists of *before* and a noun group. The prepositional phrase is an Adjunct. This structure has no passive.

*The matter **came** before the High Court by way of an application for judicial review to stay the proceedings of April 28.*

appear *7*	come *13*

V *behind* n

The verb is followed by a prepositional phrase which consists of *behind* and a noun group. The prepositional phrase is the prepositional Object in the case of *lag* and *trail*, and an Adjunct in the case of *fall in*. This structure has no passive.

The phrasal verb *fall in* has the pattern **V P *behind* n**.

*My mates and I **fell in** behind the marchers.*

*Men still **lag** behind women when it comes to buying and wearing fragrances.*

lag *1*	trail *8*
fall in *2*	

V *down* n

The verb is followed by a prepositional phrase which consists of *down* and a noun group. The prepositional phrase is an Adjunct. This structure has no passive.

*The men scaled a wall and **climbed** down scaffolding which had been erected for renovation work on the other side.*

abseil	climb *1*	roll *5*

V *past* n

The verb is followed by a prepositional phrase which consists of *past* and a noun group. The prepositional phrase is an Adjunct. This structure has no passive.

*My puppy **barged** past my legs and leapt into Jilly's welcoming arms.*

barge *3*	push *2*
brush *6*	shoulder *6*

Chapter 3: Complex Patterns

In this chapter we describe complex verb patterns in which the verb is followed by a noun group and another element, such as another noun group, an adjective group, a that-clause, or a wh-clause. Patterns in which the verb is followed by a noun group and a prepositional phrase or adverb group are described in Chapter 4.

1 V n n

The verb is followed by two noun groups. The passive pattern is **be** V-ed n.

This pattern has three main structures:

▶ Structure I: Verb with two Objects
  He gave her a present.
▶ Structure II: Verb with Object and Object Complement
  They appointed him chairman.
▶ Structure III: Verb with Object and Adjunct
  They won the game 4-2.

Structure I: Verb with two Objects

Active voice: V n n

	Verb group	noun group	noun group
Subject	**Verb**	**Object**	**Object**
I	bought	him	lunch.
Her boyfriend	gave	her	a diamond ring.
	Sing	me	a song!
I	wrote	him	a letter.

Passive voice: *be* V-ed n

	Verb group	noun group
Subject	**Verb**	**Object**
We	were brought	a salad.
Freeman	can be excused	his ignorance.
A great gift	was being offered	me.

Phrasal verbs

Active voice: V n P n, V n n P

	Verb group	noun group	Particle	noun group
Subject	Verb...	Object	...Verb	Object
They	let	him	off	his debts.
I	paid	her	back	her money.

	Verb group	noun group	noun group	Particle
Subject	Verb...	Object	Object	...Verb
I	'll give	you	seventy	back.
He	paid	them	the money	back.

Passive voice: *be* V-ed P n, *be* V-ed n P

	Verb group	Particle	noun group
Subject	Verb		Object
Students	are being turned	off	further learning.

	Verb group	noun group	Particle
Subject	Verb...	Object	...Verb
He	was given	his money	back.

Verbs with this structure belong to the following meaning groups:

I.1 THE 'GIVE' GROUP
I.2 THE 'BRING' GROUP
I.3 THE 'TELL' AND 'SEND' GROUP
I.4 THE 'COST' AND 'SAVE' GROUP
I.5 THE 'ENVY' GROUP
I.6 VERBS WITH OTHER MEANINGS

I.1 THE 'GIVE' GROUP

These verbs are concerned with giving someone something, or refusing to do so. This includes:

- giving or selling e.g. *award, sell*
- lending e.g. *lend, loan*
- bequeathing e.g. *bequeath, leave*
- transferring e.g. *hand, pass*
- allocating or committing money or resources e.g. *allocate, allot*
- allocating tasks or responsibilities e.g. *assign*
- promising
- offering e.g. *offer, proffer*
- not giving e.g. *deny, refuse*
- showing

We also include here more abstract verbs like *give* (someone a certain impression), *pay* (someone a visit), and *permit*.

> *The best way to instil in Leo a sense of discipline will be to __allot__ him some specific task which allows him to express his excellent organizing ability.*
>
> *Each patient __is assigned__ a psychiatrist from the pool of psychiatrists at McLean Hospital.*
>
> *A cloud suddenly blocked out the moon, __denying__ him his only source of light.*
>
> *That year for Christmas my parents __gave__ me a microscope kit.*
>
> *He told her that he __was not going to leave__ her anything in his will.*
>
> *Take the goods back to the retailer who __will refund__ you the purchase price.*
>
> *The club's representative had arranged to __sell__ him a ticket for the match.*

The phrasal verbs in this group have the patterns **V n n P** and **V n P n**. When they have the pattern **V n P n**, the second noun group cannot be a personal pronoun. You say *She __paid__ him __back__ the money* but you do not say *She paid him back it*.

> *She __gave__ me __back__ my ring.*

In the case of *permit 4*, the noun group following the verb is always a reflexive pronoun. This pattern is **V pron-refl n**. The verb *deny* often has this pattern as well.

> *Bob must have enjoyed it too, because he __permitted__ himself a fleeting smile at the end.*

In the case of *offer 9*, *pay 1,2,4*, and *tip*, the second noun group is always or often an **amount**. This pattern is **V n amount**.

> *They brought in an American star and __paid__ him three million pounds plus expenses.*

accord *2*	deal *2.5 (sb some cards)*	offer *1,4,5,6,7,9*	show *3,4,5,7*
advance *3*	deny *3*	pass *5*	slip *5*
afford *3*	feed *1,8*	pay *1,2,4,11*	sneak *2*
allocate	give *1.1,2,3,6,7,8,9*	permit *1,4*	spoon-feed *2 (usu passive)*
allot *(usu passive)*	give *2.1,2,3*	proffer *2*	stand *20 (sb a drink)*
allow *2,4*	grant *2*	promise *2*	throw *1*
assign *1,2,4*	hand *2.1*	refund *2*	tip *7*
assign *3 (usu passive)*	lease *2*	refuse *2*	toss *1*
award *4,5*	leave *20*	render *2*	vouchsafe
bequeath *1,2*	lend *1,2,3,5*	sell *1,2,6*	
chuck *2*	loan *3*	serve *6*	
concede *2*	make *1.1*	set *2.9*	
give back	hand back	pay back *1*	

When the verbs in this meaning group have a prepositional pattern, it is usually **V n *to* n**, as in *I gave the present to her* (see pages 418-420).

I.2 THE 'BRING' GROUP

These verbs are concerned with doing something for someone, usually something which is beneficial to them. The noun group following the verb indicates the person or people involved. These verbs are not often used in the passive.

This is a productive use: any verb which involves doing something for someone else can be used with this pattern. The verbs listed here are the ones which are most frequently used in this way.

> *They __can book__ you a room by phone and tell you how to get there.*
>
> *She asked me to __bring__ her some tea.*
>
> *They offered to __cook__ us a Swiss lunch the following day.*
>
> *She took a course in computer programming and found instant success when her communication skills __landed__ her a job as soon as she finished studying.*

In the case of *carve*, the noun group following the verb is always a reflexive pronoun. This pattern is **V pron-refl n**.

> Sagar **has carved** *himself a special niche in the world of Indian art* by creating his own style through different stages of experiments.

assure *2*	**cut** *1*	**knit** *1*	**pour** *2*
bear *1.12 (sb a child)*	**do** *2.2*	**land** *13*	**prescribe** *1*
book *3*	**fetch** *1*	**leave** *8,17*	**secure** *1*
bring *1,3,7,10*	**find** *1,2*	**make** *3.3*	**sing** *1*
buy *1,2*	**fix** *14*	**mix** *2*	**wangle**
carve *4*	**get** *2.1,3*	**order** *2.5*	
cook *1*	**guarantee** *1,3*	**play** *11,12*	

When the verbs in this meaning group have a prepositional pattern, it is usually **V n *for* n**, as in *He poured some tea for her* (see pages 366-367).

I.3 THE 'TELL' AND 'SEND' GROUP

These verbs are concerned with communicating something to someone, in spoken or written language, or non-verbally by looking or smiling. This includes sending someone something, either through the post or electronically. The noun group following the verb indicates the person or people involved.

> I am no longer allowed to be with the children, to **read** *them a story* or put them to bed.
>
> Almost as soon as he had unpacked his bag, he **sent** *his mother a postcard.*
>
> She was Carl Sagan's first wife and **taught** *him most of what he knows about biology.*
>
> Marya **told** *him the whole story of the mystery.*
>
> Emily turned with a swirl of her long dark hair and **threw** *her a suggestive grin.*

In the case of *tell 8*, the second noun group is often an **amount**. This pattern is **V n amount**.

> Being bald is a good life experience. It **tells** *you a lot about how people perceive you.*

ask *1*	**flash** *9 (sb a smile)*	**read** *2*	**throw** *10 (sb a look)*
bid *2.1 (sb farewell)*	**kiss** *1 (sb goodbye)*	**send** *1,4*	**wire** *6*
cable *5*	**mail** *3*	**shoot** *5 (sb a glance)*	**write** *2,4,6*
cast *4 (sb a look)*	**pen** *2*	**spin** *6 (sb a tale)*	
concede *1*	**post** *1.4*	**teach** *1,2,3*	
fax *2*	**quote** *4*	**tell** *1,2,8*	

I.4 THE 'COST' AND 'SAVE' GROUP

These verbs are concerned with disadvantaging someone in some way, or benefiting them in some way. We include here verbs like *charge* and *cost*, where someone has to pay for something either literally or metaphorically. The noun group following the verb indicates the person or people involved.

> How odd it was to sit here now with the man who **had caused** *her all that pain.*
>
> It was this defiant stand against Europe that finally **cost** *her the premiership.*
>
> Our son would gladly wear a sweatshirt round the clock if it **saved** *him the bother of getting washed and dressed for school.*
>
> The man's identity is not being revealed to **spare** *him further embarrassment.*

In the case of *charge*, *cost 2*, *dock*, and *take*, the second noun group is always or often an **amount**. This pattern is **V n amount**. The phrasal verb *set back* has the pattern **V n P amount**.

> The dealer had been boasting to an associate that he **charged** *me double what it was worth.*
>
> Prices are quite expensive - a basic meal will **set** *you* **back** *about eight to ten pounds.*

*It didn't turn out to be a difficult job, though it **took** me two hours.*

cause *2*	do *2.6*	intend *3*	spare *6*
charge *1*	dock *7*	lose *17*	take *2.13*
cost *2,8*	earn *3*	save *3,4,5*	win *2,5*
set back *2*			

I.5 THE 'ENVY' GROUP

These verbs are concerned with the feelings that someone has about someone else, or their attitude towards something that someone else has or has done. The noun group following the verb indicates the person or people involved.

*Whatever his many faults, we **would not begrudge** him the glory that would rightly be his.*

*She **envies** him the opportunities he will have to become big and powerful.*

*She**'d forgiven** him many things over the years because she always believed he loved her.*

(not) begrudge *1*	excuse *3*	forgive *1*
envy *2*	excuse *4 (usu passive)*	

I.6 VERBS WITH OTHER MEANINGS

There are a number of other verbs which have this structure.

*He admitted there were people who disliked him, and who **might bear** him a grudge.*

*He agreed that if what Mrs Reece alleged was true he **owed** her an apology.*

The phrasal verbs in this group only have the pattern **V n P n**. Both noun groups may be pronouns.

*Putting too much on the plate **may put** your child **off** his food.*

In the case of *set 2.9*, the noun group following the verb is always a reflexive pronoun. This pattern is **V pron-refl n**.

*He **has set** himself a particularly difficult goal, which is engineering changes in the way people behave.*

In the case of *owe 1,3*, the second noun group is often an **amount**. This pattern is **V n amount**.

*Now more and more I see I **owe** her everything.*

bear *1.13*	give *1.4*	set *2.8,9*
bet *1*	owe *1,2,3,5*	wish *8*
let off *1*	put off *3,4*	turn off *3*

Structure information: Verb with two Objects

a) Both the noun group following the verb and the second noun group are Objects.

b) This structure has a passive, with the pattern **be V-ed n**. The noun group is the Object. Either the first or the second Object of the active clause may be the Subject of the passive clause, though in most cases the human being is the Subject. Clauses like *I **was offered** a job* are more frequent than clauses like *A job **was offered** me*.

c) Phrasal verb patterns are the same, except that there also is a particle, P, which comes after the first Object, or after both Objects. Some phrasal verbs have restricted patterning, and these restrictions are mentioned under the meaning groups concerned.

d) The pattern **V n amount** has two passives, with the patterns **be V-ed n** and **be V-ed amount**. In most cases, however, the human being is the Subject, with the pattern **be V-ed amount**. Clauses like *I was owed a lot* are more frequent than clauses like *A lot was owed me*.

Structure II: Verb with Object and Object Complement

Active voice: V n n

	Verb group	noun group	noun group
Subject	**Verb**	**Object**	**Object Complement**
He	named	the child	Siddhartha.
Music magazines	proclaimed	her	their new genius.

Passive voice: *be* V-ed n

	Verb group	noun group
Subject	**Verb**	**Complement**
Cerdic the Saxon	was crowned	King of the Angles.
He	was ordained	a Catholic priest.

Most of the verbs with this structure are concerned with:

- naming or labelling e.g. *call, term*
- putting someone or something in a particular position e.g. *elect, nominate*
- thinking or considering e.g. *adjudge, deem*
- causing e.g. *make*

The noun group following the verb indicates the person or thing that is named or considered.

*In 1987, the BBC **appointed** him their Deputy Editor of News and Current Affairs.*

*My children **called** him Uncle Frankie and were always delighted to see him.*

*The Home Office **considered** him a potentially dangerous enemy alien.*

*If you **elect** me president, you will be better off four years from now than you are today.*

*If she makes a mess of this marriage she '**ll be labelled** a complete and utter failure for the rest of her life.*

*In Mexico, his writing **has made** him a well-known public figure.*

*I **make** it ten o'clock.*

*Britain's economic performance **has been rated** a C-minus virtually since 1945.*

In the case of *fancy, feel,* and *prove,* the noun group following the verb is always a reflexive pronoun. This pattern is **V pron-refl n**.

*As in the past, he **has proved** himself the master of the tactical retreat.*

In the case of *make 2.8, 6.1,* the second noun group is always an **amount**. This pattern is **V n amount**.

*A penalty goal from O'Sullivan **made** it 13-3 at half-time.*

acclaim *1 (usu passive)*	consider *1*	hail *1 (usu passive)*	rate *6*
account *6 (usu passive)*	count *7*	label *3 (usu passive)*	be rated *8*
adjudge *(usu passive)*	crown *3 (usu passive)*	make *2,3,6,8,6.1,2*	re-elect *(usu passive)*
anoint *2*	declare *1,2*	be misnamed	rename
appoint	deem	name *2,6*	rule *7*
be born *2,3*	designate *1*	nickname *2*	tag *5 (usu passive)*
brand *3*	dub *1*	nominate *2*	term *4*
call *1,2*	elect *1*	ordain *1 (usu passive)*	title *2*
christen *1 (usu passive)*	fancy *1.5*	proclaim *1*	vote *7,8*
christen *2*	feel *10*	pronounce *2*	
code-name *2 (usu passive)*	find *7,9*	prove *3*	
bring up *1*			

VERBS WITH OTHER MEANINGS

There is one other verb which has this structure.

*Two furious motorists **held** **a man prisoner in his own car** when they found him drunk on a motorway.*

> hold *3.1*

Structure information: Verb with Object and Object Complement

a) The noun group following the verb is the Object, and is very often a pronoun. The second noun group is the Object Complement.

b) This structure has a passive, with the pattern **be V-ed n**. The noun group is the Complement. Only the Object of the active clause, not the Object Complement, can be the Subject of the passive clause:

*He **was appointed** chairman.*

c) Phrasal verb patterns are the same, except that there is a particle, P, which comes after the Object. There is only one phrasal verb with this structure, *bring up*. The active pattern is **V n P n**, and the passive pattern is **be V-ed P n**:

*They **brought** him **up** a Christian.*
*He **was brought up** a Christian.*

Structure III: Verb with Object and Adjunct

Active voice: *V n amount*

	Verb group	noun group	amount
Subject	**Verb**	**Object**	**Adjunct**
The under-21 side	lost	its match	2-0 to Switzerland.
Dittmar	won	the fifth game	15-9.

Passive voice: *be V-ed amount*

	Verb group	amount
Subject	**Verb**	**Adjunct**
He	was beaten	15-10, 15-3.

The verbs with this structure are all concerned with winning or losing in sporting events. The noun group following the verb is either the name of a team or a word like *game* or *match*. The second noun group indicates the scores involved, and is always an **amount**.

> *It's the team which __thrashed__ England 40 points to 15.*

beat *9*	lose *1*	win *1*
defeat *1*	thrash *1*	

Structure information: Verb with Object and Adjunct

a) The noun group following the verb is the Object, and the second noun group, which is always an **amount**, is an Adjunct.

b) This structure has a passive, with the pattern **be V-ed amount**. The amount is an Adjunct.

Other structures

In the case of one sense of *make*, the first noun group is the Object and the second noun group is the Complement.

> *I'm very fond of Maurice and I'__d make__ him a good wife.*

make *4.1*

Other productive uses

This pattern has a productive use, in which the first noun group is the Object and the second noun group is the Complement. Any verb which indicates that someone leaves or returns somewhere can be used in this structure. The verbs most frequently found with this pattern are *depart* and *leave*.

> *Guy Harwood __should leave__ the course a happy man.*

Other related patterns

V n n that

The verb is followed by two noun groups and a that-clause from which the word *that* is often omitted. The passive pattern is **be V-ed n that**.

> *I'__ll bet__ you my next paycheck he'll be home before bedtime tonight.*

bet *1*

V n n to-inf

The verb is followed by two noun groups and a to-infinitive clause. This structure has no passive.

> *I paid £130 for all my maps to cover my 300-acre farm, which __took__ me three hours to get photocopied.*

take *2.13*

V n num

The verb is followed by a noun group and a number. The passive pattern is **be V-ed num**.

*He thinks his team **will be seeded** No. 1 for the third year in a row.*

> **rank** 3 *(usu passive)*   **seed** 5 *(usu passive)*

---

2 V n adj

The verb is followed by a noun group and an adjective group. The passive pattern is **be V-ed adj**.

This pattern has three structures:

▶ Structure I: Verb with Object
 I __like__ my tea sweet.
▶ Structure II: Verb with Object and Object Complement
 I '__ll prove__ you wrong.
▶ Structure III: Verb with Object and Complement
 The dollar __finished__ the day lower.

Structure I: Verb with Object

V n adj

	Verb group	noun group	adjective group
Subject	Verb	Object	
He	preferred	his fish	unfilleted.
He	wished	both of them	dead.

Verbs with this structure belong to the following meaning groups:

I.1   THE 'LIKE' GROUP
I.2   THE 'IMAGINE' GROUP

I.1 THE 'LIKE' GROUP

These verbs are all concerned with liking, wanting, or needing someone or something to have a particular quality or to be in a particular state. The adjective indicates that quality or state.

*The Dutch spread jam on bread for breakfast, so they **like** it smooth.*

*I wanted the house to have a lived-in feel, but I **wanted** it elegant, not too rustic.*

> like *2.1*   prefer   wish *4*
> need *1*   want *1*

I.2 THE 'IMAGINE' GROUP

These verbs are concerned with imagining someone or something to have a particular quality or to be in a particular state. The adjective indicates that quality or state.

No-one __imagined__ her capable of having an affair.

| imagine *1,2* | picture *8* |

Structure information: Verb with Object

a) The noun group and the adjective group together form the Object: they cannot be separated from each other. In the first example in the table above, what *he preferred* was his *fish* to be *unfilleted*; he did not *prefer his fish*. With this structure you can ask the question *What did he prefer?*, which makes it clear that *his fish unfilleted* is a single grammatical unit.

b) This structure has no passive.

Structure II: Verb with Object and Object Complement

Active voice: V n adj

	Verb group	noun group	adjective group
Subject	**Verb**	**Object**	**Object Complement**
The doctor	caught	her	asleep.
David	considered	her	implacable.
The darkness	could drive	a man	mad.
She	shut	her eyes	tight.

Passive voice: *be* V-ed adj

	Verb group	adjective group
Subject	**Verb**	**Complement**
I	was born	poor.
He	was found	dead.
All five crew members	are presumed	dead.
The corridors	are scrubbed	clean.

Verbs with this structure belong to the following meaning groups:

II.1 THE 'CONSIDER' AND 'CALL' GROUP

II.2 THE 'MAKE' GROUP

II.3 THE 'FIND' GROUP

II.4 THE 'BURY ALIVE' GROUP

II.5 VERBS WITH OTHER MEANINGS

II.1 THE 'CONSIDER' AND 'CALL' GROUP

These verbs are concerned with:

- considering, declaring, judging, or proving someone or something to have a particular quality e.g. *deem, pronounce*

- naming or labelling someone or something in a particular way e.g. *call, label*

The adjective indicates the quality someone or something is considered to have or what they are called.

*The journal 'Nature' **called** this book dangerous.*

*We are no longer bound to the view that the earth is the immobile center of the universe, nor even **do we consider** it stationary.*

*I **was** placed in a mental institution and **diagnosed** schizophrenic.*

*He **was** only **passed** fit to ride five minutes before declaration time.*

*Keating sampled the wine and **pronounced** it drinkable.*

*The boss has told me I don't figure in his plans, and I need to go somewhere else to **prove** him wrong.*

Some of these verbs are used only with a very restricted range of adjectives; for example *hold* is used only with *accountable, liable,* and *responsible.*

*They **held** him responsible for the brutal treatment they endured and the inhuman conditions they suffered during their detention.*

In the case of *confess, find 5, profess 2, pronounce 2,* and *prove 3,* the noun group following the verb is always a reflexive pronoun. This pattern is **V pron-refl adj.**

*He **proved** himself equally capable of coping with country life and caring deeply for his parishioners.*

account 6 *(usu passive)*	consider 1	hold 2.10	pronounce 2,3
believe 1	count 7	judge 4	prove 2,3
brand 3	declare 1,2	label 3 *(usu passive)*	rate 6
call 2	deem	pass 15 *(usu passive)*	report 1
certify 1	diagnose *(usu passive)*	presume 1 *(usu passive)*	rule 7
confess 1	find 5,8,9	profess 2	think 9

II.2 THE 'MAKE' GROUP

These verbs are concerned with having a particular effect on someone or something. The adjective indicates the final condition or attribute of something after the action has been completed. Most of these verbs indicate physical processes, while some, like *drive* and *scare*, may be psychological, and some, like *make* and *render*, may be either.

This is a highly productive use: a wide range of other verbs can be used with this meaning. The verbs listed here are the ones which are most frequently used in this way.

These verbs can be divided into seven groups:

(i) The 'pull open' group

These verbs are used with adjectives indicating the position of something after the action has been completed. The adjectives most frequently used here are *open, shut,* and *tight.* Where only one or two adjectives occur with a verb, this is indicated in the list. All the other verbs are used with both *open* and *shut,* and some are used with *tight* as well.

*In a corner, there's a safe deposit box that **has been blasted** open.*

*They **had to force** the door open to get in.*

*He rose, **opened** the window wide, and let in a blast of freezing air.*

*Miss Leon unlocked the door and he **pulled** it open.*

blast 2 (open)	kick 1	push 1	tear 2.1 (open)
blow 1.2 (open)	lever 3	shove 2	tug 1
clamp 3 (shut/tight)	nail 2 (shut)	shut 1 (tight)	wedge 1
close 1.1	open 1 (wide)	slam 1 (shut)	wrench 1 (open)
ease 5	prize 5 (open)	slide 1	yank
force 5	pry 2	spread 2 (wide)	
jam 3	pull 1	tape 7 (shut)	

(ii) The 'squash flat' group

These verbs are used with adjectives indicating the physical state of a person or thing after the action has been completed. The most frequent adjective(s) are indicated in the list.

> *A head-on collision between a bus and another passenger vehicle **has left** eighteen people dead and two more injured.*
>
> *The alsatian bit his arm before he **shook** it loose and ran off.*
>
> *Whole neighbourhoods **have been squashed** flat by shelling.*
>
> *To wash her hair she dunked it in a basin of soapy water, rinsed it and **towelled** it dry.*

batter 4 (flat)	leave 10 (dead)	set 2.4 (free) (usu passive)	stuff 3 (full)
blot 3 (dry)	pat 1 (dry)	shake 8 (loose/free)	sweep 1 (clean)
cram 1 (full)	plane 6 (flat/flush)	shoot 1 (dead)	towel 2 (dry)
draw 4 (close)	pull 4 (free)	squash 1 (flat)	wipe 1 (dry/clean)
jerk 1 (loose/free)	scrub 1 (clean) (usu passive)	squeeze 1,3 (dry)	wrench 2 (loose/free)

(iii) The 'hold steady' group

These verbs are concerned with holding or keeping someone or something in the position or state they are in. Some of the processes are concrete and some are abstract.

> *Japan **can hold** inflation steady with unemployment of less than 3 percent.*
>
> *He began to experience waves of insecurity that sometimes **kept** him awake at night.*

have 3.4	keep 1
hold 1.1,7,3.6	leave 13

(iv) The 'drive mad' group

These verbs are used with adjectives indicating someone's mental or psychological state after the action has been completed. The most frequent adjective(s) are indicated in the list.

> *He **drove the commissioners mad** with his bumbling discourse and paranoia.*
>
> *It turns out he was in a fight and **was knocked** unconscious.*

batter 2 (unconscious)	drive 13 (mad)	knock 4 (unconscious)	send 6 (mad)
beat 1 (unconscious)	jolt 2 (awake)	scare 1 (stiff/rigid)	strike 17 (dumb/blind) (usu passive)

(v) The 'turn down low' group

These verbs are used with adjectives indicating the heat, brightness, or volume of something after the action has been completed. The adjectives most frequently used here are *high*, *loud*, and *low*.

> ***Turn** the lights **down** low, turn the music on and escape to a land without cares.*
>
> *The music room is soundproofed so that you **can turn** the volume **up** really loud.*

283

> pitch 7
>
> crank up 2   turn down 2   turn up 3

(vi) The 'paint yellow' group

These verbs are used only with adjectives indicating the colour of something after the action has been completed. This pattern is **V n colour**. The passive pattern is **be V-ed colour**.

> *The petals of the plant can be chopped and used in salads or cooked with rice to __colour__ it __yellow__.*
>
> *Although white is the most common colour, you __can__ always __paint__ timber or aluminum __frames green or brown__, for instance.*

> colour 3   spray 6
> paint 3,6   turn 17

(vii) Verbs with other meanings

There are a number of other verbs with the general meaning of having a particular effect on someone or something. Most of these verbs are used with a wide range of adjectives.

> *The government considered __making such experiments illegal__.*
>
> *It contained so many errors as to __render it worthless__.*

The verb *slice* is used only with *wide*.

> *The captain swung his left foot, but __sliced the ball wide__.*

> get 1.3   render 1
> make 2.3   slice 4

II.3 THE 'FIND' GROUP

These verbs are concerned with catching or finding someone or something in a particular state.

> *'What I've been wondering,' Robina went on, 'is whether she didn't go out on some impulse, rush over to see Douglas and __find__ him dead.'*

> capture 1   catch 13   find 4,5

II.4 THE 'BURY ALIVE' GROUP

These verbs are concerned with cruel ways of killing people or animals. The adjective used with these verbs is usually *alive*.

This is a productive use: a wide range of verbs to do with killing someone can be used with this pattern, for example *boil, eat, flay, roast*, and *swallow*. The verbs listed here are the ones which are most frequently used in this way.

> *For many centuries the Christian Church __burned__ heretics __alive__.*
>
> *We feel terror at the thought of __being buried__ alive.*

Some of these verbs are sometimes used metaphorically.

> *They are fiercely competitive. If they __can skin__ us __alive__ in business, they will.*

> burn 7   bury 2   skin 5

II.5 VERBS WITH OTHER MEANINGS

There are three other verbs with this structure. They are used with a wide variety of adjectives.

All men, whites and blacks, <u>are born</u> free and equal.

You <u>can</u> boil the roots and <u>serve</u> them cold with a salad dressing.

---

be born *2*   picture *4*   serve *6*

Structure information: Verb with Object and Object Complement

a) The noun group is the Object, and the adjective group is the Object Complement.

b) This structure has a passive, with the pattern **be V-ed adj**. The adjective group is the Complement.

c) The adjective group usually comes after the noun group. Sometimes, however, the adjective group comes before the noun group, especially when the noun group is a long one. This applies particularly to the group of verbs associated with *open* and *shut*:

She <u>yanked</u> open a drawer of one filing cabinet, and pulled out a magazine.

d) Phrasal verb patterns are the same, except that there is a particle, P, which comes after the Object. There are only three phrasal verbs with this structure, *turn down, turn up*, and *crank up*. The active pattern is **V n P adj**, and the passive pattern is **be V-ed P adj**.

Structure III: Verb with Object and Complement

V n adj

	Verb group	noun group	adjective group
Subject	**Verb**	**Object**	**Complement**
Shares	ended	the day	slightly higher.
The Nikkei average	started	the day	higher.

Verbs with this structure are concerned with beginning or ending a day, or other period of time, in a particular state. Clauses with this pattern are usually about financial markets, and the adjectives are frequently *lower* and *higher*.

In Frankfurt, the dollar <u>began</u> the day lower at 1.69 German marks.

---

begin *2*   finish *4*
end *2*   start *2*

Structure information: Verb with Object and Complement

a) The noun group is the Object, and the adjective group is the Complement.

b) This structure has no passive.

Other related patterns

V n colour

See meaning group II.2 (vi) above.

3 V n -ing

The verb is followed by a noun group and an '-ing' clause. The passive pattern is **be V-ed -ing**.

This pattern has three structures:

▶ Structure I: Verb with Object
  I *remember* you saying that.
▶ Structure II: Verb with two Objects
  They *caught* him stealing.
▶ Structure III: Verb with Object and Adjunct
  I *spend* the time reading.

Structure I: Verb with Object

V n -ing

	Verb group	noun group	-ing clause
Subject	**Verb**	**Object**	
My husband	hates	me	being a businesswoman.
I	don't like	them	pointing at me.
He	resented	her	doing well.
The rain	'll save	me	having to water the garden.

Verbs with this structure belong to the following meaning groups:

I.1 THE 'LIKE' GROUP
I.2 THE 'REPORT' GROUP
I.3 THE 'ENTAIL' GROUP
I.4 THE 'STOP' GROUP
I.5 THE 'RISK' GROUP

I.1 THE 'LIKE' GROUP

These verbs are concerned with feeling or thinking. This includes:

- emotional attitudes e.g. *dread, hate, like*
- thought processes e.g. *contemplate, remember*
- imagining or envisaging e.g. *picture, visualize*
- tolerating e.g. *(cannot) bear, tolerate*

*We know how irritating an incorrectly addressed envelope can be, so we **would appreciate you letting us know if we have got it wrong.***

*One hears and sees programmes about cruelty in old people's homes, but you **don't envisage it happening in your own family.***

*'Even though I understand the need for unions, because workers need a spokesperson, I **fear them getting more power**,' she said.*

*Opal, his sixty-four-year-old wife, **didn't** really **like** him drinking so much.*

*Then he said, 'I hope you **don't mind** me calling in like this, without an appointment.'*

*When I was in my twenties and living a rather hippy existence, she **put up with** me drifting in and out of her life.*

*Nobody **can** ever **recall** him firing anybody.*

anticipate 1	envisage	like 2,3	resent
appreciate 3	favour 4	(not) mind 2.1,2	see 8
(cannot) bear 1.6	fear 4	picture 8	stand 17
(not) begrudge 2	forget 4	recall 1	tolerate 1
contemplate 1	hate 2	recollect	visualize
dislike 1	(will not) have 3.12	remember 1	want 1
dread 1	imagine 1	(not) remember 3	
put up with			

I.2 THE 'REPORT' GROUP

These verbs are concerned with speaking or writing about actions or events.

> *Parents of children who abuse volatile substances **have described** them buying five or six cans of butane at a time.*

> ***Do** the neighbours **report** anyone else going in or out?*

| describe 1 | mention 1 | report 1 |

I.3 THE 'ENTAIL' GROUP

These verbs are concerned with a logical relation between the process or thing indicated by the Subject of the verb and the process indicated by the noun group and the '-ing' clause.

> *My job **entails** me driving several thousand miles around the country each month in all traffic conditions.*

> *A move there **would involve** him taking a cut in salary.*

> *We get another customer for our hospital, and this **justifies** us spending money on new equipment.*

| entail | justify | necessitate |
| involve 1 | mean 1.6 | |

I.4 THE 'STOP' GROUP

These verbs are concerned with stopping someone doing something, or preventing something happening.

> *What they want above all is to **avoid** it degenerating into a full-scale military conflict.*

> *They signed an agreement with the National Trust which **precluded** the land being used for a bridge.*

> *The Betting, Gambling and Lotteries Act of 1963 **prohibits** any cash bet being struck on a Sunday.*

> *I think she really would have liked to **stop** us seeing each other.*

avoid 1	prohibit	stop 2
preclude 1	resist 1	
prevent 1,2	save 5	

I.5 THE 'RISK' GROUP

These verbs are concerned with someone risking something happening.

> *Glover **could not risk** four men standing up in court and telling the judge he had ordered them to kill someone.*

chance *4*	risk *5*

Structure information: Verb with Object

a) The noun group and the '-ing' clause together form the Object; they cannot be separated from each other. In the first example in the table above, what *my husband hates* is *me being a businesswoman*; he does not *hate me*. With this structure you can ask the question *What does he hate?*, which makes it clear that *me being a businesswoman* is a single grammatical unit.

b) This structure has no passive.

c) There is only one phrasal verb with this structure, *put up with*, which has two particles. The pattern is **V P P n -ing**.

Structure II: Verb with two Objects

Active voice: V n -ing

	Verb group	noun group	-ing clause
Subject	**Verb**	**Object**	**Object**
I	kept	her	waiting.
She	noticed	a man	sitting alone on the grass.
Much of the film	shows	the painter	going about his task.

Passive voice: *be* V-ed -ing

	Verb group	-ing clause
Subject	**Verb**	**Object**
Palmer	was photographed	wearing an Afghan coat.
Cans of food and groceries	were sent	flying.

Verbs with this structure belong to the following meaning groups:

II.1 THE 'SEE' GROUP
II.2 THE 'BRING' GROUP

II.1 THE 'SEE' GROUP

These verbs are concerned with perceiving, finding, or showing someone doing something.

*As she left, she **could feel** his eyes following her.*

*Men **had been observed** entering and leaving the house with large bags, the police were told.*

The Subject usually indicates a human being, but the verbs *see* and *show* sometimes have inanimate Subjects.

*The next day **saw** us cruising down endless, cactus-lined straights with vultures circling overhead.*

In the case of *catch 8*, *feel 8*, and *find 5*, the noun group is always or often a reflexive pronoun. This pattern is **V pron-refl -ing**.

*I **caught** myself wondering why we ever imagine children will bring us happiness.*

*She **felt** herself beginning to cry.*

catch *7,8*	hear *1,2*	photograph *2 (usu passive)*	show *2*
feel *7,8,9*	notice *1*	picture *4 (usu passive)*	watch *1.1*
find *4,5,6*	observe *1*	see *9*	

II.2 THE 'BRING' GROUP

These verbs are concerned with causing someone to do something or causing something to happen. We include here verbs which are concerned with keeping or leaving someone or something in a particular state.

> *Widow Edna Lawrence survived a gas blast which **brought** her home crashing down on top of her.*

> *The show generated an electric atmosphere that lit up the audience and **had** them cheering till they were hoarse.*

> *Difficulties of fuel, transport, labour and storage have meant that the grain **is left** rotting in the fields.*

> *The explosion **sent** shrapnel flying through the sides of the car on to the crowded highway.*

bring *4*	keep *7*	send *5,6*
have *3.7*	leave *6,13*	set *2.4*

Structure information: Verb with two Objects

a) Both the noun group and the '-ing' clause are Objects.

b) This structure has a passive, with the pattern **be V-ed -ing**. The '-ing' clause is the Object. The fact that you can say *A man **was noticed** sitting alone on the grass* shows that *a man* and *sitting alone on the grass* are two grammatical units. However, the verb *have* (group II.2 above) does not have a passive in this pattern, and *watch* is very infrequently passive.

Structure III: Verb with Object and Adjunct

Active voice: V n -ing

	Verb group	noun group	-ing clause
Subject	**Verb**	**Object**	**Adjunct**
The two families	ended	the day	devouring pizzas and hamburgers.
The driver	killed	time	circling the area.

Passive voice: *be* V-ed -ing

	Verb group	-ing clause
Subject	**Verb**	**Adjunct**
Nights	were passed	nursing horrible sunburns.
A lot of time	was spent	talking on the phone.

Verbs with this structure are all concerned with passing time in a particular way, or starting or ending a period of time in a particular way. The verbs *spend* and *waste* are also concerned with ways of spending or wasting money.

*Harry **passed** the time watching the waitresses as they glided discreetly around the tables.*

*Liberal Democrats **started** this day making their objections to the Republican plan clear.*

In the case of *busy* and *occupy*, the noun group is always a reflexive pronoun. This pattern is **V pron-refl -ing**.

*He **busied** himself rinsing the washcloth, soaping it again.*

begin *3*	finish *4*	pass *10*	take *2.13*
busy *4*	kill *9*	spend *1,2*	waste *1*
end *4*	occupy *5*	start *3,4*	

Structure information: Verb with Object and Adjunct

a) The noun group is the Object, and the '-ing' clause is an Adjunct.

b) Some of the verbs with this structure have a passive, with the pattern **be V-ed -ing**. The '-ing' clause is an Adjunct. The verbs that are used in the passive are *pass*, *spend*, and *waste*.

4 V n to-inf

The verb is followed by a noun group and a to-infinitive clause. The passive pattern is **be V-ed to-inf**.

This pattern has two structures:

▶ Structure I: Verb with Object
*I **need** you to be there.*
▶ Structure II: Verb with two Objects
*She **persuaded** him to leave.*

Structure I: Verb with Object

V n to-inf

	Verb group	noun group	to-infinitive clause
Subject	**Verb**	**Object**	
The English husband	hates	his wife	to stand out in a crowd.
They	would prefer	the truth	to remain untold.

Verbs with this structure are all concerned with the way someone feels about a situation, action, or event, or with what someone wants or wishes to happen.

*Treating others as you **would like** them to treat you is easier said than done.*

*I'**d love** her to go into politics or on the stage.*

*I **need** you to do something for me.*

I wouldn't wish you to view your visit to Paris with any regrets.

In the case of *will*, the noun group is often a reflexive pronoun. This pattern is **V pron-refl to-inf**.

Clenching her fists, she willed herself not to cry.

desire 2	love 9	want 1,4
hate 2	need 1	will 2,3
like 2,4,8	prefer	wish 4

Structure information: Verb with Object

a) The noun group and the to-infinitive clause together form the Object: they cannot be separated from each other. In the first example in the table above, what *the English husband hates* is *his wife to stand out in a crowd*; he does not *hate his wife*. With this structure you can ask the question *What does he hate?*, which makes it clear that *his wife to stand out in a crowd* is a single grammatical unit.

b) This structure has no passive.

Structure II: Verb with two Objects

Active voice: V n to-inf

	Verb group	noun group	to-infinitive clause
Subject	Verb	Object	Object
I	don't find	it	to be true.
My girlfriend	nagged	me	to cut my hair.
The appeals court	ordered	the trial judge	to conduct further hearings.

Passive voice: *be* V-ed to-inf

	Verb group	to-infinitive clause
Subject	Verb	Object
Leaders of divided parties	are obliged	to do one thing and say another.
The price	was reckoned	to be too high.

Phrasal verbs

Active voice: V n P to-inf, V P n (not pron) to-inf

	Verb group	noun group	Particle	to-infinitive clause
Subject	Verb...	Object	...Verb	Object
I	'm not making	him	out	to be a liar.
Time pressure	can spur	you	on	to do more.

	Verb group	Particle	noun group	to-infinitive clause
Subject	Verb		Object	Object
You	should line	up	a few extra editors	to help.

Passive voice: *be* V-ed P to-inf

	Verb group	Particle	to-infinitive clause
Subject	Verb		Object
He	was bound	over	to keep the peace.

Verbs with this structure belong to the following meaning groups:

II.1 THE 'TELL' GROUP
II.2 THE 'NAG' AND 'COAX' GROUP
II.3 THE 'CAUSE' GROUP
II.4 THE 'HELP' GROUP
II.5 THE 'TEACH' GROUP
II.6 THE 'INSPIRE' GROUP
II.7 THE 'CHOOSE' AND 'USE' GROUP
II.8 THE 'BELIEVE' GROUP
II.9 THE 'EXPECT' GROUP
II.10 THE 'OBSERVE' GROUP
II.11 VERBS WITH OTHER MEANINGS

II.1 THE 'TELL' GROUP

These verbs are concerned with communicating something to someone. This includes:

- asking, advising, or telling someone to do something e.g. *beg, order*
- communicating by gesture e.g. *beckon, motion*
- challenging someone to do something e.g. *dare, defy*
- forbidding someone to do something

She looked at him, waiting for him to __ask__ her to come with him.

A retired taxi driver who has a chronic chest disorder __challenged__ a tobacco company yesterday __to admit the link between smoking and ill-health.__

My advisers __counselled__ me to do nothing.

I was walking down the hall, looking into rooms, and this gray-haired guy __motioned__ me to come into his room.

I make no claim to being an expert with this machine and I __recommend__ all readers to follow the manufacturer's instructions.

They are expected to __be summoned__ to appear in court next month for a variety of offences.

The first Yankee soldier to ride up threw him his reins and __told__ him to hold the horse.

admonish	caution 2	forbid 1,2	recommend 2
advise 1	challenge 4,5	be given 2	remind 3
be advised 4	command 1	implore	request 2
approach 3	counsel 2	importune	summon 1 *(usu passive)*
ask 2	dare 2	instruct 1	summons 3 *(usu passive)*
beckon 1	defy 2	invite 1,2	tell 3
beg 1	direct 12	mandate 4 *(usu passive)*	warn 2
beseech	enjoin 1	motion 4	wire 5
bid 2.2	entreat	order 2.1,2	
call 5,9 *(usu passive)*	exhort	petition 3	
bind over *(usu passive)*			

II.2 THE 'NAG' AND 'COAX' GROUP

These verbs are concerned with trying to make someone do something, usually by talking to them. This includes more pleasant ways of persuasion, such as *cajole* and *coax*, as well as more unpleasant ways, such as *badger* and *pester*.

*He kept **badgering** me to go out with him, so in the end I agreed.*

*Lots of countries try to **coax** people to return bottles by insisting on a refundable deposit.*

*Over the last three or four years, they **have egged** each other **on** to agree a whole series of initiatives to tighten up immigration and asylum laws.*

*I **nagged** my father to tell me a war story, preferably one with blood and courage and drama and medals.*

*My education was the most important thing to my mother, and she **pestered** my father to pay for me to go to the best schools.*

badger *2*	encourage *3,4*	pester	prod *2*
cajole	incite	press *5*	urge *1*
chivvy	nag *1*	pressure *5*	
coax *1*	nudge *3*	pressurize	
egg on			

II.3 THE 'CAUSE' GROUP

These verbs are concerned with making or causing someone do something. This includes:

- forcing someone to do something e.g. *blackmail, coerce*
- condemning someone to do something e.g. *condemn, sentence*
- tempting someone to do something e.g. *entice, tempt*
- persuading someone to do something e.g. *convince, persuade*
- causing someone to do something or something to happen e.g. *cause, lead*

The difference between this meaning group and meaning group II.2 above is that here the action does not necessarily involve talking, and the implication is that the person concerned actually does the action indicated by the to-infinitive clause. In this meaning group, the Subject is often inanimate.

The verb *make* occurs in this pattern only in the passive: the corresponding active pattern is **V n inf** (see page 298).

*It's much easier to **bribe** the children to mow the lawn than to get down on their hands and knees pulling weeds out.*

*The force of her shove **caused** me to crack my head against someone else's.*

*There are no vested interests that **would compel** us to conceal the truth.*

*Far too many handicapped young people **have been condemned** to operate at a lower level of education and achievement than their abilities warrant.*

*It was September 1982 when his love for books **drove** him to open his own shop.*

*Kim's gnawing conscience and guilt **led** her to overeat.*

*I did nothing wrong, yet I'**m being made** to suffer like this.*

*She and Kath **were roped in** to talk to students in Blackpool about the strike.*

In the case of *bring, discipline, nerve, rouse, steel,* and *stir,* the noun group is always a reflexive pronoun. This pattern is **V pron-refl to-inf**.

*Even now she **couldn't bring** herself to tell John the whole truth.*

*I want to **discipline** myself to write more.*

*She used to be so shy, she says, she **had to steel** herself to walk into a launderette.*

bind 2	condition 7 *(usu passive)*	impel	pay 4 *(usu passive)*
blackmail 3	constrain 1 *(usu passive)*	induce 2	persuade 1
brainwash *(usu passive)*	convince 2	lead 1.13	push 6
bribe 2	discipline 5	be made 2.1,2	rouse 2
(cannot) bring 12	doom 3	manipulate 1	sentence 3
cause 2	drive 14	nerve 5	steel 3
coerce	entice	obligate	stir 5
compel 1	force 1,2	oblige 1	tempt 1,2
condemn 3	get 1.4	pay 1	
rope in			

II.4 THE 'HELP' GROUP

These verbs are concerned with allowing, enabling, helping, or qualifying someone to do something.

*Julia **was assisting** him to prepare his speech.*

*He will have a fitness test on his groin injury this morning, but is unlikely to **be cleared** to play.*

*You **helped** me to hold on and to continue to mother my own children at times when I didn't think I could even go on trying.*

*Off the east entrance we obediently awaited the signal **permitting** us to enter.*

*The basic course **does not qualify** you to practise as a therapist, but it does give you an adequate foundation.*

In the case of *permit 4*, the noun group following the verb is always a reflexive pronoun. This pattern is **V pron-refl to-inf**.

*I **do not permit** myself to be influenced away from what I think is the right thing to do.*

aid 3	clear 19 *(usu passive)*	equip 1,2	license
allow 1,3,4	empower 1	fit 1.11	permit 1,3,4
assist 1,2,3	enable 1,2,3	free 8	qualify 2
authorize	entitle 1	help 1,2,3	

II.5 THE 'TEACH' GROUP

These verbs are concerned with teaching someone to do something, or with programming or preparing someone or something to do a particular task.

*Modern roses **are bred** to flower more or less continuously throughout the summer season.*

*There are professional courses which **will prepare** students to teach in secondary schools from 11 to 16.*

*A computer **can be programmed** to keep a record of all its internal states and then to trace back through these.*

*She describes her as a 'wonderful, wise, loving woman who **taught** me to accept myself as a human being'.*

be bred 5	prime 6	ready 8	train 2.1,4,6
groom 4 *(usu passive)*	program 2	school 8	
prepare 1,2	programme 4	tailor 2	
prime 5 *(usu passive)*	programme 5 *(usu passive)*	teach 1,2	
bring up 1	gear up *(usu passive)*		

II.6 THE 'INSPIRE' GROUP

These verbs are concerned with motivating or inspiring someone to do something.

*He says the banning of his English play **decided** him to write something about censorship.*

*Jeremy Bentham's utilitarian philosophy **inspired** his followers to promote the greatest happiness of the greatest number through more efficient government.*

decide *5*	inspire *1*	move *13*	prompt *1*
incline *1*	lead *1.12*	persuade *2*	spur *1*
influence *2*	motivate *1,2*	predispose *1*	stimulate *2,3 (usu passive)*

spur on ▷*1*

II.7 THE 'CHOOSE' AND 'USE' GROUP

These verbs are concerned with appointing or choosing someone to do something, or with allocating or assigning something to a particular use.

*Belgium **chose** her to represent the country again the following year and she became a star there.*

*One usher **should be delegated** to pay special attention to the bride's mother and the groom's parents, and to escort them to their seats.*

*Reliable sources in Algeria say new men **have been nominated** to head the country's three largest banks.*

*Trish picked up a fallen branch and **used** it to lift the brambles and probe the area beneath.*

In the case of *allocate*, *budget*, and *vote*, the noun group is often an **amount**. This pattern is **V amount to-inf.**

*President Clinton **has allocated** £16 million to expand an innovative lending program in the nation's poor communities.*

allocate	choose *1*	detail *7*	intend *2 (usu passive)*
appoint	commission *1*	dispatch *1*	nominate *1,2*
assign *1*	delegate *3 (usu passive)*	earmark *1 (usu passive)*	recruit *1*
breed *2 (usu passive)*	depute *(usu passive)*	employ *1*	use *1.1*
budget *4*	be designed *8*	enlist *2*	vote *7*

line up *4*

II.8 THE 'BELIEVE' GROUP

These verbs are concerned with thinking, saying, or showing something. Some of these verbs, such as *prove* and *show*, sometimes have inanimate Subjects. The verb that most frequently occurs in the to-infinitive clause is *be*.

*The French government **is believed** to be planning to send transport helicopters to work alongside the Germans.*

*The Guardian concentrates on the likelihood that NATO leaders **will declare** nuclear weapons to be 'weapons of last resort'.*

*If Rickmore's as intelligent as I **judge** him to be, by now he'll have had to realize where our questions were leading.*

*He distrusted human reason, **knew** it to be fallible.*

*The buyer **was presumed** to be Japanese because telephone bids were negotiated by a Japanese member of staff.*

Islands __are seen__ to offer solitude, relaxation and a safe retreat, a womb of security.
She left the course by ambulance and __was thought__ to have suffered a neck injury.

In the case of *prove 3*, the noun group is always a reflexive pronoun. This pattern is **V pron-refl to-inf**.

Yeltsin __has__ above all in the last few days __proved__ himself to be a highly skilled politician.

acknowledge *1,2*	**deem** *(usu passive)*	**prove** *2,3*	**show** *1,7 (usu passive)*
adjudge *(usu passive)*	**discover** *1 (usu passive)*	**reckon** *2,4 (usu passive)*	**take** *2.25*
allege *(usu passive)*	**feel** *10*	**report** *1 (usu passive)*	**think** *1*
assume *1 (usu passive)*	**find** *7*	**be reputed**	**think** *2 (usu passive)*
believe *1*	**judge** *4,5*	**be rumoured**	**understand** *5 (usu passive)*
consider *1*	**know** *1*	**be said** *1*	
declare *1,2*	**presume** *1 (usu passive)*	**be seen** *6*	
make out *7.3*			

II.9 THE 'EXPECT' GROUP

These verbs are concerned with intentions, predictions, and expectations.

He had pinned his hopes on his friend and even after three days he __expected__ him to turn up at any minute.

The bookies __are fancying__ Brown Windsor to take first prize, while the diehard romantics favour former winner, West Tip.

He __had been scheduled__ to return to Washington, but now he clearly hoped to stay on.

He __trusted__ her to tell the truth because he knew that she always told the truth.

In the case of *pledge*, the noun group is always a reflexive pronoun. This pattern is **V pron-refl to-inf**. The verb *trust 5* often has this pattern as well.

Gathering fungi is a mystery to most Britons. Few __trust__ themselves to recognise what is safe, and they may be wise to err on the side of caution.

back *3.4*	**intend** *3*	**project** *3 (usu passive)*	**time** *19*
bill *7 (usu passive)*	**leave** *7,15*	**require** *1,2*	**timetable** *4 (usu passive)*
expect *1,3*	**mean** *1.8*	**schedule** *3 (usu passive)*	**tip** *10 (usu passive)*
(not) expect *4*	**mean** *1.11 (usu passive)*	**second** *3.0 (usu passive)*	**trust** *3,5*
fancy *1.6*	**pledge** *3*	**be slated** *4*	

II.10 THE 'OBSERVE' GROUP

These verbs are concerned with someone being heard or seen to do something. These verbs occur in this pattern only in the passive: in the case of *hear, observe,* and *see 1* the corresponding active pattern is **V n inf** (see page 298).

New mothers __have been observed__ to touch the feet and hands first, then the body, and then the baby's face.

be heard *1,2,3*	**be observed** *1*	**be seen** *1,4*

II.11 VERBS WITH OTHER MEANINGS

There are a number of other verbs which have this structure.

Mrs Mills said yesterday she __was honoured__ to have been appointed.

In the case of *trouble*, the noun group is always a reflexive pronoun. This pattern is **V pron-refl to-inf**.

'We've got some leads,' Douglas said, __not troubling__ himself to conceal the lie.

In the case of *do*, the noun group is always an **amount**. This pattern is **V amount to-inf**. The verb *take* often has this pattern as well.

> We *'ve done* a lot to improve results, and a lot more will be done.
> The treatment *takes* up to twelve months to produce worthwhile improvement.

bail 3 *(usu passive)*	**be honoured** 5	**turn** 2
be born 2	**take** 2.13	
do 2.7	**(not) trouble** 10	

Structure information: Verb with two Objects

a) Both the noun group and the to-infinitive clause are Objects.

b) This structure has a passive, with the pattern **be V-ed to-inf**. The to-infinitive clause is the Object. The fact that you can say *I was nagged to cut my hair* shows that *me* and *to cut my hair* are two grammatical units.

c) Phrasal verb patterns are the same, except that there is also a particle, P. The first Object comes either between the verb and the particle, or after the particle. When this Object comes after the particle, it cannot be a personal pronoun. You say

> The court *can bind* them *over* to control the offender
> or The court *can bind over* parents to control the offender

but you do not say *The court can bind over them to control the offender*.

Other related patterns

V n n to-inf

See page 279.

5   V n inf

The verb is followed by a noun group and a **bare infinitive** clause.

This pattern has one structure:

▶ Verb with two Objects
I *saw* him leave.

V n inf

	Verb group	noun group	infinitive clause
Subject	**Verb**	**Object**	**Object**
The voices	bade	her	go to the Dauphin.
Pemberton	felt	something	touch his knee.
She	heard	the man	laugh.

Verbs with this pattern belong to the following meaning groups:

1   THE 'SEE' GROUP
2   THE 'LET' GROUP
3   THE 'HELP' GROUP

1 THE 'SEE' GROUP

These verbs are concerned with seeing, hearing, or feeling someone or something perform an action.

*He had opened the door and was about to climb in when he __noticed__ **a figure detach itself from the shadows of the building and make its way towards him.***

*It's hard to __watch__ **youth slip away** in the mirror and realize that you're no longer growing up but growing old.*

In the case of *see 9*, there may be an inanimate Subject.

*The first half of this year __saw__ **arrears rise to record levels.***

In the case of *feel 8*, the noun group is often a reflexive pronoun. This pattern is **V pron-refl inf**.

*I __felt__ **myself grow cold** and my hands trembled as I read: We have your son. He is safe so far. If you obey orders he will soon be back with you.*

feel *7,8*	notice *1*	see *1,9*
hear *1,2,3*	observe *1*	watch *1.1*

2 THE 'LET' GROUP

These verbs are concerned with letting someone perform an action, bidding them do it, or making them do it. If the first Object is inanimate, these verbs are concerned with letting or making something happen.

*My advice is to find a knowledgeable professional who is familiar with your game and __have__ **him recommend a club that best fits your needs.***

*If you want to be saved, __let__ **others live in safety** too.*

*I wanted to find some way to __make__ **her commit herself to the group.***

*Let's see what people want, and __make__ **it happen.***

In the case of *let 1*, the noun group is often a reflexive pronoun. This pattern is **V pron-refl inf**.

*Even during his electoral campaign, he was careful never to __let__ **himself be committed to any definite promises of freedom for all.***

In the case of *let 4,5,6,7,8,9,13*, the noun group is always *me* or *us*. This pattern is **V me/us inf**. The verb is imperative.

*__Let__ **us look more closely at what else besides gender comes to us inherently at birth.***

bid *2.2*	let *1,2,4,5,6,7,8,9,10,11,12,13*
have *3.6,7*	make *2.1,2,4*

3 THE 'HELP' GROUP

This group consists of three senses of the verb *help*.

*Knowledgeable, friendly staff __can help__ **you make your choice from the hundreds of different rings available.***

help *1,2,3*

Structure information

a) Both the noun group and the infinitive clause are Objects.

b) Most of the verbs with this structure have no exact passive equivalent: when these verbs are passive, they behave like the verbs in Structure II of **V n to-inf**; that is, the to-infinitive is used, and the pattern is **be V-ed to-inf**, as in the clause *He was seen to hit out with his whip.*

There are some exceptions to this. *Let* has a passive with the pattern **be V-ed inf**. This is not very frequent, and is used mainly with *go*:

His few opponents can safely be let go.

The other exceptions are *have, notice,* and *watch,* which have no passive at all in this sense.

6 V n that

The verb is followed by a noun group and a that-clause. The passive pattern is **be V-ed that**.

This pattern has one structure:

▶ Verb with Object and Clause
I told her that there had been an accident.

Active voice: V n that

	Verb group	noun group	that-clause
Subject	**Verb**	**Object**	**Clause**
She	told	me	he'd planned to be away all that night.
I	warned	her	that I might not last out my hours of duty.

Passive voice: *be* V-ed that

	Verb group	that-clause
Subject	**Verb**	**Clause**
He	was informed	that he had been disqualified.
His father	was persuaded	that the boy should stay in school.

Most verbs with this pattern are concerned with causing someone to know or think something.

*We are pleased to **inform** you that your request for tenure has been granted.*
*I **reminded** her that on several occasions she had remarked on the boy's improvement.*
*When she called at his studio, she **was told** that he had gone to Biarritz.*

The verbs *decide* and *tell* 8 always have an inanimate Subject, and are not used in the passive.

*All other indicators **tell** us that our customers are more satisfied now with our service than they have ever been.*

The verbs *convince, remind, show,* and *teach* sometimes have an inanimate Subject.

By the time he was eighteen years old, something happened which __convinced__ him that he was destined for great things.

In the case of the following verbs, the noun group is always or often a reflexive pronoun: *assure, console, convince, delude, flatter, kid, persuade, promise, reassure, remind, satisfy, tell.* This pattern is **V pron-refl that**. These verbs indicate that someone has or acquires a particular idea or thought, often a comforting or confident one.

I __flatter__ myself I've done it all rather well.

I __have been kidding__ myself that the scoring records don't matter, but I know they will cross my mind a few times between now and Saturday.

__Remind__ yourself that the feelings will not last forever, and will become easier to cope with.

assure *1*	delude *1*	kid *6*	satisfy *2*
bet *1*	flatter *2*	notify	show *1*
caution *2*	forewarn	persuade *3*	teach *2*
console *1*	guarantee *3*	promise *1*	tell *1,4,8*
convince *1*	inform *1*	reassure	warn *1*
decide *5*	instruct *1*	remind *1,2*	

VERBS WITH OTHER MEANINGS

There are three other verbs which have this pattern.

In the case of *lay*, the noun group is always *money* or *odds*.

The sky's the limit and I'__d lay__ money he will go on to play for England.

In the case of *hit* and *strike*, the that-clause qualifies the noun *thought* rather than being part of a true verb pattern.

The thought __struck__ me that she was the wrong age for this.

hit *5*	lay *1.8*	strike *10*

Structure information

a) The noun group is the Object, and the that-clause is a new clause, with its own structure. The word *that* can be left out with the more frequent verbs. (See pages 102-103 for more information about omitting *that*.)

b) This structure has a passive, with the pattern **be V-ed that**.

Other related patterns

V n n that

See page 279.

7 V n wh

The verb is followed by a noun group and a finite wh-clause. The passive pattern is **be V-ed wh**.

This pattern has one structure:

► Verb with Object and Clause
He showed me where I should go.

Active voice: V n wh

	Verb group	noun group	wh-clause
Subject	**Verb**	**Object**	**Clause**
One boy	asked	another	what was wrong with him.
Years of working in Louisiana	have taught	him	why poor people need unions.

Passive voice: *be* V-ed wh

	Verb group	wh-clause
Subject	**Verb**	**Clause**
The woman	is being shown	how the gas cooker works.
They	haven't been told	what is planned.

Verbs with this pattern are concerned with asking, telling, teaching, or showing someone something. The Subject may be human or inanimate, with the exception of the verbs *advise* and *ask*, which always have human Subjects.

> *About seven years ago she felt she **had to ask** herself whether she really wanted to spend her life teaching.*

> *Political Economy **may instruct** us how a nation may become rich; it does not teach us how to get rich as individuals.*

> *Chernobyl mercilessly **reminded** us what all of us would suffer if a nuclear thunderstorm was unleashed.*

> *The authors wrote to them last week to **warn** them what was about to come out in the press.*

advise *1*	**instruct** *1*	**teach** *1,2*
ask *1*	**remind** *1,2*	**tell** *1,8*
inform *1*	**show** *3,5*	**warn** *1*

Structure information

a) The noun group is the Object, and the wh-clause is a new clause, with its own structure.

b) This structure has a passive, with the pattern *be* V-ed wh. The wh-clause is a new clause.

8 V n wh-to-inf

The verb is followed by a noun group and a to-infinitive clause introduced by a wh-word. The passive pattern is *be* V-ed wh-to-inf.

This pattern has one structure:

► Verb with two Objects
I 'll show you how to do it.

Active voice: V n wh-to-inf

	Verb group	noun group	wh-to-infinitive clause
Subject	**Verb**	**Object**	**Object**
He	has instructed	millions of people	how to raise their children.
I	'll show	you	what to watch out for.

Passive voice: *be* V-ed wh-to-inf

	Verb group	wh-to-infinitive clause
Subject	**Verb**	**Object**
She	was shown	how to cleanse her skin.
He	needs to be told	what to do.

Verbs with this pattern are concerned with asking, telling, teaching, or showing someone something. The Subject may be human or inanimate, with the exception of the verbs *advise* and *ask*, which always have human Subjects.

*The nurse **will advise** you how to clear up the infection quickly and easily.*

*Republicans in Congress **are asking** themselves how best to use their new-found political capital.*

*The Health Secretary, Mr Kenneth Clarke, said the aim was to **inform** the public how to get the best out of the new arrangements.*

advise 1	instruct 1	teach 1,2
ask 1	remind 1,2	tell 1,8
inform 1	show 3,5	warn 1

Structure information

a) This structure has two Objects. The noun group is the first Object, and the wh-word and the to-infinitive clause together form the second Object.

b) This structure has a passive, with the pattern *be* V-ed **wh-to-inf**. The wh-word and the to-infinitive clause together form the Object.

9 V n with quote

The verb is followed by a noun group and is used with a quote clause. The passive pattern is *be* V-ed with quote.

This pattern has one structure:

▶ Verb with Object and Clause
'I'm used to it,' I told him.

Active voice: V n with quote

The Subject, Verb, and Object can come after, within, or before the quote clause.

quote clause		Verb group	noun group
Clause	Subject	Verb	Object
'Absolutely,'	Cross	assured	her.
'We'll do it,'	she	promised	him.

quote clause...		Verb group	noun group	...quote clause
Clause...	Subject	Verb	Object	...Clause
'As you have said,'	David	reminded	him,	'the truth is the truth.'
'At one point,'	she	told	me,	'Sofia left the room.'

	Verb group	noun group	quote clause
Subject	Verb	Object	Clause
He	asked	me,	'Who are these people?'
My trainer	had warned	me:	'This guy means business.'

Passive voice: be V-ed with quote

The Subject and Verb can come after, within, or before the quote clause. They most frequently come after it, as shown below.

quote clause		Verb group
Clause	Subject	Verb
'Only include relevant achievements,'	I	was advised.
'This is considered unacceptable,'	he	was told.

Verbs with this pattern are all concerned with telling and asking. The person being addressed is indicated by the noun group.

*'It's OK,' she **was assured**. 'I know the fishermen from here and I will explain and pay.'*

*'A suite is always kept ready for me,' Loveday **informed** him with a little laugh.*

*'It changed me,' she **told** me.*

*'Don't move,' I **warned** him and took out my clasp knife.*

In the case of *tell 4*, the noun group following the verb is always a reflexive pronoun. This pattern is **V pron-refl with quote**. This verb indicates that someone thinks something, usually something encouraging.

*'I am going to make it,' I **told** myself.*

admonish	cable 5	implore	promise 1
advise 1	command 1	inform 1	remind 1
ask 1	correct 6	instruct 1	tell 1,4
assure 1	entreat	interrupt 1	urge 1
beg 1	exhort	order 2.1	warn 2

Most of the verbs with this pattern also have the pattern **V with quote**. The exceptions are *assure*, *inform*, *remind*, and *tell*.

Structure information

a) The noun group is the Object. The quote clause is a new clause, with its own structure. It may be one word, such as *yes*, or it may be much longer. The Subject and verb most frequently come after the quote clause, but they can also come before it or in the middle of it.

b) This structure has a passive, with the pattern *be* **V-ed with quote**.

Other related patterns

V n quote

The verb is followed by a noun group and a quote clause. The position of the quote clause is not variable. The passive pattern is *be* **V-ed quote**.

Verbs with this pattern belong to the following meaning groups:

1 THE 'CAPTION' GROUP
2 THE 'PRONOUNCE' GROUP

1 THE 'CAPTION' GROUP

These verbs are concerned with labelling or inscribing. The noun group indicates the thing that is labelled or inscribed.

*The photograph **is captioned** 'Farnborough, Friday, 5th September 1952'.*

*Too often he merely read a report, **marked** it 'seen' and took no action.*

The quote clause often occurs after an '-ed' form used to qualify a noun. This pattern is **V-ed quote**.

*The churchyard was full of headstones of wartime sailors whose bodies had fetched up on Colonsay beaches, some named and others **inscribed** simply 'A Sailor'.*

caption *2*	be headed *18*	label *3*
engrave	be headlined	mark *4*
be entitled *2*	be inscribed *1,2*	be subtitled *1*

2 THE 'PRONOUNCE' GROUP

These verbs indicate the way a word is pronounced or spelt.

*'This is your own Tuesday phone-in,' the DJ intoned, **pronouncing** it Chewsday.*

*Jimmy Savile, you see, he **spells** his name S A V I L E.*

pronounce *1*	spell *1*

V n *as* quote

The verb is followed by a noun group and a prepositional phrase which consists of *as* and a quote clause. The passive pattern is *be* **V-ed *as* quote**.

Verbs with this pattern indicate the way something is translated or phrased.

*The Chinese did not know what a 'naga' was so they **translated** the term as 'dragon'.*

gloss 6	render 4
phrase 3	translate 1,4

10 V n -ed

The verb is followed by a noun group and an '-ed' clause (a clause introduced by the '-ed' form of another verb). The passive pattern is **be V-ed -ed**.

This pattern has three structures:

▶ Structure I: Verb with Object
I had my car repaired.
▶ Structure II: Verb with two Objects
I 've heard the word used.
▶ Structure III: Verb with Object and Object Complement
I couldn't make myself understood.

Structure I: Verb with Object

V n -ed

	Verb group	noun group	-ed clause
Subject	**Verb**	**Object**	
I	must get	the car	serviced.
Rose	had	all her shops	decorated in pink.
I	had	three wisdom teeth	extracted.

Verbs with this structure belong to the following meaning groups:

I.1 THE 'HAVE' AND 'GET' GROUP
I.2 'ORDER'
I.3 'HAVE'
I.4 'GET' 1
I.5 'GET' 2
I.6 THE 'LIKE' GROUP

I.1 THE 'HAVE' AND 'GET' GROUP

There are only two verbs with this meaning, *have* and *get*. These verbs are concerned with arranging for someone to do something for you.

*I've got to go down to the drugstore and **get** a prescription filled.*

*A home owner who is advised to **have** a roof overhauled, when only a couple of tiles need replacing, can now sue the builder with a real prospect of success.*

get 1.5	have 3.5

There are a large number of verbs whose '-ed' forms are typically used with *have* and *get* in this structure. They include all the verbs concerned with things that someone else can do for you rather than your doing it yourself. This includes:

- things which someone does for you in order to improve your physical condition or appearance e.g. *cap* (teeth), *cut* (hair), *pierce* (ears)
- medical operations or processes which a professional does for you because they are necessary e.g. *amputate* (a limb), *extract* (a tooth), *lance* (a boil)
- repairs, services, or valuations which someone does to your house, your car, or some other piece of property e.g. *decorate, re-wire, service, value*

Where the action being done is a necessary medical operation, *have* is used rather than *get*.

> *Despite a series of operations, the finger he had injured was never very useful again, and he finally **had** it **amputated**.*
>
> *We **had** the **house done up** just before Christmas.*
>
> *A businessman who returned a pair of squeaky shoes after wearing them for a year expected to **get** them **fixed**; he got a brand-new pair instead.*
>
> *Ford believed that Violet **might have had** him **followed there** by a private detective.*
>
> *Some things I forgot about altogether, particularly emergencies, such as **having** the **car repaired**, or needing the bathroom roof fixed.*
>
> *Anastasia's parents wouldn't let her **have** her **ears pierced**. Not till she was thirteen, they said.*
>
> *If you want to sell something try to **get** it properly **valued** by a genuine dealer or ask a friend or relative for their advice.*

The following list shows which noun groups and verbs are frequently used after *get* and *have* in this pattern.

have a limb amputated	get/have something overhauled
get/have your teeth capped	have someone paged
get/have a job costed	get/have your hair permed
get/have your hair cut	get/have your ears pierced
get/have your house decorated	get/have something printed
get/have your windows double-glazed	have your stomach pumped
have a tooth extracted	get/have something remade
get/have a prescription filled	get/have something repaired
get/have something fixed	get/have your house rewired
have someone followed	get/have your car serviced
get/have yourself immunized	have someone tailed
have a boil lanced	get/have yourself vaccinated
get/have something made	get/have something valued
get/have something mended	get/have your legs waxed
get/have an animal neutered	
get/have a job costed out	get/have something printed up
get/have your house done up	get/have a tooth taken out
get/have a washing machine plumbed in	

I.2 'ORDER'

This sense of the verb *order* indicates that someone in authority orders someone else to do something to a third person. The thing that is done to them is usually unpleasant; the exception to this is ordering someone to be released from detention. The noun group refers to the third person.

> *A Philippine judge **has ordered** her **arrested** for boycotting a series of court proceedings against her.*
>
> *They were illiterate Mafiosi. At the Commonwealth Hotel, Capone **ordered** them **assassinated**.*
>
> *They were arrested by immigration officials on Monday just hours after a High Court judge **had ordered** them **freed** from detention.*

order *2.2*

I.3 'HAVE'

This sense of the verb *have* is used to indicate that something happens to you which is caused by someone else and is usually, though not always, unpleasant. The noun group indicates something which is affected by what happens or involved in what happens.

Freddie escaped a ban but was fined £110 and __had his licence endorsed with three penalty points__.

Better to ask for help now than to __have it thrust upon you__ later.

The insurance companies say that a rider under 28 is five times more likely than a 40-year-old biker to __have a motorcycle stolen__.

have *3.6*

I.4 'GET' 1

This sense of the verb *get* is concerned with causing something to happen. The noun group indicates the person or thing affected by what happens.

I now know that inadequate legal representation __can get a man killed__ and so I must see that every death-row inmate has a decent attorney for his appeals.

'Anything at all that __can get you noticed__ is good news in this business,' said Ms Swan.

It may well be that this book __will get you hooked on astrology__, and you'll want to learn more about it.

get *1.2*

I.5 'GET' 2

This sense of the verb *get* is concerned with achieving something positive.

It usually takes ten years to __get a drug approved__, which means if all goes well this could be used around the turn of the century.

How __will__ I ever __get all that cooking done__?

As a young executive, I was always impatient to __get things done__ and often felt I could do them better myself.

The noun group is often an **amount**. This pattern is **V amount -ed**.

From a girl's point of view it is easier to concentrate on our work without boys yelling out and interrupting the class. As a result we __get a lot more done__.

get *1.3*

I.6 THE 'LIKE' GROUP

These verbs are concerned with liking, wanting, or needing something to be done.

The sooner the elections are held, the better the party will do, and that's one of the reasons they __would like them brought forward__.

She came into the shop with a package saying: 'I __don't need it changed__, only re-wrapped.'

If a new idea emerges and you __want it investigated further__, ask your doctor to make the necessary calls, get the information and then discuss it with you.

like *2.1*   need *1*   want *1*

Structure information: Verb with Object

a) The noun group and the '-ed' clause together form the Object.

b) This structure has no passive.

Structure II: Verb with two Objects

V n -ed

	Verb group	noun group	-ed clause
Subject	Verb	Object	Object
I	heard	him	called Bill.
They	saw	their father	swept to his death.

These verbs are concerned with feeling, hearing, or seeing something happen.

> *'Do you remember much of the language?' Danny asked. 'No, but I love to **hear** it **spoken**.'*

> *He watched while the slings were attached to the crate, **saw** it **lifted**, swung towards the jetty and lowered onto a Ford truck.*

> *The worst part was **watching** her **wheeled away** to an operating theatre while we waited and stared at the walls.*

In the case of *feel*, the noun group is often a reflexive pronoun. This pattern is **V pron-refl -ed**.

> *Ronnie **felt** himself **dismissed**, and returned to the reception desk.*

```
feel 7,10    see 1,4,9
hear 2       watch 1.1
```

Structure information: Verb with two Objects

a) Both the noun group and the '-ed' clause are Objects.

b) This structure has no exact passive equivalent. When these verbs are passive, they behave like the verbs in Structure II of **V n -ing**: the pattern is **be V-ed -ing**, where the '-ing' clause is passive, as in *She **was seen** being wheeled away*. The exception is *feel*, which has no passive at all in this sense.

Structure III: Verb with Object and Object Complement

Active voice: V n -ed

	Verb group	noun group	-ed clause
Subject	Verb	Object	Object Complement
She	found	him	murdered.
They	kept	their hair	cut short.

Passive voice: *be* V-ed -ed

	Verb group	-ed clause
Subject	**Verb**	**Complement**
A stockbroker	was found	stabbed to death.
You	should be kept	detained.

The verbs *find* and *keep* are concerned with finding or keeping someone or something in a particular condition or situation. The verb *make* is concerned with causing yourself to be heard or understood. The verb *report* is concerned with reporting bad news, for example that people are dead or injured, or have been arrested or detained.

> *The avid fisherman can carry his or her day's catch straight to the chef and **find** it prepared to perfection at dinner that evening.*

> *Eight years before he had cruised the Caribbean with his mother, and he was careful to **keep** her informed of his progress.*

> *At least three people **were reported** killed when police opened fire in three areas of the capital.*

In the case of *make*, the noun group is always a reflexive pronoun. This pattern is **V pron-refl -ed**.

> *He had taught me a few words of his language and I **was able to make** myself understood now and then.*

find 4	**make** 2.5
keep 1	**report** 1 *(usu passive)*

Structure information: Verb with Object and Object Complement

a) The noun group is the Object, and the '-ed' clause is the Object Complement.

b) This structure has a passive, with the pattern *be* **V-ed -ed**. The '-ed' clause is the Complement.

Chapter 4: Complex Patterns with Prepositions and Adverbs

In this chapter we describe complex verb patterns in which the verb is followed by a noun group and a prepositional phrase or an adverb group. In Sections 1 to 4 we describe patterns in which the verb is followed by a noun group and either a prepositional phrase introduced by a wide variety of prepositions or an adverb group. In Sections 5 to 27 we describe patterns in which the verb is followed by a noun group and a prepositional phrase introduced by a specific preposition, such as *about, to,* or *with*. These sections are ordered alphabetically, by preposition.

1   V n prep/adv, V n adv/prep

The verb is followed by a noun group and a prepositional phrase or adverb group, or by an adverb group and a noun group. The passive pattern is *be* **V-ed prep/adv**.

The verbs described in this section are used with both adverbs and prepositional phrases, or with a variety of prepositions.

Here we treat all verbs with this pattern as having one structure:

▶ Verb with Object and Adjunct
  They fixed the shelf to the wall.

Some verbs with some prepositions have other structures, however. For example, some prepositional phrases beginning with *to* are prepositional Objects and some prepositional phrases beginning with *as* are prepositional Object Complements.

In English, most verbs with noun groups can be followed by Adjuncts of manner, time, or place. When information about manner, time, or place is not essential, the Adjunct is not part of the pattern. The verbs dealt with below are those which are always or typically used with an Adjunct.

Active voice: V n prep/adv, V adv n

	Verb group	noun group	prep. phrase/adverb group
Subject	**Verb**	**Object**	**Adjunct**
Andrew	chained	the boat	to the bridge.
I	can't picture	you	in a skirt.
	Stir	the figs	in.
You	swirl	the liquid	around your glass.

	Verb group	adverb group	noun group
Subject	Verb	Adjunct	Object
She	banged	down	the cup.
The man	spat	out	a stream of tobacco juice.
They	wired	back	a long list.

Passive voice: *be* V-ed prep/adv

	Verb group	prep. phrase/adverb group
Subject	Verb	Adjunct
The design	is printed	on linen.
Animals	are reared	in traditional ways.
I	was steered	away from dangerous sports.

Phrasal verbs

Active voice: V n P prep/adv, V P n (not pron) prep/adv

	Verb group	noun group	Particle	prep. phrase/adverb group
Subject	Verb...	Object	...Verb	Adjunct
The school bus	dropped	me	off	there.
Annette	got	herself	up	like a shepherdess.

	Verb group	Particle	noun group	prep. phrase/adverb group
Subject	Verb		Object	Adjunct
George	brought	up	his family	there.
They	have hived	off	a lot of trade	to their own office.

Passive voice: *be* V-ed P prep/adv

	Verb group	Particle	prep. phrase/adverb group
Subject	Verb		Adjunct
The results	are being posted	up	on school noticeboards.
Their bodies	were washed	up	on the shore.

Verbs with this pattern belong to the following meaning groups:

1 THE 'FASTEN' GROUP
2 THE 'PUT' GROUP
3 THE 'WRITE' GROUP

4 THE 'THROW' GROUP
5 THE 'MOVE' GROUP
6 THE 'BROADCAST' GROUP

1 THE 'FASTEN' GROUP

These verbs are concerned with attaching one thing to another. The prepositions most frequently used with verbs in this group are *into*, *onto*, and *to*. The adverbs are adverbs of place, such as *in*, *down*, *on*, and *up*. Some verbs in this group, when they are used with an adverb, are used with only one adverb. These adverbs are indicated in the list below.

*It can easily take two days or more to fit just one front wing even though they **are bolted** on.*

*Two vertical steel pins protrude from the headstone and **are cemented** into matching holes in the base.*

*As we got closer, I could see that they **were fastening** a ring to the bird's leg.*

*Apply glue to the back of this piece and **nail** it to the wall.*

*He **had pinned** up a map of Finland.*

***Screw** down any loose floorboards.*

affix *1*	couple *5 (usu passive)*	lock *4*	staple *4*
anchor *3*	fasten *2*	nail *2*	stick *2.4*
attach *1,4*	fix *1*	padlock *2*	stitch *1*
batten *2 (usu passive)*	glue *2*	paste *3*	strap *2*
bind *3*	gum *4*	peg *4*	string *7*
bind *5 (usu passive)*	harness *4 (usu passive)*	pin *2,3,7*	tack *2,5*
bolt *2 (on)*	hitch *3*	post *1.5*	tap *2*
cement *6 (usu passive)*	hook *2*	screw *2,4*	tape *7*
chain *4*	join *5*	seal *1.2 (in)*	tie *1,2,3*
clamp *3*	knit *2*	Sellotape *2*	weld *1*
clip *2*	lash *2*	sew *1,2*	
connect *1,2,3*	link *9*	solder *1*	
post up ▷*1.5*			

2 THE 'PUT' GROUP

These verbs are concerned with putting something somewhere. This includes:

- placing something so that it is positioned in a particular way e.g. *balance, loop*
- putting something somewhere carelessly or with force e.g. *bang, bung*
- putting something somewhere using an implement e.g. *ladle*
- putting something somewhere in a particular way e.g. *dab, drape*

The prepositions most frequently used with the verbs in this group are *in*, *into*, *on*, and *onto*. The adverbs are adverbs of place such as *across*, *down*, and *in*. Some verbs in this group, when they are used with an adverb, are used with only one adverb. These adverbs are indicated in the list below.

*His deputy premier **balanced** a dark green turban on his head.*

*Her furious husband **bundled** her belongings into bin liners and chucked them in the garden.*

Then he **crammed** *a hat on his head* and left the room.

Ladle *the hot soup over the noodles*.

Saturday mornings would not be complete without queuing in a bank or building society to **pay** *in cheques*.

Place *the mixture in a saucepan* and boil for 1 minute.

Bring a small pan of water to the boil, **plunge** *the eggs in* for one minute, then run the eggs under cold water.

I fill the box with various toys and he spends a happy hour taking them out, playing with them, and then **putting** *the toys back* again.

The receiver **was slammed** *down* violently.

To deter cats in your garden, save your orange peel. Cut it up finely and then **sprinkle** *it on the garden*.

As soon as Kelly was alone, she took the chair from the desk and **wedged** *it against the door* so that no one could get in.

In the case of *bury 7, embed, ensconce, install, perch, plonk 2, seat, settle*, and *station*, the noun group following the verb is always or often a reflexive pronoun. This pattern is **V pron-refl prep/adv**. The verb *embed* has an inanimate Subject.

A steel knife blade **embedded** *itself in the wall behind him*.

I was surprised when Philip **ensconced** *himself in front of the television set*.

air-drop 2	float 1	plop 3	smack 2
balance 1	fold VP (in)	plug VP2 (in)	smear 1
bang 5	force 4	plunge 2 (in)	smooth 9
bundle 5	fork 2	plunk 1 (down)	spatter
bung 2	gather 1	pop 6	splash 2
bury 1,4,6,7	grind 2	position 3	spray 3,4,5,7
channel 3	group 6	pour 1	strew
clap 2	hammer 2	pour VP (in)	spoon 3
cram 1,3	hang 1	press 1	spread 1,3
dab 1	heap 2	prop 1	sprinkle 2 (usu passive)
daub	heave 1	put 1,12	stamp 3
deposit 6,7	implant 1	ram 2 (in)	stand 6
dig VP1 (in)	install 3	replace 4	stash 1
dip 2 (in)	jab 1	rest 2.5,6	stir 1 (in)
dock 3	jam 2	rub 4	store 2
drape 1	jumble 2	run 5	stow
dribble 1	ladle 2	seat 3	stuff 2
drip 1	lay 1.1	secrete 2	superimpose 1 (usu passive)
drive 8	lay VP (down)	send 4	sweep 2
drizzle 3 (over)	lean 2	set 2.1	thread 8
drop 4,5,9	load 1,6	settle 7	throw 3
dump 1	locate 2	shove 2	thrust 1
dust 5	loop 2	shovel 3	thump 3
embed 1	nestle 1,2	site 4 (usu passive)	tip 3
ensconce	pay 8 (in)	slam 2 (down)	tuck 1
feed 6.7	perch 1	slap 3	tuck VP2 (in)
fit 1.5,6	pile 3	slather (on)	twine 2
firm 11	pivot 2	sling 2	wedge 2
flash 7	place 16	slip 4	work VP (in)
fling 4,5	plonk 1,2	slot 2	wrap 3
drop off ▷9	jumble up ▷2	prop up ▷1	

Some of the verbs in this meaning group also occur in the pattern **V n with n**, where the prepositional phrase indicates the thing that is put somewhere (see pages 442-443). Examples of both patterns are *He **would smear** some oil on his fingertips* and ***Smear** the plants* *with oil*. The verbs in this meaning group with these two patterns are: *cram, dab, daub, drape, drizzle, dust, fit, hang, load, pile, slather, smear, spatter, splash, spray, spread, sprinkle, strew, stuff, thread*, and *wrap*.

3 THE 'WRITE' GROUP

These verbs are concerned with writing or painting something somewhere. The prepositions most frequently used with the verbs in this group are *in* and *on*. The adverbs most frequently used are adverbs of place such as *there*.

He **entered** all timings *in a big diary* and nothing was missed.

He nodded from time to time, **jotting down** unnecessary notes *on the yellow, lined legal pad before him*.

I was entered into the log as captain; I **wrote** it *there* myself.

enter 8	leave 5	print 1,4 *(usu passive)*	type VP *(in)*
jot 1	paint 5	scrawl 1	write 1
jot down ▷1	write down		

4 THE 'THROW' GROUP

These verbs are concerned with making something move away from you, often with force. The adverbs used with the verbs in this group are adverbs of direction such as *away, down*, and *out*. Some verbs in this group, when they are used with an adverb, are used with only one adverb. These adverbs are indicated in the list below.

Most of the doors **have been blasted** *off their hinges*.

Anne wasn't sure what to do with the documents. She was afraid to burn them or to **flush** them *down the toilet*.

I **hurled** away *the fruit*.

Pardew **nodded** the ball *over the line*.

Jamie Hoyland **shot** the ball *past Paul Gerrard*.

The airbag is fully inflated as the driver begins to **be thrown** *forward*.

bash 3	flick 1	parachute 3	spew 1
beat 12	fling 1	pass 8	spit 3 *(out)*
blast 2,3,6,8	flip 4	pitch 3 *(usu passive)*	spout 1
blow 1.2,4,8	flush 3	pitch 4	syndicate 2 *(usu passive)*
boot 3	head 19	propel 1	throw 1
cast 8	hurl 1	push 1	toss 1
catapult 3,4	kick 2	scatter 1	volley 1
chuck 1	knock 2	shoot 4	vomit 1 *(up)*
curl 6	lob 1,2	slice 4	waft
dash 5	nod 4	sling 1	
drive 8,9,12	parachute 2 *(usu passive)*	sling 3 *(usu passive)*	

5 THE 'MOVE' GROUP

These verbs are concerned with moving something or someone somewhere. This includes:

- moving something in a particular direction e.g. *lower, raise*
- using an implement to move something e.g. *rake, winch*
- pushing someone out of your way e.g. *elbow, shoulder*
- pulling or pushing something on wheels e.g. *pull, trundle*
- sending a letter somewhere e.g. *dispatch, send*
- moving one thing so that it touches another e.g. *brush, rasp*

The adverbs used with the verbs in this group are adverbs of direction such as *aside, in, out,* and *round.* Some verbs in this group, when they are used with an adverb, are used with only one adverb. These adverbs are indicated in the list below.

It is as though my husband __was beamed up__ into space and an alien came back instead of him, using his body and wearing his clothes.

I waited while she __drew__ tobacco smoke in and out of her mouth, but she said nothing.

If the attention is not on him at a dinner table, he will put a pat of butter on his napkin and __flick__ it at the ceiling.

It's a straightforward job to __lower__ down one anchor.

He __mailed__ the stolen things back straight away.

If you have a greenhouse, __move__ the plant to a pot in September and keep it almost dry for the winter.

The nitrogen is left in the form of gas, and __is piped__ harmlessly into the atmosphere.

Wooden chairs __were ranged__ against one wall.

Someone __rasps__ his spikes on the dugout's concrete floor.

He ran forward, but the policemen rushed past him, __shouldering__ him aside.

Rod just had to settle down in the back seat as porters __trundled__ out a trolley-load of gear.

aim 7	lever 3	run 6	sweep 5
arrange 4	lift 1	scrape 2	swing 2
bounce 1,6	lower 4	send 1,5	swirl
brush 5	magnetize 2 (usu passive)	shake 8	swish 1
deflect 3	mail 4 (usu passive)	shift 1	swivel 1
diffuse 4	manoeuvre 1	shoulder 6 (aside)	tamp
discharge 3	move 1	shove 1	tip 3
dispatch 2	pass 4	shovel 2	toss 5
divert 2,3	pipe 2 (usu passive)	shunt 2	transfer 1
draw 4	pour 1	siphon 3	transpose 1
draw 9,VP3 (in)	pull 1,4	slide 1	trundle 2
elbow 2,4 (aside)	pump 2,4	slop 1	turn 2,4
flick 3	push 1	slosh 1	waltz 3
flip 3	raise 1	spill 1	wave 3
fork 4	rake 3	spread 6	whirl 1
funnel 4,5	range 6 (usu passive)	squeeze 4	winch 2
jerk 1	rasp 2	squirt 1	wrestle 3
knock 2,4	roll 1	suck 2	yank
beam down (usu passive)	**beam up** (usu passive)	**wash up** 3 (usu passive)	

6 THE 'BROADCAST' GROUP

These verbs are concerned with sending information or light somewhere. The adverbs most frequently used with the verbs in this group are general adverbs of direction and place such as *back* and *there.*

The news of Presley's death __was beamed__ around the world.

I presented a programme on Satellite TV which __was broadcast__ throughout Europe.

The moon __cast__ a pale white light on the ground.

KAL's manager in Bangkok __flashed__ the message across the airline's communication system.

If you take a glass prism and __shine__ a beam of light onto one face, it will be deviated away from the apex, with blue light being deviated more than red.

beam 3	cast 5	focus 7	shine 2
broadcast 2 (usu passive)	diffuse 1 (usu passive)	route 6	spill 5
cable 5	flash 8	send 4	wire 5,6

7 THE 'DRIVE' GROUP

These verbs are concerned with controlling a vehicle. We include here *catch* and *take*, which indicate that the Subject is a passenger on a vehicle. The adverbs used with the verbs in this group are general adverbs of direction such as *around, back*, and *there*.

*He **drove** the truck into the barn and parked it.*

*He **flew** the helicopter back last night.*

*He walked back to the main street and **caught** a bus to St. Paul's.*

*The pilot **taxied** the aircraft right into the hangar and the doors closed behind him.*

back *3.2*	nose *5*	slew *2*	take *2.30*
catch *6*	ride *1,2*	steer *1*	taxi *2*
drive *1*	row *2.0*	swing *3*	tow *1*
fly *4*	sail *3*	tack *4*	wheel *5*

8 THE 'KICK' GROUP

These verbs are concerned with moving a part of the body. The noun group indicates the part of the body. The adverb group or prepositional phrase indicates the direction of movement.

*Turning to Henry, she **flung** her arms round his neck and **hid** her face on his shoulder.*

*I **kicked** my right leg back and swept his legs clear of the ground.*

*Charles **pounded** his fist into the palm of his hand.*

*She **tilted** her head to one side.*

In the case of *drape, fling 2, hoist, pull, throw*, and *wrench*, the noun group following the verb is always or often a reflexive pronoun. This pattern is **V pron-refl prep/adv**. The phrasal verb *stretch out* has the pattern **V pron-refl P prep/adv** only. These verbs in these patterns indicate that the whole body is moved.

*By stepping on the stone blocks and grabbing the window bars to **hoist** himself up, he could look out of the tiny window.*

*Moira **stretched** herself out on the lower bench, lying on her side.*

cast *4*	hoist *1*	pound *6*	throw *2*
catch *5*	hold *1.7*	pull *4*	tilt *2*
cup *5*	hook *3*	rub *2*	toss *2*
curl *5*	jut *2*	run *6*	turn *1*
drag *5*	kick *3*	spread *2*	twist *2,3*
drape *3*	lash *8*	stamp *4*	wag *2,3*
fling *2,3*	plant *6*	sweep *3,4*	wave *1,3*
hide *3*	poke *4*	thrash *3*	wrench *2*
stretch out *1*			

9 THE 'BEND' GROUP

These verbs are concerned with changing the state of something. This includes:

- changing the shape of something e.g. *bend, twist*
- changing the configuration of something relative to something else e.g. *align, space*
- causing damage to something e.g. *pull, rip*
- changing a date or value e.g. *move, push*
- adjusting a machine e.g. *set, wind*
- changing the surface of something e.g. *slick, smooth*

The adverbs used with the verbs in this group are adverbs of direction such as *back* and *sideways*. The verb *align* is used with a prepositional phrase but not with an adverb.

You need a compass to __align__ the map with the sun's direction.

The muscle __bends__ the spine or the pelvis sideways.

The date of the talks __was moved__ forward.

Take a vegetable peeler or small knife and __pare__ back the skin.

When the young fan-shaped tree __is trained__ against a wall, the well-placed branches __must be trained__ out to form the foundation of the main branches.

align *2*	move *9*	set *2.5*	tip *2*
bend *4*	pare *1,2*	slick *5 (usu passive)*	train *2.6*
carve *5 (usu passive)*	pull *7 (apart)*	smooth *8*	twist *1*
fast forward *2*	push *4*	snap *2*	whip *7*
flip *3*	rip *4 (apart)*	space *9*	wind *2.2,4*
fold *1*	roll *8*	tear *2.1*	
lock *4*	round *4.2*	tilt *1*	

10 THE 'BATTER' GROUP

These verbs are concerned with doing harm to someone. The prepositional phrase indicates which part of the person is harmed. The adverbs most frequently used with the verbs in this group are *around* and *about*.

Sara __had been battered__ several times on her face and head.

He __knifed__ his attacker through the heart.

'If anyone __slaps__ me around again, I'm gonna kill 'em,' says the girl.

bash *2*	hit *1*	slap *1*	whack *1*
batter *2*	knife *3*	strike *3*	
butt *6*	skewer *2*	wallop	

11 THE 'HOLD' GROUP

These verbs are concerned with keeping or holding someone or something in a particular place, state, or situation. The adverbs used with the verbs in this group are adverbs of place such as *in* and *there*.

Three fans were injured as they __were crushed__ against barriers at Greenwich, south London.

She sat rigidly upright, __holding__ her handbag to her chest.

You're the one who'll need to __be kept__ out of trouble if you go around saying things like that.

He __left__ his bike there.

The verb *leave 10* has an inanimate Subject.

In Nirvana, time stops and __leaves__ you in a static state of bliss where nothing happens.

In the case of *barricade*, the noun group following the verb is always a reflexive pronoun. This pattern is **V pron-refl prep/adv**.

When I retired to my room that night I __barricaded__ myself in.

barricade *3*	hold *1.1,4,8,3.6*	manacle *2 (usu passive)*	station *5*
crush *4 (usu passive)*	keep *2,3,10*	maroon *2 (usu passive)*	
dangle *1*	leave *4,10,13*	shut *VP1 (in)*	
have *3.1*	leave *VP1 (off)*	squash *1 (usu passive)*	

12 THE 'LODGE' GROUP

These verbs are concerned with finding a place for people or animals to stay. The adverbs used with the verbs in this group are general adverbs of place such as *there*.

A further 68 prisoners __were accommodated__ temporarily in the prison hospital.

An infantry battalion, decimated in the all-day battle, <u>was billeted</u> there.

His publishers <u>have lodged</u> him in an expensive flat off Park Lane.

By October, 120,000 Polish troops <u>were quartered</u> in 265 camps in Great Britain.

accommodate 2 *(usu passive)*	**house** 12	**lodge** 6	**station** 4 *(usu passive)*
billet 1 *(usu passive)*	**lodge** 5 *(usu passive)*	**quarter** 10 *(usu passive)*	**winter** 2

13 THE 'MEET' GROUP

These verbs are concerned with seeing or meeting someone or something in a particular place or situation. We include here *catch 13*, which indicates that something happens that somone is not prepared for. The adverbs used with the verbs in this group are general adverbs of place such as *there*. The verbs *catch* and *meet* are used with a prepositional phrase, not with an adverb.

The fact that the President has taken the initiative <u>has caught</u> them by surprise.

I <u>could feel</u> a pistol against my head, because I was blindfolded.

I might have the astounding good luck to <u>find</u> him there now.

We <u>used to</u> all go up and <u>meet</u> him off the train.

Thousands of admirers at Dhaka airport <u>welcomed</u> home the man known as The Tiger.

In the case of *find 5*, the noun group following the verb is always a reflexive pronoun. This pattern is **V pron-refl prep/adv**. It indicates that the Subject is surprised at being in that place or situation.

In no time at all, they were throwing their scarcely clad bodies into freezing sea water. They emerged to <u>find</u> themselves on an isolated island, without even sheep for company.

The verbs *find 6* and *see* have Subjects that indicate a point of time.

Dawn <u>found</u> us on a cold, clammy ship drifting past the even colder iron sides of the Blacktail Spit buoy.

The last night of the course <u>saw</u> a group of us nearly in tears as we said our goodbyes.

The verb *catch 16* is usually used in the passive with *get*.

When the group split up, the three men <u>got caught</u> in a spring snowstorm that brought visibility down to zero and hampered search efforts.

catch 7,13	find 1,4,5,6	welcome 1
catch 16 *(usu passive)*	meet 5	
feel 6	see 9	
catch out		

14 THE 'CARRY' GROUP

These verbs are concerned with carrying something or someone somewhere or accompanying someone somewhere. The adverbs used with the verbs in this group are adverbs of direction such as *around*, *away*, and *down*.

I <u>will bring</u> the tape to Paris and they will be able to check what is on it.

They were building a ramshackle flotilla to <u>carry</u> them to Miami.

They use aluminum bags to <u>cart</u> away the oil-encrusted sand.

Carl <u>drove</u> him home at 12.15 and I <u>saw</u> him in.

An alternative to <u>lugging</u> a ladder around is the new 'step-stool'.

The injured man <u>had to be manhandled</u> painfully across the soft snow.

Ring leaders <u>were</u> identified and <u>taken off</u> to Hong Kong's main prison at Stanley.

accompany *1*	drive *2*	lift *9*	smuggle
airlift *2 (usu passive)*	escort *3*	lug	sneak *2*
bear *1.1*	ferry *2*	manhandle *1,2*	spirit *12 (usu passive)*
bring *1,2,4*	fly *5*	parade *4,5 (usu passive)*	stretcher *2 (usu passive)*
bus *2*	freight *3 (usu passive)*	run *18*	sweep *6*
bus *3 (usu passive)*	frog-march	rush *7*	take *2.2,3*
carry *1,3,6*	guide *4,7,8*	schlep *1*	transfer *1*
cart *2*	haul *1*	scoop *1*	transport *4*
chauffeur *2*	hoist *1,2*	see *13*	truck *3 (usu passive)*
convoy *2*	hump *4*	shepherd *2 (usu passive)*	walk *7*
drag *1,2*	lead *1.1,2*	ship *2 (usu passive)*	
take off *6*			

15 THE 'SWEEP' GROUP

These verbs are concerned with removing something from somewhere. This includes:

- removing dirt and obstructions e.g. *brush, scrub*
- removing something from a surface e.g. *peel, shave*
- taking something from somewhere by force e.g. *snatch, tear*

The adverbs used with the verbs in this group are adverbs of direction such as *off* and *away*. Some verbs in this group, when they are used with an adverb, are used with only one or two adverbs. These adverbs are indicated in the list below.

*Dry shampoos are an effective means of removing grease and **brushing** out everyday pollution dust.*

*He **dashed** the tears from his eyes.*

*Just **peel** off the adhesive backing and fix it neatly to the wall.*

*His dad **would prize** bullets out of old dead trees.*

*The Los Angeles River broke its banks and **swept** away homes and cars.*

*One price of this high-intensity farming is water pollution, as rain **washes** the fertilizers off the land and into rivers, sometimes endangering fish.*

*Fifteen policemen leapt from jeeps and **yanked** off my rucksack.*

break *VP1 (off)*	peel *3 (off/away)*	skim *1,VP (off)*	trim *VP (away/off)*
brush *2,4*	pick *4*	smooth *9*	twist *5*
clean *4*	prize *5,6*	snap *1 (off)*	wash *1,3*
clear *9*	pry *2*	snatch *1*	whip *5 (off/out)*
cross *VP (off)*	pull *2*	snip *1 (off)*	wipe *2*
cut *1*	rip *3*	suction *2*	wrench *1*
dash *5*	rub *4*	sweep *1,2*	wrest *1 (away/back)*
drain *1*	scoop *1,2*	sweep *5,10 (away/aside)*	wrest *2 (away)*
draw *12 (out)*	scrape *1*	take *2.7*	yank
flush *5*	scrub *2 (off/away)*	take *VP8 (off)*	
knock *VP2 (off)*	shave *1,2,4 (off)*	tear *2.1,3,5*	
peck *1*	siphon *1*	tip *2 (out)*	
hive off			

16 THE 'INVITE' GROUP

These verbs are concerned with causing someone or something to go somewhere. The adverbs used with the verbs in this group are adverbs of direction or place such as *along*, *back*, *out*, and *there*. The verb *call 9* is used with a prepositional phrase, not with an adverb. The verb *check VP* is used with the adverbs *in* and *out* and the prepositions *into* and *out of*. The verb *show VP* is used with the adverb *around* and the preposition *around*.

*Pugh **was assigned** to an open work camp at Clermont.*

*I waited to **be called** before the magistrate.*

*Several train-loads of mine workers arrived at dawn determined to **drive** the students from the square.*

*Many foreign-born residents **are being enticed** back to their country of origin through homesickness or because their family needs help.*

*Some Democratic members of the US Congress **have been invited** there by the government.*

*He **motioned** Arnold to a chair.*

*This was the man who **put** me in hospital for four days.*

*I never saw Daddy again. Three months later I **was summoned** home to his funeral.*

The verb *take* has an inanimate Subject.

*Work **took** me away from my children a lot when they were growing up.*

In the case of *drag 4*, the noun group following the verb is always a reflexive pronoun. This pattern is **V pron-refl prep/adv**.

*If you manage to **drag** yourself away from the luxury of the best hotel in which I have ever stayed, there are also some very cheap local restaurants.*

allow 1 *(usu passive)*	drive VP *(away/off)*	let VP1 *(out)*	show VP *(around)*
ask 7 *(out)*	entice	lure 1	shunt 1 *(usu passive)*
assign 3 *(usu passive)*	exile 4 *(usu passive)*	march 1,4	shuttle 3
beckon 1	flush 6 *(out)*	motion 4	sit 3
boo 1	force 1	move 6	steer 3
book VP *(in)*	gallop 1	nudge 2	summon 1 *(usu passive)*
call 6	get 1.8	order 2.1	take 2.4
call 9 *(usu passive)*	help 3	persuade 1	tempt 2
check 5,VP	herd 3,4	post 2.2 *(usu passive)*	throw 4
chivvy	hurry 5	post 2.4	throw VP3 *(off)*
coax 1,3	hustle 1	put 2	transfer 1
direct 9	invite 1	route 5 *(usu passive)*	urge 2
dispatch 1	jostle 1	second 3.0 *(usu passive)*	usher 1
divert 1	kick VP2 *(off)*	settle 6	warn VP *(off)*
drag 3,4	let 2,3	shoo 1	wave 2
drive 12	let VP *(in)*	show 4	whisk 1
sit down ▷3			

17 THE 'FOLLOW' GROUP

These verbs are concerned with going somewhere, physically or metaphorically. The noun group indicates a road, sign, or person. The adverbs used with the verbs in this group are adverbs of direction such as *northwards, round,* and *there*.

*Turn left when you leave here and **follow** the road round.*

*From Liverpool **take** the A567 Halsall Road towards Southport.*

*She refused to answer questions as photographers **trailed** her into the VIP lounge of Moscow airport.*

follow 1,3,8	take 2.27	trail 4

18 THE 'DIVERT' GROUP

These verbs are concerned with guiding someone through a conversation or situation, or making them think in a particular way. The noun group indicates either the person or their thoughts or attention. These verbs are most frequently used with a prepositional phrase, not with an adverb.

*The government is trying to **divert** attention from more serious issues.*

*In his latest book on the deepest and most fundamental problems in physics, he **guides** the reader through the science with skill and flair.*

There is a feeling that the powers of the presidency should be whittled down somewhat, that the emphasis __should be shifted__ more __towards Parliament__.

They fear the female vote would lean to conservatism, __tilting__ __parliament towards fundamentalism__.

The preposition is sometimes followed by an '-ing' clause.

The project __might divert__ them __from doing other activities that might not be so good for their future__.

In the case of *align*, the noun group following the verb is often a reflexive pronoun. This pattern is **V pron-refl prep**.

Britain __had to align__ itself in some degree __with other European currencies__.

align *1*	**guide** *11*	**push** *5,6*	**steer** *2*
divert *4*	**pull** *10*	**shift** *2 (usu passive)*	**tilt** *4*

19 THE 'APPORTION' GROUP

These verbs are concerned with placing blame on someone or something. They are most frequently used with a prepositional phrase or with an adverb such as *elsewhere*.

Often these women will give feeble excuses that are no more than a way to unfairly __apportion__ __blame elsewhere__.

His father __has laid__ the blame for his son's criminal behaviour __at the door of the social services__.

Everybody is trying frantically to __shift__ the blame __onto someone else__.

apportion	**place** *18*
lay *1.7*	**shift** *3*

20 THE 'VISUALIZE' GROUP

These verbs are concerned with interpreting, reacting to, or expressing something in a particular way.

The verdict __was greeted__ with uprisings over three nights from rebellious youth.

I __rate__ Tracey very highly and he will be back.

Provided politicians in the democracies __read__ the warning signs correctly, they should have several years to get ready to meet any new challenge.

It is helpful to __situate__ Marx's economics in its philosophical context.

He __takes__ bad news in much the same way as he takes good.

__Visualize__ the Court of Arthur before you as a mighty stronghold.

In the case of *express 2*, the noun group following the verb is always a reflexive pronoun. This pattern is **V pron-refl prep/adv**. The Subject is inanimate.

His passion for engineering was to __express__ itself in motor racing.

The phrasal verb in this meaning group, *look on*, has two patterns. The particle, P, always comes after the verb, not after the noun group, but the adverb group may come either after the noun group or between the verb and the particle. The noun group may be a personal pronoun. These patterns are **V P n prep/adv** and **V adv P n**.

Some people __look on__ things differently from you, Madame Fernet.

Employers __look__ favourably __on__ applicants who have any work experience, no matter what it is.

construe	list *4*	rate *6*	summarize *(usu passive)*
express *2,3*	phrase *3*	read *8*	take *2.22*
frame *10*	picture *8*	receive *4 (usu passive)*	view *3*
generalize *2*	pitch *8*	slant *3 (usu passive)*	word *11*
greet *2 (usu passive)*	place *19*	subsume *(usu passive)*	
look on			

21 THE 'CONDUCT' GROUP

These verbs are concerned with behaving in a particular way. The adverbs used with the verbs in this group are adverbs of manner such as *badly* and *well*. The noun group following the verb is a reflexive pronoun. This pattern is **V pron-refl prep/adv**.

> *These battalions went on to **acquit** themselves with great distinction during the First and Second World Wars.*

> *The Americans **comported** themselves like the pained guardians of an incorrigible adolescent.*

> *The children of marriages contracted on this day **will conduct** themselves badly.*

> *It is also important to **present** yourself in a way that is meaningful to an employer.*

acquit *2*	carry *13*	conduct *3*
bear *1.14*	comport	present *4.6*

22 THE 'END' GROUP

These verbs are concerned with starting, passing, or finishing a period of time in a particular way. The adverbs used with the verbs in this group are adverbs of manner such as *well*.

> *Philip **begins** each day with half an hour's meditation.*

> *Only two public theatres in Britain expect to **end** the year without a financial deficit.*

> *If you had the cash, Sarasota was a congenial spot in which to **pass** the time through constant eating out and shopping.*

> *The team **had started** the day well.*

The preposition is sometimes followed by an '-ing' clause.

> *I **had passed** the time by working loose all the rivets on one of the back door panels.*

begin *2,3*	finish *4*	spend *3*
end *4*	pass *10*	start *3*
live out *VP1*		

23 THE 'WANT' GROUP

These verbs are concerned with wanting or needing someone or something to be in a particular condition or place, or wanting something to be of a particular type. The prepositional phrase or adverb indicates the condition, place, or type.

> *We **need** him back as soon as possible.*

> *Given that people who like driving fast also like changing gear I thought she **would prefer** the car in a manual version instead of the automatic.*

> *Some people were poisoning the toads because they **did not want** them in their gardens.*

(would) like *2.8*	(would) prefer
need *1*	want *4,10*

24 THE 'BRING' GROUP

These verbs are concerned with causing something or someone to be in a particular state, physically or metaphorically. The prepositional phrase or adverb indicates the state.

*Cover the soup and **bring** it to the boil slowly.*

*Their continuing overweight and resultant diabetes **place** them at significantly increased risk of heart disease.*

*The Gold Coast winter bowls carnival **has been thrown** into turmoil after rain forced yesterday's programme to be abandoned.*

In the case of *declare*, the noun group following the verb is always a reflexive pronoun. This pattern is **V pron-refl prep/adv**.

*Army leader General Raoul Cedras **has declared** himself in control of Haiti at the head of a military junta.*

bring *6*	get *1.3*	push *4*	throw *7*
declare *1*	incarnate *4 (usu passive)*	put *3*	transfer *6*
draw *VP2 (in)*	place *17*	set *2.4 (usu passive)*	transport *5*

25 THE 'HANDLE' GROUP

These verbs are concerned with doing something in a particular way or in particular circumstances. This includes:

- dealing with a situation well or badly e.g. *handle, treat*
- performing an activity in a particular way e.g. *hold, rear*
- looking at someone in a particular way e.g. *eye, regard*
- dressing someone or decorating something in a particular style e.g. *do up, get up*
- managing a conversation e.g. *lead, take*

The adverbs used with the verbs in this group are adverbs of manner such as *carefully*, *properly*, and *well*. The verbs *bulldoze* and *push* are used with the preposition *through* or the adverb *through*.

*It was not in his nature just to 'dive in'. It was his custom to **approach** every problem obliquely and cautiously.*

*All people shall have the right to live where they choose and to **bring up** their families in comfort and security.*

*The opposition parties have accused the Government of **bulldozing** through the new constitution in spite of their complaints.*

*The child's dark hair **was done up** in a thousand shining ringlets.*

*You wait in an anteroom where armed security men **eye** you suspiciously.*

*When I'm tired – that's when I **handle** everything least well.*

*This car **doesn't hold** the road too well in the wet.*

*Fleck **led** the conversation into personal affairs.*

*Mr Scott has had experience of picking up undervalued assets and **has timed** the market well in the past.*

In the case of *get up* and *rig out*, the noun group following the verb is always a reflexive pronoun. This pattern is **V pron-refl P prep/adv**.

*Annette **used to have to get** herself **up** like an old-time shepherdess.*

approach *4*	handle *4*	pay *4*	steer *4*
bulldoze *3 (through)*	hold *1.14*	push *VP (through)*	take *2.23*
carry *7*	lead *1.14*	put *9*	time *19*
eye *2*	leave *19*	rear *4 (usu passive)*	treat *1*
feed *1*	manoeuvre *2*	regard *3*	wear *2*

bring up *1*	dress up *1*	rig out
do out *2.0 (usu passive)*	get up *3*	
do up *2.3 (usu passive)*	go about *1*	

26 VERBS WITH OTHER MEANINGS

There are a number of other verbs which have this pattern. There are two groups of these verbs.

(i) The adverb group or prepositional phrase indicates the degree of something or the criteria for something. The verbs *measure* and *secure* are used with a prepositional phrase, not with an adverb.

Such a system **would divide** the country on tribal lines.

A robber whose accomplice was stabbed to death by their victim **was let off** lightly yesterday.

A grammar school's success **was measured** in terms of the number of pupils who got into university and the professions.

Is the loan to **be secured** on your home or other assets?

I think I**'ve worked** you hard enough and I would like to thank you very much for coming and giving me this interview.

divide *5*	secure *9 (usu passive)*	work *19*
measure *1*	stretch *12 (usu passive)*	
let off *2*	set up *4*	

(ii) The adverb group or prepositional phrase indicates a physical or metaphorical place, or a time. We include here *make*, where the noun group indicates a place. Some verbs in this group, when they are used with an adverb, are used with only one or two adverbs. These adverbs are indicated in the list below.

I **was brought up** in Shanghai.

Protein **is found** in a wide variety of both animal and plant foods.

I do like to communicate even though it **isn't going to get** me anywhere.

Shells **had gouged** holes out of the main square tower.

Can we just **leave** it for another two weeks?

The tanker was gulping two tons of fuel an hour in order to **make** New Orleans by nightfall.

They **took** the problem to the general secretary of the Society of Authors.

He attracted attention for the brightness of his virtuosity and the vividness of his dramatic flair: qualities which quickly **took** him to the top of his profession.

In the case of *present*, the noun group following the verb is always a reflexive pronoun. This pattern is **V pron-refl prep/adv**.

Perhaps I **ought to present** myself at his door.

dangle *2*	gouge *1*	rear *4 (usu passive)*	swig *(down/back)*
enrol	leave *18*	be represented *4*	take *2.5*
factor *VP (in)*	make *5.2*	segregate	take *2.6*
be found *3*	partner *5*	situate	take *2.10 (away)*
get *1.14*	present *4.8*	spread *8*	
bring up *1 (usu passive)*			

Structure information

a) The noun group is the Object, and the adverb group or prepositional phrase is usually an Adjunct, although some prepositional phrases are prepositional Objects or prepositional Object Complements (see page 310).

b) This pattern has a passive, with the pattern **be V-ed prep/adv**. The adverb group or prepositional phrase is an Adjunct.

c) The adverb group comes before or after the noun group. The prepositional phrase usually comes after the noun group. Sometimes, however, the prepositional phrase comes before the noun group, especially when the noun group is a long one.

   A few states began to __cram__ into their constitutions details better left to legislation.

d) Phrasal verb patterns are the same except that there is also a particle, P. With most verbs, the Object comes either between the verb and the particle or after the particle. If the Object comes after the particle, it cannot be a personal pronoun. You say

   He __posted__ it __up__ on the board
   or *He __posted up__ the notice on the board*

   but you do not say *He posted up it on the board.*
   Some phrasal verbs have other restricted patterning, and these restrictions are mentioned under the meaning groups concerned.

Other related patterns

V n adv prep

The verb is followed by a noun group, an adverb group, and a prepositional phrase. The passive pattern is **be V-ed adv prep**. Many of the verbs in meaning groups 1, 2, 4, 5, 6, 7, 9, 11, 14, 15, 16, and 17 above have this pattern.

   Some time in January he __asked__ me out for a drink and I went.
   He will have to ask us to __bring__ our rubbish down to the main road.
   The record __will be mailed__ out automatically to fan club members.
   I picked up the cat and __plonked__ myself down on the sofa with him in my lap.
   Hundreds of millions of dollars __have been stashed__ away in private bank accounts.
   It was part of my job to go and __stick__ the notices up on the door.
   Wilder __threw__ the script back at him.
   They __took__ the next bus back to town.
   At the fence, she broke up the bale of hay and __tossed__ it over to the waiting cows.

V n prep prep

The verb is followed by a noun group and two prepositional phrases. The passive pattern is **be V-ed prep prep**. Many of the verbs in meaning groups 4, 5, 7, 14, 15, 16, 17, and 19 above have this pattern.

   I __have driven__ my little convertible over the Alps to Italy and back again three times.
   The barristers were trying to __shift__ the blame from one to another.

V adv n prep

The verb is followed by an adverb group, a noun group, and a prepositional phrase. The passive pattern is **be V-ed adv prep**. Some of the verbs in meaning groups 1, 2, 4, 5, 6, 7, 8, and 9 above have this pattern.

   He would be glad to discuss __moving__ up his retirement date to the middle of 1988.

V n ord

The verb is followed by a noun group and an ordinal such as *first, second,* or *last*. The passive pattern is *be V-ed ord*.

Unemployment remains the main concern for voters. The National Health Service is second. The economy is ranked third.

place 20 *(usu passive)*	**rate** 8 *(usu passive)*
rank 3 *(usu passive)*	**seed** 5 *(usu passive)*

V n ord *in/out of* n

The verb is followed by a noun group, an ordinal, and a prepositional phrase beginning with *in* or *out of*. The passive pattern is *be V-ed ord in/out of n*.

In addition to her photographic work, McKinlay writes fiction; she has just been placed third in the Dillons Short Story Competition.

place 20 *(usu passive)*	**rate** 8 *(usu passive)*
rank 3 *(usu passive)*	**seed** 5 *(usu passive)*

2 V n with adv

The verb is followed by a noun group and an adverb group, or by an adverb group and a noun group. (In this pattern, the word 'with' indicates that the adverb occurs in either position.) The passive pattern is *be V-ed adv*.

This pattern has one structure:

▶ Verb with Object and Adjunct
  Carol turned the radio off.

Active voice: V n adv, V adv n

	Verb group	noun group	adverb group
Subject	**Verb**	**Object**	**Adjunct**
The name	has served	me	well.
	Swill	your mouth	out.
He	switched	the television	on.

	Verb group	adverb group	noun group
Subject	**Verb**	**Adjunct**	**Object**
I	flicked	on	the lights.
She	whipped	off	her skis.

Passive voice: *be* V-ed adv

	Verb group	adverb group	
Subject	**Verb**	**Adjunct**	**Adjunct (optional)**
The system	is flushed	out.	
The family	is known	well	in this town.
Street lighting	has been switched	off.	

Verbs with this pattern belong to the following meaning groups:

1 THE 'SLIP' GROUP
2 THE 'CLICK' GROUP
3 THE 'EMPTY' GROUP
4 THE 'KNOW' GROUP
5 VERBS WITH OTHER MEANINGS

1 THE 'SLIP' GROUP

These verbs are concerned with putting clothes on or taking them off. They are used with the adverbs *on* and *off*.

*Erica **slipped** her damp headband **off** with one hand, shook out her wet curls, and replaced the headband.*

*Frank grabbed a paddle while Chet **tore off** his shirt and used it to plug the hole in the canoe.*

put VP1 *(on)*	**slip** 8 *(on/off)*	**tear** 5 *(off)*
rip 3 *(off)*	**take** VP *(off)*	**whip** 5 *(off)*

2 THE 'CLICK' GROUP

These verbs are concerned with turning machinery or equipment on or off. They are used with the adverbs *on* and *off*. We include here *turn (down)* and *turn (up)*, which indicate that the machine or piece of equipment is being adjusted.

*He **clicked** on the lamp.*

*Are you **going to turn** the machine **off** now?*

click 1 *(on/off)*	**put** VP *(off)*	**switch** VP *(on)*	**turn** VP1 *(on)*
flick 4 *(on/off)*	**put** VP4 *(on)*	**turn** VP2 *(down)*	**turn** VP3 *(up)*
flip 1 *(on/off)*	**switch** VP1 *(off)*	**turn** VP2 *(off)*	

3 THE 'EMPTY' GROUP

These verbs are concerned with emptying a container. They are used with the adverb *out*.

*Finally, she **emptied** the purse **out** onto the sofa.*

*Every few weeks the tank **was flushed** out.*

*Having finished his coffee, he **swilled** out the mug and left it on the draining board.*

empty 5	**flush** VP	**swill** 3

4 THE 'KNOW' GROUP

These verbs are concerned with knowing or remembering someone or something. They are used with adverbs such as *well*.

> *Did* you **know** *the house pretty well?*
> *I **can remember** it clearly, as if it were just yesterday.*

> know *2,6*   remember *1*

5 VERBS WITH OTHER MEANINGS

There are two other groups of verbs which have this pattern.

(i) Three verbs are used with the adverb *well*. These verbs are not used with the pattern **V adv n**.

> *If Robyn was nervous, she **hid** it well.*
> *He qualified as a lawyer in 1944 and his colourful language **served** him well for 40 years.*
> *I don't regret joining the society and I genuinely feel very sorry to be leaving. I **wish** them well in the future.*

> hide *4*   serve *5*   wish *8*

(ii) Three verbs are used with the adverbs *in* and *out*.

> *Myers puts his feet up on his cluttered desk and **breathes** out a swirl of cigarette smoke.*

> breathe *1 (in/out)*   count *VP (in)*   count *VP2 (out)*

Structure information

a) The noun group is the Object, and the adverb group is an Adjunct.

b) This structure has a passive, with the pattern *be* **V-ed adv**.

3   V pl-n with *together*

The verb is followed by a plural noun group and *together*, or by *together* and a plural noun group. (In this pattern, the word 'with' indicates that *together* occurs in either position.) The passive pattern is *be* **V-ed** *together*.

This pattern has one structure:

▶ Verb with Object and Adjunct
  *We **stuck** the pieces together.*

Active voice: V pl-n *together*, V *together* pl-n

	Verb group	plural noun group	*together*
Subject	**Verb**	**Object**	**Adjunct**
The two electrons	bind	the two nuclei	together.
He	lashed	her hands	together.

	Verb group	*together*	plural noun group
Subject	Verb	Adjunct	Object
He	is editing	together	excerpts of some of his films.
	Whisk	together	the egg yolks and sugar.

Passive voice: *be* V-ed *together*

	Verb group	*together*
Subject	Verb	Adjunct
Two pieces	were glued	together.
The two halves	were soldered	together.

Verbs with this pattern belong to the following meaning groups:

1 THE 'TIE' GROUP
2 THE 'GATHER' GROUP
3 THE 'COBBLE' GROUP
4 VERBS WITH OTHER MEANINGS

1 THE 'TIE' GROUP

These verbs are concerned with fastening two or more things together, physically or metaphorically.

*The Town Hall columns themselves are made up of individual drums that **are clamped together** in the ancient manner.*

*Two plastic sheets **were sandwiched** together, with a film of wax in between.*

*They pushed me down on a bed and **tied my hands together** so that I couldn't get at the blindfold.*

*Bragg **weaves** together the histories of his main characters and links in some strong personalities from the fields he knows best.*

*Paul strips the frames of the two standard bikes, **welds them together** and reassembles the finished product.*

bind *1,3,5*	**fasten** *2 (usu passive)*	**rope** *2 (usu passive)*	**tie** *1,2*
bolt *2*	**fuse** *4*	**sandwich** *2*	**weave** *6*
bond *3 (usu passive)*	**glue** *2 (usu passive)*	**sew** *1*	**weld** *1,3*
chain *4 (usu passive)*	**join** *5*	**solder** *1 (usu passive)*	**yoke** *3*
clamp *3 (usu passive)*	**knit** *2*	**stick** *2.4*	
clip *2*	**knot** *2*	**stitch** *1*	
couple *5 (usu passive)*	**lash** *2*	**tack** *5*	

2 THE 'GATHER' GROUP

These verbs are concerned with collecting a group of people or things together so that they make a single entity, physically or metaphorically. We include here *bracket* and *lump*, which indicate that two or more people or things are thought of as being very closely connected.

*Chicago and gangsters **will** always **be bracketed** together.*

*I've **gathered** together six girl dancers, six boy dancers, and a nine-piece band.*

*There are many thick liquids that **have to be mixed** together.*

*The first time I went to a yacht club I felt really uncomfortable. In those days I **couldn't string three words together**.*

The verbs *get, hold*, and *scrape* are sometimes used with a singular noun group. This pattern is **V n with** *together*.

> He **had to scrape** together the money to finance his latest film.

bracket 3 *(usu passive)*	**group** 6	**mix** 1	**throw** VP2 *(usu passive)*
edit 3	**hold** VP	**pull** VP3	**whisk** 2
gather 1,2	**jumble** 2	**scrape** VP	
get VP3	**lump** VP	**string** VP	

3 THE 'COBBLE' GROUP

These verbs are concerned with making something, usually slowly or roughly. Usually the verb is used with a singular noun group. This pattern is **V n with** *together*. The noun group indicates the thing that is made.

> Even if the politicians manage to **cobble** together a peace deal, what hope is there for refugees?
> He denied that the government **was patched** together just for a transition period.

In the case of *cobble, piece,* and *put*, the verb is sometimes followed by a plural noun group which indicates the things that go into making something.

> We got tapes of all our radio interviews and **pieced** those together to form the base of the soundtrack.
> I'**m going to put together** the bits I've assembled for a Christmas frieze.

cobble VP	**patch** VP	**put** VP1,VP2,VP3
get VP2	**piece** VP1,VP2	**throw** VP1

4 VERBS WITH OTHER MEANINGS

There are three other verbs which have this pattern.

> You'**re going to add** these numbers together.
> The spacious kitchen was achieved by **knocking** together three small rooms.
> Stretch and shake your hands, then **rub** them together to warm them.

add 2	**knock** 3	**rub** 5

Structure information

a) The noun group is the Object, and *together* is an Adjunct.

b) This structure has a passive, with the pattern **be V-ed** *together*.

---

4 V *way* prep/adv

The verb is followed by a noun group which consists of a possessive determiner, such as *my, his, her*, or *their*, and the noun *way*. This is followed by a prepositional phrase or adverb group.

This pattern has one structure:

▶ Verb with Object and Adjunct
*She **elbowed** her way through the crowd.*

V *way* prep/adv

	Verb group	*way*	prep. phrase/adverb group
Subject	**Verb**	**Object**	**Adjunct**
She	ate	her way	through a pound of chocolate.
He	is feeling	his way	into the role of successful author.
Labour	is fighting	its way	back.

This pattern is very productive and most of the verbs which are used with this pattern are not used with it often. In this section we include many of these verbs and we indicate which verbs most frequently have the pattern.

This pattern is often used with a word that is normally a noun or an adjective, but which in this pattern is a verb, for example *I finally <u>crowbarred</u> my way in*. Some of these verbs are: *crowbar, cudgel, flipper, helicopter, pickpocket, scam, strong-arm*.

Verbs with this pattern belong to the following meaning groups:

1 THE 'TALK' GROUP	10 THE 'WIND' GROUP
2 THE 'MUMBLE' GROUP	11 THE 'BORROW' GROUP
3 THE 'GOSSIP' GROUP	12 THE 'CHEAT' GROUP
4 THE 'MAKE' GROUP	13 THE 'EAT' GROUP
5 THE 'FIGHT' GROUP	14 THE 'WORK' GROUP
6 THE 'THREAD' GROUP	15 THE 'MUDDLE' GROUP
7 THE 'CHUG' GROUP	16 THE 'LAUGH' GROUP
8 THE 'CRAWL' GROUP	17 THE 'REASON' GROUP
9 THE 'OOZE' GROUP	18 VERBS WITH OTHER MEANINGS

1 THE 'TALK' GROUP

These verbs are concerned with talking persuasively, often dishonestly, in order to get into a good situation or out of an unpleasant one. The verb in this group which most frequently has this pattern is *talk*.

Men will not admit that they do not know something but <u>__will__</u> either <u>__bluff__ their way through</u> or go and find out about it.

At the end of that month, unmasked as an academic fraud who <u>__had lied__</u> her way to the top of her profession, she resigned.

The only chance was to allay the officials' suspicions: to try and somehow <u>__talk__</u> our way out of it, or see if they were open to bribery.

argue *3*	bullshit *2*	lie *2.2*	sweet talk
blag	cajole	negotiate *1*	talk *1*
bluff *3*	charm *4*	plead *1*	wheedle
bluster	con *1*	reason *4*	whinge

2 THE 'MUMBLE' GROUP

These verbs are concerned with talking, singing, or playing a musical instrument in a particular way. The noun group is most frequently followed by a prepositional phrase beginning with *through*. The prepositional phrase indicates something such as a speech, a song, or a concert. The verbs in this group which most frequently have this pattern are *croon, grunt, mumble, mutter, rap, shout, sing, slur, strum, whistle*, and *yell*.

Bono <u>has</u> just <u>__crooned__</u> his way through 'Satellite Of Love', aided by a croaking image of Lou Reed on the huge TV screens.

Our chairman <u>__mumbled__</u> his way through a couple of prayers.

*After Pauline **stammered** her way through an introduction, Nicola explained she was Ryman's wife.*

*Mark, energetically **strumming** his way through the irresistibly wistful 'Molly Malone', looks saintly.*

ad-lib *1*	groan *1*	pipe *4*	squeak *1*
babble *1*	growl *2*	purr *3*	stammer *1*
bawl *1*	grunt *1*	ramble *3*	strum
belt *VP*	holler	rap *2*	tinkle *1*
blow *1.3*	hoot *1*	shout *1*	toot
bray *2*	howl *4*	shriek *1*	wail *1*
croak *2*	hum *2*	sing *1*	warble *2*
croon *1*	jam *9*	slur *2*	whinge
curse *1*	lisp *2*	snap *4*	whisper *1*
drawl	moan *1*	snarl *2*	whistle *1,2*
drone *2*	mumble	sneer	wisecrack
enunciate *1*	mutter	splutter *1*	yell *1*

3 THE 'GOSSIP' GROUP

These verbs are concerned with talking in a particular way. The prepositional phrase or adverb group indicates a period of time that the talking is done in, a place where someone is moving while talking, or a situation that the person talking is trying to get into or out of.

*I didn't want to hear another one of his tired excuses. He **couldn't apologise** his way out of this.*

*You should feel good enough to **communicate** your way through whatever problem presents itself, and bring about a fast resolution.*

*They lived on the same street, went to the same schools, and **gossiped** their way through their teenage years.*

*Watching him **wisecracking** his way round the yard, it was difficult to take his claims of imminent disaster seriously,*

apologize	communicate *1*	haggle	rationalize *1*
bicker	debate *3*	joke *2*	verbalize
bitch *3*	gossip *2*	natter	wrangle
blather	grumble *1*	protest *1*	

4 THE 'MAKE' GROUP

These verbs, when used with *way*, are concerned with managing to get somewhere, either physically or metaphorically. The verbs in this group which most frequently have this pattern are *find* and *make*.

*Most polymers **find** their way into the electrical or electronic industries as insulators.*

*An innovation that **should be making** its way into gift shops before Christmas is a Tooth Fairy pillow.*

*Let the lad go. Let him take what food we've got left and try to **make** his way home.*

*Young artists **must pave** their way to art by drawing pictures for magazine stories that young authors write to **pave** their way to literature.*

*It was not long before they **could** no longer **see** their way out of what they had started.*

find *15*	pave *2*	retrace	sniff *2*
make *1.7*	ply *4*	see *1*	trace *2*
move *2*	pursue *2*	smell *6*	wend

5 THE 'FIGHT' GROUP

These verbs are concerned with moving somewhere with force or with difficulty, either physically or metaphorically. This includes:

- moving with energy e.g. *burst, forge, storm*
- harming people or things as you move e.g. *batter, elbow, fight, shove*
- moving with difficulty because of tiredness or obstacles e.g. *claw, plod, scramble, work*
- cutting or burrowing a path through something e.g. *bore, burrow, tunnel*

The verbs in this group which most frequently have this pattern are *claw, fight, force, push, smash*, and *work*.

*With nothing to do, the mind is unable to prevent negative thoughts from **elbowing** their way to center stage.*

*They're trying to **fight** their way towards the besieged army camp.*

*The protesters **forced** their way into the police headquarters, setting fire to parts of the building.*

*When he turned professional 11 years ago, Christie was expected to **storm** his way to a world championship.*

barge 2	crowbar	labour 3	smash 2
bash 2,3	crush 1	muscle VP	stampede 2,4
batter 2	cudgel 1	nudge 2	steamroller 2
battle 5	cut 1	plod 1	storm 4
beat 1,11	dig 1	plough VP	streak 4
blast 5	drag 4	poke 3	strong-arm
blaze 6	drill 2	power 7	struggle 6
blitz 1	elbow 3,4	press 1	stumble 1
bludgeon 1	explode 1	pummel	stutter 3
bomb 3	fight 2,4,7	punch 1	sweat 2
bore 5	force 23	push 2	sweep 7,9
break 6	forge 2	scrabble 1	tear 2.7
bulldoze 3	gatecrash	scramble 2	thrust 2
burn 1,3	grab 1	scrape 2	toil 1
burrow 2	grapple 2	scratch 2	trudge
burst 5	grasp 1	shoot 2	trundle 3
butt 6	hack 2	shoulder 6	tunnel 2
chase 6	hammer 2,7	shove 1	whack 1
chip 6	haul 1	shovel 2	win 4
chop 1	heave 1	slam 4	worm 4
claw 5	hurry 1	slash 2	wrestle 3
cleave 1	jab 1	slog 1	zap 1
crash 3	jostle 1	slug 3	zoom 1

6 THE 'THREAD' GROUP

These verbs are concerned with moving carefully or avoiding obstacles, either physically or metaphorically. The verbs in this group which most frequently have this pattern are *feel, pick*, and *thread*.

*He **edged** his way along a beam high up in the barn.*

*She reached the bottom of the stairs and, with her back pressed against the wall, **inched** her way towards the captain's cabin at the end of the corridor.*

*He **threaded** his way among the desks that cluttered the office area.*

dodge 1	inch 2	prize 5	twist 2
ease 5	manoeuvre 1	sidestep 2	weave 4
edge 3	navigate 3,5	squeeze 4	
feel 5	nose 5	steer 4	
grope 2	pick 13	thread 6	

7 THE 'CHUG' GROUP

These verbs, when used with *way*, are concerned with moving in a way that makes a particular noise.

*The launch **chugged** its way through the brown water, past a solid wall of multicoloured trees.*

buzz *1*	crunch *3*	scrape *2*	wheeze *1*
chug	grind *4*	scrunch *1*	whirr
clang	growl *3*	splutter *2*	whisper *3*
clank	rattle *1*	tap *2*	whizz
clunk *2*	roar *1*	thump *3*	
crackle	rustle	thunder *4*	

8 THE 'CRAWL' GROUP

These verbs are concerned with moving in a particular way, physically or metaphorically. This includes:

- particular modes of transport e.g. *pedal, row, sail*
- walking in a particular way e.g. *flounce, hobble, march, shuffle*
- moving in some other way e.g. *swim, wing*

*North of Port Douglas, we left the metalled roads behind us and **bumped** our way into the Daintree rain forest.*

*An injured woman caver **was crawling** her way to freedom last night after spending two days trapped inside a freezing mountain.*

*A few small privately run buses **meander** their way down roads strewn with piles of rubbish.*

*Ordinary Japanese people **had to pedal** their way about on bicycles.*

*Miriam stepped over the side, moving slowly as she **splashed** her way to the bank.*

*In northern Europe bats have never been the most popular of creatures – they're widely regarded as rather creepy and even sinister as they **wing** their way through the dusk air.*

back *3.2*	helicopter	row *2.0*	strut *1*
balance *1*	hike *2*	run *1*	swagger
bob *1*	hitch *2*	sail *3*	swim *1*
bounce *7*	hitchhike	shuffle *1*	tiptoe *1*
breeze *2*	hobble *1*	skim *2*	trample *3*
brush *6*	jack-knife	skip *1*	twirl *2*
bump *6*	leap *1*	slide *2*	wade *1*
bustle *1*	limp *1,2*	slink	walk *1*
churn *2*	lurch *1,2*	slither *1*	waltz *3,4*
clamber	march *3*	slosh *2*	wander *1*
climb *1*	meander *3*	slouch *2*	wiggle
crawl *1,3*	mince *3*	sneak *1*	wind *1*
creep *2,3*	mooch	speed *5*	wing *9*
flap *2*	nuzzle	spiral *2*	wobble *1*
float *1,2*	paddle *2*	splash *1*	wriggle *2*
flounce *1*	paw *3*	squirm *1*	zigzag *2*
gallop *1,2*	pedal *2*	stagger *1*	
glide *1*	prance *1*	straggle *1*	

9 THE 'OOZE' GROUP

These verbs typically have an inanimate Subject and indicate how something such as a liquid or an idea moves or spreads.

*The tears **dripped** their way onto his vest.*

He could seek instant guidance on complicated social issues that now take months to __ooze__ their way through journalistic filters and political processes.

drip *1*	melt *1*	percolate *3*
filter *5*	ooze *1*	waft

10 THE 'WIND' GROUP

These verbs are concerned with the shape or direction of something such as a road or a river. The verb in this group which most frequently has this pattern is *wind*.

The road climbed and __curled__ its way through skinny teak trees and tidy villages.

They followed a path that __wound__ its way through the trees.

carve *5*	snake *2*	thread *6*	weave *4*
curl *6*	spiral *2*	twist *6*	wind *2,1*

11 THE 'BORROW' GROUP

These verbs, when used with *way*, are concerned with achieving something by means of a legitimate activity. This includes:

- doing something to achieve success in sports and arts e.g. *bat, paint*
- doing something to achieve success in business, in money matters, or in a career e.g. *borrow, spend*

You must not take the route of trying to __borrow__ your way out of trouble when over-borrowing got you into this state in the first place.

Britain's capacity to __grow__ its way out of recession is severely limited.

She possessed a powerful forehand and a disconcerting ability to __hit__ her way out of crises.

adapt *1*	dive *1*	merge *1*	ski *2*
automate	earn *1*	network *2*	spend *1*
barter	export *1*	organize *1*	swim *1*
bat *2*	finance *1*	paddle *2*	tax *2*
borrow *2*	fund *3*	paint *4*	think *4*
bowl *8*	grow *11*	play *2*	trade *2*
box *9*	hit *1*	produce *2*	train *2,1*
build *1*	invest *1,2*	ride *1,2*	walk *1*
busk	jump *3*	save *2*	wrestle *2*
buy *1*	kick *2*	sell *1*	write *2*
cook *1*	manage *1*	shrink *2*	
dance *1*	market *5*	skate *3*	

12 THE 'CHEAT' GROUP

These verbs, when used with *way*, are concerned with achieving something by means of illegal, immoral, or underhand activities.

We are still saddled with the corrupt, incompetent, dishonest group of politicians who __cheated__ their way to government a year ago.

William had watched disapprovingly as Brian __insinuated__ his way into John's inner circle, becoming, in time, one of John's favourite companions.

A former paramedic __tricked__ his way into a job as a hospital doctor and killed a woman patient through lack of care.

bamboozle	fiddle *4*	massacre *2*	scheme *3*
bribe *2*	flirt *1*	mislead	steal *1*
bully *2*	gamble *3*	murder *2*	trick *2*
burgle	grovel *1*	pillage	wangle
butcher *5*	hustle *3*	pimp *2*	weasel
cheat *1*	insinuate *2*	plot *2*	wheel and deal
dominate *1*	inveigle	plunder *1*	
dupe *1*	kill *1*	rape *1*	
fake *2,4*	manipulate *1,2*	rig *1*	

13 THE 'EAT' GROUP

These verbs, when used with *way*, are concerned with consuming the whole of something. This includes:

- eating and drinking e.g. *chew, eat*
- smoking e.g. *gasp, puff, smoke*

The verb in this group which most frequently has this pattern is *eat*.

*Mrs Lorimer **chewed** her way through a large helping of apple tart.*

*If one home-owner takes steps to kill the termites, the colony simply **eats** its way through another building.*

*Fiona amazed onlookers by **puffing** her way through three cigarettes and swigging red wine and schnapps.*

*Yes, he **slurps** his way through a glass or two as he cooks for us on the television. Why not?*

booze *2*	feast *2*	munch	slurp *1*
chain-smoke *1*	gasp *2*	nibble *1,3*	smoke *3*
chew *1,4*	gnaw *1*	nosh *2*	taste *5*
chomp	graze *1*	peck *1*	work *39*
drink *1*	guzzle *1*	puff *1*	
eat *1*	lick *1*	slice *2*	

14 THE 'WORK' GROUP

These verbs, when used with *way*, are concerned with completing a long task carefully, such as reading a book or listening to a record.

*Mackenzie has made the congregation into a real family simply through **preaching** his way through the Bible.*

*Leaphorn **was thumbing** his way through the notebook a second time, making notes in his own notebook.*

*In a far corner of the bar, a pianist with a portable synthesiser **works** his way through some requests.*

leaf *VP*	read *1*	work *39*
listen *1*	sift *2*	
preach *1*	thumb *VP*	

15 THE 'MUDDLE' GROUP

These verbs are concerned with doing something in a stupid or inefficient way.

*McIver **had bumbled** his way toward success by making the right mistakes.*

*I guess somehow or other we **muddled** our way through and things worked out.*

botch *1*	bungle	muddle *VP*
bumble	fumble *1*	

16 THE 'LAUGH' GROUP

These verbs, when used with *way*, indicate that someone gets somewhere or gets through a period of time while making a sound or putting on an expression, or while doing something involuntarily. This includes:

- laughing and smiling e.g. *grin, smile*
- crying e.g. *sob, weep*
- showing a feeling in some other way e.g. *blush, shiver*

*His favourite expression is: 'There are two ways to die: you **can laugh** your way to the grave or cry yourself there.'*

*The procession **panted** its way up the steep hillside.*

*He was trembling when he opened the car door, when he ordered his steak, when he blew his nose. He **quaked** his way through the entire evening.*

*Britain is set to **shiver** its way through one of the coldest winters this century.*

blush *1*	guffaw *2*	shrug	titter
chortle	laugh *1*	shudder *1*	tut *2*
chuckle	pant	sleep *2*	twitch
cry *1*	pout *1*	smile *1*	weep *1*
gasp *2*	puff *5*	snore	yawn *1*
giggle *1*	quake *2*	sob *1*	
grin *1*	shiver	sulk	

17 THE 'REASON' GROUP

These verbs, when used with *way*, are concerned with solving a problem by thinking about it.

*She's lied to the little girl and **can't figure** her way out of it.*

*He and Dr Watson **had reasoned** their way to the structure of DNA on only the barest of evidence.*

agonize	guess *1,2*	reason *4*
(cannot) figure *11*	rationalize *1*	will *2.3*

18 VERBS WITH OTHER MEANINGS

There are a number of other verbs which have this pattern.

*The film is about four Italian Americans who **brawl** their way through life in New York's Lower East Side.*

*They **can** also **shop** their way into serious debt.*

barnstorm	meditate *2*	shop *2*
brawl *2*	party *3*	
dream *2,4*	preen *2*	

Structure information

a) The noun group following the verb is the Object and the prepositional phrase or adverb group is an Adjunct.

b) This structure has no passive.

Other related patterns

V *way* adv prep

The verb is followed by a noun group with *way*, an adverb group and a prepositional phrase. Many of the verbs in this section, especially in meaning groups 4,5,6,7,8,9, and 10, also have this pattern.

The ferry __edged__ its way out into the river.

Sam had shown that he could negotiate a complicated system of highways and waterways to __find__ his way back to Seattle.

V *way* prep prep

The verb is followed by a noun group with *way* and two prepositional phrases. Many of the verbs in this section, especially in meaning groups 4,5,6,7,8,9, and 10, also have this pattern.

He saw Benedict __limping__ his way down the path to the river.

Such exclamations __wafted__ their way from the telephone area onto the floor of the exhibition.

V *way to* -ing

The verb is followed by a noun group which consists of a possessive determiner and the noun *way*. This is followed by a prepositional phrase which consists of *to* and an '-ing' clause.

I very much hope you __will see__ your way to advising your client to sign it.

see *11*

5 V n *about* n

The verb is followed by a noun group and a prepositional phrase which consists of *about* and a noun group. With some verbs, the preposition is sometimes followed by an '-ing' clause or by a wh-clause. The passive pattern is *be* **V-ed** *about* **n.**

This pattern has one structure:

▶ Verb with Object and Adjunct
I __warned__ him about the danger.

Active voice: V n *about* n/-ing/wh

	Verb group	noun group	*about*	noun group/-ing/wh-clause
Subject	Verb	Object		Adjunct
He	advises	senior managers	about	getting the best out of their teams.
I	asked	him	about	what his record company is like.
We	used to warn	him	about	the dangers of eating too quickly.

Passive voice: *be* V-ed *about* n/-ing/wh

	Verb group	*about*	noun group/-ing/wh-clause
Subject	**Verb**		**Adjunct**
Several stars	had been contacted	about	taking part.
Players	were grilled	about	methods of payments.
They	were lectured	about	how to beat crime.
He	should be notified	about	her condition.

Verbs with this pattern belong to the following meaning groups:

1. THE 'TELL' GROUP
2. THE 'TACKLE' GROUP
3. THE 'FEEL' GROUP
4. THE 'KNOW' GROUP
5. THE 'REVEAL' GROUP
6. THE 'FOOL' GROUP
7. VERBS WITH OTHER MEANINGS

1 THE 'TELL' GROUP

These verbs are concerned with verbal communication with someone about something. This includes:

- advising
- telling
- teaching
- warning
- asking
- nagging
- scolding
- teasing

*Their husbands **were interrogated** about separatist activities.*

*His father played fiddle and **taught** him about country music.*

*They constantly **teased** her about her looks, mocking her hairstyle and the clothes she wore.*

*I liked people to **tell** me about the books they were reading.*

The preposition *about* is sometimes followed by an '-ing' clause or a wh-clause.

*He dated the decline of their marriage from the time when she had stopped **nagging** him about never being home.*

*They ruthlessly **questioned** him about why he hadn't bothered to see Christopher or even find out our address.*

advise *1*	grill *5*	pester *1*	taunt
ask *1*	inform *1*	press *5*	teach *2*
brief *6*	interrogate *1*	pump *9*	tease *1*
caution *2*	interview *4*	question *2*	tell *1*
chide	kid *5*	quiz *2*	warn *1*
consult *1*	lecture *3*	reassure	
cross-examine	nag *1*	remind *3*	
forewarn	notify	scold	

2 THE 'TACKLE' GROUP

These verbs are concerned with approaching someone about a topic, often a sensitive or controversial topic. This includes challenging and fighting someone about something.

*The other women **confronted** her about the distorted view she has of herself.*

The preposition *about* is sometimes followed by an '-ing' clause or a wh-clause.

*One of the networks **approached** him about hosting a science show.*

*I **tackled** him about how one could live amidst so much poverty.*

approach *3*	confront *5*	fight *6*
challenge *4*	contact *3*	tackle *3*

3 THE 'FEEL' GROUP

These verbs are concerned with someone's thoughts or feelings about something. They often occur in questions such as *What do you like about...?* and clauses such as *What I hate about him is...*; they do not often have ordinary Objects.

*What I **loved** about Gloria was her talent and her independence.*

*What do you **think** about this threatened strike by professional footballers, then?*

The preposition *about* is sometimes followed by an '-ing' clause.

*This is what I **hate** about mowing the lawn. I don't mind mowing the lawn but it's raking up the grass clippings afterwards.*

The preposition *about* is sometimes followed by a noun group and an '-ing' clause.

*She asked me 'What **would** your husband **feel** about you working overseas?'*

dislike *1*	hate *2*	love *5*
feel *12*	like *2.1,3*	think *1*

4 THE 'KNOW' GROUP

These verbs are concerned with knowing or finding out about something. The noun group following the verb is always an **amount**, and the pattern is **V amount *about* n**. When these verbs are used in the passive, the amount is the Subject.

*She frequented the library to **find out** all she could about the disease.*

*At the end of the conference there was general agreement that much more needs to **be found out** about the donkey.*

The preposition *about* is sometimes followed by an '-ing' clause or a wh-clause.

*He may be a brilliant 'personality', but he **knows** nothing about producing a play.*

*We**'ve learned** a lot about how to travel with kids and how not to.*

The preposition *about* is sometimes followed by a noun group and an '-ing' clause. This pattern is **V amount *about* n -ing**.

*I heard Wally **didn't know** anything about me going to Canberra and that he was upset about it.*

hear *7*	know *4*	learn *1*
find out *1*		

5 THE 'REVEAL' GROUP

These verbs indicate that something reveals a lot or a little about someone or something. The noun group following the verb is always an **amount**, and the pattern is **V amount** *about* n.

> Household interiors from the past **reveal** quite a lot about the people who lived in them.
>
> The way you present information **says** a lot about the way you do business.

> reveal *1*   say *1,7*

6 THE 'FOOL' GROUP

These verbs are concerned with having the wrong idea about something. The noun group following the verb is always a reflexive pronoun, and the pattern is **V pron-refl** *about* n/-ing/wh. The preposition *about* is usually followed by an '-ing' clause or a wh-clause.

> In our survey, nearly a quarter agreed they **deceived** themselves about what they ate.
>
> **Were** they **fooling** themselves about being in love in order to justify what they were doing?

> deceive *2*   fool *3*   kid *6*

7 VERBS WITH OTHER MEANINGS

There are three other verbs which have this pattern.

In the case of *trouble*, the noun group following the verb is always a reflexive pronoun. This pattern is **V pron-refl** *about* n.

> He seemed on the whole to be a naturally solitary person, **troubling** himself about only a few friends.

In the case of *do* and *say*, the noun group following the verb is always an **amount**. This pattern is **V amount** *about* n. The preposition *about* is sometimes followed by an '-ing' clause.

> Too many children are dying from malnutrition, preventable diseases, and neglect, and too few adults **are doing** enough about it.
>
> She **didn't say** anything about seeing a doctor.

Also in the case of *do* and *say*, the preposition *about* is sometimes followed by a noun group and an '-ing' clause. This pattern is **V amount** *about* n -ing.

> He **doesn't** really **say** much about me having HIV, but I think it makes him feel better knowing I'm going through this with him.

> do *2.5*   say *1*   (not) trouble *10*

Structure information

a) The noun group following the verb is the Object, and the prepositional phrase is an Adjunct.

b) This structure has a passive, with the pattern **be V-ed** *about* n. The prepositional phrase is an Adjunct.

c) There is only one phrasal verb with this structure, *find out*, which has the patterns **V P amount** *about* n/-ing/wh and **V amount P** *about* n/-ing/wh.

341

Other related patterns

V n amount *about* n

The verb is followed by a noun group, an **amount**, and a prepositional phrase beginning with *about*. The passive pattern is *be* **V-ed amount** *about* **n**.

   She **taught** me a lot about plants.

The preposition *about* is sometimes followed by an '-ing' clause or a wh-clause.

   He was a good man who **taught** me a lot about living on the planet and making the most of it.

In the case of *trouble*, the noun group is always a reflexive pronoun. This pattern is **V pron-refl amount** *about* **n**.

   The ordinary Frenchman **troubles** himself very little about politics.

teach *2*   tell *1*   trouble *10*

---

6   V n *against* n

The verb is followed by a noun group and a prepositional phrase which consists of *against* and a noun group. With some verbs, the preposition is sometimes followed by an '-ing' clause. The passive pattern is *be* **V-ed** *against* **n**.

This pattern has two structures:

▶ Structure I: Verb with Object and prepositional Object
   We'll *have to weigh* the responsibilities against the rewards.
▶ Structure II: Verb with Object and Adjunct
   We *insured* the house against fire.

Structure I: Verb with Object and prepositional Object

Active voice: V n *against* n

	Verb group	noun group	*against*	noun group
Subject	**Verb**	**Object**	**prepositional Object**	
The championships	will match	the professionals	against	the amateurs.
We	have to weigh	the pluses	against	the minuses.

Passive voice: *be* V-ed *against* n

	Verb group	*against*	noun group
Subject	**Verb**	**prepositional Object**	
Press freedom	has to be balanced	against	the right to privacy.
Village	is pitted	against	village.

Verbs with this structure are all concerned with considering or dealing with two or more different things, people, or groups. We include here the verbs *match*, *pit*, and *play off*, which involve making two or more people or groups compete with or fight each other.

The prospects of a better job in a higher housing cost area __would have to be balanced__ against a significant and inevitable fall in living standards.

Between 1688 and 1945 Britain participated in twelve wars in which she __was pitted__ against one or more great powers.

Union leaders __have been playing off__ one bid against another to try to secure the best possible deal.

Nobody ever said being a parent was easy. You __have to weigh__ the responsibilities against the rewards.

Sometimes the noun group following the verb is plural and the noun group following the preposition is *one another* or *each other*. In the passive, the Subject is plural.

The select committee and the judicial inquiry __are being played off__ against one another.

balance 6	**pit** 4 *(usu passive)*	**weigh** 3
cross-check *(usu passive)*	**set** VP1 *(usu passive)*	
match 8	**set** VP2	
play off VPP	**trade off** 1	

Structure information: Verb with Object and prepositional Object

a) The noun group following the verb is the Object, and the prepositional phrase is the prepositional Object.

b) This structure has a passive, with the pattern *be* V-ed *against* n. The prepositional phrase is the prepositional Object.

c) Though the prepositional phrase in this structure usually comes after the noun group, it sometimes comes before it, especially when the noun group is a long one.

He has a compulsive need to __play off__ against each other the centres of power that surround him.

d) There are only two phrasal verbs with this structure, *play off* and *trade off*. The active patterns are **V n P** *against* n and **V P n (not pron)** *against* n. The Object comes either between the verb and the particle, or after the particle. If the Object comes after the particle, it cannot be a personal pronoun. You say

She __played__ them __off__ against each other
or *She __played off__ enemies against each other*

but you do not say *She played off them against each other.*
The passive pattern is *be* V-ed P *against* n.

Structure II: Verb with Object and Adjunct

Active voice: V n *against* n

	Verb group	noun group	*against*	noun group
Subject	**Verb**	**Object**	\multicolumn{2}{c}{**Adjunct**}
She	clinked	her glass	against	his.
Your policy	insures	you	against	redundancy.

343

Passive voice: *be* V-ed *against* n

	Verb group	*against*	noun group
Subject	**Verb**		**Adjunct**
The protests	were directed	against	the central government.
Children	should be vaccinated	against	measles.

Verbs with this structure belong to the following meaning groups:

II.1 THE 'PROTECT' GROUP
II.2 THE 'STRIKE' GROUP
II.3 THE 'LEVEL' GROUP
II.4 THE 'WARN' GROUP
II.5 VERBS WITH OTHER MEANINGS

II.1 THE 'PROTECT' GROUP

These verbs are concerned with protecting someone or something against disease or any other unpleasant event, either physically or metaphorically.

*The family provides stability and support, which **cushions** members **against the disturbing effects of change**.*

*The pot or container in which the plant is growing may be vulnerable to frost and it **should be insulated** against the cold.*

*He urged people to go to the city centre to **protect** their government **against what he called a coup attempt**.*

In the case of *cover, defend, insure,* and *protect*, the preposition *against* is sometimes followed by an '-ing' clause.

*Policies **will** normally **cover** you **against having to call off your holiday because of a major crisis at home**.*

*There is no need for people who live in tower blocks to **be insured** against being struck by a juggernaut.*

In the case of *insure 2*, the noun group following the verb is always a reflexive pronoun. This pattern is **V pron-refl** *against* n. The verb *defend 1,2* often has this pattern as well.

*Women **can** now **insure** themselves **against contracting breast cancer**.*

cover 9	immunize *(usu passive)*	insulate 1,2	spray 7
cushion 4	indemnify	insure 1,2	vaccinate *(usu passive)*
defend 1,2,3	inoculate	protect 1,2	

II.2 THE 'STRIKE' GROUP

These verbs are concerned with striking or putting one thing against another.

*The Commissioner **propped** his walnut cane **against the bed** and sat down.*

*Naomi grabbed her hair, **slammed** her **against the car** and started slugging her.*

*He lashed out just once, Dean fell and **struck** his head **against the bannister**.*

In the case of *brace*, the noun group following the verb is always a reflexive pronoun. This pattern is **V pron-refl** *against* n. The verb *flatten* often has this pattern as well.

*She staggered over to her chair and slumped into it, leaning forward and **bracing** herself **against the table**.*

bang 6	dash 5	lean 2	slam 4
brace 2	drum 6	press 1	strike 5
clink	flatten 3	prop 1	

II.3 THE 'LEVEL' GROUP

These verbs are concerned with attacking someone or being hostile towards someone. The prepositional phrase indicates the person or people involved.

*The French champagne producers **brought** an action **against** the producers of the elderflower drink to stop them calling it champagne.*

*Child abuse allegations are the worst that **can be levelled** against an entertainer.*

*Dr Spencer **makes out** his case **against** Sir Arthur in a book containing new evidence based on documents and letters held by the Natural History Museum.*

bring 9	hold VP5.0	perpetrate *(usu passive)*
direct 7 *(usu passive)*	level 12	
make out 4		

II.4 THE 'WARN' GROUP

These verbs are concerned with warning someone against something. The preposition *against* is usually followed by an '-ing' clause.

*Many of his advisers **had warned** him **against** involving himself in trying to settle a complicated foreign conflict that was of little interest to most Americans.*

caution 2	warn 2

II.5 VERBS WITH OTHER MEANINGS

There are three other verbs which have this structure.

*She feared that he **would turn** her daughter **against** her.*

In the case of *steel*, the noun group following the verb is always a reflexive pronoun. This pattern is **V pron-refl *against* n**.

*She waited for the batons to strike, **steeled** herself **against** the tear gas, and said a Hail Mary.*

decide 5	steel 3	turn VP

Structure information: Verb with Object and Adjunct

a) The noun group following the verb is the Object, and the prepositional phrase is an Adjunct.

b) This structure has a passive, with the pattern **be V-ed *against* n**. The prepositional phrase is an Adjunct.

c) Though the prepositional phrase in this structure usually comes after the noun group, it sometimes comes before it, especially when the noun group is a long one.

*We want only to **defend** against its enemies that which is our priceless heritage: freedom.*

d) There is only one phrasal verb with this structure, *make out*. The active pattern is **V P n (not pron) *against* n**. The Object comes after the particle, and it cannot be a personal pronoun. You say

I __made out__ a case against him

but you do not say *I made out it against him*.
The passive pattern is *be* **V-ed P *against* n**.

---

7 V n *as* adj

The verb is followed by a noun group and a prepositional phrase which consists of the preposition *as* and an adjective group. The passive pattern is *be* **V-ed *as* adj**.

This pattern has two structures:

▶ Structure I: Verb with Object and prepositional Object Complement
I __saw__ the question as crucial.
▶ Structure II: Verb with Object and prepositional Complement
That __strikes__ me as right.

Structure I: Verb with Object and prepositional Object Complement

Active voice: V n *as* adj

	Verb group	noun group	*as*	adjective group
Subject	**Verb**	**Object**	**prep. Object Complement**	
We	accept	this premise	as	fundamental.
She	perceived	him	as	stupid.

Passive voice: *be* V-ed *as* adj

	Verb group	*as*	adjective group
Subject	**Verb**	**prepositional Complement**	
Such protection	could be considered	as	adequate.
A woman aged twenty	is described	as	critically ill.

Verbs with this structure are all concerned with labelling, interpreting, or regarding someone or something as having a particular quality. The prepositional phrase indicates a description of the Object.

Some verbs, such as *brand*, *condemn* and *scorn*, indicate that you regard someone or something as bad. Others, such as *misrepresent*, indicate that you disapprove of the way someone else labels, interprets, or regards someone or something.

There are many famous and successful people in this world who have tattoos – it __doesn't brand__ them as unfit to blend into society.

A child who __considers__ himself at least as good as other children is one that we might regard as having a reasonable measure of self-esteem.

The man gave a murmur that __could be construed__ as polite only by a leap of the imagination.

Chicken, cheese, lamb, beef, liver – all __have__ in turn __been denounced__ as dangerous to health.

Depending upon your circumstances, you __might interpret__ redundancy as welcome or unwelcome.

Her diamond rings __marked__ her __out__ as seriously rich.

In psychiatric practice much care is taken to make sure that the occasional physical illness __is not passed off__ as psychological.

The growth of free trade internationalism __was presented__ as crucial to the progress of the working man in Europe.

His government supports the idea of defining common criteria to use in deciding whether to __recognize__ states as independent.

One man __regards__ a glass of water as half full while another __views__ it as half empty.

accept *2,4,5*	construe *(usu passive)*	portray *3*
acknowledge *1*	decry	present *4.5*
acknowledge *2 (usu passive)*	denounce *1*	rank *4*
attack *2*	depict *2*	rate *6*
bill *8*	describe *2*	read *8 (usu passive)*
brand *3*	designate *1*	recognize *3,4*
certify *1*	diagnose *(usu passive)*	regard *1*
characterize *2*	dismiss *1*	remember *6 (usu passive)*
cite *1*	expose *2*	represent *8*
class *7*	interpret *1*	reveal *1 (usu passive)*
classify	label *3 (usu passive)*	scorn *2*
conceive *2*	mention *3 (usu passive)*	see *6*
condemn *1*	misrepresent	stereotype *2 (usu passive)*
confirm *7*	perceive *2*	tout *1 (usu passive)*
consider *1*	pigeon-hole *2 (usu passive)*	view *3*
mark out *2*	pass off *VPP*	write off *3*

Structure information: Verb with Object and prepositional Object Complement

a) The noun group is the Object, and the prepositional phrase is the prepositional Object Complement.

b) This structure has a passive, with the pattern *be* **V-ed** *as* **adj.** The prepositional phrase is the prepositional Complement.

c) Though the prepositional phrase in this structure usually comes after the noun group, it sometimes comes before it, especially when the noun group is a long one.

Adorno set out to __expose__ as false all claims that the 'good' or 'just' society had been achieved.

d) There are only three phrasal verbs with this structure, *mark out, pass off,* and *write off.* The active patterns are **V n P** *as* **adj** and **V P n (not pron)** *as* **adj.** The Object comes either between the verb and the particle, or after the particle. If the Object comes after the particle, it cannot be a personal pronoun. You say

I *wrote* it *off as useless*

or I *wrote off* my attempt *as useless*

but you do not say *I wrote off it as useless.*
The passive pattern is *be* V-ed P *as* adj.

Structure II: Verb with Object and prepositional Complement

V n *as* adj

	Verb group	noun group	*as*	adjective group
Subject	Verb	Object		prepositional Complement
She	impressed	the board	as	competent enough.
He	struck	me	as	young, vigorous, interesting.

Verbs with this structure are concerned with the impression that someone or something makes on a person. The Object indicates that person. The prepositional phrase indicates a description of the Subject.

Mr. White ***has impressed*** *scores of acquaintances as capable of selling anything.*

impress *4*	strike *11*

Structure information: Verb with Object and prepositional Complement

a) The noun group is the Object, and the prepositional phrase is the prepositional Complement.

b) This structure has no passive.

8 V n *as* n

The verb is followed by a noun group and a prepositional phrase which consists of *as* and a noun group. With some verbs, the preposition is sometimes followed by an '-ing' clause. The passive pattern is *be* V-ed *as* n.

This pattern has two structures:

▶ Structure I: Verb with Object and prepositional Object Complement
They <u>chose</u> *her as their representative.*
▶ Structure II: Verb with Object and prepositional Complement
He <u>struck</u> *me as a very sensible person.*

Structure I: Verb with Object and prepositional Object Complement

Active voice: V n *as* n/-ing

	Verb group	noun group	*as*	noun group/-ing clause
Subject	**Verb**	**Object**		**prep. Object Complement**
Joanna	did not dismiss	Maude	as	a fraud.
Goodliffe	mentions	this	as	being a safe alternative.
The government	has presented	these changes	as	major reforms.
He	regards	himself	as	being too old for the post.

Passive voice: *be* V-ed *as* n/-ing

	Verb group	*as*	noun group/-ing clause
Subject	**Verb**		**prepositional Complement**
A person's life	should be considered	as	beginning at the moment of birth.
A life sentence	is defined	as	being twenty-five years.
He	had been mentioned	as	a possible new Foreign Minister.
The liberators	were revealed	as	oppressors.

Phrasal verbs

Active voice: V n P *as* n/-ing, V P n (not pron) *as* n/-ing

	Verb group	noun group	Particle	*as*	noun group/-ing clause
Subject	**Verb...**	**Object**	**...Verb**		**prep. Object Complement**
She	passed	the child	off	as	her own.
You	can put	him	down	as	a sort of early idol.
They	won't show	themselves	up	as	being plain dumb.

	Verb group	Particle	noun group	*as*	noun group/-ing clause
Subject	**Verb**		**Object**		**prep. Object Complement**
They	have marked	down	Field	as	the main danger.
He	has written	off	his colleagues	as	being unsuitable for promotion.

Passive voice: *be* V-ed P *as* n/-ing

	Verb group	Particle	*as*	noun group/-ing clause
Subject	**Verb**			**prepositional Complement**
He	was marked	down	as	one of the brightest officers.
The state of Kentucky	was singled	out	as	being on the cutting edge of reform.

Verbs with this structure belong to the following meaning groups:

I.1 THE 'NAME' AND 'CONSIDER' GROUP
I.2 THE 'STAMP' GROUP
I.3 THE 'USE' GROUP
I.4 THE 'QUOTE' GROUP
I.5 VERBS WITH OTHER MEANINGS

I.1 THE 'NAME' AND 'CONSIDER' GROUP

These verbs are concerned with:

- thinking of someone in a particular way e.g. *conceive, consider*
- giving someone a role or position e.g. *appoint, ordain*
- choosing someone to have a role or position e.g. *elect, nominate*
- putting someone or something into a class e.g. *classify, pigeon-hole*
- talking to someone in a particular way e.g. *address*
- criticizing someone because they have particular qualities e.g. *denounce, reject*
- representing someone in a particular way e.g. *expose, stereotype*
- talking about someone in a particular way e.g. *brand, dub*

The Subject always indicates a human being.

Within this group some verbs have a positive meaning, such as *acclaim, hail, laud,* and *lionize.* Some verbs, such as *condemn, dismiss, scorn,* and *vilify* indicate that you regard someone or something as bad. Others, such as *caricature* and *misrepresent,* indicate that you disapprove of the way someone else labels, interprets, or regards someone or something.

The president is likely to **appoint** *a woman as secretary of the navy.*

I **would characterize** *the space station as a technology project, not as a science project.*

I **consider** *him as a friend.*

A Home Office spokesman **has described** *reports of deaths inside the prison as speculation.*

It's difficult to express concern about it without **being labelled** *as a racist or a fascist.*

An obscure engineer had been awarded a remarkable patent, **naming** *him as the inventor of the first microprocessor.*

Carter **is remembered** *as the president who wore a heavy wool sweater in the White House.*

The popular press tends to **represent** *him as an environmental guru.*

The whole story **shows** *him* **up** *as a near-criminal.*

The preposition *as* is sometimes followed by an '-ing' clause.

*Imports **have to be certified** as coming from holdings that have been free of BSE for two years.*

*I think it's too easy for bands to **be written off** as sounding like other people.*

In the case of *announce, class, disguise, establish, fancy*, and *project*, the noun group following the verb is always or often a reflexive pronoun. This pattern is **V pron-refl *as* n/-ing**. The verb *pass off* has the pattern **V pron-refl P *as* n/-ing**.

*She couldn't travel as a woman, so she **disguised** herself as a man.*

*Like most joyriders, Stuart **fancied** himself as an expert driver and a match for the police.*

*The medieval mind was fascinated by the thought of a woman **passing** herself **off** successfully as a man.*

accept *2,4,5,6*	denounce *1*	parade *10*
acclaim *1 (usu passive)*	depict *2*	perceive *2*
acknowledge *1*	describe *2*	pigeon-hole *2 (usu passive)*
acknowledge *2 (usu passive)*	designate *1,3*	pinpoint *1*
address *5*	designate *2 (usu passive)*	portray *3*
adopt *1*	diagnose *(usu passive)*	present *4.5*
announce *1,2*	dignify *2 (usu passive)*	proclaim *1*
anoint *1,2*	disguise *2*	project *4*
appoint	dismiss *1*	rank *4*
attack *2*	dub *1*	rate *6*
authenticate *1*	elect *1*	read *8 (usu passive)*
bill *8*	enthrone *1 (usu passive)*	be reborn
brand *3*	establish *4*	recognize *1,3,4*
caricature *2*	expose *2*	re-elect *(usu passive)*
cast *3*	express *2.3*	regard *1*
categorize	fancy *1.4,5*	reject *1*
certify *1*	give *1.3*	remember *6 (usu passive)*
certify *2 (usu passive)*	hail *1*	represent *8*
characterize *2*	herald *3 (usu passive)*	reveal *1 (usu passive)*
choose *1*	identify *2*	scorn *2*
cite *1*	install *2*	see *6*
class *7*	intend *3*	select *1*
classify	interpret *1*	stereotype *2 (usu passive)*
commission *8 (usu passive)*	know *10,11,12*	stigmatize
conceive *2*	label *3 (usu passive)*	tag *5*
conceptualize	laud	term *4*
condemn *1*	lionize *(usu passive)*	tout *1 (usu passive)*
confirm *7*	mention *1*	trumpet *2*
consider *1*	mention *3,4 (usu passive)*	typecast *(usu passive)*
construe	misrepresent	view *3*
count *7,8*	name *4,6*	vilify
decry	nominate *1,2,3*	visualize
define *2*	ordain *1*	
build up *3*	mark out *2*	single out
hold up *5*	pass off *VPP*	write off *3,5*
mark down *2*	put down *VPP*	
mark off *2*	show up *2*	

I.2 THE 'STAMP' GROUP

These verbs are used to indicate that something shows the nature of someone or something. Unlike the previous group, the Subject never indicates a human being.

*It was a performance that **stamped** him **as the star we had been searching for** in a season of relative mediocrity.*

The preposition *as* is sometimes followed by an '-ing' clause.

The card __identified__ him as having brown hair and eyes.

identify *4*	qualify *3*
mark *15*	stamp *8*

I.3 THE 'USE' GROUP

These verbs are concerned with the role that is assigned to something in the course of a particular action.

This is a productive use. There are a lot of verbs which are often concerned with assigning a role to something, for example: *We __bought__ the house as an investment, They __sold__ the waste as fertilizer.* The verbs listed here are the ones which are most frequently used in this way.

One recent development is the creation of lots of factories which illegally __employ__ children as cheap labour.

People __have been keeping__ parrots as indoor pets since Egyptian times.

If a substance __is marketed__ as a dietary or nutritional aid, it falls outside the regulations which control medicines.

She had moved the peanut butter jar from office to office and __used__ it as a pencil holder.

In the case of *promote* and *treat*, the preposition *as* is sometimes followed by an '-ing' clause.

Parents __should treat__ their children as being able to understand the idea of using accents appropriately.

employ *2*	market *5 (usu passive)*	train *2.1*
intend *2*	package *5 (usu passive)*	treat *1*
keep *15*	promote *2 (usu passive)*	use *1.1*

I.4 THE 'QUOTE' GROUP

These verbs are concerned with quoting someone. The preposition *as* is always followed by an '-ing' clause.

The Washington Post today __cited__ a senior Pentagon official as saying only 25 percent of the unguided bombs were accurate.

You, in fact, __quoted__ her as saying, 'My friends say I'm the white Aunt Jemima of the women's movement'.

cite *1*	quote *1*

I.5 VERBS WITH OTHER MEANINGS

There is one other verb which has this structure.

He fled to France after he __was deposed__ as president.

depose *(usu passive)*

Structure information: Verb with Object and prepositional Object Complement

a) The noun group following the verb is the Object, and the prepositional phrase is the prepositional Object Complement.

b) This structure has a passive, with the pattern *be* **V-ed** *as* **n**. The prepositional phrase is the prepositional Complement.

c) Though the prepositional phrase in this structure usually comes after the noun group, it sometimes comes before it, especially when the noun group is a long one.

*He **dismissed** as scare stories reports that teachers were being sacked because schools didn't have enough to pay them.*

d) Phrasal verb patterns are the same, except that there is also a particle, P. The Object comes either between the verb and the particle, or after the particle. If the Object comes after the particle, it cannot be a personal pronoun. You say

*She **passed** him **off** as her own*
or *She **passed off** the child as her own*

but you do not say *She passed off him as her own.*

Structure II: Verb with Object and prepositional Complement

V n *as* n

	Verb group	noun group	*as*	noun group
Subject	Verb	Object		prepositional Complement
He	began	his career	as	a wedding photographer.
She	impressed	me	as	an interesting and sensitive person.

Verbs with this structure belong to the following meaning groups:

II.1 THE 'STRIKE' GROUP
II.2 THE 'BEGIN' AND 'END' GROUP
II.3 THE 'REPLACE' GROUP
II.4 VERBS WITH OTHER MEANINGS

II.1 THE 'STRIKE' GROUP

These verbs are concerned with the impression that something or someone makes on a person. The Object indicates that person.

*He always **struck** me as a very dispassionate and calculating sort of man.*

The preposition *as* is sometimes followed by an '-ing' clause.

*The bride **has impressed** me as being equally pleasant and obviously fitted to the noble calling she has chosen.*

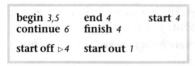

II.2 THE 'BEGIN' AND 'END' GROUP

These verbs are concerned with beginning, continuing, and ending something. They usually have a human Subject. The prepositional phrase indicates what someone or something was at the beginning or end of their life or career, or what they continue to be.

*Lloyd Wright **began** his career as a landscape architect.*

*Stephen Demainbray (1710-1782) was a Huguenot Londoner who **ended** his life as His Majesty King George III's Astronomer in charge of the Observatory at Kew.*

begin *3,5*	**end** *4*	**start** *4*
continue *6*	**finish** *4*	
start off ▷*4*	**start out** *1*	

II.3 THE 'REPLACE' GROUP

These verbs indicate that one thing or person takes the place of another.

*Turkish **replaced** Arabic as the language of the ruling elite.*

replace *1*	**supplant**

II.4 VERBS WITH OTHER MEANINGS

There is one other verb which has this structure.

*He looked for a fallen branch that **would serve** him as a crutch.*

serve *3*

Structure information: Verb with Object and prepositional Complement

a) The noun group following the verb is the Object, and the prepositional phrase is the prepositional Complement.

b) This structure has no passive.

c) There are only two phrasal verbs with this structure, *start off* and *start out*. The pattern is **V P n (not pron)** *as* **n**. The Object comes after the particle, and it cannot be a personal pronoun. You say

*He **started out** his career as a clerk*

but you do not say *He started out it as a clerk*.

Other productive uses

A prepositional phrase beginning with *as* is used with two additional meanings. These uses are productive, that is, they occur with a wide variety of verbs.

1 The prepositional phrase has the meaning 'because someone or something has a particular role'. An example is *They **burned** her as a witch*, which means that they burned her because (they thought) she was a witch.

2 The prepositional phrase has the meaning 'in his, her or its capacity as'. An example is
The book is widely consulted as an authoritative source on terrorist movements worldwide.

9 V n *as to* wh

The verb is followed by a noun group and a prepositional phrase which consists of *as to*
and a wh-clause or a noun group. The passive pattern is *be* V-ed *as to* wh/n.

This pattern has one structure:

▶ Verb with Object and Adjunct.
I informed him as to what his legal rights were.

Active voice: V n *as to* wh/n

	Verb group	noun group	*as to*	wh-clause/noun group
Subject	**Verb**	**Object**		**Adjunct**
A couple of readers	have enlightened	me	as to	standard practice.
He	was interrogating	them	as to	what they did in the war.

Passive voice: *be* V-ed *as to* wh/n

	Verb group	*as to*	wh-clause/noun group
Subject	**Verb**		**Adjunct**
He	was quizzed	as to	how he would adapt to the challenge.
Players	were warned	as to	their future conduct.

This pattern is rather formal, and is used in writing more often than in speech. Verbs with
this pattern belong to the following meaning groups:

1   THE 'ADVISE' GROUP
2   THE 'LIMIT' GROUP
3   VERBS WITH OTHER MEANINGS

1 THE 'ADVISE' GROUP

These verbs are concerned with asking for or giving advice or information.

*They **should be advised** as to how to minimize the risks.*

*Our attempts to **consult** him as to what would be a suitable site have been met evasively.*

*A second jury **would have to be** carefully **educated** as to how and why this soft-spoken
mother of five had been able to kill the father of her children.*

*Mr Bridge **has been informed** as to the full extent of the seriousness of his violation.*

Some directors were apt to take him aside and __question__ him as to the seriousness of his commitment to the theatre.

advise *1*	consult *1*	inform *1*	mislead
answer *1*	counsel *2*	instruct *1*	question *2*
ask *1*	educate *2*	interrogate	quiz *2*
challenge *4*	enlighten	misinform	warn *1*

2 THE 'LIMIT' GROUP

These verbs are concerned with limiting or restricting someone in a particular way.

Since 1883, parliamentary candidates __have been limited__ as to their election spending.

A politically appointed person can make an order against somebody, __restricting__ them as to where they can go and what they can do.

limit *5*	restrict *1*

3 VERBS WITH OTHER MEANINGS

There are two other verbs which have this pattern. The noun group following the verb is always a reflexive pronoun. This pattern is **V pron-refl *as to* wh/n**.

George's contract expires in the summer and he's yet to __commit__ himself as to what the future holds.

The buyer __should satisfy__ himself as to the condition of the bird before buying it.

commit *4*	satisfy *2*

Structure information

a) The noun group following the verb is the Object, and the prepositional phrase is an Adjunct.

b) This structure has a passive, with the patterns *be* V-ed *as to* wh and *be* V-ed *as to* n. The prepositional phrase is an Adjunct.

---

10   V n *at* n

The verb is followed by a noun group and a prepositional phrase which consists of *at* and a noun group. The passive pattern is *be* V-ed *at* n.

This pattern has three structures:

▶ Structure I: Verb with Object and prepositional Object
  He __shot__ a glance at her.
▶ Structure II: Verb with Object and prepositional Object Complement
  I __put__ the price at £1,000.
▶ Structure III: Verb with Object and Adjunct
  She __shouted__ insults at him.

Structure I: Verb with Object and prepositional Object

V n *at* n

	Verb group	noun group	*at*	noun group
Subject	**Verb**	**Object**	**prepositional Object**	
He	flashed	a loving smile	at	his new bride.
She	sneaked	a glance	at	Max.

Verbs with this structure are concerned with directing a look or a smile at someone or something.

The maid backed out, <u>throwing</u> one last cautionary look at her mistress.

dart 2	flash 9	sneak 3
direct 8	shoot 5	throw 10

Structure information: Verb with Object and prepositional Object

a) The noun group following the verb is the Object, and the prepositional phrase is the prepositional Object.

b) This structure has no passive.

c) Though the prepositional phrase in this structure usually comes after the noun group, it sometimes comes before it, especially when the noun group is a long one.

Werner at times <u>shot</u> at Anthony a look with a sly smile behind the eyes.

Structure II: Verb with Object and prepositional Object Complement

Active voice: V n *at* amount

	Verb group	noun group	*at*	amount
Subject	**Verb**	**Object**	**prep. Object Complement**	
The New York Times	put	the purchase price	at	about $200 million.
The magazine	reckoned	his personal wealth	at	£2.1 billion.

Passive voice: *be* V-ed *at* amount

	Verb group	*at*	amount
Subject	**Verb**	**prepositional Complement**	
Savings on all the programmes	are estimated	at	two million dollars.
The share price	was set	at	£1.75.

Verbs with this structure are all concerned with estimating, fixing, or maintaining the price, value, or size of something.

> *The interim dividend for the six months to June 30* **has been pegged** *at 1p and the company has promised to* **maintain** *the final dividend at 2p.*

> *The number of child workers* **was put** *at more than 4.8 million.*

estimate 1 *(usu passive)*	**peg** 5 *(usu passive)*	**reckon** 4
maintain 3	**put** 11	**set** 2.6 *(usu passive)*

Structure information: Verb with Object and prepositional Object Complement

a) The noun group following the verb is the Object, and the prepositional phrase is the prepositional Object Complement.

b) The structure has a passive, with the pattern **be V-ed** **at** **amount**. The prepositional phrase is the prepositional Complement.

c) Though the prepositional phrase in this structure usually comes after the noun group, it sometimes comes before it, especially when the noun group is a long one.

> *The resolution* **sets** *at thirty percent the ceiling of future oil revenues payable into the compensation fund*.

Structure III: Verb with Object and Adjunct

Active voice: V n *at* n

	Verb group	noun group	*at*	noun group
Subject	**Verb**	**Object**		**Adjunct**
I	sold	my house	at	a profit.
I	shook	my fist	at	him.

Passive voice: *be* V-ed *at* n

	Verb group	*at*	noun group
Subject	**Verb**		**Adjunct**
His remarks	were aimed	at	India and Israel.
The students' anger	is directed	at	the government.
Bombs	were thrown	at	shops in the capital.

Verbs with this structure belong to the following meaning groups:

III.1 THE 'POINT' GROUP

III.2 THE 'THROW' GROUP

III.3 THE 'SHOUT' GROUP

III.4 THE 'BUY' GROUP

III.5 VERBS WITH OTHER MEANINGS

III.1 THE 'POINT' GROUP

These verbs are concerned with pointing or aiming something at someone or something. The thing that is aimed may be:

- a part of your body such as your fist or finger
- a weapon
- a torch or other instrument

Sometimes, as in the case of *jab* and *stab* for example, there may be physical contact involved.

> Alan **jabbed** a finger at me.

> The 19-year-old was outside a Birmingham health centre when the boys burst into the phone box and **pointed** the gun at her.

> He **swung** a hammer at her head but missed.

aim *5*	jab *1*	point *15*	stab *2*
direct *6*	level *13*	shake *6*	swing *5*

III.2 THE 'THROW' GROUP

These verbs are concerned with throwing something at someone or something.

> He stepped away from his father and picked up a few stones, started **chucking** them at the train embankment.

> They set fire to the prison garage and to a wood store of a carpentry shop, and **hurled** roof tiles and other missiles at firemen and riot police.

> Separatists **threw** a bomb at a house owned by a woman they have accused of being a police informer.

In the case of *fling 2*, the noun group following the verb is always a reflexive pronoun. This pattern is **V pron-refl *at* n**.

> Suddenly, she **flung** herself at Andrew and buried her face in his shoulder.

chuck *1*	hurl *1*
fling *1,2*	throw *1*

III.3 THE 'SHOUT' GROUP

These verbs are concerned with directing remarks at someone, criticizing or insulting them, or shouting at them. This is a productive pattern: a large number of verbs which involve communication of some kind, usually angry or unpleasant, can be used with this pattern. The verbs listed here are the ones which are most frequently used in this way.

> These last remarks **were directed** at a small boy who had been impatiently tapping on the counter with a coin to interrupt the shopkeeper's flow of talk.

> The Defence Minister stormed out of government in June after allegations of corruption **were levelled** at him and his family.

> As several hundred soldiers advance up the hill, they **shout** and **scream** insults at the guerillas.

> I should never have told you that. I knew you**'d throw** it **back** at me.

aim 4 *(usu passive)*	**growl** 2	**level** 12	**yell** 1
bark 2	**holler**	**scream** 2	
bellow 1	**howl** 4	**shout** 1	
direct 7,8	**hurl** 2	**shriek** 2	
throw back 1			

III.4 THE 'BUY' GROUP

These verbs are concerned with buying, selling, or putting a value on something.

*Administration of the department **is budgeted** at 3.9 billion pounds.*

*Estates **may sell** property at a discount to raise money quickly for taxes.*

The noun group following the preposition is often an **amount**. This pattern is **V n at amount**.

*One day Carret **was able to buy** some bonds at $89, which he then sold at a profit.*

budget 4 *(usu passive)*	**price** 3 *(usu passive)*	**value** 4 *(usu passive)*
buy 1	**quote** 6 *(usu passive)*	
capitalize 2 *(usu passive)*	**sell** 1	

III.5 VERBS WITH OTHER MEANINGS

There are three other verbs which have this structure. In the case of *be aimed*, the preposition *at* is usually followed by an '-ing' clause rather than a noun group.

*A great deal of research **has been aimed** at developing a safe tobacco cigarette.*

In the case of *clock*, the noun group following the preposition is usually an **amount**. This pattern is **V n at amount**.

*Top winds in the storm **have been clocked** at about 50 miles an hour.*

be aimed 3	**clock** 5 *(usu passive)*	**pitch** 7

Structure information: Verb with Object and Adjunct

a) The noun group following the verb is the Object, and the prepositional phrase is an Adjunct.

b) This structure has a passive, with the pattern **be V-ed at n**. The prepositional phrase is an Adjunct.

c) Though the prepositional phrase in this structure usually comes after the noun group, it sometimes comes before it, especially when the noun group is a long one.

*Over the years they **had hurled** at each other every curse word they knew.*

d) There is only one phrasal verb with this structure, *throw back*. The active patterns are **V n P at n** and **V P n (not pron) at n**. The Object comes either between the verb and the particle, or after the particle. If the Object comes after the particle, it cannot be a personal pronoun. You say

*He **threw** it **back** at me*
or *He **threw back** my admission at me*

but you do not say *He threw back it at me*.
The passive pattern is **be V-ed P at n**.

11 V n *between/among* pl-n

The verb is followed by a noun group and a prepositional phrase which consists of *between* or *among* and a **plural noun group**. The passive pattern is *be* V-ed *between/among* pl-n.

This pattern has one structure:

▶ Verb with Object and Adjunct
He <u>divided</u> his money among his children.

Active voice: V n *between/among* pl-n

	Verb group	noun group	*between/among*	plural noun group
Subject	**Verb**	**Object**	**Adjunct**	
UN officials	have mediated	a meeting	between	the two sides.
I	would rate	him	among	the fastest bowlers.

Passive voice: *be* V-ed *between/among* pl-n

	Verb group	*between/among*	plural noun group
Subject	**Verb**	**Adjunct**	
Profits	are distributed	among	the policy holders of the fund.
The cleaning	should be shared	between	you and your partner.

Verbs with this pattern belong to the following meaning groups:

1 THE 'DIVIDE' GROUP
2 THE 'FORGE' GROUP
3 THE 'SANDWICH' GROUP
4 THE 'NUMBER' GROUP
5 VERBS WITH OTHER MEANINGS

1 THE 'DIVIDE' GROUP

These verbs are concerned with dividing something between two or more people or groups. When only two people or groups are involved, the preposition is usually *between* rather than *among*. When more than two people or groups are involved, you can use either *between* or *among*.

*Drain the noodles and **<u>divide</u> them among the individual serving bowls.***

*The tips **<u>are divided up</u>** equally **between the staff**, and then added on to their wage packet.*

*Election coverage on radio and television **<u>will be split</u>** between the party in power and the opposition parties.*

distribute 1 *(usu passive)*	**divide** 2	**split** 7 *(usu passive)*
distribute 3	**share** 2 *(usu passive)*	
divide up 2 *(usu passive)*	**share out**	**split up** 3

2 THE 'FORGE' GROUP

These verbs are concerned with forging an agreement between two people or groups.

*The programme aims to **forge** links between higher education and small businesses.*

> forge *1*   mediate *1*

3 THE 'SANDWICH' GROUP

These verbs are concerned with putting something between two or more things, either physically or metaphorically. In the case of *sandwich*, only the preposition *between* is used.

*The liquid crystal **is sandwiched** between two glass plates, each of which carries a polarising filter.*

In the case of *interpose*, the noun group following the verb is often a reflexive pronoun. This pattern is **V pron-refl *between/among* pl-n**.

*Police forces **had to interpose** themselves between the two rival groups.*

> interpose *1*   intersperse   sandwich *2*

4 THE 'NUMBER' GROUP

These verbs are concerned with considering someone or something to be in a particular group. The prepositional phrase indicates that group. Only the preposition *among* is used with these verbs.

*He **numbered** several Americans among his friends.*

> number *8*   rank *4*   rate *6*

5 VERBS WITH OTHER MEANINGS

There is one other verb which has this pattern. Only the preposition *between* is used with this verb. It is sometimes followed by two co-ordinated '-ing' clauses.

*Mothers **are caught** between wanting their girls to grow up into lovely women and hating to grow older themselves.*

> be caught *17*

Structure information

a) The noun group following the verb is the Object, and the prepositional phrase is an Adjunct.

b) This structure has a passive, with the pattern ***be* V-ed *between/among* pl-n**. The prepositional phrase is an Adjunct.

c) There are only three phrasal verbs with this structure, *divide up*, *share out*, and *split up*. The active patterns are **V n P *between/among* pl-n** and **V P n (not pron) *between/among* pl-n**. The Object comes either between the verb and the particle, or after the particle. If the Object comes after the particle, it cannot be a personal pronoun. You say

*He **split** it **up** between the children*
or *He **split up** the money between the children*

but do not say *He split up it between the children.*
The passive pattern is ***be* V-ed P *between/among* pl-n**.

Other related patterns

V n adj *among* pl-n

The verb is followed by a noun group, an adjective group, and a prepositional phrase which consists of *among* and a plural noun group. The adjective is usually *high* or *low*.

> *The paradox of the schools' success is that their teaching staff probably __rate__ academic results relatively low among their priorities.*

rank *4*	rate *6*

V n ord *among* pl-n

The verb is followed by a noun group, an ordinal number, and a prepositional phrase which consists of *among* and a plural noun group.

> *One survey __ranked__ her fifth among preferred presidential candidates.*

rank *4*

---

12 V n *by* n

The verb is followed by a noun group and a prepositional phrase which consists of *by* and a noun group. With some verbs, the preposition is sometimes followed by an '-ing' clause.

This pattern has one structure:

▶ Verb with Object and Adjunct
   He __began__ the day by taking a cool shower.

The passive pattern *be* V-ed *by* n is dealt with in this section when it is a genuine passive of a V n *by* n structure. Note, however, that *be* V-ed *by* n may also be the passive of V n. See page 58.

Active voice: V n *by* n/-ing

	Verb group	noun group	*by*	noun group/-ing clause
Subject	**Verb**	**Object**		**Adjunct**
He	began	the day	by	laying a wreath at the National Memorial.
He	grabbed	her	by	the shoulders.

Passive voice: *be* V-ed *by* n

	Verb group	*by*	noun group
Subject	**Verb**		**Adjunct**
Even first-time visitors	were called	by	their first names.
Some local trains	will be replaced	by	buses.

Chapter 4: Complex Patterns with Prepositions and Adverbs

Verbs with this pattern belong to the following meaning groups:

1 THE 'BEGIN' AND 'END' GROUP
2 THE 'GRAB' GROUP
3 THE 'CALL' GROUP
4 THE 'RAISE' AND 'LOWER' GROUP
5 VERBS WITH OTHER MEANINGS

1 THE 'BEGIN' AND 'END' GROUP

These verbs are concerned with beginning or ending a task, session, career, or period of time. The prepositional phrase indicates what someone does at the beginning or end of this period. We include here the verb *preface*, which involves saying something before making a remark or a speech; *answer*, which involves answering a question in a particular way; and *crown*, which involves finishing your career in a particularly successful way.

With these verbs, the preposition *by* is usually followed by an '-ing' clause rather than a noun group. Verbs with this meaning do not often occur in the passive.

*He **answered** the question by denying that any unusual troop movements were taking place.*

*When my father's education finished, he **began** his engineering career by building ice factories.*

*The South Korean president **has ended** his visit to Japan by inviting Emperor Akihito to pay a return visit to South Korea.*

*The senator **prefaced** his round of questions by saying that everyone makes mistakes and that the committee should be careful not to set too high a standard.*

*He **started off** this particular interview by saying, 'Yes, I think you're on to a good idea.'*

answer *11*	crown *11*	open *21*
begin *3*	end *4,6*	preface *2*
close *1.7*	finish *4*	start *3*
finish up *4*	start off *1*	start out *2*

2 THE 'GRAB' GROUP

These verbs are concerned with grabbing or holding someone by a part of their body.

*He **grabbed** Rivers by the shoulders and dragged him out of the car.*

*Sunny's father took his protesting daughter with him. He **had** her by the arm and was propelling her firmly across the gravel to the back entrance to the cafe.*

catch *3*	have *3.8*	take *2.1*
grab *1*	hold *1.4*	

3 THE 'CALL' GROUP

These verbs are concerned with calling or knowing someone by their name, or by a particular name.

*In three years I **had** never **called** him by name.*

*For some unexplained reason he seems to have been the only boy in the school who **was known** by his Christian name and not his surname.*

call *1*	know *10*

4 THE 'RAISE' AND 'LOWER' GROUP

These verbs are concerned with:

- raising or lowering a number or value by a particular amount e.g. *cut, devalue*
- multiplying or dividing a number or amount by another number e.g. *divide, multiply*

The noun group following the preposition is always an **amount**, and the pattern is **V n** *by* **amount**.

*The Irish government was forced to **devalue** its pound **by 10 percent** within the European exchange-rate mechanism.*

*The bank provides customers with a chart to estimate their year's bills and **divide** the total **by twelve**.*

*The eruption produced so much ash scientists believe it counteracted the greenhouse effect and **lowered** temperatures **by one to two degrees** worldwide.*

*Many resort town employers **have raised** salaries **by 35 to 50 percent** in the past year in an effort to attract needed help.*

cut 7	lift 10	raise 4
devalue 2	lower 5	
divide 3	multiply 3	

5 VERBS WITH OTHER MEANINGS

There are a few other verbs which have this pattern.

*He allegedly **fathered** a child **by a woman** he had met at an equestrian event in New Zealand.*

*I didn't get it. I think you**'d better run** it **by me** again.*

father 2	run VP
replace 2	surround 4

Structure information

a) The noun group following the verb is the Object, and the prepositional phrase is an Adjunct.

b) This structure has a passive, with the pattern *be* **V-ed** *by* **n**. The prepositional phrase is an Adjunct.

c) Though the prepositional phrase in this structure usually comes after the noun group, it sometimes comes before it, especially when the noun group is a long one.

*Inflation **has multiplied** by about 15 the amount of money a family needs to live on.*

d) There are only three phrasal verbs with this structure, *finish up, start off,* and *start out*. The active patterns are **V n P** *by* **-ing** and **V P n (not pron)** *by* **-ing**. The Object comes either between the verb and the particle, or after the particle. If the Object comes after the particle, it cannot be a personal pronoun. You say

*He **started** it **off** by greeting us all*
or *He **started off** the party by greeting us all*

but you do not say *He started off it by greeting us all.*

Productive uses

The pattern **V n** *by* **-ing** is productive: you can use it with a wide range of verbs involving saying or doing something. The prepositional phrase indicates the means by which something is said or done, as in *He **escaped** the law by fleeing the country.*

13 V n *for* n

The verb is followed by a noun group and a prepositional phrase which consists of *for* and a noun group. With some verbs the preposition is sometimes followed by an '-ing' clause. The passive pattern is *be* V-ed *for* n.

This pattern has two main structures:

▶ Structure I: Verb with Object and prepositional Object
She <u>bought</u> *a present for him.*
▶ Structure II: Verb with Object and Adjunct
He <u>begged</u> *his father for a loan.*

Structure I: Verb with Object and prepositional Object

Active voice: V n *for* n

	Verb group	noun group	*for*	noun group
Subject	Verb	Object		prepositional Object
She	has brought	a nice present	for	you.
They	had found	a portable high chair	for	the baby.

Passive voice: *be* V-ed *for* n

	Verb group	*for*	noun group
Subject	Verb		prepositional Object
A room	has been booked	for	him.
Bison meat	is being prescribed	for	patients with food allergies.

Verbs with this structure belong to the following meaning groups:

I.1 THE 'BUY' GROUP
I.2 THE 'EXCHANGE' GROUP

I.1 THE 'BUY' GROUP

These verbs are concerned with doing something for someone.

This is a productive use: any verb that involves doing something for someone can be used with this pattern. The verbs listed here are the ones which are most frequently used in this way.

His blue blazer and gray flannel pants **<u>had been bought</u> for him** *at Farmer's boys' department by Miss Dunn herself.*

She **<u>knitted</u> socks and sweaters for the troops**.

I followed her to the kitchen where she **<u>was making</u> coffee for all of them.**

He **<u>used to raise</u> money for charity** *by taking off all his clothes and jumping in the canal.*

In the case of *carve* and *forge*, the noun group following the preposition is always a reflexive pronoun. This pattern is **V n *for* pron-refl**.

Mark has endeavoured to **<u>carve</u> an independent career for himself.**

In the unrelenting world of National Hunt racing, Williamson, 25, **<u>has forged</u> a healthy niche for himself.**

In the case of *do*, the noun group following the verb is often an **amount**. This pattern is **V amount *for* n**.

*If you are asking others to **do** a lot **for** you, ask or suggest what you might do for them.*

book *3*	do *2.7*	knit *1*	prepare *3*
bring *3*	fetch *1*	leave *8*	prescribe *1*
buy *1*	find *1,2*	make *3.3*	raise *8*
carve *4*	fix *14*	order *2.5*	secure *1*
collect *6*	forge *1*	play *11,12*	wangle
cook *1*	get *2.1,3*	pour *2*	write *2,6*

I.2 THE 'EXCHANGE' GROUP

These verbs are concerned with exchanging one thing for another. We include here *mistake*, which involves thinking that something is something else.

*The shipment is part of a barter deal **exchanging** rice **for** coal and cement.*

*The USA nearly declared nuclear war when its computer **mistook** the rising moon **for** a missile attack.*

*Someone **swapped** the blank **for** a real bullet. He is lucky to be alive.*

barter	mistake *3*	swap *1,2*
exchange *2*	substitute *1*	trade *5*
trade off *1*		

Structure information: Verb with Object and prepositional Object

a) The noun group following the verb is an Object, and the prepositional phrase is the prepositional Object.

b) This structure has a passive, with the pattern **be V-ed *for* n**. The prepositional phrase is the prepositional Object. However, the passive is not frequent with any of the verbs in this group and with some of them, like *cook*, it does not occur at all.

c) Though the prepositional phrase in this structure usually comes after the noun group, it sometimes comes before it, especially when the noun group is a long one.

*He **secured** for them all a steady ration of clothes and beer.*

d) There is only one phrasal verb with this structure, *trade off*. The active patterns are **V n P *for* n** and **V P n (not pron) *for* n**. The Object comes either between the verb and the particle, or after the particle. If the Object comes after the particle, it cannot be a personal pronoun. You say

*He **traded** it **off** for a reduced sentence*
or *He **traded off** information for a reduced sentence*

but you do not say *He traded off it for a reduced sentence*.
The passive pattern is **be V-ed P *for* n**.

367

Structure II: Verb with Object and Adjunct

Active voice: V n *for* n/-ing

	Verb group	noun group	*for*	noun group/-ing clause
Subject	**Verb**	**Object**		**Adjunct**
I	don't blame	you	for	being upset.
	Forgive	me	for	introducing politics into this.
He	praised	the two leaders	for	their statesmanship.
I	am not going to punish	you	for	what you have just done.

Passive voice: *be* V-ed *for* n/-ing

	Verb group	*for*	noun group/-ing clause
Subject	**Verb**		**Adjunct**
He	was applauded	for	his exuberant honesty.
Six people	were arrested	for	public order offences.
Carl	was indicted	for	tampering with public records.
One member	was reprimanded	for	frolicking in the goldfish pond.

Phrasal verbs

Active voice: V n P *for* n/-ing, V P n (not pron) *for* n/-ing

	Verb group	noun group	Particle	*for*	noun group/-ing clause
Subject	**Verb...**	**Object**	**...Verb**		**Adjunct**
We	fitted	him	out	for	a trip to the Baltic.
Theresa	told	him	off	for	being such a baby.

	Verb group	Particle	noun group	*for*	noun group/-ing clause
Subject	**Verb**		**Object**		**Adjunct**
They	will fork	out	large sums	for	their pleasures.
I	was paying	out	good money	for	his services.
He	told	off	Louisa	for	fidgeting during the programme.

Passive voice: *be* V-ed P *for* n/-ing

	Verb group	Particle	*for*	noun group/-ing clause
Subject	**Verb**			**Adjunct**
He	has been singled	out	for	disciplinary action.
Harry	will be ticked	off	for	being careless with his gun.

Verbs with this structure belong to the following meaning groups:

II.1 THE 'ASK' GROUP	II.7 THE 'SELECT' GROUP
II.2 THE 'PRAISE' GROUP	II.8 THE 'PAY' GROUP
II.3 THE 'CONDEMN' GROUP	II.9 THE 'ALLOCATE' GROUP
II.4 THE 'REWARD' AND 'PUNISH' GROUP	II.10 THE 'SCHEDULE' GROUP
II.5 THE 'LEAVE' GROUP	II.11 THE 'SEARCH' GROUP
II.6 THE 'PREPARE' GROUP	II.12 VERBS WITH OTHER MEANINGS

II.1 THE 'ASK' GROUP

These verbs are concerned with asking someone for something, or trying to get money or information from them.

*They **asked** me for fresh ideas, but I had none.*

*She **begged** her father for yet another loan.*

*The Government **is being pressed** for a speedy review of an immigration ban on a Turkish waiter.*

*He **pumped** her for information.*

*Britain's biggest leisure group may be poised to **tap** its shareholders for cash, it was rumoured last night.*

ask 4	implore	press 5 *(usu passive)*	tap 4
beg 1	importune	pressure 5	touch 14
beseech	pester	pump 9	

II.2 THE 'PRAISE' GROUP

These verbs are concerned with talking or thinking about someone in a positive way, or talking to someone in a positive way, because of what they are, say, or do. The prepositional phrase indicates what they are, say, or do.

*They **have had to accept** him for what he is rather than what they would like him to be.*

*I **congratulate** him and his family for achievements in the past and wish them continued success for the next 100 years.*

*The air force and navy **are being praised** for the rescue operation.*

The preposition *for* is sometimes followed by an '-ing' clause.

*I **admired** this woman for being so persistent among these contemptuous men.*

In the case of *congratulate 3*, the noun group following the verb is always a reflexive pronoun. This pattern is **V pron-refl *for* n**.

*The President and his fellow leaders **congratulated** themselves for what they said was the most successful military and diplomatic alliance in the history of the world.*

accept 7	admire 1	commend 1	laud
acclaim 1 *(usu passive)*	applaud 2 *(usu passive)*	congratulate 1,2,3	praise 1

II.3 THE 'CONDEMN' GROUP

These verbs are concerned with talking or thinking about someone in a critical way, or talking to someone in a critical way, because of what they are, say, or do. The prepositional phrase indicates what they are, say, or do.

*He said the Security Council has a moral obligation to **condemn** the US for this incident.*

*I **was** severely **scolded** for my cowardice by Mother and Granny after I got home.*

The preposition *for* is sometimes followed by an '-ing' clause.

I think you __can't fault__ anybody for saying, OK, I want a better life, and there's got to be a better life somewhere.

She __had not__ even __reproached__ him for breaking his promise by not visiting her the night before.

Traffic police __ticked off__ a pensioner for jumping a red light but failed to spot a gunman holding a revolver to his heart.

In the case of *reproach 3*, the noun group following the verb is always a reflexive pronoun. This pattern is **V pron-refl *for* n/-ing**. The verb *despise* often has this pattern as well.

I __reproached__ myself very bitterly for having done so little about the care of this baby.

admonish	castigate	despise	scold
attack 2	censure	(cannot) fault 4	slam 3
berate	chide	rap 7	slate 5
blame 1	condemn 1	reprimand *(usu passive)*	upbraid
(not) blame 3	criticize	reproach 1,3	vilify *(usu passive)*
tell off	tick off 2		

II.4 THE 'REWARD' AND 'PUNISH' GROUP

These verbs are concerned with reacting to something that someone has done or experienced, for example by rewarding or punishing them. The prepositional phrase indicates what they have done or experienced.

The 45-year-old lorry driver __will be reported__ for careless driving, failing to stop after an accident and driving without insurance.

I __had__ generously __rewarded__ her for her services, which had delighted her.

The way things work in the United States, especially today, you __can sue__ anyone for anything.

They'__re wanted__ for murder and extortion and all other kind of heinous crimes.

The preposition *for* is sometimes followed by an '-ing' clause.

He told officers he wanted to __pay__ them __back__ for locking him up three weeks earlier.

There is really no point in trying to __punish__ your cat for hunting – it is a part of his nature.

I __must thank__ you for being so kind to me.

In the case of *console*, the noun group following the verb is often a reflexive pronoun. This pattern is **V pron-refl *for* n**.

Generous helpings of alcohol helped guests __console__ themselves for the fact that he did not turn up.

arraign *(usu passive)*	excuse 3	prosecute 1	reward 3
arrest 1	execute 1 *(usu passive)*	punish 1	sue
commit 7 *(usu passive)*	forgive 1,3	recompense 2	thank 5
compensate 1	be forgiven 2	remember 6	try 7 *(usu passive)*
console 1	indict *(usu passive)*	report 7 *(usu passive)*	want 7 *(usu passive)*
haul up ▷2 *(usu passive)*	pay back 2		

II.5 THE 'LEAVE' GROUP

These verbs are concerned with leaving someone or something. The prepositional phrase indicates the person, place, or thing that you go to instead.

Caroline's marriage ended abruptly when her husband __left__ her for another woman.

desert 5	forsake 2	leave 3

II.6 THE 'PREPARE' GROUP

These verbs are concerned with preparing someone or something for a particular task or purpose. We include here *clear*, which is usually followed by *the way* or *the path*.

*The king is expected to announce later today that he intends to **clear** the way for a multi-party democracy in his country.*

*She hastens to note that she **was not groomed** for a show-business career.*

*Sara tried hard to build up her daughter-in-law's strength, to **prepare** her for motherhood.*

*She **put** the house **up** for sale and moved to one of those army retirement homes.*

*He has mastered enough of the complexities of arrangement to write and **score** a piece for a chamber music ensemble.*

The preposition *for* is sometimes followed by an '-ing' clause.

*Volkswagen have just given the University of Munich an incredible amount of money to set up a college to **train** teachers for teaching gifted children.*

In the case of *brace, gird, prepare 2*, and *steel*, the noun group following the verb is always a reflexive pronoun. This pattern is **V pron-refl *for* n**.

*The security forces **will** probably **have to brace** themselves for more attacks and ambushes.*

brace *1*	fit *1.11*	prepare *1,2*	score *8*
clear *10*	free *8*	prime *5*	steel *3*
be designed *8*	gird	qualify *2*	train *2.3*
equip *2*	groom *4 (usu passive)*	ready *8*	transcribe *2*
fit *1.3 (usu passive)*	intend *2 (usu passive)*	revise *3*	
fit out	put up *VPP*		

II.7 THE 'SELECT' GROUP

These verbs are concerned with considering or choosing someone or something for a particular role or purpose, or with deciding not to choose them.

*Miss Halford is claiming sex discrimination after **being passed over** for promotion to a higher rank on nine occasions.*

*There was no evidence that the employer used seminar attendance to **select** employees for advancement.*

*Eighteen applicants **were shortlisted** for interviews.*

audition *2*	nominate *1,3*	seek *1 (usu passive)*
choose *1*	recommend *1*	select *1*
interview *2 (usu passive)*	recruit *1*	shortlist *2 (usu passive)*
pass over *1 (usu passive)*	rope in *(usu passive)*	single out

II.8 THE 'PAY' GROUP

These verbs are concerned with charging or paying someone for something, or with paying an amount of money for something. In the case of *bill* and *charge*, the Object indicates the person who is asked to pay. In the case of *reimburse*, the Object indicates the person who is paid. In the case of *cough up, fork out, pay out*, and *shell out*, the Object indicates the amount paid. In the case of *pay*, the Object may be the person who is paid, or the amount paid.

*The agency **bills** its clients for the employee hours spent on the campaign.*

*In 1971 the director of the Natural History Museum of Iceland **paid** nine thousand dollars for a stuffed Great Auk.*

***Pay** the gentleman for his services, please.*

The preposition *for* is sometimes followed by an '-ing' clause.

> *Hospitals caring for geriatric patients* **are reimbursed** *at a predetermined level* **for prescribing set amounts of drugs.**

In the case of *ask, cough up, fork out, pay out*, and *shell out*, the noun group following the verb is always an **amount**. This pattern is **V amount *for* n**.

> *British smokers* **cough up** **nearly twice as much for a packet of cigarettes** *as French smokers pay for their Gauloises and Gitanes.*

ask *8*	charge *1*	reimburse
bill *2*	pay *1,4*	
cough up	pay out *1*	
fork out	shell out	

The verbs *bill, charge, pay,* and *reimburse* also have the pattern **V n amount *for* n**.

> *He was shocked when the bank* **charged** *him £110* **for the manager's time.**

II.9 THE 'ALLOCATE' GROUP

These verbs are concerned with allocating time, money, or other resources for a particular purpose. The noun group is often an **amount**.

> *At their own discretion they* **can allocate** **money for research into anything interesting they think their people will be good at.**

The preposition *for* is sometimes followed by an '-ing' clause.

> *25 per cent of the funds* **is designated** **for buying shares.**

allocate	commit *3*	earmark *2 (usu passive)*
allow *5*	designate *2 (usu passive)*	reserve *1 (usu passive)*
budget *4*	earmark *1*	vote *7*

II.10 THE 'SCHEDULE' GROUP

These verbs are concerned with scheduling something to happen at a particular time.

> *The President* **has scheduled** **a news conference for this afternoon.**

reschedule *1*	slate *4 (usu passive)*
schedule *3*	time *19*

II.11 THE 'SEARCH' GROUP

These verbs are concerned with searching somewhere for something. We include here *strip-search*, which involves searching a person.

> *Seventy officers and a police helicopter* **combed** **the streets for seven-year-old Maria.**

> *Many universities say they already* **scour** **the country for qualified black undergraduates to attend graduate school.**

> *Police divers* **were** *yesterday* **searching** **a remote Scottish mountain loch for two men** *missing after a plane crashed on a training flight.*

comb *3*	scour *1*	strip-search *(usu passive)*
explore *3*	scout *3*	
scan *2*	search *2,4*	

II.12 VERBS WITH OTHER MEANINGS

There are a number of other verbs which have this structure.

*He **did not ask** me for lunch; I cannot have been very attractive.*

*Sam Smith is a perceptive operator who **exacts** swift **revenge for errors**.*

*I wouldn't say the match **holds** any more **fears for us** than any other we have played.*

*Their countries **are** now **paying** the penalty for the neglect into which their water supply and sanitation systems have fallen.*

*I **was sent** for blood tests.*

In the case of *say 8*, the noun group following the verb is always the pronoun *this* or *that*. This pattern is **V pron *for* n**.

*They've got ingenuity, I'**ll say** that **for them***

In the case of *say 9*, the noun group following the verb is always an **amount**. This pattern is **V amount *for* n**.

*Last weekend the liberals chose a new chairman, Klaus Kinkel, the foreign minister. He joined the party only two years ago, which **says** much **for its open-mindedness**.*

ask *7*	**hold** *2.2*	**sell** *1*	**touch** *12*
clear *19 (usu passive)*	**insure** *1*	**send** *2*	**treat** *2*
enter *7*	**name** *3*	**set** *2.19*	**wait** *1*
exact *4,5*	**pay** *10*	**take** *2.33*	**wire** *3 (usu passive)*
fight *3,5,9*	**sacrifice** *2*	**test** *7 (usu passive)*	
get *2.6*	**say** *8,9*	**tip** *10 (usu passive)*	
put down *VPP*			

Structure information: Verb with Object and Adjunct

a) The noun group following the verb is the Object, and the prepositional phrase is an Adjunct.

b) This structure has a passive, with the pattern **be V-ed *for* n**. The prepositional phrase is an Adjunct.

c) Phrasal verb patterns are the same except that there is also a particle, P. The Object comes either between the verb and the particle, or after the particle. If the Object comes after the particle, it cannot be a personal pronoun. You say

*He **told** them **off** for bad behaviour*
or *He **told off** the students for bad behaviour*

but you do not say *He told off them for bad behaviour.*

Other structures

In the case of two verbs, *know* and *take*, the prepositional phrase is a prepositional Object Complement.

*After all these years, **do** you **take** me for a fool?*

know *11*	**take** *2.25*

Other related patterns

V n amount *for* n

See meaning group II.8 above.

14 V n *from* n

The verb is followed by a noun group and a prepositional phrase which consists of *from* and a noun group. With some verbs, the preposition is sometimes followed by an '-ing' clause. The passive pattern is *be* V-ed *from* n.

This pattern has one structure:

► Verb with Object and Adjunct
I borrowed the money from my father.

Active voice: V n *from* n/-ing

	Verb group	noun group	*from*	noun group/-ing clause
Subject	**Verb**	**Object**		**Adjunct**
He	borrowed	money	from	friends.
The years	have not erased	the signs of war	from	the landscape.
The embargo	prevents	them	from	selling oil.

Passive voice: *be* V-ed *from* n/-ing

	Verb group	*from*	noun group/-ing clause
Subject	**Verb**		**Adjunct**
They	should be discouraged	from	harbouring grudges.
The top seeds	have been eliminated	from	the World Doubles Championship.
He	was extradited	from	the United States.
Three foxes	were saved	from	being savagely ripped apart.

Phrasal verbs

Active voice: V n P *from* n, V P n (not pron) *from* n

	Verb group	noun group	Particle	*from*	noun group
Subject	**Verb...**	**Object**	**...Verb**		**Adjunct**
Darren's hair style	marks	him	out	from	the crowd.
What characteristics	set	us	apart	from	other animals?

	Verb group	Particle	noun group	*from*	noun group
Subject	**Verb**		**Object**		**Adjunct**
Ozone	filters	out	harmful radiation	from	sunlight.
The black night	had taken	away	the colour	from	all things.

Passive voice: *be* V-ed P *from* n

	Verb group	Particle	*from*	noun group
Subject	**Verb**			**Adjunct**
The side alley	was walled	off	from	the back garden.
A trawler	was warned	away	from	the area.

Verbs with this pattern belong to the following meaning groups:

1 THE 'DEMAND' AND 'GET' GROUP
2 THE 'REMOVE' GROUP
3 THE 'TRANSFER' GROUP
4 THE 'SEPARATE' GROUP
5 THE 'STOP' GROUP
6 THE 'DEFLECT' GROUP

7 THE 'CONCEAL' GROUP
8 THE 'PROTECT' GROUP
9 THE 'RESCUE' GROUP
10 THE 'MAKE' GROUP
11 THE 'ABSOLVE' GROUP
12 VERBS WITH OTHER MEANINGS

1 THE 'DEMAND' AND 'GET' GROUP

These verbs are concerned with acquiring something from someone or somewhere. This includes:

- taking something away from its owner e.g. *confiscate*
- asking someone for something e.g. *demand*
- trying to get something from someone or something e.g. *coax*
- getting information from someone or from somewhere e.g. *glean*

*Police **confiscated** video tape **from** television crews and prevented photographers and reporters from approaching the house.*

*Italian judges and lawyers are staging a one-day national strike to **demand** more support **from the government** in the fight against crime.*

*It would be dangerous to **draw** too many conclusions **from** these statistics.*

*Angina can occur as the heart finds it difficult to **extract** enough oxygen **from the blood** it receives.*

*Inheritance tax will be cut so people **can inherit** houses **from their parents** without large penalties.*

*Conclusive evidence emerged this week that money **can be stolen from** cash dispensers with forged cash cards.*

*They **took** comfort **from the familiar words of the prayer.***

The preposition *from* is sometimes followed by an '-ing' clause.

*There are plenty of people in this world who **get** pleasure **from** hurting other people.*

In the case of *learn*, the noun group following the verb is often an **amount**. This pattern is **V amount *from* n**.

*Well, my father is a carpenter. I **learned** a lot **from him**.*

acquire *1*	deduce	gain *2*	pump *9*
borrow *2,3*	demand *1*	get *2.1,2,9*	salvage *4*
cadge	derive *1,2*	glean	seek *3*
charm *5*	distil *2*	hustle *3*	select *1*
choose *1*	distil *3 (usu passive)*	infer *1*	solicit *1*
coax *2*	draw *10,12,16,17*	inherit *1,2,3*	steal *1*
collect *3*	exact *4*	learn *4*	take *2.16*
confiscate	excerpt *2 (usu passive)*	make *3.6*	wheedle
conjure *1*	extort *1*	milk *5*	wrest *1,2*
copy *2,4*	extract *1,4,5,6*	plunder *1*	wring *1*
crib *2*	extract *7 (usu passive)*	poach *2*	
cull *1*	extrapolate	propagate *2*	

2 THE 'REMOVE' GROUP

These verbs are concerned with removing someone or something from somewhere, either physically or metaphorically. We include here verbs like *deduct* and *subtract*, which are concerned with taking something away from a total.

> He **was deported** from Britain *after serving part of a 12-year prison sentence.*
>
> *He's in a stable condition after having surgery to* **remove** *a blood clot from the brain.*
>
> *The proper way to measure the real interest rate is to* **subtract** *expected inflation from the* **nominal interest rate.**
>
> *He stood up and lifted his hand to* **wipe** *the rain and the sweat from his brow.*

In the case of *absent*, the noun group following the verb is always a reflexive pronoun. This pattern is **V pron-refl** *from* **n**. The phrasal verb *tear away* often has the pattern **V pron-refl P** *from* **n**.

> *He* **absented** *himself from the conference debate to visit a local building society.*
>
> *With a great wrench, he* **tore** *himself* **away** *from everything that he held most dear.*

In the case of *clip 8, cut, deduct,* and *subtract*, the noun group following the verb is always or often an **amount**. This pattern is **V amount** *from* **n**.

> *If you order three items, you* **can deduct** *£15 from the total.*

absent *3*	dismiss *2*	exile *2*	purge *1*
abstract *7*	disqualify	exile *4 (usu passive)*	remove *1,3,4*
avert *2*	distract	expunge	roust
banish *1*	divert *1*	extract *2*	shave *5*
banish *3 (usu passive)*	drain *6*	extradite *(usu passive)*	skim *1*
chase *4,5*	drain *7 (usu passive)*	flick *2*	squeeze *6*
clear *9*	eject *1*	hound *3 (usu passive)*	strike *19*
clip *5,8*	eliminate *1*	mop *3*	subtract
crop *9*	eliminate *2 (usu passive)*	pare *1*	take *2.7*
cut *7*	erase *1,2*	peel *3*	unload *1*
deduct	evict	pluck *1,2*	wipe *2*
deport *(usu passive)*	excise *2*	prize *5*	withdraw *1,2,3*
dislodge	exclude *1,2*	pull *2*	
strip away *2*	tear away		
take away *1,2*	turn out *6,7*		

3 THE 'TRANSFER' GROUP

These verbs are concerned with moving someone or something from one place to another. We include here verbs concerned with transferring someone from one job or level to another.

> *Its broadcasts* **will be relayed** *from a transmitter in the Taiwan port of Keelung.*
>
> **Transferring** *funds from a Barclays account using a telegraphic transfer would cost a minimum of £17 for the first £4,400.*

divert *2*	promote *3 (usu passive)*	send *1,2 (usu passive)*	transplant *3*
forward *10*	relay *2*	transfer *1,2,4,5,7*	transpose *1*
pass *6 (usu passive)*	relay *4 (usu passive)*	transfer *8 (usu passive)*	

All the verbs in this group usually have the pattern **V n** *from* **n** *to* **n** or the pattern **V n** *from* **n** *into* **n**. The verb is followed by a noun group and two prepositional phrases, the first beginning with *from* and the second beginning with *to* or *into*. The passive pattern is **be V-ed** *from* **n** *to/into* **n**.

> *He quickly embraced the American work ethic and* **was promoted** *from the shop floor to the* **position of head buyer for the shoe department.**

We can even arrange for your bank to __transfer__ funds from your account into the trust account each month.

4 THE 'SEPARATE' GROUP

These verbs are concerned with separating someone or something from something, either physically or metaphorically.

Unfortunately, he appears unable to __distinguish__ fantasy from reality.

It is far preferable to __isolate__ young offenders from their own peer group and not put them in the company of 40 or 50 other persistent young offenders.

Her independence of spirit __marked__ her __out__ from her male fellow officers.

While it grieved Elaine to __be separated__ from her son, she had agreed, at least during the summer holidays, to send him to her family.

An alternative method for smoking cessation is homeopathy, in which you are given capsules or pills with small quantities of nicotine to __wean__ you __from__ the habit.

In the case of *detach 2,3, disassociate 1, disengage, disentangle 2,3, dissociate 1, distance, shut off,* and *wean 2,* the noun group following the verb is always or often a reflexive pronoun. This pattern is **V pron-refl** *from* n, or in the case of *shut off,* **V pron-refl P** *from* n.

It is hard for mothers and daughters to __disentangle__ themselves from the emotional web that binds them.

It's obvious that you're not in a position to __shut__ yourself __off__ from what needs to be faced.

alienate *2*	disassociate *1,2*	distance *6*	part *2.4*
decouple	disconnect *3*	distinguish *1,2*	separate *3,4,6,7,8*
demerge	disengage *1*	divide *4*	tell *6*
detach *1,2,3*	disentangle *1,2,3*	divorce *4*	wean *1,2*
differentiate *1,2*	dissociate *1,2*	isolate *1,2,3,4,5*	
filter out	separate out ▷*7*	wall off *(usu passive)*	
mark off *2*	set apart		
mark out *2*	shut off *2*		

5 THE 'STOP' GROUP

These verbs are concerned with stopping someone from doing something. This includes:

- trying to stop someone from doing something
- prohibiting someone from a place or activity

The preposition *from* is usually followed by an '-ing' clause rather than a noun group.

She has been under house arrest for nearly a year and __is banned__ from the elections.

Reports allege that the airport ground crew tried to __dissuade__ the pilot from taking off, fearing problems with the left hand engine.

Senate ethics rules __prohibit__ a senator from taking contributions from someone he knows is trying to obtain his influence.

Always when things are dull, something new turns up to challenge us and to __stop__ us from settling into a rut.

ban *3 (usu passive)*	discourage *2*	keep *4*	proscribe
bar *10 (usu passive)*	dissuade	preclude *2*	restrain *2*
debar *(usu passive)*	enjoin *2*	prevent *1,2*	restrict *2*
deter	inhibit *2*	prohibit	stop *2*
warn away			

6 THE 'DEFLECT' GROUP

These verbs are concerned with changing someone's focus of attention or course of action from something.

> The war **did not deflect** him from the path he had long ago taken.

The preposition *from* is sometimes followed by an '-ing' clause.

> 'We're not going to allow anything to **sidetrack** us from achieving our goals,' he said.

deflect *2*	divert *4*	sidetrack

7 THE 'CONCEAL' GROUP

These verbs are concerned with hiding or keeping something, usually information, from someone.

> She quickly realized that it was virtually impossible to **conceal** her family background from her fellow students.

> What is at issue is how much of the information **can be** disguised and **kept** from the other superpower.

conceal *2*	keep *6*
hide *4*	withhold

8 THE 'PROTECT' GROUP

These verbs are concerned with protecting someone or something from danger or harm.

> Germany's inter-city trains are sealed and pressurised like aircraft to **insulate** passengers from the changes in pressure outside.

> Law is designed to **protect** society from abuses of power and guarantee citizens and their organizations their rights and freedoms.

> A temperature of at least 16 degrees C is needed and the plant **must be shaded** from direct sunshine.

cocoon *4*	insulate *1,2*	safeguard *1*	shade *4*
cushion *3*	protect *1*	shade *3 (usu passive)*	shield *2*

9 THE 'RESCUE' GROUP

These verbs are concerned with freeing or rescuing someone from danger or difficulty. We include here *excuse* and *exempt*, which involve freeing someone from a particular payment or obligation.

> She has a doctor's certificate and **has been excused** from games.

> Thousands of giant clams **have been rescued** from a tiny island off the coast of Queensland in one of the Australian navy's most unusual operations.

The preposition *from* is sometimes followed by an '-ing' clause.

> Fire-fighting ships are still trying to **save** a Norwegian supertanker from sinking off the coast of Texas.

In the case of *extricate 1*, the noun group following the verb is often a reflexive pronoun. This pattern is **V pron-refl** *from* **n**.

> He was quite confident of being able to **extricate** himself from the mess he had got into.

deliver *7*	free *3,8*	release *1 (usu passive)*	spare *5 (usu passive)*
excuse *4 (usu passive)*	heal *2 (usu passive)*	release *3*	spare *6*
exempt *2*	liberate *2*	rescue *1*	
extricate *1,2*	pluck *6,7 (usu passive)*	save *1,5*	

10 THE 'MAKE' GROUP

These verbs are concerned with making something from a particular material or thing.

*Father explained how to **make glass from sand**.*

*Neither Japanese, Chinese, nor any other types of chopsticks **are manufactured** from hardwoods derived from rainforests.*

carve *1*	fabricate *2*	machine *2 (usu passive)*	print *7*
construct *1,2 (usu passive)*	fashion *4*	make *3.1 (usu passive)*	produce *2*
create *1*	hew *2 (usu passive)*	manufacture *1 (usu passive)*	

11 THE 'ABSOLVE' GROUP

These verbs are concerned with saying that someone is not guilty.

*She felt that she **was absolved** from sin, that the entire family had received a benediction and was free.*

*In his report, Justice Louis Harms **exonerates** the police from involvement in the alleged death squads.*

absolve	exonerate

12 VERBS WITH OTHER MEANINGS

There are a number of other verbs which have this pattern.

***Omitting** the bacon from the recipe turns it into a simple side dish.*

In the case of *rouse 2*, the noun group following the verb is always a reflexive pronoun. This pattern is **V pron-refl** *from* n.

*Christabel **roused** herself from her stupor. 'What happened?' she said in a whisper.*

deflect *1*	draw *20*	rouse *1,2*
dispossess	omit *1*	
take away *VPP*		

Structure information

a) The noun group following the verb is the Object, and the prepositional phrase is an Adjunct.

b) This structure has a passive, with the pattern ***be* V-ed *from* n**. The prepositional phrase is an Adjunct.

c) Though the prepositional phrase in this structure usually comes after the noun group, it sometimes comes before it, especially when the noun group is a long one.

*Try to **exclude** from your diet anything which contains sugar.*

d) Phrasal verb patterns are the same except that there is also a particle, P. The Object comes either between the verb and the particle, or after the particle. If the Object comes after the particle, it cannot be a personal pronoun. You say

*Ozone **filters** it **out** from sunlight*

or *Ozone **filters out** harmful radiation from sunlight*

but you do not say *Ozone filters out it from sunlight.*

Other related patterns

V n *from* amount *to* amount

The verb is followed by a noun group and two prepositional phrases, the first beginning with *from* and the second beginning with *to*. Each preposition is followed by an **amount**. The passive pattern is **be V-ed *from* amount *to* amount**. The phrasal verb patterns are the same except that there is a particle following the verb. These verbs are concerned with increasing or decreasing an amount.

*The bank **lowered** its discount rate from 3.75 per cent to 3.25 per cent.*

*The pensionable age for men and women **was raised** from 60 to 65.*

decrease 1	lower 5	reduce 1
increase 1	raise 4	widen 4
whittle down		

V n *from* colour *to* colour

The verb is followed by a noun group and two prepositional phrases, the first beginning with *from* and the second beginning with *to*. Each preposition is followed by a colour word.

*Blood **turned** his suit from beige to red.*

turn 17

V n *from* n *to* n

See **V n *from* n *into* n** below, and meaning group 3 above.

V n *from* n *into* n

The verb is followed by a noun group and two prepositional phrases, the first beginning with *from* and the second beginning with *into*. The passive pattern is **be V-ed *from* n *into* n**. These verbs are concerned with changing something from one thing into another.

*Ford was the builder who **transformed** the automobile from an expensive curiosity for the wealthy into a commodity for the masses.*

change 3	transform 1	turn 15
metamorphose	translate 1	

See also meaning group 3 above.

The verbs *change*, *transform*, and *turn* also have the pattern **V n *from* n *to* n**.

*She **changed** her name from Blanca to Bianca.*

15 V n *in* n

The verb is followed by a noun group and a prepositional phrase which consists of *in* and a noun group. With some verbs, the preposition is sometimes followed by an '-ing' clause, a wh-clause, a fraction, or a number. The passive pattern is *be* V-ed *in* n.

This pattern has two structures:

▶ Structure I: Verb with Object and prepositional Object Complement
  We cut the rope in half.
▶ Structure II: Verb with Object and Adjunct
  He dipped a biscuit in his tea.

Structure I: Verb with Object and prepositional Object Complement

Active voice: V n *in* n

	Verb group	noun group	*in*	noun group/fraction
Subject	Verb	Object	prep. Object Complement	
You	may split	it	in	half.
	Tie	the rope	in	knots.

Passive voice: *be* V-ed *in* n

	Verb group	*in*	noun group/fraction
Subject	Verb	prepositional Complement	
They	will be divided	in	groups of four.
The branch	was snapped	in	half.

Most of the verbs with this structure are concerned with dividing something into pieces. The prepositional phrase indicates the result. We include here *fold*.

> *Break the cake in pieces and place in a food processor bowl.*
> *The market is split in two halves.*

The preposition *in* is sometimes followed by a fraction or number. These patterns are **V n *in* fraction** and **V n *in* num**.

> *Divide the pastry in half.*
> *Next he tore a blank page from his notebook and folded it in two.*

break *1*	cut *1*	slice *2*	split *1*
carve *3*	divide *1,4*	snap *1*	
chop *1 (usu passive)*	fold *1*	sort *3*	

VERBS WITH OTHER MEANINGS

There is one other verb which has this structure.

> *It was tied in a knot.*

tie *4*

Structure information: Verb with Object and prepositional Object Complement

a) The noun group is the Object, and the prepositional phrase is the prepositional Object Complement.

b) This structure has a passive, with the pattern *be* V-ed *in* n. The prepositional phrase is the prepositional Complement.

c) The prepositional phrase usually comes after the noun group. Sometimes, however, the prepositional phrase comes before the noun group, especially when the noun group is a long one.

He <u>sliced</u> *in half the huge lemons with their greenish tinge*, and squeezed them.

Structure II: Verb with Object and Adjunct

Active voice: V n *in* n

	Verb group	noun group	*in*	noun group
Subject	Verb	Object		Adjunct
The bolt	embedded	itself	in	the turf.
His wife	shot	him	in	the foot.
The bouquet	stirred	memories	in	George.

Passive voice: *be* V-ed *in* n

	Verb group	*in*	noun group
Subject	Verb		Adjunct
The coastline	was cloaked	in	mist.
He	is confirmed	in	his suspicions.
A hole	was drilled	in	the drawers.

Phrasal verbs

Active voice: V n P *in* n, V P n (not pron) *in* n

	Verb group	noun group	Particle	*in*	noun group
Subject	Verb...	Object	...Verb		Adjunct
She	couldn't put	it	down	in	writing.
They	have tangled	themselves	up	in	a blanket.

	Verb group	Particle	noun group	*in*	noun group
Subject	Verb		Object		Adjunct
	Put	down	their names	in	big letters.
I	had been turning	over	the same thoughts	in	my mind.

Passive voice: *be* V-ed P *in* n

	Verb group	Particle	*in*	noun group
Subject	Verb			Adjunct
They	might be caught	up	in	fighting.
The agency	was tangled	up	in	legal red tape.

Verbs with this structure belong to the following meaning groups:

II.1 THE 'DRAPE' GROUP

II.2 THE 'IMMERSE YOURSELF' GROUP

II.3 THE 'DIP' GROUP

II.4 THE 'INFUSE' GROUP

II.5 THE 'ENSNARE' GROUP

II.6 THE 'KICK' GROUP

II.7 THE 'BORE' GROUP

II.8 THE 'CARVE' GROUP

II.9 THE 'JOIN' GROUP

II.10 THE 'INVOLVE' GROUP

II.11 THE 'GROUND' GROUP

II.12 THE 'ENCAPSULATE' GROUP

II.13 THE 'TRAIN' GROUP

II.14 THE 'AROUSE' GROUP

II.15 THE 'SEE' GROUP

II.16 VERBS WITH OTHER MEANINGS

II.1 THE 'DRAPE' GROUP

These verbs are concerned with decorating, covering, or enclosing something in something, either physically or metaphorically.

*Although the rocks **were bathed** in yellow light fifty feet above our heads, we were standing in deepening gloom.*

*He rested his head against her, letting her **cradle** him in her arms like an infant.*

*I told her once that I would like to **drape** her in black velvet.*

*Naomi led me to her bedroom on the second floor where she pointed to her desk which **was framed** in a patch of wintery light.*

*The copper piping **is** itself **sheathed** in armoured plastic hosing, so that if there is a leak, it is contained.*

The verb *plaster* often has the pattern **V pron-refl *in* n**.

*A lot of women that I know, who are really beautiful women, **plaster** themselves in make up.*

bathe *5*	cradle *5*	entomb *1*	swathe *3*
bind *4 (usu passive)*	cup *6*	festoon *(usu passive)*	take *2.1*
catch *3*	douse *2*	frame *8 (usu passive)*	wrap *1*
cloak *4*	drape *2*	immerse *2 (usu passive)*	wreathe *1*
coat *3*	encase	plaster *4*	wreathe *2 (usu passive)*
cocoon *4*	enclose *1*	seal *1.1*	
cover *3 (usu passive)*	enfold *1,2*	sheathe *1 (usu passive)*	
cover *4*	enshroud	shroud *3 (usu passive)*	

II.2 THE 'IMMERSE YOURSELF' GROUP

These verbs are concerned with concentrating very hard on something, so that you do not notice anything else. The noun group following the verb is always a reflexive pronoun, and the pattern is **V pron-refl *in* n**.

*I **immersed** myself in the writings of this remarkable Japanese writer.*

*Imaginative children **lose** themselves in fantasy worlds through stories.*

bury *9,10*	lose *15*
immerse *1*	submerge *2*

II.3 THE 'DIP' GROUP

These verbs are concerned with putting or moving something somewhere, either physically or metaphorically.

*The fighting **is** apparently **concentrated** in the west and south-east of the city.*

*Wash the fish fillets and dry them, then **dip them in the beaten egg**.*

*You might try to **inculcate** a few ideas in him, to show him how wrong he's been acting.*

*I have had a series of operations to **insert** metal rods in the bones to strengthen them.*

*The founding fathers decreed that all executive power **should be vested** in the president of the United States.*

In the case of *lodge*, the noun group following the verb is often a reflexive pronoun. This pattern is **V pron-refl** *in* **n**.

*An unforgettable fragrance has the capacity to **lodge** itself in the soul forever.*

concentrate 2 *(usu passive)*	fix 10	jot 1	slot 2
dip 1	implant 1,4	land 9	stick 2.2
draft 4	inculcate	lodge 8	throw 5
dunk 1,2	insert 2	pack 2	tuck 1,VP2
embed 1	instil	place 19,22,25	vest 3 *(usu passive)*
enter 8	invest 1,2,3,4	settle 7	

II.4 THE 'INFUSE' GROUP

These verbs are concerned with preparing food. The prepositional phrase indicates what the food is placed in.

*If you like a strong garlic flavour, **infuse the garlic clove in the lemon juice** for an hour or two before making the dip.*

*Mix the flour with the spice powder and seasoning, then **toss the liver in this seasoned flour**.*

dilute 1	infuse 3	marinate
flambée	macerate	toss 6

II.5 THE 'ENSNARE' GROUP

These verbs are concerned with trapping someone somewhere, either physically or metaphorically.

*The tumultuous times naturally **ensnared many a young couple in romantic notions of love and duty**, which inspired impetuous romances and ill-conceived marriages.*

*'You **will** go upstairs and **lock yourself in your room**,' he repeated.*

ensnare 1,2	lock 3	tangle 2 *(usu passive)*
entangle 1,2	shut VP	
tangle up 1		

II.6 THE 'KICK' GROUP

These verbs are concerned with doing harm to someone. The prepositional phrase indicates the part of the body that is harmed.

*The fiery actress punched him on the nose and **kicked** him in the shins.*

*He survived the attack despite **being stabbed** in the neck, abdomen and arms.*

bite *1*	hit *1*	punch *1*	stab *1*
blast *4*	kick *1*	shoot *1*	strike *3,5*
boot *3*	knee *5*	slap *1*	thump *2*
catch *4*	knife *3*	smack *1*	
elbow *2*	poke *1*	smash *2*	

II.7 THE 'BORE' GROUP

These verbs are concerned with making a hole in something, either physically or metaphorically.

> To **bore** *a hole **in** a bean*, *the weevil needs to support itself against a firm surface.*
>
> *We took eighteen tyres with us, having used a sledge hammer to **punch** three holes **in** each.*

bore *5,6*	gouge *1*	punch *4*
drill *2*	prick *1*	

II.8 THE 'CARVE' GROUP

These verbs are concerned with writing or making marks in a surface. In the case of *etch 3*, *imprint*, and *turn over*, the meaning is metaphorical.

> *True to his word, Brian **had carved** their initials **in** the tree trunk.*
>
> *He repeated the names, as if to **imprint** them **in** his mind.*
>
> *I think that you **should put** your questions **down** **in** writing.*

carve *2*	etch *1*	imprint *2 (usu passive)*
engrave	etch *3 (usu passive)*	
put down *1*	turn over *3*	

II.9 THE 'JOIN' GROUP

These verbs are concerned with taking part in an activity along with someone else. The prepositional phrase indicates the activity.

> *Why **do** you **not join** your friends **in** the fight against Fascism?*

The preposition *in* is sometimes followed by an '-ing' clause.

> *These leaders **will assist** the Commission **in** identifying which voters are eligible.*
>
> *The leader strikes a bell three times and **leads** the others **in** chanting something **in** a foreign language.*

assist *2*	join *3*	lead *1.7*

II.10 THE 'INVOLVE' GROUP

These verbs are concerned with making someone become involved in an activity. The prepositional phrase indicates the activity. We include here *implicate*, which is concerned with making someone appear to be involved in an illegal or immoral activity.

> *The President's habit of **embroiling** his government **in** seemingly pointless fights has isolated him from all except his military chiefs.*
>
> *In the tape Amos gave to his brother he **implicates** Stewart **in** the scheme.*
>
> *Reflexology **involves** the patient **in** their own healing.*

The preposition *in* is sometimes followed by an '-ing' clause.

> *Riding in the car offers a wonderful opportunity to **engage** your child **in** observing the surroundings.*

In the case of *involve 3*, the noun group following the verb is always a reflexive pronoun. This pattern is **V pron-refl *in* n**.

*He has already started to **involve** himself in the country's domestic political issues.*

embroil	engage *3*	include *2*
employ *1,3 (usu passive)*	implicate	involve *3,4,5*
be caught up *5*		

II.11 THE 'GROUND' GROUP

These verbs are concerned with providing a physical or metaphorical foundation for something. The prepositional phrase indicates what the foundation is.

*Until two decades ago, the church's special relationship to the government **was enshrined** in the constitution.*

*Her books sell because she **grounds** her ideas in everyday realities, draws her characters compellingly and knows how to tell a good story.*

anchor *5 (usu passive)*	enshrine
embed *2 (usu passive)*	ground *12*

II.12 THE 'ENCAPSULATE' GROUP

These verbs are concerned with representing something or someone in some way. This includes:

- talking or writing about someone or something e.g. *couch, render*
- representing the essential nature of something e.g. *capture, encapsulate*
- showing something e.g. *incarnate, manifest*

*The argument **will** probably **be couched** in the pompous language which newspapers enjoy so much.*

*His ideas **were** later **encapsulated** in a book called Democratic Ideals and Reality.*

*The iniquities of the regime **are incarnated** in one man.*

*The tragedy **is rendered** in tough, everyday language that assaults the audience with its realism.*

capture *4*	couch *3 (usu passive)*	encapsulate	manifest *2*
cast *10*	embody *2 (usu passive)*	incarnate *3 (usu passive)*	render *4*

II.13 THE 'TRAIN' GROUP

These verbs are concerned with teaching someone. The prepositional phrase indicates the subject that is taught.

*You **will** kindly **not instruct** me in elementary physics.*

*Attempting to **tutor** an adolescent in reading yourself, at home, is not recommended.*

The preposition *in* is sometimes followed by an '-ing' clause.

*Court welfare officers **must be trained** in communicating with children.*

The preposition *in* is sometimes followed by a to-infinitive clause introduced by a wh-word.

*It is important that people **are trained** properly in how to use the system.*

instruct *2*	train *2.1*
school *8*	tutor *3*

II.14 THE 'AROUSE' GROUP

These verbs are concerned with causing an emotion in someone.

*He urged people to avoid any action which **could arouse** fear or passion in others.*

arouse 2	stir 7

II.15 THE 'SEE' GROUP

These verbs are concerned with emotions and qualities. The noun group following the verb indicates the emotion or quality. This includes:

- finding an emotion such as comfort in an activity or situation
- putting an emotion such as faith in a person or thing
- seeing a quality in a person or thing

We also include here *hold*, where the noun group following the verb indicates a person or thing and the prepositional phrase indicates the emotion.

*Her parents **will find** comfort in the fact that they have been blessed with a large family.*

*Little by little you'll come to hate me and **hold** me in contempt.*

*Small wonder that little faith **has been placed** in the project's findings.*

In the case of *find* and *see 6*, the preposition *in* is sometimes followed by an '-ing' clause.

*The militants **see** no contradiction in using violence to bring about a religious state.*

The verb *see 7* is often used in questions such as *What do you see in him?*

*Mr Meredith, **what do** you **see** in David Duke?*

find 10	place 18	see 6,7
hold 2.5	put 5	take 2.16

II.16 VERBS WITH OTHER MEANINGS

There are a number of other verbs which have this structure.

*Quite often a fox'll go across the road in front of me and I'll just **catch** it in the headlights.*

*The experience gained from a master seaman was invaluable, and **confirmed** him in his intention to leave school at the earliest opportunity and take to the sea.*

*Throughout the Seventies she **was ranked** in Britain's top ten.*

*Ken Loach, whose films include Cathy Come Home and Kes, **has been rebuffed** in his plans to produce Britain's first left-wing soap opera.*

*They **toasted** one another in champagne.*

In the case of *assist*, *interest*, and *lead*, the preposition *in* is sometimes followed by an '-ing' clause.

*The following forms are to **assist** you in understanding the possible risks.*

*Some salesmen tried to **interest** me in buying property here.*

assist 3	interest 4	rank 3 *(usu passive)*	remand 1
catch 20	keep 13	rebuff *(usu passive)*	toast 4
confirm 5	lead 1.7	reflect 3 *(usu passive)*	

The verb *rank* also has the pattern **V n ord *in* n**. The verb is followed by a noun group, an ordinal, and a prepositional phrase beginning with *in*. The passive pattern is ***be* V-ed ord *in* n**.

Gul __is ranked__ eighth in the world.

Structure information: Verb with Object and Adjunct

a) The noun group following the verb is the Object, and the prepositional phrase is an Adjunct.

b) This structure has a passive, with the pattern **be V-ed *in* n**. The prepositional phrase is an Adjunct.

c) The prepositional phrase usually comes after the noun group. Sometimes, however, the prepositional phrase comes before the noun group, especially when the noun group is a long one.

   Philip now __saw__ in Arthur the means of John's downfall.

d) Phrasal verb patterns are the same except that there is also a particle, P. The Object comes either between the verb and the particle, or after the particle. If the Object comes after the particle, it cannot be a personal pronoun. You say

   He __set__ it __down__ in writing
   or *He __set down__ the ruling in writing*

   but you do not say *He set down it in writing*.

Phrasal prepositions with *in*

There are some phrasal prepositions which consist of *in*, a noun group, and another preposition. The phrasal prepositions *in the form of, in the light of, in the role of,* and *in terms of* often follow a verb and a noun group, and so appear to be part of the pattern **V n *in* n**.

   Surely Magda __hadn't__ now __cast__ Paula in the role of desirable daughter-in-law?

   An allergic food reaction __can manifest__ itself in the form of sickness and vomiting.

   Film __has to present__ ideas in terms of characters.

The prepositional phrase formed with one of these phrasal prepositions is a prepositional Complement or a prepositional Object Complement. These phrasal prepositions follow verbs which indicate that something is expressed in a particular way or that someone or something is given a particular role, such as *cast, manifest,* or *present.*

Other related patterns

V amount *in* n

See page 73.

V n *in* num

The verb is followed by a noun group and a prepositional phrase consisting of *in* and a number such as *hundreds* or *thousands*. The passive pattern is **be V-ed *in* num**.

   You could easily believe that his personal friends __are numbered__ in the tens of thousands.

> **number** 5 *(usu passive)*

See also Structure I above.

V n *in* fraction

See Structure I above.

V n ord *in* n

See meaning group II.16 above.

16   V n *into* n

The verb is followed by a noun group and a prepositional phrase which consists of *into* and a noun group. The passive pattern is **be V-ed *into* n.**

This pattern has two structures:

▶ Structure I: Verb with Object and prepositional Object Complement
 She changed the prince into a frog.
▶ Structure II: Verb with Object and Adjunct
 He frightened them into silence.

Structure I: Verb with Object and prepositional Object Complement

Active voice: V n *into* n

	Verb group	noun group	*into*	noun group
Subject	**Verb**	**Object**		**prep. Object Complement**
He	will convert	the Tudor kitchens	into	a living museum.
We	will divide	early language development	into	two stages.
	Shape	the dough	into	an oblong.

Passive voice: *be* V-ed *into* n

	Verb group	*into*	noun group
Subject	**Verb**		**prepositional Complement**
The course	was compressed	into	two years.
Intent	has to be translated	into	action.

Phrasal verbs

Active voice: V n P *into* n, V P n (not pron) *into* n

	Verb group	noun group	Particle	*into*	noun group
Subject	**Verb...**	**Object**	**...Verb**		**prep. Object Complement**
The drugs	chop	DNA	up	into	small pieces.
	Split	them	up	into	two groups.

	Verb group	Particle	noun group	*into*	noun group
Subject	Verb		Object	prep. Object Complement	
You	should break	down	the activity	into	simple stages.
The board	might break	up	the group	into	constituent parts.

Passive voice: *be* V-ed P *into* n

	Verb group	Particle	*into*	noun group
Subject	Verb		prepositional Complement	
The army	is divided	up	into	about 50 regiments.
The carbon sample	is smashed	up	into	its constituent atoms.

Verbs with this structure belong to the following meaning groups:

I.1   THE 'CHANGE' GROUP
I.2   THE 'BREAK' GROUP

I.1 THE 'CHANGE' GROUP

These verbs are concerned with changing something into something new, or changing its form or shape. We include here verbs such as *amalgamate* and *weld*, which are concerned with putting parts together to make a whole. The prepositional phrase indicates the new thing, form, or shape.

*He said he would work to **change** the alliance into an economic and political grouping.*

*Brain and offal tissue from sheep **is made** into meat meal and bone meal, which has been fed to cattle as a protein supplement.*

*He turned away, **screwed** the paper into a ball and tossed it into the fire.*

*He is well on the way to **welding** some 130 staff into an efficient, courteous whole.*

In the case of *form 8*, the noun group following the verb is always a reflexive pronoun. This pattern is **V pron-refl *into* n**.

*Diodorus also told of the warrior women of Libya who **formed** themselves into armies and invaded other lands.*

aggregate 3 *(usu passive)*	**group** 6	**process** 3 *(usu passive)*	**transform** 1,2
amalgamate	**knit** 1,2	**render** 4	**translate** 1
change 3,14	**knock** 3	**reorganize**	**translate** 3 *(usu passive)*
compress 2,3 *(usu passive)*	**make** 2.7	**roll** 6	**transmute**
condense 1,2	**merge** 1	**screw** 2,4,5,6	**turn** 15
convert 1,2,3	**metamorphose**	**scrunch** 2	**weave** 1
distil 3	**mould** 3,4	**sculpt** 2	**weld** 3
dub 2 *(usu passive)*	**mutate** 1	**shape** 5,6	**work** 24
form 3,8	**organize** 3	**sublimate**	

Many of the verbs in this group also have the pattern **V n *from* n *into* n**. The verb is followed by a noun group and two prepositional phrases, the first beginning with *from* and the second beginning with *into*. The passive pattern is *be* V-ed *from* n *into* n.

*He has helped to **transform** Labour from a disorganised, demoralised rabble into a force which must again be taken seriously.*

I.2 THE 'BREAK' GROUP

These verbs are concerned with breaking or dividing something into smaller pieces.

> The impact __broke__ the truck *into three pieces.*
>
> Traditionally, the English-speaking theatre __has been carved up__ *into fairly clear spheres of influence.*
>
> __Cut up__ the lamb *into bite-size pieces,* reserving the liver, and start to fry.
>
> The old farms along our road __were subdivided__ *into two-acre building lots.*

break *1*	cut *1*	separate *10*	sort *3*
carve *3*	divide *1,3,4*	shatter *1*	split *1*
chop *1*	resolve *4*	slice *2*	subdivide *(usu passive)*
compartmentalize	rip *4*	smash *1*	
break down *3,4*	chop up	slice up ▷*3*	
break up *1*	cut up *1*	smash up *1*	
carve up *1*	divide up *1*	split up *3*	

Structure information: Verb with Object and prepositional Object Complement

a) The noun group following the verb is the Object, and the prepositional phrase is the prepositional Object Complement.

b) This structure has a passive, with the pattern *be* V-ed *into* n. The prepositional phrase is the prepositional Complement.

c) Phrasal verb patterns are the same except that there is also a particle, P. The Object comes either between the verb and the particle or after the particle. If the Object comes after the particle, it cannot be a personal pronoun. You say

> __Cut__ it __up__ *into pieces*
> or __Cut up__ the lamb *into pieces*

but you do not say *Cut up it into pieces.*

Structure II: Verb with Object and Adjunct

Active voice: V n *into* n

	Verb group	noun group	*into*	noun group
Subject	**Verb**	**Object**		**Adjunct**
The case	has frightened	staff and students	into	silence.
His debut album	sent	critics	into	fits of rapture.
The tiger	sank	its teeth	into	his leg.
They	trapped	him	into	a confession.

Passive voice: *be* V-ed *into* n

	Verb group	*into*	noun group
Subject	**Verb**		**Adjunct**
The firm	has been absorbed	into	a much larger international firm.
One side	was being blackmailed	into	compliance.
I	was drafted	into	the Air Force.
He	has been rushed	into	concessions on political pluralism.

Phrasal verbs

Active voice: V n P *into* n, V P n (not pron) *into* n

	Verb group	noun group	Particle	*into*	noun group
Subject	Verb...	Object	...Verb	Adjunct	
The government	is going to plough	the money	back	into	road building.
He	worked	himself	up	into	a temper.

	Verb group	Particle	noun group	*into*	noun group
Subject	Verb		Object	Adjunct	
The ringleader	would whip	up	the others	into	a frenzy.

Passive voice: *be* V-ed P *into* n

	Verb group	Particle	*into*	noun group
Subject	Verb		Adjunct	
Religious concepts	are carried	over	into	political life.
Stainless steel operations	were hived	off	into	a joint venture.

Verbs with this structure belong to the following meaning groups:

II.1 THE 'FORCE', 'TRICK', AND 'CHARM' GROUPS

II.2 THE 'SEND' GROUP

II.3 THE 'PUT' GROUP

II.4 THE 'INCORPORATE' GROUP

II.5 THE 'BREATHE' GROUP

II.6 VERBS WITH OTHER MEANINGS

II.1 THE 'FORCE', 'TRICK', AND 'CHARM' GROUPS

These verbs are all concerned with making someone do something or get involved in something. The prepositional phrase indicates what they are made to do. Many of the verbs in this group are more frequently found in the pattern **V n *into* -ing** (see pages 396-399). They can be divided into five groups.

(i) The 'force' group

These verbs are concerned with making someone do something or get involved in something by using insistent verbal persuasion, force, or violence.

Behind the kidnappings, it's thought, is an attempt by the drug barons to __force the__ __government into peace talks.__

Smith is serving life without parole for __goading Fox into the killing.__

He deliberately __provoked you into argument__ because he wanted to hear you stand up for the idealism which he fears the war has destroyed.

The British and the French have been very careful not to __be sucked__ into the conflict.

This conversation in 1932 seems to have been the last attempt the King made seriously to influence his son, or to __talk__ him into marriage.

*Paul Hallbrook spent 15 years in jail for a bombing in Guildford which he did not commit, because police **terrified** him into a false confession.*

*Occasionally you'd get a ringleader who **would whip up** the others into a frenzy.*

badger 2	coerce	nag 1	railroad 2
blackmail 3	cow 4	panic 3	scare 1
bludgeon 2	drag VP	press 5	stampede 4
bounce 9	dragoon 2	press-gang 1,2 (usu passive)	steamroller 2
browbeat	force 1,2	pressure 5 (usu passive)	suck 3 (usu passive)
bulldoze 3	frighten VP	prod 2	talk VP1
bully 3	goad 1	provoke 1	terrify 1
chivvy	intimidate	push 6	whip 8
whip up 1			

(ii) The 'trick' group

These verbs are concerned with making someone do something by tricking or deceiving them.

*Luisa, a small-time crook, **inveigles** Paco into a plot to swindle Trini out of her savings, and to murder her.*

*The radar will reduce the risk of the international community **being tricked** into military intervention.*

bamboozle	dupe 1	inveigle	trick 2
con 1	entrap	lure 1	
deceive 1	fool 3	trap 4	

(iii) The 'charm' group

These verbs are concerned with making someone do something by being nice to them in some way or by saying something that pleases them.

*The ingredient he brought to the job was a talent for marketing his policies and **charming** his opponents into submission.*

*The government has changed the law in order to **tempt** foreign companies into exploration for gas and oil.*

cajole	seduce 2	tempt 2
charm 3	sweet talk	

(iv) The 'spur' group

These verbs indicate that a person, situation, or event persuades someone to do something, or motivates them to do it.

*Dealers suggested the market will be soft and sluggish all this week unless unforeseen events **galvanize** it into action.*

*The friendship could be extremely good for her, for she will catch the enthusiasm and energy and **be spurred** into action.*

galvanize	persuade 1	spur 1	tempt 1
jolt 2	propel 2	steer 2	
nudge 3	seduce 1	stir 5	

(v) Other verbs

There are a number of other verbs that are also concerned with ways of making someone do something.

The intention was to __shame__ young drivers into better behaviour on the roads with the threat of a return to L-plates.

chasten *(usu passive)*	manoeuvre 2	sidetrack
condition 7 *(usu passive)*	rush 8 *(usu passive)*	
lull 2,3	shame 5	

II.2 THE 'SEND' GROUP

These verbs are concerned with putting someone or something into a particular state or situation.

Vandals had damaged the electricity sub-station, __plunging the streets into darkness.__

Because teenagers associate driving with maturity, the slightest criticism from a parent is likely to __send__ them into a funk.

In the case of *fling, insinuate, launch, plunge 4, talk, throw,* and *work up,* the noun group following the verb is always or often a reflexive pronoun. This pattern is **V pron-refl *into* n**, or in the case of *work up,* **V pron-refl P *into* n**.

She __flung__ herself into anti-racist work, picketed town halls, opposed the Vietnam War, joined the Black Panthers.

He __has talked__ himself into a position where he will have no option but to go.

He glared at him malevolently, then __worked__ himself __up__ into another rage.

draw *VP2*	get 1.3	plunge 3,4	throw 11
drive 13	insinuate 2	send 6	
fling 6	launch *VP*	talk *VP2*	
work up 1			

II.3 THE 'PUT' GROUP

These verbs are concerned with putting something or someone into something, either physically or metaphorically. This includes investing money in something. The prepositional phrase indicates the place where they are put.

I drove the Cooper and Bruce McLaren __beat__ me into second place in his similar car.

He __had booked__ both of us into the local hotel.

Graham handed her the card and she __fed__ the name into a computer.

She __gulped__ air into her lungs and rose to her feet, pressing back despair.

A needleful of his white blood cells __was injected__ into me.

'If anyone can afford to __put__ their money into furniture, now is a very good time to do so,' says Charles Walford of Sotheby's.

absorb 1 *(usu passive)*	dig 3,*VP1*	gulp 3	pack *VP1*
air-drop 2	dip 1,2	implant 1	pack *VP2 (usu passive)*
beat 9	draft 3 *(usu passive)*	infiltrate 2	pay 8
book *VP*	draft 4	inject 1,3	plough *VP2*
build 2 *(usu passive)*	drag *VPP*	insert 1,2	plug *VP1,2,4*
channel 4	draw 9	interpolate *(usu passive)*	plunge 2
check *VP1*	dump 10	introduce 1	poke 2
copy 3	enter 9	jab 1 *(usu passive)*	pour *VP*
crowd 4	feed 12	leak 1	pull *VP*
decant	fold *VP*	load 1,6	pump 8,10
deliver 3	fork 2	lock 3	put 7,8,11

scan *4 (usu passive)*	stick *2.2*	transpose *3*	weave *6*
shoehorn *2*	stir *1*	transpose *3*	work *VP*
sink *11,13*	thread *7*	tuck *VP2*	write *VP*
slot *2*	throw *5*	type *VP*	
carry over *(usu passive)*	hive off *(usu passive)*	plough back *(usu passive)*	

II.4 THE 'INCORPORATE' GROUP

These verbs are concerned with incorporating or absorbing someone or something into a system or organization.

> One needs to learn how to **build** *enjoyment into what happens day in, day out.*

> During the patient's fourth week, he/she attends a continuing care group to **be hooked** *into after-care.*

> Medical schools are only now beginning to **incorporate** *significant geriatric training into their curricula.*

absorb *3 (usu passive)*	build *5*	factor *VP*	induct *2*
accept *6,7*	conscript *2 (usu passive)*	hook *6 (usu passive)*	integrate *1,2*
assimilate *1*	co-opt *2 (usu passive)* ·	incorporate *2*	yoke *3*

II.5 THE 'BREATHE' GROUP

These verbs are concerned with causing someone to have a quality or an idea, or causing something to have a quality. The prepositional phrase indicates the person or thing involved.

> Tentative efforts were made two or three years ago to **breathe** *some new life into these fossilized organisations.*

> Now scientists believe that memories **are etched** *into our brains* with the help of proteins.

> Grace did her best to **inject** *a note of welcome into her voice.*

> The massive blast **struck** *terror into thousands of innocent office workers and tourists.*

breathe *4*	hammer *4*	inject *2*
drum *VP (usu passive)*	implant *4*	instil
etch *3 (usu passive)*	infuse *1*	strike *16*

II.6 VERBS WITH OTHER MEANINGS

There are a number of other verbs which have this structure.

> I only had an hour to **get changed** *into my dress.*

> They describe how society first victimised them inside its children's homes, which **inducted** *them into a life of crime.*

> I **can let** *you into the secret*, but don't tell anyone else.

In the case of *read*, the noun group following the verb is often an **amount**. This pattern is **V amount *into* n**.

> The Employment Secretary said: 'We must be careful not to **read** *too much into one month's figures.'*

get changed *5*	follow *14*	let *VP*	read *VP*
etch *1*	induct *1*	permit *1 (usu passive)*	slam *4*
etch *2 (usu passive)*	initiate *2,3*	put *6*	stretch *5 (usu passive)*

Structure information: Verb with Object and Adjunct

a) The noun group following the verb is the Object, and the prepositional phrase is an Adjunct.

b) This structure has a passive, with the pattern **be V-ed *into* n**. The prepositional phrase is an Adjunct.

c) Though the prepositional phrase in this structure usually comes after the noun group, it sometimes comes before it, especially when the noun group is a long one.

*We **must incorporate** into the budgets this possible increase in sales.*

d) Phrasal verb patterns are the same except that there is also a particle, P. The Object comes either between the verb and the particle, or after the particle. If the Object comes after the particle, it cannot be a personal pronoun. You say

*He **whipped** them **up** into a frenzy*
or *He **whipped up** the crowd into a frenzy*

but you do not say *He whipped up them into a frenzy.*

Other related patterns
V n *from* n *into* n

See meaning group I.1 above.

---

17 V n *into* -ing

The verb is followed by a noun group and a prepositional phrase which consists of *into* and an '-ing' clause. The passive pattern is **be V-ed *into* -ing**.

This pattern has one structure:

▶ Verb with Object and Adjunct
  *She **nagged** him into cutting his hair.*

Active voice: V n *into* -ing

	Verb group	noun group	*into*	-ing clause
Subject	**Verb**	**Object**		**Adjunct**
Richard's mother	badgered	him	into	taking a Spanish wife.
She	bullied	the printers	into	rushing through the invitations.

Passive voice: *be* V-ed *into* -ing

	Verb group	*into*	-ing clause
Subject	**Verb**		**Adjunct**
Joan's son	was coerced	into	giving evidence against her.
The government	should not be pressured	into	making hasty decisions.

Verbs with this pattern belong to the following meaning groups:

1 THE 'FORCE' GROUP
2 THE 'TRICK' GROUP
3 THE 'CHARM' GROUP
4 THE 'SPUR' GROUP
5 VERBS WITH OTHER MEANINGS

1 THE 'FORCE' GROUP

These verbs are concerned with making someone do something by using insistent verbal persuasion, force, or violence.

> Scientists use film role models to **brainwash** *fussy youngsters into liking spinach and broccoli.*

> His elder brother literally **forced** *him into cutting his hair.*

> He tried to **frighten** *people into doing what he wanted.*

> The advert's principal task is to **nag** *the user into buying a copy of the program.*

> This **provoked** *the team into rethinking their diagnosis and ordering a number of investigations.*

> Gretchen realized that it had been a mistake to let Molly **talk** *her into coming all the way down to New Orleans.*

In the case of *talk*, the noun group following the verb is often a reflexive pronoun. This pattern is **V pron-refl *into* -ing**.

> When you're not feeling as well as you would like, at least **talk** *yourself into feeling well.*

badger 2	**coerce**	**nag** 1	**railroad** 2
blackmail 3	**co-opt** 2 (usu passive)	**panic** 3	**scare** 1
bludgeon 2	**cow** 4	**press** 5	**shock** 5
bounce 9	**dragoon** 2	**press-gang** 1 (usu passive)	**stampede** 4
brainwash	**force** 1,2	**pressure** 5 (usu passive)	**steamroller** 2
browbeat	**frighten** VP	**pressurize** (usu passive)	**talk** VP1
bulldoze 3	**goad** 1	**prod** 2	**terrify** 1
bully 3	**intimidate**	**provoke** 1	
chivvy	**manipulate** 1	**push** 6	

2 THE 'TRICK' GROUP

These verbs are concerned with making someone do something by tricking or deceiving them.

> We**'ve deluded** *ourselves into thinking that the actual point of life is to be comfortable.*

> Can a machine be built that **could fool** *a human judge into thinking it was a person?*

> A small business went bankrupt after **being trapped** *into paying for two machines* when the first one broke down.

> It is easy to **be tricked** *into thinking that just because twins look alike, their characters are the same.*

con *1*	entrap	lure *1*	trick *2*
deceive *1*	fool *3*	mislead	
delude *1,2*	hoodwink	sucker *3*	
dupe *1*	inveigle	trap *4*	

3 THE 'CHARM' GROUP

These verbs are concerned with making someone do something by flattering them or by being nice to them in some way.

*Henry **charmed** and **cajoled** people into parting with thousands of pounds.*

beguile *2*	charm *3*	flatter *1*
bribe *2*	coax *1*	sweet talk
cajole	entice	tempt *2*

4 THE 'SPUR' GROUP

These verbs indicate that a person, situation, or event persuades someone to do something, or motivates them to do it.

*Some new acquaintances **persuaded** us into spending the summer near Kiev.*

*Dining out is a bit of a treat and a psychological boost which **can spur** you into keeping up with your diet the following week.*

*If you're cleaning the plates of others, **don't be tempted** into taking even the smallest taste of any leftover uneaten food.*

galvanize	nudge *3*	seduce *1*	stimulate *2 (usu passive)*
jolt *2*	persuade *1*	spur *1*	stir *5*
lead *12*	propel *2*	steer *2*	tempt *1*

5 VERBS WITH OTHER MEANINGS

There are a number of other verbs that are also concerned with ways of making someone do something.

*Somehow the authorities **have to manoeuvre** the markets into demanding a cut in interest rates.*

chasten *(usu passive)*	embarrass *1*	manoeuvre *2*	shame *5*
condition *7 (usu passive)*	lull *2*	rush *8 (usu passive)*	sidetrack *(usu passive)*

The verb *put* also has this pattern, but it does not have the same meaning as the other verbs.

*The Seychelles **have put** a lot of effort into training teachers both at home and abroad.*

put *6*

Structure information

a) The noun group is the Object, and the prepositional phrase is an Adjunct.

b) This structure has a passive, with the pattern **be V-ed *into* -ing**. The prepositional phrase is an Adjunct.

---

18   V n *of* n

The verb is followed by a noun group and a prepositional phrase which consists of *of* and a noun group. With some verbs, the preposition is sometimes followed by an '-ing' clause. The passive pattern is **be V-ed *of* n**.

This pattern has one structure:

▶ Verb with Object and Adjunct
They <u>convicted</u> him of theft.

Active voice: V n *of* n/-ing

	Verb group	noun group	*of*	noun group/-ing clause
Subject	**Verb**	**Object**		**Adjunct**
The settlement	absolved	the company	of	all criminal responsibility.
	Clear	your mind	of	other thoughts.
They	suspected	him	of	doing away with Beryl.

Passive voice: *be* V-ed *of* n/-ing

	Verb group	*of*	noun group/-ing clause
Subject	**Verb**		**Adjunct**
People	were cheated	of	their retirement cash.
They	were convicted	of	handling explosives.

Verbs with this pattern belong to the following meaning groups:

1   THE 'ROB' AND 'FREE' GROUP
2   THE 'INFORM' GROUP
3   THE 'ACQUIT' AND 'CONVICT' GROUP
4   VERBS WITH OTHER MEANINGS

1 THE 'ROB' AND 'FREE' GROUP

These verbs are concerned with taking something away from someone, either physically or metaphorically. These include verbs with a positive meaning, like *cleanse, cure,* and *free,* as well as those with a negative meaning, like *dispossess* and *rob.* The noun group indicates the person from whom something is taken.

*The family of a sick Nigerian boy are appealing to the public to help them raise funds for an operation to <u>**cure**</u> him of a crippling disease.*

*The Opposition leaders warned that the Bill <u>**might deprive**</u> citizens of fundamental rights.*

*The realization that you truly can't control anyone else's actions or feelings <u>**can**</u> also <u>**free**</u> you of unnecessary guilt.*

*They <u>**were robbed**</u> of their wristwatches and shot during the course of the robbery.*

*Heart attacks occur because blockages in blood vessels <u>**starve**</u> heart muscle of oxygen and nutrients.*

In the case of *divest 1,3*, *rid 4*, and *unburden*, the noun group following the verb is always or often a reflexive pronoun. This pattern is **V pron-refl** *of* **n**.

> *Gilles finally confesses to the affair, **unburdening** himself of a secret which his wife has known from the very beginning.*

absolve	defraud	**drain** 6 *(usu passive)*	**rid** 3,4
break 11	**denude** 1,2	**free** 3,8	**rob** 1 *(usu passive)*
cheat 3	deprive	**plunder** 1	**rob** 2
cleanse 1	disabuse	**purge** 1,2	**starve** 3
clear 5,9	dispossess	**relieve** 2,3	**strip** 8
cure 2,6	**divest** 1,2,3	**relieve** 5 *(usu passive)*	unburden

2 THE 'INFORM' GROUP

These verbs are concerned with talking or writing, for example giving someone information, warning someone about something, or reminding someone of something.

> *They seemed mightily pleased, shook hands and **assured** us of their help if it was ever needed.*

> *The Prime Minister's new year broadcast totally **convinced** me of the need to improve our education system.*

> *The spokesman said that the army was not obliged to **inform** the federal government of its actions.*

advise 3	**convince** 1	notify	**remind** 1,4
apprise	forewarn	**persuade** 3	**warn** 1
assure 1	**inform** 1	reassure	

3 THE 'ACQUIT' AND 'CONVICT' GROUP

These verbs are concerned with declaring or thinking that someone has or has not committed a crime. The noun group indicates the person, and the prepositional phrase indicates the crime.

The preposition *of* is usually followed by an '-ing' clause.

> *His change of fortune began on the day last June when he **was acquitted** of assaulting a man in Milwaukee.*

> *She **was cleared** of attempting to murder and causing grievous bodily harm to a 73-year-old woman and a 15-year-old boy.*

> *A 15-year-old boy is being held in a special wing at Cardiff prison pending sentence after Newport magistrates **convicted** him of breaking a teacher's nose.*

accuse 1,2	**clear** 20 *(usu passive)*	**suspect** 2
acquit 1 *(usu passive)*	**convict** 1	

4 VERBS WITH OTHER MEANINGS

There are a number of other verbs which have this pattern.

> *If Leo could **make** a true friend of Victor, then his ties with the army would be strong indeed.*

The verbs *make VP* and *think 1,14* have this pattern only when they occur in a question or clause beginning with *what*.

> *'**What** did you **think** of the video?' 'Well, it's not that bad really.'*

In the case of *avail*, the noun group following the verb is always a reflexive pronoun. This pattern is **V pron-refl** *of* **n**.

> *She **is unable to avail** herself of legal aid services because her husband's income is taken into account.*

In the case of *ask 2, expect, hear, see,* and *think,* the noun group following the verb is always or often an **amount**. This pattern is **V amount *of* n**.

> *His business was not doing too well so I __didn't see__ much of him, and we were under a lot of financial pressure.*

The verbs *ask, expect, hear,* and *see* are occasionally used in the passive. The pattern is **be V-ed *of* n**, where the amount is the Subject.

> *A lot __was expected__ of Fernando Redondo in midfield, but he failed to reproduce the form he showed with Tenerife.*
>
> *Why __has__ so little __been heard__ of the 'fundamental reviews' of government spending?*

The verb *think* also has a passive with the pattern **be V-ed amount *of***.

> *His artistic sketches __were thought__ a lot of locally, Tom said.*

In the case of *think,* the **amount** is often an adverb.

> *Neil __thinks__ very highly of him indeed.*

ask *1,2*	be born *1*	make *1.2,2.3,9*	see *14*
assure *2*	expect *3*	make *VP*	think *1,10,14*
avail *2*	hear *7*	require *2*	

The verbs *compose, comprise,* and *make up* do not have the active pattern **V n *of* n**, but they have the passives *be composed of, be comprised of,* and *be made up of* something (see page 15).

Structure information

a) The noun group following the verb is the Object, and the prepositional phrase is an Adjunct.

b) This structure has a passive, with the pattern **be V-ed *of* n**. The prepositional phrase is an Adjunct.

c) Though the prepositional phrase in this structure usually comes after the noun group, it sometimes comes before it, especially when the noun group is a long one.

> *This vain battle for identity and for love __made__ of him a new human being.*

---

19   V n *off* n

The verb is followed by a noun group and a prepositional phrase which consists of *off* and a noun group. The passive pattern is **be V-ed *off* n**.

This pattern has one structure:

▶ Verb with Object and Adjunct
I __crossed__ her off my list.

Active voice: V n *off* n

	Verb group	noun group	*off*	noun group
Subject	**Verb**	**Object**		**Adjunct**
I	'll borrow	some money	off	my family.
They	'd cleared	all the snow	off	the carpark.

Passive voice: *be* V-ed *off* n

	Verb group	*off*	noun group
Subject	**Verb**		**Adjunct**
Light from the lenses	is bounced	off	the mirrors.
Two schools	were crossed	off	the list.

Verbs with this pattern belong to the following meaning groups:

1 THE 'PEEL' GROUP
2 THE 'CADGE' GROUP
3 THE 'REFLECT' GROUP
4 VERBS WITH OTHER MEANINGS

1 THE 'PEEL' GROUP

These verbs are concerned with removing something or someone from somewhere, either physically or metaphorically. This includes taking an amount of money or time off something such as a debt or a record. It also includes omitting someone or something from a list.

*He threatened to boycott the wedding when his estranged wife **was left** off the guest list.*

*Leo stood by the dresser **peeling** the foil off a bottle of champagne.*

In the case of *clip*, *cut 7*, and *shave 5*, the noun group following the verb is always an amount. This pattern is **V amount *off* n**.

*Members of the House and Senate are trying to design a budget which would **shave £500 billion off the federal deficit** in five years.*

break *VP1*	cross *VP*	leave *VP1*	shave *4,5*
chase *4*	cut *7,VP1*	lop *VP2*	skim *1,VP*
clean *4*	flick *2*	peel *3*	strike *VP*
clear *9*	kick *VP4*	pluck *2*	take *VP2.8*
clip *8*	knock *VP2*	scrape *1*	trim *VP*

2 THE 'CADGE' GROUP

These verbs are concerned with acquiring something from someone.

*He**'s been cadging** meals off me under false pretences for the past two months.*

borrow *2*	cadge

3 THE 'REFLECT' GROUP

These verbs are concerned with bouncing or reflecting light or sound off a surface.

*Most holograms on public display can be seen when white light **is reflected** off them.*

bounce *3*	reflect *2*

4 VERBS WITH OTHER MEANINGS

There are a few other verbs which have this pattern.

> *We kind of **bounce** ideas off each other.*
>
> *Bill's sister was there to **meet** them off the train that autumn afternoon.*

bounce *8*	pull *VP2*	warn *VP*
meet *5*	throw *VP3*	wean *1,2*

Structure information

a) The noun group following the verb is the Object, and the prepositional phrase is an Adjunct.

b) This structure has a passive, with the pattern **be V-ed *off* n**. The prepositional phrase is an Adjunct.

---

20 V n *on* n

The verb is followed by a noun group and a prepositional phrase which consists of *on* and a noun group. With some verbs, the preposition is sometimes followed by an '-ing' clause or a wh-clause. The passive pattern is **be V-ed *on* n**.

With some verbs, the preposition is sometimes *upon* instead of *on*. Upon is a more formal or literary word.

This pattern has one structure:

▶ Verb with Object and Adjunct
  *He **played** a trick on her.*

Active voice: V n *on* n

	Verb group	noun group	*on*	noun group
Subject	**Verb**	**Object**		**Adjunct**
I	don't force	vegetarianism	on	patients.
The rebels	have inflicted	heavy losses	on	government forces.
He	lavished	attention	on	her.
We	will put	pressure	on	the authorities.
McClaren	sprang	a new idea	on	him.
Bitter youngsters	have turned	their anger	on	police.

Passive voice: *be* V-ed *on* n

	Verb group	*on*	noun group
Subject	**Verb**		**Adjunct**
Every detail	was imprinted	on	his memory.
Hostile acts	were being perpetrated	on	the community.
Cheese	can be sprinkled	on	egg or vegetable dishes.

Phrasal verbs

Active voice: V n P *on* n, V P n (not pron) *on* n

	Verb group	noun group	Particle	*on*	noun group
Subject	**Verb...**	**Object**	**...Verb**		**Adjunct**
I	can fill	him	in	on	the background.
She	took	her anger	out	on	me.

	Verb group	Particle	noun group	*on*	noun group
Subject	**Verb**		**Object**		**Adjunct**
	Pin	down	suppliers	on	delivery dates.
None of them	will put	down	anything	on	paper.

Passive voice: *be* V-ed P *on* n

	Verb group	Particle	*on*	noun group
Subject	**Verb**		**Adjunct**	
This worthless paper	was palmed	off	on	the state-owned banks.
The young Humes	were thrown	back	on	their own resources.

Verbs with this pattern belong to the following meaning groups:

1 THE 'BESTOW' GROUP
2 THE 'IMPOSE' GROUP
3 THE 'QUESTION' GROUP
4 THE 'PLACE' GROUP
5 THE 'FOCUS' GROUP
6 THE 'PULL A GUN' GROUP
7 THE 'BANG' GROUP
8 THE 'PAT ON THE BACK' GROUP
9 THE 'CARVE' GROUP
10 THE 'BASE' GROUP
11 THE 'GAMBLE' GROUP
12 THE 'SPEND' GROUP
13 THE 'MODEL' GROUP
14 VERBS WITH OTHER MEANINGS

1 THE 'BESTOW' GROUP

These verbs are concerned with giving something to someone, or doing something pleasant to them.

Good looks are used in advertisements and films to __confer prestige and power on those who possess them__, and this is a value that has been absorbed into our system.

Japanese car bosses __have heaped__ praise on British workers who accelerated their factory into profit a year early.

It involves a substantial amount of money __being settled__ on that child.

The preposition is sometimes *upon* instead of *on*.

The King and Queen __bestowed__ their grateful thanks upon Lancelot.

bestow	heap *3*	press *8*
confer *2*	lavish *3*	settle *5*

2 THE 'IMPOSE' GROUP

These verbs are concerned with giving something unpleasant to someone, or doing something unpleasant to them. This includes:

- blaming something on someone
- inflicting or imposing something on someone e.g. *dump, perpetrate*
- wishing something bad on someone
- playing a trick on someone e.g. *play, pull*
- serving a writ on someone

*He said the republics **brought trouble on themselves** by ignoring his presidential decisions and by disregarding the Soviet constitution.*

*Rob **dumped his children on the grandparents** but my family does not live nearby.*

*Rose grieved privately with her immediate family and **did not impose** her grief on friends.*

*I did not bring this case to **lay blame on my husband**. It was the only way to get the insurance.*

*There are consistent reports of electrical torture **being practised** on inmates.*

*A Home Office spokeswoman said last night: 'We **have served** a writ on Central Television to prevent the programme being screened.'*

*I didn't mean to **take my anger out** on him, but I couldn't help myself.*

*He told his son that he'd spent his life doing things he hated, and he **wouldn't wish** that on anyone.*

The preposition is sometimes *upon* instead of *on*.

*The reality is that a good therapist or counsellor will not try to **foist anything upon a 'client'**.*

In the case of *impose 5*, the noun group following the verb is always a reflexive pronoun. This pattern is **V pron-refl *on* n**.

*Mrs Griffin said they **could not** possibly **impose themselves on her** for dinner, but if they might, they'd just stay for a drink and a chat.*

blame *1*	impose *1,2,3,5*	practise *3 (usu passive)*	vent *2*
bring *7*	inflict	pull *14*	be visited *4*
dump *9*	lay *1.7*	revenge *2*	wish *7*
exact *5,6*	perpetrate *(usu passive)*	serve *9*	
foist *VP*	pin *5*	spring *9*	
force *3*	play *5*	thrust *VP*	
palm off	take out *VPP*		

3 THE 'QUESTION' GROUP

These verbs are concerned with speaking or writing about a particular topic. The noun group indicates the person involved. This includes:

- advising someone e.g. *advise, counsel*
- instructing someone e.g. *instruct, lecture*
- questioning someone e.g. *cross-examine, grill*
- commending someone e.g. *compliment, congratulate*
- criticizing someone e.g. *pick up*
- accepting an offer or suggestion e.g. *take up*

*This guide **will brief you on sightseeing and shopping**.*

*I **congratulated** Katherine on her decision to advance her education.*

*Witnesses **were cross-examined** on only those parts of the statements considered controversial.*

*He **wouldn't be drawn** on numbers, but said the Saudis would be given all the troops they needed.*

*His hosts will clearly want to **question** him closely **on what he said in Dublin**.*

*I'**ll tell** my mummy **on you**!*

The preposition *on* is sometimes followed by an '-ing' clause or a wh-clause.

*The prime minister **complimented** him **on leading what she described as the only Conservative government in Eastern Europe**.*

*BR made it clear that it would **consult** its legal advisers **on whether court action could be taken to prevent the strikes**.*

In the case of *congratulate 3*, the noun group following the verb is always a reflexive pronoun. This pattern is **V pron-refl *on* n**.

*She **congratulated** herself **on her own business acumen**.*

advise *2*	congratulate *1,2,3*	grill *5*	press *5 (usu passive)*
brief *6*	consult *1*	harangue *1*	question *2*
challenge *4*	counsel *3*	instruct *2*	quiz *2*
commend *1*	cross-examine	lecture *2,3*	tell *VP*
compliment *2*	(not) draw *23 (usu passive)*	poll *2*	update *3*
fill in *3*	pin down *2*		
pick up *13*	take up *VPP1,2*		

4 THE 'PLACE' GROUP

These verbs are concerned with putting or fastening something somewhere, either physically or metaphorically. This includes:

- concrete actions e.g. *perch, sprinkle*
- abstract actions e.g. *cast (doubt), throw (light)*
- putting a value or a tax on something

*The top nature photographer explains how to **capture** iridescent peacock plumes **on film**.*

*The World Bank **has cast** doubt **on reports in Argentina** that it is to extend loans to the government of four thousand million dollars.*

*The taxes **are levied** **on energy** irrespective of the polluting potential of the technology and fuel used to generate that energy.*

*As they all piled in, Kai Lee **perched** herself **on the driver's seat**. She could just reach the pedals.*

*The fact that people are willing to pay to reduce risks shows that they **set** an implicit value **on human life**.*

*The next Budget **should slap** a massive tax surcharge **on any car with an engine capacity above, say, 1,500cc**.*

The preposition is sometimes *upon* instead of *on*.

*The Prime Minister **placed** great weight **upon the American role in the Atlantic community**.*

In the case of *cast, place, put 4*, and *throw 9*, the preposition *on* is sometimes followed by an '-ing' clause or a wh-clause.

*The prosecutors want to **cast** doubt **on whether Smith has a good character**.*

*He said 'I **have placed** particular emphasis **on establishing a good rapport and effective dialogue with British industry**.'*

capture *4*	impale	place *18*	slap *4*
cast *6*	levy *2*	plunk *1*	sprinkle *1 (usu passive)*
centre *8*	load *6*	prop *1*	throw *8,9*
clip *2*	mount *7*	put *4,11,VP8*	
cram *3*	perch *3*	set *2.7,VP*	
throw back *2 (usu passive)*			

5 THE 'FOCUS' GROUP

These verbs are concerned with focusing your attention, your feelings, or your efforts on someone or something.

> *The public housing authorities were encouraged to **concentrate** their efforts on slum clearance and redevelopment rehousing.*

> *Scientists now **pin** their hopes on treatment with combinations of drugs – but these hopes are not high.*

> *She **projected** her desires on you.*

The preposition is sometimes *upon* instead of *on*.

> *These writers assume the historical truth of the crucifixion of Jesus and **focus** their attention upon its significance.*

In the case of *turn*, the feeling you focus on someone is usually aggressive.

> *The crowd then **turned** their anger on the Prime Minister and began to wave banners declaring 'Spend more money on health.'*

The preposition *on* is sometimes followed by an '-ing' clause or a wh-clause.

> *The debate **is centred** on whether the country's president should be elected directly by the people or by parliament.*

centre 9 *(usu passive)*	fasten 3	pin 6
concentrate 1	fix 7,9	project 5
direct 6	focus 1,5	turn 10

6 THE 'PULL A GUN' GROUP

These verbs are concerned with directing a weapon at someone. In the case of *fix* and *train*, the object that is directed may also be a camera or radar.

> *I reminded him that Feld **had pulled** a gun on me and, most probably, had later ransacked my apartment.*

fix 11	train 2.5
pull 8	turn 10

7 THE 'BANG' GROUP

These verbs are concerned with striking one thing on another, or catching one thing on another. We include here the verb *wipe*.

> *He shouted out loud in his anger, and **banged** his fists on the steering wheel.*

> *He **caught** his shirt on a nail.*

> *I stared at the phone and **drummed** my fingers on my desk.*

> *She set down the serving fork and **wiped** her hands on a dish towel.*

bang 5,6	hammer 3	snag 2
catch 5	rap 4	strike 5
drum 6	slap 3	wipe 1

8 THE 'PAT ON THE BACK' GROUP

These verbs are concerned with touching or hitting someone, either in a friendly way or in a violent way. The noun group following the verb indicates the person you touch or hit. The prepositional phrase indicates which part of their body you touch or hit. We include here *land* and *plant*, where the noun group is *a blow* or *a kiss*, for example.

To *pat someone on the back* may also be metaphorical, meaning to praise someone. When a reflexive pronoun is used (see below), the action is always metaphorical.

> *His fist lashed out, __caught__ her on the side of her face and knocked her down.*

> *One by one the uncles rose and shook his hand, __patted__ him on the back and welcomed him home.*

> *Mary Ann leaned over and __pecked__ him on the cheek.*

> *Marvin tried to __plant__ a Valentine's Day kiss on Ruth's cheek but his peck landed on the side of her neck.*

In the case of *pat*, the noun group following the verb is often a reflexive pronoun. This pattern is **V pron-refl *on* n.**

> *The industry __is patting__ itself on the back for being incredibly successful.*

beat *1*	clout *1*	pat *1*	slap *2*
catch *4*	hit *1*	peck *2*	
clap *3*	land *14*	plant *10*	

9 THE 'CARVE' GROUP

These verbs are concerned with writing something somewhere, or with etching or carving something onto a surface. In the case of *carve, engrave, etch, impress,* and *imprint*, the process is metaphorical – someone impresses something on someone's mind.

> *He will say your name as often as he can, thus __engraving__ it on his memory.*

> *I wish to thank my friend Theresa King who encouraged me to develop my ideas and __put them down__ on paper.*

The preposition is sometimes *upon* instead of *on*.

> *His rune __was carved__ or __scratched__ upon warriors' swords to bring them luck in battle.*

In the case of *impress 3*, the noun group following the verb is often a reflexive pronoun. This pattern is **V pron-refl *on* n.**

> *Details in the room were beginning to __impress__ themselves on his mind.*

carve *2*	impress *2,3*	print *3*	write *1*
engrave	imprint *2 (usu passive)*	scratch *2*	
etch *1,2,3 (usu passive)*	inscribe *1*	superimpose *1,2 (usu passive)*	
put down *1*			

10 THE 'BASE' GROUP

These verbs are concerned with basing one thing on another, for example basing a theory on facts.

> *They tried to __build__ an empire on shaky foundations.*

The preposition is sometimes *upon* instead of *on*.

> *A practical program leading toward the abolition of nuclear weapons __must be based__ upon firm principles.*

The preposition *on* is sometimes followed by an '-ing' clause.

*The whole thing **is predicated** on whipping up demand for the tournament hotline.*

The preposition *on* is sometimes followed by a noun group and an '-ing' clause. This pattern is **V n *on* n -ing**.

*My feminist understanding **is predicated** on me being a woman and seeing the world through the eyes of a woman in a society that is dominated by men.*

base *7*	ground *12 (usu passive)*	be premised
build *4*	predicate *2 (usu passive)*	

11 THE 'GAMBLE' GROUP

These verbs are concerned with gambling. The noun group indicates the stake, that is, what it is that you gamble, such as *a pound* or *your life*.

*I'**ll bet** a quid on anything, but never more than a fiver.*

*Having decided to **wager** their lives on a toss of the dice, what value might they attach to the lives of others?*

The preposition *on* is sometimes followed by an '-ing' clause.

*She **gambled** a small fortune on hiring a top American publicist to plug her talents.*

In the case of *bet, gamble, lay,* and *stake,* the preposition is sometimes followed by a noun group and an '-ing' clause. This pattern is **V n *on* n -ing**.

*You wouldn't want to **stake** your life on the signal being picked up.*

bet *1*	place *24*	wager *1*
gamble *2*	put *VP7*	
lay *1.8*	stake *3*	

12 THE 'SPEND' GROUP

These verbs are concerned with spending, saving, and wasting time, money, or resources.

*'I **do spend** a lot on expensive jewelry and clothing,' she admits.*

*My father thought a university education **was wasted** on a woman.*

The preposition *on* is sometimes followed by an '-ing' clause.

*She **blew** part of the cash on furnishing her flat.*

blow *1.9*	spend *1*	waste *5 (usu passive)*
save *3*	waste *1*	
fork out	shell out	

13 THE 'MODEL' GROUP

These verbs are concerned with modelling something on something else, or modelling yourself on someone else.

*Their organizational structure **was patterned** on the World War II underground resistance movement.*

In the case of *model 8*, the noun group following the verb is often a reflexive pronoun. This pattern is **V pron-refl *on* n**.

*As far as their preferences and dislikes are concerned, most children tend to **model** themselves on their parents.*

model *7,8*	pattern *2 (usu passive)*

14 VERBS WITH OTHER MEANINGS

There are a number of other verbs which have this pattern.

*Thomas Jefferson **sold** Congress on the idea of the decimal system for currency.*

*He took the opportunity again to **urge** restraint on the Soviet government in its handling of the crisis.*

*She is a true couturier in that she wants to **work** individual magic on her clients.*

In the case of *commit, gorge, preen,* and *pride,* the noun group following the verb is always or often a reflexive pronoun. This pattern is **V pron-refl *on* n.**

*It isn't their diplomatic style to **commit** themselves on such a delicate issue.*

(not) commit 5	gorge 2	preen 2	sell 6
decide 5	indict	pride 4	urge 3
feed 1	judge 4	remand 1	work 15
let in VPP			

Structure information

a) The noun group following the verb is the Object, and the prepositional phrase is an Adjunct.

b) This structure has a passive, with the pattern ***be* V-ed *on* n.** The prepositional phrase is an Adjunct.

c) Though the prepositional phrase in this structure usually comes after the noun group, it sometimes comes before it, especially when the noun group is a long one. Verbs in meaning group 1 above have this ordering very frequently.

*Expensive clothes **do not** necessarily **bestow** upon the wearer style or distinction.*

*Five Alsatian dogs from a private security firm were brought in to **impress** on the men the seriousness of the situation, and in this they were most successful.*

d) Phrasal verb patterns are the same except that there is also a particle, P. The Object comes either between the verb and the particle, or after the particle. If the Object comes after the particle, it cannot be a personal pronoun. You say

*She **took** it **out** on me*
or *She **took out** her anger on me*

but you do not say *She took out it on me.*

21　V n *onto* n, V n *on to* n

The verb is followed by a noun group and a prepositional phrase which consists of *onto* or *on to* and a noun group. The passive pattern is ***be* V-ed *onto* n.**

This pattern has one structure:

▶ Verb with Object and Adjunct
*He **projected** his feelings onto her.*

Active voice: V n *onto* n

	Verb group	noun group	*onto*	noun group
Subject	**Verb**	**Object**		**Adjunct**
I	clipped	the camera	on to	the tripod-head.
The telescope mirror	focuses	light	onto	the small adaptive mirror.

Passive voice: *be* V-ed *onto* n

	Verb group	*onto*	noun group
Subject	**Verb**		**Adjunct**
The skin	has to be grafted	onto	the burns.
The image	is scanned	on to	a photo-sensitive drum.

Verbs with this pattern belong to the following meaning groups:

1 THE 'STICK' GROUP
2 THE 'SCAN' GROUP
3 THE 'FOCUS' GROUP
4 VERBS WITH OTHER MEANINGS

1 THE 'STICK' GROUP

These verbs are concerned with attaching or joining something to something else.

*I like to use cut-outs of cartoon characters and **sew** them onto jeans.*

*Some manufacturers **stick** plywood strips on to a large sheet of glass to give the impression of separate panes.*

attach *1*	connect *1*	sew *1*	tape *7*
bolt *2*	graft *2,3 (usu passive)*	solder *1*	tie *2*
clamp *2*	hitch *3*	stick *2.4*	weld *1*
clip *2*	hook *2*	tack *2*	yoke *3*

2 THE 'SCAN' GROUP

These verbs are concerned with transferring information from one medium to another or one form to another.

*He then **printed** the picture onto grade five paper with a soft focus filter under the enlarging lens.*

*The photographer needs only to **scan** the images onto the computer and then manipulate them until they are perfect.*

*The seeing eye robots pick out the clones they are programmed to select and **transfer** them onto tapes.*

copy *2*	scan *4 (usu passive)*
print *7*	transfer *6*

3 THE 'FOCUS' GROUP

These verbs are concerned with focusing or projecting light or an image onto a surface.

*The system uses large curved mirrors to **focus** the sun's rays onto a glass pipe.*

*Once a specimen has been selected, its microscopic image **is** automatically **projected** onto a television-sized screen where it can be easily focused and viewed.*

focus 7	reflect 2
project 6	throw 8

4 VERBS WITH OTHER MEANINGS

There are a few other verbs which have this pattern.

Johanna did not view herself as having difficulties and tended to __project__ much of the blame and responsibility onto others.

A colleague at the 'Independent' __put__ me __onto__ the story.

co-opt 2 *(usu passive)*	project 5
offload 1	put VP

Structure information

a) The noun group following the verb is the Object, and the prepositional phrase is an Adjunct.

b) This structure has a passive, with the pattern *be* V-ed *onto* n. The prepositional phrase is an Adjunct.

c) Though the prepositional phrase in this structure usually comes after the noun group, it sometimes comes before it, especially when the noun group is a long one.

We are prone to __project__ onto the other person feelings and reactions which are essentially our own.

22 V n *out of* n

The verb is followed by a noun group and a prepositional phrase which consists of *out of* and a noun group. With some verbs, the preposition is sometimes followed by an '-ing' clause. The passive pattern is *be* V-ed *out of* n.

This pattern has one structure:

▶ Verb with Object and Adjunct
 I __dragged__ the information out of him.

Active voice: V n *out of* n/-ing

	Verb group	noun group	*out of*	noun group/-ing clause
Subject	Verb	Object		Adjunct
He	fished	a timetable	out of	the drawer.
She	couldn't get	any more information	out of	Ted.
People	shouldn't make	money	out of	running prisons.

Passive voice: *be* V-ed *out of* n/-ing

	Verb group	*out of*	noun group/-ing clause
Subject	**Verb**		**Adjunct**
They	were conned	out of	several hundred pounds.
His voice	will be edited	out of	the final film.
Some	were talked	out of	leaving.

Verbs with this pattern belong to the following meaning groups:

1 THE 'CHEAT' GROUP
2 THE 'SCREW' GROUP
3 THE 'GET' GROUP
4 THE 'PLUCK' GROUP
5 THE 'FORCE' GROUP
6 THE 'TALK' GROUP
7 THE 'SHUT' GROUP
8 THE 'BAIL' GROUP
9 THE 'MAKE' GROUP
10 VERBS WITH OTHER MEANINGS

1 THE 'CHEAT' GROUP

These verbs are concerned with fraudulently taking something, usually money, away from someone. The noun group indicates who is deprived of something, and the prepositional phrase indicates what is taken from them.

A businessman __cheated__ the Inland Revenue out of £150 million, a court heard yesterday.

He __swindled__ clients out of millions before FIMBRA caught him out.

bilk	con *1*	do *VPP*	swindle
cheat *3*	defraud	fleece *3*	trick *2*

2 THE 'SCREW' GROUP

These verbs are concerned with getting something from someone with some difficulty. The noun group indicates what is obtained, and the prepositional phrase indicates who it is obtained from.

This is a productive use: any verb which indicates a way of persuading someone or applying pressure can be used with this pattern. The verbs listed here are the ones which are most frequently used in this way.

The families soon discovered that every piece of information __had to be dragged__ out of them.

The company has a monopoly position that it uses to __screw__ more money out of people.

He didn't try to __worm__ secrets out of you the way so many grown-ups did.

charm *5*	get *2.1*	tease *VP*	wring *1*
coax *2*	prize *6*	wheedle	
con *1*	screw *10*	winkle *VP1*	
drag *VP2*	squeeze *6*	worm *VPP*	

413

3 THE 'GET' GROUP

These verbs are concerned with gaining something from an activity or thing.

The attempt to __make__ money out of the historic find has caused outrage.

The preposition *out of* is sometimes followed by an '-ing' clause.

You __might get__ a lot of pleasure out of refurnishing and re-equipping a new home.

In the case of *get*, the noun group following the verb is often an **amount**. This pattern is **V amount *out of* n**.

'Would you recommend the course to other people?' 'Yes, I feel I __got__ a lot out of it.'

> get *2.9*   make *3.6*

4 THE 'PLUCK' GROUP

These verbs are concerned with removing something from a place or thing. We include here *pull VP3*, which indicates that a country takes their troops out of an area.

Relief workers are still trying to __dig__ people out of the rubble.
He __plucked__ a cube of sugar out of the bowl and placed it on his tongue.
He said that the Americans and their allies __should pull__ their forces out of the area.

In the case of *elbow*, the noun group is usually followed by *out of the way*.

He __elbowed__ Crook out of the way and advanced on Woods, his massive beer-gut quivering with indignation.

clip *5*	elbow *2*	prize *5*	write *VP2*
cut *VP1,2*	filter *VP*	pull *2, VP3*	
dig *VP1*	fish *VP*	take *2.7*	
edit *VP*	pluck *2*	turn *VP7*	

5 THE 'FORCE' GROUP

These verbs are concerned with forcing someone to leave a place, position, activity, or state.

This is a productive use: any verb which indicates the use of force or pressure can be used with this pattern. The verbs listed here are the ones which are most frequently used in this way.

He said he would oppose moves to __force__ the president out of office.
She fears the authorities __might kick__ her out of Barbados.
The sixth seed, Michael Chang, __has been knocked__ out of the Australian Indoor Championship in the third round.
This was apparently enough to __shake__ Haig out of his complacency.

bomb *VP (usu passive)*	drum *VP (usu passive)*	kick *VP*	throw *VP3*
boot *VP*	flush *6*	knock *VP2*	turf *VP*
chase *4,5*	force *1,2*	order *2.1*	turn *VP6*
chuck *VP2*	hound *3 (usu passive)*	put *VP7*	vote *VP*
drive *12*	jolt *2*	shake *12*	winkle *VP2*

6 THE 'TALK' GROUP

These verbs are concerned with persuading someone to leave a place or state, or persuading someone not to do something.

This is a productive use: any verb which indicates a way of persuading someone can be used with this pattern. The verbs listed here are the ones which are most frequently used in this way.

> *David Gower **has been coaxed** out of retirement to captain the Earl of Carnarvon's XI against South Africa.*

In the case of *talk*, the preposition *out of* is sometimes followed by an '-ing' clause.

> *My mother tried to **talk** me out of getting a divorce.*

coax *1*	persuade *1*	talk *VPP1*

7 THE 'SHUT' GROUP

These verbs are concerned with excluding someone or something. We include here *block* and *blot*, which indicate that someone excludes a thought from their mind.

> *You know it can happen but you **have to block** it out of your mind.*
> *They were concerned that they **were being left** out of the decision-making process.*
> *She also bombarded him with cruel abuse and **locked** him out of the house at night.*
> *American semiconductor firms **were** virtually **shut** out of the Japanese market.*

block *VP1*	edge *VP*	lock *VP1*	shut *VP1,3*
blot *VP2*	freeze *VP*	put *VP7*	squeeze *VP (usu passive)*
cut *VP5*	leave *VP*	rule *VP*	

8 THE 'BAIL' GROUP

These verbs are concerned with rescuing someone from a bad situation.

> *We**'d bail** him out of trouble when he owed money.*

In the case of *talk*, the noun group following the preposition is always a reflexive pronoun. This pattern is **V pron-refl *out of* n**. This verb sometimes indicates that someone gets themselves out of a good situation rather than a bad one.

> *I always have the sense that I **can talk** myself out of trouble.*
> *He **talked** himself out of a job.*

bail *VP1*	pull *VP4*
get *1.3*	talk *VPP2*

9 THE 'MAKE' GROUP

These verbs are concerned with making something. The prepositional phrase indicates the materials or things that are used to make the thing. We include here *be born*, which indicates that something abstract is created from or produced by something else.

> *His quest for justice **was born** out of the violence and racism he encountered in his youth.*
> *Joe remained as immobile as if he **had been carved** out of rock.*
> *He was very clever with his hands and he enjoyed **making** new things out of old bits and pieces.*

be born *5*	construct *1,2 (usu passive)*	fashion *4*	manufacture *1*
carve *1,5 (usu passive)*	create *1*	hew *2 (usu passive)*	
conjure *1*	cut *1*	make *3.1*	
conjure up ▷*1*			

10 VERBS WITH OTHER MEANINGS

There are three other verbs which have this pattern.

*Soon it was time to go, and we **got changed** out of our swimming gear.*
*Schools **knock** the creative impulse out of their students.*

> get changed 5   check *VP1*   knock 5

Structure information

a) The noun group following the verb is the Object, and the prepositional phrase is an Adjunct.

b) This structure has a passive, with the pattern *be* V-ed *out of* n.

c) The prepositional phrase in this structure usually comes after the noun group. Sometimes, however, the prepositional phrase comes before the noun group, especially when the noun group is a long one.

> *It didn't take long before she'**d wormed** out of him confessions of his other infidelities.*

23 V n *over* n

The verb is followed by a noun group and a prepositional phrase which consists of *over* and a noun group. The passive pattern is *be* V-ed *over* n.

This pattern has one structure:

▶ Verb with Object and Adjunct
Spoon the sugar over the fruit.

Active voice: V n *over* n

	Verb group	noun group	*over*	noun group
Subject	**Verb**	**Object**	**Adjunct**	
	Brush	melted butter	over	the pastry.
The youths	poured	kerosene	over	the floor.

Passive voice: *be* V-ed *over* n

	Verb group	*over*	noun group
Subject	**Verb**	**Adjunct**	
A portion of his ashes	was scattered	over	the Channel.
Cooling water	was sprayed	over	the engines.

Most of the verbs with this pattern are concerned with pouring or sprinkling a substance over a surface or over something else.

> *Place the stoned mirabelle plums in the mould and **drizzle the liqueur over them**.*
> ***Sprinkle the wheat grains** liberally **over the soil**, water them in, then cover with wet newspaper.*

The preposition *over* is sometimes preceded by *all*.

*The racoons knock over the rubbish bins in search of food, and **strew** the contents all over the ground.*

brush *3*	drizzle *3*	spoon *3*	strew
distribute *4*	pour *1*	spray *3*	
dribble *1*	scatter *1*	sprinkle *1*	

VERBS WITH OTHER MEANINGS

There are three other verbs which have this pattern.

***Did** Laura know something and **hold** it over Felicity?*

fight *3*	hold *VP1*	rap *7*

Structure information

a) The noun group following the verb is the Object, and the prepositional phrase is an Adjunct.

b) This structure has a passive, with the pattern *be* V-ed *over* n. The prepositional phrase is an Adjunct.

24　V n *to* n

The verb is followed by a noun group and a prepositional phrase which consists of *to* and a noun group. With some verbs, the preposition is sometimes followed by an '-ing' clause. The passive pattern is *be* V-ed *to* n.

This pattern has three structures:

▶ Structure I: Verb with Object and prepositional Object
*I **lent** some money to my father.*
▶ Structure II: Verb with Object and prepositional Object Complement
*He **changed** his name to Adam.*
▶ Structure III: Verb with Object and Adjunct
*She **devoted** a whole chapter to the subject.*

Structure I: Verb with Object and prepositional Object

Active voice: V n *to* n

	Verb group	noun group	*to*	noun group
Subject	**Verb**	**Object**		**prepositional Object**
We	explained	the situation	to	him.
Building societies	lend	money	to	housebuyers.
She	rented	rooms	to	university students.
I	showed	the sketches	to	my producer.

Passive voice: *be* V-ed *to* n

	Verb group		*to*	noun group
Subject	**Verb**			**prepositional Object**
The wall paintings	have been attributed		to	a 16th century Sicilian painter.
Personal details	were being forwarded		to	the authorities.
Minimum wages	are to be indexed		to	inflation.
The car	must be restored		to	its rightful owner.

Phrasal verbs

Active voice: V n P *to* n, V P n (not pron) *to* n

	Verb group	noun group	Particle	*to*	noun group
Subject	**Verb...**	**Object**	**...Verb**		**prepositional Object**
He	married	his daughter	off	to	a peasant farmer.
I	have passed	my information	on	to	the police.

	Verb group	Particle	noun group	*to*	noun group
Subject	**Verb**		**Object**		**prepositional Object**
He	made	out	a cheque	to	his wife.
Pregnant women	may pass	on	the disease	to	their unborn children.

Passive voice: *be* V-ed P *to* n

	Verb group	Particle	*to*	noun group
Subject	**Verb**			**prepositional Object**
The evidence	was handed	over	to	the German authorities.
Mops and brooms	were loaned	out	to	the staff.

Verbs with this structure belong to the following meaning groups:

I.1   THE 'GIVE' GROUP
I.2   THE 'PROMISE' GROUP
I.3   THE 'COMMUNICATE' GROUP
I.4   THE 'TRANSMIT' GROUP
I.5   THE 'SHOW' GROUP
I.6   THE 'SELL' GROUP
I.7   THE 'LINK' GROUP
I.8   THE 'IMPART' GROUP
I.9   THE 'ATTRIBUTE' GROUP
I.10 VERBS WITH OTHER MEANINGS

I.1 THE 'GIVE' GROUP

These verbs are concerned with giving or transferring something to someone. This includes:

- giving e.g. *award, feed, grant*
- bequeathing e.g. *leave, will*

- lending e.g. *lend, loan*
- transferring something e.g. *hand, pass*
- transferring responsibility for something e.g. *delegate, subcontract*
- allocating or committing money or resources e.g. *allot, assign*
- conceding e.g. *cede, yield*
- introducing ideas or systems e.g. *export, introduce*
- marrying someone to someone
- dedicating something such as a book or a building to someone

*The seats **are allotted** to candidates who have won the most votes according to their parties' percentages.*

*With fewer than twenty agents on the case he **couldn't assign** this distasteful task to a junior agent.*

*Just before Charles died in November 1700 the court persuaded him to **bequeath** his whole empire intact **to Louis's grandson, Philip of Anjou**.*

*Willis was a target for criticism after Liverpool **conceded** three first half goals to the champions.*

*He took the money home at the end of the week and **gave** it to his mother to keep shoes on his feet and chickens in the pot.*

*He pledged to **introduce** real democracy to Chad.*

*I became a dancer. Otherwise I **would have been married off** to a rich industrialist.*

*The commander in chief said he expected his forces to **surrender** their arms to United Nations peace-keeping forces early next week.*

*Most scientists here believe that it is at least theoretically possible for the disease to **be transmitted** to humans.*

The preposition *to* is sometimes followed by an '-ing' clause when the verb involves committing money or resources to a particular cause or activity.

*NBC Radio's embattled president **had committed** all available resources to fixing his disastrous prime time schedule.*

In the case of *arrogate*, the noun group following the preposition is always a reflexive pronoun. This pattern is **V n *to* pron-refl**.

*Such non-Catholic religious persons were thereby invisibly tied to the official church, which **arrogated** jurisdiction over them to itself.*

accord *2*	dedicate *3 (usu passive)*	introduce *1*	sacrifice *1*
administer *1,2*	delegate *2*	leave *20*	sell *6*
allocate	deliver *1,3*	lend *1,2,3*	serve *6*
allot *(usu passive)*	devolve	license	slip *5*
arrogate	dispense *1,3*	loan *3*	subcontract *1*
assign *1,2,3*	distribute *1*	marry *3*	submit *2*
award *4,5*	donate *1*	pass *5,8*	supply *1*
bequeath *1,2*	entrust	pass *6 (usu passive)*	surrender *2*
bring *3,5,10*	export *3*	pay *1,11*	transfer *2,7*
cede	extend	present *4.1,11*	transmit *2,3*
commit *3*	feed *1,8,12*	reallocate	vouchsafe
concede *2,4,5*	give *1.2,2.1,2,3*	remit *2*	will *2.5*
contribute *1,2*	grant *2*	render *2*	yield *2*
dedicate *2*	hand *2.1*	restore *4 (usu passive)*	
contract out *1*	hand back *2.0*	make over *7.0*	turn over *4,5*
deal out *2.0*	hand on *2.0*	marry off	
farm out	hand over *2.2,3*	pass on *1,2*	
give back *3.0*	loan out ▷*3*	pay out *1*	

I.2 THE 'PROMISE' GROUP

These verbs are concerned with offering or promising something to someone.

*Banks in many areas **offer** free checking accounts to older people or reduce the minimum balance requirements.*

*The company's management **will promise** higher returns to stockholders.*

offer *1,5,6,7,9*	proffer *1,2*
pledge *2*	promise *2*

I.3 THE 'COMMUNICATE' GROUP

These verbs are concerned with communicating something to someone verbally or in writing. The noun group following the verb may indicate the communication, e.g. *address remarks, pen a note*, or the content of the communication, e.g. *break the news, communicate our ideas*. It may also indicate the person involved, e.g. *introduce someone, unburden yourself*. The prepositional phrase indicates the person who you speak or write to.

We include here *nod* and *wave*, which indicate non-verbal communication.

*She turned and **addressed** her next remarks to Mary Ann.*

*On 4th December 1700, Philippe **bade** farewell to the King and his court.*

*Police **were** last night **breaking** the news of the tragedy to Faye's parents, who were away on holiday.*

*Words are the tools, the transmitters, by which we **communicate** our ideas to one another.*

*The contents of any interview with a foreign journalist **are divulged** immediately to Japanese journalists covering the same story.*

*It's not uncommon for attorneys and other professionals to act as intermediaries and **introduce** clients to each other.*

*If you feel that your home circumstances necessitate a period of convalescence, **mention** this to the Ward Sister.*

*Usually, psychologists and psychiatrists agree on a diagnosis and **present** their findings to the presiding judge.*

*Less than three weeks before he died, Chekhov **wrote** a letter to his mother in which he told her his health was on the mend.*

In the case of *address 4* and *unburden*, the noun group following the verb is often a reflexive pronoun. This pattern is **V pron-refl to n.**

*Children soon discover that it is much safer to **unburden** yourself to a member of the family than just a friend.*

address *2 (usu passive)*	disclose	offer *4*	repeat *2*
address *4*	divulge	pass *7*	report *1*
admit *1*	explain *1,2*	pen *2*	reveal *1*
announce *1*	express *1*	pencil *2*	say *1*
bid *2.1*	give *1.3*	present *4.4*	suggest *1*
break *18*	impart *1*	propose *6*	teach *1,4*
commend *2*	intimate *7*	put *9,10*	tell *1,2*
communicate *2*	introduce *3*	read *2*	unburden
confess *2*	leak *3*	recommend *1*	wave *1*
confide	mention *1*	relate *4*	write *4*
describe *1*	murmur *1*	relay *4 (usu passive)*	
dictate *2*	nod *3*	remember *7*	
call out	pass on ▷*7*		
make out *5*	report back *3*		

I.4 THE 'TRANSMIT' GROUP

These verbs are concerned with sending something such as a message to someone or to a place, for example through the post or by fax.

*He handed over his report to his secretary, who **faxed** it **to Martin**.*

*Controllers barked orders by telephone which **were relayed** **to pilots** by radio.*

*Life on board the boats **has been transmitted** by video **to the world's television screens**, with scenes of icebergs at dawn, of small yachts ploughing through massive seas.*

cable *5*	mail *3*	return *4*	telex *4*
fax *2*	post *1,4*	send *1,4*	transmit *1*
forward *10*	relay *2*	telegraph *2*	wire *6*

I.5 THE 'SHOW' GROUP

These verbs are concerned with showing something to someone.

*She **displayed** the new baby **to a group of admiring friends**.*

*He promised me I'd admire this part of the country, wanted to **show** it **to me**.*

demonstrate *4*	display *2*	show *3*

I.6 THE 'SELL' GROUP

These verbs are concerned with selling, auctioning, or renting something to someone.

*France and Germany announced they were planning to **export** reprocessing plants **to Pakistan and Brazil**.*

*Originally the land **was leased** either **to the aristocracy, the governing monarch or the monasteries**, who then **sub-leased** it **to the people**.*

*If prices dropped today, **would** you **sell** your house **to me**?*

auction *2 (usu passive)*	let *14*	sub-lease
export *1*	rent *2*	sublet
lease *2*	sell *1*	
sell on		

I.7 THE 'LINK' GROUP

These verbs are concerned with linking two or more things or people, or making a connection between them.

*The Cuban musicians themselves often **liken** their musical movement **to the works of Bob Dylan and Leonard Cohen**.*

*The President appeared to **link** a solution to the Gulf crisis **to talks on other Middle East disputes**.*

*America's future as a superpower **is tied** **to social justice at home, to a healthy economy and good trading relations with other nations**.*

The preposition *to* is sometimes followed by an '-ing' clause. Also, in the case of *compare* and *liken*, the verb is sometimes followed by an '-ing' clause instead of a noun group.

*I like to **compare** undergoing bypass surgery **to paying taxes**. The longer it is comfortably and safely put off, the better.*

anchor *5 (usu passive)*	correlate *1 (usu passive)*	link *2,7*	tie *8 (usu passive)*
compare *2*	index *4 (usu passive)*	match *3,5*	
connect *7,8*	liken	relate *2*	
match up ▷*3*			

I.8 THE 'IMPART' GROUP

These verbs are concerned with adding a particular quality to a thing, event, or situation.

*Their political differences only **added** spice to their relationship.*

*Butter **imparts** a full, rich taste to a cake.*

*Earle was improving in health, and this fact alone **lent** a brighter hue to life and its duties.*

```
add 4      impart 2
bring 7    lend 5
```

I.9 THE 'ATTRIBUTE' GROUP

These verbs are concerned with ascribing or attributing a particular thing, feature or quality to someone or something.

*Society **is** now **assigning** no positive value to suffering and is becoming more oriented toward a culture of comfort.*

*The gulf separating him from other children **could not be attributed** to class differences alone.*

*The fact that witch-hunting flourished in very different religious cultures should make us wary of **imputing** great significance to any one set of beliefs.*

The preposition *to* is sometimes followed by an '-ing' clause.

*Kelly **attributes** her coping ability to growing up in a big family.*

The preposition *to* is sometimes followed by a noun group and an '-ing' clause. This pattern is **V n to n -ing**.

*Some officials **attribute** this to people not knowing where to go.*

```
ascribe 1,2,3   attribute 1,2              impute
assign 4        attribute 3 (usu passive)
attach 3        credit 7

put down VPP
```

I.10 VERBS WITH OTHER MEANINGS

There are a few other verbs which have this structure.

*The Puritans hated bear-baiting, not because it **gave** pain to the bear, but because it **gave** pleasure to the spectators.*

*Conventional, fixed-rate loans **present** major risks to lenders.*

In the case of *lend*, the noun group following the verb is always a reflexive pronoun. This pattern is **V pron-refl to n**.

*NASA says the current schedule of upcoming shuttle missions **does not lend** itself to another attempt at a night landing in Florida any time within the foreseeable future.*

In the case of *owe 3,4* the noun group following the verb is always an **amount**. This pattern is **V amount to n**.

*Their mother worked two jobs, 14 hours a day, to pay for her children's education. 'We **owe** a lot to our mother,' Julie said.*

```
give 1.7    owe 1,2,3,4,5    present 4.2,7
lend 4      pledge 3
```

Structure information: Verb with Object and prepositional Object

a) The noun group following the verb is the Object, and the prepositional phrase is the prepositional Object.

b) This structure has a passive, with the pattern **be V-ed *to* n**. The prepositional phrase is the prepositional Object.

c) Though the prepositional phrase in this structure usually comes after the noun group, it sometimes comes before it, especially when the noun group is a long one.

> *The State **has arrogated** to itself the power and will to reform the moral character of the delinquent and even of the criminal.*

> *I am eager to **demonstrate** to you the extent of our far-flung scientific endeavor.*

d) Phrasal verb patterns are the same except that there is also a particle, P. The Object comes either between the verb and the particle, or after the particle. If the Object comes after the particle, it cannot be a personal pronoun. You say

> *He **passed** it **on** to the police*
> or *He **passed on** the information to the police*

> but you do not say *He passed on it to the police.*

Structure II: Verb with Object and prepositional Object Complement

Active voice: V n *to* n

	Verb group	noun group	*to*	noun group
Subject	Verb	Object		prep. Object Complement
She	changed	her name	to	Caroline.
He	converted	the note	to	cash.
He	raised	his voice	to	a shriek.

Passive voice: *be* V-ed *to* n

	Verb group	*to*	noun group
Subject	Verb		prepositional Complement
Their sentences	have been commuted	to	life imprisonment.
He	has been promoted	to	senior vice president.

Verbs with this structure are all concerned with changing something to something else. We include here the verbs *demote* and *promote* when the prepositional phrase indicates a person's new status, as in *They **promoted** him to non-executive Director*. We also include *keep*, which involves letting something stay at the same level.

This is a productive use: any verb which involves change can be used with this pattern. The verbs listed here are those which are most frequently used in this way.

> *Obtain the rate of exchange from your local bank on the day you order and use that figure to **convert** the pounds to dollars.*

> *He had a tendency to **drop** his voice to a whisper.*

> *Security **was kept** to a minimum this year and the protest passed off peacefully.*

abbreviate	decrease *1*	keep *VP4*	reduce *2,4 (usu passive)*
change *3*	demote *1*	lower *4,5,8*	shorten *3*
commute *3*	drop *8*	promote *3*	swell *1*
convert *1,4*	increase *1*	raise *1,4,6*	turn *15*
cut down ▷*7*	narrow down	whittle down	

Many of the verbs with this structure also have the pattern **V n *from* n *to* n**. The verb is followed by a noun group and two prepositional phrases, the first beginning with *from*, and the second beginning with *to*. The first prepositional phrase indicates what the person or thing originally was, and the second indicates what he, she, or it becomes. The passive pattern is **be V-ed *from* n *to* n**. The phrasal verb patterns are **V n P *from* n *to* n**, **V P n (not pron) *from* n *to* n**, and **be V-ed P *from* n *to* n**.

Pope Urban **commuted** *Galileo's sentence from prison to house arrest.*

Structure information: Verb with Object and prepositional Object Complement

a) The noun group following the verb is the Object, and the prepositional phrase is the prepositional Object Complement.

b) This structure has a passive, with the pattern **be V-ed *to* n**. The prepositional phrase is the prepositional Complement.

c) There are only three phrasal verbs with this structure, *cut down, narrow down*, and *whittle down*. The active patterns are **V n P *to* n** and **V P n (not pron) *to* n**. The Object comes either between the verb and the particle, or after the particle. If the Object comes after the particle, it cannot be a personal pronoun. You say

*The police **narrowed** it **down** to four*
or *The police **narrowed down** their list of suspects to four*

but you do not say *The police narrowed down it to four.*
The passive pattern is **be V-ed P *to* n**.

Structure III: Verb with Object and Adjunct

Active voice: V n *to* n

	Verb group	noun group	*to*	noun group
Subject	**Verb**	**Object**		**Adjunct**
She	banished	him	to	the upstairs attic room.
He	challenged	the officer	to	a duel.
A woman	denounced	her	to	the police.

Passive voice: *be* V-ed *to* n

	Verb group	*to*	noun group
Subject	**Verb**		**Adjunct**
I	was admitted	to	the Duke Hospital.
He and his colleagues	were brought	to	trial.
He	was condemned	to	death.
The team	was relegated	to	Division Two.

424

Phrasal verbs

Active voice: V n P *to* n, V P n (not pron) *to* n

	Verb group	noun group	Particle	to	noun group
Subject	Verb...	Object	...Verb		Adjunct
She	brought	him	round	to	her way of thinking.
One of the men	hooked	the stereo speakers	up	to	the TV.
That	takes	me	back	to	my childhood.

	Verb group	Particle	noun group	to	noun group
Subject	Verb		Object		Adjunct
They	put	off	the match	to	Friday.
You	can tack	on	another 20 percent	to	those estimates.

Passive voice: *be* V-ed P *to* n

	Verb group	Particle	to	noun group
Subject	Verb			Adjunct
The children	were packed	off	to	school.
Modern hypnosis	can be traced	back	to	the late eighteenth century.

Verbs with this structure belong to the following meaning groups:

III.1 THE 'DEVOTE' GROUP	III.11 THE 'ALERT' AND 'BLIND' GROUP
III.2 THE 'LIMIT' AND 'EXTEND' GROUP	III.12 THE 'INCITE' GROUP
III.3 THE 'ATTACH' GROUP	III.13 THE 'CONDEMN' GROUP
III.4 THE 'ATTRACT' GROUP	III.14 THE 'BEAT TO DEATH' GROUP
III.5 THE 'PREFER' AND 'SUBJUGATE' GROUP	III.15 THE 'DRAW ATTENTION' GROUP
III.6 THE 'BANISH' GROUP	III.16 THE 'POSTPONE' GROUP
III.7 THE 'APPOINT' GROUP	III.17 THE 'CREDIT' GROUP
III.8 THE 'LEAD' GROUP	III.18 THE 'CONVERT' GROUP
III.9 THE 'BETRAY' GROUP	III.19 VERBS WITH OTHER MEANINGS
III.10 THE 'INVITE' GROUP	

III.1 THE 'DEVOTE' GROUP

These verbs are concerned with devoting or dedicating yourself, your time, or your energy to a particular cause or activity. This includes restricting or tying yourself to one particular activity.

> With her household now running comparatively smoothly, Eleanor **was able to devote** still more time to worthy projects outside her home.

The preposition *to* is sometimes followed by an '-ing' clause.

> I wouldn't like to **be tied** to catching the last train home.

In the case of *abandon, address, apply, commit, confine, dedicate, devote, limit, pledge,* and *restrict,* the noun group following the verb is always or often a reflexive pronoun. This pattern is **V pron-refl *to* n/-ing**.

> The Guardian **addresses** itself to the question of how the Labour opposition should act over the issue.

425

We don't want to __commit__ ourselves to doing anything that might require too much strength, endurance, or time.

The report recommended that council members __confine__ themselves to debating broad issues of social policy, leaving the professionals responsible for the detailed execution.

The government will continue to __dedicate__ itself to peace.

In his preface to The Story of Art, Sir Ernst makes it clear that he __limits__ himself to real works of art and does not consider mere specimens of fashion.

Chomsky is not interested in linguistic variation. He __restricts__ himself to grammar, and in particular to core grammar.

abandon 4	confine 2	limit 6	tie 9 (usu passive)
address 6	dedicate 1	pledge 3	
apply 2	devote 1	restrict 3	
commit 4	enslave 2	rivet 1 (usu passive)	
give over VPP (usu passive)			

III.2 THE 'LIMIT' AND 'EXTEND' GROUP

These verbs are concerned with:

- limiting or restricting yourself or someone else to a particular amount of something
- limiting a thing or activity to a particular person, thing, or idea
- extending or generalizing something so that it affects more people or things

He now wants to __extend__ his law to all private and public buildings.

The American Psychoanalytic Association chose to __limit__ normal membership to licensed physicians.

In the case of *limit 6, ration,* and *restrict 1,* the noun group following the preposition is often an **amount**. This pattern is **V n to amount**. Where the noun group following the verb is a reflexive pronoun, the pattern is **V pron-refl to amount**.

When our children were young, viewing __was rationed__ to about three times a week.

He told him that an excess of sweeteners was aggravating his mother's condition and made him promise to see she __restricted__ herself to six a day.

broaden 2	generalize 2 (usu passive)	ration 2 (usu passive)
extend 8	limit 5,6,7	restrict 1,3,4
boil down VPP (usu passive)		

III.3 THE 'ATTACH' GROUP

These verbs are concerned with attaching, adding, or joining something to something else, either physically or metaphorically.

For your free safety check and tyre gauge, __affix__ two different numbered tokens to the coupon.

The lawyers argue that, by __attaching__ conditions to public arts funding, Congress suppresses freedom of expression.

Tendons are tough fibrous bands of elastic tissue which __connect__ muscles to the bone.

Another difference with this year's Williams car is that its engine __is coupled__ to a semi-automatic gearbox.

He ran a wire under his bedroom carpet and __soldered__ it to the telephone terminal so he could continue dialling into networks at other people's expense.

Security experts __wired up__ dozens of expensive plants to the main alarm system at his mansion.

In the case of *attach 2,4*, the noun group following the verb is often a reflexive pronoun. This pattern is **V pron-refl *to* n**.

This molecule __attaches__ itself to titanium atoms but not to carbon atoms.

add *1*	clamp *2*	knit *2*	stick *2.4*
affix *1*	clip *2*	lash *2*	tack *2*
annex *1*	connect *1,2,3*	link *4*	tape *7*
append *(usu passive)*	couple *5 (usu passive)*	padlock *2*	tether *3*
attach *1,2,4,5*	harness *4 (usu passive)*	rope *2*	tie *2*
bind *1*	hitch *3*	sew *1*	weld *1*
bolt *2*	hook *2*	shackle *1,2*	yoke *3*
chain *4*	join *5*	solder *1*	
connect up ▷*2*	link up *2 (usu passive)*	wire up ▷*3*	
hook up *1*	tack on		

III.4 THE 'ATTRACT' GROUP

These verbs are concerned with attracting someone to a person or thing. In the case of *attract* and *draw*, the noun group following the verb indicates the person who is attracted. In the case of *commend, endear,* and *recommend*, it indicates the thing that someone is attracted to. We include here *attract 5*, which involves one object attracting another object.

Financially, any company wants to __attract__ investors to something new.

In the case of *recommend*, the Subject always indicates a quality.

The qualities that __recommended__ him to the electorate – his apparent diffidence and lack of ambition – may make him vulnerable as prime minister.

In the case of *commend* and *endear*, the noun group following the verb is often a reflexive pronoun. This pattern is **V pron-refl *to* n**.

He is the kind of bluff, witty figure who __can endear__ himself to ordinary men and women.

attract *1,2,5*	commend *3*	endear
attract *3 (usu passive)*	draw *22*	recommend *3*

III.5 THE 'PREFER' AND 'SUBJUGATE' GROUP

These verbs are concerned with thinking of something as being better or worse than something else, or with acting as though something is more important than something else.

The modern executive woman has probably worked hard at __subjugating__ her maternal instinct to the pursuit of ambition and the extension of her intellectual capacity.

The preposition *to* is sometimes followed by an '-ing' clause. In the case of *prefer*, the noun group following the verb is sometimes replaced by an '-ing' clause as well.

The goalkeeper seemed to __prefer__ dribbling the ball up the field to defending his goal.

prefer	subjugate *2 (usu passive)*	subordinate *4*

III.6 THE 'BANISH' GROUP

These verbs are concerned with sending or taking someone or something to a place. We include here verbs concerned with allowing someone to enter a place or organisation.

The US Navy owns most of the island, and __has banished__ the inhabitants to a narrow central strip.

*When a reporter asked me how to find a cheap airfare to Boston, I ended up **directing** him to a cut-rate travel agent in San Bruno.*

*A cameraman **was plucked** to safety yesterday after being trapped for two days inside an active volcano.*

*He borrowed heavily to **send** his three sons to the best schools.*

admit 2,3 *(usu passive)*	**confine** 1	**pluck** 7 *(usu passive)*	**transfer** 1
admit 4	**confine** 3 *(usu passive)*	**refer** 4 *(usu passive)*	**transfer** 8 *(usu passive)*
assign 3 *(usu passive)*	**consign**	**refer** 6	**transplant** 3
banish 1	**deport**	**relegate** 1	
bring 9 *(usu passive)*	**direct** 9	**restrict** 3	
commit 6 *(usu passive)*	**extradite** *(usu passive)*	**send** 2,3	
bundle off	**pack off**	**take out** 2,3	

Many of the verbs in this group also have the pattern **V n *from* n *to* n**. The verb is followed by a noun group and two prepositional phrases, the first beginning with *from*, and the second beginning with *to*. The first prepositional phrase indicates the original location of the person or thing, and the second indicates where he, she, or it is sent or moved to. The passive pattern is **be V-ed *from* n *to* n**.

> *Twelve of the member countries in the league decided to **transfer** the organisation's headquarters from Tunisia to Cairo.*

III.7 THE 'APPOINT' GROUP

These verbs are concerned with appointing someone to a position, or with moving them from one job or role to another. We include here the verb *accredit*, which involves the recognition that someone has a particular job or position.

> *The proposal is seen as a compromise, following resistance within the police of an earlier plan to **appoint** graduates to senior police positions.*
>
> *He **was apprenticed** to a clock-maker in Wick and invented the first electric clock.*
>
> *Archbishop Tutu said: 'I am more convinced than ever that theologically and socially it is right to **ordain** women to the priesthood.'*

accredit 2 *(usu passive)*	**demote** 1,2	**promote** 3,4 *(usu passive)*	**relegate** 2 *(usu passive)*
appoint	**nominate** 2	**recall** 5	**transfer** 4,5
apprentice 2 *(usu passive)*	**ordain** 1	**recruit** 1	**upgrade** 2 *(usu passive)*

Many of the verbs in this group also have the pattern **V n *from* n *to* n**. The verb is followed by a noun group and two prepositional phrases, the first beginning with *from*, and the second beginning with *to*. The first prepositional phrase indicates the person's original position, and the second indicates their new position. The passive pattern is **be V-ed *from* n *to* n**.

> *Aston Villa **had** just **been relegated** from the First Division to the Second, but the new manager was able to lift them back.*

III.8 THE 'LEAD' GROUP

These verbs are concerned with leading someone somewhere metaphorically, for example to a point in the conversation or to a time in the past.

> *This **leads** me to my third point. Issues of control.*

bring 11	**lead** 1.15
take back 2.4	

III.9 THE 'BETRAY' GROUP

These verbs are concerned with telling people in authority that someone has done something wrong. The prepositional phrase indicates who the authority is. The implication is usually that the person referred to by the Subject betrays the other person by giving this information.

> The unnamed protagonist of the drama is a student on the run from his own revolutionary comrades, **having betrayed** them **to the police** under torture.

> My parents didn't talk to me because I **grassed** him **up to the police**.

In the case of *turn in*, the noun group following the verb is often a reflexive pronoun. This pattern is **V pron-refl P *to* n**.

> The third suspect **turned** himself **in** to the police department later that afternoon.

betray *2*	report *7*
denounce *2*	shop *5*
grass up ▷*4*	turn in *2*

III.10 THE 'INVITE' GROUP

These verbs are concerned with inviting someone to take part in something.

> She **invited** us **to a lavish party** to celebrate her fiftieth birthday.

ask *7*	challenge *5*	invite *1*

III.11 THE 'ALERT' AND 'BLIND' GROUP

These verbs are concerned with changing someone's awareness of or attitude to a situation. This includes:

- making someone aware of something e.g. *awaken, sensitize*
- blinding or desensitizing someone to something e.g. *blind, inure*
- adapting yourself to something e.g. *acclimatize, accustom*
- resigning yourself to a situation e.g. *reconcile, resign*

> He stopped for a moment to try to **adjust** his vision **to the faint starlight** of the night.

> In the old days he would have been executed for failing to **alert** the army **to the ambush**, but the colonel was not in a mood to add blood to blood.

> His quest to get to the bottom of each case **may have blinded** him **to the practicalities** of getting the best deal for the hapless victims.

The preposition *to* is sometimes followed by an '-ing' clause.

> After that night almost a year earlier, she **had reconciled** herself **to never seeing** him **again**, and after Sophie's birth, she had stopped wanting to see him.

In the case of *acclimatize, accommodate, accustom, adapt 1, adjust, desensitize, reconcile*, and *resign*, the noun group following the verb is always or often a reflexive pronoun. This pattern is **V pron-refl *to* n**.

> It takes time to **acclimatize** yourself **to retirement**.

> He was using his relaxation sessions to **desensitize** himself **to the trauma of his journey**.

acclimatize	adjust *1*	desensitize	sensitize *1*
accommodate *5*	alert *4*	inure	
accustom	awaken *2*	reconcile *4*	
adapt *1,2*	blind *5*	resign *2*	

III.12 THE 'INCITE' GROUP

These verbs are concerned with putting someone or something in a particular state, or making them behave in a particular way.

> The party agreed not to threaten armed action, to train its soldiers inside the country, or to **incite** its supporters **to** violence.

> There is enough evidence to suggest that factors such as personality, attitude and moral sense **predispose** some individuals **to** criminal behaviour.

> The presence of a committed fifth member **has spurred** the band **on** to their most adventurous effort to date.

The preposition *to* is sometimes followed by an '-ing' clause.

> In some areas, the UN team found that communities **were reduced to** eating wild plants and had access only to very limited supplies of water.

In the case of *work up*, the noun group following the verb is always a reflexive pronoun. This pattern is **V pron-refl P *to* n**.

> He **had worked** himself **up** to such a pitch of indignation that he had to tell me the whole story.

drive *13,14*	incline *1*	move *9,14*	reduce *3 (usu passive)*
incite	lull *3*	predispose *1,2*	rouse *3 (usu passive)*
bring round *2*	spur on ▷*1*		
put up *VPP*	work up *1*		

III.13 THE 'CONDEMN' GROUP

These verbs are concerned with making someone experience something unpleasant.

> The main aim must be to find these children families and **not condemn** them **to** institutions.

In the case of *put*, the prepositional phrase is always *to death*.

> Looking back over the recently ended holocaust, Voltaire claimed that one hundred thousand witches **had been put to death.**

In the case of *subject*, the noun group following the verb is often a reflexive pronoun. This pattern is **V pron-refl *to* n**.

> White, not content to train his mind, **has** also **subjected** himself **to** a strict diet.

condemn *2 (usu passive)*	doom *3*	sentence *3*
condemn *3*	put *3*	subject *9*

III.14 THE 'BEAT TO DEATH' GROUP

These verbs are concerned with:

- ways of injuring or killing someone
- ways of affecting someone very strongly e.g. *bore, frighten*

The verbs concerned with killing or injuring are usually used in the passive. With these verbs, the most frequent prepositional phrase that occurs is *to death*. The verb *bore* also occurs with the prepositional phrase *to tears*.

This is a very productive use: any verb involving injuring or killing can be used with this pattern. The verbs listed here are the ones which are most frequently used in this way.

> A subsequent investigation revealed the two men **had been beaten to death.**

> I wish Alex would take me out, but I'm afraid I **bore** him **to death.**

*Campaigners working on behalf of the family of a man who **was crushed** to death by a police car are furious that the officers involved are still on duty.*

In the case of *drink*, the noun group following the verb is always a reflexive pronoun. This pattern is **V pron-refl *to* n**. The verb *starve* often has this pattern as well.

*He is now on the third day of his hunger strike. He says he **will starve** himself to death unless his activists are released from prison.*

batter 2 *(usu passive)*	**choke** 2 *(usu passive)*	**gore** 1 *(usu passive)*	**shoot** 1 *(usu passive)*
beat 1 *(usu passive)*	**club** 7 *(usu passive)*	**kick** 1 *(usu passive)*	**spear** 2 *(usu passive)*
blast 4 *(usu passive)*	**crush** 4 *(usu passive)*	**knife** 3	**stab** 1 *(usu passive)*
bore 2	**drink** 2	**peck** 1	**starve** 2
burn 7 *(usu passive)*	**frighten** 2	**scare** 1	**torture** 1 *(usu passive)*

III.15 THE 'DRAW ATTENTION' GROUP

These verbs are concerned with directing your own or someone else's attention to something or someone.

*I'm dipping into the culture, pointing a finger, **directing** attention to what's there.*

*I want to **draw** your attention once again to the opportunity of borrowing from individual investors.*

*We **have given** some thought to the problem of motor traffic, which is clearly one of the biggest sources of pollution.*

The preposition *to* is sometimes followed by an '-ing' clause.

*Landscape painting finally became a subject in its own right and great artists began to **turn** their undivided attention to developing this form of painting.*

direct 7	**give** 1.9	**turn** 12
divert 4	**pay** 11	
draw 19	**switch** 3	

Many of the verbs in this group also have the pattern **V n *from* n *to* n**. The verb is followed by a noun group and two prepositional phrases, the first beginning with *from*, and the second beginning with *to*. The first prepositional phrase indicates where the person's attention was orginally focused, and the second indicates its new focus.

*One thing the Democrats have to do is to **switch** people's attention from the Gulf to the economy and domestic problems.*

III.16 THE 'POSTPONE' GROUP

These verbs are concerned with postponing or rescheduling something to a particular time or date.

*If I don't use all my holiday allowance one year, **can** I **carry** it **over** to the next year?*

*The date for price reform **has been postponed** to January 2nd – it was actually supposed to happen this month.*

*The Alton Water Junior Championships **has been rescheduled** to Saturday, October 2.*

backdate	**postpone** *(usu passive)*	**reschedule** 1
carry over	**put back** *(usu passive)*	**put off** 1

The verb *postpone* also has the pattern **V n *until* n**. The passive pattern is **be V-ed *until* n**. The phrasal verbs *put back* and *put off* have the patterns **V n P *until* n**, **V P n (not pron) *until* n**, and **be V-ed P *until* n**.

*The album was originally due out before Christmas but **has** now **been put back** until the beginning of next year.*

III.17 THE 'CREDIT' GROUP

These verbs are concerned with charging, crediting, or debiting something to a bank account.

> *The preferential overdraft is only available to young workers who **credit** their salary to their Maxim account.*

charge *2*	credit *3*	debit *1*

III.18 THE 'CONVERT' GROUP

These verbs are concerned with changing the condition or circumstances of someone or something in some way. The prepositional phrase indicates the nature of the change or the new condition or circumstances.

> *As he **braked** the car to a halt, he became aware that something was in the vehicle with him.*
> *We trudged back through the snow, which was filtering down over the top of my boots and **chilling** my legs to the bone.*
> *He **was converted** to Christianity and renounced his wealth.*
> *Villages and farms **were razed** to the ground.*
> *In his songs he **set** poetic texts to music.*

brake *2*	elevate *2*	relegate *1*	tune *5 (usu passive)*
chill *3*	grind *3*	restore *2*	
convert *3,5,7*	raze *(usu passive)*	set *2.21*	
turn over *VPP*			

III.19 VERBS WITH OTHER MEANINGS

There are many other verbs which have this structure.

> *Gently **apply** the cream to the affected areas.*
> *Under the blueprint to be implemented from October, the area around the famous monuments **will be barred** to all tourist vehicles*
> *I **had to** decide very quickly what was significant and **commit** it to paper.*
> *The guidebooks **devoted** a paragraph or two to the subject.*
> *What **have** they **done** to Sam's hair?*
> *At worst, wearing a helmet **may expose** cyclists to greater danger, says Doctor Hillman.*
> *I'**m going to hold** you to your promise, so don't you forget.*
> *This is not the first time the work of the grand jury has become public, even though members **are sworn** to secrecy about the proceedings.*

In the case of *draw up, help, lower,* and *treat,* the noun group following the verb is always or often a reflexive pronoun. This pattern is **V pron-refl *to* n,** or in the case of *draw up,* **V pron-refl P *to* n.**

> *He **drew** himself **up** to his full height.*
> ***Do help** yourself to another drink.*

In the case of *leave 7,* the noun group following the preposition is always a reflexive pronoun. This pattern is **V n *to* pron-refl.**

> *The giant panda **is** never **left** to himself. People keep making him get on jets and meet eligible young females.*

In the case of *leave 16* and *mean 1.3,* the noun group following the verb is always an **amount.** This pattern is **V amount *to* n.**

Our mothers' approval __means__ a lot to us.

apply *4,6*	**devote** *2*	**(not) lower** *7*	**stretch** *5 (usu passive)*
apply *5 (usu passive)*	**do** *2.6,8*	**get married** *1*	**swear** *4 (usu passive)*
bar *10 (usu passive)*	**expose** *3,4*	**mean** *1.3*	**tailor** *2*
beat *9*	**help** *7,8*	**mould** *5*	**trace** *1,2*
be born *1*	**hold** *3.16*	**pip** *2*	**transfer** *1*
commit *8*	**introduce** *2*	**refer** *5,8*	**treat** *4*
date *2*	**leave** *7,15,16,18*	**sacrifice** *2*	
draw up *3*	**make up** *VPP*	**pin down** *1,2*	
hold up *5.5 (usu passive)*	**open up** *2*	**trace back** ▷*1*	

Structure information: Verb with Object and Adjunct

a) The noun group following the verb is the Object, and the prepositional phrase is an Adjunct.

b) This structure has a passive, with the pattern *be* **V-ed** *to* **n**. The prepositional phrase is an Adjunct.

c) Though the prepositional phrase in this structure usually comes after the noun group, it sometimes comes before it, especially when the noun group is a long one.

You authorise us to __debit__ to your account any applicable premium or charge.

d) Phrasal verb patterns are the same except that there is also a particle, P. The Object comes either between the verb and the particle, or after the particle. If the verb comes after the particle, it cannot be a personal pronoun. You say

I __packed__ them __off__ to school
or *I __packed off__ the children to school*

but you do not say *I packed off them to school.*

Other related patterns

V n adv *to* amount

The verb is followed by a noun group, the adverb *down, off,* or *up,* and a prepositional phrase which consists of the preposition *to* and an **amount**.

The latter is the money left over when dividends __are rounded__ down to the nearest five cents.

round *4.2*

V n *from* n *to* n

See Structure II and meaning groups III.6, 7, and 15 above.

V n *until* n

See meaning group III.16 above.

25 V n *towards/toward* n

The verb is followed by a noun group and a prepositional phrase which consists of *towards* or *toward* and a noun group. With some verbs, the preposition is sometimes followed by an '-ing' clause. The passive pattern is *be* V-ed *towards/toward* n.

This pattern has one structure:

▶ Verb with Object and Adjunct
She is now directing her talents towards music.

Active voice: V n *towards/toward* n/-ing

	Verb group	noun group	*towards/toward*	noun group/-ing clause
Subject	Verb	Object	Adjunct	
They	contributed	$3	toward	costs.
He	directed	his efforts	towards	helping people.

Passive voice: *be* V-ed *towards/toward* n/-ing

	Verb group	*towards/toward*	noun group/-ing clause
Subject	Verb	Adjunct	
We	are drawn	towards	a life of simplicity.
The savings	were put	towards	reducing the deficit.

Verbs with this pattern belong to the following meaning groups:

1 THE 'DIRECT' GROUP
2 THE 'PUSH' GROUP
3 THE 'CONTRIBUTE' GROUP
4 VERBS WITH OTHER MEANINGS

1 THE 'DIRECT' GROUP

These verbs are concerned with aiming something at someone or something, usually metaphorically.

This show __is geared__ towards younger viewers.

The preposition *towards* is sometimes followed by an '-ing' clause.

Planning __is__ therefore largely __directed__ towards improving or preserving existing living conditions.

---

direct 6   direct 7,8 *(usu passive)*   gear 6 *(usu passive)*

---

2 THE 'PUSH' GROUP

These verbs are concerned with causing someone to do something, be attracted to something, or have a particular opinion.

O'Keeffe __was drawn__ towards art from an early age.

This, coupled with his wife's death, __pushed__ him towards resignation in 1983.

| draw 22 *(usu passive)* | incline 1 | push 6 |

3 THE 'CONTRIBUTE' GROUP

These verbs are concerned with providing part of a sum of money. The prepositional phrase indicates what the money has been or will be spent on.

*The money will come in very handy. I'__ll__ spend it on the house or **put** it towards a holiday.*

The preposition *towards* is sometimes followed by an '-ing' clause.

Any spare money __is put__ towards buying a flock of sheep.

The noun group following the verb is often an **amount**. This pattern is **V amount towards/toward** n.

The City of Paris is to __contribute__ nine million dollars towards the cost of the French challenger for the Americas Cup.

| contribute 2 | put 7 |

4 VERBS WITH OTHER MEANINGS

There is one other verb which has this pattern.

He __feels__ no bitterness towards the British.

| feel 1 |

Structure information

a) The noun group following the verb is the Object, and the prepositional phrase is an Adjunct.

b) This structure has a passive, with the pattern *be* **V-ed** *towards/toward* n. The prepositional phrase is an Adjunct.

26 V n *with* n

The verb is followed by a noun group and a prepositional phrase which consists of *with* and a noun group. With some verbs, the preposition is sometimes followed by an '-ing' clause. The passive pattern is *be* V-ed *with* n.

This pattern has two structures:

▶ Structure I: Verb with Object and prepositional Object
  He __has confused__ fact with fiction.
▶ Structure II: Verb with Object and Adjunct
  They __covered__ the walls with wallpaper.

Structure I: Verb with Object and prepositional Object

Active voice: V n *with* n

	Verb group	noun group	*with*	noun group
Subject	**Verb**	**Object**		**prepositional Object**
	Blend	the spinach	with	the egg yolks.
Many people	confuse	a severe cold	with	flu.
You	can intersperse	periods of running	with	periods of walking.

Passive voice: *be* V-ed *with* n

	Verb group	*with*	noun group
Subject	**Verb**		**prepositional Object**
Education	is correlated	with	income.
The offer	was coupled	with	a warning.

Phrasal verbs

Active voice: V n P *with* n, V P n (not pron) *with* n

	Verb group	noun group	Particle	*with*	noun group
Subject	**Verb...**	**Object**	**...Verb**		**prepositional Object**
He	has muddled	me	up	with	Ian Ogilvy.
She	paired	me	off	with	her brother.

	Verb group	Particle	noun group	*with*	noun group
Subject	**Verb**		**Object**		**prepositional Object**
He	matches	up	the descriptions	with	the actual places.
The book	muddles	up	real characters	with	invented ones.

Passive voice: *be* V-ed P *with* n

	Verb group	Particle	*with*	noun group
Subject	**Verb**			**prepositional Object**
Europe	cannot be lumped	together	with	the US.
Their sons	had been paired	up	with	unsuitable women.

Verbs with this structure belong to the following meaning groups:

I.1   THE 'COMPARE' GROUP
I.2   THE 'COMBINE' GROUP
I.3   THE 'ALTERNATE' GROUP
I.4   THE 'JUXTAPOSE' GROUP
I.5   VERBS WITH OTHER MEANINGS

I.1 THE 'COMPARE' GROUP

These verbs are concerned with considering two people, things, or groups as being the same or different, or with treating them as if they were the same or different.

*Once you've defined what you want to be, you'll need to **compare** yourself **with the competition** to determine your strengths and weaknesses.*

*Many of these buildings are excellent, but they **have been** condemned and **lumped together with the worst and most unpopular examples of the modern movement**.*

*I **couldn't square** what I was doing **with the view of the world I have tried to transmit to my son**.*

The preposition *with* is sometimes followed by an '-ing' clause. Also, the verb is sometimes followed by an '-ing' clause instead of a noun group.

*Again and again, we seem to **confuse** talking about an issue **with doing something about it**.*

associate *1*	confuse *1*	dovetail *1*	pair *4 (usu passive)*
balance *3*	connect *7*	equate	reconcile *1*
bracket *3 (usu passive)*	contrast *5*	identify *6*	square *8*
compare *1*	correlate *1 (usu passive)*	link *2,7*	
conflate	correlate *2*	match *5*	
lump together *(usu passive)*	mix up *1*		
match up *▷5*	muddle up *2*		

I.2 THE 'COMBINE' GROUP

These verbs are concerned with joining or mixing two or more things, physically or metaphorically.

*Try to **combine** career and financial aspirations **with spiritual values**.*

*The most interesting programmes, however, are those that try to **fuse** technology **with culture**.*

*In this context, the question of crime **is interlinked with the question of human rights**.*

*You can treat coco-peat in exactly the same way as you would treat ordinary peat. So you **can mix** it **up with fertiliser** and use it for potting.*

*My husband **is** constantly **thrown together with young people** through his work.*

In the case of *combine*, *link*, and *mix*, the preposition *with* is sometimes followed by an '-ing' clause. Also, the verb is sometimes followed by an '-ing' clause instead of a noun group.

*Singer Eileen manages to **combine** shimmying across the stage **with sending her voice soaring up to heaven**.*

amalgamate	couple *4 (usu passive)*	integrate *1,2*	link *4*
blend *1,2*	cross-breed *1*	interconnect	merge *1*
bond *2,6*	entangle *1,2*	interface *4*	mesh *2*
combine *1,2,3,4,5*	entwine *1*	interlink *(usu passive)*	mix *1,5*
conjoin	fuse *4,5*	intertwine *1*	unify
connect *4,8*	hybridize	interweave	
mix up *2*	pair up	tie in *VPP*	
pair off	throw together *2*		

I.3 THE 'ALTERNATE' GROUP

These verbs are concerned with doing two or more things alternately.

*The meetings were organized to **alternate** a speaker with an open meeting.*

*Originally the intention was to **intersperse** the historical scenes with modern ones.*

*The cooking sessions **are punctuated** with visits to bakeries, chocolate makers, farms and markets.*

In the case of *alternate* and *juggle*, the preposition *with* is sometimes followed by an '-ing' clause.

*Leslie has managed to **juggle** a successful career with bringing up Joseph, 5, and Max, 21 months.*

alternate *1*	intersperse	punctuate *(usu passive)*
intercut	juggle *1*	

I.4 THE 'JUXTAPOSE' GROUP

These verbs are concerned with placing two people, ideas, words, or things together, either physically or in an abstract way. We include here *synchronize*, which indicates that two activities are done at the same time.

*This book neatly **juxtaposes** Van Gogh's letters with his paintings.*

*The camera's shutter mechanism means that flash **can be synchronised** with the camera at any shutter speed.*

juxtapose	partner *5 (usu passive)*	synchronize
match *3*	rhyme *1*	twin *4 (usu passive)*
line up *3*	match up ▷*3*	

I.5 VERBS WITH OTHER MEANINGS

There are three other verbs which have this structure.

*He **was reconciled** with his wife and daughters in his final illness.*

In the case of *ally* and *associate*, the noun group following the verb is always a reflexive pronoun. This pattern is **V pron-refl with n**.

*He **can** swallow his pride and **ally** himself with his political enemies.*

ally *4*	associate *2*	reconcile *2,3*

Structure information: Verb with Object and prepositional Object

a) The noun group following the verb is the Object, and the prepositional phrase is the prepositional Object.

b) This structure has a passive, with the pattern **be V-ed with n**. The prepositional phrase is the prepositional Object.

c) Phrasal verb patterns are the same except that there is also a particle, P. The Object comes either between the verb and the particle, or after the particle. If the Object comes after the particle, it cannot be a personal pronoun. You say

They **mixed** them **up** with someone else's
or They **mixed up** my results with someone else's

but you do not say *They mixed up them with someone else's.*

Structure II: Verb with Object and Adjunct

Active voice: V n *with* n/-ing

	Verb group	noun group	*with*	noun group/-ing clause
Subject	Verb	Object		Adjunct
I	console	myself	with	writing up my notes.
You	can exchange	information	with	other computer users.
He	plays	football	with	the staff.

Passive voice: *be* V-ed *with* n

	Verb group	*with*	noun group
Subject	Verb		Adjunct
The paper	will be printed	with	your own name.
A deal	has been struck	with	the authorities.

Phrasal verbs

Active voice: V n P *with* n, V P n (not pron) *with* n

	Verb group	noun group	Particle	*with*	noun group
Subject	Verb...	Object	...Verb		Adjunct
She	patched	things	up	with	her son.
They	are taking	the matter	up	with	the school.

	Verb group	Particle	noun group	*with*	noun group
Subject	Verb		Object		Adjunct
We	load	up	the car	with	guns.
Stock	up		your cupboard	with	tins of tomatoes.

Passive voice: *be* V-ed P *with* n

	Verb group	Particle	*with*	noun group
Subject	Verb			Adjunct
The products	are padded	out	with	fat and water.
They	were weighed	down	with	serious debts.

Verbs with this structure belong to the following meaning groups:

Chapter 4: Complex Patterns with Prepositions and Adverbs

II.1 THE 'PROVIDE' GROUP

These verbs are concerned with giving something to someone or something. The prepositional phrase indicates the thing that is given. This includes:

- supplying someone with something that they want or need e.g. *arm, provide*
- giving someone too much of something, or something they do not want e.g. *deluge, land*
- giving someone something that is not what is needed e.g. *fob off, palm off*
- giving a particular kind of thing, or giving in a particular way e.g. *dose, inject*
- showing approval of someone by giving them something or doing them a service e.g. *honour, oblige*

*Old ladies have to like their companions, because they **entrust** **them with their jewels and their personal mail and stuff**.*

*Any individual who incites another to commit murder, who **furnishes** **him with the lethal weapon to kill someone**, is guilty of the crime as much as the killer is.*

*The government planned to **honour** **him with a brass band concert in his garden**.*

*The scientists decided to **inject** **the chimpanzees with a strong dose of live HIV**.*

*Too many solicitors are failing to give their clients a clear idea of their charges – until they **land** **them with a huge bill**.*

*Joseph Smith made sure that he **was** never **palmed off** **with inferior stuff**.*

*Many additives help to **provide** **us with good and safe food**.*

arm *2.2,3*	fix *3*	lavish *3*	regale
deluge *2 (usu passive)*	furnish *2*	leave *5,9*	saddle *5*
dope *2*	honour *6*	lumber *VP (usu passive)*	serve *9*
dose *3*	infect *1*	mail *3*	supply *1*
endow *2*	inject *1*	oblige *2*	treat *2*
entrust	inundate *1*	outfit *3*	vest *3 (usu passive)*
equip *1,2*	invest *6*	ply *1,2*	
feed *1,8*	issue *5 (usu passive)*	present *4.1,2,4*	
fit *6*	land *10*	provide *1*	
dose up ▷*3*	fob off *(usu passive)*	palm off *0,VPP (usu passive)*	
fit out	kit out *(usu passive)*		
fix up *3*	load down		

II.2 THE 'IMBUE' GROUP

These verbs are concerned with giving someone or something a quality, feeling, or idea. The prepositional phrase indicates the quality, feeling, or idea.

*If evolution **has endowed** **us with rich and different personalities**, that is probably because such diversity was once good for our survival.*

*He spent a lot of time amongst actors trying to **imbue** **them with a radical spirit**.*

endow 1 *(usu passive)*	**imbue**	**infuse** 1
fire 1.8 *(usu passive)*	**infect** 3	**invest** 5 *(usu passive)*

II.3 THE 'AGREE' GROUP

These verbs are concerned with doing something jointly with another person. The prepositional phrase indicates the other person involved. This includes:

- arguing or negotiating with someone e.g. *agree, conclude, fight, negotiate*
- playing a game with someone
- sharing things with someone
- taking joint responsibility with someone e.g. *co-author*

All the verbs in this group are **reciprocal verbs** or **ergative reciprocal verbs** (see Chapter 6 and Chapter 8).

*The university might acquire some more property if it **can agree** a deal with the city council.*

*Alien scientists were transmitting messages to **establish** contact with other beings.*

*Further talks **are being held** with the protest leaders.*

*Many prefer to **talk** these issues **through** with a careers adviser or close friend.*

agree 3	**conclude** 4	**finalize**	**renew** 2
argue 4	**debate** 3	**forge** 1	**reopen** 3,4
bandy	**dispute** 3	**hold** 2.6	**share** 2,3,4,6
clinch 1	**establish** 2	**negotiate** 1	**strike** 13
clink	**exchange** 1	**normalize** 2	**swap** 1
co-author 2	**fight** 3	**play** 2	**trade** 5,6,7
patch up 1	**talk over**	**talk through** 1	

II.4 THE 'SHARE' GROUP

These verbs are concerned with talking or doing something with someone, but unlike the previous group they are not reciprocal verbs. The activity is not mutual, and only the person indicated by the Subject is responsible for what is done.

*But who would choose to **pick** a fight **with this man**?*

*Yvonne was delighted with her prize and plans to **share** her payout **with daughter-in-law Eileen**.*

*Some parents have had success by **taking** the matter **up** with the school.*

In the case of *ingratiate*, the noun group following the verb is always a reflexive pronoun. This pattern is **V pron-refl** *with* n.

*This is the sorry sight of someone trying to **ingratiate** himself with everyone.*

check 1	**ingratiate**	**share** 7,8
cross-check	**pick** 6	**square** 9
take up 2.2		

II.5 THE 'DECORATE' GROUP

These verbs are concerned with changing the appearance of something by adding things to it. This includes:

- putting a decoration on something e.g. *decorate, garland*
- putting a mark on something e.g. *brush, daub, smear*
- cutting or printing the surface of something e.g. *etch, imprint*

The prepositional phrase indicates the additions made.

Their blood was used to __daub__ the walls with slogans.

The wall facing him __was decorated__ with elaborate dark wood carvings.

Each photo __is__ automatically __printed__ with the date on which it was taken.

accessorize	etch *1 (usu passive)*	print *3,5 (usu passive)*
brush *3*	festoon *(usu passive)*	smear *1*
dab *1*	frame *8*	spread *3*
daub	furnish *1*	stamp *3*
deck *5*	garland *2 (usu passive)*	stencil *2*
decorate *1*	girdle *2 (usu passive)*	streak *2 (usu passive)*
drape *2*	grace *5 (usu passive)*	thread *7*
embellish *1 (usu passive)*	hang *4 (usu passive)*	trim *5 (usu passive)*
embroider *1 (usu passive)*	imprint *4 (usu passive)*	wreathe *2 (usu passive)*
engrave *(usu passive)*	mark *4*	

Some of the verbs in this group also occur in the pattern **V n prep/adv**, where the prepositional phrase or adverb indicates where the addition is put. Examples of both patterns are *We draped the walls with banners* and *We draped banners across the walls*. The verbs in this meaning group with these two patterns are: *dab, daub, drape, hang, smear, spread*, and *thread*. See pages 313-314.

II.6 THE 'COVER' GROUP

These verbs are concerned with putting something around or on top of something, or with covering the surface of something, physically or metaphorically. We also include here *line*, which indicates that the inside surface of something is covered.

In the middle of the table, which __was covered__ with a starched, lace-edged cloth, stood a large bowl of jelly.

Every reform __was hedged about__ with pages of rules.

The polished floorboards __are overlaid__ with old rugs.

The main method for treating waste on site is to __top__ it __with an impermeable cap__.

In the case of *surround 4*, the noun group following the verb is always a reflexive pronoun. This pattern is **V pron-refl with n**.

Her technique was to __surround__ herself with strong women and weak men.

cap *9*	cover *3 (usu passive)*	overlay *1,3 (usu passive)*	top *14*
carpet *4 (usu passive)*	douse *2*	plaster *3*	wrap *1*
coat *3*	encase	slather	
cover *1,4*	line *33*	surround *1,2,4*	
hedge about *(usu passive)*	wrap up ▷*1*		

The verbs *plaster* and *slather* also occur in the pattern **V n prep/adv**, where the prepositional phrase or adverb indicates where the addition is put (see pages 313-314).

II.7 THE 'FILL' GROUP

These verbs are concerned with filling something, physically or metaphorically. The prepositional phrase indicates the things that are put into the container or other thing that is filled.

The third drawer __was cluttered__ with an assortment of unconnected items.

When we are at the sea we tend to breathe more deeply to __fill__ our lungs with fresh air.

Then it was time to pack the bags, __load up__ the vehicles with bikes and trophies, and make for the airport.

The air in these caves __is saturated__ with water vapour.

In the case of *fill 10* and *stuff 4*, the noun group following the verb is always a reflexive pronoun. This pattern is **V pron-refl *with* n**. The phrasal verb *fill up* has the pattern **V pron-refl P *with* n**.

> *When your life is filled with interesting activities, you won't need to <u>fill yourself up</u> with food.*

choke 3 *(usu passive)*	**flood** 6	**pack** 10	**stuff** 3,4
clutter 2 *(usu passive)*	**glut** 2 *(usu passive)*	**pile** 4 *(usu passive)*	**suffuse** 2 *(usu passive)*
cram 1	**impregnate** 1	**saturate** 1 *(usu passive)*	
encumber 2 *(usu passive)*	**load** 1,6	**soak** 2	
fill 1,3,4,5,6,10	**overload** 2	**stack** 4	
clutter up ▷2	**fill up** 1	**load up** ▷1	

Some of the verbs in this group also occur in the pattern **V n prep/adv**, where the prepositional phrase or adverb indicates where the things are put. Examples of both patterns are *He loaded the van with cartons* and *He loaded cartons into the van*. The verbs in this meaning group with these two patterns are: *cram, load, pile,* and *stuff*. See page 313.

II.8 THE 'FLAVOUR' GROUP

These verbs are concerned with adding a small or measured amount of something into or on to something, physically or metaphorically. The prepositional phrase indicates the thing that is added.

> *Prepare the custard and <u>flavour</u> it with orange-flower water.*

> *Compiled by perfume expert Sheila Pickles, the book <u>is scented</u> with Elizabethan Rose fragrance.*

> *Each camel trainer has his own ideas about what else to add, and <u>may supplement</u> this diet with honey, date seeds, lemons, local plants, and spices.*

> *The seriousness of the president's economic message <u>was tempered</u> with a few light moments.*

dilute 1	**fortify** 2 *(usu passive)*	**perfume** 4	**spice** 2
drizzle 3	**lace** 4,5	**perfume** 5 *(usu passive)*	**supplement** 1
dust 5	**lard** 2,3	**scent** 2	**sweeten** 1,2
flavour 3	**leaven** 1	**season** 8	**temper** 3
pad out			

II.9 THE 'SHOWER' GROUP

These verbs are concerned with scattering objects or a liquid around a place. The prepositional phrase indicates the objects or liquid.

> *Outside, the road <u>was peppered</u> with glass.*

> *He will be disfigured for life after <u>being showered</u> with blazing petrol.*

> *I would far rather have weeds in my garden than <u>strew</u> the ground with bark or coconut shell chips.*

pepper 4 *(usu passive)*	**spatter**	**spray** 3,4,5	**sprinkle** 2 *(usu passive)*
shower 8 *(usu passive)*	**splash** 2	**spray** 6 *(usu passive)*	**squirt** 2
shower 9	**splatter**	**sprinkle** 1	**strew**

Some of the verbs in this group also occur in the pattern **V n prep/adv**, where the prepositional phrase or adverb indicates where the thing is scattered. Examples of both patterns are *I splashed my face with water* and *I splashed water on my face*. The verbs in this meaning group with these two patterns are: *spatter, splash, spray, sprinkle,* and *strew*. See pages 313-314.

II.10 THE 'POPULATE' AND 'STOCK' GROUP

These verbs are concerned with providing or populating a place with people or things.

*It seemed to **be** entirely **peopled** with men and women in blue or green suits.*

*His style is typical of the ruling families who **populate** the foreign ministry with their offspring.*

*Most fields **have been sown** with rye grass or abandoned to thistles.*

*She **stocked** her little cupboard with biscuits and snacks.*

people 4,5 *(usu passive)*	**restock** 1,2	**stock** 5
plant 3	**sow** 1.1 *(usu passive)*	
populate 2	**staff** 3 *(usu passive)*	
stock up 5		

II.11 THE 'GREET' GROUP

These verbs are concerned with thinking about or reacting towards something or someone in a particular way.

*She tried to **fix** me with an honest gaze.*

*First published in France some time ago, the novel **was greeted** with considerable acclaim.*

*I asked them to **treat** me with respect.*

*Any newcomers **are** always **viewed** with suspicion.*

acknowledge 5	**fix** 8	**meet** 8	**treat** 1
answer 11	**greet** 2 *(usu passive)*	**regard** 2,3	**view** 3

II.12 THE 'BORE' GROUP

These verbs are concerned with giving someone a particular feeling or telling them something that makes them feel a particular way. The prepositional phrase indicates the cause of the feeling. We include here *acquaint* and *familiarize*, which indicate only that someone is told something; *face*, which indicates that someone is forced to think about something; and *confront*, which indicates that someone is accused of something.

This is a productive use: any verb which involves making someone think or feel something can be used with this pattern. The verbs listed here are the ones which are most frequently used in this way.

*The salesmen did everything they could to **acquaint** the clerks with the details of their products.*

*I **won't bore** you with private matters.*

*I pulled on a coat and boots and went round right away to **confront** Muriel with her stupidity and cowardice.*

In the case of *console*, *content*, and *familiarize*, the noun group following the verb is always or often a reflexive pronoun. This pattern is **V pron-refl with n**.

*I think it's extremely important nowadays to **familiarize** oneself with computers.*

In the case of *console* and *content*, the preposition *with* is sometimes followed by an '-ing' clause.

*Amy wanted to run round the table and hug her sister, but she **contented** herself with squeezing her fingers.*

acquaint	confront 5	face 2.5	tempt 1
amaze	console 1	familiarize	traumatize
bore 1	content 3	strike 12 (usu passive)	
bother 5	dazzle 1	surprise 4	
burden 3	excite 3	tantalize	

II.13 THE 'BESET' GROUP

These verbs indicate that someone has problems. The prepositional phrase indicates the problem.

> The oil and gas industries **_are beset_ with labour production problems**.

> I **_was racked_ with envy and then guilt for feeling jealous**.

In the case of *confront* and *face*, the preposition *with* is sometimes followed by an '-ing' clause.

> In a country where it was the norm to combine family and career, women **are** suddenly **_being confronted_ with making a choice – working or staying at home to take care of the kids**.

> In 1955 my wife and I **_were faced_ with making the journey from Birmingham to the Isle of Wight** following our wedding.

barrage 3 (usu passive)	**confront** 1 (usu passive)	**face** 2.4 (usu passive)
beset (usu passive)	**encumber** 1 (usu passive)	**rack** 2 (usu passive)
weigh down 2 (usu passive)		

II.14 THE 'BUSY' GROUP

These verbs are concerned with spending your time or energy doing something. The noun group following the verb is always a reflexive pronoun, and the pattern is **V pron-refl *with* n**.

> The other women **_occupied_ themselves with their perpetual sewing**.

> Why **_trouble_ yourself with small details**?

The preposition *with* is sometimes followed by an '-ing' clause.

> She snapped on the lights and **_busied_ herself with preparing a quick dinner**.

busy 4	**occupy** 5
concern 7	**trouble** 10
be taken up VPP2	

II.15 THE 'BE BORN' GROUP

These verbs are concerned with having an illness or handicap. The prepositional phrase indicates the illness or handicap.

> Wilson **_has been afflicted_ with knee trouble**.

> I **_was born_ with cerebral palsy**.

> He **has** just **_been diagnosed_ with leukaemia**.

afflict (usu passive)	**be born** 2	**diagnose** (usu passive)
lay up (usu passive)		

II.16 THE 'BEGIN' AND 'END' GROUP

These verbs are concerned with beginning or ending a period of time or an event in a particular way.

*He **began** the day with a seven o'clock breakfast.*

*Then he **closes** the show with a simple line, 'Shane, we love you,' and walks offstage.*

*In 1950, Butler **crowned** an impressive career with victory in the national 24-hour championship.*

*You may want to **end** the session with a hug.*

begin *3*	crown *11*	finish *4*	start *2*
close *2.7*	end *6*	open *21*	

II.17 THE 'FOLLOW' GROUP

These verbs are concerned with arranging two things so that one comes before or after the other.

*He **followed** college with a few months in Hollywood.*

*It's about time he started **following** his big words **up** with actions.*

*Each section **is prefaced** with a clear introductory essay by one of the editors.*

follow *5*	preface *2*	be prefixed
follow up ▷*5*		

II.18 THE 'REPLACE' GROUP

These verbs are concerned with exchanging one person or thing for another.

*Red meat **can be interchanged** with cheese, eggs, and pulses as a source of protein.*

*They now seem to be setting out to **replace** the people with robots.*

In the case of *interchange* and *replace 2*, the preposition *with* is sometimes followed by an '-ing' clause.

*His balance was good enough to eliminate the usual exercise programme and **replace** it with walking up and down hill.*

interchange *2*	replace *1 (usu passive)*	replace *2*

II.19 THE 'HELP' GROUP

These verbs are concerned with helping someone. The prepositional phrase indicates what the help relates to.

*You **might be able to help** us with a problem.*

*I opened the door, gave her a sympathetic smile, and **helped** her **off** with her coat.*

In the case of *assist* and *help*, the preposition *with* is sometimes followed by an '-ing' clause.

*I was then asked to **assist** them with raising the profile of the club.*

*I also visit local schools and **help** young people with applying for jobs.*

assist *1,3*	help *1*
help off *VPP*	help on *VPP*

II.20 THE 'CHARGE' GROUP

These verbs are concerned with believing or saying that someone has done a particular thing or has a particular characteristic.

*He **must credit** me with strength I don't have.*

The preposition *with* is sometimes followed by an '-ing' clause.

*We**'re going to charge** you with allowing your premises to be used to supply heroin.*

charge *5,6*	credit *7,8*

II.21 VERBS WITH OTHER MEANINGS

There are a number of other verbs which have this structure.

*I **blackmailed** him with the fact that he was carrying out illegal operations.*

*Steve **caught** me with a great punch.*

*Her spare time **is taken up** with an MBA course and canoeing.*

*The group lists 29 breeds of donkeys, cattle, goats, horses, sheep and swine that **are threatened** with extinction.*

In the case of *threaten* and *trust*, the preposition *with* is sometimes followed by an '-ing' clause.

*Residents who complain to the police suffer abuse in the street and **are threatened** with being petrol-bombed.*

*The party has changed sufficiently to **be trusted** with governing the country.*

In the case of *concern*, the noun group following the verb is always a reflexive pronoun. This pattern is **V pron-refl** *with* n.

*Chapter 2 **concerns** itself with the methodological difficulties of measuring criminal victimization.*

In the case of *do*, the noun group following the verb is always an **amount**. This pattern is **V amount** *with* n.

*You **can do** quite a lot with quite a little money if you channel it in the right direction.*

blackmail *3*	do *2.4*	match *4,8*	threaten *2 (usu passive)*
catch *4*	dump *9 (usu passive)*	take *2.2*	trust *4*
concern *8*	leave *4*	threaten *1*	
take up *5*			

Structure information: Verb with Object and Adjunct

a) The noun group is the Object, and the prepositional phrase is an Adjunct.

b) This structure has a passive, with the pattern *be* **V-ed** *with* n. The prepositional phrase is an Adjunct.

c) Though the prepositional phrase usually comes after the noun group, it sometimes comes before it, especially when the noun group is a long one.

*Sceptics are right to **treat** with caution the results produced using this method.*

d) Phrasal verb patterns are the same except that there is also a particle, P. The Object comes either between the verb and the particle, or after the particle. If the Object comes after the particle, it cannot be a personal pronoun. You say

He _followed_ it _up_ with another record
or He _followed up_ this success with another record

but you do not say He followed up it with another record.

Other productive uses

A prepositional phrase beginning with _with_ is often used to indicate what someone uses to do something. An example is _An ordinary wooden door has been reinforced with steel plates_, which means that the steel plates have been used to reinforce the door.

---

27 Less frequent patterns

There are some patterns with noun groups and prepositions which apply to a very small number of verbs. They are collected together in this section.

V n _after_ n

The verb is followed by a noun group and a prepositional phrase which consists of _after_ and a noun group. The noun group following the verb is the Object, and the prepositional phrase is an Adjunct. This structure has a passive, with the pattern _be_ **V-ed** _after_ n.

> London's socialist boroughs have delighted in **_naming_ their estates after deeply obscure local politicians and barely pronounceable freedom fighters.**

In the case of _model 8_, the noun group following the verb is often a reflexive pronoun. This pattern is **V pron-refl** _after_ n.

> The girls **_had to model_ themselves after their mother** and tend the home.

model _7,8_   name _3_   be patterned _2_

V n _around/round_ n

The verb is followed by a noun group and a prepositional phrase which consists of _around_ or _round_ and a noun group. The noun group following the verb is the Object, and the prepositional phrase is an Adjunct. This structure has a passive, with the pattern _be_ **V-ed** _around/round_ n.

> She flung herself at him, **_grabbing_ him around the collar.**
> For barbecues, **_wrap_ bacon around banana chunks**, thread on to skewers and grill.

centre _9_   mould _5_
grab _1_   wrap _3,4_

V n _before_ n

The verb is followed by a noun group and a prepositional phrase which consists of _before_ and a noun group. The noun group following the verb is the Object and the prepositional phrase is an Adjunct. This structure has a passive, with the pattern _be_ **V-ed** _before_ n.

> Later that day he **_was brought_ before a magistrate** and charged with causing grievous bodily harm.

The phrasal verb _haul up_ has the active patterns **V n P** _before_ n and **V P n (not pron)** _before_ n. The passive pattern is _be_ **V-ed P** _before_ n.

*He **was hauled up** before a magistrate at Munich Airport Police Station and ordered to pay DM1,600.*

---

bring *9*   dangle *2*   haul *2 (usu passive)*

haul up ▷*2*

The verbs *bring* and *haul* also have the pattern **V** n *in front of* n. The passive pattern is *be* **V-ed** *in front of* n.

*He **was hauled** in front of the Cabinet to explain the blunders.*

V n *through* n

The verb is followed by a noun group and a prepositional phrase which consists of *through* and a noun group. The noun group following the verb is the Object, and the prepositional phrase is an Adjunct. This structure has a passive, with the pattern *be* **V-ed** *through* n.

*The second Duke, as Queen Anne's High Commissioner, **piloted** the 1707 Act of Union through Parliament.*

---

bulldoze *3*   run *7*   thread *7*
pilot *6*   stick *2.2*

Chapter 5: Link Verbs

In this book, we use the term **link verb** to refer to verbs like *be*, *become*, and *seem* which need to be followed by a Complement. Complements can be noun groups, adjective groups, adverb groups, prepositional phrases, or clauses. They describe the person or thing indicated by the Subject. Verbs of this kind have the label **V-LINK** in the Collins Cobuild English Dictionary.

There are other verbs which are sometimes followed by Complements, but they are not generally considered to be link verbs because they have a complete meaning in themselves, for example they indicate an action such as moving or leaving. These verbs are dealt with in Chapter 1, Sections 2 and 6 (see pages 14-16 and 74-80).

When verbs such as *be* and *stay* are followed by prepositional phrases and adverbs indicating place, they are not considered to be link verbs: see page 130.

Some link verbs are used in various patterns with **introductory *it*** as Subject: see Chapter 9, Section 1.

Link verb meanings

Link verbs can be divided into three main meaning groups.

1 THE 'BE' GROUP

These verbs indicate that a person or thing is something, or has a particular quality. The verb *be* is by far the most frequent of these. We include here *keep*, *remain*, and *stay*, which indicate that a person or thing remains something, or continues to have a particular quality.

A few of these verbs have passives. These are given in the list below.

average *6*	cover *3*	lie *1.4*	remain *1,8*
be *2.1,2,9*	equal *6*	make *4.1,3*	represent *5*
compose *1*	extend *1*	measure *3*	be represented by *5*
be composed of *1*	feel *1*	number *5*	stand *11,14*
comprise *1,2*	form *6,7*	pass *19*	stay *3*
be comprised of *2*	be formed by *6*	prove *1*	total *4*
constitute *1,2*	go *2.2,3*	rank *4*	weigh *1*
be constituted by/of *2*	keep *1*	rate *6*	
make up *1*	be made up of *1*	work out *3*	

A few verbs are used with the general meaning 'be' only when talking about the level of share prices or currencies:

close *1.9*	finish *4*
end *7*	open *22*

2 THE 'BECOME' GROUP

These verbs indicate that a person or thing becomes something, or comes to have a particular quality.

become 1	form 3	go 2.1	turn 15,16,17,18
come 6	be formed by 3	grow 7	
fall 9	get 1.1,2	make 4.2	
come out 4	end up 2	turn out 1	
come over 2	finish up 1	wind up 3	

A few verbs are used with the general meaning 'become' only when talking about the level of share prices, currencies, or other amounts:

creep 4	edge 3	move 11
drift 2	inch 2	

3 THE 'SEEM' GROUP

These verbs indicate that a person or thing seems to be something, or seems to have a particular quality. We include here *act* and *play*, which indicate that someone pretends to be something.

act 5	look 2.1,4	smell 3
appear 1,2	play 9	sound 7,8,9
feel 1,2,3	seem 1	taste 4

Prepositional link verbs

The following combinations of verbs and prepositional phrases can be considered to be link verbs followed by Complements. See the sections on **V as n**, **V to n**, etc in Chapter 2.

act 4 as sth	double 11 as sth	parade 10 as sth	run 32 at sth
amount 2,VP to sth	end 4 as sth	pass 20 as/for sth	run VP4 into sth
begin 3,5 as sth	figure 13 as sth	pose 3 as sth	shade 7 into/to sth
come 14 to sth	finish 4,5 as sth	serve 3 as/for sth	stand 13 at sth
come 20 as sth	function 3 as sth	rank 4 as sth	start 4 as sth
consist 1 of sth	lie 1.6 as sth	rate 6 as sth	transmute into sth
consist 2 in sth	masquerade 1 as sth	remain 1 as sth	turn 15 into/to sth
continue 6 as sth	operate 2 as sth	reside 2 in sth	
convert 1 into/to sth	originate as sth	resolve 4 into sth	
add up VPP to sth	come over 3 as sth	go down VPP as sth	weigh in 2 at sth
average out at/to sth	double up ▷11 as sth	shape up 1 as sth	work out 3 at sth
clock in VPP at sth	end up 2 as sth	start off ▷4 as sth	
come across 2 as sth	finish up 1 as sth	start out 1 as sth	

Link verb patterns

Link verbs have the following patterns. Many of these patterns are dealt with in other chapters because they also occur with verbs that are not link verbs.

1 V n

The verb is followed by a noun group.

*His father **was** an accountant.*

*I **felt** such a fool.*

See pages 14-16.

2 V amount

The verb is followed by a word or phrase indicating an amount.

*Twenty-four minus five **is nineteen**.*

Other related patterns are:

V amount adj

*The tunnel **is six hundred metres long**.*

V amount adv

*The parasols **measure 3 metres across**.*

V amount *in* n

*Each aviary **will be 5 metres in width** and 3.5 metres high.*

See pages 69 and 73.

3 V adj

The verb is followed by an adjective group.

*All the lights **were out**.*
*She **looked worried**.*
*It **smells nice**.*

Other related patterns are:

V colour

*Her lips **were turning blue**.*

V -ed

*The style **became known as art deco**.*

See pages 74-76, 79 and 80.

4 V to-inf

Some verbs which are link verbs are also followed by a to-infinitive, as in *She seemed to be looking for someone*. However, here the verbs are considered to be **in phase**, rather than to be a link verb and its Complement. See page 88, meaning group I.2.

5 V as if, V as though

The verb is followed by a clause beginning with *as if*, *as though*, or, in informal English, *like*.

*He **looked** as if he hadn't slept for a week.*

See page 121.

6 V prep

The verb is followed by a prepositional phrase that describes the Subject and is therefore similar to an adjective in function.

*Her husband **is from Guyana** and they have one son.*
*If you **are in debt**, you can get practical help from the Citizens Advice Bureau.*
*I **was out of work** for three months.*

Many of them will need retraining to cope with new technology if they are not to **end up** on the **human scrapheap**.

He **had fallen** in love with another woman.

Within two years the pact **lay** in ruins.

The neck **looks** a bit on the long side to my way of thinking.

Drug therapy **had proved** of little value and Jackie's only relief was to go to bed and try to sleep.

Franks joined us and **seemed** in a worse mood than usual.

appear 1,2	feel 1	lie 4	seem 1
be 2.1	get 1.2	look 2.1	sound 8
come 6	go 2.1	prove 1	stay 3
fall 9	keep 1	remain 1	
come out 4	finish up 1		
end up 2	wind up 3		

7 V *like* n

The verb is followed by a prepositional phrase consisting of *like* and a noun group.

It **looks** like a small bear.

See pages 209-210.

8 V *of* n

The verb is followed by a prepositional phrase consisting of *of* and a noun group.

The kitchen **smelled** of onions and bad meat.

See page 212, meaning group 4.

9 Clause as Complement

The verb *be* can be followed by a variety of clauses which identify the Subject. The Subject indicates something abstract such as a problem or an aim. This structure is often used to focus on a fact or situation.

These patterns are **V -ing**, **V to-inf**, **V that**, **V wh**, and **V wh-to-inf**. The verbs *become* and *remain* also occasionally have these patterns.

The biggest problem **was** getting them close enough to the wall.

Our broad aim **is** to raise people's visual awareness and appreciation of life.

The important thing **is** that the book comes out.

The question **is** whether or not it is cost effective.

The problem **is** where to start looking.

The most pressing question for Mr Brooke **remains** how to find a formula that will satisfy all parties and allow the talking to begin.

be 1.4	become 1	remain 8

10 Complement followed by *to* and a noun group

With verbs meaning 'seem', a prepositional phrase beginning with *to* is sometimes used after the Complement to indicate or emphasize whose viewpoint you are giving.

These patterns are **V adj/n** *to* n and **V** *like* n *to* n.

It __sounds__ crazy to me.

Life __seemed__ a great joke to her.

He __didn't look__ like a fisherman to me.

Sometimes the prepositional phrase beginning with *to* comes directly after the verb.

This is a situation which __seems to me extraordinary__.

11 Link verbs used without a following Complement

Verbs meaning 'seem' can be used by themselves, without a following Complement, in comparative clauses beginning with *as* or *than*. This structure is used when you are making a comparison between what someone or something appears to be like and what they are really like.

He is much more astute than he __seems__.

This is not as simple as it __sounds__.

The verb *be* is used by itself in comparative clauses, and also when confirming or contradicting a statement and in short answers to questions.

He's smarter than I __am__.

'Pat Norton is your brother-in-law?' 'Yes, he __is__.'

Be is also used to form question tags, which ask the hearer or reader to confirm a statement. The verb follows a clause and is followed by a noun group, which is its Subject.

You're not from here, __are__ you?

It's very difficult, __isn't__ it?

Be is also used after *so*, *nor*, or *neither* to indicate a situation that is similar to one mentioned in a previous clause. The verb is followed by a noun group, which is its Subject.

They're strong, yes, but so __are__ we.

'I'm not worried about Mrs Parfitt.' 'Neither __am__ I.'

Chapter 6: Reciprocal Verbs

Reciprocal verbs describe actions or processes in which two or more people, groups, or things do the same thing to each other, have a relationship, or are linked because they are participating jointly in an action or event. Verbs of this kind have the label **V-RECIP** in the Collins Cobuild English Dictionary.

Reciprocal verbs have two basic patterns:

1 They can be used with a plural Subject – that is, a Subject consisting of a **plural noun group**. When they are used with this plural Subject, the meaning is that the people, groups, or things involved are interacting with each other. For example, two people can *quarrel*, can *have a chat*, or can *meet*.

2 They can also be used with a Subject which refers to one of the participants and a prepositional Object, Adjunct, or Object which indicates the other participant, as in *She quarrelled with her sister*, *I had a chat with him*, and *I met him at university*. This structure is used to focus on the involvement of the first participant mentioned, or to imply that they have a more active role or greater responsibility for what happens. Usually the action or process is reciprocal even when this structure is used, so *She quarrelled with her sister* implies that her sister also quarrelled with her. However, with some verbs and some noun groups, the action or process may not in fact be reciprocal, as when, for example, someone *kisses* a baby or a car *collides* with a tree: in these instances the baby does not kiss the person and the tree does not collide with the car.

A number of reciprocal verbs can be used with a singular Subject in patterns where the other participant is not mentioned, as in *I agree* and *I was still negotiating for the best rate*. These verbs are listed in the relevant sections in Chapters 1 and 2, for example **V** or **V for n**, and are labelled 'also non-recip' in the lists below.

Some verbs are **ergative** as well as reciprocal. These verbs are explained and listed separately in Chapter 8.

Pattern combinations

A reciprocal verb has one of these three pattern combinations:

▶ Pattern combination 1: pl-n V; V *with* n
  We *quarrelled*.
  He *quarrelled* with his father.
▶ Pattern combination 2: pl-n V n; V n *with* n
  We *have reached* a compromise.
  France *has reached* a compromise with Britain.
▶ Pattern combination 3: pl-n V; V n
  We *embraced*.
  He *embraced* her.

Pattern combination 1: pl-n V; V *with* n

These verbs have two patterns:

- **pl-n V**: The verb is used with a plural Subject.

- **V *with* n**: The verb is used with a Subject referring to one participant and followed by a prepositional phrase indicating the other. In most cases, the prepositional phrase consists of *with* and a noun group; in a few cases, the preposition is *from*, *to*, *against*, or *into*.

pl-n V

plural noun group	Verb group	
Subject	**Verb**	**Adjunct (optional)**
Those values	don't conflict.	
They	were gossiping	intently.

V *with* n

	Verb group	*with*	noun group
Subject	**Verb**	**prepositional Object**	
Their views	conflicted	with	those of the President.
Eva	gossiped	with	Sarah.

Phrasal verbs

pl-n V P

plural noun group	Verb group	Particle	
Subject	**Verb**		**Adjunct (optional)**
They	fell	out	over tax reform.
The boys and Fred	get	on	very well.

V P *with* n

	Verb group	Particle	*with*	noun group
Subject	**Verb**		**prepositional Object**	
He	fell	out	with	his bosses.
She	gets	on	with	everybody.

Verbs with this combination of patterns belong to the following meaning groups:

1.1 THE 'TALK' GROUP
1.2 THE 'FIGHT' GROUP
1.3 THE 'FRATERNIZE' GROUP
1.4 THE 'TEAM UP' AND 'BREAK UP' GROUP
1.5 THE 'GET ON' GROUP
1.6 THE 'COLLABORATE' GROUP
1.7 THE 'TALLY' AND 'CLASH' GROUP
1.8 THE 'DIFFER' GROUP
1.9 THE 'INTERSECT' GROUP
1.10 THE 'INTERACT' GROUP
1.11 VERBS WITH OTHER MEANINGS

1.1 THE 'TALK' GROUP

These verbs are concerned with speaking and communicating. This includes:

- having a conversation
- arguing
- agreeing and disagreeing

Her parents never **argued**.
*He **was arguing** with his girlfriend and she hit him with a frying pan.*
*We **chatted** for a while.*
*On deck, he appeared happy and relaxed as he **chatted** with the crew and gazed out to sea.*
*Owens and his boss **are** still **negotiating**.*
*She repeated her long-held belief that no country **can negotiate** with terrorists.*

The verbs *chat, natter, speak 1*, and *talk 2,6,7* also have the pattern **V to n**.

*I**'ve been talking** to Jim Hoffman. He suggested that I call you.*

The verbs *(not) speak 6* and *talk 3* have the pattern **V to n**, not the pattern **V with n**.

*Yesterday the couple **were** no longer **speaking to his mum**. And she **was** certainly **not speaking to them**.*

The verb *agree 3* has the patterns **pl-n V on n** and **V on n with n**, not the patterns **pl-n V** and **V with n**.

*However, **we agreed** on a compromise.*
*Yesterday Health Minister Graham Richardson said he **was going to agree** on a figure with the committee.*

agree 1 *(also non-recip)*	**correspond** 2	**natter** *(also non-recip)*
agree 3	**dicker**	**negotiate** 1 *(also non-recip)*
argue 4,5	**differ** 2	**parley** 2
banter 2	**disagree** 1 *(also non-recip)*	**quarrel** 3
bicker *(also non-recip)*	**fight** 6	**quibble** 1
chat	**flirt** 1 *(also non-recip)*	**row** 3.3
clash 1	**gossip** 2 *(also non-recip)*	**spar** 2
communicate 1	**haggle** *(also non-recip)*	**speak** 1
concur *(also non-recip)*	**huddle** 3	**(not) speak** 6
confer 1	**interact** 1	**squabble**
consult 2	**joke** 2	**talk** 2,3,6,7 *(also non-recip)*
converse 1	**meet** 7	**wrangle**

1.2 THE 'FIGHT' GROUP

These verbs are concerned with fighting, either physically or metaphorically, or competing. We include here *draw* and *tie*, which indicate that neither person or team wins in a contest.

*The worst sufferers this week have been **companies** which **are competing** in world markets – chemicals, motors and aerospace.*
*Apple's introduction of the new printers is seen as an effort to **compete** with Hewlett-Packard.*
*Did he say why **they were fighting**?*
*A man was injured after he **fought** with a would-be thief tampering with his neighbour's BMW yesterday.*
*We **struggled** and she fell to the ground.*
*After the judgment, Mr Hill **struggled** with prison officers and swore at the judges as he was led from the dock.*

The verbs *battle, compete*, and *draw* also have the pattern **V against n**.

*Increasingly, local government **is competing** against the private sector.*

The verb *fight 3* has the pattern **V against n**, not the pattern **V with n**.

*Under the Duke of Marlborough, The Royal Scots **fought against the French** in the War of the Spanish Succession.*

When the verbs *contend*, *tussle 2*, and *vie* are used with a plural Subject, they do not have the simple pattern **pl-n V**. Instead, *contend* has the pattern **pl-n V *for* n**; *tussle* has the pattern **pl-n V *for/over* n**; *vie* has the patterns **pl-n V to-inf** and **pl-n V *for* n**.

*The capital has become a wreck, as **rival forces contend** for power.*

*Behind him came Robin Seymour and Chris Young, while **Fred Salmon and Paul Lasenby tussled** for seventh place ahead of Barrie Clarke.*

*To keep customers loyal, **the two firms are vying** to provide the best sales and service back-up.*

The verb *draw* usually has the pattern **pl-n V amount**, rather than **pl-n V**.

*The two sides **drew** 1-1 in Germany a fortnight ago.*

battle 4	duel 3 *(also non-recip)*	joust 1,2	tussle 1,2
brawl 2	feud 2	scuffle 2	vie
clash 1,5	fight 3,5	skirmish 2	wrestle 2 *(also non-recip)*
compete 1,2 *(also non-recip)*	grapple 2	spar 1	
contend 3	jockey 2	struggle 4	
draw 24 *(also non-recip)*	jostle 2	tie 11	

The verbs *battle*, *fight*, and *wrestle* also have the pattern **V n**: see meaning group 3.3.

1.3 THE 'FRATERNIZE' GROUP

These verbs are concerned with associating with someone or engaging in sexual activity with them.

*It may be that **some couples cohabit** initially because they are uncertain about the strength of their relationship.*

*Widows' benefits are not payable if the widow remarries or if she **is cohabiting with a man** as his wife.*

*On a rainy evening before a game between the Leones and the Tigres, **players of both clubs are fraternizing** in the Tigres dugout.*

*At these conventions, executives **fraternized with key personnel of other banks**.*

*We'**d** only **been going out** for about six months at the time.*
*He **used to go out** with Kylie Minogue.*

In the case of *mingle* and *mix*, the preposition *with* is always followed by a plural noun group. This pattern is **V *with* pl-n**.

*In these institutions, guards **mingle with prisoners** in open day rooms, rather than patrol long lines of cells.*

The verb *cuddle up* also has the pattern **V P *to* n**.

*'When I met Kev, I thought, mmm, nice,' laughs Paula, as she **cuddles up to her man**.*

The passive verb *get married* has the patterns **pl-n get V-ed** and **get V-ed *to* n**.

*She gave a little party for me and Alexander after **we got married**.*
*I'**m getting married to my American girlfriend, Ginny**, in September.*

breed 3	fraternize *(also non-recip)*	neck 4
canoodle	intermarry	rendezvous 3
cohabit *(also non-recip)*	get married 1 *(also non-recip)*	smooch
copulate	mate 5 *(also non-recip)*	snog
elope	mingle 2 *(also non-recip)*	
fornicate *(also non-recip)*	mix 6	
cuddle up	make out 7	
go out 2	meet up ▷2	

The verb *snog* also has the pattern **V n**: see meaning group 3.1 below.

1.4 THE 'TEAM UP' AND 'BREAK UP' GROUP

These verbs are concerned with starting or ending a relationship of some kind. We include here *make up*, which indicates that people resume a relationship.

*His demands increased until **we** finally **broke up**.*
*Just before Penny's marriage I **broke up** with a man I'd been seeing for over a year.*

***Mary Stuart Masterson, Madeline Stow and Drew Barrymore** **team up** to star in 'Bad Girls', the Western that focuses on females.*
*What it lacks is a base in America. To provide it, the company **may team up** with Sprint.*

The verbs *part* and *separate* have the pattern **V from n**, not the pattern **V with n**.

*I **have parted** from my wife by mutual agreement.*

The passive verb *get divorced* has the patterns **pl-n get V-ed** and **get V-ed from n**.

*When **my parents got divorced**, I didn't really register how much it bothered me at the time.*
*He **is getting divorced** from his wife of 11 years.*

get divorced 2 *(also non-recip)*	**part** 2.3	**separate** 5
break up 2	**join up** 2	**meet up** ▷1
fall out 2	**link up** 1	**shack up**
hook up 2	**make up** 6	**team up**

1.5 THE 'GET ON' GROUP

These verbs indicate that two or more people have a good relationship.

***They** **clicked** immediately. They loved the same things – oddball things, far-out things, avant-garde things.*
*In any team there are always people more likely to **click** with one player than another.*

***We** **get on** pretty well, all in all.*
*If the job you're after involves working as part of a team, put down any hobbies that show you are versatile and **can get on** with people.*

click 3	**connect** 9	
communicate 3	**gel** 1 *(also non-recip)*	
get along 1	**get on** 1	**rub along**

1.6 THE 'COLLABORATE' GROUP

These verbs indicate that people work together or take part in an activity or venture together.

*Redway was as eager to publish Waite as Waite was to write for him, and **they** **collaborated** happily for four years from 1896 to 1899.*
*In 1976, the firm **collaborated** with the Victoria and Albert Museum in staging an exhibition of Minton wares from 1798 to 1910.*

***They** **danced** as though they had been dancing together all their lives.*
*In the living room, Al **was dancing** with Mary, both of them frowning, intense, comical.*

When the verbs *connive*, *conspire*, and *co-star* are used with a plural Subject, they do not have the simple pattern **pl-n V**. Instead, *connive* and *conspire* have the pattern **pl-n V to-inf**, and *co-star* has the pattern **pl-n V in n**.

*A grand jury has been investigating whether **officials at Southern Co. conspired** to cover up their accounting for spare parts to evade federal income taxes.*

*Robin Wright, 25, and Sean Penn, 31, met when **they** **co-starred** in the movie 'State Of Grace'.*

collaborate 1	conspire 1	dance 3 (also non-recip)
collude	co-operate 1 (also non-recip)	liaise (also non-recip)
connive 1	co-star 2	trade 2

Verbs which indicate specific kinds of dancing, such as *jive*, *tango*, and *waltz* also sometimes have these patterns.

1.7 THE 'TALLY' AND 'CLASH' GROUP

These verbs indicate that two or more things are similar or compatible, or are not similar or compatible.

*Anxious mothers still consult Jennifer to make sure **their party dates <u>don't clash</u>**.*
*The unfortunate thing is that the final at Hickstead **<u>will clash</u> with the Junior European Championships**.*

*Hornby cites one instance where the case evaporated because **the child interview videos and written transcripts <u>did not tally</u>**.*
*The figure **<u>tallied</u> with the payments into her building society account**.*

The verb *correspond* also has the pattern **V** *to* **n**.

*That number **<u>corresponds</u> to a telephone number on this list he gave me**.*

The verb *go* usually has the pattern **pl-n V** *together* rather than **pl-n V**.

***All natural colors <u>go</u> together**.*

agree 5,8	coincide 2	converge 3	harmonize 1
blend 3	collide 2	correlate 1	jibe 3
clash 2,3,4	conflict 5	correspond 1 (also non-recip)	tally 2
cohere (also non-recip)	contrast 6	go 3.4 (also non-recip)	

1.8 THE 'DIFFER' GROUP

These verbs are concerned with being or becoming different. All the verbs in this group have the pattern **V** *from* **n** or **V P** *from* **n**, not **V** *with* **n** or **V P** *with* **n**.

*People **<u>differ</u>** in the amount of time they need on their own.*
*Britain **<u>differs</u> from most European countries** in having no statutory minimum wage.*

differ 1	diverge 1,2
grow apart	

1.9 THE 'INTERSECT' GROUP

These verbs indicate that two or more things occur together, are in contact, or come into contact.

*If you want to know how fish farming works or how **fish and marine plants <u>coexist</u>**, this museum will show you.*
*Grey squirrels probably do not kill red squirrels, but they **<u>cannot coexist</u> with them**, except perhaps in dense pine and spruce forests.*

***The two Skyhawk jets** apparently **<u>collided</u>** in mid-air as they were practising takeoffs.*
*Twenty-two people were killed yesterday when the bus they were travelling in **<u>collided</u> with a lorry** outside Cairo.*

*There are **two main corridors** which **<u>intersect</u>** at the very heart of the building.*
*It then became paved road just north of Tahoma, until it **<u>intersected</u> with Highway 89**, where we turned south.*

The verb *merge* also has the pattern **V** *into* **n**.

*The closer to the edges and the woodland, the more natural is the planting, so that the garden seamlessly **<u>merges</u> into the woodland**.*

coexist	collocate 2	intertwine 2	overlap 2
coincide 1	intermingle	merge 2	
collide 1	intersect 1,2	mingle 1	

The verbs *intersect 1* and *overlap* also have the pattern **V n**: see meaning group 3.4 below.

1.10 THE 'INTERACT' GROUP

These verbs indicate that two or more things have an effect on each other.

> *A lot is already known about the factors that give rise to these violent storms, but there's still much to learn about how **they interact**.*
> *However, X-rays have their limitations because they **interact** with the electron cloud surrounding the nuclei of atoms.*

| interact 3 | react 4 |

1.11 VERBS WITH OTHER MEANINGS

There are two other verbs with this combination of patterns. *Compromise* has the pattern **V with n**. *Diverge* has the pattern **V from n**.

> *Three directors decided the theatre should stop trading immediately. The remaining three decided it should carry on. Finally, **they compromised**.*
> *The government **has compromised** with its critics over tight fiscal and monetary policies.*

> *If the lens is small and the wavelength of light large, **the light waves diverge** as they pass through the lens.*
> *Cornish arrived there at 13.39 when the tug was seaward of the Hakai Passage on a course that **diverged** from the Calvert Island coastline.*

| compromise 2 *(also non-recip)* | diverge 3 *(also non-recip)* |

Structure information: Pattern combination 1

a) In the pattern **V with n**, the prepositional phrase is the prepositional Object.

b) There is a passive pattern, **be V-ed with**, but it does not often occur, and is not possible with some verbs.

c) Phrasal verb patterns are the same, except that there is a particle, P, which comes after the verb.

Pattern combination 2: pl-n V n; V n *with* n

These verbs have two patterns:

- **pl-n V n**: The verb is used with a plural Subject and is followed by a noun group.
- **V n *with* n**: The verb is used with a Subject referring to one participant and is followed by a noun group and a prepositional phrase indicating the other participant. The prepositional phrase consists of *with* and a noun group.

  The passive patterns are **be V-ed**, **be V-ed *with* n**, and **be V-ed *by/between* n**.

Active voice

pl-n V n

plural noun group	Verb group	noun group
Subject	Verb	Object
MPs	have been debating	the issue.
Sam and Debbie	swap	stories of life in their homelands.

V n *with* n

	Verb group	noun group	*with*	noun group
Subject	Verb	Object		Adjunct
I	am not going to debate	the issue	with	you.
I	could swap	data	with	them.

Passive voice

be V-ed

	Verb group
Subject	Verb
Glances	were exchanged.
A compromise	was reached.

be V-ed *with* n

	Verb group	*with*	noun group
Subject	Verb		Adjunct
New ties	were established	with	countries in Latin America.
No final agreement	has been reached	with	Washington.

be V-ed *between/by* pl-n

	Verb group	*between/by*	plural noun group
Subject	Verb		Adjunct
A pitched battle	is being fought	between	Croat militia and Serb fighters.
An alliance	has been forged	between	seven of the factions.

Phrasal verbs

Active voice

pl-n V n P, pl-n V P n (not pron)

plural noun group	Verb group	noun group	Particle
Subject	Verb...	Object	...Verb
The two of us	are fighting	it	out.
She and her father	have patched	things	up.

plural noun group	Verb group	Particle	noun group
Subject	Verb		Object
Andy Forbes and Andy Naylor	fought	out	an enthralling battle.
Mr Clinton and Mr Brown	patched	up	their quarrel.

V n P *with* n, V P n (not pron) *with* n

	Verb group	noun group	Particle	*with*	noun group
Subject	Verb...	Object	...Verb	Adjunct	
I	can't break	it	off	with	her.
I	talked	it	over	with	my dad.

	Verb group	Particle	noun group	*with*	noun group
Subject	Verb		Object	Adjunct	
The Americans	should break	off	their dialogue	with	the organization.
She	talked	over	the problem	with	her doctor.

Passive voice

be V-ed P

	Verb group	Particle	
Subject	Verb		Adjunct (optional)
Diplomatic ties	were broken	off	in 1939.
Issues involving commitment	should be talked	through.	

Verbs with this combination of patterns belong to the following meaning groups:

2.1 THE 'DISCUSS' GROUP
2.2 THE 'AGREE' AND 'NEGOTIATE' GROUP
2.3 THE 'HOLD' GROUP
2.4 THE 'FORGE' AND 'BREAK OFF' GROUP
2.5 THE 'EXCHANGE' GROUP
2.6 THE 'FIGHT' GROUP
2.7 VERBS WITH OTHER MEANINGS

2.1 THE 'DISCUSS' GROUP

These verbs are concerned with discussing something. The noun group following the verb indicates what people are discussing.

> *We __discussed__ her options.*
> *For his part, Mr Perez de Cuellar welcomed the news and said he __would discuss__ the matter with the Iraqi ambassador.*
> *The report's findings and recommendations __would be discussed__ with consumer groups and retailers, he said.*

argue *4*	discuss *1 (also non-recip)*
debate *3*	dispute *3 (also non-recip)*
talk over *(also non-recip)*	talk through *1 (also non-recip)*

2.2 THE 'AGREE' AND 'NEGOTIATE' GROUP

These verbs indicate that two people or groups agree on future arrangements, or are trying to agree on them.

> *Tottenham and Norway __have agreed__ a compromise deal in the row over the availability of goalkeeper Erik Thorstvedt.*
> *He was determined to __agree__ terms with the French and then to impose them on his allies.*
>
> *The US and Canada then __negotiated__ an agreement that was completed in 1987.*
> *The city's Peace Officers Association __is__ currently __negotiating__ a new contract with the city.*

The verbs *do* and *make* can be used with a wide range of noun groups, but are reciprocal only when used with noun groups such as *an agreement* and *a deal*.

> *'I came in here thinking we __were going to do__ a deal,' Roberts said.*
> *He __has done__ a deal with Customs and Excise to allow selected VAT-free shops beyond the customs barrier.*

agree *3*	finalize *(also non-recip)*	reach *7*
conclude *4*	make *1.1 (also non-recip)*	sign *6 (also non-recip)*
do *2.1 (also non-recip)*	negotiate *1 (also non-recip)*	strike *13 (also non-recip)*

2.3 THE 'HOLD' GROUP

These verbs are used with noun groups such as *talks* and *a conversation* to indicate that two or more people talk to each other.

> *The ANC leader and Mr de Klerk __held__ talks at the weekend before Mr Mandela left for his six week international tour.*
> *He's also scheduled to __hold__ talks in Geneva __with Jordanian officials__ before returning to Washington.*
> *Talks __are being held__ between the unions and the government at the moment but no agreement looks likely.*

The verb *have* can be used with a wide range of noun groups, but is reciprocal only when used with noun groups of the kind mentioned above. It has no passive.

> *The two fishermen __were having__ a conversation, and though they were at least a quarter of a mile away from us, we could hear every word.*
> *I __have had__ a brief conversation with my client, who still maintains his innocence.*

have *2.1,2 (also non-recip)*	hold *2.6 (also non-recip)*

2.4 THE 'FORGE' AND 'BREAK OFF' GROUP

These verbs are concerned with having, beginning, ending, or renewing contact or a relationship.

>*The two West African states **had broken off** relations two years ago after bloody clashes erupted in the frontier area.*
>*The Soviet Union **broke off** relations with Israel in 1967 at the time of the Six Day War.*
>
>*After years locked in confrontation, they **can** now make a new beginning, **forge** a new partnership and a sturdy peace.*
>*A top ANC official has called on British people to **forge** closer links with Black South Africans.*

The verbs *resolve* and *settle* are usually followed by a noun such as *dispute* or *differences*.

>*Unless **France and Britain can resolve** their differences there will be no treaty on political union.*
>*The former captain **has** now **resolved** his differences with team officials.*

In the case of *break off* and *make up*, when the noun group comes directly after the verb, it is always *it*.

>*Then did she come here to **make** it **up** with him – to make peace with him, anyway?*

establish *2*	have *2.1,2 (also non-recip)*	resolve *1 (also non-recip)*
forge *1 (also non-recip)*	renew *2*	settle *1*
form *10 (also non-recip)*	reopen *4*	
break off *3 (also non-recip)*	make up *6*	patch up *1 (also non-recip)*

2.5 THE 'EXCHANGE' GROUP

These verbs indicate that people give, say, or do things of the same kind to each other. They often have the patterns **pl-n V pl-n** and **V pl-n *with* n**.

>*We **exchanged** addresses, and as a result of our meeting he has given much needed financial assistance to the team.*
>*The separatists **exchanged** fire with security forces at two places in the old city area.*
>
>*The Daily Mirror says the three candidates **traded** insults and blew their own trumpets yesterday as each one claimed to be heading for victory.*
>*He was too reckless, too willing to challenge the odds and to **trade** punches with a larger opponent when he should have walked away.*

The verb *bandy* is used mainly with the noun *words*.

>*He was tired of **bandying** words with the man.*

bandy *(also non-recip)*	swap *1*
exchange *1*	trade *5,6,7*

2.6 THE 'FIGHT' GROUP

These verbs are concerned with fighting and competing.

>*The allies **have** turned on each other and **fought** a running battle for the past four days.*
>*At the weekend police **fought** a gun battle with a gang which used military hand grenades against them.*

The verb *have* can be used with a wide range of noun groups, but is reciprocal only when used with noun groups like *a fight*. It has no passive.

>*We **had** a fight yesterday, and he walked out.*
>*Surprisingly enough, readers, I got horrendously drunk and **had** a fight with Graham Poppie in the bar of the hotel.*

In the case of *fight out*, the noun group following the verb is usually *it*.

*He spent his first week lying on the floor of his elegant residence while **the guerrillas and the army <u>fought</u> it <u>out</u>** in his back street.*

---

fight *3 (also non-recip)*   **have** *2.1 (also non-recip)*   **play** *2 (also non-recip)*

fight out *(also non-recip)*

2.7 VERBS WITH OTHER MEANINGS

There are two other verbs with this combination of patterns.

They <u>dance</u> a tango.
*You should see me <u>dance</u> **the tango with a girl who knows her paces.***

My sister and I <u>shared</u> a bedroom until I was seven.
*For once Livy wished she <u>wasn't sharing</u> **a room with Caroline.***

---

dance *3 (also non-recip)*   **share** *2,3,4,6 (also non-recip)*

There are a number of phrases which are like reciprocal verbs of this type and their Objects. See 'Reciprocal phrases' at the end of this chapter.

Structure information: Pattern combination 2

a) In both the **pl-n V n** pattern and the **V n *with* n** pattern, the noun group following the verb is the Object. In the **V n *with* n** pattern, the prepositional phrase is an Adjunct.

b) There are three passive patterns. In the pattern **be V-ed**, neither participant is mentioned. In the pattern **be V-ed *with* n**, one of the participants is mentioned in the prepositional phrase after the verb. In the pattern, **be V-ed *between/by* pl-n**, both participants are mentioned in the prepositional phrase.

c) Phrasal verb patterns are the same except that there is also a particle, P. The Object comes either between the verb and the particle, or after the particle. If the Object comes after the particle, it cannot be a personal pronoun. You say

He <u>talked</u> them <u>through</u> with a colleague
or *He <u>talked through</u> his ideas with a colleague*

but you do not say *He talked through them with a colleague.*

Productive uses

Many verbs are reciprocal and are used with these patterns when they have the prefix *co-*, for example *co-author*, *co-found*, *co-host*, *co-sponsor*, and *co-write*.

Pattern combination 3: pl-n V; V n

These verbs have two patterns:

- **pl-n V**: The verb is used with a plural Subject.
- **V n**: The verb is used with a Subject referring to one participant and followed by a noun group referring to the other. The passive pattern is **be V-ed**.

Active voice

pl-n V

plural noun group	Verb group
Subject	**Verb**
They	embraced.
Their eyes	met.

V n

	Verb group	noun group
Subject	**Verb**	**Object**
She	embraced	Jack.
Her eyes	met	Harry's.

Passive voice

be V-ed

	Verb group	
Subject	**Verb**	**Adjunct (optional)**
It	is intersected	by another arterial road.
He	was kissed	by them all.

Verbs with this combination of patterns belong to the following meaning groups:

- 3.1 THE 'KISS' GROUP
- 3.2 THE 'MARRY' AND 'DIVORCE' GROUP
- 3.3 THE 'FIGHT' GROUP
- 3.4 THE 'INTERSECT' GROUP
- 3.5 VERBS WITH OTHER MEANINGS

3.1 THE 'KISS' GROUP

These verbs are concerned with affectionate or sexual contact. When these verbs are used with a Subject referring to one participant, the meaning is usually that the other participant does not do the same thing back – the action is not reciprocal. Some informal verbs referring to sexual intercourse also have this pattern.

> *We __hugged__ and cried.*
> *He wanted to __hug her__.*
> *She gave a fractional smile. __They kissed__. She drove away.*
> *She __kissed__ me and turned out the light.*

cuddle	hug *1*	snog
embrace *1*	kiss *1*	

The verb *kiss* also has the patterns **pl-n V n** and **V n n**. The noun group which follows the verb, or follows the first noun group, is something such as *goodbye* or *goodnight*.

> *They __kissed goodnight__ before splitting up to avoid photographers who spotted them.*

*He **kissed** me **goodnight** and then went off to check on something in the kitchen.*

The verb *snog* also has the pattern **V *with* n**: see meaning group 1.3 above.

3.2 THE 'MARRY' AND 'DIVORCE' GROUP

These verbs are concerned with marriage, divorce, or romantic relationships.

> *They **divorced** in 1976.*
> *She **divorced** her Army husband at 23.*
> *The front page of the Sun this morning has a story about a guy who**'s being divorced** by his bride because he likes buses.*
>
> *When **we married** we vowed to be together, to live together, and to die together, she said.*
> *She **married** a barrister, and died childless in 1864.*

court *2.1*	**divorce** *2 (also non-recip)*
date *10 (also non-recip)*	**marry** *1 (also non-recip)*

3.3 THE 'FIGHT' GROUP

These verbs are concerned with fighting or competing.

> *When **my brother and I used to fight**, Mother would become hysterical and shriek that we were going to kill each other.*
> *I **had to fight** him even though I hate violence.*
>
> *The two sides **meet** at Goodison Park on Saturday in what promises to be an explosive clash.*
> *The winner of the India-West Indies tie in Melbourne tomorrow **will meet** Australia in the final.*

battle *4*	**meet** *18*
fight *3,5*	**wrestle** *2 (also non-recip)*

The verbs *battle*, *fight*, and *wrestle* also have the pattern **V *with* n**: see meaning group 1.2.

3.4 THE 'INTERSECT' GROUP

These verbs indicate that two or more things are in contact. We include here *overlap*, where the meaning is metaphorical.

> *As he paused where **the three galleries intersected**, another thought occurred to him.*
> *It was well after noon and the gas gauge was almost at E before the road **intersected** a larger highway.*
>
> *The drive leads through thick woods, over boulders and a stream to a crossing where **four paths meet**.*
> *Where bones **meet** other bones to form a moving joint there is a protective covering of cartilage over the surface of the bone which stops them wearing away.*
>
> *Although each person is assigned to one area of the shop, **their roles** often **overlap**.*
> *It is not uncommon for a mother's life to **overlap** her daughter's by 70 years or more.*

In the case of *criss-cross*, the noun group following the verb is always a reciprocal pronoun.

> *The roads here are quite a maze, **criss-crossing** one another in a fashion that at times defies logic.*

criss-cross *2*	**join** *7*	**overlap** *2*
cross *1.3*	**meet** *14 (also non-recip)*	
intersect *1*	**meet** *16,17*	

The verbs *intersect 1* and *overlap* also have the pattern **V *with* n**: see meaning group 1.9.

3.5 VERBS WITH OTHER MEANINGS

There are a few other verbs with this combination of patterns.

> *John and I <u>met</u> in high school.*
> *I told you. We were friends. I <u>met</u> her about a month ago.*

> *Like charges <u>repel</u>.*
> *One way to reduce the problem is to use positrons instead of electrons, as they <u>repel</u> positive ions.*

> attract 5   meet 1,2,15
> consult 2   repel 2

Structure information: Pattern combination 3

a) In the **V n** pattern, the noun group following the verb is the Object.

b) There is a passive pattern *be* **V-ed**. However, it does not often occur.

Other patterns of reciprocal verbs

1 Patterns with 'pl-n'

In the following patterns, the verb is used with a plural Subject. These patterns are dealt with in other chapters.

pl-n V to-inf

The verb is followed by a to-infinitive clause.

> *He alleged that **the major oil companies** <u>**conspired**</u> **to fix gasoline prices** from the 1950s till the early 1970s.*

See page 94, meaning groups III.1 and III.3.

pl-n V that

The verb is followed by a that-clause.

> *Experts <u>**agree**</u> that one cause of poverty among the young is the dramatic rise in the number of single-parent families.*

See pages 98-100, meaning groups 1 and 4.

pl-n V wh

The verb is followed by a finite wh-clause.

> *The Germans <u>**are**</u> now <u>**debating**</u> whether that constitutional provision should be changed.*

See pages 106-107, meaning group 1.

pl-n V wh-to-inf

The verb is followed by a to-infinitive clause introduced by a wh-word.

> *They are waiting while **federal authorities** <u>**debate**</u> **what to do about them**.*

See page 112, meaning group 3.

pl-n V *about* n

The verb is followed by a prepositional phrase which consists of *about* and a noun group.

People still __argue__ about the costs and benefits of that development.

See pages 147-148, meaning group II.1.

pl-n V *against* n

The verb is followed by a prepositional phrase which consists of *against* and a noun group.

*But British newspapers alleged that **the government and royal family __were conspiring__ against her**, fearing she would embarrass them.*

See page 154, meaning group 1.

pl-n V *for* n

The verb is followed by a prepositional phrase which consists of *for* and a noun group.

More than 2300 candidates from 93 political parties __are competing__ for 486 seats.

See pages 178-179, meaning group II.2.

pl-n V *into* n

The verb is followed by a prepositional phrase which consists of *into* and a noun group.

The fights __coalesced__ into a battle that raged the long length of the street.

See page 204, meaning group I.1.

pl-n V *on* n

The verb is followed by a prepositional phrase which consists of *on* and a noun group.

*Even when **people __disagree__ on issues**, trust builds bridges and everyone benefits.*

See page 218, meaning group II.3, and page 223, meaning group II.17.

pl-n V *over* n

The verb is followed by a prepositional phrase which consists of *over* and a noun group.

The two sides __are squabbling__ over issues of citizenship, gold reserves and international treaties.

See pages 235-236, meaning group I.1.

2 Patterns with '*with* n'

In the following patterns, the verb is followed by a prepositional phrase beginning with *with*.

V *with* n to-inf

The prepositional phrase is followed by a to-infinitive clause which indicates what two or more people or groups are trying to do.

It said she __conspired__ with others to perform illegal campaign services.

collaborate *1*	conspire *1*
connive *1*	vie

V *with* n that

The prepositional phrase is followed by a that-clause which indicates the topic or issue involved.

*Many **would agree** with him that intelligence is something with which one is born (or not, as the case may be).*

agree *1*	concur	joke *2*

V *with* n *about* n, V *about* n *with* n

The prepositional phrase beginning with *with* is followed by another prepositional phrase beginning with *about* which indicates the topic or issue involved. The prepositional phrases may come the other way round.

*I actually **agree** with you about the gun situation.*

***Talk** about it with your partner.*

agree *1*	consult *2*	haggle	spar *2*
argue *4,5*	converse *1*	joke *2*	speak *1*
banter *2*	correspond *2*	meet *7*	squabble
bicker	dicker	natter	talk *2,6*
chat	disagree *1*	negotiate *1*	
communicate *1*	fight *6*	quarrel *3*	
confer *1*	gossip *2*	row *3.3*	

V *with* n *for* n, V *for* n *with* n

The prepositional phrase beginning with *with* is followed by another prepositional phrase beginning with *for* which indicates what two or more people or groups are trying to get. The prepositional phrases may be the other way round.

*Defence **had to compete** for money with other government services.*

*Turlington **has jostled** with Linda Evangelista, Claudia Schiffer and Naomi Campbell for the earnings crown in the past three years.*

compete *1,2,3*	jostle *2*	vie
contend *3*	struggle *4*	
jockey *2*	tussle *2*	

V *with* n *on* n, V *on* n *with* n

The prepositional phrase beginning with *with* is followed by another prepositional phrase beginning with *on* which indicates the topic or project involved. The prepositional phrases may be the other way round.

*Yes, I **do agree** with you on that.*

agree *1,3*	differ *2*
collaborate *1*	disagree *1*

V *with* n *over* n

The prepositional phrase beginning with *with* is followed by another prepositional phrase beginning with *over* which indicates the topic or issue involved.

He also __fought__ with Reagan over cutbacks in social programs.

argue *4*	fight *6*	quarrel *3*	squabble
compromise *2*	haggle	row *3.3*	wrangle

Emphasizing reciprocity

There are three ways of emphasizing the reciprocity of an action or process when using a reciprocal verb with a plural Subject.

a) With most reciprocal verbs, a **reciprocal pronoun** (*each other* or *one another*) can be used after the appropriate preposition or after the verb. These patterns are **pl-n V *with* pron-recip, pl-n V n *with* pron-recip,** and **pl-n V pron-recip.**

*All across the world today **people __are fighting__ with each other** and killing each other because of their racial and religious differences.*

The fans __would exchange__ information with one another.

They __hugged__ each other.

b) With a number of reciprocal verbs, a prepositional phrase consisting of *among* or *amongst* and a plural reflexive pronoun can be used, when there are more than two participants involved. A prepositional phrase consisting of *between* and a plural personal pronoun or reflexive pronoun is also sometimes used, and in this case there may be just two participants.

*The more **they __argue__ among themselves**, the better.*

Small groups around the room __discussed__ theories amongst themselves, looking from one suspect to another.

She tried to persuade him to eat what was left of their food but he couldn't manage it, and so the driver and Amy __shared__ it between them.

These patterns most frequently occur with the following verbs:

agree *1*	co-operate *1*	joke *2*	share *2,3 (something)*
agree *3 (something)*	debate *3 (something)*	make *1.1 (an agreement)*	sign *6 (an agreement)*
argue *4,5*	differ *1*	meet *7*	speak *1*
battle *4*	disagree *1*	quarrel *3*	squabble
bicker	discuss *1 (something)*	reach *7 (an agreement)*	swap *1 (things)*
chat	feud *2*	resolve *1 (your differences)*	talk *2,6*
compete *1,2*	fight *5,6*	row *3.3*	wrangle
confer *1*	interact *3*	settle *1 (your differences)*	

c) With a few reciprocal verbs, the adverb *together* can be used for emphasis. This pattern is **pl-n V *together*.**

Members of the group __meet__ together once a week to check their weight, discuss healthy eating and do some exercises.

They often __play__ tennis together, and share a love of Sixties music.

dance *3*	play *2 (a game)*	talk *2,6*	
meet *2,7*	share *2,3 (something)*		
merge *2*	speak *1*		

Other verbs with reciprocal meanings

a) Many verbs not mentioned in this chapter can have a reciprocal meaning. This happens when they are used with a plural Subject and followed by a reciprocal pronoun (*each other* or *one another*), as in *They hated each other*, or by a prepositional phrase containing a reciprocal pronoun, as in *They looked at each other*. These are not, however, true reciprocal verbs because they cannot be used on their own with a plural Subject, or do not have a reciprocal meaning when they are used like this. For example, you do not say *They hated*, and if you say *They looked*, you do not mean that they looked at each other.

b) Verbs which have the patterns **V pl-n** and **V** *with* **n**, **V** *to* **n**, or **V** *from* **n** have a reciprocal meaning when they are used in the passive. For example, two things *can be distinguished*, or one thing *can be distinguished from another*.

c) Some verbs with the pattern **pl-n V** *together* are similar in meaning to reciprocal verbs, but they are not regarded as true reciprocal verbs because they must be followed by the adverb *together* when used with a plural Subject. See pages 139-141.

Reciprocal phrases

There are a number of phrases which behave like reciprocal verbs and have a reciprocal meaning.

Most of them consist of a verb and a noun group, and are like the combinations of verbs and noun groups found in Pattern combination 2. A few consist of a verb and a prepositional phrase or an adverbial phrase.

They all have the patterns **pl-n PHR** and **PHR** *with* **n**.

All political parties <u>should bury the hatchet</u> and work together to help drag Australia out of the recession.
Kevin Keegan last night <u>buried the hatchet</u> with Bobby Robson, the man who upset him so much when he was dropped by England.

The police are sure to link us when they <u>compare notes</u>.
What Michelle is missing most is the chance to <u>compare notes</u> with other suffering mothers, said Marion.

<u>We'd lost touch</u> 34 years ago, when George joined the RAF.
Then after graduation Zach went to Europe, and I <u>lost touch</u> with him.

Both men were grinning as they <u>shook hands</u>.
The boy came out to meet me and I <u>shook hands</u> with him.

battle it out	go to bed	link arms	pass the time of day
bury the hatchet	go to war	lock horns	see eye to eye
change places	have it away	lose contact	settle accounts
chew the fat	have it off	lose touch	shake hands
compare notes	have it out	make contact	shoot the breeze
cross swords	have sex	make friends	shoot the bull
do battle	have words	make love	slog it out
do business	hit it off	make peace	slug it out
fall in love	hold hands	mend fences	
go hand in hand	join forces	part company	

Chapter 7: Ergative Verbs

Introduction

What an ergative verb is

An ergative verb has the following features:

- it has two patterns
- only one of these patterns has a noun group following the verb
- the person or thing indicated by that noun group may also be indicated by the Subject of the other pattern

For example, the verb *break* has two patterns, **V** and **V n**. Only one of these patterns, **V n**, has a noun group following the verb. An example of the pattern **V n** is *John broke the vase*. The noun group following the verb, *the vase*, may also be the Subject of the verb: *The vase broke*.

Combinations of patterns with ergative verbs

Some ergative verbs have symmetrical combinations of patterns. For example, the verb *break* has a combination of two patterns, **V** and **V n**. This combination is symmetrical because the only difference between the two patterns is that one has a noun group following the verb and the other does not. You say

*The stick **broke***
and *She **broke** the stick*.

Some ergative verbs have combinations of patterns that are asymmetrical, that is, the patterns are different in more ways than the presence or absence of a noun group. For example, the verb *puff* has the pattern **V n** but not the pattern **V**. Instead, it has the pattern **V prep/adv**. Therefore, you say

*The chimney **puffed** smoke*
and *Smoke **puffed** out of the chimney*

but you do not say *Smoke puffed*.

What the patterns indicate

When you use an ergative verb, you have a choice between two (or more) patterns. These patterns allow you to talk about the world in very different ways. For example, you can choose to indicate that something just happens, perhaps as a natural occurrence, without indicating that someone or something is responsible for it. Or you can indicate that someone or something is the cause of what happens and so is responsible for it. Compare the examples below. (Unlike the other examples in this book, these and the following examples in this Introduction have been invented to illustrate the differences in meaning between the patterns.)

> *The vase **broke**.*
> *John **broke** the vase.*
> *The volume often **varies**.*
> *The technician **can vary** the volume.*
> *Many factories **closed**.*
> *The government's policies **closed** many factories.*

In the first example in each pair there is only one noun group. This noun group indicates something that does something or has something happen to it: the vase breaks, the volume varies, and the factories close. We can call the vase, the volume, and the factories the 'doer'. In these examples with only a 'doer', you are not told what the cause of the action is. In fact, you may understand that the action has no cause. You may think, for example, that the vase broke by itself. Or you may understand that there is a cause but that the speaker or writer has chosen not to mention it. You may think, for example, that someone caused the vase to break but that the speaker or writer is deliberately hiding that information.

In the second example in each pair there are two noun groups. One of them is the 'doer' and the other indicates the person or thing that causes the action: John causes the vase to break, the technician causes the volume to vary, and the government's policies cause the factories to close. We can call John, the technician, and the government's policies the 'causer'. In these examples with both a 'doer' and a 'causer', you can understand the clause in only one way: that someone or something caused something to happen.

How the 'doer' and the 'causer' relate to the action depends on who or what they are. Here are some more examples:

(i) 'Doer' and 'causer' are both animate

Where the 'doer' and the 'causer' are both animate and the action is something that is under the control of the 'doer', the exact roles of the 'doer' and the 'causer' vary according to the verb.

The 'causer' may be someone in authority who encourages or orders the 'doer' to do the action.

> The horse **_galloped_** down the hill.
> The rider **_galloped_** his horse down the hill.
>
> The squad **_marched_** down the hill.
> The sergeant **_marched_** the squad down the hill.

The 'causer' may provide conditions that allow the 'doer' to do the action.

> The cows **_grazed_** in the water meadows.
> The farmer **_grazed_** the cows in the water meadows.

The 'doer' and the 'causer' may both be involved in the action, with different responsibilities.

> She **_auditioned_** on Tuesday.
> I **_auditioned_** her on Tuesday.
>
> He **_enrolled_** on a two-year course.
> The tutor **_enrolled_** him on a two-year course.

(ii) 'Doer' is inanimate, 'causer' is animate

Where the 'doer' is inanimate, or is animate but the action is not under their control, and the 'causer' is animate, the exact roles of the 'doer' and 'causer' vary according to the verb.

The 'causer' may hold ultimate responsibility for the action, even though he or she does not intend to cause the action.

> The vase **_broke_** when it fell on the floor.
> He **_broke_** the vase when he dropped it on the floor.
>
> The car **_crashed_**.
> He **_crashed_** his car.

The 'causer' may provide the conditions in which a natural process takes place.

> Raspberries **_freeze_** well.
> She **_froze_** some raspberries.

The 'causer' may not cause the action at all, but may be affected by the action, for example by suffering an injury.

*His leg **fractured**.*
*He **fractured** his leg.*

The 'doer' may not do anything, but may be affected by the action.

*The bucket **filled** in two minutes.*
*He **filled** the bucket in two minutes.*

(iii) 'Doer' may be animate or inanimate depending on the verb, 'causer' is inanimate

When the 'causer' is inanimate, it may be the immediate cause of the action.

*The vase **broke**.*
*The impact **broke** the vase.*

Alternatively, the 'causer' may be an indirect cause of the action.

*Her spirits **lifted** as if by magic.*
*The party **lifted** her spirits as if by magic.*

Patterns with reflexive pronouns

With many ergative verbs, the noun group following the verb is sometimes a reflexive pronoun. When this is the case, the 'doer' and the 'causer' are the same person or thing. Sometimes this means that there is little difference in meaning between this pattern and the pattern which mentions only the 'doer'. For example, the first two examples below mean almost the same thing, although they have different patterns, but the third example has a different meaning.

*The symptoms of the illness **manifested** ten days later.*
*The symptoms of the illness **manifested** themselves ten days later.*
*She **manifested** all the symptoms of the illness.*

Sometimes, however, the pattern with a reflexive pronoun emphasizes that the Subject of that pattern is the cause of an event and also the person or thing that is affected by it. This is true particularly when the verb involved indicates that a person suffers harm. For example, the first example below suggests that the drowning was an accident, the second example suggests that it was suicide, and the third example suggests that it was murder.

*He **drowned** in the river.*
*He **drowned** himself in the river.*
*She **drowned** him in the river.*

The following ergative verbs often have a reflexive pronoun following the verb.

acclimatize	beach 2	hang 5	plunge 4
assimilate 1	disengage 1	manifest 2	resolve 4
attach 4	drown 1	overstretch	

Ergative verbs and the passive

In patterns where there is a noun group (the Object) following the verb, the 'causer' is indicated by the Subject and the 'doer' is indicated by the Object. If that structure is made passive, however, the 'doer' becomes the Subject and the 'causer' may not be mentioned. Compare the following examples:

*The vase **broke**.*
*John **broke** the vase.*
*The vase **was broken**.*

The third example is the passive of the second example. We said above that in the first example, you may understand that the vase broke by itself or that someone caused the vase to break, whilst in the second example, you must understand that John caused the vase to break. In the third example, you understand that the vase did not break by itself, but do not know who caused the breakage. The Subjects of the first and the third examples are the same, but the meanings are different.

Actual and potential events

Most ergative verbs can be used to indicate events that have taken place (actual events), or events that might take place (potential events). An example of an actual event is:

*The glass **broke**.*

Examples of potential events are:

*This kind of glass tends to **break** in cold weather.*
*This kind of glass **breaks** easily.*

Some ergative verbs, in the pattern with the 'doer' as Subject, are usually used only to indicate potential events. The pattern with the 'causer' as Subject can be used to indicate both actual and potential events.

*This cream smells clean and fresh, and **applies** easily.*
*After you have stepped from a warm bath, **apply the cream** evenly over your body.*

*These eye shadows **won't fade** or crease and contain herbal extracts to soften the skin.*
*Ultraviolet light **will fade the colours in organic materials**.*

These verbs are indicated in the meaning groups described below.

Ergative link verbs

There are a few verbs which are ergative and which in one of their patterns only are **link verbs** (see also Chapter 5). For example, the verb *turn*, in the pattern **V colour**, is a link verb. It also has the pattern **V n colour**, in which it is not a link verb.

*The feet start to burn, feel hot to the touch, and **turn** bright red.*
*She experienced a tremendous flush, **turning** her bright red.*

The following verbs are **ergative link verbs**.

form *3*	rank *4*	turn *17*
keep *1*	rate *6*	

About this chapter

In this chapter you will find information about all the combinations of patterns that occur with ergative verbs. As in the other chapters, information about clause structure is given here. This information is less detailed than in the other chapters, however. For example, we do not here show the patterns or structures of passives, or of phrasal verbs, although we do include examples of passives and phrasal verbs.

If you want to find out more about the patterns and structures described in this chapter, look in the relevant sections in Chapters 1-4.

Pattern Combinations

There are six symmetrical combinations of patterns.

▶ Pattern combination 1: V; V n
*The vase **broke**.*
*John **broke** the vase.*
▶ Pattern combination 2: V prep/adv; V n prep/adv
*The boat **sailed** up the river.*
*We **sailed** the boat up the river.*

▶ Pattern combination 3: V adj; V n adj
  The door _slammed_ shut.
  She _slammed_ the door shut.

▶ Pattern combination 4: V *as* adj; V n *as* adj
  That score _counts_ as successful.
  We _count_ that score as successful.

▶ Pattern combination 5: V to-inf; V n to-inf
  She _trained_ to compete.
  They _trained_ her to compete.

▶ Pattern combination 6: V ord prep; V n ord prep
  They _rank_ sixth in the world.
  Most people _rank_ them sixth in the world.

There are four asymmetrical combinations.

▶ Pattern combination 7: V prep/adv; V n; V n prep/adv
  Light _reflects_ on the water.
  The mirror _reflects_ light.
  The glass _reflected_ light onto the wall.

▶ Pattern combination 8: V prep/adv; V n
  Smoke _puffed_ out of the chimney.
  The chimney _puffed_ smoke.

▶ Pattern combination 9: V adv; V n
  This carpet _cleans_ easily.
  We _cleaned_ the carpet.

▶ Pattern combination 10: V adj; V n
  The chair _folds_ flat.
  He _folded_ the chair.

Pattern combination 1: V; V n

In the pattern **V**, the verb can be used on its own, without anything following it. In the pattern **V n**, the verb is followed by a noun group. This pattern combination is symmetrical.

This combination of patterns has one combination of structures:

▶ Verb; Verb with Object
  The window _broke_.
  They _broke_ the window.

V

	Verb group	
Subject	**Verb**	**Adjunct (optional)**
The pattern	altered.	
The foghorn	blasted.	
My spirits	lifted.	
That meeting	will reconvene	in two weeks.

V n

	Verb group	noun group	
Subject	**Verb**	**Object**	**Adjunct (optional)**
All creatures	alter	their own environment	a little.
Some motorists	blast	their horns	in support.
Sunlight	can lift	the spirits.	
Ministers	will reconvene	their meeting	today.

Verbs with this combination of patterns belong to the following meaning groups:

Groups of verbs concerned with change

1.1 THE 'CHANGE' GROUP	1.9 THE 'CLOG UP' GROUP
1.2 THE 'BREAK' GROUP	1.10 THE 'BLUR' GROUP
1.3 THE 'DISSOLVE' AND 'SOLIDIFY' GROUP	1.11 THE 'DIVIDE' GROUP
1.4 THE 'COOK' GROUP	1.12 THE 'QUICKEN' AND 'SLOW DOWN' GROUP
1.5 THE 'EXPAND' AND 'COMPRESS' GROUP	1.13 THE 'OPEN' AND 'CLOSE' GROUP
1.6 THE 'IMPROVE' AND 'WORSEN' GROUP	1.14 THE 'CALM DOWN' GROUP
1.7 THE 'BLISTER' GROUP	1.15 THE 'WEAKEN' AND 'STRENGTHEN' GROUP
1.8 THE 'BLEACH' GROUP	

Groups of verbs concerned with movement and action

1.16 THE 'DETACH' GROUP
1.17 THE 'REVERSE' GROUP
1.18 THE 'SPURT OUT' GROUP
1.19 THE 'CLENCH' AND 'RELAX' GROUP
1.20 THE 'ASSEMBLE' AND 'DISBAND' GROUP
1.21 THE 'OVERWORK' GROUP
1.22 THE 'LEAK' GROUP

Groups of verbs concerned with starting something

1.23 THE 'START' AND 'STOP' GROUP
1.24 THE 'DEVELOP' GROUP
1.25 THE 'AWAKEN' GROUP
1.26 THE 'HOOT' GROUP
1.27 THE 'DETONATE' AND 'PLAY' GROUP

1.28 VERBS WITH OTHER MEANINGS

1.1 THE 'CHANGE' GROUP

In the pattern **V**, these verbs are concerned with something changing. In the pattern **V n**, they are concerned with someone or something bringing about a change. The verbs in this group have general meanings. More specific kinds of change are dealt with in other meaning groups below.

> *As society **has changed** in Java, the ways in which dancers are taught **have** also **changed**. Those who wish to **change** society have to create an active, political community.*

alter	change *3*	metamorphose	vary *2*

1.2 THE 'BREAK' GROUP

These verbs are concerned with something breaking or being damaged. They may be divided into two groups:

(i) In the pattern **V**, these verbs indicate that something breaks or shows damage of some kind. In the pattern **V n**, they indicate that someone or something breaks or damages something or someone. The Subject in the pattern **V n** is the person or thing that causes the damage.

> *He slammed the door with such force that a window **broke**.*
> *They threw stones and **broke** the windows of buses.*

> *While children can swallow many small objects without ill effect, batteries can cause severe damage if they **corrode** inside the body.*
> *It is claimed that chewing gum helps prevent tooth decay by stimulating saliva, which neutralises the acids that **can corrode** teeth.*

> *In due time, Carey would go free while his accomplices **hanged**.*
> *The convicted men were due to **be hanged** this week, having lost their appeal recently.*

With some of these verbs, the pattern **V** is usually used to indicate that something often happens (a potential event), rather than to indicate an actual event.

> *Men tend to **bruise** far more than women, because of the way their fat is arranged on the body.*

These verbs are often followed by an adverb such as *easily*. This pattern is **V adv** (see also page 137).

> *I keep a jar of comfrey ointment which clears up bruises fast. I **bruise** very easily and the ointment is brilliant.*

break *1,3,4*	crack *1.1*	fuse *2*	scuff *1*
bruise *2,3*	crumble *1*	hang *5*	shatter *1*
buckle *3*	deform	jam *3*	short-circuit *1*
burn *11,12*	derail *2*	mark *2*	snap *1*
burst *1,2*	drown *1*	puncture *4*	split *5*
chip *6*	erode *1*	rip *1*	suffocate *1,2*
choke *1*	flake *3*	rupture *4*	tear *2.1*
corrode *1*	fray *1*	scorch *2*	warp *1*
blow up *1*	burn up *1*	wear down *1*	
burn down	wear away	wear out *1*	

(ii) In the pattern **V**, these verbs indicate that something breaks or shows damage of some kind. In the pattern **V n**, they indicate that something is broken or damaged. The Subject of the pattern **V n** may be someone or something that suffers damage to a part of themselves, as in *I fractured my skull*, or it may be someone who is responsible for the thing at the time that it is damaged, as in *I crashed my car*.

> *A couple of fuses **had blown**, so I had to trot over the road to Halfords.*
> *When I tried to factor in the extra odds, my computer **blew** a fuse.*

> *When Julie was a baby they had to literally wrap her up in cotton wool to make sure no bones **broke**.*
> *Suzanne ran anxiously down the path assuming he'**d broken** a leg.*

blow *1.11,12 (a fuse or tyre)*	crash *2*	overstretch
break *2 (a bone)*	crash-land	rupture *2*
burn *5*	fracture *2*	tear *2.4*

1.3 THE 'DISSOLVE' AND 'SOLIDIFY' GROUP

In the pattern **V**, these verbs are concerned with something changing in some physical way. In the pattern **V n**, they are concerned with someone or something causing a physical change in something. The Subject in the pattern **V n** may be a person who makes a process happen, or provides conditions for a process to happen, as in *The scientist condensed the vapor*, or something that takes part in the process, as in *The cold atmosphere condensed the vapor*. In the case of some verbs, such as *ripen, ripple*, and *rot*, the second kind of Subject is more frequent.

*Stir the mixture with a metal spoon until the sugar **has dissolved**.*
***Dissolve** the sugar in the warm water and add the dried yeast.*

*The seed **will** only **germinate** when the weather is warm and damp.*
*First, the researchers **germinated** the plantain seeds.*

*The engineers filled the glasses with water and gunned the engine to 157 miles per hour. The water in the glasses **didn't** even **ripple**.*
*The surface of the water **was rippled** by a sudden wind.*

*Silicon **solidifies** as it cools.*
*The latest snowfall was soft, but the bitter cold **had solidified** the layers beneath it.*

*After a few minutes, the clumps of trees started to **thin out**, and Nancy realized she was heading uphill.*
*The trees **had been thinned out** for cooking fires. They were able to move fast.*

burn 4 *(fuel)*	dull 8	liquefy	solidify 1
chill 1	empty 6	loosen 3	spoil 4
coarsen 1	emulsify	melt 1	stabilize
condense 2	evaporate 1	mutate 1	steady 5
cool 5	fatten 1	naturalize 1	tarnish 2
crystallize 2	ferment 2	overheat 1	thaw 3
curdle	fill 1	oxidize	thicken 1
decompose	flood 2	perish 3	thin 11
deepen 4 *(a sound)*	fossilize 1	regenerate 2	tighten 2
defrost 2 *(a freezer)*	freeze 1	ripen	toughen 1
digest 1	germinate 1	ripple 2,3	turn 20
dilute 1	harden 1	root 2	vaporize
dissipate 1	hatch 2	rot 1	weather 2
dissolve 1	heal 1	shrivel	
drain 2,3	improve 1	singe	
dry 2	incubate 2	soften 1	
boil away	dry out 1	firm up 1	thaw out 2,▷3
cool down ▷5	dry up 1	grow out *(a hairstyle)*	thin out ▷11
cool off	even out	light up 1	warm up 1
dry off	fill up ▷1	liven up 1	

1.4 THE 'COOK' GROUP

In the pattern **V**, these verbs indicate that food cooks. In the pattern **V n**, they are concerned with someone cooking food. The Subject of the pattern **V n** is usually the person who cooks the food, but it is sometimes the fuel or cooking equipment that is used.

*While the water **boiled**, I picked up the shopping and put it away.*
*Milwaukee residents have been advised to **boil** their tap water or drink bottled water.*

*Buffalo meat **cooks** faster than beef.*
*I have to have cakes and pastries in my life; fortunately my wife **cooks** them brilliantly.*
*The heat from the coals **cooks** the food.*

*Stir until the soup **is** just **simmering**.*
***Simmer** the vegetables in the lemon juice and stock for 10 minutes.*

In the case of *boil 2*, the Subject of the **V** pattern and the Object of the **V n** pattern is the container of the food or liquid.

*Ann and Mrs Kelly were standing awkwardly in the kitchen waiting for the kettle to **boil**.*
*You will almost certainly want to **boil** a kettle within minutes of arrival.*

In the case of *freeze*, the pattern **V** is used to indicate that a particular food does not come to harm when it is frozen.

*The Iced Apricot and Almond Cream and Iced Maple and Pistachio Cream **will freeze**.*

The verb is often followed by the adverb *easily* or *well*. This pattern is **V adv** (see meaning group 9.1 below for other verbs with this pattern and use).

*Marrows **don't freeze** well, but they can be stored by hanging in nets.*

bake *2*	crisp *2*	macerate	percolate *2*
boil *1,2,4*	defrost *1*	marinade *2*	reduce *5 (a liquid)*
brown *5*	dissolve *1*	marinate	simmer *1*
char *1*	freeze *2*	mature *6*	steam *3*
cook *2*	infuse *3*	melt *1*	thaw *3*
boil away	thaw out *2,▷3*	warm up *1*	

1.5 THE 'EXPAND' AND 'COMPRESS' GROUP

In the pattern **V**, most of these verbs are concerned with the size, degree, shape, or configuration of something changing. The verbs *bend, curl, curve, kink,* and *taper 1* indicate what shape something is, rather than how a shape changes. In the pattern **V n**, these verbs are concerned with someone or something changing the size, degree, shape, or configuration of something.

*When we breathe in, the lymphatic vessels in the abdomen **compress**.*
*The implosion **would compress** any metal at its core.*

*I tried to concentrate on the qualities I admired in him: his confidence, his charm, the way his hair **curled** at the nape of his neck.*
*He spent hours on end **curling** a strand of his hair with his fingertips and looking stupid.*

*The hot weather has caused the track to **expand** slightly.*
*This old-fashioned wooden Shoe Stretcher has special attachments that **expand** the leather in the specific spots where your foot needs more room.*

*With the use of random drug testing, the chance of being caught **has increased**.*
*Just one severe sunburn in childhood **can increase** the chances of developing skin cancer.*

*Fighting **has** also **intensified** in other cities throughout the republic.*
*In recent weeks, the guerrillas **have intensified** their attacks.*

*Relax your muscles and feel your spine **straighten out**.*
*Osteopathy is gentle – **straightening out** the pelvis and lower back to improve movement and breathing.*

In the case of *compress, crease, tangle, tie, unzip,* and *zip up*, the patterns **V** and **V P** are usually used to indicate that something may happen or often happens, rather than to describe an actual occurrence.

*I don't use Styls lines because they tend to **tangle** in the wind.*

bend *5*	deflate *2*	halve *1*	redouble *(efforts)*
coil *6*	diminish *1*	increase *1*	shorten *1,2*
compress *1*	double *9*	inflate *1,2*	shrink *2*
concertina *2*	ease *4*	intensify	slacken *1*
contract *3*	elongate	kink *2*	snag *2*
crease *2*	enlarge *1*	lengthen *1,2*	straighten *3*
crumple *1*	erode *2,3*	lessen	stretch *8,10*
curl *3*	escalate	moderate *5*	swell *1*
curve *2*	expand *1,2*	multiply *1*	swivel *1*
decrease *1*	flatten *1*	narrow *5*	tangle *2*
deepen *1*	grow *2,3,4,5,12*	quadruple *1*	taper *1,2*

tie 5	uncoil	unravel 3	unzip
treble 1	unfold 3	unroll	widen 1,2,4
triple 2	unfurl 1	unwind 2	wrinkle 4
build up ▷8,1	ease off	fold up ▷4	slim down 1 (a company)
bulk up	fan out 2	ratchet up	straighten out ▷3
crumple up ▷1	flatten out ▷1	ruck up	zip up

1.6 THE 'IMPROVE' AND 'WORSEN' GROUP

In the pattern **V**, these verbs are concerned with something changing in some abstract way. In the pattern **V n**, they are concerned with someone or something causing an abstract change in something.

> In South Asia, the region most usually associated with mass poverty, the situation **is** now **improving** quite rapidly.
> We are convinced that he **could improve** the political situation.

> As our economy **strengthens**, our government will be able to recreate the caring services and the decent standards to which I believe a civilised society rightly aspires.
> Optimists believe that this **will strengthen** the companies' revenue.

> In 1991 the Oklahoma plant began to **wind down**.
> The recession went on and on, and I slowly **wound down** the business.

> In addition to the problem of poverty of the old, there is concern over the problem of family poverty, which continues to **worsen**.
> The Pope said that war would be a disaster for all of humanity and **would** only **worsen** the problems of the region.

bounce 10 (a cheque)	globalize	sharpen 3 (a disagreement)
brighten 4	heal 3 (a situation)	soften 3
broaden 2	improve 1,2	solidify 2
clear 18 (a cheque)	industrialize 1	sour 5 (a relationship)
depreciate (a currency)	loosen 2,6	strengthen 3,4,6
develop 4,7	normalize 1	thaw 4 (relations)
dim 8 (hope)	ossify	tighten 3 (its grip)
dissolve 5	overheat 2 (an economy)	unravel 2
drop 1	petrify 2	weaken 1
dull 8	relax 4 (a rule)	worsen
float 10 (a currency)	reunite 2	
fossilize 2 (an idea)	revive 1	
bog down	even out	rev up 2 (a situation)
brighten up ▷4	firm up 2	sharpen up
broaden out 1	liven up 1	turn around/round 3
calm down 2	move along 2	wind down 3 (a business)
clear up 3	open up 2	
ease off	perk up 3	

1.7 THE 'BLISTER' GROUP

In the pattern **V**, these verbs are concerned with someone experiencing something physically. In the pattern **V n**, they are concerned with something having a physical effect on someone. The Subject in the pattern **V n** is often inanimate. The Object in that pattern, and the Subject in the pattern **V**, is a part of the body.

> My left hand is dead to sensation. I could accidentally pick up scalding cups of coffee and not feel a thing although my hand **would blister**.
> Some persons are able to endure fire, for example, handle, walk on, or roll in hot coals without **being blistered**.

> Coughing and hacking, her eyes **stinging**, she backed out of Joe's room.
> Sand **stung** his eyes.

age 4	cloud 5	dilate	sharpen 1
blister 2	constrict 1	dim 9	stiffen 2
blur 4	convulse	distend	sting 4
chafe 1	crease 3	knot 5	wrinkle 2
churn 3	dehydrate 2	mend 2	

stiffen up ▷2

1.8 THE 'BLEACH' GROUP

In the pattern **V**, these verbs are concerned with a colour or degree of brightness changing. In the pattern **V n**, they are concerned with someone or something making a colour or degree of brightness change.

The verbs in this group, when used in the pattern **V**, often indicate that something may change colour or has a tendency to change colour (a potential event), rather than that a colour has actually changed.

*It is forbidden to cut indigo, make charcoal, or put cloth out to **bleach** in the sun.*
*We make our own yarn, we weave it, we **bleach** it, we cut and sew.*

*Don't worry if the bananas **discolour** slightly – even when sliced at the last minute, they tend to turn brown.*
*This furniture should be stored indoors, because rust **will discolour** the metal and the fabrics.*

blacken 1	darken 1	discolour	redden
bleach 2	deepen 3	fade 1	whiten
brighten 5	dim 7	lighten 1	

1.9 THE 'CLOG UP' GROUP

In the pattern **V P**, these verbs are concerned with something such as a pipe becoming blocked. In the patterns **V n P** and **V P n (not pron)**, they are concerned with something blocking something such as a pipe.

*I could stop worrying about my arteries **clogging up** so quickly again.*
*Too much butter will start to **clog up** the arteries and lead to excess body fat.*

block up	freeze up	silt up
clog up	fur up	

1.10 THE 'BLUR' GROUP

In the pattern **V**, these verbs are concerned with a glass or image becoming cloudy or distorted. In the pattern **V n**, they are concerned with something making a glass or image cloudy or distorted. In the pattern **V n**, the Subject indicates the cause of the cloudiness or distortion.

*Alex frowned at the white figure; it was beginning to **blur**.*
*This creates a spectrum of colours at the edges of objects which **blurs** the image.*

blur 2	distort 2	mist 2
cloud 6	fog 4	

fog up ▷4

1.11 THE 'DIVIDE' GROUP

In the pattern **V**, these verbs are concerned with a thing, organization, or group of people dividing into two or more parts. In the pattern **V n**, they are concerned with someone or something dividing a thing, organization, or group of people in this way.

*The gene causes a problem in the way cells **divide**.*
*The suggestion that I proposed to **divide** the city is absolute nonsense.*

*This inbred world **is** dividing and **polarising**.*
*He **has to polarize** the electorate.*

*When the Soviet Union **split up**, Sahlins lost touch with the theater completely.*
*One of the largest commuter airlines in the country **may be split up**.*

degrade *3*	fracture *3*	split *2*
demerge	fragment *2*	
divide *1*	polarize	
break down *4*	break up *1*	split up *3*

1.12 THE 'QUICKEN' AND 'SLOW DOWN' GROUP

In the pattern **V**, these verbs are concerned with something happening more quickly or more slowly. In the pattern **V n**, they are concerned with someone or something making something happen more quickly or more slowly.

*The pace of unification began to **quicken** at the beginning of this year.*
*The crisis has at least indirectly forced the President to **quicken** the pace of change.*

*The car never **slowed down**. Its tires squealed as it sped round the corner and out of sight.*
*The idea was dreamed up to **slow down** traffic and protect cyclists in built-up areas.*

accelerate *1*	quicken	slow *5*
slow down *1*	slow up	speed up *1,2*

1.13 THE 'OPEN' AND 'CLOSE' GROUP

In the pattern **V**, these verbs are concerned with something opening or closing. In the pattern **V n**, they are concerned with someone or something opening or closing something.

*Rumbelows said 200 of its 500 shops **may close** within two years.*
*Business was so bad Lynn McCourtney got a job out of town and **is closing** the shop.*

*The door **opened** and Mrs MacMahon, carrying a tray, entered.*
*Before anyone realised what was happening he **opened** the door and jumped onto the track.*

close *1.1,4,5*	reopen *1,6*
open *1,3,12,18,19,20,26*	shut *1,4*
close down ▷*1.5*	open up ▷*3,*▷*12*
close up *1,2*	shut down

1.14 THE 'CALM DOWN' GROUP

In the pattern **V**, these verbs are concerned with someone starting to have a feeling or emotion. In the pattern **V n**, they are concerned with someone or something making someone feel an emotion.

*Just **calm down** and tell me what's happened.*
*Frannie spent two hours on the phone with Dede, trying to **calm her down**.*

*All the passengers in the aircraft got up and sort of ran to the front of the plane as the stewardesses were yelling, '**Don't panic!**'*

*Cats **could** easily **panic** the birds and cause the eggs to be broken.*

(not) budge *1*	mellow *3*	suffocate *3*
freak *5*	panic *3*	tire *1*
heal *2*	relax *1*	worry *1,2*
calm down *1*	cool down *2*	perk up *1*
cheer up	crease up	warm up *4*

1.15 THE 'WEAKEN' AND 'STRENGTHEN' GROUP

In the pattern **V**, these verbs are concerned with someone experiencing something mentally. In the pattern **V n**, they are concerned with something affecting someone's mind or attitudes. The Subject in the pattern **V n** is often inanimate. The Object in that pattern, and the Subject in the pattern **V**, is an aspect of the mind, thoughts, or emotions.

*But later, the acid returns to Ryder's tongue, he hunches over the table, and his mood appears to **darken** once more.*
*Nothing **was going to darken** his mood today.*

*Nationalist feeling **has strengthened**.*
*Economic blockades **may strengthen** nationalist feeling.*

*When other men asked me out, the healthy part of me accepted, but as the day wore on, resolve **would weaken**.*
*No act of defiance **will weaken** our resolve or shake our determination.*

boggle	dim *10 (memory)*	lift *5*	stir *4 (memory)*
build *6 (confidence)*	fray *2*	lighten *3*	strengthen *7*
cool *6 (an emotion)*	harden *2 (attitudes)*	melt *4*	weaken *2*
crystallize *1 (opinion)*	heighten *(a feeling)*	sharpen *1*	
darken *2*	jangle *2*	stiffen *3*	
build up ▷*6 (confidence)*	wear out *3 (a welcome)*		

1.16 THE 'DETACH' GROUP

In the pattern **V**, these verbs are concerned with someone or something moving, but not under their own control. In the pattern **V n**, they are concerned with someone or something moving someone or something, or putting someone or something somewhere. We include here *accrue* and *accumulate*, where the movement is sometimes metaphorical.

Many of these verbs also have patterns with adverbs or prepositional phrases (see meaning group 2.8 below), and for most of them those patterns are more frequent.

*Her six-monthly statements would have revealed how little interest **was accruing**.*
*It has promised that the bank's customers will not lose their money, which will continue to **accrue** interest.*

*A cable connects the seat to the aircraft. When this is pulled tight, it **detaches** and ignites the rocket pack below the seat.*
*One night we unscrew every screw and unplug every plug and **detach** every wire and then that night we put in new systems.*

*Dark, dusty alleys separated the buildings, and lines of brightly colored clothes **flapped** like flags on clotheslines stretched across the rooftops.*
*Icy wind **flapped** his overcoat and he turned his back to escape its knife-like pain on his face.*

*The first stone fitted exactly over the other stone, and then they **would** both **revolve**.*
*Karlov picked up a round ruler like a baton and **revolved** it slowly between his long fingers.*

In the case of *recline*, the pattern **V** is used to indicate that something such as a chair has a particular quality which can be made use of rather than to indicate an actual occurrence.

*Air France first-class seats **recline** almost like beds.*

*Charles **had reclined** his seat and was lying back smoking.*

accrue *1,2*	flap *1*	refract *(light)*	swirl
accumulate	flutter *1*	revolve *4*	tilt *1*
balance *8*	fly *7*	rewind *1*	turn *3,4*
bounce *1,4*	ground *15*	rock *5*	twirl *1*
(not) budge *2*	jar *5*	rotate *1*	unscrew *1*
circulate *1,2*	jolt *1*	settle *8*	unstick
collect *4*	jumble *2*	shake *7*	vibrate
detach *1*	land *14*	shift *1*	waggle
disengage *1*	move *1*	slop *1*	whirl *1*
disperse *1*	overturn *1*	slosh *1*	wiggle
engage *6 (a mechanism)*	part *2.1*	spin *1*	
entwine *2*	recline *2*	submerge *1*	
break off *1*	jumble up ▷*2*	shear off	turn over *1*
double up	pile up *1*	tip over	
get away *3*	pour in	tip up	
hang up ▷*1*	rain down ▷*4*	turn around *2*	

1.17 THE 'REVERSE' GROUP

In the pattern **V**, these verbs are concerned with a vehicle moving. In the pattern **V n**, they are concerned with someone driving or operating a vehicle. We include here *capsize*, *refuel*, and *sink*.

> *The authorities in Japan said the ship would not be allowed to **dock**.*
> *Carpenter **docked** his ship and turned over his command.*

> *The van came to a halt, **reversed**, halted again.*
> *A gunman opened fire as PC Whitehouse **reversed** the car in a desperate attempt to escape.*

> *Then my engine **stalled**, and had to be restarted.*
> *She **stalled** the engine, and restarted it.*

In the case of *capsize*, *halt*, and *sink*, the Subject in the pattern **V n** may be inanimate.

> *Two anglers died when a wave **capsized** their 17ft boat off Cresswell, Northumberland.*

Most of these verbs have another **V** pattern in which the Subject indicates the person driving or operating the vehicle.

> *When she got out, the driver **reversed**, crushing her against the patrol car.*

anchor *2*	dock *2*	rev *1*	start *6*
back *3.2*	halt *1*	reverse *4*	stop *5*
beach *2*	land *7*	sail *3*	swerve
capsize	navigate *1*	sink *3*	tack *4*
ditch *4*	refuel	stall *4*	
rev up ▷*1*	start up ▷*6*	warm up *3*	

1.18 THE 'SPURT OUT' GROUP

These verbs are concerned with liquids, gases, or flames coming out of a container. In the pattern **V**, the Subject indicates the liquid, gas, or flame. In the pattern **V n**, the Subject indicates the container.

> *Bake the lemon in the oven at a moderate heat until it begins to crack open and the juice starts to **exude**.*
> *The dandelion is composed of a tapering root and green serrated leaves, both of which **exude** a milky juice when cut.*

> *The point of the blade slipped further in and a few drops of blood **spurted out**.*
> *So now when the washing machine **spurts out** water at least we can mop it up.*

> exude 2   leak 1   spurt 1
>
> spurt out ▷1

1.19 THE 'CLENCH' AND 'RELAX' GROUP

These verbs are concerned with movements of part of the body, or changes in behaviour. In the pattern **V**, the Subject indicates the part of the body or aspect of behaviour. In the pattern **V n**, the Subject indicates the person whose body or behaviour is involved.

*He got suddenly angry. His fists **clenched**.*
*She **clenched** her fists. She stared at him fiercely.*

*Your ears **prick up** when you hear discouraging or nasty remarks.*
*The dog **pricked up** its ears, wagged its tail, and scrambled into the back of the truck.*

*The tensed muscles of the animal slowly **relaxed**.*
*These tapes will help you to **relax** each muscle in your body.*

*Her speech **was slurring**. She was tired and said she was dying.*
*I **was slurring** my words a bit.*

*Jill's voice **softened**, and her eyes were normal again.*
*She was unable to **soften** her voice.*

In the case of *loosen up*, *tense up*, and *twitch*, in the patterns **V** and **V P**, the Subject may indicate a part of the body or a person.

*His face **tensed up** a bit once more.*
*Baxter **tensed up**.*

adjust 4	deepen 5	narrow 3	soften 4
arch 4,5	drop 8	open 4	tan 2
beat 8	flail 1	pucker	tauten
bend 3	flap 2	relax 2	thrash 3
clench 1	flare 5	retract 2	tighten 1
close 1.3	focus 5	roll 9	twitch
coarsen 2	furrow 4	ruffle 4	work 27
contort	jut 2	shut 3	wrinkle 5
crinkle 1	loosen 5	slacken 2	
curl 5,9	lower 8	slur 2	
ball up 3	prick up	tense up ▷4	
loosen up 2	screw up 1		

1.20 THE 'ASSEMBLE' AND 'DISBAND' GROUP

These verbs are concerned with a group of people moving or doing something together. This includes:

- forming a group e.g. *assemble, organize*
- splitting a group up e.g. *demobilize, disband*
- going somewhere as a group e.g. *pull out, relocate*
- behaving in a particular way as a group e.g. *bunch up, rotate*

In the pattern **V**, the Subject indicates the group of people. In the pattern **V n**, the Subject indicates someone who organizes the group or something that motivates the group to do something.

*Monks **should assemble** at the full and new moons for a form of private mutual confession.*
*While in his twenties he **had** bought a boat, **assembled** a crew, and sailed round the world.*

*On November 17th the group voted quietly to **disband**.*
*At the end of 1780 Washington **had to disband** part of his army for lack of clothing.*

*We**'re going to unite** and we're going to win the next general election.*
*Opposition to the government **unites** soldiers and civilians.*

In the case of *rotate*, the Subject of the pattern **V** and the Object of the pattern **V n** is sometimes inanimate.

> *If there is a leader __will__ the leadership __rotate__ among the members?*
> *The new party rules __rotate__ the leadership.*

assemble *1*	mobilize *1,3*	regroup	rotate *2*
demobilize	muster *2*	relocate	scatter *2*
disband	organize *5 (workers)*	reorganize	settle *6*
disperse *2*	reassemble *2*	resettle	unite
mass *9*	redeploy *1*	reunite *1*	withdraw *2*
bunch up	pull back *2*	turn back *1*	
hold together	pull out *3*		
line up *1*	split up *2*		

1.21 THE 'OVERWORK' GROUP

These verbs are concerned with a person or animal going somewhere or doing something, under their own control. In the pattern **V**, the Subject indicates the person or animal who moves or does something. In the pattern **V n**, the Subject indicates the person or group of people who:

- makes the person or animal move or do something
- encourages the person or animal to move or do something
- provides conditions that allow the person or animal to move or do something

> *A jolly baby __may feed__ eagerly, but after the first three or four months may keep breaking off to have a little 'chat' or a giggle with you.*
> *The simplest thing to do is to __feed__ your baby.*

> *I push myself too hard. I __overwork__ a lot.*
> *He blamed his heart attack on his employer for __overworking__ him.*

> *If only I had taken better care of him, if only I had insisted he __slow down__, or eat more sensibly.*
> *Meanwhile, Maria refused to let pregnancy __slow__ her __down__.*

> *As the distribution started the crowd __stampeded__ and many were crushed or trampled underfoot.*
> *The next moment Joe yelled, 'They__'re stampeding__ the herd!'*

assimilate *1*	hush *2*	quiet *10*	retrain
feed *4*	integrate *1*	quieten *1*	run *3 (a horse)*
graze *1*	nurse *6*	rearm	stampede *2*
hatch *1 (a bird)*	overwork	reform *3*	train *2.1,3*
dry out *2*	move along *1*	quieten down	sober up
hold back *1*	pull up *3*	shut up	trip up
liven up *2*	quiet down	slow down *2*	

1.22 THE 'LEAK' GROUP

These verbs are concerned with something moving metaphorically. In the pattern **V**, the Subject indicates the thing that 'moves'. In the pattern **V n**, the Subject indicates someone or something that makes the thing 'move'.

> *NBC Radio was afraid that the news __would leak__.*
> *It would help calm the furious row if details of the trip __were leaked__.*

> *Perhaps, after ten years in office, it is inevitable that problems __pile up__.*
> *We sometimes waste our energy __piling up__ and dwelling on __years of worries__.*

leak *3*	shift *2*	spread *5*
pile up *2*	spill out	

1.23 THE 'START' AND 'STOP' GROUP

In the pattern **V**, these verbs are concerned with an activity starting or stopping. In the pattern **V n**, they are concerned with someone or something starting or stopping an activity.

> At one stage during the day there was every chance that the meeting **might break up** without any resolution being passed at all.
> The meeting **was broken up** and was called again at six o'clock this morning.

> The blaze **started** in the kitchens of the thirty-six floor hotel.
> The following year she **started** a blaze at her husband's parents' home.

> For now, the fighting **has stopped**, but the guns haven't.
> We're doing what must be done if we**'re going to stop** the fighting.

adjourn	convene	reconvene	start 2
begin 2	end 2	restart	still 2.4 (a sound)
commence	halt 2	resume 1	stop 4
continue 2,4	recommence	stall 1	terminate 1
break up 3,4	strike up 2 (a tune)		
kick off 2	taper off ▷2		

1.24 THE 'DEVELOP' GROUP

In the pattern **V**, these verbs are concerned with something coming into existence or becoming noticeable. In the pattern **V n**, they are concerned with someone or something making something come into existence, making it noticeable, or noticing it.

In the pattern **V n**, the Subject may indicate:

- someone who brings something into being, as in *The children formed a circle*
- someone or something that is the unconscious source or cause of something, as in *She manifests self-confidence*
- someone who is affected by what is brought into being, as in *He developed measles*

> Concepts **develop** in parallel and even the greatest thinkers see their initial thoughts developed by others.
> He **has developed** the concept of a teaching programme for unborn children.

> Fear about my blindness **didn't register**, as I was in such a state with the pain.
> She **had** quickly **registered** the difference between Archie's run-down residence and the opulent garage, but said nothing.

> A pair of pliers **turned up** in the pocket of a borrowed jacket.
> He **turned up** a frightening arsenal of licensed and unlicensed guns.

develop 8 (an illness)	form 3,9	obtrude	register 4,7
develop 11 (an idea)	form 10 (a relationship)	premiere 2	run 30 (Newspaper...a story)
evolve 2	manifest 2	re-form	show 6,7
brew up 2 (a situation)	open up 3 (opportunities)	turn up 2	
get across (an idea)	show up 1		

1.25 THE 'AWAKEN' GROUP

In the pattern **V**, these verbs are concerned with someone waking up. In the pattern **V n**, they are concerned with someone or something making someone wake up.

> The tea dishes must be done before the old woman **awakened**.
> The sound of the door opening **awakened** her.

> One woman fans her with a magazine, another gets some water, and she finally **revives**.
> Alan tried to give Natalie the kiss of life but failed to **revive** her.

> We **have to wake up** early.

*Imagine **being woken up** by the smell of burning coming from downstairs.*

awake 3	revive 3	wake 1
awaken 3	rouse 1	waken
wake up ▷1	waken up ▷	

1.26 THE 'HOOT' GROUP

In the pattern **V**, these verbs are concerned with something making a noise. In the pattern **V n**, they are concerned with someone or something doing something that makes a noise, either deliberately or by accident.

*The coal dust **crunched** with gritty familiarity under his feet.*
*She ran for her car, **crunching** old branches underfoot and making far too much noise.*

*Somewhere in the distance a siren **hooted**.*
*As he drove away he **hooted** his horn.*

*The horses wheeled together again, stirrup irons **jingling** under the riders' black boots as the police regrouped for another charge.*
*If your baby seems fascinated by a mobile, **do** you **jingle** it even more?*

bang 3	clack	jingle 1	tinkle 2
beat 4	click 1	ratchet 2	toll 1
beep 2	crack 1.2	rattle 1	toot
blare	crunch 2	ring 1.3	twang 1
blast 7	honk 1	rustle 1	
blow 1.6	hoot 1	slam 1	
chink 3	jangle 1	sound 1.5	
blare out ▷	blast out	boom out ▷6	

1.27 THE 'DETONATE' AND 'PLAY' GROUP

In the pattern **V**, these verbs are concerned with a machine or device working or a natural process happening. In the pattern **V n**, they are concerned with someone or something operating the machine or device or providing conditions that allow the natural process to happen.

*Two days later nine firebombs went off in shops in Manchester city centre, while four more failed to **detonate**.*
*He threatened to **detonate** an explosive device, and told the pilot to take the plane to Taiwan.*

*The normal clutch is four white eggs which usually **hatch** after about 14 days.*
*This pair was for many years kept in a cage indoors, where they laid eggs and even **hatched** them, but always failed to rear the young.*

*A taped message from his mother **plays** in the background.*
*At first Livy **had played** the records everyone played those days.*

detonate	flush 2	light 1.7	run 12,13,14
explode 1	hatch 2 (an egg)	operate 1,3	
flash 2	ignite 1	play 11,12	

1.28 VERBS WITH OTHER MEANINGS

There are a number of other verbs that have this combination of patterns.

*Is there any reason he **can't audition**?*
*Casting directors usually **do not audition** actors who themselves have mental disabilities to play such roles.*

Each year we draw up a schedule for opening and closing branches and they normally __balance out__.

You need to __balance out__ all the costs before committing yourself to a particular environment.

The winters were long and cold, while roads, electricity, drainage and schools __were__ largely __lacking__.

He suggested that while Lithuania was theoretically self-sufficient in food, in two weeks time it __could lack__ the means to bring that food to the shops.

The vet rang to say that the puppy's condition had miraculously improved, that he just __might pull through__ after all.

We all hoped that proper treatment __would pull__ him __through__.

audition *2*	enrol	interview *2*	sign *7*
enlist *1*	graduate *4*	lack *2*	substitute *1*
add up ▷*2*	balance out	pull through	strike out *4*

Pattern combination 2: V prep/adv; V n prep/adv

In the pattern **V prep/adv**, the verb is followed by a prepositional phrase or an adverb group. In the pattern **V n prep/adv**, the verb is followed by a noun group and a prepositional phrase or adverb group. This pattern combination is symmetrical.

This combination of patterns has four combinations of structures, depending on whether there is a prepositional phrase or an adverb group in the pattern, and on what the preposition is:

▶ Structure combination (i): Verb with prepositional Complement; Verb with Object and prepositional Object Complement
The prince <u>changed</u> into a frog.
The magician <u>changed</u> the prince into a frog.
▶ Structure combination (ii): Verb with prepositional Object; Verb with Object and prepositional Object
Beauty <u>equates</u> with goodness.
He <u>equated</u> beauty with goodness.
▶ Structure combination (iii): Verb with prepositional Object; Verb with Object and Adjunct
She <u>converted</u> to Christianity.
He <u>converted</u> them to Christianity.
▶ Structure combination (iv): Verb with Adjunct; Verb with Object and Adjunct
The coach <u>halted</u> in front of the ballroom.
The footman <u>halted</u> the coach in front of the ballroom.

Structure combination (i):
Verb with prepositional Complement;
Verb with Object and prepositional Object Complement

V prep

	Verb group	prepositional phrase
Subject	**Verb**	**prepositional Complement**
These fashions	parade	as modern movements in art.
The stick	snapped	in half.
You	'll turn	into everyone's dogsbody.

V n prep

	Verb group	noun group	prepositional phrase
Subject	Verb	Object	prep. Object Complement
He	paraded	them	as stars.
Fierce storms	snapped	the tanker	into two parts.
Parents	can't turn	their house	into a fortress.

Structure combination (ii): Verb with prepositional Object; Verb with Object and prepositional Object

V prep

	Verb group	prepositional phrase
Subject	Verb	prepositional Object
Charity	would equate	with interference.
This policy	didn't square	with an accident.

V n prep

	Verb group	noun group	prepositional phrase
Subject	Verb	Object	prepositional Object
They	equated	disease	with vice and sin.
He	couldn't square	his dreams	with reality.

Structure combination (iii): Verb with prepositional Object; Verb with Object and Adjunct

V prep

	Verb group	prepositional phrase
Subject	Verb	prepositional Object
A high priority	attaches	to science and technology.
The country	plunged	into civil war.
They	qualify	for extra aid.

V n prep

	Verb group	noun group	prepositional phrase
Subject	Verb	Object	Adjunct
You	can attach	blame	to people.
This	plunged	the country	into turmoil.
This	qualifies	them	for aid.

Structure combination (iv): Verb with Adjunct; Verb with Object and Adjunct

V prep/adv

	Verb group	prep. phrase/adverb group
Subject	**Verb**	**Adjunct**
A larger ship	anchored	offshore.
His gun	still dangled	from his hand.
The display	ends	with a flyby of military aircraft.
You	enrol	on a full-time course.
We	marched	across the surface of the moon.

V n prep/adv

	Verb group	noun group	prep. phrase/adverb group
Subject	**Verb**	**Object**	**Adjunct**
We	anchored	the boat	in six feet of water.
She	dangles	the cigarette	from her lips.
Thomas	ended	his remarks	with this statement.
He	enrolled	his daughter	in a public school.
She	marched	the girls	back to school.

Verbs with this combination of patterns belong to the following meaning groups:

2.1　THE 'CHANGE' GROUP	2.9　THE 'SAIL' GROUP
2.2　THE 'DIVIDE' GROUP	2.10　THE 'DROP' GROUP
2.3　THE 'COUNT' GROUP	2.11　THE 'GALLOP' GROUP
2.4　THE 'EQUATE' GROUP	2.12　THE 'THUMP' GROUP
2.5　THE 'AWAKEN' GROUP	2.13　THE 'DRAIN' GROUP
2.6　THE 'ACCLIMATIZE' GROUP	2.14　THE 'BEGIN' AND 'END' GROUP
2.7　THE 'FOCUS' GROUP	2.15　VERBS WITH OTHER MEANINGS
2.8　THE 'DETACH' GROUP	

2.1　THE 'CHANGE' GROUP

These verbs are concerned with change. In the pattern **V prep**, the Subject indicates the person or thing that changes. In the pattern **V n prep**, the Subject indicates the person or thing that causes the change. The prepositional phrase indicates the result of the change. The verb *change* also has the patterns **V** and **V n** (see meaning group 1.1 above).

The prepositions most frequently used with the verbs in this group are *into* and *to*. With these prepositions, the verbs in this meaning group belong to Structure combination (i). Otherwise, they belong to Structure combination (iii) or (iv).

> In the event, the scandal **_blew up_ into a major political furore**.
> No good purpose would be served if the unfortunate death of Miss Oates **_was blown up_ into front-page news for the Tory gutter press**.

> His skin dried up like leather and his face **_changed_ into a grinning skull**.
> We**_'ve got to change_ this world into a world of love**.

If broken, toughened glass __forms__ into safe pellet-like pieces rather than lethal shards.
O'Brien __formed__ the men into a ragged line.

This Dracula __can metamorphose__ into rats or a wolf as well as a bat.
She jolts upright, __metamorphoses__ her face into a macabre parody of her mother and suddenly fills the hushed room with a terrible blood-curdling cry.

After 30 minutes the powder __will swell__ to its maximum capacity, forming a transparent gel.
There is a small herb-rich meadow in the wood which helps to __swell__ the plant list to over 120 species.

change *3*	form *3*	swell *1*
convert *1*	metamorphose	transmute
evolve *2*	mutate *1*	turn *15*
blow up *5*		

2.2 THE 'DIVIDE' GROUP

In the pattern **V prep**, these verbs are concerned with something breaking or dividing. In the pattern **V n prep**, they are concerned with someone or something making something break or divide. When the verbs in this group are used with *into*, they belong to Structure combination (i). When they are used with other prepositions, they belong to Structure combination (iii).

If you have lots of children in the car, you might want to __divide__ into two or three groups and sing simple songs.
Patients __are divided__ into groups, each group with a primary counselor.

It was decided to __separate__ into two groups.
The police wanted to __separate__ them into smaller groups, but they insisted on staying together.

I was just explaining that the ornament was of no great value when I dropped it. It __shattered__ into tiny pieces.
Kelly turned her head to see the truck plow through the phone booth, __shattering__ it into a thousand pieces.

divide *1*	resolve *4*	snap *1*
fragment *2*	separate *10*	split *1*
polarize	shatter *1*	tear *2.1*
break up *1*		

2.3 THE 'COUNT' GROUP

These verbs are concerned with one thing being thought of or presented as another thing. In the pattern **V prep**, the Subject indicates one of the two things; the other thing is indicated by the prepositional phrase. In the pattern **V n prep**, the Subject in most cases indicates the person or group of people who thinks of one thing as being another, or who presents one thing as another. The preposition most frequently used with the verbs in this group is *as*, but *boil down* is used with *to*. This group belongs to Structure combination (i).

A few words scrawled on a piece of paper, or a simple gesture, __could count__ as art.
I __count__ him as my best friend.

In the case of *qualify*, the Subject in the pattern **V n prep** is something that makes people think the comparison is valid.

Jeff Campbell sat through the program and was won over, but still __doesn't qualify__ as a strong supporter.
His loyalty and good works helped __qualify__ him as a candidate for sainthood in the Catholic Church.

In the case of *translate*, the pattern **V *as* n** is used to indicate that a particular translation is possible, not that it was actually used on a particular occasion.

495

The Arc valley is better known as the Maurienne, a name combining the patois words of 'mau'
*and 'riau' which **translate** as 'wicked river'.*
*The Celtic word 'geis' **is** usually **translated** as 'taboo', but actually carried connotations not*
borne by that word.

count *7*	qualify *3*	translate *4*
parade *10*	rank *4*	
boil down *VPP*		

2.4 THE 'EQUATE' GROUP

These verbs are concerned with two things being thought of or presented as similar or
compatible, or with something being compared with a group of things. In the pattern **V**
prep, the Subject indicates one of the two things; the other thing is indicated by the
prepositional phrase. In the pattern **V n prep**, the Subject indicates the person or group of
people who thinks of the two things as being comparable, or who presents the two things
as comparable. The preposition most frequently used with the verbs in this group is *with*.
This group belongs to Structure combination (ii).

*In relation to several important criteria, hostel accommodation fails to **equate** with the*
housing preferences of lone migrant workers.
*Many people **equate** conflict with war and seek peace by designing the 'perfect' society.*

equate	square *8*
match up ▷3	tie in *VPP*

2.5 THE 'AWAKEN' GROUP

In the pattern **V prep**, these verbs are concerned with someone coming to feel or think
something. In the pattern **V n prep**, they are concerned with someone or something
making someone feel or think something. The prepositions most frequently used with
the verbs in this group are *to* and *towards*. This group belongs to Structure combination
(iii).

*Today many more people **are awakening** to deeper issues and taking responsibility.*
*His 1979 film, 'Cambodia: The Year Zero', did much to **awaken** the world to the horrors of*
the four previous years of rule by the Khmer Rouge.

*Corti was unable to decide whether Bugno's troubles lay in his head or his legs, but **was***
***inclining** towards the latter.*
*It becomes important to identify the other factors which **incline** us towards the particular*
beliefs we hold.

awaken *2*	incline *1*
convert *5*	tilt *4*
wake up *VPP*	

2.6 THE 'ACCLIMATIZE' GROUP

In the pattern **V prep**, these verbs are concerned with somebody becoming involved in or
used to a place, society, or activity. In the pattern **V n prep**, they are concerned with
someone or something making somebody do this or creating the conditions where they
are able to do this. This group belongs to Structure combination (iii).

The troops and tanks have had time to <u>acclimatise</u> to the desert, and are ready for action.
The mountaineers advanced from camp to camp to <u>acclimatise</u> themselves to the thinning oxygen at higher altitudes.

<u>Don't rush</u> into this decision unless you are in desperate need of money.
Wright is resisting the temptation to <u>rush</u> her straight into the other big roles of the repertoire.

acclimatize *(to)*	**plunge** *3,4 (into)*	**train** *2.3 (for)*
hook *6 (into)*	**qualify** *2 (for)*	
integrate *1 (into/with)*	**rush** *8 (into)*	

2.7 THE 'FOCUS' GROUP

In the pattern **V prep**, these verbs are concerned with something focusing on a particular thing. In the pattern **V n prep**, they are concerned with someone or something making something focus on a particular thing. This group belongs to Structure combination (iii).

Discussion is expected to <u>centre</u> on expanding the role of the United Nations.
Ortega <u>centred</u> his farewell speech on a call for all Nicaraguans to work for the disarmament of the Contras.

Inevitably attention <u>will focus</u> on the appearances by Oscar Peterson.
The case <u>focused</u> much international attention on Brazil.

attach *3 (to)*	**fix** *7 (on)*	**switch** *3 (to)*
centre *9 (on/around)*	**focus** *1,5 (on)*	
fasten *3 (on)*	**shift** *2*	

2.8 THE 'DETACH' GROUP

In the pattern **V prep/adv**, these verbs are concerned with someone or something moving somewhere, but not under their own control. In the pattern **V n prep/adv**, they are concerned with someone or something moving someone or something, or putting someone or something somewhere. We include here *catch*, which indicates that something becomes entangled in something. This group belongs to Structure combination (iv), except for *dig, hook, pass, sink, strike,* and *transfer,* which belong to Structure combination (iii).

Many of these verbs also have the patterns **V** and **V n** (see meaning group 1.16 above). Some verbs with similar meanings are found in Pattern combination 7 below.

Dead and dying cells <u>had detached</u> from the flask and drifted into the fluid.
Pick apples and pears when they <u>can be detached</u> easily from the branches.

The wind <u>funnelled</u> down power lines, blew out windows and damaged several roofs.
The towers are topped by wind catchers that <u>funnel</u> air into them.

Tree limbs which <u>rub</u> together can cause weakness through deformation.
Nancy <u>rubbed</u> her palms together and got ready to push again.

It developed into a huge game with water <u>splashing</u> everywhere.
Leaning over the fountain, Joanna <u>splashed</u> water upon her face.

In the case of *clip*, the pattern **V prep/adv** is usually used to indicate that something has a particular quality, that is, it can be clipped somewhere, rather than that something actually happens.

When not in use, the blade is protected by a sheath which <u>clips</u> on to the handle of the knife.

balance *1*	flick *1*	settle *8*	squeeze *4*
beam *3*	flip *3*	shift *1*	squirt *1*
bind *5*	float *1*	shoot *4*	stick *2.2 (in)*
blow *1.2*	funnel *4*	shuttle *3*	strike *5 (against/on)*
bounce *1*	hang *1*	sink *11 (into)*	swill *2 (around/about)*
bounce *3 (off)*	hook *2 (onto)*	slide *1*	swing *2*
bus *2*	inch *2*	slop *1*	swirl
catapult *3,4*	keep *2*	slosh *1*	swivel *1*
catch *5*	leak *1*	slot *2*	tilt *1*
clip *2*	lock *4*	smash *3*	tip *2*
coil *6*	mould *5*	snag *2*	transfer *1,2 (from/to)*
curl *6*	move *1*	snap *2*	trickle *1*
dangle *1*	nestle *1,2*	spatter	twine *2*
detach *1*	pass *6 (to)*	spew *1*	uncoil
diffuse *4*	peel *3 (off/from)*	spill *5*	waft
dig *3 (into)*	rain *4 (blows) (on)*	spin *1*	wash *3*
disengage *1*	rest *2.6*	splash *2*	whirl *1*
dribble *1*	roll *1*	splatter	winter *2*
drip *1*	rub *5 (together)*	spray *3,4*	withdraw *2 (from)*
drop *4*	screw *2,4*	spread *6*	
pour into	rain down ▷*4 (on)*		

Most of the verbs in this group also have the patterns **V adv prep**, **V prep prep**, **V n adv prep**, and **V n prep prep**.

> *A friend and I **bussed** from New York City to New Jersey without any certainty we'd be able to see our friend.*
> *Many supporters **are bussed** in from across the country.*

The verbs *spatter, splash, splatter,* and *spray* also have a pattern **V n**, with the substance that moves as Subject.

> *Rain **was spattering** the windscreen.*

2.9 THE 'SAIL' GROUP

These verbs are concerned with vehicles moving. In the pattern **V prep/adv**, the Subject indicates the vehicle. In the pattern **V n prep/adv**, the Subject indicates the driver of the vehicle or someone or something that makes the driver move the vehicle somewhere. This group belongs to Structure combination (iv). Some of the verbs in this group also have the patterns **V** and **V n** (see meaning group 1.17 above).

> *The plane finally glided down and **taxied** towards the terminal.*
> *The pilot **taxied** the plane to the end of the runway.*

Most of these verbs have another **V prep/adv** pattern in which the Subject indicates a person driving or travelling in the vehicle.

> *On day three we **sailed** to Poole.*

In the case of *navigate*, the pattern **V n prep/adv** sometimes has the vehicle as Subject and a place as Object.

> *There was a time when small boats **could navigate** the creek all the way to the point where Newell Road crosses.*

anchor *2*	dock *2*	reverse *4*	tack *4*
back *3.2*	halt *1*	sail *3*	taxi *2*
beach *2*	land *7*	slew *2*	
crash *2 (into)*	navigate *1*	swerve	
ditch *4*	nose *5*	swing *3*	

Most of the verbs in this group also have the patterns **V adv prep**, **V prep prep**, **V n adv prep**, and **V n prep prep**.

*Nothing prepared us for the sight of Santorini as we **sailed** into the bay from Crete.*
*The boatman **nosed** his launch up against what appeared to be a thick wall of jungle foliage.*

2.10 THE 'DROP' GROUP

These verbs are concerned with part of someone's body moving. In the pattern **V prep/adv**, the Subject indicates the part of the body that moves. In the pattern **V n prep/adv**, the Subject indicates either the person who moves, or someone or something that causes that movement. This group belongs to Structure combination (iv).

*Freddy's eyes roll up in their sockets and his head **drops** into his chest.*
*McGregor slumped, **dropping** his open palms onto his legs.*

*When he's into a song, Jones' jaw **juts** forth.*
*Father **jutted** his jaw toward the people sitting across the aisle, and I gave a silent nod.*

ball *3*	drop *8*	poke *4*	twist *2*
curl *5*	jut *2*	sweep *4*	
drop *5*	lash *8*	tighten *1*	

2.11 THE 'GALLOP' GROUP

These verbs are concerned with a person, group of people, or animal going somewhere or doing something, under their own control. In the pattern **V prep/adv**, the Subject indicates the person, group, or animal who moves or does something. In the pattern **V n prep/adv**, the Subject indicates the person or group of people who:

- makes the person, group, or animal move or do something
- encourages the person, group, or animal to move or do something
- provides conditions that allow the person, group, or animal to move or do something

This group belongs to Structure combination (iv).

*A riderless horse **galloped** in panicked circles, adding immeasurably to the confusion.*
*Staff officers **galloped** fine horses down the road's wide verges.*

*He **parachuted** to safety.*
*He **was parachuted** in.*

The verbs *canter*, *gallop*, *trot*, and *walk*, which, in the pattern **V n prep/adv**, indicate that someone rides a horse at a particular speed, also have another **V prep/adv** pattern with the rider as Subject.

*The Duke **galloped** along the right of his line.*

canter	group *6 (together)*	settle *6*	walk *1*
crowd *4 (into)*	march *1*	transfer *4,5,8 (from/to)*	
gallop *1*	parachute *2*	trot *2*	
gather *1*	pull *VP3 (out of)*	unite	
beam down	beam up		

2.12 THE 'THUMP' GROUP

These verbs are concerned with someone or something making a noise while moving. In the pattern **V prep/adv**, the Subject indicates the person or thing that moves and makes the noise. In the pattern **V n prep/adv**, the Subject indicates the person or thing that moves someone or something somewhere. This group belongs to Structure combination (iv).

A couple of cars __swished__ by, spray hissing up from their tyres.
They then swamped the dunes on horseback in an attempt to scare people away, __swishing__ their whips through the grass as they went.

She carried her drink out to the kitchen, her heavy shoes __thumping__ on the polished floor.
She made a fist and __thumped__ it on the counter as hard as she could.

rasp *2*	scrape *2*	thump *3*
rattle *1*	swish *1*	

2.13 THE 'DRAIN' GROUP

These verbs are concerned with metaphorical movement. In the pattern **V prep/adv**, the Subject indicates the thing that 'moves'. In the pattern **V n prep/adv**, the Subject indicates the person or thing that makes it 'move'. This group belongs to Structure combination (iv), except for *get across*, which belongs to Structure combination (iii).

Memory __drained__ out of him in the heat.
Relief __drained__ the strength from his muscles as Charley Lunn's head appeared round the half-open kitchen door.

Then a memory __stirs__ in you and you start feeling anxious.
This __might stir__ many emotions in me, but I am afraid that understanding is not one of them.

centre *10*	keep *3 (away/off)*	spread *5*
drain *7*	land *9 (in)*	stir *7 (in)*
carry over	get across *(to)*	

2.14 THE 'BEGIN' AND 'END' GROUP

These verbs are concerned with activities or periods of time beginning or ending in a particular way. In the pattern **V prep/adv**, the Subject indicates the activity or period of time. In the pattern **V n prep/adv**, the Subject indicates the person or thing whose behaviour is indicated in the prepositional phrase or adverb group. The verbs in this group are most frequently used with prepositional phrases beginning with *with*, *in*, and *on*, and with prepositional phrases consisting of *by* and an '-ing' clause. This group belongs to Structure combination (iv).

Sunday __will begin__ with a full breakfast, followed by a beauty presentation from Rene Guinot.
Clinton __began__ his week in California, a state crucial to his electoral success in November.

A meeting between Turkey, Iraq and Syria to discuss the sharing of waters from the river Euphrates __has ended__ in disagreement.
Environment ministers from Eastern and Western Europe __have ended__ a one-day meeting in Dublin with agreement that protection of the environment is one of the most urgent political priorities on the agenda.

begin *3*	end *4,6*	open *21*
close *1.7*	finish *4*	start *2*

2.15 VERBS WITH OTHER MEANINGS

There are a number of other verbs which have this combination of patterns. Of these verbs, *train* belongs to Structure combination (i), *turn* belongs to Structure combination (ii), *connect, fill, pull, open up*, and *translate* belong to Structure combination (iii), and the other verbs belong to Structure combination (iv).

*The phrase 'proceeding gingerly' has nothing to do with the spice but **derives** from the old French word 'gensour', meaning 'daintily' or 'with refinement'.*
*Etak, which **derives** its name from the Polynesian word for navigation, was founded by Stan Honey.*

*The screen **fills** with grainy black and white newsreel footage.*
*On a nice day, **fill** a bucket with soapy water outside and let your child scrub down toys, outdoor furniture, or just the patio.*

*Britain's ethnic communities have suffered injustices and degradations which **would meet** with outrage if they occurred elsewhere.*
*All new ideas **are met** with hesitancy, most will have teething troubles.*

*Tables have been constructed so that each life event can be rated as to how disturbing it would usually be to a person. Losses by death or divorce, or gains by marriage or birth always **rate** highly.*
*I was told he **rated** me highly, which is a real compliment.*

*The roots of this plant **can substitute** for potatoes.*
*In no case **should** you **substitute** alcohol for other foods.*

*His parents wanted him to **train** as a doctor.*
*They **train** the young women as seamstresses.*

*If fine words **were to translate** into deeds, a massive campaign of Biblical re-education now had to be mounted among the white population.*
*If this mood **is translated** into votes, the Democrats must strengthen their grip on Congress.*

connect 6 *(to)*	fill 1 *(with)*	rank 3 *(in)*	translate 3
decrease 1	hold 3.6	rate 6	turn VP *(against)*
derive 2 *(from)*	increase 1	stretch 5 *(into)*	widen 4
enlist 1 *(in/as)*	meet 8 *(with)*	substitute 1 *(for)*	
enrol	pull VP4 *(out of)*	train 2.1 *(as)*	
fill up ▷1 *(with)*	open up 2 *(to)*		

Pattern combination 3: V adj; V n adj

In the pattern **V adj**, the verb is followed by an adjective group. In the pattern **V n adj**, the verb is followed by a noun group and an adjective group. This pattern combination is symmetrical.

This combination of patterns has one structure combination:

▶ Verb with Complement; Verb with Object and Object Complement
*The door **slammed** shut.*
*She **slammed** the door shut.*

V adj

	Verb group	adjective group
Subject	**Verb**	**Complement**
The twigs	jerked	free.
The door	slammed	shut.
The lock	snapped	shut.

501

V n adj

	Verb group	noun group	adjective group
Subject	**Verb**	**Object**	**Object Complement**
The boy	jerked	himself	free of Andrew's grasp.
She	slammed	the door	shut.
The Major	snapped	his box	shut.

Verbs with this combination of patterns belong to the following meaning groups:

3.1 THE 'SLAM SHUT' GROUP

3.2 THE 'WORK FREE' GROUP

3.3 VERBS WITH OTHER MEANINGS

3.1 THE 'SLAM SHUT' GROUP

In the pattern **V adj**, these verbs are concerned with something opening or closing, usually noisily or violently. In the pattern **V n adj**, they are concerned with someone or something opening or closing something, usually noisily or violently. The adjectives most frequently used with the verbs in this group are *open* and *shut*.

Passengers complained when automatic doors on a new train __jammed__ open.
They just __jam__ the door open with a brick.

He peered warily up the staircase just as the door upstairs opened, then __slammed__ shut.
He managed to drag her back inside the vehicle and __slam__ the door shut.

Her eyes __squeezed__ shut and tears appeared under the lashes.
Hart __squeezed__ his eyes tight shut, but the tears fell anyway.

bang 3 *(shut)*	**slam** 1 *(shut)*	**spring** 5	**tear** 2.1 *(open)*
blow 1.2	**slide** 1	**squeeze** 3 *(shut)*	
jam 3	**snap** 2	**swing** 1	

3.2 THE 'WORK FREE' GROUP

In the pattern **V adj**, these verbs are concerned with someone or something becoming detached from something. In the pattern **V n adj**, they are concerned with someone pulling or shaking someone or something so that they become detached. The adjectives most frequently used with the verbs in this group are *free* and *loose*.

He shook his head back and forth, and tried to __pull__ free.
She struggled to __pull__ herself loose.

The chair may topple backwards when sat upon and the armrests __can work__ loose.
He pulled his key ring from his pocket and __worked__ one key free of it.

jerk 1	**shake** 2	**wrench** 2
pull 4	**work** 23	

3.3 VERBS WITH OTHER MEANINGS

There are three other verbs which have this combination of patterns. The adjective most frequently used in each case is indicated in the list below.

Ticket and subscription sales __have held__ steady and fund-raising is even up slightly.
They had achieved their aim of __holding__ numbers steady.

The woman's eyes __opened__ wide.
She __opened__ her eyes very wide.

freeze *1,2 (solid/hard)*   hold *2.7,3.6 (steady)*   open *1,4 (wide)*

Pattern combination 4: V *as* adj; V n *as* adj

In the pattern **V *as* adj**, the verb is followed by a prepositional phrase which consists of *as* and an adjective group. In the pattern **V n *as* adj**, the verb is followed by a noun group and a prepositional phrase which consists of *as* and an adjective group. This pattern combination is symmetrical.

This combination of patterns has one combination of structures:

▶ Verb with prepositional Complement; Verb with Object and prepositional Object Complement
He <u>qualified</u> as unemployed.
This <u>qualified</u> him as unemployed.

V *as* adj

	Verb group	*as*	adjective group
Subject	**Verb**		**prepositional Complement**
Many women	count	*as*	unemployed.
His joy	qualifies	*as*	genuine.

V n *as* adj

	Verb group	noun group	*as*	adjective group
Subject	**Verb**	**Object**		**prep. Object Complement**
I	count	myself	*as*	old-fashioned.
This	qualified	him	*as*	young in spirit.

In the pattern **V *as* adj**, these verbs are all concerned with something having a particular attribute. In the pattern **V n *as* adj**, they are concerned with someone considering someone or something to have a particular attribute, or something causing someone or something to be considered in that way.

> *The events of 16th January **must rank** as equivalent to a coronation.*
> *The respondents also **ranked** their local competition as weak, moderate, or strong.*

count *7*   qualify *3*   rank *4*

Pattern combination 5: V to-inf; V n to-inf

In the pattern **V to-inf**, the verb is followed by a to-infinitive clause. In the pattern **V n to-inf**, the verb is followed by a noun group and a to-infinitive clause. This pattern combination is symmetrical.

This combination of patterns has two combinations of structures:

▶ Structure combination (i): Verbs in phase; Verb with two Objects
I <u>incline</u> to think he is wrong.
This <u>inclined</u> me to think he was wrong.
▶ Structure combination (ii): Verb with Adjunct; Verb with two Objects
She <u>qualified</u> to teach children.
Her course <u>qualified</u> her to teach children.

Only one verb, *incline*, has Structure combination (i). The other verbs have Structure combination (ii).

> It is true that conservationists **incline** to adopt a people-centred language.
> Their political ideas **incline** them to romanticise the idea of working-class solidarity.
>
> The policewomen only **qualify** to carry arms on duty when they reach a high standard.
> Clive has had an hour's lesson on a dry slope, which **qualifies** him to advise the rest of us by shouting 'snowplough!' at the top of his voice all the time.

---

incline *1*   qualify *2*   train *2.1*

Pattern combination 6: V ord prep; V n ord prep

In the pattern **V ord prep**, the verb is followed by an ordinal number and a prepositional phrase. In the pattern **V n ord prep**, the verb is followed by a noun group, an ordinal number, and a prepositional phrase. In both patterns, the prepositional phrase usually begins with *among*, *in*, or *out of*. This pattern combination is symmetrical.

There is only one verb with this combination of patterns. The pattern **V ord prep** has the structure Verb with two Adjuncts; the pattern **V n ord prep** has the structure Verb with Object and two Adjuncts.

> The second-best British player, Michael Adams, already **ranks** 20th in the world.
> The junior team **is ranked** third in the world.

---

rank *3*

Pattern combination 7: V prep/adv; V n; V n prep/adv

In the pattern **V prep/adv**, the verb is followed by a prepositional phrase or adverb group. In the pattern **V n**, the verb is followed by a noun group. In the pattern **V n prep/adv**, the verb is followed by a noun group and a prepositional phrase or adverb group.

This combination is asymmetrical because in the structure without an Object the verb must be followed by a prepositional phrase or adverb group, whereas in the structure with an Object the verb may be followed by a noun group alone.

This combination of patterns has one combination of structures:

▶ Verb with Adjunct; Verb with Object; Verb with Object and Adjunct
> The boat **rocked** up and down.
> Huge waves **rocked** the boat.
> The waves **rocked** the boat up and down.

For structure tables, see Pattern combinations 1 and 2.

Verbs with this combination of patterns are concerned with something moving, or someone or something making something move.

> A court at Peking has sentenced a hijacker to eight years in prison for forcing a plane to **divert** to Japan last December.
> NASA have offered to **divert** the Space Shuttle Columbia on its next mission to help.
> Planners fight gridlock by simplifying traffic patterns as well as by trying to **divert** cars away from the problem area.
>
> The light **reflected** off the ochre stone, creating a golden glow he found entrancing.
> The curved surface of the mirror **reflects** the sun's rays so they form a spot of light one centimetre across.
> The dish **reflects** radio waves to an antenna suspended at its focus 150 metres above.

In the case of *spout*, the Subject in the patterns **V n** and **V n prep/adv** is a container holding a liquid or gas.

> *An underground labyrinth of corridors leads to a pool where water **spouts from the mouths of carved lions**.*
> *He replaced the Rayburn when the last one began to **spout flames**.*
> *Ickes jotted down the license plate numbers of cars **spouting black smoke from their exhaust pipes**.*

In the case of *angle*, the pattern **V prep/adv** indicates the configuration of something, rather than a movement.

> *The path **angled downhill and northward**.*
> *Charles reached out for the driving mirror and **angled it** so that he could see back along the track we'd driven.*
> *The lock is the smallest on the river but, by **angling the boat across the width**, we just scraped through.*

angle 6	fasten 1	reflect 2	swing 1
brush 5	flash 7	rock 4	swivel 3
divert 1	jerk 1	spill 1,3	trail 6
drain 1	pan 4	spout 1	

Pattern combination 8: V prep/adv; V n

In the pattern **V prep/adv**, the verb is followed by a prepositional phrase or adverb group. In the pattern **V n**, the verb is followed by a noun group.

This combination is asymmetrical because in the structure without an Object the verb does not occur alone.

This combination of patterns has three combinations of structures:

▶ Structure combination (i): Verb with prepositional Complement; Verb with Object
The glass splintered into pieces.
The blow splintered the glass.
▶ Structure combination (ii): Verb with prepositional Object; Verb with Object
His heart hardened against her.
The years hardened my heart.
▶ Structure combination (iii): Verb with Adjunct; Verb with Object
Water gushed out of the hole.
The hole gushed water.

For structure tables, see Pattern combinations 1 and 2.

Verbs with this combination of patterns belong to the following meaning groups:

8.1 THE 'SMASH' GROUP

8.2 THE 'OBSESS' GROUP

8.3 THE 'BENEFIT' GROUP

8.4 THE 'TOPPLE' GROUP

8.5 THE 'BELCH' GROUP

8.6 THE 'DIFFUSE' GROUP

8.7 THE 'ORIGINATE' AND 'CONCLUDE' GROUP

8.8 VERBS WITH OTHER MEANINGS

8.1 THE 'SMASH' GROUP

These verbs are concerned with damage. In the pattern **V prep/adv**, the Subject indicates the person or thing that is damaged. In the pattern **V n**, the Subject indicates the person or thing that causes the damage. This group belongs to Structure combination (i).

*When you fire at a clay pigeon and it **smashes** into lots of little pieces, it's a real thrill.*
*The bottle **smashed** the window, but did not go into the house.*

smash *1*   splinter *2*

8.2 THE 'OBSESS' GROUP

These verbs are concerned with someone feeling an emotion about something. In the pattern **V prep/adv**, the Subject indicates the person who feels the emotion. In the pattern **V n**, the Subject indicates the cause or topic of the emotion. This group belongs to Structure combination (ii), except for *thrill*, which belongs to Structure combination (iii).

*If you **obsess** about small things, it keeps you from **obsessing** about the really big things.*
*As Rebecca's death grew closer, the lack of a child started to **obsess** him.*

*Coleridge has written a book for those who **thrill** to the scene in Citizen Kane where Charles declares 'I think it would be fun to run a newspaper'.*
*It was a sight that never failed to **thrill** her.*

bother *4 (about)*	**obsess** *(about/over)*
harden *4 (against)*	**thrill** *2 (at/to)*

8.3 THE 'BENEFIT' GROUP

These verbs are concerned with something being an advantage to someone. In the pattern **V prep/adv**, the Subject indicates the person who gains the advantage. In the pattern **V n**, the Subject indicates the thing that is advantageous. This group belongs to Structure combination (ii).

*It is hoped that hundreds of youngsters **will benefit** from the charity.*
*We need to persuade employers that equal opportunities **can benefit** them as well as us.*

benefit *3 (from)*   profit *3 (from/by)*

8.4 THE 'TOPPLE' GROUP

In the pattern **V prep/adv**, these verbs are concerned with someone or something moving somewhere. In the pattern **V n**, they are concerned with someone or something moving something or someone in a particular direction. This group belongs to Structure combination (iii).

*I **toppled** onto the floor.*
*Protestors tried to **topple** a bust of Stalin.*

spiral *2*   splay   topple *1*

8.5 THE 'BELCH' GROUP

These verbs are concerned with liquids or gases coming out of something. In the pattern **V prep/adv**, the Subject indicates the liquid or gas. In the pattern **V n**, the Subject indicates what it comes out of. This group belongs to Structure combination (iii).

*Traffic roared by and smoke **belched** from the steelworks in the background.*
*The old van had slowly become a big polluter, wasting gasoline and **belching** black smoke.*

The man staggered back, blood __spurting__ from his hand.
A gash just above the eye __was spurting__ so much blood that he was all but blinded.

---

belch *2 (from/out of)*   **haemorrhage** *4 (from)*   **puff** *2*
gush *1*   **ooze** *1*   **spurt** *1*

belch out ▷*2*

8.6 THE 'DIFFUSE' GROUP

These verbs are concerned with something moving metaphorically. In the pattern **V prep/adv**, the Subject indicates the thing that 'moves'. In the pattern **V n**, the Subject indicates the person or thing that makes the thing 'move'. This group belongs to Structure combination (iii).

My advice to anyone about to launch a new technology is to look at how a new innovation __diffuses__ through the populace.
The Society's declared object was to collect and __diffuse__ knowledge of the laws which govern the universe.

Even the restive military __rallied__ to Mr Clinton yesterday morning when he chose Fort McNair for his morning jog.
In trying to __rally__ voters, they've focused on dissatisfaction with the government.

---

devolve *(upon/on)*   **drain** *9*   **exude** *1 (from)*
diffuse *1*   **emanate** *1 (from)*   **rally** *2 (to)*

8.7 THE 'ORIGINATE' AND 'CONCLUDE' GROUP

These verbs are concerned with something starting, coming into existence, or concluding. In the pattern **V prep/adv**, the Subject indicates the thing that starts, comes into existence, or concludes. In the pattern **V n**, the Subject indicates the person who makes something start or conclude, or the source of something. This group belongs to Structure combination (iii).

Whales __must have originated__ from a land mammal which moved around on front and hind legs.
Dr Stevenson __did not__ really __originate__ this type of test.

---

conclude *3*   **originate**   **sprout** *5,6*

8.8 VERBS WITH OTHER MEANINGS

There are a few other verbs which have this combination of patterns. The verbs *average out* and *sign up (as)* belong to Structure combination (i). *Sign up (for)* belongs to Structure combination (ii). The verbs *climax* and *put up* belong to Structure combination (iii).

There were reportedly 'important differences of view' between head teacher and governors which __climaxed__ in the head leaving.
The victory __climaxed__ a perfect season for UCLA, which won all 30 of its games.

He decided that he would drive back at once instead of __putting up__ for the night __at the hotel__.
The company __will put__ you __up__ when you're between tours.

---

climax *2*

average out   **put up** *6*   **sign up** *(as/for)*

Pattern combination 9: V adv; V n

In the pattern **V adv**, the verb is followed by an adverb group. In the pattern **V n**, the verb is followed by a noun group.

This combination is asymmetrical because in the structure without an Object the verb must be followed by an adverb.

This combination of patterns has one combination of structures:

▶ Verb with Adjunct; Verb with Object
The dress <u>washes</u> easily.
She <u>washed</u> the dress.

For structure tables, see Pattern combinations 1 and 2.

In the pattern **V adv**, the verb often focuses on a quality or feature of the person or thing indicated by the Subject, rather than on something that has actually happened.

Verbs with this combination of patterns belong to the following meaning groups:

9.1   THE 'CLEAN' GROUP
9.2   THE 'SCARE' GROUP
9.3   THE 'FISH' GROUP

9.1 THE 'CLEAN' GROUP

In the pattern **V adv**, these verbs indicate that something has a desirable quality, such as being easily cleaned, prepared, or moved. In the pattern **V n**, they indicate that something is affected in some way, such as being cleaned, prepared, or moved.

Most of the pans <u>cleaned</u> easily with hot, soapy water and a soft cloth.
These products are a much safer bet than caustic soda, although not as effective in actually <u>cleaning</u> the surface.

I've put the vine in a raised bed that <u>drains</u> freely.
Tulip trees have masses of roots that lie just below the surface and <u>drain</u> the surrounding soil.

The door was closed but only with a wooden bar which <u>lifted</u> easily.
She <u>lifted</u> the lid.

The knitwear <u>sold</u> well.
It's a regular market. I mean they <u>sell</u> food there, they <u>sell</u> clothing.

apply *6*	display *1,4*	glue *2*	read *1,6*
clean *4*	drain *2*	grill *4*	sell *1,4*
cut *1*	fold *4*	lift *1*	wash *1*

9.2 THE 'SCARE' GROUP

In the pattern **V adv**, these verbs indicate that someone feels an emotion often or easily. In the pattern **V n**, they indicate that someone or something makes someone feel an emotion.

This use is productive: any verb which has the pattern **V n** and indicates that someone is made to feel an emotion can be used with the pattern **V adv**. However, there are only two verbs for which the pattern **V adv** is frequent.

Although they are a young team, they <u>do not scare</u> easily.
'Things are starting to <u>scare</u> me,' I said.

scare *1*   spook *3*

9.3 THE 'FISH' GROUP

In the pattern **V adv**, these verbs indicate that a place used for a sport allows the sport to be enjoyable. In the pattern **V n**, they indicate that someone takes part in that sport at that place.

> *The beach is a south-west-facing venue that **fishes well** when there is a strong breeze blowing directly onto the beach.*
> *Chatting to other anglers who **fish the water** can also be a great help.*

> *The cross-country course **rode well**, although the water jump caused problems.*
> *Ryan **rode the 13-fence show-jumping course at Barcelona** as if he were David Broome.*

fish *4*   ride *1*

Pattern combination 10: V adj; V n

In the pattern **V adj**, the verb is followed by an adjective group. In the pattern **V n**, the verb is followed by a noun group. This pattern combination is asymmetrical.

For structure tables, see Pattern combinations 1 and 4.

There is only one verb with this combination of patterns.

> *These easy-to-clean non-stick racks **fold flat** for easy storage.*
> *Brian rose, picked up his copy of 'Jitterbug Perfume', **folded the lawn chair**.*

fold *4*

Chapter 8: Ergative Reciprocal Verbs

There are some verbs which are both **ergative** and **reciprocal**. Verbs of this kind have the label **V-RECIP-ERG** in the Collins Cobuild English Dictionary.

A typical ergative reciprocal verb has the following features:

1 Like an ergative verb, it has both patterns where the verb is not followed directly by a noun group (for example **pl-n V** and **V** *with* **n**) and patterns where the verb is followed directly by a noun group (for example **V pl-n** and **V n** *with* **n**). The person or thing indicated by the Subject of the first kind of pattern may also be indicated by the noun group following the verb in the second kind of pattern. For example: *The oil <u>mixes</u> with the other ingredients; She <u>mixed</u> the oil with the other ingredients.*

2 Like a reciprocal verb, it has a pattern where the verb is used with a plural Subject indicating the participants in an action (for example **pl-n V**), and one or more patterns where one participant is indicated by the Subject and the other is indicated by the Object, prepositional Object, or Adjunct (for example **V** *with* **n**). For example: *The salt water and fresh water <u>mix</u>; The salt water <u>mixes</u> with the fresh water.*

Ergative reciprocal verbs all indicate that two or more people, groups, or things join together or are linked in some way, or that someone or something causes two or more people, groups, or things to join together or be linked.

Pattern combinations

An ergative reciprocal verb has one of these three pattern combinations:

▶ Pattern combination 1: pl-n V; V *with* n; V pl-n; V n *with* n
The liquids <u>will blend</u> to make a rich sauce.
The chocolate <u>blends</u> with the coffee.
<u>Blend</u> the remaining ingredients.
<u>Blend</u> the butter with the sugar.

▶ Pattern combination 2: V; pl-n V n; V n *with* n
The peace talks <u>will reopen</u> tomorrow.
The two groups <u>reopened</u> talks yesterday.
They <u>have reopened</u> negotiations with the government.

▶ Pattern combination 3: pl-n V; V n; V pl-n; V n *to/with* n
The chairs all <u>matched</u>.
Her hat <u>matched</u> her coat.
<u>Match</u> the two lengths of cloth.
We <u>will match</u> the fabric to your existing furnishing.

Pattern combination 1: pl-n V; V *with* n; V pl-n; V n *with* n

These verbs have four patterns. Two patterns are reciprocal:

- **pl-n V**: The verb is used with a plural Subject.

- **V *with* n**: The verb is used with a Subject indicating one participant and is followed by a prepositional phrase indicating the other. In most cases, the prepositional phrase consists of *with* and a noun group; in a few cases, the preposition is *from*, *to*, or *against*.

Two patterns are not reciprocal:

- **V pl-n**: The verb is followed by a **plural noun group**.
- **V n *with* n**: The verb is followed by a noun group and a prepositional phrase. In most cases, the prepositional phrase consists of *with* and a noun group; in a few cases, the preposition is *from*, *to*, or *against*.

pl-n V

plural noun group	Verb group
Subject	Verb
The values of exports and imports	should balance.
Oil and water	don't mix.

V *with* n

	Verb group	*with*	noun group
Subject	Verb	prepositional Object	
The flash	should balance	with	the normal lighting.
The smell of sage	mixed	with	the salt air.

V pl-n

	Verb group	plural noun group
Subject	Verb	Object
Planners	must balance	these two demands.
	Mix	the dry ingredients.

V n *with* n

	Verb group	noun group	*with*	noun group
Subject	Verb	Object		prepositional Object
He	is balancing	the classics	with	a variety of modern works.
	Mix	the flour	with	the sugar.

Verbs with this combination of patterns belong to the following meaning groups:

1.1   THE 'MERGE' GROUP
1.2   THE 'INTERTWINE' GROUP
1.3   THE 'SEPARATE' GROUP
1.4   THE 'DOVETAIL' GROUP
1.5   THE 'ALTERNATE' GROUP

1.1 THE 'MERGE' GROUP

In the patterns **pl-n V** and **V *with* n**, these verbs indicate that two or more things or people join together or touch. In the patterns **V pl-n** and **V n *with* n**, they are concerned with someone or something joining things or people, or making them touch.

> *A short distance from where **these two creeks merge**, a duck emerged from the water.*
> *It **has** since **merged with other parties** to form the Janata Dal that is now in power in Delhi.*
> *Rob Farbrother, chief of Nexus, says consumers will force companies who issue cards to **merge their systems**, so that most cards will be accepted by everyone.*
> *He seemed to want to do something drastic with the paper, but what? Close it down, **merge** it **with another publication**?*
> *The orchestra is to **be merged** with **the orchestra of Scottish Opera** to create the National Orchestra of Scotland.*

The verb *connect* has the patterns **V *to* n** and **V n *to* n**, not the patterns **V *with* n** and **V n *with* n**.

> *His project involves compact disc players that **connect to personal computers** and play images as well as music.*
> *Tendons are tough fibrous bands of elastic tissue which **connect muscles to the bone which that muscle moves**.*

The verb *clink* has the patterns **V *against* n** and **V n *against* n**, not the patterns **V *with* n** and **V n *with* n**.

> *The rifle **clinked against a rock** as it swung in front of his chest.*
> *She **clinked** her **glass against his**.*

The phrasal verbs *pair off* and *pair up* usually have the passive patterns **pl-n *be* V-ed P** and ***be* V-ed P *with* n**, rather than the active equivalents. All their patterns are shown here.

> *We sort of **paired up** properly in the Lower Fourth because we found we shared a taste for making a nuisance of ourselves.*
> *She has no immediate desire to **pair up with someone**, preferring to concentrate on her career as a photographer.*
> ***Non-smokers are paired up**.*
> *In Greece, a group of male contestants' mothers protested that their sons **had been paired up with unsuitable women**.*

amalgamate	combine *2,5*	entwine *1*	interlock *1*
blend *1*	conjoin	fuse *4,5*	merge *1*
bond *2,6*	connect *1*	hybridize	mix *1*
clink	cross-breed *1*	integrate *2*	unify
pair off	pair up		

1.2 THE 'INTERTWINE' GROUP

In the patterns **pl-n V** and **V *with* n**, these verbs indicate that two or more things or people have a connection. In the patterns **V pl-n** and **V n *with* n**, they are concerned with someone or something connecting things or people.

> *Sautet's flowing, unfussy style brings each of these figures into clear focus as **their lives intertwine**.*
> *As you will see, each of these factors **intertwines with the other two**.*
> *This is appropriate, for **advertising and market research are** closely **intertwined**.*
> *She had learned many strange and terrible things since some trick of her genes **had intertwined her life** so utterly **with Jonty Thrale's**.*

The verbs *interconnect* and *interlock* usually have the passive pattern **pl-n *be* V-ed**, rather than the active patterns **V pl-n** and **V n *with* n**.

> *They are ideally suited to organisation-wide work-group computing, where **all users are interconnected**.*

*Students cannot identify world leaders or the capitals of other countries at a time when **the destinies of all nations <u>are interlocked</u>**.*

The verb *correlate* has the pattern **V *to* n** as well as the pattern **V *with* n**. It has the passive patterns **pl-n *be* V-ed** and ***be* V-ed *with* n**, not the active patterns **V pl-n** and **V n *with* n**.

*The performance of a side **<u>does not</u>** necessarily **<u>correlate</u> to the ability of its leader**.*
*Also, we were never totally convinced that **the two effects <u>were correlated</u>**.*
*It has also been shown conclusively that these mind-related changes **<u>are correlated</u> with healthful changes in the body**.*

The verb *relate* has the patterns **V *to* n** and **V n *to* n**, not the patterns **V *with* n** and **V n *with* n**.

*In any society there will be reasonably clear cultural differences which **<u>relate</u> to features of its social structure**.*
*Sociologists **<u>might relate</u>** these films to violence on the street.*

combine *1*	interconnect	interlock *2*	interweave
connect *4*	interface *4*	interrelate	relate *2*
correlate *1*	interlink	intertwine *1*	

1.3 THE 'SEPARATE' GROUP

In the patterns **pl-n V** and **V *from* n**, these verbs indicate that two or more things or people move apart or stop being connected, physically or metaphorically. In the patterns **V pl-n** and **V n *from* n**, they are concerned with someone or something moving things or people apart or ending a connection between them.

*This mascara is easy to apply. **The eyelashes <u>separate</u>** nicely; it doesn't clump or flake.*
*The forward part of the fuselage and cockpit **<u>separated</u> from the main body of the aircraft** within two to three seconds of the blast.*
*A scuffle developed. The women's teenage girls tried to **<u>separate</u> them**.*
*Undercooking makes it impossible to **<u>separate</u> the meat from the bones***; overcooking destroys the texture and flavor.*

The verb *split up* has the patterns **pl-n V P**, **V P *with* n**, and **V n P**.

*When **Ellen and her husband <u>split up</u>**, she took her three teenaged children and moved back to her hometown.*
*She **<u>split up</u> with her husband** more than two years ago and now wants to divorce him.*
*It's obvious she's being malicious and trying to **<u>split us up</u>** but it's not working.*

separate *3,4*
split up *1*

1.4 THE 'DOVETAIL' GROUP

In the patterns **pl-n V** and **V *with* n**, these verbs indicate that two or more things are similar or compatible in some way. In the patterns **V pl-n** and **V n *with* n**, they are concerned with someone or something using or putting two or more similar or compatible things together, or putting them together successfully.

We include here *line up*, which is concerned with putting two or more things in the right position relative to each other.

*Despite the fact that most of his assumptions were based on guesswork, **they** all **<u>dovetailed</u>** so neatly that there must be some underlying truth.*
*The company is interested in routes which **<u>would dovetail</u> with its bus operations**.*
*Pearson **<u>might be able to dovetail</u> the schedules of BSkyB and UK Gold** to attract viewers away from ITV to satellite.*
*The management of local affairs **<u>should dovetail</u> regional interests with those of the entire country**.*

The phrasal verb *match up* also has the patterns **V P *to* n** and **V n P *to* n**.

> *Under new EC law, package tour operators must pay compensation if the holiday they have sold you **doesn't match up to the one you receive**.*
> *Some are graduates who have not been able to get jobs, while others are in the middle of doing their studies. We **match them up to the appropriate levels**.*

balance *3*	dovetail *1*	mesh *2*	rhyme *1*
co-ordinate *2*	match *4,5*	(do not) mix *5*	synchronize
line up *3*	match up ▷*5*		

1.5 THE 'ALTERNATE' GROUP

In the patterns **pl-n V** and **V *with* n**, these verbs indicate that two or more things occur or do something alternately or swap roles or places. In the patterns **V pl-n** and **V n *with* n**, they are concerned with someone or something using two or more things alternately or swapping them over.

> *That evening just before sundown Jozsef went into an alarming series of attacks, **the tremors and the coma alternating** without any interval between.*
> *Depression **can alternate** with high spirits, noisy outbursts and even euphoria.*
> *Make a fan-like design with the apple and liver inside the ring, **alternating the liver and apple**.*
> *The text **alternates** naturalistic dialogue with surreal, comic train announcements and passionate monologues.*

alternate *1*	interchange *2*

Pattern combination 2: V; pl-n V n; V n *with* n

These verbs have three patterns. Two patterns are reciprocal:

- **pl-n V n**: The verb is used with a plural Subject and is followed by a noun group.
- **V n *with* n**: The verb is used with a Subject indicating one participant and is followed by a noun group. This is followed by a prepositional phrase consisting of *with* and a noun group which indicates the other participant.

One pattern is not reciprocal:

- **V**: The verb need not be followed by anything.

V

	Verb group
Subject	**Verb**
The peace negotiations	have reopened.

pl-n V n

plural noun group	Verb group	noun group
Subject	**Verb**	**Object**
Caterpillar Inc. and its striking union	reopened	negotiations.

V n *with* n

	Verb group	noun group	*with*	noun group
Subject	**Verb**	**Object**		**Adjunct**
Zuckerman	reopened	talks	with	Pete Hamill.

Verbs with this combination of patterns belong to the following meaning groups:

2.1   THE 'NORMALIZE' GROUP
2.2   THE 'CLINK' GROUP

2.1 THE 'NORMALIZE' GROUP

These verbs indicate that two or more countries, groups, or people start communicating with each other again.

*The government invited him to become its exclusive business agent in the United States when relations **normalized**.*
*They say Japan already made formal apologies to China when **the two countries normalized** relations 20 years ago.*
*Baker said that Washington **will normalize** economic relations with Cambodia as soon as the United Nations team begins implementing the new peace treaty.*

> normalize *2*   reopen *3*

2.2 THE 'CLINK' GROUP

These verbs indicate that two or more people put their drinking glasses together or touch each other. They have the patterns **pl-n V**, **pl-n V pl-n**, and **V pl-n *with* n**.

*Their glasses **clinked**, their eyes met.*
*The two **clinked** glasses like a pair of Red Army colonels downing a toast of vodka, then refilled their glasses from a Lalique decanter on Paco's coffee table.*
*Politicians and businessmen **clinked** glasses with him at the Leipzig trade fairs.*

> clink   touch *2*

Pattern combination 3: pl-n V; V n; V pl-n; V n *to/with* n

These verbs have four patterns. Two patterns are reciprocal:

- **pl-n V**: The verb is used with a plural Subject.
- **V n**: The verb is used with a Subject indicating one participant and is followed by a noun group indicating the other.

Two patterns are not reciprocal:

- **V pl-n**: The verb is followed by a **plural noun group**.
- **V n *to/with* n**: The verb is followed by a noun group and a prepositional phrase consisting of *to* or *with* and a noun group.

pl-n V

plural noun group	Verb group
Subject	**Verb**
Cats' territories	may overlap.

V n

	Verb group	noun group
Subject	Verb	Object
The second toe	overlaps	the third toe.

V pl-n

	Verb group	plural noun group
Subject	Verb	Object
	Overlap	the strips.

V n *to/with* n

	Verb group	noun group	*to/with*	noun group
Subject	Verb	Object	prepositional Object	
	Overlap	your right hand	with	your left.

There are five verbs with this combination of patterns. The verbs *match* and *overlap* have the pattern **V n *with* n**. The verbs *marry*, *match* and *touch* have the pattern **V n *to* n**.

> He compared the sequence of visits entered in the appointments diary with the dates quoted at the back of the file. *They **matched**.*
>
> They told him he couldn't board the plane unless the name on his ticket ***matched** the one on his passport.*
>
> Magnetic boards are also very popular because the children ***can match** shapes, animals and numbers,* effectively developing their memory skills.
>
> Mr Wright's task is to ***match** graduates **with** firms.*
>
> She held out her hand and ***their fingers touched**.*
>
> Smoothly lower the bar so that it ***touches** the middle of your chest,* then press it upwards to arm's length again.
>
> Laura and I ***touched** knees* again.
>
> She ***touched** her glass to his.*

The verb *wed* has the passive pattern **pl-n *be* V-ed**, not the active patterns **V pl-n** or **V n *to/with* n**.

> We ***were wed*** in 1928 and had a very happy marriage.

marry 1,2	overlap 1	wed
match 3,5	touch 2	

Emphasizing reciprocity

When ergative reciprocal verbs are used in patterns with a plural Subject, they can be emphasized with phrases in the same way as ordinary reciprocal verbs (see page 472). With most of them, a **reciprocal pronoun** (*each other* or *one another*) can be used after the appropriate preposition or after the verb.

> The third possibility is that *building societies **may merge** with **each other***.
>
> These muscles ***overlap** each other*.

With the verbs listed below, the adverb *together* can be used for emphasis.

> Given enough speed, *nuclei **fuse** together* and make a new, heavier element.
>
> Biological, psychological, and cultural factors all ***mesh** together* to produce illness.

blend *1*	dovetail *1*	mesh *2*
bond *2,6*	fuse *4,5*	
clink	merge *1*	

Chapter 9: Patterns with *it*

In this chapter we describe verb patterns in which the Subject or Object is always the word *it*. In these patterns *it* has two basic uses. It may function as a 'dummy' Subject or Object pointing forward to a clause somewhere else in the sentence, in which case we call it **introductory** *it*. Or it may refer vaguely to a general situation, and not point anywhere else in the sentence. In this case we call it **general** *it*. This chapter contains the following sections:

1 Introductory *it* as Subject
2 Introductory *it* as Object
3 General *it* as Subject
4 General *it* as Object

1 Introductory *it* as Subject

In all the patterns described here, the clause begins with **introductory** *it*, which is the Subject of the clause. Although it is the Subject, it does not contribute to the meaning of the clause, and is often known as a 'dummy' Subject. English prefers to have old information at the beginning of a clause and new information at the end of a clause. If a clause does not contain any old information, having *it* as Subject allows all the new information to be placed at the end of a clause. For example, the clause *It is difficult to see what you mean* has two pieces of new information: *difficult* and *to see what you mean*. You could say *To see what you mean is difficult*, but then some of the new information would be at the beginning of the clause. In the clause beginning with *it*, none of the new information comes at the beginning of the clause.

In spoken English, the word *it* is sometimes omitted, especially with the verbs *look, seem* and *sound*, e.g. *Looks as if we're out of luck*, *Seems he knows all the answers*, *Sounds as if it runs in the family*. The same thing occurs with the phrase *it stands to reason*, e.g. *Stands to reason he stole it*. In the case of *be*, some nouns and adjectives sometimes occur without *it is*, e.g. *Pity you didn't let me know*.

All the patterns described here contain a clause such as a that-clause or a to-infinitive clause. All these are new clauses, with their own structures.

The patterns with introductory *it* as Subject fall into six pattern groups:

▶ Pattern group 1: *it* V clause
▶ Pattern group 2: *it* V *to* n clause
▶ Pattern group 3: *it* V prep clause
▶ Pattern group 4: *it be* V-ed clause
▶ Pattern group 5: *it* V n clause
▶ Pattern group 6: *it* V adj clause

Pattern group 1: *it* V clause

There are five patterns in this group, each consisting of *it*, the verb, and a type of clause:

- 1.1 *it* V that
  It seemed that I was right.
- 1.2 *it* V to-inf
  It helps to talk.

- 1.3 *it* V wh
  It doesn't matter what you think.
- 1.4 *it* V when/if
  It hurts when you forget to write.
- 1.5 *it* V as if/as though/like
  It sounds as if they made a dreadful mistake.

1.1 *it* V that

The verb is followed by a that-clause.

it	Verb group	that-clause
Subject	**Verb**	**Clause**
It	emerged	that smoking reduces life-expectancy.
It	seemed	that he would keep his word.
It	transpired	that the gunman had been released from jail.

Verbs with this pattern belong to the following meaning groups:

1 THE 'EMERGE' GROUP
2 THE 'APPEAR' GROUP
3 THE 'HURT' GROUP

1 THE 'EMERGE' GROUP

These verbs indicate that something happens or becomes known, or that something is logically the case. With some verbs the word *that* is often omitted, as in *It happened I was there at the time.*

*It never really **clicked** that I was homeless until I had been on the streets a couple of months.*

*It **emerged** that he had a violent criminal record, of which the welfare agencies had been unaware.*

*Doug was a good man when I knew him, but that had been a lot of years ago. And it **figured** that there was a solid case against him.*

*Since sound is actually the motion of molecules, it **follows** that the fastest speed with which the air molecules can get out of the way is the speed of sound.*

*It **happened** that we had a number of very competent women so it was not difficult to pick a woman to do it.*

There are five phrasal verbs with this meaning, listed below. Their pattern is *it* **V P that**.

*How **did** it **come about** that a man so shrewd and wise as David should fall for such a blatantly obvious confidence trick?*

*What'll happen is, it'**ll come out** that he didn't shoot himself, Jack shot him.*

*If it **does turn out** that the inspectors have found highly enriched uranium, this raises a number of questions.*

click *2*	figure *12*	happen *4*
emerge *3*	follow *6*	transpire *1*
come about	get around/round *3*	turn out *3*
come out *2*	leak out ▷*3*	

The old-fashioned verb group *come to pass* also has this pattern.

After the war, it __came to pass__ that he did not resume his medical studies.

2 THE 'APPEAR' GROUP

These verbs are concerned with what a situation is, or seems to be. They are all **link verbs** (see Chapter 5). The word *that* is often omitted, as in *It seems you understand me.*

A police spokesman said it __appeared__ that the bag had contained two tubes filled with pieces of lead which flew into the air injuring the eleven people.

The verb *be* is not usually used alone in the affirmative in this pattern. The following types of clause are frequent: negative clauses; clauses in which *be* follows a modal; and clauses including an adverb such as *just* or *simply*.

He was to be a priest, so, she thought, it __could not be__ that he was interested in her.

This doesn't necessarily mean that sport can improve your emotional health; it __could__ simply __be__ that people with a more extrovert personality are more likely to enjoy sports in the first place.

> appear *1*   be *2.2*   seem *1*

3 THE 'HURT' GROUP

These verbs indicate how someone feels about the event indicated by the that-clause.

Hundreds of people attended the wake and funeral. It __helped__ that so many people cared. I felt stronger when people were around.

I have been wanting to write to you since day one. It __hurts__ that you cannot see this.

The bigger the cost, the more it __matters__ that the money should not be wasted.

> help *2*   matter *9*
> hurt *5*   rankle

1.2 *it* V to-inf

The verb is followed by a to-infinitive clause.

it	Verb group	to-infinitive clause
Subject	**Verb**	**Clause**
It	may help	to talk about it.
It	hurt	to breathe.
It	pays	to shop around for the best deals.

Three of the verbs with this pattern indicate that something is helpful to someone, or is a good thing.

Different building societies offer different services so it __pays__ to shop around.

The verb *do* usually occurs in negative clauses.

I'm learning the language. A career diplomat has to. It __doesn't do__ to have to use translators all the time.

> (not) do *2.22*   help *2*   pay *9*

There are two other verbs with this pattern.

Though his case was far from complete, he was convinced he was right. ***It <u>remained</u> to convince his superiors.***

> hurt *2,5*   remain *1*

1.3 *it* V wh

The verb is followed by a wh-clause. There is only one verb with this pattern.

> *I don't think* ***it <u>matters</u> what you really are, it <u>matters</u> what you do.***

> matter *9*

1.4 *it* V when/if

The verb is followed by a clause beginning with *when* or *if*, which indicates a situation that occurs or may occur.

> ***It <u>didn't help</u> when he tried to cover his mistake.***

> help *2*   hurt *5*

1.5 *it* V as if, *it* V as though, *it* V like

The verb is followed by a clause beginning with *as if* or *as though*. In informal English, the clause sometimes begins with *like*. Some people think these clauses are incorrect, but we include them here because they occur frequently.

it	Verb group	as if/as though/like-clause
Subject	**Verb**	**Clause**
It	looks	as if there will be a rebellion.
It	seemed	like his dream had come true.
It	sounds	as though she is leading an invalid life.

Verbs with this pattern are concerned with what a situation seems or feels like. They are all **link verbs** (see Chapter 5).

> *There was smoke coming up at the bottom of the hill.* ***It <u>appeared</u> as if there had been a bonfire or something.***
>
> *Chess experts are awe-struck by Fischer's play.* ***It <u>is</u> as if he had never stopped playing chess.***
>
> *The band played.* ***It <u>felt</u> as though the room were a moving vehicle and had just crashed up against a wall of sound.***

> appear *1*   feel *2*   seem *1*
> be *2.2*   look *2.4*   sound *9*

Pattern group 2: *it* V *to* n clause

There are four patterns in this group, each consisting of *it*, the verb, a prepositional phrase beginning with *to*, and a type of clause:

- 2.1 *it* V *to* n that
  It _seems_ to me that I had done everything I could.
- 2.2 *it* V *to* n to-inf
  It _fell_ to me to organize the event.
- 2.3 *it* V *to* n wh
  It _matters_ to me what happens to you.
- 2.4 *it* V *to* n as if/as though/like
  It _sounds_ to me as if you don't want to help her.

2.1 *it* V *to* n that

The verb is followed by a prepositional phrase beginning with *to*, and a that-clause. The prepositional phrase always indicates a human being. The prepositional phrase is the prepositional Object.

it	Verb group	*to*	noun group	that-clause
Subject	**Verb**	**prepositional Object**		**Clause**
It	came	to	him	that the car following him was the same one.
It	didn't occur	to	him	that he might win.
It	seemed	to	me	that there was absolutely no hope.

The word *that* is often omitted, as in *It seems to me you're lying.*

Verbs with this pattern belong to the following meaning groups:

  1 THE 'SEEM' GROUP
  2 THE 'OCCUR' GROUP
  3 VERBS WITH OTHER MEANINGS

1 THE 'SEEM' GROUP

These verbs are concerned with what a situation seems like to someone. They are also found without the prepositional phrase, in the pattern **it V that**. Of the verbs in this meaning group, *seem* occurs much more frequently than any of the other verbs.

All the verbs in this group are **link verbs** (see Chapter 5).

It _seemed_ to me that the book tried to say something in a different way than it had been said before.

appear *1*	look *2.4*	sound *9*
feel *2*	seem *1*	

2 THE 'OCCUR' GROUP

These verbs indicate that an idea occurs to someone. These verbs are not found in the pattern **it V that**: they occur only with a prepositional phrase, for example *to me* or *to my attention*.

Quite recently it _came_ to my attention that I am older than the Prime Minister.

She seemed to be asleep. Then it _occurred_ to him she might be dead.

come *11*	occur *3*

3 VERBS WITH OTHER MEANINGS

There is one other verb with this pattern.

Her husband appealed to the public yesterday: 'It __matters__ to everyone that the killer is still around.'

> matter 9

2.2 *it* V *to* n to-inf

The verb is followed by a prepositional phrase beginning with *to*, and a to-infinitive clause. The prepositional phrase always indicates a human being. The prepositional phrase is the prepositional Object.

it	Verb group	*to*	noun group	to-infinitive clause
Subject	Verb	prepositional Object		Clause
It	appeals	to	bankers	to keep supporting a strong franc.
It	hadn't occurred	to	me	to bring a cheque-book.

There are only three verbs with this pattern.

It __fell__ to Malcolm to care for her, but he had less and less time.

It __occurred__ to me to wonder how other animals that live in highly-organised societies, like human beings, cope with their diseases.

> appeal 6   fall *VP1*   occur 3

2.3 *it* V *to* n wh

The verb is followed by a prepositional phrase beginning with *to*, and a wh-clause. The prepositional phrase always indicates a human being. The prepositional phrase is the prepositional Object.

it	Verb group	*to*	noun group	wh-clause
Subject	Verb	prepositional Object		Clause
It	came	to	me	what Pop had forgotten.
It	didn't matter	to	her	what happened to us.

Two of the verbs with this pattern indicate that an idea occurs to someone.

It __occurred__ to me how truly blessed we are to live in a town that's just chock-full of so many interesting races, creeds and colors.

> come 11   occur 3

There is one other verb with this pattern.

It __doesn't matter__ to them whether or not they sell your product.

> matter 9

2.4 *it* V *to* n as if, *it* V *to* n as though, *it* V *to* n like

The verb is followed by a prepositional phrase beginning with *to*, and a clause beginning with *as if* or *as though*. In informal English, the clause sometimes begins with *like*. Some people think these clauses are incorrect, but we include them because they occur frequently.

The prepositional phrase is the prepositional Object.

it	Verb group	*to*	noun group	as if/as though/like-clause
Subject	**Verb**	**prepositional Object**		**Clause**
It	felt	to	me	like the war was coming closer and closer.
It	looked	to	me	as if this gun had been used close up.
It	sounds	to	me	as though you've tried your best.

All the verbs with this pattern are concerned with what a situation seems or feels like to someone. These verbs are also found without the prepositional phrase, in the pattern *it* V **as if**. All the verbs in this group are **link verbs** (see Chapter 5).

*You have many skills and capabilities. All in all **it seems** to me as though you could be very useful to us.*

```
appear 1    look 2.4    sound 9
feel 2      seem 1
```

Pattern group 3: *it* V prep clause

Patterns in which the preposition is *to* and the prepositional phrase indicates a human being have been described in Pattern group 2 above. Here we describe the patterns which contain other prepositional phrases.

There are two patterns in this group, each consisting of *it*, the verb, a prepositional phrase, and a type of clause:

- 3.1 *it* V prep that
  It <u>came</u> to light that he had not been telling the truth.
- 3.2 *it* V prep to-inf
  It <u>was</u> up to me to decide what to do.

3.1 *it* V prep that

The verb is followed by a prepositional phrase and a that-clause. The prepositional phrase is the prepositional Complement with the verbs *be, come,* and *count*, and an Adjunct with the other verbs.

it	Verb group	preposition	noun group	that-clause
Subject	**Verb**	**prepositional Complement**		**Clause**
It	is	to	our credit	that people are now healthier.
It	counts	as	an achievement	that he was able to resign.

it	Verb group	preposition	noun group	that-clause
Subject	**Verb**	**Adjunct**		**Clause**
It	came	to	light	that the plane had not been insured.
It	goes	without	saying	that most gardeners love the outdoor life.

Verbs with this pattern have a variety of meanings. Most of them occur within fairly fixed phrases.

> **It _is_ to his credit that the bitterness he felt over his recent failure did not alter his determination to carry out his regimental duties to perfection.**

> **It _is not_ for nothing that sports people call their clothes their 'strip'.** Athletes now wear clinging, black garments that leave nothing to the imagination.

> **It _came_ as little surprise that the twelve ministers found much to criticise in the reform proposals.**

> Since alcohol is drying, it _stands_ to reason that those products marketed for women with dry skin have little or no alcohol.

There is one phrasal verb with this pattern, *creep up*. Its pattern is *it V P on n* that.

> It's hard to say at first why Ed is so remarkable but then it _creeps up_ on you that this is top-quality song-writing.

---

be 2.2   **come** (to) (see light 14)   **go** (without) (see say 18)
come 20 (as)   **count** 7 (as)   **stand** 28
creep up VPP

3.2 *it* V prep to-inf

The verb is followed by a prepositional phrase and a to-infinitive clause. The prepositional phrase is the prepositional Complement with *be* and *come*, and an Adjunct with *accord*.

it	Verb group	preposition	noun group	to-infinitive clause
Subject	**Verb**	**prepositional Complement/Adjunct**		**Clause**
It	accords	with	the public interest	to prosecute.
It	is	up to	them	to stay competitive.

Verbs with this pattern have a variety of meanings.

> If there are any surplus resources, it _is not_ in the interests of the government to keep them.

> **It _comes_ as no surprise to learn that magistrates in England and Wales dislike the new Criminal Justice Act and are now seeking to modify it.**

---

accord 3   **be** 2.2   **come** 20

Pattern group 4: *it be* V-ed clause

There are three patterns in this group, each consisting of *it*, a verb in the passive, and a type of clause. Although in these patterns *it* is the Subject in a passive clause, we include them here because there is no active equivalent containing *it*.

- 4.1 *it be* V-ed that
  > It _is thought_ that the temple was used in the third century.

- 4.2 *it be* V-ed to-inf
  It *was decided* to cancel the meeting.
- 4.3 *it be* V-ed wh
  It *is not known* what causes the disease.

4.1 *it be* V-ed that

The verb is followed by a that-clause.

it	Verb group	that-clause
Subject	Verb	Clause
It	was admitted	that the tests were all wrong.
It	was agreed	that a new treaty would be signed.
It	is estimated	that a hundred people have now died.

This pattern is used to indicate that something is said, thought, or discovered, without indicating who said, thought, or discovered it. The implication is that this is a group of people, people in general, or occasionally an unspecified individual: the context has to determine which of these alternatives applies.

This is a productive pattern and occurs occasionally with a large number of verbs concerned with saying, knowing, and thinking, such as *add, affirm, appreciate, compute, decree, deduce, deem, hint, hypothesize, maintain, mention, moot, perceive, postulate, speculate,* and *stipulate.* The verbs listed below are the ones which are most frequently used in this way.

The word *that* is often omitted, as in *It was said he had a good head for business.*

Verbs with this pattern belong to the following meaning groups:

1 THE 'REPORT' GROUP
2 THE 'THINK' AND 'DISCOVER' GROUP

1 THE 'REPORT' GROUP

These verbs are concerned with what is spoken and written. This includes something that is:

- agreed or conceded
- suggested or recommended
- announced, reported, or disclosed
- rumoured or alleged
- argued or denied

We also include here *demonstrate* and *show*, which do not necessarily involve speaking or writing.

Eventually it was agreed that the present laws would continue to apply in the same areas for two years.

It is claimed that running helps to unleash hidden energies, both psychic and physical.

In 1990, it was disclosed that he had contracted the AIDS virus.

A short time ago, it was reported that demonstrators had broken through the police lines and more vehicles were set alight.

It is rumoured that his farmhouse resembles a fortress, with a panic-button to alert the police in the event of intruders breaking in.

Until it is shown that the tape is genuine, we have to remain sceptical.

*It **is suggested** that teachers should design activities which will keep the class actively and constructively engaged.*

There are two phrasal verbs with this meaning, given below. Their pattern is *it be* **V-ed P that**.

*When it **was pointed out** that she would need considerable journalistic experience she agreed she didn't have it.*

These verbs are sometimes used with a **modal** such as *must* or *can* to indicate that the speaker feels obliged or able to say something, not that someone else has said something.

*It **can be argued** that human health would not suffer if we were to stop most animal research.*

*Though it **cannot be denied** that appearance is the first step towards attraction, it is similarity of attitude that is often a deciding factor when it comes to pursuing a relationship.*

*It **must be emphasized** that goat's and sheep's milk also contain lactose.*

*It **must be said** that the success has been solid rather than spectacular.*

be acknowledged *1*	be conceded *1*	be held *2,1*	be said *1*
be admitted *1*	be confirmed *2*	be proposed *1*	be shown *1*
be agreed *1,3*	be contended *2*	be recommended *2*	be stated *8*
be alleged	be demonstrated *1*	be recorded *2*	be stressed *1*
be announced *1*	be denied *1*	be reported *1*	be suggested *1*
be argued *1*	be disclosed	be revealed *1*	be trumpeted *2*
be asserted *1*	be emphasized	be ruled *7*	be whispered *2*
be claimed *1*	be explained *1*	be rumoured	
be laid down *2*	be pointed out *2*		

2 THE 'THINK' AND 'DISCOVER' GROUP

These verbs are concerned with what is thought. This includes something that is:

- expected, hoped, or feared
- thought or believed
- decided or intended
- remembered or forgotten
- known or suspected
- discovered

*It **is accepted** now that drinking water in many areas contains certain pollutants which are undesirable.*

*At one time it **was believed** that an addict couldn't quit until she hit bottom and lost everything. That's true for many people but, it turns out, not for everybody.*

*It **was concluded** that the aircraft was flying at the maximum permitted speed when the leading edge of the wing opened up, ripping the wing apart.*

*Inquiries were made and it **was decided** that there were no grounds for further investigation.*

*They became concerned when it **was discovered** that more than nine-thousand ballot papers had been forged.*

*It **is estimated** that up to two million people around the country suffer from various forms of asthma.*

*It **is expected** that by the weekend, air traffic, garbage collection and mail delivery will be back in full operation.*

*At first it **was feared** that a bomb had caused the blast but now it appears that the explosion may have been triggered accidentally.*

*It **was felt** that valuable work could be carried out in establishing a good working relationship between the groups.*

It should be remembered that the success rate of Alcoholics Anonymous stands second to none.

From the stories related in this book, it can be seen that the average age of those women marrying is 17.

It has long been thought that aluminium was a poisonous substance and it has been linked to cancer of the stomach, though there is no evidence for this.

It is understood that damage estimated at more than a hundred thousand pounds has been caused to furniture, fittings and equipment in the Embassy building.

be accepted *2,4*	be envisaged *1*	be implied *1*	be realized *1*
be anticipated *1*	be established *3*	be intended *1*	be reckoned *4*
be assumed *1*	be estimated *1*	be judged *4*	be recognized *2*
be believed *1*	be expected *1*	be known *1*	be regretted *1*
be calculated *1,2*	be feared *4*	be learnt *2*	be remembered *5*
be concluded *1*	be felt *10*	be noted *9*	be seen *4*
be considered *1*	be found *7*	be noticed *1*	be supposed *2*
be decided *1,2,4*	be forgotten *2*	be predicted	be suspected *2*
be determined *2,3*	be hoped *1*	be presumed *1*	be thought *1*
be discovered *1*	be imagined *2*	be proven *2*	be understood *5*

4.2 *it be* V-ed to-inf

The verb is followed by a to-infinitive clause.

it	Verb group	to-infinitive clause
Subject	**Verb**	**Clause**
It	was hoped	to use helicopters to evacuate refugees.
It	is proposed	to allow cameras into courts.

Verbs with this pattern are concerned with a course of action being proposed, hoped for, recommended, or decided upon.

At an emergency meeting of teachers and parents, it was agreed to send home all 300 pupils at Chigwell county primary, Essex, until further notice.

She was actually too old for foster care, but because she was so upset emotionally, it was decided to place her with a foster family.

A spokesman said that it was intended to complete the evacuation of the remaining 1,700 citizens by January 10th.

be agreed *3*	be hoped *1*	be planned *2*
be decided *1*	be intended *1*	be proposed *2*

4.3 *it be* V-ed wh

The verb is followed by a wh-clause.

it	Verb group	wh-clause
Subject	**Verb**	**Clause**
It	is being asked	why you did not make your views known earlier.
It	was not disclosed	how much the sale will raise.

The verbs with this pattern are concerned with information being asked for, discovered, explained, understood, or doubted.

It *has to be clarified* **whether the radicals are holding two of the soldiers, as they say, or three, as other reports have suggested.**

It *was* never *established* **whether the motor failed or the take-off was aborted.**

Many theories exist, but it *is not known* **what causes endometriosis, or how the disease can trigger infertility.**

Another top Tory is under pressure to quit after it *was revealed* **how a company he ran cost taxpayers £200,000.**

It *is* pretty well *understood* **what controls the flow of carbon dioxide in and out of the atmosphere today.**

be asked *1*	be discovered *1*	be imagined *2*	be seen *4*
be clarified	be doubted *2*	be known *1*	be shown *1*
be decided *1*	be established *3*	be learned *1*	be understood *5*
be determined *2*	be explained *1*	be questioned *3*	
be disclosed	be found *7*	be revealed *1*	

Pattern group 5: *it* V n clause

There are eleven patterns in this group, each consisting of *it*, the verb, a noun group, and a type of clause. Patterns 5.8 to 5.11 contain other elements as well.

- 5.1 *it* V n that
  It *struck* me that the story would make a good film.
- 5.2 *it* V n to-inf
  It *worries* me to see you unhappy.
- 5.3 *it* V n wh
  It *beats* me why sales are falling.
- 5.4 *it* V n when/if
  It *worries* me when you come home late.
- 5.5 *it* V n -ing
  It's no fun working all weekend.
- 5.6 *it* V n/amount before/since
  It's only a matter of time before he finds out.
- 5.7 *it* V n for n to-inf
  It *took* months for them to answer my letters.
- 5.8 *it* V n n to-inf
  It *took* me ages to finish my work.
- 5.9 *it* V amount for n that
  It *said* a lot for him that he was able to apologize.
- 5.10 *it* V n adj that
  It *drove* him crazy that he couldn't do anything to help.
- 5.11 *it* V n adj to-inf
  It *makes* me sick to think about all the thefts.

5.1 *it* V n that

The verb is followed by a noun group and a that-clause. The noun group is the Complement in group 1, and the Object in groups 2 and 3.

it	Verb group	noun group	that-clause
Subject	**Verb**	**Complement**	**Clause**
It	is	a shame	that the press ignored these events.
It	became	a rule	that visitors could not leave their cars.

it	Verb group	noun group	that-clause
Subject	**Verb**	**Object**	**Clause**
It	bothered	her	that he hadn't asked for her.
It	hit	me	that I was going off on my own.

Verbs with this pattern belong to the following meaning groups:

1 THE 'BE' GROUP
2 THE 'ANNOY' AND 'PLEASE' GROUP
3 THE 'STRIKE' GROUP

1 THE 'BE' GROUP

These verbs are concerned with what a situation is, seems, or becomes. All the verbs in this group are **link verbs** (see Chapter 5). The word *that* is often omitted, as in *It's a pity you can't come.*

*You can name your own price. It's almost **a foregone conclusion that you'll get what you want.***

*It remains **a subject of fascination that one family produced three exceptional writers: Charlotte, Anne, and Emily Bronte.***

be *2.2*	remain *1*
become *1*	seem *1*

2 THE 'ANNOY' AND 'PLEASE' GROUP

These verbs indicate how a situation makes someone feel. The noun group always indicates a human being.

This is a productive use and occurs occasionally with a large number of verbs indicating the emotional effect of something, such as *alarm, anger, awe, baffle, bemuse, confuse, depress, enrage, fascinate, frustrate, horrify, intrigue, offend, stagger,* and *upset.* The verbs listed here are the ones which are most frequently used in this way.

It amuses me that every 22-year-old now wants to own property. I was 38 before I could afford my first flat.

It annoyed me that I didn't have time to do more ironing, but I will get it done.

It frightens me that kids are now walking around with guns.

In a dormitory I saw a notice: 'It pleases God that children should be respectful to their elders.'

It puzzles me that people are willing to pay any taxes at all to this Government.

It saddens me that almost all my anxieties have been confirmed. I wish I had been proved wrong.

Does it surprise you that the polls are showing currently that this initiative will be approved by the voters?

amaze	concern 2	gall 2	please 5
amuse 1	disappoint	hurt 5	puzzle 1
annoy	distress 3	infuriate	sadden
appal	disturb 2	irk	shock 4
astonish	embarrass 1	irritate 1	surprise 3
bother 4	frighten 1	pain 3	worry 2

3 THE 'STRIKE' GROUP

These verbs indicate either that an idea occurs to someone, or that they fail to notice something. The noun group usually indicates a human being. In the case of *escape*, it may be something such as *my attention* or *their notice*.

> *They so obviously enjoyed life, enjoyed the things they did together, that it almost <u>escaped</u> their attention that some people did not approve of the family.*

> *Didn't it <u>strike</u> you that he was awfully uptight and tense?*

There is one phrasal verb with this meaning, *dawn on*. The pattern is **it V P n that**.

> *I noticed that he was soaking wet, and for the first time it <u>dawned on</u> me that he had come down across the fields from the hill.*

escape 5	hit 5	strike 10
dawn on		

Other productive uses

This pattern is productive: a wide range of verbs concerned with the consequences or implications of situations and events sometimes have this pattern. For example, it occurs in sentences like *It <u>destroyed</u> our credibility that we didn't know what was going on within our own team.*

In addition, there are a few fairly fixed phrases with this pattern.

> *It <u>broke my heart</u> that she could shut out my pain so easily.*

> *He seemed less surly, more comfortable about being polite and ordinary. So it <u>crossed my mind</u> that I might give him another chance.*

> *It <u>never entered her head</u> that their divorce would go through without a financial settlement having been made.*

> *Most of the evidence was against him, and so it <u>makes sense</u> that he was found guilty.*

> *It <u>made no difference</u> that we tried to talk to her, she just looked straight ahead and didn't answer us.*

5.2 *it* V n to-inf

The verb is followed by a noun group and a to-infinitive clause. The noun group is the Complement in group 1, and the Object in groups 2, 3, and 4.

it	Verb group	noun group	to-infinitive clause
Subject	**Verb**	**Complement**	**Clause**
It	became	policy	to increase the number of magistrates.
It	seemed	a pity	to break up the peaceful scene.

it	Verb group	noun group	to-infinitive clause
Subject	**Verb**	**Object**	**Clause**
It	amused	him	to see her furious.
It	takes	time	to learn about finance.

Verbs with this pattern belong to the following meaning groups:

1 THE 'BE' GROUP
2 THE 'PAIN' AND 'PLEASE' GROUP
3 THE 'PAY' GROUP
4 VERBS WITH OTHER MEANINGS

1 THE 'BE' GROUP

These verbs are concerned with what a situation is, seems, or becomes. All the verbs in this group are **link verbs** (see Chapter 5).

It __is__ a crime to listen in on private conversations with scanners.

James had often said that while it __was__ one thing to have children dependent upon you, it was intolerable to be materially dependent on them.

It __remains__ our aim to maintain its real value over a run of years.

be *2.2*	**remain** *1*
become *1*	**seem** *1*

2 THE 'PAIN' AND 'PLEASE' GROUP

These verbs indicate how a situation makes someone feel. The noun group always indicates a human being or a human attribute such as *feelings* or *heart*.

This is a productive use and occurs occasionally with a large number of verbs indicating the emotional effect of something, such as *anger, astonish, awe, bore, choke, confuse, dismay, embarrass, enrage, jar, reassure, repulse*, and *soothe*. The verbs listed here are the ones which are most frequently used in this way.

I don't suppose it __bothered__ the Platts to know that the money wasn't honestly come by.

It __disturbs__ me to see you unhappy, darling.

As a nurse it __frightened__ her to contemplate the procedure and its risks.

It __gladdens__ my heart to see you again.

It __hurts__ my pride to depend on her for our daily bread.

I'm jealous, but it __kills__ me to admit that I am.

You are always in my thoughts and it __pains__ me to think of you struggling all alone.

It __pleased__ him to see that he'd delighted her with his choice.

alarm *2*	disturb *2*	infuriate	scare *1*
amaze	fascinate	interest *3*	shame *3*
amuse *1*	frighten *1*	intrigue *2*	shock *4*
annoy	gall *2*	irk	surprise *3*
bother *4*	gladden *1*	kill *5*	tickle *3*
comfort *5*	grieve *2*	pain *3*	touch *10*
delight *4*	horrify	please *5*	upset *2*
depress *1*	hurt *5*	sadden	worry *2*

3 THE 'PAY' GROUP

These verbs indicate that an action is helpful or useful to someone.

> *Clearly it __pays__ banks to take big risks with our money.*
> *For some peculiar reason it __suited__ her to live like a character in a Victorian melodrama.*

benefit *3*	pay *9*	suit *4*
help *2*	profit *3*	

4 VERBS WITH OTHER MEANINGS

There are a few other verbs which have this pattern.

> *Reforms seldom come from the top down so it __behoves__ us to put pressure on the decision makers.*
> *It __takes__ courage to face the unknown.*

In the case of *cost, mean,* and *take 2.13*, the verb is always or often followed by an **amount**. This pattern is ***it* V amount to-inf**.

> *It __costs__ a fortune to fly these people in from all over the country.*
> *It __means__ a lot to win the World Cup.*

In the case of *mean*, a prepositional phrase beginning with *to* often occurs after the verb. This pattern is ***it* V amount *to* n to-inf**.

> *She'd begun composing as a child in Berlin, so it __meant__ a lot to her to have her music performed here.*

behove	mean *3*
cost *2*	take *2.13,14*

Other productive uses

This pattern is productive, and occurs with a wide range of verbs concerned with the consequences or implications of actions and events. For example, it occurs in sentences like *It __accentuates__ wrinkles to fill them with face-powder* and *It __put__ a strain on his heart to reach up high.*

In addition, there are a few fairly fixed phrases with this pattern.

> *It __broke my heart__ to see him go.*
> *It __crossed my mind__ to phone her.*
> *It __never entered her head__ to question him.*
> *It __makes a world of difference__ to be dying for your ideas.*
> *It __made sense__ to delay the meeting, as there were no concrete proposals on the table.*
> *It __serves no purpose__ to disclose what happens for those who haven't seen the film.*

5.3 *it* V n wh

The verb is followed by a noun group and a wh-clause. The noun group is the Complement in group 1, and the Object in groups 2, 3, and 4.

it	Verb group	noun group	wh-clause
Subject	**Verb**	**Complement**	**Clause**
It	is	a mystery	how they do that.
It	remains	a puzzle	why these evils have gone unnoticed.

it	Verb group	noun group	wh-clause
Subject	**Verb**	**Object**	**Clause**
It	doesn't bother	me	whether you agree with me.
It	worries	me	what the future holds.

Verbs with this pattern belong to the following meaning groups:

1 THE 'BE' GROUP
2 THE 'AMAZE' AND 'SADDEN' GROUP
3 THE 'STRIKE' GROUP

1 THE 'BE' GROUP

These verbs are used when describing a situation or question. Both of these verbs are **link verbs** (see Chapter 5).

It <u>is</u> a mystery why anyone should want to shoot him.

be *2.2*   remain *1*

2 THE 'AMAZE' AND 'SADDEN' GROUP

These verbs indicate how a situation or question makes someone feel. This includes making them feel puzzled because they cannot understand something or do not know how to answer a question. The noun group always indicates a human being.

This is a productive use and occurs occasionally with a large number of verbs indicating the emotional effect of something, such as *anger, astonish, astound, baffle, confuse, fascinate, infuriate, interest, intrigue, shake, startle,* and *trouble*. The verbs listed below are those for which this pattern is frequent.

It <u>amazes</u> me how many plastic shopping bags are given out by cashiers in large supermarkets.

It <u>beats</u> me why sales, particularly in a recession, are still running at £300 million a year.

You believed in something bigger: your own sense of morality. **It <u>didn't concern</u> you whether a thing was illegal or dangerous but whether it was right.**

It <u>saddened</u> me how these children have accepted life in detention as normal.

amaze	bug *7*	pain *3*	surprise *3*
amuse *1*	concern *2,9*	please *5*	upset *2*
annoy	hurt *5*	puzzle *1*	worry *3*
beat *17*	irritate *1*	sadden	
bother *4*	kill *5*	scare *1*	

3 THE 'STRIKE' GROUP

These verbs indicate that an idea occurs to someone. The noun group always indicates a human being.

It <u>struck</u> her how self-centred she'd been, *considering only her sorrow, not his.*

There is one phrasal verb with this meaning, *dawn on*. Its pattern is *it* V P n wh.

It <u>dawned on</u> them what happened in Nagasaki in 1945 and what it must have been like.

hit *5*	strike *10*
dawn on	

534

In addition, the phrase *make a difference* has this pattern.

As far as learning is concerned, **it *doesn't make any difference* how old you are.**

5.4 *it* V n when/if

The verb is followed by a noun group and a clause beginning with *when* or *if*, which indicates a situation that occurs or may occur. The noun group is the Complement in group 1 and the Object in groups 2 and 3.

it	Verb group	noun group	when/if clause
Subject	**Verb**	**Complement**	**Clause**
It	is	his tough luck	if he doesn't understand the risks.
It	's	the team's problem	if they're not strong enough.

it	Verb group	noun group	when/if clause
Subject	**Verb**	**Object**	**Clause**
It	wouldn't surprise	me	if she left.
It	upsets	me	when you say things like that.

Verbs with this pattern belong to the following meaning groups:

1 THE 'BE' GROUP
2 THE 'AMUSE' AND 'IRRITATE' GROUP
3 VERBS WITH OTHER MEANINGS

1 THE 'BE' GROUP

These verbs are concerned with what a situation is or may be. Both of these verbs are **link verbs** (see Chapter 5).

'I would like to speak to them but **it *is not* the end of the world if I do not,**' he added.

> be 2.2   remain 1

2 THE 'AMUSE' AND 'IRRITATE' GROUP

These verbs are concerned with how a situation makes someone feel. The noun group always indicates a human being.

When I was still innocent, **it *amused* me when my father joked about men who trade in their 41-year-old wives for two 20-year-olds.**

It *irritates* me when I'm asked to do things that are not part of my job.

It always *pleases* me when guests compliment me on the look of my food.

Sometimes **it *scares* me when I think that people may recognise me and that one day my past could catch up with me.**

It *wouldn't worry* me if he came to my house, but I don't know if I would go out of my way to ask him.

amaze	bug *7*	pain *3*	surprise *3*
amuse *1*	concern *2*	please *5*	upset *2*
annoy	hurt *5*	puzzle *1*	worry *3*
beat *17*	irritate *1*	sadden	
bother *4*	kill *5*	scare *1*	

In addition, the phrase *break someone's heart* has this pattern.

> *It **breaks my heart** when all the little girls say they want to be nurses. I say, 'Have you thought of being a doctor?' but they look blank.*

3 VERBS WITH OTHER MEANINGS

There are two other verbs with this pattern.

> *It **would help** everyone if we got that issue sorted out.*

In the case of *mean*, the verb is always followed by an **amount**. This pattern is *it* **V amount when/if**.

> *It's best for her to be in America to earn money, she deserves that. But it **would mean** a lot if just once she would say she remembers us, that we were her friends.*

help *2*	mean *3*

5.5 *it* V n -ing

The verb is followed by a noun group and an '-ing' clause. The noun group is the Complement when the verb is *be*, and Object when the verb is *bother*, *worry*, or *take*.

it	Verb group	noun group	-ing clause
Subject	**Verb**	**Complement**	**Clause**
It	is	no fun	doing things alone.
It	is	no use	complaining.

it	Verb group	noun group	-ing clause
Subject	**Verb**	**Object**	**Clause**
It	must take	nerve	marrying into a family like that.
It	worries	me	seeing him so helpless.

Two of the verbs with this pattern are concerned with something bothering or worrying someone.

> ***Does** it **bother** them being typecast mainly as Italian heavies or cops?*

bother *4*	worry *2*

There are two other verbs with this pattern.

> *It **is** no use putting all the blame on young drivers for the high number of accidents.*
> *It **took** ages getting through customs as they searched my belongings for drugs.*

be *2.2*	take *2.13,14*

5.6 *it* V n/amount before/since

The verb is followed by a noun group or an **amount**, and a clause beginning with *before* or *since*. The noun group or amount is the Complement with the verbs *be* and *seem*, and the Object with the verb *take*.

There are only three verbs with this pattern. The verbs *be* and *seem* are **link verbs** (see Chapter 5).

> *It is only a matter of time before other Asian women bands emerge.*
>
> *We ought to get out of here fast; it won't be long before they send more troops after us.*
>
> *It seems an age since only the Post Office supplied our phones.*
>
> *It took several months before Janice's condition could be stabilized.*

> be *2.2*   seem *1*   take *2.13*

5.7 *it* V n *for* n to-inf

The verb is followed by a noun group and a clause which consists of the preposition *for*, a noun group, and a to-infinitive clause. The noun group following the verb is the Complement with *be* and *become*, and the Object with *take*.

There are only three verbs with this pattern. The verbs *be* and *become* are **link verbs** (see Chapter 5).

> *It has become common practice for winemakers to add acid to some sun-ripe wines to boost freshness.*
>
> *Sometimes it takes courage for us to approach the subject of the death with another survivor.*

In the case of *take 2.13*, the first noun group following the verb is often an **amount**. This pattern is *it* **V amount** *for* **n to-inf**.

> *It didn't take too long for everyone to catch on to the real meaning behind the doublespeak.*

> be *2.2*   become *1*   take *2.13,14*

In addition, the phrase *make sense* has this pattern.

> *'Maybe it does make sense for us to get together,' he said.*

5.8 *it* V n n to-inf

The verb is followed by two noun groups and a to-infinitive clause. Both noun groups are Objects.

it	Verb group	noun group	noun group/amount	to-infinitive clause
Subject	**Verb**	**Object**	**Object**	**Clause**
It	cost	me	a fortune	to renovate the house.
It	will do	me	good	to have a rest.

There are four verbs with this pattern.

> *She enjoyed the warmth of Rosie's company and it gave her genuine pleasure to perform little acts of kindness for her.*

In the case of *cost 8*, the second noun group is always an **amount**. This pattern is *it* **V n amount to-inf**. The verbs *cost 2* and *take 2.13* often have this pattern as well.

It <u>cost</u> him a lot to admit he needed help.

It <u>took</u> them a long time to reach the other shore.

cost *2,8*	give *1.7*
do *2.6*	take *2.13,14*

5.9 *it* V amount *for* n that

The verb is followed by an *amount*, a prepositional phrase beginning with *for*, and a that-clause. The amount is the Object, and the prepositional phrase is an Adjunct.

There is only one verb with this pattern.

It <u>says</u> a lot for her culinary skills that so many of her recipes have stood the test of time.

say *8*

5.10 *it* V n adj that

The verb is followed by a noun group, an adjective group, and a that-clause. The noun group is the Object and the adjective group is the Object Complement.

There are only two verbs with this pattern.

It <u>makes</u> me sick that young people commit offences time after time and never seem to get punished.

drive *13*	make *2.3*

5.11 *it* V n adj to-inf

The verb is followed by a noun group, an adjective group, and a to-infinitive clause. The noun group is the Object and the adjective group is the Object Complement.

There are only two verbs with this pattern.

I was sure he was thinking, you'll never pin this on me, Meg. And it <u>drove</u> me crazy to think that he might be right.

drive *13*	make *2.3*

Pattern group 6: *it* V adj clause

There are seven patterns in this group, each consisting of *it*, the verb, an adjective group, and a type of clause. Patterns 6.6 and 6.7 have a prepositional phrase as well.

- 6.1 *it* V adj that
  It <u>seems</u> likely that she will leave soon.
- 6.2 *it* V adj to-inf
  It <u>is</u> difficult to see in the dark.

- 6.3 *it* V adj wh
  It <u>became</u> apparent how ill she was.
- 6.4 *it* V adj when/if
  It <u>is</u> nice when people compliment you.
- 6.5 *it* V adj -ing
  It <u>is</u> interesting seeing what happens here.
- 6.6 *it* V adj *of* n to-inf
  It <u>'s</u> nice of you to come.
- 6.7 *it* V adj *for* n to-inf
  It <u>is</u> impossible for me to arrive any earlier.

6.1 *it* V adj that

The verb is followed by an adjective group and a that-clause. The adjective group is the Complement.

it	Verb group	adjective group	that-clause
Subject	**Verb**	**Complement**	**Clause**
It	is	important	that you say exactly what you mean.
It	seems	certain	that elections will go ahead.

These verbs are concerned with what a situation is, seems, or becomes. All the verbs in this group are **link verbs** (see Chapter 5). The word *that* is often omitted, as in *It is certain he will be there.*

I think it<u>'s</u> important that you get to know them beforehand.

It quickly <u>becomes</u> apparent that he is not mad at all.

It <u>looks</u> increasingly likely that the three national parties may form a government of national unity.

Though the course of events which led to the cataclysm is well known, it <u>remains</u> astonishing that a whole society was overthrown so easily.

appear *1*	become *1*	look *2.4*	remain *1*
be *2.2*	feel *2*	prove *1*	seem *1*

6.2 *it* V adj to-inf

The verb is followed by an adjective group and a to-infinitive clause. The adjective group is the Complement.

it	Verb group	adjective group	to-infinitive clause
Subject	**Verb**	**Complement**	**Clause**
It	feels	good	to have finished a piece of work.
It	would look	pretty silly	to turn the proposal down.

These verbs are concerned with what an action is, seems, or becomes. All the verbs in this group are **link verbs** (see Chapter 5).

It <u>appears</u> reasonable to assume that most hostel tenants would prefer single to shared rooms.

It *has proven* difficult to infiltrate small terrorist cells, *which often are held together by family relationships.*

appear *1*	become *1*	look *2.4*	remain *1*
be *2.2*	feel *2*	prove *1*	seem *1*

6.3 *it* V adj wh

The verb is followed by an adjective group and a wh-clause. The adjective group is the Complement.

it	Verb group	adjective group	wh-clause
Subject	**Verb**	**Complement**	**Clause**
It	is not	clear	who will get the money.
It	remains	uncertain	how many snipers were involved.

These verbs are concerned with what a situation or question is, seems, or becomes. All the verbs in this group are **link verbs** (see Chapter 5).

It *appeared* **unclear whether the council would do much for the rebels beyond expressing outrage.**

In the end the government did raise taxes as it *became* **clear how much money needed to be spent in the East.**

appear *1*	become *1*	seem *1*
be *2.2*	remain *1*	

6.4 *it* V adj when/if

The verb is followed by an adjective group and a clause beginning with *when* or *if*, which indicates a situation or event that occurs or may occur. The adjective group is the Complement.

it	Verb group	adjective group	when/if clause
Subject	**Verb**	**Complement**	**Clause**
It	feels	good	when our tastes are similar.
It	seems	so unfair	when these things happen.

These verbs are used when describing an event or experience. They are all **link verbs** (see Chapter 5).

When you're part of a team it *feels* weird *if you leave for a while.*

As my wife was supposed to be suffering from a migraine it *would have looked* odd *if I had failed to leave the palace early.*

be *2.2*	look *2.4*	seem *1*
feel *2*	prove *1*	

6.5 *it* V adj -ing

The verb is followed by an adjective group and an '-ing' clause. The adjective group is the Complement.

it	Verb	adjective group	-ing clause
Subject	**verb group**	**Complement**	**Clause**
It	gets	very boring	talking about racing all the time.
It	seemed	so dramatic	calling at this hour.

These verbs are used when describing something you do or might do. They are all **link verbs** (see Chapter 5).

> It *is* worthwhile spending time reading biographies and articles about important and powerful people.
> It *feels* wrong having a physical relationship with someone you can't talk to.

be *2.2*	get *1.1*	seem *1*
feel *2*	look *2.4*	

6.6 *it* V adj *of* n to-inf

The verb is followed by an adjective group and a clause which consists of the preposition *of*, a noun group, and a to-infinitive clause. The adjective group is the Complement.

There is only one verb with this pattern.

> It *is* kind of you to come to see me.

be *2.2*

6.7 *it* V adj *for* n to-inf

The verb is followed by an adjective group and a clause which consists of the preposition *for* and a to-infinitive clause. The adjective group is the Complement.

it	Verb group	adjective group	*for*	noun group	to-infinitive clause
Subject	**Verb**	**Complement**			**Clause**
It	was	easy	for	me	to get there on foot.
It	remains	possible	for	them	to finish the course.

These verbs are used when describing an action or situation. They are all **link verbs** (see Chapter 5).

> It *was becoming* quite difficult for me to commute the fifty miles from my home and office in Chicago several times a week.
> It *looks* bad for a civilized country to have these kinds of problems.
> It *seems* almost impossible for me to find myself in a relationship without wanting to get away at some point.

appear *1*	become *1*	look *2.4*	remain *1*
be *2.2*	feel *2*	prove *1*	seem *1*

Other phrases

The following fairly fixed phrases also have introductory *it* as Subject.

> <u>*Far be it from me*</u> *to criticise, but shouldn't Susan take a share of the blame?*

> <u>*It came home to him*</u> *that after his long period of deskwork, he had put on weight, and was out of combat condition.*

> <u>*It remains to be seen*</u> *whether the agreement will stick.*

Using *it* and the verb *be* to focus

When you want to focus on an element of the sentence, you can put *it* and a form of the verb *be* at the beginning, followed by the element you want to focus on, then a relative pronoun such as *who, which,* or *that,* then the rest of the sentence. Thus instead of saying *John got married last week,* you can focus on *John* and say *It was John who got married last week.* The meaning of this is often contrastive: *It was John, not Paul, who got married last week.*

> *Her height is striking enough but* **it is her face which amazes everyone.** *(Her face amazes everyone.)*

> *He was at Hove yesterday, and it was a fair bet that* **it was Alan Wells who he had gone to watch.** *(He had gone to watch Alan Wells.)*

2 Introductory *it* as Object

In all the patterns given in this section, **introductory** *it* is the Object of the clause. Although it is the Object, it does not contribute to the meaning of the clause, and is often known as a 'dummy' Object.

Many of these patterns are combinations of introductory *it* as Subject and other patterns. For example, if the clause *it is difficult to understand you* is preceded by the verb *find,* you get a clause like *I find it difficult to understand you.* However, some patterns with introductory *it* as Object cannot be explained in this way. For example, *I hate it when she's away* has no equivalent pattern with introductory *it* as Subject.

The patterns with introductory *it* as Object fall into five pattern groups:

▶ Pattern group 1: V *it* clause
▶ Pattern group 2: V *it to* n clause
▶ Pattern group 3: V *it as* n/adj clause
▶ Pattern group 4: V *it* n clause
▶ Pattern group 5: V *it* adj clause

Pattern group 1: V *it* clause

There are two patterns in this group, each consisting of the verb, *it,* and a type of clause:

- 1.1 V *it* that
  I <u>*loved*</u> *it that he cared enough to ask.*
- 1.2 V *it* when/if
  I <u>*hate*</u> *it when she's away.*

1.1 V *it* that

The verb is followed by *it* and a that-clause.

Verbs with this pattern belong to the following meaning groups:

1 THE 'LOVE' AND 'HATE' GROUP
2 THE 'ARRANGE' GROUP
3 VERBS WITH OTHER MEANINGS

1 THE 'LOVE' AND 'HATE' GROUP

These verbs indicate how a situation makes someone feel. These verbs have no equivalent passive pattern.

*I really **appreciate** it that you raised me in such a warm and happy family.*

*I **hate** it that you can paint contentedly while I'm feeling restless and bored.*

*One of his major attractions was that he took charge. She **loved** it that he made all the decisions.*

*I **can't stand** it that he wears a Sea World tee shirt!*

appreciate 3	like 3	(cannot) stand 16
(cannot) bear 6	love 5	
hate 2	resent	

2 THE 'ARRANGE' GROUP

These verbs are concerned with plans and arrangements. They are usually used in the passive. The passive pattern is **it be V-ed that**, where *it* is the Subject of the clause.

*It **was arranged** that I should go along to the inn to see him.*

*It **is planned** that these hostages will be released in phases over three months up to late March.*

arrange 2 *(usu passive)*	plan 2 *(usu passive)*

The verb *arrange* also has the pattern **V *it* so that**.

*The League **have arranged** it so that all games are played before the Cup final.*

3 VERBS WITH OTHER MEANINGS

There are three other verbs with this pattern.

*Rumour **has** it that Britain's universities are jam-packed full of bright ideas struggling to escape from those ivory towers.*

*You have a reputation for extreme discretion. **Can** I **take** it that what I am going to reveal will remain strictly between the two of us?*

One of the verbs is a phrasal verb. Its pattern is **V *it* P that**.

*Then she undermined him, destroyed his confidence in his own talent, **put** it **about** that he was unreliable, a troublemaker.*

In the case of *put about*, there is a passive pattern **it be V-ed P that**, where *it* is the Subject of the clause.

*When the introduction of charges for directory inquiries was suggested, **it was put about** by BT that this was the only way of dealing with 'misuse' of the facility.*

have 3.13	take 2.43
put about	

1.2 V *it* when/if

The verb is followed by *it* and a clause beginning with *when* or *if*.

Most of the verbs with this pattern indicate how a situation or possible situation makes someone feel or react.

> '*You **can't bear** it if I know things that you don't,*' she said.
>
> *I **couldn't believe** it when she said I should do something about my appearance and wear more make-up.*
>
> '*I really **hate** it when you cry like that,*' Oliver said.
>
> *How **would** you **like** it if your ninety-year-old self came walking through the door?*
>
> *Frankly, we'**d prefer** it if you could find an adequate excuse to leave the country for the time being.*
>
> *He was so easy and friendly I **didn't resent** it when he asked me straight out the purpose of my trip.*

In the case of *appreciate*, there is a passive pattern *it be* **V-ed when/if**, where *it* is the Subject of the clause.

> *It **would be appreciated** if those who can, would stay on here for another night or so.*

accept *4*	(cannot) endure *1*	love *5*	(cannot) take *2.11*
adore *2*	enjoy *1*	(not) mind *2.1*	understand *4*
appreciate *4*	handle *3*	prefer	welcome *3*
(cannot) bear *1.6*	hate *2*	regret *1*	
(cannot) believe *6*	like *3*	resent	
dislike *1*	loathe	(cannot) stand *16*	

There is one other verb with this pattern.

> *I **can't help** it if you think I'm odd.*

(cannot) help *10*

Pattern group 2: V *it to* n clause

There are two patterns in this group, each consisting of the verb, *it*, a prepositional phrase beginning with *to*, and a type of clause:

- 2.1 V *it to* n that
  *I **put** it to him that he may have been wrong.*
- 2.2 V *it to* n to-inf
  *I **owe** it to my parents to work hard.*

2.1 V *it to* n that

The verb is followed by *it*, a prepositional phrase beginning with *to*, and a that-clause. The prepositional phrase always indicates the person who someone addresses.

> *They'**d** already **broken** it to the troops that there was to be no brief period in reserve as promised.*
>
> *When I interviewed him again I **put** it to him that he'd lied to you and to me about not seeing his wife that afternoon. And he just caved in.*

In the case of *put*, there is a passive pattern ***it be* V-ed *to* n that**, where *it* is the Subject of the clause.

> *He was rattled when it <u>was put</u> to him that his power has diminished.*

The verb *drum* has the patterns **V *it into* n that** and ***it be* V-ed *into* n that**.

> *They <u>drummed</u> it <u>into</u> me that you were not to know.*

> **break** *18*   **drum** *VP*   **put** *14*

2.2 V *it to* n to-inf

The verb is followed by *it*, a prepositional phrase beginning with *to*, and a to-infinitive clause. The prepositional phrase usually indicates a human being, but in the case of *owe* it may be a country or institution.

> *You just shut your eyes, and <u>left</u> it to the other people to clear up the mess!*
>
> *I <u>owe</u> it to my country to fight for what's right.*

In the case of *leave*, there is a passive pattern ***it be* V-ed *to* n to-inf**, where *it* is the Subject of the clause.

> ***It <u>was left</u> to him to assess the needs of the various underground groups and disperse the cash according to these needs.***

In the case of *owe*, the noun group is often a reflexive pronoun. This pattern is **V *it to* pron-refl to-inf**.

> *You were born to be happy and healthy and you <u>owe</u> it to yourself to achieve this goal.*

> **leave** *7*   **owe** *6*

Pattern group 3: V *it as* n/adj clause

There are three patterns in this group, each consisting of the verb, *it*, a prepositional phrase which consists of *as* and a noun group or an adjective group, and a type of clause:

3.1 V *it as* n/adj that
He <u>regards</u> it as significant that the Government is suggesting cuts.
3.2 V *it as* n/adj to-inf
They <u>accept</u> it as their responsibility to educate the public.
3.3 V *it as* n/adj when/if
He <u>would take</u> it as an insult if I left.

3.1 V *it as* n/adj that

The verb is followed by *it*, a prepositional phrase which consists of *as* and a noun group or an adjective group, and a that-clause.

Most of the verbs with this pattern are concerned with how someone sees or interprets a situation.

> *Have we grown up <u>accepting</u> it as fact that there always have been and always will be starving children in Africa?*
>
> *I <u>regard</u> it as an affront to civil liberty that any person going about his lawful business should be stopped randomly by any authority.*
>
> *I <u>see</u> it as a serious flaw that a report can have that kind of ambiguity.*

The passive pattern is ***it be* V-ed *as* n/adj that**, where *it* is the Subject of the clause.

It is seen as ironic that after saying he was the only person who could hold the country together, he is now trying to create a federation.

accept *2*	**see** *6*	**view** *3*
regard *1*	**take** *2.22*	

There is one other verb with this pattern. The preposition *as* is followed by a noun group, not an adjective group.

The professor has given it as his opinion that the expedition took place about the era of Magnus Maximus (380-390).

give *3*

3.2 V *it as* n/adj to-inf

The verb is followed by *it*, a prepositional phrase which consists of *as* and a noun group or an adjective group, and a to-infinitive clause.

Verbs with this pattern are concerned with how someone sees or interprets an action or state.

The Romans regarded it as undignified to compete naked in front of spectators.

He saw it as his duty to further the aims of the Party.

They say the West views it as legitimate to intervene in areas where they feel their economic interests are threatened.

The passive pattern is *it be* V-ed *as* n/adj to-inf, where *it* is the Subject of the clause.

In the late 1980s, it was regarded as almost trendy to be a non-stop single-minded workaholic yuppie.

accept *2*	**see** *6*	**view** *3*
regard *1*	**take** *2.22*	

3.3 V *it as* n/adj when/if

The verb is followed by *it*, a prepositional phrase which consists of *as* and a noun group or adjective group, and a clause beginning with *when* or *if*.

Verbs with this pattern are concerned with how someone sees or interprets a situation or possible situation. These verbs have no equivalent passive pattern.

I take it as a compliment when people call me aggressive.

The public expect us to have three finalists in every championship and view it as abnormal when we don't.

regard *1*	**take** *2.22*
see *6*	**view** *3*

Pattern group 4: V *it* n clause

There are three patterns in this group, each consisting of the verb, *it*, a noun group, and a type of clause.

4.1 V *it* n that
I <u>thought</u> it a pity that she didn't get the job.
4.2 V *it* n to-inf
They <u>felt</u> it their duty to visit her in hospital.
4.3 V *it* n when/if
I <u>'d consider</u> it a compliment if you accepted.

4.1 V *it* n that

The verb is followed by *it*, a noun group, and a that-clause.

Most of the verbs with this pattern are concerned with how someone evaluates or judges a situation.

*The pilot **<u>called</u>** it a miracle that no one was killed.*
*He **<u>considered</u>** it a good thing that the parliaments would be involved.*
*Ann **<u>felt</u>** it an injustice that she had been automatically blamed.*
*Tom **<u>thought</u>** it a tragedy that she had settled for marrying Joe Scully.*

These verbs are occasionally used in the passive with this pattern. The passive pattern is *it be* V-ed n that, where *it* is the Subject of the clause.

*There were a number of new faces there and so **it <u>was thought</u>** a good idea that we all just say who we are beforehand.*

believe *1*	**consider** *1*	**find** *7,9*
call *2*	**feel** *10*	**think** *2*

There is one other verb with this pattern.

*If you are getting a mortgage, the lender **<u>will make</u>** it a condition of the loan that the property is insured, and will usually arrange cover.*

make *2.3*

4.2 V *it* n to-inf

The verb is followed by *it*, a noun group, and a to-infinitive clause.

Most of the verbs with this pattern are concerned with how someone evaluates or judges a situation.

*Drivers still **<u>consider</u>** it a challenge to negotiate the long, desolate stretches of road with few services.*
*I **<u>deemed</u>** it a great honor to be granted an interview with him.*
*I sometimes **<u>find</u>** it a strain to be responsible for the mortgage and household bills each month.*

The passive pattern is *it be* V-ed n to-inf, where *it* is the Subject of the clause.

*It **<u>is considered</u>** a snub to leave work before the most senior person.*

consider *1*	**feel** *10*	**think** *2*
count *7*	**find** *7,9*	
deem	**reckon** *1*	

There is one other verb with this pattern. This verb has no equivalent passive pattern.

*He **<u>has</u>** always **<u>made</u>** it his business to know about these things.*

> make *2.3*

4.3 V *it* n when/if

The verb is followed by *it*, a noun group, and a clause beginning with *when* or *if*.

Most of the verbs with this pattern are concerned with how someone evaluates or judges a situation or possible situation.

> *I <u>would consider</u> it a favour if you would ask me home again next weekend.*
> *She said she <u>would not find</u> it a problem if she never appeared on TV again.*

The passive pattern is *it be* V-ed n when/if, where *it* is the Subject of the clause.

> *America's divorce rate may be falling while Japan's is rising, but it <u>would be considered</u> a major social triumph if Americans stayed married as enthusiastically as Japanese still do.*

> consider *1*   find *7,9*   think *2*

Pattern group 5: V *it* adj clause

There are four patterns in this group, each consisting of the verb, *it*, an adjective group, and a type of clause.

5.1 V *it* adj that
He <u>made</u> it clear that he would not negotiate.
5.2 V *it* adj to-inf
I <u>find</u> it hard to understand your motives.
5.3 V *it* adj wh
He <u>left</u> it unclear whether he would resign or not.
5.4 V *it* adj when/if
I <u>think</u> it best if you tell him the truth.

5.1 V *it* adj that

The verb is followed by *it*, an adjective group, and a that-clause.

Most of the verbs with this pattern are concerned with how someone evaluates or judges a situation.

> *Although people <u>have believed</u> it possible that planets exist orbiting around suns similar to our own, it has been thought unlikely that neutron stars would have their own planets.*
> *I <u>consider</u> it essential that the photographer should do his own printing.*
> *I <u>find</u> it remarkable that my lad seems unaffected by the insecurity he's lived with for most of his life.*
> *Having been fortunate enough to see his immaculate garden, I <u>think</u> it highly unlikely that he shares my relaxed approach to weeds.*

The passive pattern is *it be* V-ed adj that, where *it* is the Subject of the clause.

> *It <u>is considered</u> unlikely that any of the Cabinet changes will represent any major changes in policy.*

> believe *1*   feel *10*   think *2*
> consider *1*   find *7,9*
> deem   imagine *2*

There is one other verb with this pattern, *make*. The adjective that most frequently occurs with this verb is *clear*.

From the very beginning he __had made__ it clear that he did not have marriage in mind.

The passive pattern is ***it be* V-ed adj that**, where *it* is the Subject of the clause.

It __was made__ clear that there was no place for superstition in the new society.

make *2.3*

5.2 V *it* adj to-inf

The verb is followed by *it*, an adjective group, and a to-infinitive clause.

Verbs with this pattern belong to the following meaning groups:

1 THE 'CALL' GROUP
2 THE 'MAKE' GROUP
3 VERBS WITH OTHER MEANINGS

1 THE 'CALL' GROUP

These verbs are concerned with how someone evaluates or judges an action or state. We include here *declare* and *rule*, which involve someone in authority making an official statement, usually that something is illegal.

The Senator __calls__ it wasteful to give free immunizations to those who can afford to pay.

They __deem__ it more important to privatise state property quickly than to settle in advance the details of a market economy.

He suspected that Samantha had attended such parties previously and __had not felt__ it necessary to tell him.

Most people __find__ it hard to understand how living with one's own children could be lonely.

She dodged into the nearest toilet and remained there until she __judged__ it safe to emerge.

Courts in Scotland __have ruled__ it illegal to clamp a car parked on private ground and then to demand a fine.

The passive pattern is ***it be* V-ed adj to-inf**, where *it* is the Subject of the clause.

An official source said 'It __has been felt__ necessary to remove the five secretaries in order to maintain administrative discipline.'

believe *1*	declare *2*	find *7,9*	think *2*
call *2*	deem	judge *4*	
consider *1*	feel *10*	rule *7*	

2 THE 'MAKE' GROUP

These verbs are concerned with causing a particular situation.

The reflection of the sun on the surface of the water __made__ it impossible to see the bottom.

He argues that federal subsidies __have rendered__ it hard to differentiate between good farmers and bad.

The passive pattern is ***it be* V-ed adj to-inf**, where *it* is the Subject of the clause.

It __should be made__ impossible to overrule a minority with anything less than 75% of the votes in the Council of Ministers.

> make *2.3*   render *1*

3 VERBS WITH OTHER MEANINGS

There is one other verb with this pattern.

*Neil Mitchell, of Friends of the Earth: 'We **haven't left** it too late to survive, but we**'ve left** it too late to have the world as we used to know it.'*

> leave *18*

5.3 V *it* adj wh

The verb is followed by *it*, an adjective group, and a wh-clause.

These verbs are concerned with leaving a situation unclear or doubtful, or making it clear or obvious.

*The failure of many republics to take part **leaves** it unclear whether any laws passed by this new Parliament will be valid throughout the country.*

*On the very first day, the United Nations **made** it absolutely clear what he should do.*

The passive pattern is **it be** V-ed adj wh, where *it* is the Subject of the clause.

*It **has not been made** clear whether the invitation was extended before or after the coup.*

> leave *18*   make *2.3*

5.4 V *it* adj when/if

The verb is followed by *it*, an adjective group, and a clause beginning with *when* or *if*.

Most of the verbs with this pattern are concerned with how someone evaluates or judges a situation or possible situation.

*I **find** it ridiculous when people keep analysing their marriage, forever questioning whether it will turn out to be a success.*

*I **think** it best if you leave at once.*

The passive pattern is **it be** V-ed adj when/if, where *it* is the Subject of the clause.

*It **is considered** even better if preventative health care for a child begins before the child is born.*

> consider *1*   find *7,9*   think *2*

Other phrases

The following fairly fixed phrases also have introductory *it* as Object.

*I **had it in mind** to write a book about how much one should strive for perfection.*

*Officials **let it be known** that they were hoping to get more than two thirds of the members together.*

*I **wouldn't put it past your father** to insist that this behaviour is kept secret from you.*

*The institutions simply **took it for granted** that the debtor countries should honour their debts in full.*

We grabbed sleep when we could and <u>took it in turns</u> to keep watch.

In the phrase *see to it that*, the prepositional phrase *to it* is the prepositional Object.

Lennie stopped the concert, shouted for a doctor, and <u>saw to it</u> that the player was given medical attention.

3 General *it* as Subject

Sometimes the pronoun *it* does not refer to something that has been explicitly mentioned, and does not point forwards to a clause giving new information. In these cases, either it does not refer to anything at all, or it refers very vaguely to the general situation. We call this **general *it***. In all the patterns described in this section, **general *it*** is the Subject.

1 *it* V

The verb can be used on its own, without anything following it.

it	Verb group	
Subject	**Verb**	**Adjunct (optional)**
It	's raining.	
It	snowed	all afternoon.

Verbs with this pattern are all concerned with the weather.

Outside it <u>was drizzling</u> steadily and the city looked grey.

There is one phrasal verb with this pattern. The pattern is *it* V P.

It <u>will brighten up</u> in the next few days.

The to-infinitive form of these verbs is sometimes part of a **complex verb group**, in phase with another verb such as *begin* or *come on*.

It <u>began to snow</u>.

It <u>was coming on to rain</u> when finally Mac's lorry arrived.

drizzle *2*	hail *3*	rain *3*	be spitting *6*
freeze *4*	pour *4*	snow *3*	thunder *2*
brighten up ▷*6*			

The verb *pour* is sometimes followed by the prepositional phrase *with rain*. This pattern is *it* V *with rain*. Two other verbs have this pattern but do not have the pattern *it* V.

If it <u>hadn't been bucketing down</u> with rain, I would have had a glorious view of Bantry Bay from my bedroom window.

It <u>was pouring</u> with rain and rivers of brick-coloured water ran down the streets.

pelt *3*	pour *4*
bucket down	

2 *it* V adj

The verb is followed by an adjective group.

it	Verb group	adjective group
Subject	**Verb**	**Complement**
It	was	very windy.

Most of the verbs with this pattern are used when indicating what the weather, the temperature, or the light is like.

It _**was**_ **chilly**, *and he was glad of his coat and scarf.*

It _**was**_ **hot and stuffy** *in the classroom even though two of the windows had been opened.*

We arrived just as it _**was getting**_ **dark**.

There is one phrasal verb with this pattern, *turn out*. The pattern is *it* **V P adj**. The adjective is usually *nice*.

If we forecast bad weather and it _**turns out**_ **nice**, *nobody accuses us of getting it wrong.*

One verb, *get 1.15*, is used with the adjective *late*.

Well, it _**'s getting**_ **late**. *I guess your wife will be wondering where you are.*

be *2.2*   get *1.1,15*

turn out *2*

3 *it* V adj prep/adv

The verb is followed by an adjective group and a prepositional phrase or adverb group. The prepositional phrase or adverb group is an Adjunct.

There is one verb with this pattern, *be*. It is used to indicate your opinion of being in a place.

It_**'s**_ **nice here**.

It _**was**_ **awful in hospital**.

be *2.2*

4 *it* V n

The verb is followed by a noun group. In the case of *be* and *come*, the noun group is the Complement; in the case of *be blowing*, it is the Object.

There are three verbs with this pattern.

It _**was**_ **four o'clock in the morning**.

We get called out in all weathers – usually when it_**'s blowing**_ **a gale**.

When it _**came**_ **time to think about a new career path**, *he was at a loss.*

be *2.2*   be blowing *1.1*   come *9*

5 *it* V *to* n

The verb is followed by a prepositional phrase which consists of *to* and a noun group. The prepositional phrase is the prepositional Object.

Two senses of the verb *get* have this pattern.

> **It _got_ to the point where we just couldn't bear to be in the same room as each other**.

> Then **it _got_ to 3.30, 4.30**. *Eventually at 6 o'clock my eldest son was getting fidgety*.

There is one phrasal verb with this pattern, *come down*. The pattern is **it V P to n/wh**.

> **It _comes down_ to business**. *I'd love to play but I have too many commitments*.

> At the end of the day **it _comes down_ to whether you are delivering your product to the customer at the right price at the right time**.

> **get** *1.13,15*
>
> **come down** *VPP*

The verb *get 1.15* also has the pattern **it V *towards* n**.

> **It _was getting_ towards evening** *when we got back*.

6 *it* V prep/adv that

The verb is followed by a prepositional phrase or an adverb group, and a that-clause.

There is only one verb with this pattern. It is used when indicating what is written somewhere.

> **It _says_ here they have live music**.

> **say** *3*

This verb also has the pattern **it V prep/adv with quote**. The verb is used with a quote clause, which can come before the Subject or after the prepositional phrase or adverb group.

> **'If we cannot compete, we can achieve nothing,'** **it _says_ in a recent report from the European Round Table of Industrialists**.

4 General *it* as Object

In all the patterns described in this section, **general *it*** is the Object. Many of these combinations of a verb and *it* are sometimes considered to be phrases. Most of them are informal English.

1 V *it*

The verb is followed by *it*.

	Verb group	*it*
Subject	**Verb**	**Object**
They	didn't make	it.
	Don't push	it.

Phrasal verbs: V *it* P

	Verb group	*it*	Particle
Subject	**Verb...**	**Object**	**...Verb**
She	's coining	it	in.
	Cut	it	out!

Verbs with this pattern belong to the following meaning groups:

1 THE 'CUT IT OUT' GROUP
2 THE 'LEG IT' GROUP
3 THE 'BLOW IT' AND 'MAKE IT' GROUP
4 THE 'ROUGH IT' GROUP
5 VERBS WITH OTHER MEANINGS

1 THE 'CUT IT OUT' GROUP

These verbs are concerned with stopping doing something. We include here *snuff it*, which means 'die' and *end it all*, which means 'kill yourself'.

'One of them was so bad,' said Chernikov, 'we thought he __had snuffed__ it.'

The verbs *cool, hold, cut out*, and *knock off* are always or usually used in the imperative.

'I'm warning you, Fatso,' his persecutor said. '__Cut it out__. Or else.'

'__Hold__ it, Mom. Better not call the cops,' Frank said quickly.

The verbs *end, chuck in*, and *chuck up* are always or usually used with *it all*, rather than *it*.

I wouldn't fall on the floor in surprise if he suddenly announced one day that he __was chucking it all up__.

I'd just had enough, and I just wanted to __end it all__.

cool *13*	hold *2.5*
end *19*	snuff *2*
chuck in	cut out *4*
chuck up	knock off *(see knock 10)*

2 THE 'LEG IT' GROUP

These verbs indicate that someone leaves a place.

It's already past your bedtime. __Hop it__.

One of them pulled a Thompson sub-machine gun from inside his coat and suddenly all hell broke loose. Well, I __legged__ it.

hop *7*	leg *7*

3 THE 'BLOW IT' AND 'MAKE IT' GROUP

These verbs are concerned with failure, success, and risk-taking.

> *The moment I faced him all your years of teaching went down the drain. I'm afraid I **blew** it.*
> *Andy knew there would be random testing. I cannot believe he **would have chanced** it.*
> *You**'ll make** it, don't worry.*
> *A drink or two is fine but **don't overdo** it.*

blow *10*	(cannot) hack *10*	make *5.3,4*	push *10*
bottle *8*	have had *(see had 4)*	(cannot) make *5.5*	
chance *5*	lose *3*	overdo *1,2*	

4 THE 'ROUGH IT' GROUP

These verbs indicate how comfortable or well-off someone is.

> *But if you are prepared to **rough** it then make the trek over to the Rocky Shore and try from there.*
> *He left Washington and he's now in Hawaii, **living** it **up** on his share of the money.*

be coining *3*	rough *11*	slum *2*
be coining in *▷3*	live up *1.12*	

5 VERBS WITH OTHER MEANINGS

There are a number of other verbs which have this pattern.

> *And if you are caught or if people complain, simply argue that 'everyone does it' and **brazen** it **out**.*
> *They come up for sentence early next week, and **won't** they **cop** it?*
> *They **were** just **trying** it **on**, applying a little pressure in the hope that they would squeeze something out of me.*
> ***Watch** it, Sam. You're going to spill that if you're not careful.*

The verb *say* is followed by *it all*, rather than *it*.

> *Their blank looks **say** it **all**.*

clinch *2*	mix *8*	settle *1*
cop *2*	say *13*	watch *10*
brazen out	keep up *(see keep 25)*	try on *2*
camp up *(see camp 8)*	stick out *3*	
hurry up	sweat out *(see sweat 6)*	

Productive uses

It is used after various swear words, in the imperative form, to form exclamations, for example *damn it* and *bugger it*.

2 pl-n V *it* P; V *it* P *with* n

All these verbs are **reciprocal verbs** (see Chapter 6). They have two patterns:

- **pl-n V *it* P**: The verb is used with a plural Subject and is followed by *it* and a particle.

- **V *it* P *with* n**: The verb is used with a Subject referring to one participant and followed by *it*, a particle, and a prepositional phrase beginning with *with* which indicates the other participant.

pl-n V *it* P

plural noun group	Verb group	*it*	Particle
Subject	Verb...	Object	...Verb
She and her mother	made	it	up.
Reformers and conservatives	slugged	it	out.

V *it* P *with* n

	Verb group	*it*	Particle	*with*	noun group
Subject	Verb...	Object	...Verb		Adjunct
I	'll make	it	up	with	him.
He	tries to slug	it	out	with	bigger, stronger men.

Verbs with this combination of patterns belong to the following meaning groups:

1 THE 'BATTLE IT OUT' GROUP
2 THE 'HIT IT OFF' GROUP

1 THE 'BATTLE IT OUT' GROUP

These verbs are concerned with fighting, competing, or arguing.

> *The two men who **will** now **battle** it **out** for the post of President used to be close allies.*
> *He flew in specially for the sale and **battled** it **out** with a telephone bidder.*

battle out *(see battle 11)*	**have out** *(see have 3.18)*	**slug out** *(see slug 5)*
fight out	**slog out** *(see slog 5)*	

2 THE 'HIT IT OFF' GROUP

These verbs are concerned with having, beginning, or ending a relationship.

> *In a second interview she did admit to being his girlfriend but claimed **they broke** it **off** after his engagement.*
> *I believed she was about to **break** it **off** with me.*

> *Despite an age gap of more than 30 years, **they hit** it **off** straight away.*
> *Introductions had already been made, and he saw that Colonel Johns **had hit** it **off** with Mr Clark.*

break off 3 *(also non-recip)*	**have off** *(see have 3.16)*	**make up** 6
have away *(see have 3.16)*	**hit off** *(see hit 8)*	

3 V *it* prep/adv

The verb is followed by *it* and a prepositional phrase or adverb group. The prepositional phrase or adverb group is an Adjunct.

Verbs with this pattern belong to the following meaning groups:

1 THE 'HOT-FOOT' GROUP
2 THE 'LOVE' AND 'HATE' GROUP

1 THE 'HOT-FOOT' GROUP

These verbs indicate that someone goes somewhere.

> *Seconds later a cacophony of sirens began and I **hot-footed** it home.*

hop *7*	hot-foot	leg *7*

2 THE 'LOVE' AND 'HATE' GROUP

These verbs indicate someone's opinion of being in a place.

> *My family **hated** it in Southampton.*
> *I **love** it here. Everybody is so polite.*

enjoy *1*	like *3*	prefer
hate *2*	love *5*	(cannot) stand *16*

4 V *it* adj/adv

The verb is followed by *it* and an adjective group or adverb group.

	Verb group	*it*	adjective/adverb group
Subject	**Verb**	**Object**	**Adjunct**
	Play	it	safe.
You	could strike	it	lucky.

Verbs with this pattern belong to the following meaning groups:

1 THE 'STRIKE IT RICH' GROUP
2 THE 'PLAY IT COOL' GROUP

1 THE 'STRIKE IT RICH' GROUP

These verbs indicate that someone is successful or lucky.

In the case of *strike*, the word after *it* is *lucky* or *rich*.

> *She says the graduates' perception is that commerce offers more opportunities to **strike** it rich.*

In the case of *make*, the word after *it* is always *big*.

> *He warned Dean his private life would disappear if he **made** it big as an actor.*

make *(see big 10)*	strike *27*

2 THE 'PLAY IT COOL' GROUP

These verbs are concerned with behaviour.

> ***Do** you **play** it cool after the first date?*

In the case of *make*, the word after *it* is always *snappy*. *Make* is usually used in the imperative. The adjective is an Object Complement.

> ***Make** it snappy! I've got a deadline.*

In the case of *take*, the word after *it* is always *easy*.

> *The seven astronauts aboard the space shuttle Columbia **are taking** it easy today, following six full days of medical research.*

There is one phrasal verb with this pattern, *lay on*. The pattern is **V *it* P adj/adv**. The word after the particle is always *thick* or *thickly*.

> **<u>Don't lay</u> it <u>on</u> too thick**, *but make sure they are flattered enough to take up an invitation to meet their 'admirer'.*

> **make** *(see snappy 4)*   **play** *10*   **take** *(see easy 13)*
>
> **lay on** *(see lay 1.11)*

5 V *it* n

The verb is followed by *it* and a noun group. The noun group is the Object Complement.

There are two verbs with this pattern. The verb *call* is used with *a day* or *quits* to indicate that someone stops doing something.

> *Maybe in ten years or so when I'm not winning any more I'<u>ll call</u> it a day and retire.*

The verb *make 6.2* is used when indicating or asking the time.

> *'What time <u>d'you make</u> it?' 'Thirteen past.'*

In the case of *make 6.1*, the noun group following *it* is always an **amount**. This pattern is **V *it* amount**.

> *She heard Sam ask, 'How many shots has she got left?' and Paul answer, 'I <u>make</u> it two.'*

> **call** *(see day 7, quit 4)*   **make** *6.1,2*

6 V *it* -ed

The verb is followed by *it* and the '-ed' form of another verb.

There is only one verb with this pattern, *have*. The '-ed' form is always *made*.

> *Sure I had to help her. I had a job, didn't I? Compared to her and everyone else in my family, I <u>had</u> it made.*

> **have** *(see made 3)*

7 V *it* inf

The verb is followed by *it* and the infinitive form of another verb.

There is only one verb with this pattern, *let*. It is followed by *it all* and the infinitive form *hang out*.

> *This was a chance for them to stretch – to explore different themes and <u>let</u> it all hang out.*

> **let** *(see hang 12)*

8 V *it* over n

The verb is followed by *it* and a prepositional phrase beginning with *over*. The prepositional phrase is the prepositional Object.

There is only one verb with this pattern.

> *In Egypt priests were a privileged class, **lording** it **over common folk**.*

> **lord** *11*

9 V *it to* n

The verb is followed by *it* and a prepositional phrase beginning with *to*. The prepositional phrase is the prepositional Object.

There is only one verb with this pattern.

> *I **have to hand** it **to you**, you do have a knack for making plans.*

> **(have to) hand** *2.2*

10 V *it* P P n

The verb is followed by *it*, two particles, and a noun group.

There are two verbs with this pattern.

> *There are plenty of people who **have** it **in for me**. I know that. I've never gone out of my way to propitiate people.*
> *I know how badly I've behaved. I'd like to **make** it **up to you**, Cathy.*

> **have in for** *(see have 3.14)*   **make up to**

11 V prep *it*

The verb is followed by a prepositional phrase ending in *it*. The preposition that comes after each verb is indicated in the list.

	Verb group	preposition	*it*
Subject	**Verb**	**prepositional Object**	
I	ran	for	it.
	Snap	out of	it!

Verbs with this pattern have a variety of meanings.

> *If anyone can do this range of distances, Morceli can. He **should go** for it while he's at the right age.*
> *Did he actually say, 'Just give me five years and we'**ll be rolling** in it'?*
> *We'**ll have to step** on it to get to Winchester by eight.*

The verb *wait* is used only in the imperative.

> *It is a 10-second advertisement for a new magazine about feelings and emotions, which is called, **wait** for it, 'Let's Share'.*

There is one phrasal verb with this pattern, *get away*. Its pattern is **V P from it all**.

> *It is a favorite retreat of power brokers, the social, and the celebrated who want to **get away** from it all.*

go *3.16 (for it)*	**run** *50 (for it)*	**wait** *9,10 (for it)*
keep *21 (at it)*	**snap** *VPP (out of it)*	
be rolling *3 (in it)*	**step** *13 (on it)*	
get away *(from it all)*		

12 V n *for it*

The verb is followed by a noun group and the prepositional phrase *for it*.

There is only one verb with this pattern.

> *The two men **made a run for it** as Sally Wright shouted: 'Stop, thief!'*

make *(see bolt 10, break 31, run 50)*

Chapter 10: Patterns with *there*

There are two verb patterns that begin with the word *there*. Like **introductory it**, *there* does not carry any meaning in these patterns. English prefers to have old information at the beginning of a clause and new information at the end of a clause. If a clause does not contain any old information, having *there* at the beginning allows all the new information to be placed at the end of a clause. For example, the clause *There were lizards on the floor* has two pieces of new information: *lizards* and *on the floor*. You could say *Some lizards were on the floor*, but then some of the new information would be at the beginning of the clause. In the clause beginning with *there*, none of the new information comes at the beginning of the clause.

There are two ways of forming a negative in patterns with *there*. The verb may be made negative, for example with *not*, or the noun group may be made negative, for example with *no*. You can say *There wasn't any evidence* or *There was no evidence*.

The two patterns beginning with *there* are:

▶ Pattern I: *there* V n
  There <u>was</u> no hope.
▶ Pattern II: *there* V n prep/adv
  There <u>are</u> dangers here.

The verb *be* is by far the most frequent of the verbs that have these patterns.

Pattern I: *there* V n

The verb follows *there* and is followed by a noun group.

The noun group is the Subject. It agrees in number with the verb group: if the noun group is singular, the verb group is singular, and if the noun group is plural, the verb group is plural. However, if the noun group is a co-ordinated noun group, the verb group remains singular, as in *There <u>is</u> a computer, a printer, and a photo-copying machine.*

there	Verb group	noun group	
There	**Verb**	**Subject**	**Adjunct (optional)**
There	appeared	a completely new problem.	
There	was	no moon	that night.
There	remain	deep differences.	
There	seems	little hope of success.	

The noun group is usually indefinite: it begins with a determiner such as *a* or *some*, or a quantifier such as *any* or *a few*. If the noun group is plural, there is often no determiner at all. When the noun group is definite, beginning with a determiner such as *the*, this may be for one of three reasons:

1 It is used to change to a topic that is new in the conversation or writing but already known to the hearer or reader. The sentence often begins with *And, Firstly,* or *Then*.

  *And then **there <u>is</u> the leadership crisis**.*

2 It is used when the noun group must be definite, for example because it includes a superlative adjective.

  *You have to send your horses where **there <u>are</u> the best opportunities** and that often means overseas.*

3 It is used with *always* to indicate that something good or bad may happen, or that the hearer or reader has the opportunity to do something.

Be positive. **There _is_ always the chance that it may get better.**

There _is_ always the risk of a more serious injury *if you use a spray.*

And, of course, **there _is_ always the 'off' button.** *You can always turn the television off.*

In this pattern the noun group often includes a clause such as a relative clause, a that-clause, or a to-infinitive clause, or an adjective group following the noun. When the head of the noun group is a pronoun such as *enough, little,* or *more,* there is usually a clause following the pronoun.

Granted **there _are_ a great many who are extremely lean and wiry,** *but others can certainly become overweight.*

Are there any exercises that will achieve this?

They get pleasure from the thought that **there _are_ whales swimming freely about.**

In every love affair or marriage **there _comes_ a time when romance abates and only compatibility, affection, generosity and goodwill hold it all together.**

And **there _are_ signs that the richer nations are waking up to the broader problem.**

There _was_ something strange about the flickering blue light.

There _are_ only 100 places available, *so book now.*

There _is_ never enough to go round *and tempers are frayed.*

The noun group may be the '-ing' form of a verb. In this case, it is always negative.

There'_s_ no denying that beautiful make-up looks better on beautiful skin.

Verbs with this pattern belong to the following meaning groups:

I.1   THE 'BE' GROUP
I.2   THE 'EMERGE' GROUP

I.1 THE 'BE' GROUP

These verbs are concerned with something existing or something happening. We include here *follow,* which indicates that something happens after something else.

Thousands are wounded. Yet **there _appears_ little early prospect of a mass evacuation.**

Was there any genuine prejudice?

Although **there _is_ no certain evidence to prove the origins of Gypsies,** *the earliest are usually thought to have moved westwards from India about nine centuries ago.*

There _exist_ some absolute limits to what human beings can know about their surroundings.

There _followed_ months of research.

There _remains_ one difficulty: how to describe the new wines from South Africa.

The verb *seem* is usually followed by a noun group beginning with *little* or *no,* or with the pronoun *nothing.*

There _seems_ little point in adopting a different system.

appear *1*	follow *7*	seem *1*
be *2.3*	occur *1*	
exist *1*	remain *3*	

The verb *be* is often used with a modal verb such as *may,* with a **phrasal modal verb** such as *be bound to* or *be supposed to* (see Chapter 11), or with a phrase with an adjective group such as *be certain/likely/sure/unlikely to.*

There _was bound to be_ an increase in job losses.

There was certain to _be_ speculation.

The to-infinitive form of the verb *be* is often used following a verb such as *appear, continue, happen, need, seem,* or *tend,* or following the passive of a verb such as *believe, estimate, expect, know, reckon, report, rumour, say, see, think,* or *understand.* The two verbs are **in phase** and form a **complex verb group.** The to-infinitive form of the verb *exist* is sometimes used with *appear* and *seem.*

> **There appeared _to be_ no progress following today's talks.**
>
> **There are reckoned _to be_ thirty-seven different groups.**
>
> **There were understood _to be_ no injuries.**
>
> **There seems _to exist_ a large and impressive body of evidence that points to reincarnation.**

I.2 THE 'EMERGE' GROUP

These verbs are concerned with something coming into existence or starting to be seen.

> Then **there _appear_ a number of teachers with circles of devotees and students.**
>
> **There _arises_ no question of loyalty to one's employers.**
>
> **There _emerges_ a picture of a woman who cares deeply for her man.**

appear *3,4*	come *9*	emerge *3,5*
arise *1,3*	develop *1,2*	grow *2,10*
grow up *3*		

Pattern II: *there* V n prep/adv

The verb follows *there* and is followed by a noun group. There is also a prepositional phrase or adverb group which usually comes after the noun group. Most of these verbs also have the pattern ***there* V n.**

The noun group is the Subject and the prepositional phrase or adverb group is an Adjunct.

there	Verb group	noun group	prep. phrase/adverb group
There	**Verb**	**Subject**	**Adjunct**
There	was	no one	there.
There	occurs	discord	in the marriage.
There	remained	a risk	in such a situation.

Sometimes the prepositional phrase or adverb group comes before *there,* as in *For every action there _is_ an equal and opposite reaction,* or after the verb, as in *There _was_ in the flat an ancient wood-burning stove.*

The noun group is usually indefinite: it begins with a determiner such as *a* or *some,* or a quantifier such as *any* or *a few.* If the noun group is plural, there is often no determiner at all, as in *There are schools in the rural areas.*

Verbs with this pattern belong to the following meaning groups:

II.1 THE 'BE' GROUP

II.2 THE 'EMERGE' GROUP

II.1 THE 'BE' GROUP

These verbs are concerned with something existing or something happening. This is a productive use: any verb which indicates where someone or something is, or how they move, can be used with this pattern, for example *Near our camp there _flowed_ a beautiful stream.* We include in the list here those verbs, such as *lie* and *stand,* which are most frequently used in this way.

I just think there <u>are</u> great sources of pain in everyone.

In Brighton there <u>exists</u> an ancient custom of playing a Boxing Day game of bowls using oranges.

There <u>seemed</u> a note of venom in what he said.

In the case of *lie, stand,* and other verbs used productively in this way, the prepositional phrase or adverb group usually comes immediately after the verb or at the beginning of the clause, rather than after the noun group.

There <u>lay</u> between them something unspoken.

At one end of the room there <u>stood</u> a grand piano.

be *2.3*	occur *1*	stand *4*
exist *1*	remain *3*	
lie *1,2,4*	seem *1*	

The verb *be* is often used with a modal verb, such as *may*, with a phrasal modal, such as *be bound to* or *be supposed to*, or with a phrase with an adjective group, such as *be certain/likely/sure/unlikely to.*

There <u>may be</u> a deeper truth here.

There<u>'s supposed to be</u> a state of emergency in the city.

The to-infinitive form of the verb *be* is often used following *appear* or *seem*, or following the passive of a verb such as *believe, estimate, expect, know, reckon, report, rumour, say, see, think,* or *understand*. The two verbs are **in phase** and form a **complex verb group**.

There appeared <u>to be</u> a woman in the car, accompanied by a man.

There were reported <u>to be</u> wounded on both sides.

II.2 THE 'EMERGE' GROUP

These verbs are concerned with something coming into existence or starting to be seen.

There <u>appeared</u> another little girl in her fantasy.

From amidst the disillusioned masses there <u>arose</u> a man who was to change the face of twentieth century history.

Out of all this there <u>emerged</u> many things that were positive, if also uncomfortable.

appear *3,4*	come *9*	emerge *3,5*
arise *1,3*	develop *1,2*	grow *2,10*
grow up *3*		

Chapter 11: Auxiliaries, Modals, and Phrasal Modals

In this chapter we describe the patterns of two kinds of verbs which form part of the verb group: auxiliaries and modals. We also include here phrasal modals, that is, phrases which behave like modal verbs. This chapter contains:

1 Auxiliary verbs: *be, do, get,* and *have*
2 Modal verbs e.g. *may, must, should, will*
3 Phrasal modals e.g. *be able to, had better, would rather*

---

1 Auxiliaries

There are four verbs which are sometimes auxiliary verbs: *be, do, get,* and *have*. They are used mainly to add meaning to a main verb, for example by forming a continuous tense, a passive, a negative, or an interrogative. They are also used to add meaning to a clause, for example by helping to form question tags.

Like other verbs, auxiliaries have tenses, some of which are formed with other auxiliaries. For example, in the clause *She has been singing for two hours*, the auxiliary *be* is used in the pattern **AUX -ing**, that is, *been singing*. However, the auxiliary *be* itself has a tense formed by the auxiliary *have* in the pattern **AUX -ed**, that is, *has been*.

	been	*singing*
	AUX	-ing
has	*been*	
AUX	-ed	

Another example is the clause *Our boat was being thrown around like a toy*, where the auxiliary *be* is used in the passive pattern **AUX -ed**, that is, *being thrown*. However, that auxiliary itself has a tense formed by the auxiliary *be* in the pattern **AUX -ing**, that is, *was being*. The verb group in this clause therefore contains two forms of the auxiliary verb *be*.

	being	*thrown*
	AUX	-ed
was	*being*	
AUX	-ing	

Looking at this from another point of view, when an auxiliary is followed by an '-ing' form, an '-ed' form, or a to-infinitive form, that form may itself be that of an auxiliary verb which is followed by another verb. For example, in the clause *She has been arrested*, the auxiliary *have* is used in the pattern **AUX -ed**, that is, *has been*. However, *be* is also an auxiliary, used here in the pattern **AUX -ed**, that is, *been arrested*.

	has	*been*
AUX	-ed	
	been	*arrested*
	AUX	-ed

In this chapter, we use the terms '-ing' form, '-ed' form, and to-infinitive form to indicate either a single main verb with that form, such as *liking*, *liked*, or *to like*, or an auxiliary with that form together with the main verb following it, such as *being liked*, *been liked*, or *to be liked*.

Auxiliary verbs are made negative by putting *not* after them, as in *She is not swimming*, *They did not know*, or *He has not written to you*. In spoken English and informal written English, *not* is usually contracted to *n't* and is added to the auxiliary: *He hasn't written to you.*

The interrogative of verb groups formed with auxiliary verbs is made by placing the Subject after the auxiliary verb, as in *Is she swimming?* or *Has he not written to you?* If the *n't* form of the negative is used, the Subject comes after that: *Hasn't he written to you?*

Auxiliary verbs have the following patterns:

▶ AUX -ing
He is swimming.

▶ AUX to-inf
She is to arrive at six.

▶ AUX neg inf
Don't go!

▶ AUX n inf
Did they remember?

▶ AUX inf
Do come in.

▶ AUX -ed
She got knocked down.

▶ AUX
She's probably earning more than I am.

▶ cl AUX n
She hasn't finished, has she?

▶ so/nor/neither AUX n
...so do I.

▶ AUX n -ed
Had I known...

AUX -ing

The auxiliary verb *be* is followed by the '-ing' form of another verb. The auxiliary and the other verb together form the verb group.

Subject	Auxiliary	-ing form	Completive
		Verb	
I	am	being punished.	
He	was	driving	too quickly.
She	is	writing	a novel.

This pattern is used to form continuous tenses.

> *Darkness was coming, a pink glow above the rooftops.*
> *He was being questioned at a police station in London.*
> *Everybody is complaining about the recession.*
> *An air and sea rescue operation has been going on all day for the crew of a fishing trawler which sank in the English Channel.*

AUX to-inf

The auxiliary verb *be* is followed by the to-infinitive form of another verb. The two verbs are **in phase** and form a **complex verb group**.

	Auxiliary verb	to-infinitive	
Subject	**Verb**		**Completive**
The talks	are	to begin	tomorrow.
She	is	to be congratulated.	
He	was	to become	President.

This pattern is used to talk about something that will happen, something that should happen, something that would happen under certain conditions, or something that has happened, seen from the viewpoint of a time before it happened, and when it was not expected.

*The Prime Minister **is to get** a full briefing on the release of the hostages next week.*

*She said if she didn't get back by six, I **was to call** the police.*

*What **is to be done**?*

*If you **were to rub** a piece of plastic with a cloth, you would produce static electricity.*

*He needs to pull his socks up if he **is to make** a success of his England career.*

*Other reformers such as Thomas Spence, who **was to become** a more significant radical influence at a later date, substituted phonetic for conventional spellings in their writings.*

AUX neg inf

The auxiliary verb *do* is followed by the negative *not* and the **bare infinitive** form of another verb. The auxiliary and the other verb together form the verb group.

	Auxiliary verb	negative	infinitive	
Subject	**Verb...**	**Negative**	**...Verb**	**Completive**
He	did	not	like	cakes.
	Do	not	open	the box.

This pattern with *do* is used to make negative forms of verbs in the simple present and the simple past tenses, and to make negative imperatives.

*Franklin **did not want** Wilson to resign.*

*He **does not have** a name until much later in the story.*

***Don't** ever **call** this number again.*

AUX n inf

The auxiliary verb *do* is followed by a noun group and the **bare infinitive** form of another verb. The auxiliary and the other verb together form the verb group. The noun group is the Subject.

Auxiliary verb	noun group	infinitive	
Verb...	**Subject**	**...Verb**	**Completive**
Do	you	like	chocolate?
Did	she	break	her leg?

This pattern with *do* is used to make questions with verbs in the simple present and the simple past tenses.

*What **do** you **mean**?*

__Does__ she love you?
Where __did they find__ the money?

AUX inf

The auxiliary verb *do* is followed by the **bare infinitive** of another verb. The auxiliary and the other verb together form the verb group.

Subject	Auxiliary verb	infinitive	Completive
	Verb		
I	do	understand.	
	Do	have	another biscuit.

This pattern is used to add emphasis to a verb in the simple present or the simple past tense, for example because it contrasts with something that has previously been said or implied. It is also used to invite someone politely to do something.

He doesn't say too much, but what he __does__ say either enhances the absurd humour or the spectacle.

Well, as a matter of fact, I __did want__ to talk to you about something.

__Do sit down.__

AUX -ed

The auxiliary verb is followed by the '-ed' form of another verb. The auxiliary and the other verb together form the verb group.

Subject	Auxiliary verb	-ed form	Completive
	Verb		
They	were	eaten	by rats.
We	got	married	in September.
He	has	finished	his work.

This pattern has four uses.

1 The auxiliaries *be* and *get* are used with this pattern to form the passive. *Be* is used much more frequently in this way than *get*.

Doctors believe more research __is needed__ into the spread of the disease.

No suspects __have been__ picked up yet by police.

'Did I get you into trouble?' she asked. He laughed. 'No. I __got teased__ a bit,' he added.

2 The auxiliary *have* is used with this pattern to form perfect tenses.

Mount Pinatubo __has blanketed__ the countryside with volcanic ash, up to half a meter deep.

Jupe picked one of the magazines up and leafed through it. Someone __had inserted__ a slip of paper halfway through to mark a place.

__Having established__ his business in San Francisco in the 1960s, he travelled to England with the simple objective of catching up with contemporary British design.

The verb *have* is also used with the '-ed' form of the auxiliary *be* to form perfect continuous tenses. This pattern is **AUX been -ing**.

So far Indonesia __has been__ accepting all boat people arriving on its shores – some twelve hundred each month.

568

3 The auxiliary *get* is used with this pattern, but without making a passive, to indicate that an action, usually something difficult, is successfully achieved. This is an informal use.

*He spoke in a hasty, nervous way, as if once he **had got** **started** he was afraid that he might be interrupted.*

*Until I **get** **warmed up** it's difficult to run and there's pain.*

4 The to-infinitive form of the auxiliary verb *be* is used with this pattern, usually with the verbs *found, heard,* or *seen* to indicate that people can find, hear, or see something somewhere.

*Most of his works are **to be** **found** in the area around Arezzo.*

*There's hardly a tree **to be** **seen**.*

AUX

The auxiliary verb is used with nothing following it, or with just *not* following it, when confirming or contradicting a statement, in short answers to questions, or following comparatives. This pattern is used with the auxiliaries *be, do* and *have*.

*'I'm keeping my piranhas,' Paul said. 'No you**'re not**,' said his mother. 'Yes I **am**,' said Paul.*

*'Is Debbie coming to see us tomorrow?' 'Yes, she **is**.'*

*'Governor Clinton never indicated during the campaign that he supported a gasoline tax.' 'No, he **didn't**.'*

*You'd imagine that I'd learn with age but I **don't**.*

*'You've never even seen it!' 'Yes I **have**,' snapped Betty.*

*My grandparents were very poor and they wanted their kids to do better than they **had**.*

cl AUX n

The auxiliary verb follows a clause and is followed by a noun group. The noun group is the Subject of the auxiliary verb. It is a personal pronoun.

clause	Auxiliary verb	noun group
Clause	**Verb**	**Subject**
She isn't laughing,	is	she?
You live in Birmingham,	don't	you?
They hadn't been arrested,	had	they?

This pattern is used with *be, do,* and *have* to form question tags, which ask the hearer or reader to confirm a statement. A negative statement is always followed by a positive question tag. A positive statement may be followed by a negative or a positive question tag. A negative question tag following a positive statement indicates that the information is considered to be shared. A positive question tag following a positive statement indicates that the information is not considered to be shared, but is something that the hearer alone has the right to confirm or deny.

In the case of *be* and *have*, the clause before the question tag contains a verb group formed with *be* or *have* as an auxiliary. In the case of *do*, the clause contains a verb group formed with *do* as an auxiliary, or a verb without an auxiliary.

*He isn't wearing shorts, **is** he?*

*Ah, you're making an assumption there, **are** you?*

*You liked Gil, **didn't** you?*

*They'd moved up here before you were born, **had** they?*

so/nor/neither AUX n

The auxiliary verb follows one of the conjunctions *so, nor*, or *neither* and is followed by a noun group. The noun group is the Subject of the auxiliary verb.

so/nor/neither	Auxiliary verb	noun group
Conjunction	Verb	Subject
So	am	I.
Nor	did	he.
Neither	had	they.

This pattern is used with *be, do*, and *have* to indicate a situation that is similar to one mentioned in a previous clause, but with a different person involved.

> *'I'm working at home on Wednesday.' '**So am** I.'*

> *He never spoke of my mother; **nor did** my aunt or my grandmother.*

> *'I've never been to Alcatraz.' '**Neither have** I.'*

This pattern, with *nor*, is also used to confirm a previous clause. This is a formal use. In spoken English, the stress is on the auxiliary rather than the Subject.

> *He confirmed there and then: 'I will never race again.' **Nor did** he.*

AUX n -ed

The auxiliary verb *had* is followed by a noun group and the '-ed' form of another verb. The noun group is the Subject. This pattern is always used with another clause, which comes before or after this one.

Auxiliary	noun group	-ed	
Verb...	Subject	...Verb	Completive
Had	I	known...	
Had	she	remembered	her lines...

This pattern is used to indicate a situation that might have happened but did not. Its meaning is similar to the meaning of a clause beginning with *if*, but this pattern is more formal.

> *The captain of the boat did not want to leave; he wanted to remain on his vessel and try and do something. **Had he remained**, he would have gone down with his boat.*

> *Kay didn't know of the affair he was having with a younger woman, but she probably would not have done anything about it **had she known**.*

2 Modals

There are eleven modal verbs in English. They are used to add meaning to a main verb, for example to indicate how certain or possible something is, or how frequently something happens, or whether a course of action is recommended or allowed.

can	may	need	will
could	might	shall	would
dare	must	should	

Unlike ordinary verbs and auxiliary verbs, modal verbs do not change their form depending on the Subject. For example, you say *I must* and *He must*.

Unlike ordinary verbs and auxiliary verbs, modal verbs do not change their form to indicate tense, although *could, should,* and *would* are sometimes considered to be the past equivalents of *can, shall,* and *will*. It is better, however, to think of these words as different verbs, not as different forms of the same verb, because they have very different meanings. The pattern **MODAL *have* -ed** is sometimes used to talk about something in the past, as in *She must have seen him.*

Modal verbs are made negative by putting *not* after them, as in *She might not be happy,* or *You should not go.* In spoken and informal written English, *not* is usually contracted to *n't* and is added to the modal: *You shouldn't go.* The negative form of *can* is *cannot.* In spoken and informal written English this is usually contracted to *can't.* Similarly, *shall not* is usually contracted to *shan't* and *will not* to *won't.*

The interrogative of verb groups formed with modal verbs is made by placing the Subject after the modal verb, as in *Might she be happy?* or *Should you not go?* If the *n't* form of the negative is used, the Subject comes after that: *Shouldn't you go?*

The modal verbs *dare* and *need* also occur as main verbs. In *He doesn't dare climb the tree,* *dare* is a main verb, but in *He dare not climb the tree,* *dare* is a modal verb.

There are two main patterns associated with modal verbs:

▶ MODAL inf
  She <u>must</u> be mad.

▶ MODAL *have* -ed
  She <u>must</u> have missed the bus.

MODAL inf

The modal verb is followed by the **bare infinitive** form of another verb. The two verbs together form the verb group. The bare infinitive may be *be* followed by an '-ed' form or an '-ing' form.

	Modal verb	infinitive	
Subject	**Verb**		**Completive**
I	can't	tell	you that.
She	could not	lie	to him.
We	may	be facing	a catastrophe.
Final decisions	shall	be taken	in the future.
The building	should	reopen	soon.

All the modal verbs are used with this pattern, with a variety of meanings. These include:

- expressing certainty or uncertainty about a situation e.g. *could, might, must*
- saying what sometimes happens e.g. *can, may*
- talking about an obligation e.g. *must, need, should*
- talking about ability e.g. *can, could*
- saying what someone dare do

- talking about future possibilities e.g. *may, shall, will*
- talking about permission e.g. *can, may, might*
- talking about something hypothetical e.g. *should, would*

*Insect stings **can** be nasty but they aren't usually dangerous.*

*The British Airways desk clerk said she **could not** accept me on to the plane unless I showed my passport.*

*We **dare not** let that happen again.*

*And many thanks to Debbie Licorish for her calm manner and eye for detail. Finally, **may** I **thank** Tony Green for all his support and good humour during the most trying of times.*

__Might__ I ask what you're doing here?

*He had decided she **must** have some idea of what was going on.*

*Only those who have been misbehaving or who have something to hide **need worry**.*

*If you don't want to talk to me, I **shan't try** to force you to.*

*Maybe you **should see** a doctor, get something to help you sleep.*

*So **will** interest rates **keep** rising?*

*If this became known, he **would** be lucky to escape with his life.*

MODAL *have* -ed

The modal verb is followed by *have* and the '-ed' form of another verb. The three verbs together form the verb group. The '-ed' form may be of the auxiliary verb *be*, with another verb following it. In this chapter we treat the auxiliary *be* and the following verb together as the '-ed' form. (See Section 1 above.)

	Modal verb	*have*	-ed	
Subject	**Verb**			**Completive**
He	must	have	forgotten	his lunch.
She	should	have	remembered	his name.
I	would	have	been told	earlier.

This pattern is used with all the modal verbs except *dare*, with a variety of meanings. These include:

- drawing a conclusion about the past e.g. *can(not), may*
- drawing a conclusion about the present e.g. *will, would*
- talking about something that was possible but did not happen e.g. *could, might*
- talking about something that will be true in the future e.g. *shall, should*
- talking about something that you think was unnecessary or that you disapprove of e.g. *need (not), would (not)*

*If Jane had shouted back, she **could** have **won** the day. Sadly, she didn't.*

*The picture came out of a magazine or newspaper. Some kids got hold of it and it **may have been passed** around the school.*

*If this had happened, he **might** have **drunk** less and been a better statesman.*

*At one time Berti's place **must** have **been** part of the cottage.*

*She **needn't** have **worried**.*

*I **would** never have **done** what they did.*

Other related patterns

In addition to the two patterns described above, modal verbs are used in two patterns that are the same as those used with auxiliary verbs.

MODAL

The modal verb is used with nothing following it, or with just *not* following it, when confirming or contradicting a statement, in short answers to questions, or following comparatives. All the modal verbs except *dare* and *need* are used in this pattern.

*His mother could no more relax than he **could**.*

*'You'll never see it,' he said. 'Yes, he **will**,' said a voice.*

cl MODAL n

The modal verb follows a clause and is followed by a noun group which is the Subject. This forms a question tag. (See **cl AUX n** in Section 1 above.) All the modal verbs are used in this pattern.

*You'll look after me, **won't** you, Mama?*

3 Phrasal modals

Phrasal modals are phrases which form a single verb group with another verb and which affect the meaning of that verb in the same way that a modal verb does. In the Collins Cobuild English Dictionary they have the label **PHR-MODAL**.

Some phrasal modals begin with *be* or *have*: *be able to, be bound to, be going to, be liable to, be meant to, be supposed to, be sure to, be unable to, have got to,* and *have to*. The first word in these phrases changes its form depending on the Subject and the tense, in the way that *be* and *have* normally do. You say *I **am** liable to panic* and *She **is** liable to panic, We **have** to leave tonight* and *They **had** to leave last night*. The other phrasal modals do not change in this way. You say *I would rather go by bus* and *He would rather go by bus*.

Most phrasal modals are made negative by putting *not* after the first word in the phrase, as in *He **is** not **able to** be with us* or *You **ought** not **to** eat so quickly*. However, *had best, had better, would rather, would just as soon,* and *would sooner* are made negative by putting *not* after the whole phrase, as in *You **had best** not go by yourself* or *I **would just as soon** not go by myself*. The negative of *would do well to* is made by putting *not* after *well*, as in *She **would do well** not **to** forget that*. The phrasal modal *used to* has three negative forms: *used not to, didn't used to,* and *didn't use to*.

The interrogative of verb groups formed with most phrasal modals is made by placing the Subject after the first word in the phrase, as in ***Have** you **got to** go?* or ***Would** you **sooner** stay?* The interrogative form of *have to* is *do you have to*, as in ***Do** you **have to** go?* The interrogative form of *used to* is *did you used to*, as in ***Did** you **used to** eat sweets?*

Phrasal modals have the following patterns:

► MODAL inf
*I **have to** go.*

► MODAL
*Go if you **have to**.*

► MODAL inf *than/as* inf
*I'**d rather** die than surrender.*

► MODAL that
*I'**d rather** you didn't.*

MODAL inf

The phrasal modal is followed by the **bare infinitive** of another verb. The phrasal modal and the infinitive together form the verb group.

	Phrasal modal	infinitive	
Subject	Verb		Completive
She	is able to	sit up	in a wheelchair.
They	were going to	shoot	something.
He	used to	shout	at people.

All the phrasal modals have this pattern.

> The deep-sea diving **is bound to** take me away a good deal, but I know when it's time to settle down, then I'll be looking to come back here.
>
> 'Maybe we **ought to** explore the mountain a little,' said Ginger to Steve.
>
> It **was supposed to** last for a year and actually lasted eight.
>
> We need good health and circulation of our blood and we **would do well not to** add salt to our food at all.

be able to	have got to	would rather	be unable to
had best	have to	would just as soon	used to
had better	be liable to	would sooner	would do well to
be bound to	be meant to	be supposed to	
be going to	ought to	be sure to	

MODAL

The phrasal modal is used with nothing following it, when the verb it refers to is clear from the immediately preceding context.

> 'It's not really improving anything.' 'No, but perhaps it**'s not meant to**.'
>
> I've never had a tremendous social life; I tend not to put that first. I **ought to**, but politics comes first.
>
> I felt I could no longer bully and whip people into line like a foreman **is supposed to**.
>
> I wish I could run about like I **used to**, and I love dancing. Well, I can't do that any more.

In the case of would rather and would sooner, the phrasal modal is usually followed by not, and the pattern is **MODAL not**.

> 'Don't tell me if you**'d rather not**,' he said.
>
> They'll be delighted if you'd like to come, but of course we'll understand it if you**'d sooner not**.

be able to	have got to	would rather	be unable to
had better	have to	would sooner	used to
be bound to	be meant to	be supposed to	
be going to	ought to	be sure to	

MODAL inf than/as inf

The phrasal modal is followed by the **bare infinitive** of another verb, than, and the **bare infinitive** of another verb. In the case of would just as soon, as is used instead of than. The phrasal modal and the two infinitives form co-ordinated verb groups.

	Phrasal modal	infinitive		than/as	infinitive	
Subject	Verb		Completive	Co-ordinator	Verb	Completive
I	would rather	die		than	surrender.	
He	'd just as soon	dance		as	eat.	
They	would sooner	buy	sweets	than	eat	a proper meal.

This pattern is used with phrasal modals which indicate what someone prefers.

> I **would rather** be honest with people **than mislead** them that there is going to be some pot of gold at the end of the rainbow.
>
> The average villain today **would just as soon** kill you **as look** at you.
>
> I **would sooner** give up sleep **than miss** my evening class.

---
would rather   would just as soon   would sooner

MODAL that

The phrasal modal is followed by a that-clause. The phrasal modal by itself is the verb group and the that-clause is a new clause, with its own structure.

	Phrasal modal	that-clause
Subject	Verb	Clause
I	would rather	that the theory was stated.
I	'd sooner	we said it.

This pattern is used to indicate what someone would like to happen.

> Most of what he's marked on the printout has behind it the opinion: I **would rather** that the broadcasters had not said this.

In the case of would just as soon and would sooner, the that-clause never begins with the word that.

> I**'d just as soon** you put that thing away.
>
> I**'d sooner** he grinned and bore it. He can have a two month rest in the summer.

In this pattern the that-clause is often co-ordinated with another clause using than or as.

> The police **would rather** you played safe than ended up being sorry.

---
would rather   would just as soon   would sooner

Chapter 12: Combinations of Patterns

Many verbs have more than one pattern. For example, *boast* has the patterns **V *about* n** and **V that**; you can boast about something you have done, or boast that you have done something. Verbs that have the same basic meaning may also share a combination of patterns. For example, *argue* and *complain*, like *boast*, have the patterns **V *about* n** and **V that**.

In this chapter, we give the most important combinations of patterns. The patterns in each pattern combination are ordered alphabetically, so, for example, we give the combination **V *in* n; V *on* n**, not the combination **V *on* n; V *in* n**. Under each pattern combination, we give examples showing both patterns, and a list of the verbs which have that combination of patterns. The examples indicate whether the two patterns perform a similar function, as in *argue about something* and *argue over something*, or whether they perform different functions, as in *campaign against something* and *campaign for something*. We sometimes give two examples of one pattern, to show its two possible meanings with a particular verb. The verbs with one combination of patterns may all have the same basic meaning, or they may have different meanings: for example, some of the verbs with the combination **V *at* n; V n *at* n** are concerned with shouting, and some with pointing.

The pattern combinations themselves are also presented in alphabetical order. For example, **V *in* n; V n *in* n** comes before **V *in* n; V *on* n**. If you know which combination of patterns you want to look at, you can find it in its alphabetical place. If, on the other hand, you are interested in, for example, any combination of patterns with **V that**, look up **V that** in its normal alphabetical place: you will find some combinations there, and cross-references to the other combinations.

Although most of the combinations we give involve two patterns, the combinations of three and four patterns are particularly interesting. In this chapter you will find the following combinations of three patterns:

V *about* n; V *at* n; V with quote
V *about* n; V *on* n; V *over* n
V *about* n; V *over* n; V that
V *about* n; V that; V with quote
V *about* n; V wh; V wh-to-inf
V *against* n; V *for* n; V *in favour of* n
V *at* n; V that; V with quote
V *for* n; V that; V to-inf
V n *about* n; V n wh; V n wh-to-inf
V n adj; V n *as* adj; V n *as* n
V n adj; V n *as* n; V n n
V n *as* adj; V n *as* n; V n n
V n *into* -ing; V n *into* n; V n to-inf
V n to-inf; V n with quote; V with quote
V n to-inf; V that; V with quote
V n with quote; V that; V with quote
V *on* n; V that; V with quote
V that; V to-inf; V with quote
V that; V *to* n; V with quote
V that; V wh; V with quote
V that; V *with* n; V with quote

There is one combination of four patterns:

V n adj; V n *as* adj; V n *as* n; V n n

The patterns **V** and **V n** are particularly frequent, and very many verbs that have other patterns also have the pattern **V** or **V n**. For example, *boast*, *argue*, and *complain* have the pattern **V** as well as **V *about* n** and **V that**. We do not show combinations with **V** or **V n**, except for the combination **V; V n** itself.

V; V n

The examples and list below contain only verbs which are among the 400 most frequently occurring verbs in the Bank of English. Many verbs that have the patterns **V** and **V n** are **ergative verbs**, for example *A window broke, They broke the window*. These verbs are not listed or exemplified here but are described in Chapter 7.

*To our great relief, she **accepted**.*
*He offered to help me, and I **accepted** the offer.*

*Unable to have children of their own, Penny and Rodney decided to **adopt**.*
*Persons who wish to **adopt** a child may contact their local social services department.*

*The question was directed at the Russian, but I **answered**.*
*You **didn't answer** my question.*
*He **didn't answer** me.*

*Bob kneeled by his side, hovering over his wounded friend, as the guards **approached**.*
*Cross **approached** the door and looked out.*

*I was taught to **cook** by the nuns at my convent school.*
***Cook** the carrots, onions, celery and diced bacon until golden.*

*Caine learned to **drive** only a few years ago.*
*They **drive** a grey Buick station wagon.*

*When he was almost level with the deck, his strength **failed** and he fell back into the sea.*
*My courage **failed** me.*

*But what if Jay **found out**?*
*We **found out** a funny thing about the kids.*

***Have** you **finished**?*
*There were further cheers when the old man **had finished** his speech.*

*He took his pistol and **fired.***
*Hood **fired** an air rifle from his bedroom and hit a 13-year-old boy in the head.*
*With a gentle squeeze of the trigger he **fired** a single bullet.*

*I wouldn't let my children **go without**.*
*My mother and I **had to go without** food sometimes.*

*He talked softly so that nobody **could hear**.*
*Dennis **heard** a metallic clatter.*

*So you think the government actually **could** step in and **help out**?*
*The more experienced players **are not helping out** the youngsters.*

*Cocaine **can kill**.*
*A series of explosions **have killed** three soldiers and wounded at least three others.*

*He never **married**.*
*He **married** a local woman.*

*Many of the families have vowed not to **move**.*
*She doesn't want to **move** house at all.*

*We **opened up** at nine.*
*They **opened up** the church and began ringing the church bells.*

*He **paid** and went out.*
*He **paid** his bill without complaint.*

*Tony grabbed the wire and **pulled**.*
*Reggie put a gun to his head and **pulled** the trigger.*

*You helped him once before, **do** you **remember**?*
*I **remember** the day he was born.*

*France's defence minister **resigned** today.*
*David **resigned** his directorship in December 1973.*

*She**'ll ring back** later.*
*I**'ll ring** you **back** in the morning.*

*Chief Buthelezi **was speaking** at a news conference in Hong Kong.*
*Severn pulled his face away and Keats **spoke** his last words.*

*The chauffeur **survived** and identified Garcia.*
*A baby girl **survived** a 20ft fall from a second-floor window yesterday.*

*He **has taught** at Princeton, Harvard and Yale.*
*She **taught** English Literature.*

*Almost as soon as he learnt to **write**, he handed his parents a note which read, 'I wish to become a painter.'*
*He's beginning to read and **can write** his own name.*

accept *1*	eat *1*	miss *2.1,2*	run *1,2*
accuse *1*	enter *1,6*	move *5*	save *2*
act *8*	explain *1,2*	negotiate *1*	score *1,12*
adopt *2*	fail *9*	notice *1*	see *1*
answer *1,4,6*	fight *4,9*	order *2.5*	sell *5*
approach *1*	finish *1,3*	paint *3,4*	serve *6,8,11*
ask *1*	fire *2.1*	pass *1,13*	settle *2*
attack *1,5*	fit *1.7*	pay *1*	share *7*
attend *1,2*	fly *4*	perform *3*	shoot *9*
be expecting *5*	follow *1,4,13,15*	play *2,13*	sing *1*
call *4*	hear *1*	please *5*	speak *1*
change *5,9*	help *1,2*	promise *1*	start *1*
charge *1*	hold *3.4*	propose *6*	steal *1*
check *1*	hurt *4,5*	publish *2*	stop *1*
choose *1*	indicate *6*	pull *1*	strike *6,18*
claim *9*	injure	push *1*	study *1*
cook *1*	investigate	read *3*	suffer *1*
count *2*	kill *1*	realize *1*	survive *1,2,3*
defend *3*	know *1*	recall *1*	teach *3*
deliver *1,2*	lay *1.5*	receive *5*	travel *1*
demand *2*	lead *1.1,4*	remember *1*	turn *1*
dominate *1,2*	learn *1*	repeat *5*	visit *1*
draw *1,24*	leave *1,2,3*	report *1*	wait *1*
drink *1*	lose *1*	resign *1*	watch *1.1,3*
drive *1*	marry *1*	ring *1.1*	win *1*
earn *1*	(not) mind *2.1*	rule *5*	write *1*
answer back	drop by	hit back *1*	sell up
back up *6*	fall behind *1*	hold back *5*	shoot up *2*
call back	find out *1*	last out *13*	sign off *2*
call up *1*	follow through	lead off *2*	sign on
carry on *1*	get off *4*	leave off *2*	spread out *1,2*
clear away	get through *6,7*	move down	start over
clear up *1*	give over	move up *2*	stop by
cut back	give up *1*	open up *5*	take over *3*
cut down *1*	go without	pass by	turn off *1*
do without *1*	hang up *2*	report back *1*	
drink up	help out	ring back	

V *about* n; V *at* n

*I **shouldn't grumble** about Mum. She's lovely really.*
*The men **grumbled** at the rebuke.*
*I keep **grumbling** at them.*

*Amnesty International **has protested** about the treatment received by the prisoners.*

He **protested** *at police brutality during peaceful anti-government demonstrations.*

carp 2	grumble 1	rage 3	snigger
fume 2	protest 1	rant 1	yap 2
go on 8			

V *about* n; V *at* n; V *with* quote

Reporters **have been grumbling** *about their limited access to President Clinton.*
He noted in his autobiography that his wife was a great success as a camper in that she never **grumbled** *at hardships.*
All night Ray **had grumbled** *at me.*
'I'm sure we should have been nearer the front,' Charlotte **grumbled.**

Mr Bright sounds like the type of schoolboy who **sniggered** *about sex at the back of the class.*
The old woman **sniggered** *at such a humorous sight.*
'It couldn't happen to a nicer bunch of chaps,' **sniggered** *the man.*

fume 2	rage 3	snigger
grumble 1	rant 1	

V *about* n; V n *about* n

In the case of *hear, know, learn,* and *find out,* the noun group following the verb in the pattern **V n *about* n** is always an **amount**.

I think he was a bit taken aback when I **asked** *about his family history.*
He **asked** *me about my illness.*

Perhaps other people **knew** *about our affair and didn't regard it seriously.*
Technical people often complain that translators **know** *nothing about the specialised subject they are supposed to be translating.*

ask 1	hear 7	learn 1
fight 6	know 4	
find out 1		

V *about* n; V *on* n

His colleagues in Parliament **have been deliberating** *about constitutional change.*
The government **was deliberating** *on an urgent question of policy.*

Doctors **differ** *about her condition.*
Mr Hurd said they **differed** *on a number of issues.*

It is virtually impossible to **generalize** *about the state of the country's health.*
I am always a little nervous to **generalize** *on youth attitudes.*

I **talked** *about things which interested me.*
We also **talked** *on Catholicism and curiously enough, all my objections sounded awfully lame to me.*

agree 1	disagree 1	pontificate 1	waver 1
brood 3	discourse 3	ruminate 1	write 3
cogitate	generalize 1	speculate 1	
deliberate 3	muse 1	talk 4	
differ 2	philosophize	waffle 2	
sound off			

V *about* n; V *on* n; V *over* n

The two sides __disagree__ about the number of victims.
All are committed to market reform but they __disagree__ on essential details.
We __disagreed__ over a few points, but the committee seemed reasonably satisfied.

Several times she __had speculated__ about the extent of his involvement.
He said it was too early to __speculate__ on a motive for the killing.
While dealers __speculate__ over the future of gold, most people seem to have forgotten to inquire after the health of gold's poorer relation, silver.

brood *3*	disagree *1*	speculate *1*
deliberate *3*	muse *1*	waffle *2*
differ *2*	ruminate *1*	waver *1*

V *about* n; V *over* n

The contenders __argued__ about human rights, democracy and foreign investment.
Mrs Ford and the children __have been arguing__ over the inheritance ever since.

I __had fantasized__ about food for nearly three agonizing weeks.
Brett is gorgeous, so let people __fantasise__ over the lovely boy.

Judy __frets__ about her aged parents.
Gilmour said he had spent the day __fretting__ over the accident.

agonize	disagree *1*	gloat	rhapsodize
argue *4,5*	dither	gush *3*	row *3.3*
bicker	enthuse *1*	haggle	ruminate *1*
brood *3*	equivocate	muse *1*	speculate *1*
crow *3*	fantasize *2*	obsess	squabble
deliberate *3*	fight *6*	puzzle *2*	waffle *2*
dicker	fret *1*	quarrel *3*	waver *1*
differ *2*	fume *2*	quibble *1*	

V *about* n; V *over* n; V *that*

My mother and I __disagree__ about music.
Washington and the EC still __disagree__ over agricultural subsidies.
No one __will disagree__ that dictionaries are useful.

He toured the world, conducting, teaching, and generally __enthusing__ about his art.
Her mother __enthused__ over her youthful acting.
His publicist __enthuses__ that the book contains some of the best one-liners in modern fiction.

crow *3*	enthuse *1*	muse *1*
disagree *1*	fret *1*	speculate *1*

V *about* n; V *that*

A lot of people __complain__ about the lack of new writers in television.
The critics __complain__ that public transport has not been able to cope adequately with the travel boom.

The bomb killed five people, including a seven-month-old baby. The majority of the country's newspapers __speculated__ about a possible terrorist link.
Officials __speculated__ that the dolphins might have been poisoned.

agree *1*	dream *2,4*	hear *7*	speculate *1*
bleat *3*	enthuse *1*	joke *2*	testify *1*
boast *1*	fantasize *1*	know *1,8*	theorize
brag	forget *2,4*	moan *2*	wail *2*
burble *2*	fret *1*	muse *1*	whine *2*
complain *1*	groan *3*	mutter	worry *1*
crow *3*	grouse *2*	preach *2*	
disagree *1*	grumble *1*	read *1*	
find out *1*			

V *about* n; V that; V with quote

*He was cheeky and he loved to **boast** about his crimes.*
*Mr Turner **boasts** that CNN will soon have total global coverage.*
*'We're the toughest crew in the world,' he **boasted.***

*The chairman **grumbled** about recent falls in the company's share price.*
*He **is** still **grumbling** that he wished he had stayed at home.*
*'The whole thing is becoming a circus,' Barbara **grumbled**.*

*The desperate mother **wails** about the lack of safety for her daughter.*
*Primrose began to **wail** that she was hungry.*
*'Have I done wrong?' she **wailed.***

agree *1*	complain *1*	joke *2*	read *1*
boast *1*	enthuse *1*	moan *2*	speculate *1*
brag	grouse *2*	muse *1*	wail *2*
burble *2*	grumble *1*	mutter	whine *2*

V *about* n; V wh; V wh-to-inf

*We already **know** about the importance of a clean body, clean hair and clean nails.*
*We **knew** what we wanted.*
*Some people just **don't know** how to plan a budget.*

argue *4*	know *1*	think *4*
ask *1*	learn *1*	
find out *1*		

V *about* n; V with quote

*I **inquired** about the provision of home care services in the Canadian program.*
*'Has she lived here a long time?' Nancy **inquired**.*

*It embarrassed her when friends insisted she was beautiful. They **raved** about her high cheekbones and perfect nose.*
*Sheila Rix, 29, **raved**: 'It was really great. It's one of the maddest things I have ever seen.'*

*Kay sometimes found herself **wondering** about his motives.*
*'Why's she weeping?' he **wondered**.*

agree *1*	fume *2*	mutter	speculate *1*
ask *1*	grouse *2*	philosophize	twitter *2*
boast *1*	grumble *1*	rage *3*	wail *2*
brag	gush *3*	rant *1*	whine *2*
burble *2*	inquire *1*	rave *2*	whinge
call *3*	joke *2*	rhapsodize	wonder *1*
complain *1*	moan *2*	sing *1*	
enthuse *1*	muse *1*	snigger	

V *against* n; V *for* n

*Beregovoy promised to **campaign** against corruption.*
*They actively **campaigned** for the vote and for equal opportunities in all areas of life.*

*You **can insure** against injury, illness or redundancy.*
*St Margaret's Trust seemed to offer the best deal so I **insured** for the full market value.*

*A wife **can't testify** against her husband, they tell me.*
*Ken's former wife and children **had** already **testified** for the prosecution.*

argue *2*	demonstrate *3*	lobby *1*	stand *19*
campaign *2*	fight *4*	retaliate	strike *2*
compete *1*	insure *1*	run *8*	testify *1*
crusade *2*	legislate	spy *3*	vote *5*

V *against* n; V *for* n; V *in favour of* n

*As a lawyer Mr Mohammed often **argued** against apartheid legislation.*
*Women also **argued** for changes in domestic life and work.*
*In his speech the Governor **argued** in favour of financial liberalisation.*

argue *2*	demonstrate *3*
campaign *2*	vote *5*

V *against* n; V *in favour of* n

*Thousands of people **demonstrated** against the resurgence of racism.*
*25,000 women paraded in New York to **demonstrate** in favour of women's suffrage.*

*The Church of England **has ruled** against the ordination of practising homosexuals.*
*On May 24th a New York judge **ruled** in favour of Mr Jett's request that his case be heard before an arbitration panel.*

argue *2*	demonstrate *3*	vote *5*
campaign *2*	discriminate *2*	
decide *1*	rule *7*	
come out *5*	speak out	

V *against* n; V n *against* n

*It remains to be seen if the vaccine **will protect** against different strains of AIDS virus.*
*It's always important to **protect** your skin against the sun.*

*The rising water arrived at the moment my right toe **struck** against a submerged rock.*
*Dean fell and **struck** his head against the bannister.*

*Miles **warned** against hasty alterations to the rules.*
*He **had warned** his team against complacency.*

caution *2*	insure *1,2*	slam *4*	strike *5*
clink	protect *1,2*	spray *7*	warn *2*

V *against* n; V *that*

*She thought about inviting Roger to stay for lunch but **decided** against it.*
*Eventually, David **decided** it would be best if he lived on his own.*

*After bribed witnesses **testified** against her, she was executed.*
*Several witnesses **testified** that they saw the officers hit Green.*

advise 1	decide 1	rule 7
caution 2	preach 2	testify 1

V *against* n; V to-inf

She **battled** *against cancer* for 19 months.
Firemen **battled** *to bring* 100ft flames under control.

He wanted to call Langley, but **decided** *against it*.
I rather quickly **decided** *to seek a second interview with Pollard*.

There were rumours that at least one faction in the party **was plotting** *against him*.
Prosecutors in the trial allege the defendants **plotted** *to overthrow the government*.

battle 4,5	conspire 1,2	plot 2	vote 5
campaign 2	decide 1	scheme 3	
compete 1	legislate	struggle 1	
gang up			

V *against* n; V with quote

He saw several doctors about his problem, many of whom **advised** *against surgery*.
'Don't let the devil distract you from your work,' she **advised.**

Although he maintained an essentially Western life-style and possessed a vast knowledge of Western culture, he **raged** *against Japan's imitation of the West*.
'Do you want to ruin me?' she **raged.**

advise 1	rage 3	warn 2
caution 2	rant 1	

V *as* n; V *for* n

After two and a half years of hard study he spoke Tibetan well enough to **pass** *as a native*.
She **could pass** *for a man* in bad light.

She **volunteered** *as a nurse* in a soldiers' rest home.
He **volunteered** *for service* with the army.

pass 20	serve 3	volunteer 3
run 8	stand 19	work 1
sign up		

V *as* n; V n *as* n

What **began** *as an attempt at artistic creation* has turned into a marketable commodity.
'Cuore' **began** life *as a supplement to 'l'Unita'*, the former Communist Party daily.

He hardly **rates** *as a strong leader*, but appears to offer what the public wants.
He **rates** Richard *as one of the best central defenders in the world* after his performances in the European Championship finals.

An old wooden manger unearthed in the barn **serves** *as a coffee table*.
The old drawing room **serves** her *as both sitting room and study*.

begin 3,5	end 4	qualify 3	serve 3
continue 6	finish 4,5	rank 4	start 4
count 7	parade 10	rate 6	train 2.1
start off 4	start out 1		

V *at* n; V n *at* n

McGregor lifted the revolver from his side and **aimed** **at Hughes**.
He **aimed** **the gun at two pupils** and pulled the trigger.
As he read, Molotov interrupted and **shouted** **at him** furiously.
They stood there and **shouted** **abuse at me** as I walked down the street.

aim 5	holler	shout 1	swing 5
bark 2	jab 1	shriek 2	yell 1
bellow 1	scream 2	stab 2	

V *at* n; V *over* n

He **chuckled** **at my expression of dismay**.
Donald Sinclair **was** still **chuckling** **over the letters** when the telephone rang.
Kelly **fumed** **at his own stupidity**.
Hill **is fuming** **over the absence of compensation from the authorities in Britain**.

chuckle	drool 1	grieve 1	seethe 1
coo 2	fume 2	salivate 2	smart 6

V *at* n; V *that*

People all over the world **are rejoicing** **at the fall of dictatorships**.
I am an environmentalist but I actually **rejoice** **that people have more cars**.
I **shouted** **at my husband** if he was not home on time.
The demonstrators **shouted** **that they wanted security and food**.

bellow 1	guess 1	rejoice 1	sneer
exclaim	hint 2	scream 2	wonder 2
grumble 1	marvel 1	shout 1	yell 1

V *at* n; V *that*; V *with quote*

Nancy and Ned **marvelled** **at the clarity of the colours on the screen**.
He **marvelled** **that his father's voice was much like his own**.
'Wow,' I **marvel**, 'men who talk about their feelings – just what women want.'
I felt I **was screaming** **at Jeremy and Emily** all the time.
Marian **screamed** **that he was selfish**.
Miller, 19, burst into the store and **screamed**: 'Give me the money'.

bellow 1	guess 1	rejoice 1	sneer
exclaim	hint 2	scream 2	wonder 2
grumble 1	marvel 1	shout 1	yell 1

V *at* n; V *to* n

Annual nursing home fees **average out** **at more than £17,000**.
Unemployment in 1992 **averaged out** **to 7.4 percent of the work force**.
He **nodded** **at the two men** and went out through the double doors.
Cross **nodded** **to Dr. Stockton**.
Every sinew in Fanny's body **thrilled** **at a brisk knock on her door**.
Maus **had thrilled** **to the atmosphere of the 1886 Impressionist Exhibition**.

nod 3	thrill 2	whistle 2
point 14	wave 1	
average out		

V *at* n; V *with* n

The dollar __finished__ at 127.23 yen.
Moorer __finished__ with 25 points.

Elizabeth __laughed__ at Gretchen's description of Jerry.
Endo __laughed__ with real pleasure.

beam 1	cackle	finish 4	seethe 1
bristle 5	end 7	laugh 1	shudder 1

V *at* n; V *with* quote

Burke turned and __beamed__ at her admiringly.
'How kind,' __beamed__ Frannie.

We __can__ only __guess__ at Elsie's state of mind.
'How many Saturdays will there be in December?' 'Four,' he __guessed__.

They __marvelled__ at her efficiency.
'I don't know how she does it,' __marvelled__ great-niece Eveline Wharton.

The priest __scoffed__ at us and called us Quakers.
They __scoffed__ at my suggestion.
'Aw, come on,' Pete __scoffed__. 'Nobody believes in gnomes any more.'

bark 2	exult	marvel 1	snarl 2
bawl 1	fume 2	rage 3	sneer
beam 1	grumble 1	rant 1	snigger
bellow 1	guess 1	scoff 1	wince
cackle	guffaw 2	scream 2	yell 1
chuckle	holler	screech 2	
coo 2	jeer 1	shout 1	
exclaim	laugh 1	snap 4	

For other combinations with the pattern V *at* n, see V *about* n.

V *between* pl-n; V *from* n or V *from* n *to* n

All these verbs have the pattern **V *between* pl-n**. The verbs *range*, *vary*, and *waver* also have the pattern **V *from* n *to* n**. The verb *choose* also has the pattern **V *from* n**. The verb *commute* has all three patterns.

Alison Fairlie had made her career at a time when women often __had to choose__ between family and profession.
Students __can choose__ from a wide range of subjects.

The temperatures __range__ between 102.5 and 106 degrees Fahrenheit.
Prices __range__ from £15 to £150 with many options in between.

choose 1	range 4	waver 1
commute 1	vary 1	

V *by* -ing; V n *by* -ing

Penelope Fitzgerald __began__ by reading an extract from the book.
The president __began__ the summit by welcoming his guests.

begin 3	end 6	open 21
close 1.7	finish 4	start 3
start off 1	start out 2	

V for n; V n for n

He **begged** *for water and there was not a drop to be had.*
He broke into tears and **begged** *his captors for his life.*

She **paid** *for the taxi when I arrived.*
He **paid** *£120,000 for the property.*
The company **isn't paying** *me for this.*

Last year she **played** *for the prince at Salisbury Cathedral.*
They were kind enough to **play** *some guitar for me.*

Now that he is 65 and he **qualifies** *for the old-age pension, he feels he has his dignity back.*
Students tend to demand training that **qualifies** *them for the rewards society offers.*

Nothing **can substitute** *for the health advice your doctor can provide.*
To make this salad egg-free, **substitute** *more yoghurt for the mayonnaise.*

ask 4	explore 3	prepare 2	train 2.3
audition 2	insure 1	qualify 2	wait 1
beg 1	pay 1,10	scout 3	
collect 6	play 11	substitute 1	
cough up	fork out	shell out	

V for n; V that

Everybody **hoped** *for a peaceful solution to the crisis.*
His mother **hoped** *that he would become a priest.*

I **testified** *for the husband in a custody case.*
She **testified** *that she had witnessed Larry Plover taking cocaine.*

beg 1	plead 1	testify 1
check 1	pray 1,2	
hope 1	shout 1	

V for n; V that; V to-inf

The government **is hoping** *for a vote of confidence in the elections.*
I **hope** *that this new edition, too, will be a best-seller.*
The banks said they **hope** *to offer better services to customers.*

beg 1	plead 1
hope 1	pray 1

V for n; V to-inf

We **hope** *for an end to the violence.*
I **hope** *to see you in two weeks.*

The President **had opted** *for a peaceful solution.*
She **has opted** *to do a degree in Japanese.*

The woman **paid** *for her purchases and left.*
I **am paying** *to see that game, and I'm looking forward to it.*

During the war the first floor was occupied by the Ministry of Food and it was there that we all **had to queue up** *for our ration books.*

About two thousand Soviet citizens __queued up__ to tour the ship.

ache 3	be dying 8	opt	scrabble 2
aim 1	fight 2	pay 1	scramble 3
apply 1	hanker	petition 3	serve 3
beg 1	hope 1,2	plan 2	strive
bid 1.3	hunger 4	plead 1	vie
campaign 2	itch 2	pray 1	volunteer 3
care 5	jockey 2	prepare 2	vote 5
clamour 1	legislate	qualify 2	wait 1,3
compete 1,2	live 1.3	queue 3	wish 2
crave	negotiate 1	register 2	yearn
queue up	stand by 1		
shell out	wait around		

V *for* n; V *with* quote

He quickly __apologized__ for his mistake.
'Sorry I'm late,' he __apologized__. 'Mr. Traynor kept me a while.'

There was blood everywhere and people __were__ screaming and __shouting__ for help.
'Rory!' he __shouted__, but there was no answer.

apologize	plead 1	scream 2
beg 1	pray 1	shout 1
holler	roar 4	

For other combinations with the pattern V *for* n, see V *against* n, V *as* n.

V *from* n or V *from* n *into* n; V *into* n

All these verbs have the pattern **V *into* n**. The verbs *change*, *metamorphose*, and *turn* also have the pattern **V *from* n *into* n**. The other verbs have all three patterns.

He is likely to find that the atmosphere __has changed__ from loving concern into something more highly charged and dangerous.
Why, after all those years of marriage, __did__ I __change__ into someone else?

Birds __are supposed to have evolved__ from reptiles.
Thousands of species appeared on the scene, some of which eventually __evolved__ into the flora and fauna we see around us today.

change 3	evolve 1,2	metamorphose	turn 15
develop 1	fade 3,4	retreat 3	vanish 1

V *from* n; V n *from* n

To fund new investments they have little alternative but to __borrow__ from banks.
He wanted to get the property for himself, so he __borrowed__ money from friends.

The blood __drained__ from his face.
A deadly gray pallor __had drained__ all life from his face.

Not all companies __gain__ from devaluation.
He slowly __gained__ confidence from his political success.

Fry until the oil __separates__ from the spice mixture.
Cereals are harvested and threshed to __separate__ the seeds from the rest of the plant.

borrow 2	detach 1	gain 2	transfer 1,2,4,5,8
choose 1	divert 1	learn 4	withdraw 2
crib 2	drain 6	peel 3	
derive 2	extrapolate	separate 3,4	

V *from* n or V *from* n *to* n; V *to* n

All these verbs have the pattern **V *to* n**. The verbs *change, graduate, move, pass, switch*, and *turn* also have the pattern **V *from* n *to* n**. The other verbs have all three patterns.

> I **commute** *from Crawley* every day, which takes me two hours.
> Mike is a graphic designer and **commutes** *to London* every day.

> Judge Jefferies was captured in 1688 trying to **escape** *to Hamburg*.
> Crito had tried to convince Socrates to **escape** *from Athens* rather than kill himself with the poison.

> Licences to grow peanuts are jealously guarded privileges that **pass** *from father to son*.
> After Alice Boyd's death in 1897, the castle **passed** *to three spinster sisters*.

ascend 7	escape 1	pass 6	turn 14,15
change 3	extend 3	return 1	withdraw 2
commute 1	graduate 5	rise 1	
defect 2	immigrate	switch 2	
divert 1	move 7,8	transfer 1,2,4,5,8	
change over	rise up 1	run away 1	

For other combinations with V *from* n, see V *between* pl-n.

V *in favour of* n: see V *against* n.

V -ing; V n -ing

> Perhaps he had locked the door to **avoid** *being disturbed* during his meal.
> The couple are trying for a second time to agree on a divorce settlement to **avoid** *their case going to public court*.

> I **like** *doing competitions* but I never win anything.
> My mum **doesn't like** *me cycling* 'cos of all the heavy traffic.

> He won't offend you if it **means** *offending me*.
> He said he would not reverse his decision even if it **meant** *him losing power*.

> She **remembered** *having heard the story* from her mother.
> I **remember** *her smiling*.

anticipate 1	entail	like 2.3	recall 1
appreciate 3	envisage	mean 1.6	recollect
avoid 1	favour 4	mention 1	remember 1,3
(cannot) bear 1.6	forget 4	mind 2.2	report 1
(not) begrudge 2	hate 2	(not) mind 2.1	resent
contemplate 1	imagine 1	necessitate	risk 5
describe 1	involve 1	preclude 1	save 5
dislike 1	justify	prevent 1	visualize
dread 1	keep 7	prohibit	

V -ing; V that

> Mr Righton **denied** *making the videos himself*.
> Mary flatly **denied** *that there was any problem*.

> Some people in Moscow **propose** *abolishing the union presidency altogether*.

In that report, we also **proposed** that all high school seniors write an essay on a consequential topic.

I deeply **regret** having offended you last November.
She **regrets** that there was any criminal activity involved.

acknowledge 1	dread 1	mention 1	recommend 2
admit 1	envisage	(not) mind 2.1	regret 1
advise 1	fantasize 1	prefer	remember 1
advocate 1	forget 4	propose 1	report 1
anticipate 1	imagine 1	recall 1	suggest 1
deny 1	intend 1	recollect	

V -ing; V to-inf

I soon **began working** with them as their resident musician.
I **began to laugh.**

He dotes on his children and **hates being away** from them.
Politicians **hate to admit** they were wrong.

Have you **tried contacting** your local councillor?
He **tried to smile.**

begin 1	deserve 1	hate 2	omit 2
(not) bother 1	dread 1	intend 1	prefer
cease 2	fear 8	like 2.1,3	start 1
commence	forbear	love 5	try 1
continue 1	go 1.4	need 2	

V -ing; V with n

He **continued looking** at me for a while.
The surprise display over, the general **continued with** his address.

It was quite incredible the way he **fell about laughing.**
Back in the bar two girls in pink silk pyjamas **are falling about with laughter.**

(not) bother 1	continue 1,3
carry on 1	go on 1
fall about	start off 1

V in n; V n in n

He **invested** heavily **in shares** after retiring from a bank he part-owned eight years ago.
He **invested the money in real estate.**

Everyone present **joined in the singing.**
More than 100 villagers **joined police in a search.**

He **trained in law** at Turin university.
We **were able to train** them **in some very basic techniques.**

assist 2,3	land 9	stick 2.2	tutor 3
invest 1,2,3	lodge 8	stir 7	
join 3	slot 2	train 2.1	

V in n; V on n

More than 200 performers **will collaborate in a three-day sound and light show.**
Ms. Rudner and Mr. Bergman **have collaborated on several writing projects.**

It is also interesting to note that golf hardly __features__ in sports magazines.
The song __features__ on the soundtrack of Myers' latest movie.

Mary __didn't ride__ in the car with her.
John __rode__ on the bus with Lisa.

appear *6*	collaborate *1*	lecture *2*	sit *6*
catch *5*	feature *4*	ride *3*	speculate *2*

V *into* n; V n *into* n

In Greek legend, the goddess Daphne __changes__ into a laurel tree.
Drugs __changed__ him into a person we didn't recognize.

Barry __dipped__ into the plastic bag.
She __dipped__ a hand into the jar of toffees and pulled one out.

The class __divides__ into groups of two, a boy and a girl in each, to carry on the guesswork.
Roger and Gary began to __divide__ the mushrooms into seven equal portions.

We __are plunging__ into a depression.
The defeat __plunged__ the country into confusion.

amalgamate	dip *2*	plunge *3,4*	smash *1*
assimilate *1*	divide *1*	resolve *4*	split *1*
break *1*	form *3*	rush *8*	stretch *5*
change *3*	hook *6*	separate *10*	translate *3*
condense *2*	integrate *1*	shatter *1*	transmute
convert *1*	merge *1*	sink *11*	turn *15*
crowd *4*	metamorphose	slam *4*	
dig *3*	mutate *1*	slot *2*	
carry over			

V *into* n; V *out of* n

Participants say the talks never __developed__ into serious dialogue.
Modern Pentecostalism __developed__ out of the revivalist movement.

Edgar __fell__ into a deep sleep for four hours.
Nasser's system of centralised economic management __has fallen__ out of favour.

change *5*	fall *9*	slip *8*
condense *2*	get *1.2*	
develop *1*	pile *6*	

V *into* n; V *to* n

Additional guests can sleep in the library, where a sofa __converts__ into an extra bed.
The saloon is big enough for the settees to __convert__ to single beds.

Maybe I'__m regressing__ into second childhood.
I seem to __have regressed__ to my post-college days.

ascend *6*	convert *1*	regress	throng *2*
build *8*	cross *1.1*	shade *7*	turn *15*
change *3*	crumble *2*	spring *6*	withdraw *4*
come *6*	mushroom *2*	stretch *5*	
carry over	get back *1*		

For other combinations with the pattern V *into* n, see V *from* n.

V n *about* n; V n *on* n

Tour companies __are briefing__ vacationers about the city's dangers.
Captain Ramirez __had briefed__ them on the execution of their current mission.

They refused even to __challenge__ the government about the situation of young people.
I __challenged__ him on the hypocrisy of his political attitudes.

Morgan __has consulted__ a barrister about his case.
He fails to __consult__ her on major decisions that affect her life.

brief 6	cross-examine	press 5
challenge 4	grill 5	question 2
consult 1	lecture 3	quiz 2

V n *about* n; V n *that*

The government are mounting a number of new initiatives to __inform__ the public about diet and health.
Officers closed in and __informed__ him that he was being arrested on suspicion of murder.

caution 2	kid 6	teach 2
forewarn	notify	tell 1
inform 1	reassure	warn 1

V n *about* n; V n wh; V n wh-to-inf

The army __informs__ all recruits about the dangers of drug taking.
He __did not inform__ anyone there what he was looking for.
The aim was to __inform__ the public how to get the best out of the new arrangements.

advise 1	inform 1	tell 1
ask 1	teach 2	warn 1

V n *about* n; V with quote

I made a mental note to __ask__ Eileen about Kintail's background.
'You really are serious about this, aren't you?' he __asked__, nearly incredulous.

advise 1	caution 2	say 1	tease 1
ask 1	challenge 4	scold	warn 1

For other combinations with the pattern V n *about* n, see V *about* n.

V n adj; V n *as* adj

Kitson __was branded__ greedy.
Since the album made its debut in May, lyrics in several songs __have been branded__ as racist.

brand 3	consider 1	label 3
certify 1	diagnose	rate 6

V n adj; V n *as* adj; V n *as* n

Parker died aged 34; the doctor who __certified__ him dead thought he was twice that age.
The UN on Saturday __certified__ the election as 'free and fair'.
Gallup __certified__ her as the most popular actress in America.

brand 3	consider 1	label 3
certify 1	diagnose	rate 6

V n adj; V n *as* adj; V n *as* n; V n n

They __labelled__ his work 'naive'.
Just because she isn't thin, she __labels__ herself as 'much too fat'.
According to the prison psychiatrist they're wrong to try and __label__ him as a psychopath.
The following day's headlines __labelled__ her a saint.

brand 3	label 3
consider 1	rate 6

V n adj; V n *as* n; V n n

I suppose I __must count__ myself lucky.
I __count__ him as my best friend.
You__'d better count__ yourself a privileged lady, Frau Eckdorf!

brand 3	count 7	rate 6
consider 1	label 3	

V n adj; V n n

Jesse __was born__ handicapped and it was thought he'd never talk.
'The Sun' reported last week that their baby __had been born__ a drug addict.

The organisers are considering whether to __declare__ the lottery void.
The government __declared__ the area a national reserve.

account 6	consider 1	find 9	prove 3
be born 2	count 7	label 3	rate 6
brand 3	declare 1,2	make 2.3	rule 7
call 2	deem	pronounce 2	serve 6

V n *against* n: see V *against* n.

V n *as* adj; V n *as* n

The company __attacked__ the proposals as unjustified and unnecessary.
The Reagan administration __attacked__ Social Security as a drain on the budget.

The Minister for Home Affairs __described__ the death as unfortunate.
Most working women __describe__ their employment as a job rather than as a career.

I __rate__ him as very special.
I __rate__ him as the best coach in the game.

accept 2,4,5	class 7	denounce 1	interpret 1
acknowledge 1,2	classify	depict 2	label 3
attack 2	conceive 2	describe 2	mention 3
bill 8	condemn 1	designate 1	perceive 2
brand 3	confirm 7	diagnose	pigeon-hole 2
certify 1	consider 1	dismiss 1	portray 3
characterize 2	construe	expose 2	present 4.5
cite 1	decry	impress 4	rank 4

rate 6	remember 6	see 6	view 3
read 8	represent 8	stereotype 2	
recognize 3,4	reveal 1	strike 11	
regard 1	scorn 2	tout 1	
mark out 2	write off 3		

V n *as* adj; V n *as* n; V n n

*There is no scriptural reason to **consider** women as inferior.*
*We **should consider** today as a memorable historic day.*
*I **will** always **consider** him a good friend of mine.*

brand 3	designate 1	rate 6
consider 1	label 3	

For other combinations with the pattern V n *as* adj, see V n adj.

V n *as* n; V n *for* n

*In the preview of the fall campaign, Simpson **attacked** Bill Clinton as a draft dodger.*
*Candidates regularly **attack** their opponents for statements made in advertising.*

*He **nominated** David Gower as his chief executive officer.*
*Democrats in California **have nominated** a woman for this November's election for governor.*

*I think he'**ll be remembered** as the greatest dancer of our lifetime.*
*Woody Guthrie **is remembered** for the songs he wrote about the Great Depression.*

acclaim 1	condemn 1	laud	select 1
attack 2	designate 2	nominate 1,3	vilify
choose 1	intend 2	remember 6	
single out			

V n *as* n; V n -ing

*She **began** her career as a dancer.*
*She **began** her broadcasting career working on commercials with Alan Parker.*

*Mr Pehuoa also **mentioned** the economy as an area of disagreement.*
*You **mentioned** Milan Stevens being fond of you.*

begin 3	finish 4	start 4
end 4	mention 1	visualize

V n *as* n; V n n

*He caused uproar when he **branded** the jobless as 'layabouts'.*
*They **branded** her an opportunist.*

*In Japan today, the Parliament **elected** Kiichi Miyazawa as the country's 49th prime minister.*
*If you **elect** me President you will be better off four years from now than you are today.*

acclaim *1*	dub *1*	label *3*	re-elect
anoint *2*	elect *1*	name *6*	tag *5*
brand *3*	fancy *5*	nominate *2*	term *4*
consider *1*	give *1.3*	ordain *1*	
count *7*	hail *1*	proclaim *1*	
designate *1*	intend *3*	rate *6*	

For other combinations with the pattern V n *as* n, see V *as* n, V n adj, V n *as* adj.

V n *at* n: see V *at* n.

V n *for* n; V n n

*Look, little one, she**'s brought** a nice present for you.*
*When I was ill he **brought** me flowers.*

*All the doors upstairs are broken. I'm scared to ask them to fix it; they **might charge** me for that.*
*It would be insulting to **charge** them a fee.*

*Ireland never **forgave** Cromwell for his harsh treatment of towns that resisted him.*
*'You **forgave** me my unusual way of life,' he told them. 'I thank you.'*

acclaim *1*	cook *1*	knit *1*	prescribe *1*
allocate	excuse *3*	leave *8*	secure *1*
book *3*	fetch *1*	make *3.3*	sell *1*
bring *3*	find *1,2*	order *2.5*	vote *7*
buy *1*	fix *14*	pay *1,4*	wangle
carve *4*	forgive *1*	play *11,12*	write *2,6*
charge *1*	get *2.1,3*	pour *2*	

V n *for* n; V n to-inf

*The Olympic Committee yesterday **chose** Nagano for the 1998 winter games.*
*Churchill **chose** Cripps to be his messenger to India.*

*They **paid** cash for almost everything.*
*I **paid** £80 to have my car radio fixed.*

*I know he gets fed up with people **pestering** him for money.*
*The cat had got lost and the kids **pestered** me to go look for it.*

*Previous experience **had** hardly **prepared** him for this type of war.*
*His sleeves were rolled up to his elbows as if he **had prepared** himself to do some dirty work.*

admonish	do *2.7*	nominate *1*	ready *8*
allocate	earmark *1*	pay *1*	recruit *1*
beg *1*	equip *2*	pester	schedule *3*
beseech	fit *1.11*	prepare *1,2*	steel *3*
budget *4*	free *8*	press *5*	take *25*
choose *1*	groom *4*	pressure *5*	tip *10*
clear *19*	importune	prime *5*	vote *7*
be designed *8*	intend *2*	qualify *2*	
rope in			

For other combinations with the pattern V n *for* n, see V *for* n, V n *as* n.

V n *from* n or V n *from* n *into* n; V n *into* n

All these verbs have the pattern **V n *into* n**. The verbs *change*, *metamorphose*, *transform*, and *translate* also have the pattern **V n *from* n *into* n**. The verbs *distil*, *divide*, and *sidetrack* also have the pattern **V n *from* n**. The verb *transplant* has all three patterns.

> These people have a tendency to try to **sidetrack** you **from** your task.
> He **was** sometimes **sidetracked** into power struggles.

> By late 1917, London **had been transformed** from an open city into a defended location.
> The old offices and storerooms **were transformed** into classrooms and workshops.

change *3*	divide *4*	sidetrack	translate *1*
distil *3*	metamorphose	transform *1*	transplant *3*

V n *from* n; V n *out of* n

> He **carves** his figures from white pine and yellow poplar.
> The younger of the girls asks Andrew to **carve** a pendant out of a piece of a driftwood.

> When Johnny **couldn't** beg or **charm** a meal from a civilian, he at times would stoop to stealing.
> They **have charmed** money out of the pockets of credulous citizens.

> She flew at him and actually **chased** him from the house.
> He **chased** them out of the camp and across the desert.

carve *1*	construct *1,2*	make *3.1,6*	take *2.7*
charm *5*	create *1*	manufacture *1*	wheedle
chase *4,5*	fashion *4*	pluck *2*	wring *1*
clip *5*	get *2.1,9*	prize *5*	
coax *2*	hew *2*	pull *2*	
conjure *1*	hound *3*	squeeze *6*	

V n *from* n or V n *from* n *to* n; V n *to* n

All these verbs have the pattern **V n *to* n**. The verb *change* also has the pattern **V n *from* n *to* n**. The other verbs have all three patterns.

> They **were banished** from the country, seemingly never to return.
> Five years later he **was banished** to Upper Egypt.

> We decided to **change** our name from National Marriage Guidance to Relate.
> She **changed** her name to Joanna.

> Pamela Counter **has been promoted** from account executive.
> He **was promoted** to lieutenant general.

banish *1*	extradite	promote *3*	transplant *3*
bar *10*	forward *10*	relay *2,4*	
change *3*	pass *6*	send *1,2*	
deport	pluck *7*	transfer *1,2,4,5,7,8*	

For other combinations with the pattern V n *from* n, see V *from* n.

V n inf; V n -ing

> Seeing that the girl was in pain, Mrs Dambar **had** her sit down.
> We **had** him working at CBS within three weeks.

> Wade glanced up and **saw** her disappear.
> I **saw** him coming along the path.

feel *7,8*	notice *1*	watch *1.1*
have *3.7*	observe *1*	
hear *1,2*	see *1,9*	

V n -ing: see V -ing, V n *as* n, V n inf.

V n *in* n; V n *into* n

Peel the onions and <u>cut</u> them *in half* lengthwise.
<u>Cut</u> the potatoes *into strips* and fry rapidly in hot oil.

They<u>'d throw</u> me *in jail* if I did that.
They<u>'ve thrown</u> them *into prison* without a trial!

break *1*	divide *1,4*	lock *3*	split *1*
carve *3*	draft *4*	render *4*	stick *2.2*
chop *1*	etch *1,3*	slice *2*	throw *5*
cut *1*	implant *1,4*	slot *2*	
dip *1*	instil	sort *3*	

V n *in* n; V n *on* n

His face <u>is etched</u> *in my memory*.
Every detail of the attack <u>is etched</u> *on the captain's memory*.

Joseph <u>instructs</u> a class *in woodwork*.
The video <u>instructs</u> them *on body language*.

capture *4*	engrave	hit *1*	place *18*
carve *2*	etch *1,3*	imprint *2*	remand *1*
catch *4*	ground *12*	instruct *2*	strike *5*
put down *1*			

For other combinations with the pattern V n *in* n, see V *in* n.

V n *into* -ing; V n *into* n

He claimed the police <u>had bullied</u> him *into admitting the crime*.
His wife Sonia <u>could bully</u> him *into silence*.

Policewoman Joanne Field was praised yesterday for <u>charming</u> a gunman *into handing over his rifle*.
His uncompromisingly honest songs <u>charm</u> you *into rapt attention*.

The experience <u>has lulled</u> citizens *into accepting dismal levels of public service*.
His absence <u>had lulled</u> Felicity *into a sense of security*.

She <u>might be able to shame</u> her friends *into lending her the money*.
He <u>could</u> well <u>shame</u> other nations *into action*.

badger *2*	coerce	intimidate	pressure *5*
blackmail *3*	con *1*	inveigle	prod *2*
bludgeon *2*	condition *7*	jolt *2*	propel *2*
bounce *9*	cow *4*	lull *2*	provoke *1*
browbeat	deceive *1*	lure *1*	push *6*
bulldoze *3*	dragoon *2*	manoeuvre *2*	put *6*
bully *3*	dupe *1*	nag *1*	railroad *2*
cajole	entrap	nudge *3*	rush *8*
charm *3*	fool *3*	panic *3*	scare *1*
chasten	force *1,2*	persuade *1*	seduce *1*
chivvy	galvanize	press *5*	shame *5*
co-opt *2*	goad *1*	press-gang *1*	sidetrack

spur 1	steer 2	tempt 1,2	trick 2
stampede 4	stir 5	terrify 1	
steamroller 2	sweet talk	trap 4	

V n *into* -ing; V n *into* n; V n to-inf

She is trying to <u>force</u> me into marrying Desmond Featherstone.
She'd had a relationship with a man who virtually <u>forced</u> her into a life of crime.
He pulled the boy's arms from around his neck and <u>forced</u> him to sit back on his chair.

badger 2	coerce	nudge 3	prod 2
blackmail 3	condition 7	persuade 1	push 6
cajole	force 1,2	press 5	spur 1
chivvy	nag 1	pressure 5	tempt 1,2

V n *into* -ing; V n to-inf

I've just <u>got to persuade</u> my dad into letting me having a season ticket.
He <u>persuaded</u> Ferranti to set up the first British Computer Service Bureau.

You should try to support her and not <u>pressurize</u> her into being superwoman.
Who's <u>pressurizing</u> you to keep up your grades?

badger 2	coerce	nudge 3	prod 2
blackmail 3	condition 7	persuade 1	push 6
brainwash	force 1,2	press 5	spur 1
cajole	manipulate 1	pressure 5	tempt 1.2
chivvy	nag 1	pressurize	

V n *into* n; V n *out of* n

He has scotched rumours that the selector's decision <u>will force</u> him into early retirement.
The accident <u>forced</u> the Frenchman out of the race.

get changed 5	cut 1	get 1.3	persuade 1
con 1	force 1,2	jolt 2	trick 2

V n *into* n; V n to-inf

I <u>wouldn't push</u> couples into marriage if they were uncertain of their strength of commitment.
He <u>had pushed</u> her to buy a new car.

Don't let greed for power <u>tempt</u> you into waters that are too deep.
Don't let credit <u>tempt</u> you to buy something you can't afford.

badger 2	condition 7	persuade 1	spur 1
blackmail 3	force 1,2	press 5	tempt 1,2
cajole	nag 1	pressure 5	
chivvy	nudge 3	prod 2	
coerce	permit 1	push 6	

V n *into* n; V n *to* n

The restorers <u>converted</u> the signals into digital code.
A light bulb <u>converts</u> electrical energy to heat energy.

His family <u>were driven</u> into exile in 1921.
Sarah's father <u>was driven</u> to suicide by debts of £10 million.

beat 9	drive 13	lull 3	turn 15
change 3	feed 12	scare 1	yoke 3
convert 1,3	introduce 1	stretch 5	
deliver 3	knit 2	transplant 3	
carry over	work up 1		

For other combinations with the pattern V n *into* n, see V *into* n, V n *from* n, V n *in* n.

V n n; V n *to* n

She could help him or she **could do** him a considerable amount of harm.
'Trick or treat' is a threat that you**'ll do** something terrible to the occupants of the house if they don't give you a gift.
Nobody phoned the police or ambulance service, though one woman **offered** him a towel.
He tasted the wine himself before **offering** it to his friends.
They liked him, they thought he was a war hero, he **told** them some kind of story.
But this much I'll give my word on, I**'ll not tell** one story to you and another somewhere else.

accord 2	do 2.6	offer 1,4,5,6,7,9	send 1,4
allocate	fax 2	ordain 1	serve 6
allot	feed 1,8	owe 1,2,3,5	show 3
appoint	give 1.2,3,2.1,2,3	pass 5	slip 5
assign 1,2,3,4	grant 2	pay 1,11	teach 1
award 4,5	hand 2.1	pen 2	tell 1,2
beat 9	lease 2	post 1.4	vouchsafe
bequeath 1,2	leave 20	proffer 2	wire 6
bid 2.1	lend 1,2,3,5	promise 2	write 4
bring 3,7,10	loan 3	read 2	
cable 5	mail 3	render 2	
concede 2	nominate 2	sell 1,6	

For other combinations with the pattern V n n, see V n adj, V n *as* adj, V n *as* n, V n *for* n.

V n *on* n; V *on* n

She **advises** companies on investment strategies in Latin America.
A doctor should be on the premises to monitor and **advise** on medication.
He **bet** £10 on three horses called Bartisan, Your Fancy and Merry Dance at Lewes races.
I **bet** on American football.
We **focus** our attention on people who are ill.
Robert's counselling **focuses** on positive energy and humour to fight the mounting tension.
The couple **had forked out** £2774 on a special trip to celebrate Mick's 50th birthday.
You**'ll have to fork out** on publicity.

advise 2	counsel 3	gamble 2	save 3
bet 1	drum 6	gorge 2	snag 2
catch 5	fasten 3	hammer 3	wager 1
centre 9	fix 7	lecture 2	
concentrate 1	focus 1,5	rap 4	
fork out	shell out		

For other combinations with the pattern V n *on* n, see V n *about* n, V n *in* n.

V n *out of* n: see V n *from* n, V n *into* n.

V n that; V n to-inf

The death of my son __taught__ me that life is very fragile.
The harsh lessons of the war __had taught__ me to defend myself.

caution 2	instruct 1	teach 2
decide 5	show 1	

V n that; V n wh

They __told__ me they'd call the cops.
__Tell__ me how it happened.

inform 1	remind 1,2	tell 1,8
instruct 1	teach 2	warn 1

V n that; V n with quote

Hopkins privately __assured__ Churchill that Roosevelt and the American people would stand by Britain no matter what the danger.
'You can happily drink my wines within a year of bottling,' he __assured__ me.

I __promised__ the children we'd go for a boat ride in the pond.
'We'll manage,' she __promised__ him.

assure 1	instruct 1	remind 1
inform 1	promise 1	tell 1,4

V n that; V that

The Japanese Prime Minister __has__ already __promised__ him that aid worth four billion dollars will soon be on its way.
I __promise__ I'll explain everything as soon as I can.

caution 2	instruct 1	show 1
guarantee 3	promise 1	warn 1

For other combinations with the pattern V n that, see V n *about* n.

V n to-inf; V n with quote

I grabbed him by both shoulders and __begged__ him to calm down.
She __begged__ her father: 'Please look after the cats for me.'

Finally Stalin __instructed__ Zhukov to go to the Kremlin.
'Go home and ask your father what he thinks,' Scott __instructed__ him.

admonish	command 1	implore	urge 1
advise 1	entreat	instruct 1	warn 2
beg 1	exhort	order 2.1	

V n to-inf; V n with quote; V with quote

He __commanded__ his men to retreat.
An urgent voice from the gloom __commanded__ me: 'Stop! Don't move.'
'Open it,' she __commanded__.

I genuinely believed Carling was best-suited for the job and I __implored__ him not to give it up.
'Sing it one time!' Stevie __implores__ the audience.
'Can't you do something?' he __implored__.

advise *1*	entreat	instruct *1*	warn *2*
beg *1*	exhort	order *2.1*	
command *1*	implore	urge *1*	

V n to-inf; V that

I __asked__ Beryl to drop in.
The Attorney __asked__ that Mr. Rough be sentenced to no more than a year in jail.

They __would have preferred__ me to be a doctor or a lawyer.
I __would prefer__ that you pronounce my name correctly.

They __understand__ him to be unharmed.
I __understand__ he spends most of his time in Europe and America.

acknowledge *1*	command *1*	instruct *1*	require *2*
advise *1*	consider *1*	know *1*	show *1,7*
allege	declare *1,2*	order *2.2*	think *2*
ask *2*	direct *12*	prefer	understand *5*
assume *1*	discover *1*	presume *1*	wish *4*
beg *1*	expect *1*	prove *2,3*	
believe *1*	feel *10*	recommend *2*	
caution *2*	find *7*	report *1*	

V n to-inf; V that; V with quote

I __advised__ her to make the trip.
When his condition worsened, doctors __advised__ that he should be transferred to a private room at St Mary's hospital.
'Be careful, boys!' he __advised__.

Myrna Blyth __declared__ her to be the greatest media personality of the decade.
The ministers __declared__ that the recent decline of the yen had undesirable consequences for the world economy.
'To be honest, I hate children,' __declares__ Bob.

advise *1*	beg *1*	command *1*	instruct *1*
allege	caution *2*	declare *1*	report *1*

V n to-inf; V to-inf

I __will beg__ her to come back.
He __begs__ to come in the house, but we can't allow it.

The Bank __expects__ inflation to rise this year.
I __didn't expect__ to find Monica at the flat because she works in the mornings.

I jumped when the telephone rang, __preparing__ myself to receive bad news.
She __was preparing__ to go to Manchester to film an episode of 'Cluedo'.

beg 1	help 1,2	need 1	qualify 2
desire 2	incline 1	pay 1	train 2.1
expect 1,3	like 2.4,8	petition 3	(not) trouble 10
(not) expect 4	love 9	prefer	want 1,4
hate 2	mean 1.8	prepare 2	

V n to-inf; V with quote

I __would caution__ you to read the fine print.
He __cautioned__, however: 'There is still an awful lot of bad news to come.'

Eight republics __have__ now __declared__ themselves to be independent.
'To run an efficient international organisation you cannot skimp,' he __declares.__

advise 1	challenge 4	exhort	request 2
allege	command 1	implore	urge 1
beg 1	counsel 2	instruct 1	warn 2
beseech	declare 1	order 2.1	
caution 2	entreat	report 1	

For other combinations with the pattern V n to-inf, see V n *for* n, V n
into -ing, V n *into* n.

V n *to* n; V n *with* n

We __can connect__ this suspect to the other shootings in the Columbia Heights area.
Nothing was found to __connect__ them with the robbery.

Leica __has__ always __supplied__ equipment to armed forces throughout the world.
The Soviets __supplied__ Finland with all its oil in return for Finnish manufactured goods.

connect 7,8	entrust	mail 3	supply 1
correlate 1	feed 1,8	match 3,5	
credit 7	link 2,4,7	present 4.1,2,4	
match up 3			

V n *to* n; V pl-n with *together*

There had always been the strong ties that __bound__ her to Rachel, Chris and Caroline.
You can enjoy the understanding that __binds__ you and your lover together.

Lightly gather the material, then pin and __sew__ it to the ribbon.
Normally I __sew__ the pages together by machine.

bind 1	couple 5	rope 2	tie 2
bolt 2	join 5	sew 1	weld 1
chain 4	knit 2	solder 1	yoke 3
clip 2	lash 2	stick 2.4	

V n *to* n; V *to* n

Keegan __adapted__ himself to a change of routine.
The data will help scientists learn how the body __adapts__ to the absence of gravity.

He __admitted__ the crime to his father's twin brother.
He also __admitted__ to mistakes in his economic policy.

You can hear stereo sound on the VCR if you __connect__ it to an audio stereo system.
A short curly lead __connects__ to the camcorder's external mike socket.

In twelve months time I __will have increased__ my salary to £30,000 per year.

Italy's deficit __increased__ to £14.5 billion.

I sometimes sit and __read__ the newspaper to her.
My mother __read__ to us every evening until we were 18.

acclimatize	commit 4	incline 1	stretch 5
accommodate 5	confess 2	increase 1	swell 1
adapt 1	connect 1	lend 1	switch 3
adjust 1	contribute 1,2	mould 5	telegraph 2
admit 1	convert 1,5	nod 3	transfer 1,2,4,5,8
attach 3,4	correlate 1	pass 6,8	transmit 1
awaken 2	decrease 1	propose 6	turn 12,15
brake 2	dictate 2	read 2	write 4
change 3	drop 8	relate 2	
clip 2	give 2.1	sell 1	
carry over	match up 3	open up 2	

V n *to* n; V *that*

We shyly __admitted__ our plan to friends.
He __admitted__ he had been lying.

More than a third of people __prefer__ bungalows to houses.
The two leaders __prefer__ that a vote occur after next week's meeting.

admit 1	disclose	murmur 1	reveal 1
announce 1	divulge	pledge 2	say 1
confide	explain 1,2	prefer	submit 2
dictate 2	mention 1	report 1	suggest 1

V n *to* n; V *with quote*

Tony cried then, but he __wouldn't admit__ it to the press.
'I do like being tall now,' she __admits__, 'but when I was growing up, I disliked it.'

So he only __suggested__ the idea to you once.
'Perhaps a little cognac for everyone,' he __suggested__ meekly.

admit 1	explain 1,2	report 1	telegraph 2
cable 5	murmur 1	say 1	
confide	read 2	suggest 1	

For other combinations with the pattern V n *to* n, see V n *from* n, V n *into* n.

V n *wh*; V n *wh-to-inf*

I was embarrassed when he __asked__ me who my father was.
They __asked__ him how to get in touch with Julie's family.

I'll __show__ you what I've done.
He __showed__ me how to fix the camera and tripod.

advise 1	instruct 1	teach 1,2
ask 1	remind 1,2	tell 1,8
inform 1	show 3,5	warn 1

V n wh; V n with quote

Hi, <u>can</u> you <u>tell</u> us where King's Square is, please.
'The only thing I need is a tape player so I can listen to music,' she <u>told</u> us.

advise *1*	inform *1*	remind *1*
ask *1*	instruct *1*	tell *1*

For other combinations with the pattern V n wh, see V n *about* n, V n that.

V n wh-to-inf: see V n *about* n, V n wh.

V n *with* n; V *with* n

He<u>'s assisting</u> us with the investigation.
Everyone is expected to <u>assist</u> with camp chores.

Nagano <u>ended</u> the concert with the full version of Stravinsky's Firebird ballet.
The rally <u>ended</u> with spectacular fireworks.

By the time Diana appeared I<u>'d filled</u> the bath with water.
Behind him his tracks <u>filled</u> with snow.

assist *1*	equate	integrate *1*	open *21*
begin *3*	fill *1*	juggle *1*	square *8*
check *1*	finish *4*	meet *8*	
end *6*	help *1*	oblige *2*	
fill up *1*			

For other combinations with V n *with* n, see V n *to* n.

V n with quote; V that; V with quote

'I'll be back by noon,' he <u>promised</u> the clerk.
The President <u>promised</u> that the reforms would be carried out within two years.
'I'll do what I can for you at the trial,' I <u>promised.</u>

advise *1*	command *1*	promise *1*
beg *1*	instruct *1*	

V n with quote; V with quote

'What did you do at school today?' a mother <u>asked</u> her 12-year-old daughter.
'Who are you?' I <u>asked.</u>

'You're making a big mistake,' he <u>warned</u> me.
'I'd like to get closer if I could,' he said. '<u>Forget it!</u>' <u>warned</u> Pete. 'Those beasts are dangerous.'

advise *1*	command *1*	implore	promise *1*
ask *1*	correct *6*	instruct *1*	urge *1*
beg *1*	entreat	interrupt *1*	warn *2*
cable *5*	exhort	order *2.1*	

For other combinations with the pattern V n with quote, see V n that, V n to-inf, V n wh.

V *on* n; V *over* n

*The government **has backed down** on performance-related contracts.*
*The Allies **had backed down** over the 1936 re-militarization of the Rhineland.*

*He **brooded** on his failure to avert the confrontation in the woods.*
*Christine **brooded** over the cause of her broken marriage.*

*A gloomy silence once again **descended** on the room.*
*A deathly hush **descended** over Rome's Olympic Stadium.*

*Murdock **tripped** on the last step and nearly landed flat on his face.*
*Nancy **tripped** over a tree root and went sprawling.*

brood *3*	disagree *1*	prevaricate	trip *2*
compromise *2*	fall *12,14*	procrastinate	waffle *2*
deliberate *3*	fawn *3*	ruminate *1*	waver *1*
descend *2*	muse *1*	speculate *1*	
differ *2*	ponder	stall *2*	
back down	climb down	trip up *2*	

V *on* n; V *that*

*International airlines **are betting** on a return to profits this year.*
*Despite the problems caused by German unification, many economists **are** still **betting** that Europe's economies will outshine America's over the next few years.*

*The government has refused to **comment** on such questions.*
*He **commented** that I spoke French with a Swiss accent.*

agree *1,3*	disagree *1*	muse *1*	rule *7*
bet *3*	gamble *2*	pronounce *3*	speculate *1*
comment *1*	insist *1,2*	remark *1*	
report back *1*			

V *on* n; V *that*; V *with quote*

*I feel I **must comment** on the statement made by Boris Yeltsin.*
*One official **commented** that Hurricane Andrew damaged every building in the town.*
*'There are some aspects that worry me,' he **commented**.*

*Simply **insist** on your point of view in a gentle but resolute manner.*
*He **insisted** he was feeling fine and asked everyone to go on drinking and talking as before.*
*'I hope our fears are ill-founded but we have to err on the side of caution,' he **insisted**.*

agree *1*	muse *1*	speculate *1*
comment *1*	pronounce *3*	
insist *2*	remark *1*	

V *on* n; V *to*-inf

*The leaders **agreed** on the need for extra debt relief for the poorest countries.*
*It's not clear if the two sides **have agreed** to ban the development of nuclear weapons.*

*I felt they **were** all **ganging up** on me.*
*The big institutional shareholders **ganged up** to push the deal through.*

agree *3*	fail *1*	survive *2*
collaborate *1*	legislate	vote *5*
gang up	shell out	

V *on* n; V with quote

*He **would break in** on her conversation with clients to ask her to make him some tea.*
*'Hey, wait!' Joe **broke in** unexpectedly. 'What about Ian?'*

*Although some scientists **have mused** on the question of how to get rid of sonic booms,*
they have not yet found satisfactory answers.
*'I ought to reconsider her offer to move in,' he **mused**.*

agree *1*	insist *2*	philosophize	remark *1*
comment *1*	muse *1*	pronounce *3*	speculate *1*
break in *2*	butt in	cut in	

For other combinations with the pattern V *on* n, see V *about* n, V *in* n, V n *on* n.

V *out of* n: see V *into* n.

V *over* n; V with quote

I have been a subscriber to 'The Oldie' almost from the beginning and have spent many hours
***chuckling** over some of the articles and cartoons.*
He said he spent his time in detention reading. 'It was a good opportunity for me to get
*some reading done,' he **chuckled**.*

*Mae West was astonished when an admirer **enthused** over an old film of hers he had seen*
at New York's Museum of Modern Art.
*'With my brains and your looks we'll be the perfect partnership!' she **enthused**.*

chuckle	enthuse *1*	gush *3*	rhapsodize
coo *2*	fume *2*	muse *1*	speculate *1*

For other combinations with the pattern V *over* n, see V *about* n, V *at* n, V *on* n.

V that; V to-inf

*He seemed to **have forgotten** that the rest of us were present.*
*I'm sorry I'm late, John. I **forgot** to set my alarm and I overslept.*

*I'm quite sure that the pilot **didn't intend** that we should hear him.*
*The factory **intended** to use only 2,000 workers.*

agree *2,3*	determine *4*	plead *1*	regret *3*
arrange *2*	dread *1*	pledge *2*	resolve *2*
ask *3*	expect *1*	pray *1*	swear *2*
beg *1*	forget *2*	prefer	threaten *1*
claim *1*	guarantee *3*	pretend *1,2,3*	venture *3*
decide *1*	hope *1*	profess *1*	vow *1*
demand *1*	intend *1*	promise *1*	

V that; V to-inf; V with quote

*The police **are claiming** that the situation in the capital is serious.*
*The leader of the cult **claimed** to be Jesus Christ.*
*'I never touched it,' he **claimed**.*

*Jordan **pleaded** that food and medicines were permitted on humanitarian grounds.*
*She **pleaded** to be released and not be hurt.*
*'Please help me,' she **pleaded**.*

beg *1*	demand *1*	pray *1*	venture *3*
claim *1*	plead *1*	promise *1*	vow *1*

V that; V *to* n

He __admits__ he has had a problem with drug and alcohol dependency.
They openly __admitted__ to the murder of Surrendra Paul.

We repeatedly heard faculty members __complain__ that their students are unprepared to do college-level work.
He will urge the Board to __complain__ to the European Athletics Association.

admit *1*	complain *1*	object *5*	signal *2*
attest	confess *1*	pray *1*	swear *3*
boast *1*	dictate *2*	reply *1*	testify *1*
brag	mutter	respond *1*	whisper *1*
report back *1*			

V that; V *to* n; V *with* quote

Members of the federal government __objected__ that such an arrangement would reduce central authority to a shell.
Teachers __objected__ to the prospect of being compelled to work longer hours.
'You've no right to jump to conclusions,' Armstrong __objected__.

admit *1*	brag	mutter	reply *1*
attest	complain *1*	object *5*	respond *1*
boast *1*	confess *1*	pray *1*	whisper *1*

V that; V wh

I __couldn't believe__ that the man I'd been so happy with for years had done this.
I __can't believe__ how hard this course is.

Experts at the United Nations __estimate__ that 10 percent of the earth's people have already been affected to some extent by desertification.
You __must__ now __estimate__ how much capital is needed.

__Imagine__ you are sending someone a picture postcard of where you live. What does it look like?
It's easy to __imagine__ how the current fighting could escalate.

accept *2,4*	determine *2,3*	foresee	realize *1*
acknowledge *1*	dictate *2,3*	foretell	recall *1*
advise *1*	discern *1*	guess *1,2*	recognize *2*
affirm *1*	disclose	hear *7*	recollect
agree *1,3*	discover *1,3*	hint *2*	recommend *2*
announce *1,2,3*	dispute *2*	hypothesize	recount *1*
anticipate *1*	divine *4*	illustrate *1*	reflect *5*
appreciate *2*	divulge	imagine *1*	register *7*
argue *1*	doubt *2*	indicate *1,2,5*	remain *8*
ascertain	emphasize	intimate *7*	remark *1*
(cannot) believe *6*	envisage	know *1*	remember *1*
calculate *1,2*	envision	learn *2*	report *1*
check *1*	establish *3*	marvel *1*	resolve *2*
(cannot) conceive *1*	estimate *1*	mention *1*	reveal *1*
confess *1*	explain *1,2*	note *9,11*	say *1*
confirm *1,2*	fantasize *1*	notice *1*	see *1,4,5,16*
conjecture *2*	figure *11*	predict	sense *2*
decide *1,4*	find *7*	prove *2*	show *1*
demonstrate *1*	forecast *2*	read *1*	signal *4*

606

speculate *1*	suggest *1*	twig *2*	warn *1*
state *8*	surmise *1*	underline *1*	worry *1*
stipulate	suspect *2*	underscore *1*	
stress *1*	suss	verify *1*	
figure out	let on	work out *1*	
find out *1*	put down *1*		

V that; V wh; V with quote

Ms Andreyevna **guesses** that in fact 50 per cent of the working population is on short time or paid leave.
I bet you **can't guess** what I'm going to do.
'How many of them are there?' he asked. 'Six hundred?' Sharpe **guessed**.

Naomi **recalled** that the beginning of the war felt exciting.
He **could recall** how terrible he'd felt.
'I met Conrad Black years ago in Palm Beach,' Brooke Astor **recalled.**

Greenspan **said** he expects the economy to recover quickly from the current recession.
I **said** how sorry I was to ring him at midnight.
'I love you, Lee,' he **said**.

advise *1*	deduce	predict	speculate *1*
affirm *1*	demand *1*	proclaim *2*	state *8*
agree *1*	estimate *1*	read *1*	stress *1*
announce *2*	explain *1,2*	recall *1*	suggest *1*
argue *1*	guess *1*	remark *1*	warn *1*
confess *1*	marvel *1*	report *1*	
declare *1*	note *11*	say *1*	

V that; V *with* n; V with quote

Derrida **responded** that such a project was impossible.
She **responded** with a letter in which she thanked him.
'Well, things almost turned out just the way you wanted,' Nancy **responded**.

agree *1*	joke *2*	respond *1*
counter *4*	plead *1*	

V that; V with quote

He **added** that most of the information is already available.
'She's planning to start at Berkeley in September,' Pete **added**.

The government **has promised** the elections will be fair.
'I'll be here,' she **promised**.

My uncle **said** he was going to take the blame.
After a while she **said**, 'Fielding, why aren't you at school?'

I **suggest** you have a leisurely meal and then perhaps go for a drive.
'Let's take a taxi,' Chet **suggested**.

He was so arrogant that he **thought** he could talk his way out of everything.
I have to do as my father says, he **thought**, there's no choice.

add 5	conclude 1	lament 1	repeat 1
admit 1	concur	maintain 2	reply 1
advise 1	confess 1	marvel 1	report 1
affirm 1	confide	moan 2	respond 1
agree 1	contend 2	murmur 1	retort
allege	counter 4	muse 1	say 1,3
announce 2	cry 2	note 11	scream 2
answer 1	declaim	object 5	shout 1
argue 1	declare 1	observe 3	sneer
assert 1	deduce	opine	speculate 1
attest	demand 1	plead 1	squawk 2
aver	enthuse 1	pray 1	state 8
beg 1	estimate 1	predict	stress 1
bellow 1	exclaim	proclaim 2	suggest 1
boast 1	explain 1,2	promise 1	venture 3
brag	go 3.5	pronounce 3	volunteer 4
burble 2	grouse 2	protest 3	vow 1
caution 2	grumble 1	quip 2	wail 2
chant 3	guess 1	read 1	warn 1
claim 1	hazard 3	reason 4	whine 2
command 1	insist 2	recall 1	whisper 1
comment 1	instruct 1	reiterate	write 5
complain 1	interject	rejoin 4	yell 1
concede 1	joke 2	remark 1	
cry out 2			

For other combinations with the pattern V *that*, see V *about* n, V *against* n, V *at* n, V *for* n, V -ing, V n that, V n to-inf, V n *to* n, V n with quote, V *on* n.

V to-inf; V with quote

She **offered** to accompany Mr Snabel on his hike.
'We could play golf this afternoon,' he **offered**.

beg 1	offer 2	promise 1
claim 1	plead 1	venture 3
demand 1	pray 1	vow 1

For other combinations with the pattern V to-inf, see V *against* n, V *for* n, V -ing, V n to-inf, V *on* n, V that.

V *to* n; V *with* n

All youth groups **will have to affiliate** to the National Youth Agency.
He said he wanted to **affiliate with a U.S. firm** because he needed expert advice and counsel in legal affairs.
The Institute's diet plans **conform** to guidelines of the American Heart Association.
An inquiry could find no fault with the structure of the ship. It **conformed with all the necessary regulations**.
The Secretary General **spoke to reporters** in Amman.
As Laurie **spoke with Forstmann**, her husband was on the other line with Cohen.

affiliate 2	connect 5	natter	speak 1
bind 5	correlate 1	resound 2	talk 2,6,7
chat	correspond 1	respond 1	
conform 1,2	equate	sign 7	
cuddle up	match up ▷5	sing along	

V *to* n; V *with* quote

I _assented_ to the request of the American publishers to write this book.
'I think you're right,' Pantieri _assented_.

The guards _muttered_ to each other, ignoring Vangelis.
'Sometimes Bess doesn't have much sense,' she _muttered_.

admit 1	brag	object 5	sing 1
apologize	complain 1	pray 1	telegraph 2
assent 2	confess 1	read 2	whisper 1
attest	mumble	reply 1	
boast 1	mutter	respond 1	

For other combinations with the pattern V *to* n, see V *at* n, V *from* n,
V *into* n, V n *to* n, V *that*.

V wh; V wh-to-inf

I _have decided_ what the course content is going to be at the start of the course.
A writer or poet _decides_ what to say and then chooses the most beautiful words to express it.

When they were going I suddenly _realized_ who they were.
I think, finally, with this record, I_'ve realized_ how to write songs.

I _can't remember_ what the programme was called.
I just _couldn't remember_ how to spell the most simple of words.

advise 1	determine 2,3	investigate	reveal 1
argue 4	discover 1,3	judge 4	say 1
ask 1	discuss 1	know 1,7	see 1,5,10
assess 1,2	establish 3	learn 1,2,3	show 2
calculate 1	explain 1	plan 2	specify 1
check 1	figure 11	ponder	suggest 1,2
consider 2	forget 1	realize 1	think 4,6,8
debate 3,4	guess 1,2	recall 1	understand 1,3,4
decide 1,4	illustrate 1	rehearse 2	
demonstrate 4	imagine 1	remember 1	
describe 1	indicate 1	(cannot) remember 3	
figure out	puzzle out	work out 1	
find out 1	weigh up 3		

V wh; V *with* quote

Around eleven, Father Gregory phoned to _ask_ how she was.
'Where have you been all this time?' Bess _asked_ anxiously.

You can use a chart to _note_ when your next injection is due.
I _noted_ in my diary, 'I must say this car really is a little beauty.'

I _was thinking_ how lovely this house is.
Pamela was right, she _thought._

advise 1	deduce	predict	state 8
affirm 1	demand 1	proclaim 2	stress 1
agree 1	estimate 1	query 3	suggest 1
announce 2	explain 1,2	recall 1	think 8
argue 1	guess 1	remark 1	warn 1
ask 1	inquire 1	report 1	wonder 1
confess 1	marvel 1	say 1	
declare 1	note 11	speculate 1	

For other combinations with the pattern V wh, see V *about* n, V that.

V wh-to-inf: see V *about* n, V wh.

V *with* n; V with quote

I **_do agree_** with you absolutely.
Many European governments **_agree_** with these proposals.
'I don't look sixty-seven,' she added. 'No,' he **_agreed_**, 'you don't.'

As a boy, he had arms and legs that were long and straight and brown, and he **_laughed_** with
pleasure when people said he looked like an Indian.
Liam **_laughed_** with his friends who were taking a break from playing cricket.
'You never know,' **_laughed_** Dr Holly, 'just when the past will catch up with you!'

The number of smokers is falling, but those who **_persist_** with the habit are smoking more.
'You haven't answered me,' she **_persisted_**.

agree *1*	crow *4*	groan *2*	persist *2*
beam *1*	end *6*	interrupt *1*	plead *1*
cackle	explode *2*	joke *2*	respond *1*
counter *4*	expostulate	laugh *1*	squeal
butt in	chime in	chip in *2*	

For other combinations with the pattern V *with* n, see V *at* n, V -ing,
V n *with* n, V that, V *to* n.

V with quote: see V *about* n, V *against* n, V *at* n, V *for* n, V n *about* n, V n to-inf, V n *to* n, V n with quote, V *on* n, V *over* n, V that, V to-inf, V *to* n, V wh, V *with* n.

Appendix: Different forms of a pattern

In the English that you read or hear, the elements of a verb pattern may not appear as they do in the basic pattern given as a heading in this book, or in the simple examples given in the structure tables. Below we explain the different forms of a pattern that may occur.

1 Subject not before verb

Although in a basic example of a pattern the Subject comes immediately before the verb, in some examples the Subject comes earlier in the clause, or is not explicitly mentioned in the clause. For example, the verb being exemplified may itself be part of the pattern of another verb and be in the to-infinitive form or the '-ing' form. In these cases, the Subject of the main verb is the Subject of this verb too.

> I'm sorry, love, I didn't mean to **_snap_ at you** like that.
> As a youngster he loved **_dressing up_ as Superman**.

In the following examples, the verb is in the to-infinitive form and the Subject is understood from the context, or has been mentioned in a previous sentence.

> Their aim is to **_profit_ by buying replacement shares later at a lower price**.
> The proper way to measure the real interest rate is to **_subtract_ expected inflation from the nominal interest rate**.

There is usually no Subject if the verb is in the imperative.

> **_Don't generalize_ from one example**. It's bad science.

2 Different word orders

When describing a pattern, we usually give the elements in the order in which they occur in an ordinary active clause. For example, the pattern **V _about_ n** means that in an ordinary active clause the verb is followed by the preposition *about* and a noun group. However, in actual speech and writing, the order of elements in a pattern may be different.

Two of these changed orders sometimes appear in the examples in this book:

1 Passive voice

Some verbs which, in an active clause, are followed by a noun group, or by a preposition and a noun group, can be passivized. If they can, the passive pattern is given in the same section as the active pattern, usually with a table. For example, the passive of **V n** is **be V-ed**; the passive of **V n n** is **be V-ed n**; and the passive of **V _for_ n** is **be V-ed _for_**:

> One civilian and one soldier **_were killed_**.
> After six months, Capra **_was offered_ a better contract**.
> The tests **_are paid_ for** by the National Health Service.

In any group of examples, there may be both active and passive examples.

2 Questions and reported questions

There are two kinds of question. In a 'yes/no' question, the order of elements in the verb pattern is the same as in an ordinary clause, except that the Subject usually comes between two parts of the verb group. For example, the 'yes/no' question form of the pattern **V n** is shown in the following example:

Did you see that?

In the kind of question that begins with a wh-word, the order of elements is normal if the question relates to the Subject of the verb. The following example shows the pattern **V of n**:

Who thought of it first?

However, if the question relates to the Object or Complement of the verb, a wh-word or a noun group beginning with a wh-word is used as the Object or Complement, and this occurs at the beginning of the clause. The Subject usually comes between two parts of the verb group. For example, the wh-question form of the pattern **V n** is shown in the following example:

What did you say?

This is the wh-question form of the pattern **V n n**:

What did you tell her?

In the case of the verb *be*, with the pattern **V n**, the Subject comes after the verb.

Who is she?

In the case of verbs which are followed by a preposition and a noun group in the basic pattern, the noun group occurs at the beginning of the clause and the preposition remains after the verb. For example, the wh-question form of the pattern **V for n** is shown in the following example:

What are you looking for?

This is the wh-question form of the pattern **V as n**:

What did he train as?

Similarly, adjuncts such as *where* and *how* come first in a question. For example, the wh-question form of the pattern **V prep/adv** is shown in the following example:

Where does she live?

With reported questions, the wh-word comes first but the word order is normal after that - that is, the Subject comes before the whole verb group. For example, the reported question form of the pattern **V n** is shown in the following example:

They asked me who I could trust.

This is the reported question form of the pattern **V for n**:

Perhaps in the back of my mind I knew what I was looking for.

There are eight other circumstances in which the order of the elements in a pattern is changed. We have generally avoided using examples of these in this book, to minimize confusion.

1 Relative clauses

In general, relative clauses begin with a relative pronoun (*who, whom, which, that*) or the determiner *whose*. They occur immediately after the noun group they are qualifying. This does not affect the normal order of the elements in a pattern when the relative pronoun is the Subject of the verb in the relative clause.

The man who shot him was immediately overpowered.

However, when the relative pronoun is the Object or Complement of the verb, the normal order is changed. The relative pronoun comes before the Subject; the order of the other elements is unchanged. The following example shows the pattern **V n**:

Most of the people that I met were academics.

This example shows the pattern **V n n**:

*Inside the ticket hall he dialled the number **that** Mr Furniss **had given** him.*

This example shows the pattern **V n adv**:

*He tapped the file on Baum **which** Fox **had brought** in.*

A similar thing happens with prepositional phrases. In formal English, the whole prepositional phrase is often used to begin the relative clause, but in other contexts just the noun group belonging to the preposition comes first. The following example shows the pattern **V prep/adv**, with the whole prepositional phrase beginning the relative clause:

*The feeling of timelessness was just as strong at the farmhouse **in which** we **stayed**.*

This example shows the pattern **V for n**, with the noun group first in the relative clause and the preposition last:

*We have put together several lists of plants **that** you **may be looking** for.*

Often, no relative pronoun is used as the Object or Complement of the verb in the relative clause. In these cases, part of the pattern is missing, though understood. The following examples show the pattern **V n**:

*The people I **met** at Fairbanks appeared very capable.*

*What would the boy I **was** make of the person he **has become**?*

A similar thing happens with prepositional phrases. The preposition comes after the verb.

The following example shows the pattern **V for n**:

*It sounded exactly like the small town I **was looking** for.*

In the case of verbs with the pattern **V that**, the Subject may be preceded by a relative pronoun which is part of the that-clause. This relative pronoun may be the Subject, Object, or Complement of the verb in the that-clause. As with other relative clauses, the relative pronoun *that* can be omitted when it is the Object or Complement.

*I shall invite both written and oral observations from any person **who** I **think** can help me.*

*His contract finishes at the end of the season but he has an option **which** he **says** he will probably take up.*

*That is the breathing space they **claim** they need to get themselves ready for battle.*

*Far from being the self-assured and mature man I **thought** he was, his diary showed him to be an unhappy man, beset by problems.*

2 '-ing' form or to-infinitive as part of a Complement

If a non-finite verb form is used after an adjective or noun as part of a Complement, that verb 'loses' a noun group from its pattern. In the following example, *ready for printing* is the Complement of the verb *be*. The verb *print* has the pattern **V n** (as in *They printed the book*), but in this example the noun group which the verb relates to occurs as the Subject of the clause.

*The book is ready for **printing**.*

Here are some more examples:

*Strawberries are easy to **propagate**.*

*Gina seemed very likeable and looked easy to **talk** to.*

*The battle will be fun to **watch**.*

3 To-infinitive as qualifier of a noun group

If the to-infinitive form of a verb is used after a noun group, that verb 'loses' a noun group from its pattern. In the following example, *to play* is qualifying the noun group *a rotten trick*. The verb *play* has the pattern **V n** (as in *He played a trick*), but in this example the noun group which the verb relates to occurs before the verb.

*It was **a rotten trick** <u>to play</u>.*

Here are some more examples:

*We were given **a card** <u>to put up</u>.*
*You need **a case** <u>to put</u> your clothes in.*

4 Fronted elements

Normally the first element in a clause is the Subject. However, other elements can be put first in order to emphasize them or focus on them. When this is done, the element that comes first is said to be **fronted**.

The next three examples show a fronted Object or prepositional Object.

This example shows the pattern **V n**:

***This** I <u>could</u> never <u>have anticipated</u>.*

This example shows the pattern **V *of* n**:

*I became known among my friends as the boy who took drugs. **This** I really <u>bragged</u> of.*

This example shows the pattern **V n prep/adv**:

*He put the hat into his holdall. **The gun** he <u>put</u> in the pocket of his raincoat.*

The next three examples show a fronted Complement or Object Complement.

This example shows the pattern **V adj**:

***Terrible** he <u>was</u>. Horrible man.*

This example shows the pattern **V n n**:

***The Butcher**, they <u>called</u> him.*

This example shows the pattern **be V-ed n**:

***Lucky Alexander** he <u>was called</u>.*

The next two examples show a fronted Adjunct. Note that there is usually inversion – that is, the Subject comes after the verb – except when the Subject is a pronoun. These examples show the pattern **V prep/adv**.

*In the middle of all this, **in** <u>walked</u> Maggie.*
*Taking a deep breath, **in** he <u>went</u>, hoping that his beating heart and weak knees were not outwardly visible.*

The next two examples show a fronted wh-clause. This kind of fronting occurs when the speaker is saying that someone does not know something. These examples show the pattern **V wh**.

***Why** I did this I <u>cannot say</u>.*
***How** he got in I <u>don't know</u>.*

5 Cleft structures

If you want to focus on a noun group, you can use a cleft structure instead of using that noun group as the Subject or Object. In a cleft structure, the Subject is *it*, the verb is *be*, and the noun group you are focusing on is the Complement. The noun group is followed by a relative clause giving the rest of the information. For example, instead of saying *Dick suggested it*, you can say *It was Dick who suggested it*.

*He found a telephone and dialled the Kent number. **It was Bird** who <u>answered</u>.*

As with ordinary relative clauses, when the noun group you are focusing on is the Object of the verb, the normal word order is changed. The Subject comes after the relative pronoun if there is one, or after the Object. The following examples show the pattern **V n**.

*If it's **gossip** you <u>want</u>, you've come to the right place.*

*It was you I came to **see**.*

6 Clauses beginning with *what* and *all*

A clause beginning with *what* can be used as the Subject of the verb *be* to focus on new information that comes after the verb. The word *what* can be the Subject or Object of the clause, but always comes first. If *what* is the Subject, the word order is normal. If *what* is the Object, it comes before the Subject. The following examples show the pattern **V n**.

*What **worries** me is that there has been a huge influx of drivers with very little experience.*
*What we **need** is democracy.*

A clause beginning with *all* can be used in a similar way, but *all* is always the Object of the clause.

*All they **want** is a quiet life.*

7 Comparisons

When a comparative noun group is followed by a clause beginning with *than*, there is no noun group after the auxiliary, verb, or preposition in the clause. The following examples show the pattern **V n**:

*They knew more than we **did** about the problems ahead!*
*I have much more money than I **need**.*
*It may be a better job than it **looks**.*

This example shows the pattern **V for n**:

*We got far more than we **had bargained** for.*

When a noun group beginning with *as* is followed by a clause beginning with *as*, there is no noun group after the auxiliary, verb, or preposition in the clause. The following examples show the pattern **V n**.

*Please give as much notice as you **can** before you vacate the premises.*
*Alternatively, fit a Venetian blind which can be angled to let in as little or as much light as you **want**.*

This example shows the pattern **V for n**:

*We have as much support as we **ask** for.*

A similar thing happens when an adjective group or adverb group is followed by a clause beginning with *than* or *as*. There is no adjective or adverb after the verb or auxiliary in the clause. The following examples show the pattern **V adj**:

*He's smarter than I **am**.*
*This is not as simple as it **sounds**.*

This example shows the pattern **V adv**:

*They did better than we **did**.*

These examples show the pattern **V that**. There is no that-clause after the verb.

*Obtaining access to Wu took a little longer than she **had promised**.*
*I'm not as disheartened as people **think**.*

8 Other clauses beginning with *as*

Some of the more frequent verbs which have the pattern **V that** are used in clauses beginning with *as* and ending with the verb. These clauses usually come before or within a main clause. This structure implies that, in your opinion, what was said or thought is true, or turned out to be true.

*As Eamonn McCabe **says**, now it's up to the industry to prove him wrong.*
*He had, as he **predicted**, immediately assumed an non-executive chairmanship.*

Meaning Finder

This Finder will tell you which patterns are used to express particular ideas, and where to look in this book to find these patterns. For each pattern, the relevant page number(s) are given, and, where necessary, the name of the meaning group(s) concerned. In some cases only some of the verbs in a meaning group can be used to express the idea indicated. If only one or two verbs in a meaning group can be used in this way, these verbs are shown in brackets.

Attacking and doing harm
See also **Changing something, Fighting and competing, Physical contact**
V n 19 'KILL'
V pron-refl 63 'HANG'
V *at* n 168 'EAT AWAY', 'SHOOT', 169 'HIT BACK'
V *on* n 220 'POUNCE'
V *through* n 240 'SMASH'
V n adj 284 'BURY ALIVE'
V n prep/adv, V n adv/prep 316 'BEND', 317 'BATTER'
V n *against* n 345 'LEVEL'
V n *in* n 384 'KICK', 385 'BORE'
V n *on* n 405 'IMPOSE', 408 'PAT ON THE BACK'
V n *to* n 430 'BEAT TO DEATH'
V, V n 480 'BREAK', 483 'BLISTER', 484 'CLOG UP'
V prep/adv, V n prep/adv 506 'SMASH'

Beginning, continuing, and ending: events, periods of time
See also **Sequence of events**
V 8 'BEGIN' AND 'STOP', 9 'OCCUR'
V prep/adv, V adv/prep 133 'BEGIN' AND 'END'
V *as* n 161 'BEGIN' AND 'END'
V *in* n 201 'BEGIN' AND 'END'
V n adj 285
V n -ing 289-290
V n *with* n 446 'BEGIN' AND 'END'
V, V n 490 'START' AND 'STOP'
V prep/adv, V n prep/adv 500 'BEGIN' AND 'END'

Behaving in a particular way
V n 16 'ACT', 57
V pron-refl 63 'FLAUNT', 64 'DEMEAN', 'EXERT', 'COMPOSE', 66 'ENJOY', 68 Other structures (*be*)
V *as if* 121 'ACT'
V prep/adv, V adv/prep 132 'BEHAVE'
V *like* n 210
V n prep/adv, V n adv/prep 322 'CONDUCT'
V n *with* n 444 'GREET'
V pron-refl *with* n 445 'BUSY'
V *it* adj/adv 557 'PLAY IT COOL'

Bodily functions and movements
See also **Movement**
V 11 'LAUGH'
V n 44 'OPEN YOUR EYES'
V pron-refl 67 'OTHER MEANINGS' (*relieve*)
V *with* n 267 'TREMBLE'
V, V n 488 'CLENCH' AND 'RELAX'
V prep/adv, V n prep/adv 499 'DROP'
V adj, V n adj 502 'OTHER MEANINGS' (*open*)

Buying something
See **Giving, getting, and paying for things**

Changing
See also **Dividing into parts**
V 5 'CHANGE'

V n 47 'DEVELOP'
V pron-refl 64 'COMPOSE'
V amount 72 'INCREASE'
V prep/adv, V adv/prep 132 'LURCH'
V prep 143 'RISE' AND 'DROP'
V *by* amount 173 'INCREASE' AND 'DECREASE'
V *from* n *to* n 193 'CHANGE'
V *from* amount *to* amount 193
V *in* n 198 'ERUPT', 200 'INCREASE' AND 'DECREASE'
V *into* n 204 'TURN', 206 'CHANGE', 208 'FADE'
V *on* n 221 'BACK-PEDAL'
V *out of* n 233 'CHANGE', 'GROW'
V *over* n 237 'BACK DOWN'
V *to* n 242 'CHANGE', 242 'INCREASE' AND 'DECREASE', 248 'PROGRESS' AND 'SWITCH', 249 'ADAPT', 253 'BLEED TO DEATH'
V, V n 479 'CHANGE', 481 'DISSOLVE' AND 'SOLIDIFY', 482 'EXPAND' AND 'COMPRESS', 483 'IMPROVE' AND 'WORSEN', 484 'BLEACH', 'BLUR'
V prep/adv, V n prep/adv 494 'CHANGE'
V adj, V n adj 502 'OTHER MEANINGS'

Changing something, or changing its state
See also **Attacking and doing harm**
V n 21 'CHANGE', 29 'CHANGE'
V *at* n 168 'EAT AWAY'
V *with* n 264 'DABBLE'
V n n 277-278
V n adj 283 'SQUASH FLAT', 'DRIVE MAD', 'TURN DOWN LOW', 284 'PAINT YELLOW'
V n prep/adv, V n adv/prep 316 'BEND', 323 'BRING'
V n *with* adv 327 'CLICK', 'EMPTY'
V n *by* n 365 'RAISE' AND 'LOWER'
V n *from* amount *to* amount 380
V n *from* n *into* n 380
V n *from* n *to* n 380, 424
V n *into* n 390 'CHANGE', 394 'SEND', 395 'BREATHE'
V n *to* n 422 'IMPART', 423-424, 429 'ALERT' AND 'BLIND', 432 'CONVERT'
V n *with* n 440 'IMBUE', 441 'DECORATE', 442 'FILL', 443 'FLAVOUR'
V, V n 479 'CHANGE', 481 'DISSOLVE' AND 'SOLIDIFY', 482 'EXPAND' AND 'COMPRESS', 483 'IMPROVE' AND 'WORSEN', 484 'BLEACH', 'BLUR'
V prep/adv, V n prep/adv 494 'CHANGE'
V adj, V n adj 502 'OTHER MEANINGS'
V *it* adj to-inf 549 'MAKE'
V *it* adj wh 550

Communication 1: talking, writing, and gesturing
V 10 'SPEAK', 11 'CALL'

V n 54 'SAY', 55 'DESCRIBE'
V pron-refl 65 'EXPLAIN'
V -ing 84 'RECOMMEND'
V to-inf 91 'PROMISE', 92 'CLAIM'
V that 98 'SAY', 99 'ADD', 'SCREAM', 101 'GO'
V wh 106 'ASK'
V wh-to-inf 111 'DESCRIBE', 112 'DECIDE'
V with quote 114 'SAY', 115 'ADD', 'SCREAM',
116 'GASP', 'SNEER',117 'GO'
V so/not 119-121
V prep/adv, V adv/prep 131 'LOOK' AND
'GESTURE'
V prep 143 'SHOOT', 144 'DELIBERATE'
V about n 147 'TALK'
V against n 155 'PREACH'
V around n 157 'SKATE'
V as to wh 163 'INQUIRE', 'ADVISE', 'AGREE'
V at n 166 'GRUMBLE', 167 'REJOICE'
V for n 178 'ASK', 180 'ARGUE'
V from n 190 'OTHER MEANINGS' (dissent)
V in favour of n 202 'SPEAK'
V of n 211 'TALK'
V on n 217 'COMMENT', 218 'ENLARGE', 220
'POUNCE', 221 'INFORM'
V on to n 230 'GET'
V over n 235 'ARGUE'
V to n 245 'ADMIT', 'SWEAR', 'REFER', 246
'AGREE', 248 'TURN'
V to n as n 245 'REFER'
V with n 262 'AGREE' AND 'DISAGREE', 268 'CHIP
IN'
V n n 277-278
V n -ing 287 'REPORT'
V n to-inf 295 'BELIEVE'
V n prep/adv, V n adv/prep 314 'WRITE'
V way prep/adv 331 'TALK', 'MUMBLE', 332
'GOSSIP'
V n as n 350 'NAME' AND 'CONSIDER', 352
'QUOTE'
V n by n 364 'CALL'
V n for n 369 'PRAISE', 'CONDEMN'
V n from n 379 'ABSOLVE'
V n in n 385 'CARVE'
V n on n 404 'BESTOW', 408 'CARVE'
V n with n 447 'CHARGE'
it be V-ed that 526 'REPORT'
it be V-ed wh 528
V it adj to-inf 549 'CALL'
it V prep/adv that 553
pl-n V it P, V it P with n 556 'BATTLE IT OUT'

Communication 2: mentioning the hearer
See also **Making someone do something or telling someone to do something, Stopping or preventing something happening**
V n 56 'CALL'
V into n that 104
V on/upon n that 104
V to n that 105
V of n wh 110
V on/upon n wh 110
V to n wh 110
V after n with quote 117
V at n with quote 118
V of n with quote 118
V to n with quote 118
V adv 138 'PHONE'

V at n 166 'SHOUT', 'WINK'
V in n 199 'OTHER MEANINGS' (confide)
V to n 244 'TALK', 246 'CONDESCEND', 'BECKON'
V to n for n 255
V with n 262 'REMONSTRATE'
V n n 275 'TELL' AND 'SEND'
V n that 299-300
V n wh 300-301
V n wh-to-inf 301-302
V n with quote 302-305
V n about n 339 'TELL', 340 'TACKLE'
V n amount about n 342
V n against n 345 'WARN'
V n as n 350 'NAME' AND 'CONSIDER'
V n as to wh 355 'ADVISE'
V n at n 359 'SHOUT'
V n for n 369 'ASK', 'PRAISE', 'CONDEMN'
V n of n 400 'INFORM'
V n on n 405 'QUESTION', 410 'OTHER MEANINGS'
(urge, let in)
V n to n 419 'PROMISE', 420 'COMMUNICATE',
'TRANSMIT', 429 'BETRAY', 'INVITE'
V n with n 441 'AGREE', 'SHARE', 444 'BORE', 447
'CHARGE', 'OTHER MEANINGS' (blackmail,
threaten)
pl-n V, V with n 457 'TALK', 459 'GET ON'
pl-n V n, V n with n 464 'DISCUSS', 'AGREE' AND
'NEGOTIATE', 464 'HOLD', 465 'EXCHANGE'
V with n that 471
V with n about n 471
V with n on n 471
V with n over n 472
V it to n that 544

Competing See **Fighting and competing**
Damaging something
See **Attacking and doing harm**
Decisions See **Plans and decisions**
Difference: making someone or something different
See **Changing something or changing its state**
Difference: being different
See **Sameness and difference**
Directing something at or towards someone or something
V prep 143 'SHOOT'
V at n 168 'SHOOT'
V n prep/adv, V n adv/prep 315 'BROADCAST'
V n at n 359 'POINT'
V n on n 407 'FOCUS', 'PULL A GUN'
V n on to n 411 'FOCUS'
V n to n 431 'DRAW ATTENTION'
V n towards/toward n 434 'DIRECT'
Dividing into parts
V 5 'CHANGE' (divide)
V n 21 'CHANGE'
V pl-n 61 'COMBINE' AND 'SEPARATE'
V n between pl-n 361 'DIVIDE'
V n from n 377 'SEPARATE'
V n in n 381-382
V n into n 391 'BREAK'
pl-n V, V with n, V pl-n, V n with n 459 'TEAM
UP' AND 'BREAK UP'
V, V n 485 'DIVIDE'
V prep/adv, V n prep/adv 495 'DIVIDE'
Drinking
See **Eating, drinking, and smoking**

Duration: how long something lasts
V n 45 'TAKE THREE DAYS'
V amount 71 'OTHER MEANINGS' (*allow*), 73 'OTHER MEANINGS' (*last*)
V prep/adv, V adv/prep 134 'LAST'
V *for* n 183 'LAST'
V *from* n *to* n 193 'LAST'
V *to* n 253 'STRETCH'
V n amount 275 'COST' AND 'SAVE'
V n n to-inf 79
it V n -ing 536 (*take*)
it V n/amount before/since 537

Eating, drinking, and smoking
V 12-13 'OTHER MEANINGS'
V n 20 'EAT'
V *at* n 168 'CHEW'
V *from* n 188 'DRINK'
V *into* n 205 'BITE'
V *on* n 224 'FEED'
V *way* prep/adv 336 'EAT'
V n *on* n 410 'OTHER MEANINGS' (*feed, gorge*)

Ending an event or period of time
See Beginning, continuing, and ending

Exchanging things
V n 23 'BRING' (*change*)
V pl-n 61 'ALTERNATE'
V n *for* n 367 'EXCHANGE'
V n *with* n 446 'REPLACE'
V prep/adv, V n prep/adv 500 'OTHER MEANINGS' (*substitute*)

Failure See Success and failure
Feelings See Thinking and feeling

Fighting and competing
See also Attacking and doing harm
V 4 'COMPETE'
V n 33 'BEAT', 36 'WIN', 41 'DO' AND 'TAKE'
V amount 73 'WIN'
V to-inf 94 'VIE'
V ord 139
V *against* n 154 'COMPETE'
V *by* amount 173 'WIN' AND 'LOSE'
V *for* n 178 'COMPETE'
V *for* n *with* n 179 'COMPETE'
V *with* n *for* n 179 'COMPETE'
V n amount 278-279
pl-n V, V *with* n 457 'FIGHT'
pl-n V n, V n *with* n 465 'FIGHT'
pl-n V, V n 468 'FIGHT'
V *with* n *for* n, V *for* n *with* n 471
pl-n V *it* P, V *it* P *with* n 556 'BATTLE IT OUT'

Financial transactions
See Giving, getting, and paying for things

Giving, getting, and paying for things
V n 22 'FEED', 24 'BUY'
V amount 70 'PAY', 71 'GAIN' AND 'LOSE'
V to-inf 95 'PAY' AND 'CHARGE'
V *for* n 182 'PAY'
V *from* n 188 'BORROW'
V *from* n *to* n 193 'OTHER MEANINGS'
V *to* n 248 'COME', 250 'LEND'
V *with* n 265 'ABSCOND'
V n n 273 'GIVE'
V n amount 275 'COST' AND 'SAVE'
V n *at* amount 360 'BUY'
V n *for* n 366 'BUY', 367 'EXCHANGE', 371 'PAY'
V n *from* n 375 'DEMAND' AND 'GET'
V n *of* n 399 'ROB' AND 'FREE'

V n *off* n 402 'CADGE'
V n *on* n 404 'BESTOW', 409 'SPEND'
V n *out of* n 413 'CHEAT', 'SCREW'
V n *to* n 418 'GIVE', 421 'SELL'
V n *towards/toward* n 435 'CONTRIBUTE'
V n *with* n 440 'PROVIDE'

Helping someone or doing something for someone
V n 22 'PROTECT', 32 'HELP'
V *for* n 179 'WORK', 'DEPUTIZE'
V *in* n 198 'PARTICIPATE'
V *in favour of* n 203 'DISCRIMINATE'
V *to* n 249 'ATTEND'
V *with* n 260 'HELP', 265 'ASSIST'
V n n 274 'BRING', 275 'COST' AND 'SAVE'
V n to-inf 294 'HELP'
V n -ed 305 'HAVE' AND 'GET'
V n *for* n 366 'BUY'
V n *in* n 385 'JOIN'
V n *out of* n 415 'BAIL'
V n *with* n 446 'HELP'
V prep/adv, V n 506 'BENEFIT'
it V n to-inf 520

Hurting someone
See Attacking and doing harm

Joining: two things joining, joining one thing to another
V pl-n 61 'COMBINE' AND 'SEPARATE'
V *on to* n 230 'HOLD'
V *to* n 247 'CLING', 'AFFILIATE'
V n prep/adv, V n adv/prep 312 'FASTEN'
V pl-n *with* *together* 329 'TIE', 'GATHER'
V n *on to* n 411 'STICK'
V n *to* n 426 'ATTACH'
V n *with* n 437 'COMBINE'
pl-n V, V *with* n 460 'INTERSECT'
pl-n V, V *with* n, V pl-n, V n *with* n 512 'MERGE', 512 'INTERTWINE'

Learning and finding out
V n 50 'HEAR'
V to-inf 93 'OTHER MEANINGS' (*learn*)
V *that* 100 'DISCOVER'
V *wh* 107 'DISCOVER'
V *wh*-to-inf 111 'DISCOVER'
V *about* n 148 'LEARN'
V *into* n 205 'INQUIRE'
V *of* n 212 'KNOW'
V *on* n 219 'READ UP'
V *to* n 250 'COTTON ON'
V n *about* n 340 'KNOW'
it be V-ed *that* 527 'THINK' AND 'DISCOVER'
it be V-ed *wh* 528

Liking, disliking, and wanting
See also Opinions
V n 50 'HEAR'
V -ing 83 'LIKE' AND 'DISLIKE', 84 'DREAD' AND 'LOOK FORWARD TO'
V to-inf 92 'HOPE', 'LIKE'
V *that* 99 'THINK'
V adj/adv *about* n 150
V *after* n 152 'HANKER'
V *at* n 167 'REJOICE', 167 'BALK' AND 'JUMP'
V *for* n 180 'YEARN', 181 'CARE'
V *for* n to-inf 185 'LONG'
V *in* n 197 'DELIGHT'
V *of* n 213 'OTHER MEANINGS' (*tire, weary*)
V *towards/toward* n 257 'STRIVE'

V n adj 280 'LIKE'
V n to-inf 290-291
V n -ed 307 'LIKE'
V n prep/adv, V n adv/prep 322 'WANT'
V n *about* n 340 'FEEL'
V n *to* n 427 'PREFER' AND 'SUBJUGATE'
V *it* that 543 'LOVE' AND 'HATE'
V *it* when/if 544
V *it* prep/adv 557 'LOVE' AND 'HATE'

Logical relations

V n 48 'SHOW', 49 'ALLOW', 'IDENTIFY'
V -ing 85 'INVOLVE'
V that 101 'SHOW', 'ARRANGE', 'OTHER MEANINGS' (*presume, presuppose*)
V wh 108 'SHOW', 'DETERMINE'
V *from* n 187 'RESULT'
V *in* n 196, 199 'OTHER MEANINGS' (*result*)
V *of* n 213 'OTHER MEANINGS' (*permit*)
V *on* n 222 'DEPEND'
V *out of* n 233 'ARISE'
V *to* n 245 'POINT', 251 'RELATE'
V n -ing 287 'ENTAIL'
V n -ed 307 'GET 1'
V amount *about* n 341 'REVEAL'
V n *on* n 408 'BASE'
it V that 519 'EMERGE'

Making someone do something or telling someone to do something

See also Communication 2, Stopping or preventing something happening
V n 33 'CALL OUT'
V to-inf 92 'DEMAND'
V *at* n to-inf 171
V *for* n to-inf 185 'ASK'
V *on/upon* n to-inf 229 'CALL'
V *with* n to-inf 269
V n -ing 289 'BRING'
V n to-inf 292 'TELL', 293 'NAG' AND 'COAX', 'CAUSE', 295 'INSPIRE'
V n inf 298 'LET'
V n prep/adv, V n adv/prep 319 'INVITE'
V n *against* n 345 'WARN'
V n *in* n 385 'INVOLVE'
V n *into* n 392 'FORCE', 393 'TRICK', 'CHARM', 'SPUR', 394 'OTHER VERBS'
V n *into* -ing 397 'FORCE', 'TRICK', 398 'CHARM', 'SPUR', 'OTHER MEANINGS'
V n *out of* n 414 'FORCE', 'TALK'
V n *to* n 427 'BANISH', 430 'INCITE'
V n *towards/toward* n 434 'PUSH'
V, V n 488 'ASSEMBLE' AND 'DISBAND', 489 'OVERWORK'

Making something

V n 28 'BUILD', 39 'FORM'
V n with *together* 330 'COBBLE'
V n *for* n 366 'BUY'
V n *from* n 379 'MAKE'
V n *out of* n 415 'MAKE'
V, V n 490 'DEVELOP'

Movement: change of place, position or posture

See also Bodily functions and movements
V 2 'MOVE', 3 'TURN', 'LEAVE'
V n 27 'FOLLOW'
V pron-refl 66 'STRETCH OUT', 67 'ABSENT'
V amount 72 'WALK'
V to-inf 94 'FLOCK'

V prep/adv, V adv/prep 126 'GO', 'WANDER', 127 'WALK', 128 'DRIVE', 129 'FLOW', 'FLOCK', 'ROAR', 130 'TURN'
V adv prep 135
V prep prep 135
V adv 137 'SWING'
pl-n V *together* 140 'CLUSTER'
V prep 143 'RECEDE'
V *across* n 150
V *around* n 158 'CIRCLE', 'CROWD', 'MOVE'
V *for* n 183 'HEAD'
V *from* n 191-192
V *into* n 207 'INFILTRATE', 208 'DIP'
V *on* n 227 'CONVERGE'
V *out of* n 234
V *through* n 241 'FILTER'
V *to* n 252 'MOVE'
V *down* n 270
V *past* n 271
V n prep/adv, V n adv/prep 320 'FOLLOW'
V *way* prep/adv 322 'MAKE', 333 'FIGHT', 'THREAD', 334 'CHUG', 'CRAWL', 'OOZE'
V n *for* n 370 'LEAVE'
V, V n 486 'DETACH', 487 'REVERSE', 'SPURT OUT', 488 'ASSEMBLE' AND 'DISBAND', 489 'OVERWORK', 'LEAK'
V prep/adv, V n prep/adv 497 'DETACH', 498 'SAIL', 499 'GALLOP', 'THUMP'
V adj, V n adj 502 'SLAM SHUT', 'WORK FREE'
V prep/adv, V n, V n prep/adv 504
V prep/adv, V n 506 'TOPPLE', 'BELCH'
V *it* 554 'LEG IT'
V *it* prep/adv 557 'HOT-FOOT IT'

Moving something or controlling a vehicle

V n 23 'BRING', 26 'OPERATE', 'COVER'
V n adj 282 'PULL OPEN'
V n prep/adv, V n adv/prep 312 'FASTEN', 314 'THROW', 'MOVE', 316 'DRIVE', 'KICK', 318 'CARRY', 319 'SWEEP'
V n adv prep 325
V n prep prep 325
V n with adv 327 'SLIP'
V n *at* n 359 'THROW'
V n *from* n 376 'REMOVE', 'TRANSFER'
V n *in* n 384 'DIP'
V n *into* n 394 'PUT'
V n *off* n 402 'PEEL', 'REFLECT'
V n *on* n 406 'PLACE', 'BANG'
V n *on to* n 411 'SCAN'
V n *out of* n 414 'PLUCK', 'FORCE'
V n *over* n 416-417
V n *to* n 427 'BANISH'
V n *with* n 442 'COVER', 'FILL', 443 'SHOWER', 444 'POPULATE' AND 'STOCK'
V, V n 486 'DETACH', 487 'REVERSE', 488 'ASSEMBLE' AND 'DISBAND', 489 'OVERWORK', 'LEAK'
V prep/adv, V n prep/adv 497 'DETACH', 498 'SAIL', 499 'GALLOP', 'THUMP'
V adj, V n adj 502 'SLAM SHUT', 'WORK FREE'
V prep/adv, V n, V n prep/adv 504
V prep/adv, V n 506 'TOPPLE'

Not doing something or getting out of a situation

V 3 'LEAVE', 5 'BACK OUT'
V -ing 82 'AVOID'

'CONTROL', 38 'COUNT AGAINST', 45 'FACE', 46 'TOP', 47 'DEVELOP', 48 'INCLUDE', 53 'GIVE AN IMPRESSION'
V amount 69 'EQUAL', 'MEASURE', 70 'HOLD', 'DO'
V amount adj/adv 73
V adj 74-80
V to-inf 88 'APPEAR'
V as if 121 'LOOK'
V prep/adv, V adv/prep 130 'LIVE', 131 'FACE', 133 'COME OVER'
V adv 137 'CLEAN', 'BRUISE', 'SCARE'
V as n 160 'FUNCTION', 161 'RANK', 'MASQUE-RADE'
V at n 164 'STAND', 'PEAK'
V for n 176-177, 183 'LAST'
V in n 198 'ABOUND'
V like n 209-210
V of n 212 'REEK'
V on n 219 'IMPINGE'
V on to n 230 'BACK'
V over n 238
V to n 253 'STRETCH'
V with n 261 'BRIM', 'GLISTEN', 262 'ECHO', 'FIT IN', 266 'RANKLE'
V among pl-n 270
V adj among pl-n 270
V way prep/adv 335 'WIND'
V prep/adv, V n prep/adv 496 'EQUATE', 500 'OTHER MEANINGS'
V as adj, V n as adj 503
V ord prep, V n ord prep 504
V adv, V n 508 'CLEAN', 'SCARE', 509 'FISH'
pl-n V, V with n, V pl-n, V n with n 513 'DOVE-TAIL'
it V as if/as though/like 521
it V n to-inf 532 'BE'
it V n wh 534 'BE'
it V n when/if 535 'BE'
it V n -ing 536
it V adj that 539
it V adj to-inf 539
it V adj when/if 540
it V adj -ing 541
it V adj for n to-inf 541
it V adj 552
it V adj prep/adv 552

Responding
V 12 'OTHER MEANINGS'
V n 37 'ANSWER'
V at n 169 'HIT BACK'
V by -ing 175 'RECIPROCATE'
V to n 249 'REACT'
V with n 268 'RESPOND'
V n for n 370 'REWARD' AND 'PUNISH'
pl-n V n, V n with n 465 'EXCHANGE'

Sameness and difference
See also **Opinions, Qualities**
V pl-n 61 'COMPARE'
V between pl-n 172 'DIFFERENTIATE'
V from n 189 'DIFFER'
V to n 251 'CORRESPOND'
V pl-n with together 329 'GATHER'
V n to n 421 'LINK'
V n with n 437 'COMPARE'
pl-n V, V with n 460 'TALLY' AND 'CLASH', 'DIFFER'

V prep/adv, V n prep/adv 495 'COUNT'

Seeing and hearing
See also **Directing something at or towards someone or something**
V 10 'THINK' AND 'WATCH'
V n 50 'HEAR', 52 'INTEREST', 53 'EYES FOLLOW'
V that 100 'DISCOVER'
V wh 107 'DISCOVER'
V wh-to-inf 111 'DISCOVER'
V prep/adv, V adv/prep 131 'LOOK' AND 'GESTURE'
V on n 221 'SPY', 225 'FOCUS'
V over n 236 'PORE'
V to n 250 'LISTEN'
V n -ing 288 'SEE'
V n to-inf 296 'OBSERVE'
V n inf 298 'SEE'
V n -ed 308
V amount of n 401 'OTHER MEANINGS'
it be V-ed that 527 'THINK' AND 'DISCOVER'

Sequence of events: something happens first or last in a sequence
See also **Beginning, continuing, and ending**
V -ing 86-87
V prep/adv n 135
V by -ing 175 'START' AND 'FINISH'
V in n 201 'BEGIN' AND 'END'
V with n 268 'BEGIN' AND 'END'
V n -ing 289-290
V n as n 354 'BEGIN' AND 'END'
V n by n 364 'BEGIN' AND 'END'

Shape See **Qualities**

Showing something
V n 28 'RECORD'
V n n 273 'GIVE'
V n wh 300-301
V n wh-to-inf 301-302
V n as n 351 'STAMP'
V n to n 421 'SHOW'
it be V-ed wh 528

Size See **Qualities**

Speaking See **Communication 1**

Starting, stopping, or continuing to do something or to be in a particular state
V 4 'CARRY ON', 8 'START' AND 'BREAK', 'BEGIN' AND 'STOP'
V n 30 'END', 40 'START' AND 'STOP'
V -ing 81 'START' AND 'STOP'
V to-inf 88 'BEGIN'
V prep/adv, V adv/prep 132 'LURCH'
V as n 161 'BEGIN' AND 'END'
V for n 182 'STOP'
V in n 195 'PERSIST'
V into n 206 'ENTER'
V on n 216, 226 'START'
V out of n 233 'FALL'
V to n 250 'KNUCKLE DOWN'
V with n 259 'PROCEED', 264 'CONTINUE', 265 'BREAK'
V n in n 385 'JOIN'
V pron-refl to -ing 425 'DEVOTE' (address)
pl-n V, V with n 459 'TEAM UP' AND 'BREAK UP'
V it 554 'CUT IT OUT'

Stopping doing something
See **Starting, stopping, or continuing to do something**

Stopping or preventing something happening

See also **Making someone do something or telling someone to do something**

V n 40 'START' AND 'STOP'
V *against* n 154 'CAMPAIGN'
V *on* n 220 'POUNCE', 221 'BACK-PEDAL'
V n -ing 287 'STOP'
V n *from* -ing 377 'STOP', 378 'DEFLECT'
V n *out of* n 414 'TALK'
V n *to* n 431 'POSTPONE'

Success and failure

V 7 'SUCCEED' AND 'FAIL'
V n 31 'BEAT AN ILLNESS', 36 'BREAK A RECORD', 'WIN'
V pron-refl 65 'EXCEL'
V amount 73 'WIN'
V to-inf 89 'MANAGE'
V prep/adv, V adv/prep 133 'SHAPE UP'
V adv 136 'DO WELL'
V ord 139
V *by* amount 173 'WIN' AND 'LOSE'
V *in* n 195 'OTHER MEANINGS', 198 'SUCCEED'
V *on* n 228 'OTHER MEANINGS'
V *out of* n adv/prep 234
V *through* n 239 'LIVE'
V *with* n 263 'COPE'
V n amount 278-279
V n -ed 307 'GET 2'
V n prep/adv, V n adv/prep 323 'HANDLE'
V *way* prep/adv 331 'TALK', 335 'BORROW', 'CHEAT'
V *it* 555 'BLOW IT' AND 'MAKE IT'
V *it* adj/adv 557 'STRIKE IT RICH'

Talking See Communication

Teaching someone or preparing someone for something

V n 55 'DESCRIBE'
V n n 275 'TELL' AND 'SEND'
V n to-inf 294 'HELP', 'TEACH'
V n wh 300-301
V n wh-to-inf 301-302
V n *about* n 339 'TELL'
V n *for* n 371 'PREPARE'
V n *in* n 386 'TRAIN'
V prep/adv, V n prep/adv 500 'OTHER MEANINGS' (*train*)
V to-inf, V n to-inf 503

Telling someone to do something

See **Making someone do something**

Thinking and feeling

See also **Liking, disliking, and wanting, Opinions**

V 10 'THINK' AND 'WATCH'
V n 50 'HEAR', 52 'INTEREST', 53 'GIVE AN IMPRESSION'
V -ing 84 'CONSIDER', 84 'REMEMBER'
V to-inf 91 'PROMISE', 92 'HOPE'
V that 99 'THINK', 100 'DISCOVER'
V *the fact* that 104
V wh 107 'THINK', 'DISCOVER'
V wh-to-inf 112 'DECIDE', 'REMEMBER'
V with quote 117 'THINK'
V *so/not* 119-121

V prep/adv, V adv/prep 131 'LOOK' AND 'GESTURE' (*wander*)
V adv 137 'SCARE'
V prep 144 'DELIBERATE'
V *about* n 148 'THINK'
V *at* n 167 'REJOICE'
V *for* n 181 'CARE'
V *in* n 197 'BELIEVE', 200 'RISE'
V *of* n 212 'THINK', 213 'OTHER MEANINGS'
V *on* n 218 'REFLECT'
V *over* n 236 'GRIEVE'
V *through* n 241 'FLASH'
V *to* n 248 'COME'
V *towards/toward* n 257 'COOL'
V *with* n 262 'AGREE' AND 'DISAGREE', 263 'SYMPATHIZE'
V n n 276 'ENVY'
V n -ing 286 'LIKE'
V n to-inf 296 'EXPECT'
V n with adv 328 'KNOW'
V *way* prep/adv 337 'REASON'
V n *at* amount 357-358
V pron-refl *in* n 383 'IMMERSE YOURSELF'
V n *towards/toward* n 435 'OTHER MEANINGS'
V, V n 485 'CALM DOWN', 486 'WEAKEN' AND 'STRENGTHEN'
V prep/adv, V n prep/adv 496 'AWAKEN'
V prep/adv, V n 506 'OBSESS'
V adv, V n 508 'SCARE'
it V that 520 'HURT'
it V *to* n that 522 'OCCUR', 523 'OTHER MEANINGS'
it V *to* n to-inf 523
it V *to* n wh 523
it be V-ed that 527 'THINK' AND 'DISCOVER'
it be V-ed wh 528
it V n that 530 'ANNOY' AND 'PLEASE', 531 'STRIKE'
it V n to-inf 532 'PAIN' AND 'PLEASE'
it V n wh 534 'AMAZE' AND 'SADDEN', 'STRIKE'
it V n when/if 535 'AMUSE' AND 'IRRITATE'
it V n -ing 536
it V n adj that 538
it V n adj to-inf 538

Time: length of time

See **Duration**

Touching See Physical contact

Trying

V -ing 82 'TRY'
V to-inf 89 'TRY'
V *towards/toward* n 257 'STRIVE'

Vehicles

See **Moving something or controlling a vehicle**

Wanting something

See **Liking, disliking, and wanting**

Work

V prep 144 'WORK'
V *at* n 169 'WORK'
V *on* n 223 'WORK'
V *over* n 237 'OTHER MEANINGS'
V *with* n 263 'ASSOCIATE'
pl-n V, V *with* n 459 'COLLABORATE'

Writing See Communication

Structure Finder

There are 22 structures:

1 Verb
The meeting had ended.
2 Verbs in phase
The number of victims continues to rise.
3 Verb with Complement
I was hungry.
4 Verb with prepositional Complement
His smile turned into a grin.
5 Verb with Object
The thieves broke a window.
6 Verb with prepositional Object
They swore at him.
7 Verb with Adjunct
The train emerged from the tunnel.
8 Verb with Clause
I said that I would do it.
9 Verb with Complement and Adjunct
It was nice there.
10 Verb with Complement and Clause
It's no fun working all weekend.
11 Verb with prepositional Complement and Clause
It is to our credit that people are now healthier.
12 Verb with Object and Complement
The dollar finished the day lower.

13 Verb with Object and prepositional Complement
That strikes me as right.
14 Verb with Object and Object Complement
They appointed him chairman.
15 Verb with Object and prepositional Object Complement
He changed his name to Adam.
16 Verb with two Objects
He gave her a present.
17 Verb with Object and prepositional Object
She bought a present for him.
18 Verb with Object and Adjunct
Spoon the sugar over the fruit.
19 Verb with Object and Clause
He showed me where I should go.
20 Verb with prepositional Object and Clause
It seems to me that I had done all I could.
21 Verb with Adjunct and Clause
It was up to me to decide what to do.
22 Co-ordinated verbs
Go and find him.

1 Verb
V 1, 478, 514
pl-n V 456, 467, 511, 515
it V 551

2 Verbs in phase
V -ing 81
V to-inf 87, 503
V inf 96
V *and* v 122
V *about* n 146
V *from* n 186
V *in* n 194
V *on* n 216
V *out of* n 231
V *with* n 259

3 Verb with Complement
V n 14
V pron-refl 68
V amount 68
V adj 74, 501, 509
it V adj 552
it V n 552

4 Verb with prep. Complement
V *as* adj 159
V *as* n 160
V *at* n 164
V *for* n 176
V *in* n 196
V *into* n 203
V *like* n 209
V *of* n 213
V *to* n 242
V prep 492, 505

5 Verb with Object
V n 16, 467, 479, 504, 505, 508, 509
pl-n V n 462
V pl-n 60, 511, 516
V pron-refl 63
V amount 69
V -ing 83
V to-inf 91
V wh-to-inf 110
V *so/not* 120
V n adj 280
V n -ing 286
V n to-inf 290
V n -ed 305
it V n 552
V *it* 554
pl-n V *it* P 556

6 Verb with prep. Object
V prep 142
V *about* n 146
V *after* n 151
V *against* n 153
V *around/round* n 156
V *as to* wh 162
V *at* n 165
V *between* pl-n 171
V *for* n 177
V *from* n 187
V *in* n 196
V *in favour of* n 202
V *into* n 205
V *like* n 210
V *of* n 211
V *off* n 214

V *on* n 216
V *on to* n, V *onto* n 230
V *out of* n 232
V *over* n 235
V *through* n 239
V *to* n 243
V *towards/toward* n 256
V *under* n 258
V *with* n 260, 456, 511
V prep/adv 493, 505
it V *to* n 553
V prep *it* 559

7 Verb with Adjunct
V n 57
V amount 71
V -ing 86
V to-inf 93, 503
V prep/adv, V adv/prep 125, 494, 504, 505
V adv 136, 508 pl-n
V *together* 140
V prep 142
V *about* n 149
V *across* n 151
V *around/round* n 157
V *at* n 170
V *by* amount 173
V *by* -ing 175
V *from* n 191
V *in* n 199
V *into* n 207
V *like* n 210
V *off* n 215
V *on* n 227
V *out of* n 234

623

V *over* n 238
V *through* n 240
V *to* n 252
V *with* n 267

8 Verb with Clause
V that 97
V wh 105
V with quote 113
V *as if*, V *as though* 121
it V that 519
it V to-inf 520
it V wh 521
it V when/if 521
it V *as if/as though/like* 521

9 Verb with Complement and Adjunct
it V adj prep/adv 552

10 Verb with Complement and Clause
it V n that 529
it V n to-inf 531
it V n wh 533
it V n when/if 535
it V n -ing 536
it V n/amount before/since 537
it V n *for* n to-inf 537
it V adj that 539
it V adj to-inf 539
it V adj wh 540
it V adj when/if 540
it V adj -ing 541
it V adj *of* n to-inf 541
it V adj *for* n to-inf 541

11 Verb with prep. Complement and Clause
it V prep that 524
it V prep to-inf 525

12 Verb with Object and Complement
V n n 279
V n adj 285

13 Verb with Object and prep. Complement
V n *as* adj 348
V n *as* n 353

14 Verb with Object and Object Complement
V n n 277
V n adj 281, 502
V n -ed 308
V *it* n 558
V *it* -ed 558

15 Verb with Object and prep. Object Complement
V n *as* adj 346, 503
V n *as* n 349
V n *at* n 357
V n *for* n 373
V n *in* n 381
V n *into* n 389
V n *to* n 423
V n prep 493

16 Verb with two Objects
V n n 272
V n -ing 288
V n to-inf 291, 503
V n inf 297
V n wh-to-inf 302
V n -ed 308
V *it* inf 558

17 Verb with Object and prep. Object
V n *against* n 342
V n *at* n 357
V n *for* n 366
V n *to* n 417, 516
V n *with* n 436, 511, 516
V n prep 493
V *it over* n 558
V *it to* n 559

18 Verb with Object and Adjunct
V n n 278
V n -ing 289
V n prep/adv, V n adv/prep 310, 494, 504
V n with adv 326
V pl-n with *together* 328
V *way* prep/adv 331
V n *about* n 338
V n *against* n 343
V n *as to* wh 355

V n *at* n 358
V n *between/among* pl-n 361
V n *by* n 365
V n *for* n 368
V n *from* n 374
V n *in* n 382
V n *into* n 391
V n *into* -ing 396
V n *of* n 399
V n *off* n 401
V n *on* n 403
V n *onto* n, V n *on to* n 411
V n *out of* n 412
V n *over* n 416
V n *to* n 424
V n *towards/toward* n 434
V n *with* n 439, 515
V *it* P *with* n 556
V *it* prep/adv 556
V *it* adj/adv 557

19 Verb with Object and Clause
V n that 299
V n wh 301
V n with quote 303
it V n that 530
it V n to-inf 532
it V n wh 534
it V n when/if 535
it V n -ing 536
it V n/amount before/since 537
it V n *for* n to-inf 537
V *it* that 543
V *it* when/if 544

20 Verb with prep. Object and Clause
it V *to* n that 522
it V *to* n to-inf 523
it V *to* n wh 523
it V *to* n as if/as though/like 524

21 Verb with Adjunct and Clause
it V prep that 524
it V prep to-inf 525
it V prep/adv that 553

22 Co-ordinated verbs
V *and* v 123

Pattern Finder

Verb patterns

AUX 569
AUX *been* -ing 568
AUX -ed 568
AUX inf 573
AUX -ing 566
AUX n -ed 570
AUX neg inf 567
AUX n inf 567
AUX to-inf 566
be V-ed 14-57, 68-73, 461-469
be V-ed *about* 145-150
be V-ed *about* n -ing 340, 341
be V-ed *about* n/-ing/wh 338-341
be V-ed adj 280-285, 501-503
be V-ed adv 310-326
be V-ed adv prep 325
be V-ed *after* 151-153
be V-ed *after* n 448
be V-ed *against* 153-156
be V-ed *against* n/-ing 342-346
be V-ed *among* pl-n 361-362
be V-ed amount 274-279
be V-ed amount *about* n/-ing/wh 342
be V-ed amount *of* 401
be V-ed *around/round* n 448
be V-ed *as* adj 346-348, 503
be V-ed *as* n/-ing 348-355
be V-ed *as* quote 304
be V-ed *as to* wh/n 355-356
be V-ed *at* 163-170
be V-ed *at* amount 357-358, 360
be V-ed *at* n 356-360
be V-ed *before* n 448
be V-ed *between* pl-n/-ing 361-362
be V-ed *by* amount 365
be V-ed *by/between* n 461-466
be V-ed *by* n 58
be V-ed *by* n/-ing 363-365
be V-ed colour 284
be V-ed -ed 305-309
be V-ed *for* 176-184
be V-ed *for* n/-ing 366-373
be V-ed *from* 186-192
be V-ed *from* amount *to* amount 380
be V-ed *from* n/-ing 374-379
be V-ed *from* n *into* n 376, 380, 390
be V-ed *from* n *to* n 376, 380, 424, 428
be V-ed *in* 194-201
be V-ed *in* fraction 381
be V-ed *in front of* n 449
be V-ed -ing 286-290
be V-ed *in* n/-ing 381-388
be V-ed *in* num 381
be V-ed *into* 203-209
be V-ed *into* -ing 396-399
be V-ed *into* n 389-396
be V-ed n 272-279
be V-ed n that 279
be V-ed num 280
be V-ed *of* 211-213
be V-ed *of as* n/-ing/adj 213

be V-ed *off* n 401-403
be V-ed *of* n 15
be V-ed *of* n/-ing 399-401
be V-ed *on* -ing 409
be V-ed *on* n/-ing/wh 403-410
be V-ed *on to* n 410-412
be V-ed *onto* n 410-412
be V-ed *on/upon* 215-228
be V-ed *on/upon as* n/-ing/adj 228
be V-ed *on/upon for* 222
be V-ed *on/upon* to-inf 229
be V-ed ord 326
be V-ed ord *in* n 387
be V-ed *out of* n/-ing 412-416
be V-ed *over* 234-238
be V-ed *over* n 416-417
be V-ed prep 125-135, 141-145
be V-ed prep/adv 310-326, 492-501, 504-505
be V-ed prep prep 325
be V-ed quote 304
be V-ed that 299-300
be V-ed *through* 239-241
be V-ed *through* n 449
be V-ed *to* 241-254
be V-ed *to* amount 426
be V-ed *together* 328-330
be V-ed to-inf 290-297
be V-ed *to* n/-ing 417-433
be V-ed *towards/toward* n/-ing 434-435
be V-ed *to/with* n 515-516
be V-ed *until* n 431
be V-ed wh 300-301
be V-ed wh-to-inf 301-302
be V-ed *with* 259-269, 510-514
be V-ed *with* n 461-466, 510-515
be V-ed *with* n/-ing 435-448
be V-ed *with* quote 302-304
cl AUX n 569
cl MODAL n 573
get V-ed 58-59
get V-ed *from* n 459
get V-ed *to* n 458
it be V-ed adj that 548
it be V-ed adj to-inf 549
it be V-ed adj wh 550
it be V-ed adj when/if 550
it be V-ed *as* n/adj that 545
it be V-ed *as* n/adj to-inf 546
it be V-ed *into* n that 545
it be V-ed n that 547
it be V-ed n to-inf 547
it be V-ed n when/if 548
it be V-ed that 526, 543
it be V-ed to-inf 528
it be V-ed *to* n that 545
it be V-ed *to* n to-inf 545
it be V-ed wh 528
it be V-ed when/if 544
it V 551
it V adj 552
it V adj *for* n to-inf 541

625

it V adj -ing 541
it V adj *of* n to-inf 541
it V adj prep/adv 552
it V adj that 539
it V adj to-inf 539
it V adj wh 540
it V adj when/if 540
it V amount *for* n that 538
it V amount *for* n to-inf 537
it V amount to-inf 533
it V amount *to* n to-inf 533
it V amount wh 536
it V as if 521
it V as though 521
it V like 521
it V n 552
it V n adj that 538
it V n adj to-inf 538
it V n/amount before/since 537
it V n amount to-inf 538
it V n *for* n to-inf 537
it V n -ing 536
it V n n to-inf 537
it V n that 529
it V n to-inf 531
it V n wh 533
it V n when/if 535
it V prep/adv that 553
it V prep/adv with quote 553
it V prep that 524
it V prep to-inf 525
it V that 522
it V to-inf 520
it V *to* n 553
it V *to* n as if 524
it V *to* n as though 524
it V *to* n like 524
it V *to* n that 522
it V *to* n to-inf 523
it V *to* n wh 523
it V *towards* n 553
it V wh 521
it V when/if 521
MODAL 573, 574
MODAL *have* -ed 572
MODAL inf 571, 574
MODAL inf *than/as* inf 574
MODAL *not* 574
MODAL that 575
pl-n *be* V-ed 59-62, 510-514, 515-516
pl-n *get* V-ed 458, 459
pl-n V 455-461, 466-469, 510-514, 515-516
pl-n V *about* n 470
pl-n V *against* n 470
pl-n V amount 458
pl-n V *for* n 458, 470
pl-n V *in* n 459
pl-n V *into* n 470
pl-n V n 461-466, 514-515
pl-n V *on* n 457, 470
pl-n V *over* n 470
pl-n V pl-n 470
pl-n V pron-recip 472
pl-n V that 469
pl-n V *together* 139-141, 460, 472
pl-n V to-inf 458, 459, 469
pl-n V wh 469

pl-n V wh-to-inf 469
pl-n V *with* pron-recip 472
so/nor/neither AUX n 570
there V n 561-563
there V n prep/adv 563-564
V 1-14, 478-492, 514-515
V *about* 138
V *about* -ing 145-149
V *about* n 145-150
V *about* n -ing 147, 148, 149
V *about* n *to* n 245
V *about* n *with* n 471
V *about* wh 145-149
V *across* n 150-151
V adj 74-79, 501-503
V adj/adv *about* n 150
V adj *among* pl-n 270
V adj/n *to* n 454
V adj prep 75
V adv 136-139, 480, 482, 508-509
V adv *for* n 136
V adv n 310-326, 326-328
V adv n prep 325
V adv prep 135, 498
V adv/prep 125-135
V adv *with* n 137
V *after* n 151-153
V *after* n with quote 117
V *against* n 153-156, 457, 512
V *ahead* 138
V *among* pl-n 270
V amount 68-73
V amount *about* n -ing 340, 341
V amount *about* n/-ing/wh 340, 341
V amount adj 80
V amount adj/adv 73
V amount -ed 307
V amount *for* n 367, 372, 373
V amount *from* n 375, 376
V amount *in* n 73
V amount *into* n 395
V amount *off* n 402
V amount *of* n 401
V amount *out of* n 414
V amount to-inf 414
V amount *to* n 422, 432
V amount *towards/toward* n 435
V amount *with* n 447
V *and* inf 123, 124
V *and* v 122-124
V *around* 138
V *around* n 156-158
V *as* adj 158-159, 495
V as if 121-122
V *as if* to-inf 122
V *as* -ing 161
V *as* n 159-162
V *as* quote 119
V as though 121-122
V *as to* n 162-163
V *as to* wh 162-163
V *at* amount 164
V *at* -ing 165-170
V *at* it 559
V *at* n 163-170
V *at* n -ing 167
V *at* n prep/adv 170

V *at* n to-inf 171
V *at* n with quote 118
V *at* wh 170
V *away* 138
V *back* 138
V *before* n 270
V *behind* 138
V *behind* n 270
V *between* pl-amount 172
V *between* pl-n 171-172
V *by* 138
V *by* amount 173-174
V *by* amount prep 174
V *by* amount to-inf 174
V *by* -ing 174-176
V *by* n 176
V colour 75, 79, 477
V *down* 138
V *down* n 270
V -ed 80
V-ed quote 304
V *for* adj 177
V *for* amount 183, 184
V *for* -ing 177-184
V *for* it 559
V *for* n 176-184
V *for* n prep/adv 132, 184
V *for* n to-inf 185
V *for* n *to* n 255
V *for* num 177
V *for* n *with* n 471
V *for* pron-refl 179, 184
V *from* amount 194
V *from* amount *to* amount 193
V *from* colour *to* colour 193
V *from* -ing 186-191
V *from* n 186-192, 459, 460, 461, 473, 513
V *from* n -ing 188
V *from* n *into* n 193
V *from* n *to* n 192
V how 105-109
V if 105-109
V *in* 138
V inf 96-97
V *in favour of* -ing 201-203
V *in favour of* n 201-203
V -ing 80-87
V *in* -ing 194-196, 197, 198
V *in* it 559
V *in* n 194-201
V *in* n *from* amount *to* amount 201
V *in* n *from* n/adj/colour *to* n/adj/colour 201
V *in* n -ing 199
V *in* poss *favour* 201-203
V *into* -ing 206
V *into* n 203-209, 460
V *into* n that 104
V it 553
V it adj/adv 557
V it adj that 548
V it adj to-inf 549
V it adj wh 550
V it adj when/if 550
V it amount 558
V it *as* n/adj that 545
V it *as* n/adj to-inf 546
V it *as* n/adj when/if 546

V it -ed 558
V it inf 558
V it *into* n that 545
V it n 558
V it n that 547
V it n to-inf 547
V it n when/if 548
V it *over* n 558
V it prep/adv 556
V it *so* that 543
V it that 543
V it *to* n 559
V it *to* n that 544
V it *to* n to-inf 545
V it *to* pron-refl to-inf 545
V it when/if 544
V like 121-122
V like -ing 209, 210
V like n 209-211
V like n *to* n 454
V *me/us* inf 298
V n 14-57, 466-469, 478-492, 504-509, 515-516
V n *about* -ing 338-341
V n *about* n 338-341
V n *about* n -ing 340
V n *about* wh 338-341
V n adj 280-285, 501-503
V n adj *among* pl-n 363
V n adv prep 325, 498
V n adv/prep 310-326
V n adv *to* amount 433
V n *after* n 448
V n *against* -ing 344, 345
V n *against* n 342-346
V n *among* pl-n 361-363
V n amount 274-279
V n amount *about* n/-ing/wh 342
V n amount *for* n 372
V n *around* n 448
V n *as* adj 346-348, 503
V n *as* -ing 348-353
V n *as* n 348-355
V n *as* quote 304
V n *as* to n 355-356
V n *as* to wh 355-356
V n *at* amount 357-358, 360
V n *at* n 356-360
V n *before* n 448
V n *between* pl-n 361-362
V n *by* amount 365
V n *by* -ing 363-365
V n *by* n 363-365
V n colour 284, 477
V n -ed 305-309
V n *for* -ing 368-373
V n *for* it 560
V n *for* n 366-373
V n *for* pron-refl 366
V n *from* amount *to* amount 380
V n *from* colour *to* colour 380
V n *from* -ing 374-379
V n *from* n 374-379
V n *from* n *into* n 376, 380, 390
V n *from* n *to* n 376, 380, 424, 428
V n inf 297-299
V n *in* fraction 381
V n *in front of* n 449

Phrasal verb patterns

V n P *by* n/-ing 363-365
V n P *for* n/-ing 366-373
V n P *from* n/-ing 374-379
V n P *from* n *to* n 424
V n P *in* n/-ing 381-388
V n P *into* n 389-396
V n P n 274, 276
V n P *on* n/-ing/wh 403-410
V n P prep/adv 310-326, 492-501, 504-505
V n P *to* amount 426
V n P to-inf 290-297
V n P *to* n/-ing 417-433
V n P *until* n 431
V n P *upon* n/-ing/wh 403-410
V n P *with* n 461-466, 510-516
V n P *with* n/-ing 435-449
V P 1-14, 478-492
V P *about* n/-ing/wh 145-150
V P adj 74-79
V P adv/prep 125-135
V P *after* n 151-153
V P *against* n 153-156
V P amount 68-73
V P amount *about* n/-ing/wh 340
V P *and* v 122-124
V P *as* adj 158-159
V P *as* n/-ing 159-162
V P *at* amount 164
V P *at* n 163-170
V P *at* n to-inf 171
V P *behind* n 270
V P *by* amount 173-174
V P *by* -ing 174-176
V P *for* n 176-184
V P *for* n to-inf 185
V P *from* amount *to* amount 193
V P *from it all* 559
V P *from* n/-ing 186-192
V P *from* n *to* n 192
V P *in favour of* n/-ing 201-203
V P -ing 80-87
V P *in* n 194-201
V P *in* poss *favour* 201-203
V P *into* n 203-209
V pl-n P 59-62, 510-514
V P n 14-57
V P n (not pron) 14-57, 478-492, 504-509
V P n (not pron) *against* n 342-346
V P n (not pron) *as* adj 346-348
V P n (not pron) *as* n/-ing 348-355
V P n (not pron) *at* n 356-360

V P n (not pron) *before* n 448
V P n (not pron) *between/among* pl-n 361-362
V P n (not pron) *by* n/-ing 363-365
V P n (not pron) *for* n/-ing 366-373
V P n (not pron) *from* n/-ing 374-379
V P n (not pron) *from* n *to* n 424
V P n (not pron) *in* n/-ing 381-388
V P n (not pron) *into* n 389-396
V P n (not pron) *on* n/-ing/wh 403-410
V P n (not pron) prep/adv 310-326, 492-501, 504-505
V P n (not pron) to-inf 290-297
V P n (not pron) *to* n/-ing 417-433
V P n (not pron) *until* n 431
V P n (not pron) *with* n 461-466
V P n (not pron) *with* n/-ing 435-448
V P n prep/adv 310-326
V P *on to* n 230-231
V P *onto* n 230-231
V P *on* n/-ing 215-228
V P *over* n 234-238
V P P -ing 86
V P pl-n 59-62, 510-514
V P pl-n (not pron) 59-62
V P P n 14-57
V P P n 288
V P prep 141-145
V P prep/adv 125-135, 492-501, 504-507
V P pron-refl 62-68
V pron-refl P *as* n/-ing 351
V pron-refl P *from* n 376, 377
V pron-refl P *into* n 394
V pron-refl P prep/adv 316, 323
V pron-refl P *to* n 429, 430, 432
V pron-refl P *with* n/-ing 443
V P *that* 97-104
V P *to* amount 242, 243
V P to-inf 87-96
V P *to* n 514
V P *to* n *for* n 255
V P *to* n/-ing 241-254
V P *to* n *that* 105
V P *to* n wh 110
V P *to* n with quote 118
V P *under* n 258
V P *upon* n/-ing 215-228
V P wh 105-109
V P wh-to-inf 110-112
V P *with* n 455-461, 510-514
V P *with* n/-ing 259-269
V P with quote 113-117

Verb Index
and frequency information

As well as showing where to find information on each verb mentioned in this book, this index indicates how frequent each verb is, using black diamonds. The most frequent verbs have five diamonds (♦♦♦♦♦) and the least frequent have no diamonds. Phrasal verbs are not given separate frequency information, unless there is no entry for the verb without a particle.

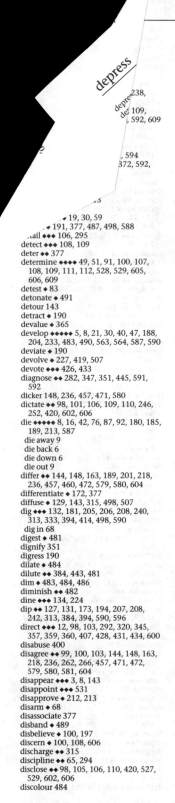